Implementing SAP® CRM

The Guide for Business and Technology Managers

Implementing SAP® CRM

The Guide for Business and Technology Managers

Vivek Kale

CRC Press
Taylor & Francis Group
Boca Raton London New York

CRC Press is an imprint of the
Taylor & Francis Group, an **informa** business

AN AUERBACH BOOK

CRC Press
Taylor & Francis Group
6000 Broken Sound Parkway NW, Suite 300
Boca Raton, FL 33487-2742

First issued in paperback 2019

© 2015 by Vivek Kale
CRC Press is an imprint of Taylor & Francis Group, an Informa business

No claim to original U.S. Government works

ISBN-13: 978-1-4822-3142-7 (hbk)
ISBN-13: 978-0-367-37805-9 (pbk)

Library of Congress Cataloging-in-Publication Data

Kale, Vivek.
    Implementing SAP* CRM : the guide for business and technology managers / Vivek Kale.
       pages cm
    Includes bibliographical references and index.
    ISBN 978-1-4822-3142-7 (hardcover : alk. paper) 1. SAP* CRM. 2. Customer
    relations--Management--Computer programs. 3. Customer relations--Data processing. 4.
    Management information systems. I. Title.

    HF5415.5.K35 2015
    658.8'12028553--dc23   2014033351

Visit the Taylor & Francis Web site at
http://www.taylorandfrancis.com

and the CRC Press Web site at
http://www.crcpress.com

To

My wife, Girija, and our beloved daughters, Tanaya and Atmaja, for all their love and support.

Without them, I would not be where I am in my life today.

Contents

SECTION III PRE-IMPLEMENTATION STAGE

SECTION IV   IMPLEMENTATION STAGE

13   SAP ASAP Methodology

SECTION VI   SAP CRM IMPLEMENTATION AND BEYOND

15   Valuing the Relationship-Based Enterprise 443

Preface

As customer-facing applications, CRM systems are expected to be implemented by companies as the top-most priority. However, the reality is quite different. CRM implementations usually follow in the wake of ERP implementation. Not all companies go as far as implementing an enterprise-wide CRM strategy and application(s). Of the several reasons for this apparent lack of enthusiasm for implementing the most critical customer-oriented application, a major one is the nonavailability of a single-point resource on all aspects of implementing a CRM system like SAP® CRM. This book attempts to fill that gap.

SAP CRM is one of the best CRM systems in the market. Its advanced architecture and design provides for comprehensive and flexible adoption and also permits the development and release of functional upgrades of individual modules without disrupting the already functioning systems at various customer installations in a major way.

Adopting CRM not only means a new way of looking at a business's operational processes, but also requires a nearly complete overhaul of the company's Information Technology (IT) systems. This book helps technologists and managers come to grips with the vision, concept, and technology of CRM, particularly SAP CRM. It provides a framework for making the optimal decisions necessary for the successful implementation of SAP CRM in organizations. The book begins with laying down the groundwork for understanding CRM by explaining the concept and context of CRM and the tangible business benefits of adopting CRM. Then, it demonstrates the professional approach to the evaluation and selection of SAP CRM as the best CRM suite of applications and its technology, architecture, functionality, project cycle, plan and methodology of implementation, development and customization, project management, and support and administration. Besides, it provides detailed Critical Success Factors (CSFs) and patterns and antipatterns for successful SAP CRM implementation.

From there, the book scans an overview of SAP CRM:

- SAP CRM Enterprise applications, including marketing, sales, service, interaction center, partner channel management, and mobile applications
- SAP E-Business, including E-Marketing, E-commerce, E-Service, and Web Channel Analytics
- Vertical market applications, including Consumer Goods, Finance, and Insurance
- SAP NetWeaver environment, covering people integration, information integration, process integration, and application integration
- SAP tools and programming environment, including ABAP and Java custom development

The book provides details of the SAP ASAP methodology for the implementation of SAP CRM within an enterprise. The last section deals with the Balanced ScoreCard (BSC) for companies and concludes with a discussion of other important CRM-related aspects like *relationships on demand*.

What Makes This Book Different

This book studies the 1990s phenomenon of the emergence of Customer Relationship Management (CRM) systems from both business and technological perspectives. It tries to demystify CRM systems like SAP CRM and their power and potential to transform business enterprises. Unlike customary works on CRM systems, which seldom discuss the key differentiator of SAP CRM from earlier mission-critical systems, this book brings to the fore the fact that with CRMs like SAP, companies are, for the first time, able to treat customer-related information not merely as a *records of information* but as *customer relationships*. This importance of customer relationships is based on a simple fact: it can cost four to seven times more to replace a customer than it does to retain one. A major step in retaining a customer is to realize that whereas customer relationships are not all about information, all customer-related information is certainly about customer relationships. Hence, Chapter 1, the longest chapter of the book, provides a reference framework for business operations based on customer relationships rather than the traditional four Ps (product, positioning, price, and promotion).

This is also one of the first books to focus on a company's internal operations and business processes to show how they greatly impact external, that is, customer-facing strategies, services, and relationships. It further spells out strategies to configure internal business processes and operations (via SAP CRM) in order to improve customer-facing strategies, services, and relationships.

Many companies have been struggling with the implementation of CRM projects primarily because they have misunderstood CRM implementations to be technology projects that are confined to only certain aspects and areas of the enterprise's operations. Nothing could be further from the truth. CRM implementations can add significant value to a company's bottom lines only if the company first transforms itself into a customer-centric and customer-responsive enterprise. The book thus begins with an overview of what it means to be a customer-centric and customer-responsive enterprise and then discusses the technology of CRM systems in subsequent chapters.

Second, this book recommends that CRM implementation be undertaken as an enterprise-wide effort. In the big-bang approach to CRM implementation adopted in the book, all facets of CRM relevant for an enterprise's operations are implemented at the same time. Thus, CRM implementations should entail enterprise-wide communication, participation, planning, resourcing, risk and change management, quality checking, and training.

This book also touches upon certain aspects of SAP CRM implementation that would be of particular interest to company executives and decision-makers, for instance, the ROI of implementing CRM is covered in Section VI.

Far from developing in isolation from the IT industry, the design and architecture of SAP have picked on the best developments in IS/IT in the latter half of the twentieth century. Hence, at relevant stages, the book highlights SAP's connections with parallel developments in software development technologies and methodologies to make the context of several outstanding features of SAP more meaningful.

The book has used many concepts for the first time in the context of CRM systems, such as Collaborative Enterprise, Extended Collaborative Enterprise (ECE), Critical Value Determinants

(CVDs), and Management by Collaboration (MBC). But some new terms and concepts have also been introduced, such as the concept of *infosphere*, that is, the cloud (Chapter 1), or the vision of *Decisions on Desktops* or *Relationships on Demand* (Chapter 16).

Quite a few people have asked me: why a SAP specific book? For highlighting the real significance of CRM, it was important to consider a specific enterprise system that also has a major presence in the market. This book focuses on SAP because

- SAP is closest to what a canonical enterprise system should be: it enables the enterprise to operate as an integrated, enterprise-wide, process-oriented, information-driven, and real-time enterprise.
- In the past few years, all other competing systems have fallen way behind SAP in the market; currently, SAP is the predominant ERP system in the market with more than 70% share of the installed base (both large enterprises and small and medium businesses) across the world.

How This Book Is Organized

Section I: Setting the Stage

Chapters in the first section give the context and significance of CRMs in general and SAP CRM in particular for increasing the competitiveness of organizations. Chapter 1 describes the customer relationship management (CRM) business initiatives; it introduces the key idea: information is relationship. Chapter 2 defines the customer relationship management (CRM) systems and their characteristic features. Chapters 3 and 4 present a framework for the evaluation and selection of CRMs. Chapter 5 demonstrates SAP CRM as the best CRM system in the market. Chapter 6 presents an overview of a SAP CRM implementation project. Chapter 7 touches on the Business Process Re-Engineering (BPR) aspects of any CRM implementation project.

Section II: SAP CRM Applications

This section has four chapters that cover the main components of SAP CRM applications. Chapter 8 presents an overview of the SAP CRM Enterprise Applications addressing functionality in the areas of marketing, sales, service and support, interaction or contact center, partner channel management, and so on. Chapter 9 describes SAP E-Business applications. Chapter 10 deals with SAP's operating NetWeaver environment and related products. Chapter 11 is on SAP tools and programming environments that cater to ABAP and Java custom development.

Section III: Pre-Implementation Stage

This section presents various activities that are prerequisites to starting a SAP CRM project. Chapter 12 discusses various activities and tasks necessary for SAP CRM implementation.

Section IV: Implementation Stage

This section presents in detail SAP's ASAP implementation methodology through all its phases. Chapter 13 introduces the concept and context of ASAP and details the five stages of ASAP methodology, namely, Project Preparation, Business Blueprint, Realization, final Preparation, and Go-Live support.

Section V: Post-Implementation Stage

In this section, Chapter 14 gives a brief overview of the post-implementation issues associated with the support of a SAP system in production. It also describes future SAP CRM enhancements, including the areas of Mobile Applications, Big Data Analytics, and SAP HANA.

Section VI: SAP CRM Implementation and Beyond

Chapter 15 presents various aspects related to valuing the ROI of SAP CRM implementation using the method of Balance Scorecard (BSC). The last chapter of the book, Chapter 16, presents prospects for intelligent customer-centric enterprises as also the vision of *relationships on demand* that has the potential for enabling provisioning of *instant Relationships*!

Who Should Read This Book

All those who are involved with any aspect of a SAP CRM project—Sales, Marketing, Service and Support personnel, SAP CRM implementation project and IS/IT personnel—will profit from using this book as a roadmap to make a more meaningful contribution to the success of their SAP CRM implementation project.

This complete and comprehensive guide to SAP CRM has been designed to be read selectively with a view to understanding specific components of the system relevant to the reader's purpose.

Following are the sets of chapters that can be recommended for reading to different categories of stakeholders:

1. Chapters 1 through 7, 12, 15, and 16 for Executives and business managers
2. Chapters 1, 2, 4 through 9, 12, and 14 through 16 for Operational Managers
3. Chapters 1 through 6, 8, 9, 15, and 16 for CRM Evaluation and Selection team members
4. Chapters 1, 2, 5 through 10, and 12 through 14 for Project Managers and module leaders
5. Chapters 1 through 9 and 12 through 16 for functional members of the SAP CRM team and for students of management courses
6. Chapters 1 through 6, 8 through 14, and 16 for Technical Managers
7. Chapters 1 through 3, 5, 6, and 8 through 14 for technical members of the SAP CRM team
8. Chapters 1, 2, 5 through 9, 12, 13, 15, and 16 for professionals interested in SAP CRM
9. Chapters 1 through 16 for students of computer courses
10. Chapters 1, 2, 5 through 9, 12, 15, and 16 for general readers interested in CRM and SAP CRM

Acknowledgments

I would like to thank all those who have helped me with their clarifications and criticism, and who were patient enough to read the entire or parts of the manuscript and made many valuable suggestions. During the formative years of this book, I had gained immensely from my discussions and correspondence with Prof. Frank Davis of University of Tennessee, Prof. Jagdish Sheth of Emroy University, and Jill Dyche from Baseline Consulting. As before, I continue to get valuable support for research and reference from Dr. B. Srinivas, Nilesh Acharya, and Rajeev Ganatra; my heartfelt thanks to them.

At Taylor & Francis, I thank John Wyzalek for making this book happen as also the extended publishing team consisting of Edward Curtis, Jessica Vakili, S. Vinithan, Vijay Bose, and a host of other people who were involved with the production of this book.

I thank my beloved daughters Tanaya and Atmaja for their understanding and support. They have made my past worthwhile and my future hopeful. Finally, I owe my greatest thanks to my wife, Girija, without whose continuing love, support, and sacrifice, this book would not have been possible. For this and much more, I am deeply and forever grateful to her.

Vivek Kale
Mumbai, India

Author

Vivek Kale has more than two decades of professional IT experience, during which he has handled and consulted on various aspects of enterprise-wide information modeling, enterprise architectures, business process redesign, and e-business architectures.

He has been Group CIO of Essar Group, the steel, oil, and gas major of India, as well as Raymond Ltd., the textile and apparel major of India. He is a seasoned practitioner in transforming the business of IT, facilitating business agility, and enabling the Process-Oriented Enterprise.

He is the author of *Implementing SAP R/3: The Guide for Business and Technology Managers* (2000), *A Guide to Implementing the Oracle Siebel CRM 8.x* (2009), *Guide to Cloud Computing for Business and Technology Managers: From Distributed Computing to Cloudware Applications* (2014), and *Inverting the Paradox of Excellence: How Companies Use Variations for Business Excellence and How Enterprise Variations Are Enabled by SAP* (2014).

SETTING THE STAGE

I

This part lays the background and context of undertaking a Customer Relationship Management (CRM) implementation project within a company.

The phenomenon of CRMs like SAP CRM that is being witnessed in the last few years is fascinating. Technically, there have always been several application software systems to cater to all aspects of organizational interaction with its customers. Thus, one may be intrigued by the question of what is so special about CRMs in the 2000's? I feel that the answer lies in the fact that CRMs, for the first time, are able to treat customer-related information not merely as records of customer interactions, expectations, and transactions, but also as relationships. This enables CRMs to leverage the totality of this information, across all channels and customer touch points, to manage customer relationships more effectively and optimize the realized customer value throughout the entire life cycle of the customer. The importance of customer relationships is based on a simple fact: it can cost four to seven times more to replace a current customer than it does to retain one. A major step in this direction is to realize that whereas customer relationships are not all about information, all customer-related information is certainly about customer relationships.

Chapters in first part of this book give the context and significance of CRMs and SAP CRM in particular, for increasing competitiveness of organizations. Chapter 1 introduces a reference framework based on customer relationships rather than traditional one based 4Ps (Products/Positioning/Price/Promotion). Chapters 1 and 2 introduces the key idea of customer information is relationship. Chapter 1 and Chapter 2 unravel the mystery of CRMs like SAP CRM, and their power and potential to transform customer relationships.

Chapters 3 and 4 present a framework for evaluation and selection of CRMs. Chapter 5 presents support on claim that SAP CRM is the best CRM system that there is on the market. Chapter 6 presents an overview of a SAP implementation project. This would help in understanding how all other pieces, discussed in the following chapters, fit into the overall scheme. Chapter 7 touches upon enterprise-wide Business Process Re-Engineering (BPR), which is an important aspect of any CRM implementation project.

Chapter 1: The Relationship-Based Enterprise
Chapter 2: Customer Relationship Management (CRM) System
Chapter 3: CRM Evaluation
Chapter 4: CRM Selection
Chapter 5: SAP CRM Solution
Chapter 6: SAP CRM Implementation Project Cycle
Chapter 7: SAP CRM and Enterprise Business Process Re-Engineering

Companies have a wealth of knowledge in the files and records that customer-facing employees have on customer and customer interactions. The best way to leverage this knowledge is to free it from the shackles of experience, institutionalize it, and transfer it in real time to all employees, so that they are empowered to build relationships with customers.

Enterprises routinely miss altogether or underestimate the power and potential for enterprise change management enabled by enterprise systems like SAP ERP. Initiating change and confronting change are the two most important issues facing the enterprises of today. The ability to change business processes contributes directly to the innovation bottom line. The traditional concept of change management is usually understood as a one-time event or at least a nonfrequent event. But if an enterprise is looking for the capability not only to handle change management, but also management of changes on a continual basis, then establishing an enterprise system like SAP is a must!

Chapter 1

The Relationship-Based Enterprise

Customer Relationship Management (CRM) is a holistic approach to identifying, attracting, and retaining customers. CRM deals with creating a customer-centric enterprise. This involves two major aspects: customer centricity and customer responsiveness. All activities must eventually add value to the customer reflected in their willingness to pay for the products and/or services; non-value-adding elements should be excised swiftly in Internet time because customers have numerous other choices. This entails focusing all strategies, plans, and actions on the customer rather than the traditional focus on the products and/or services. As originally proposed by Fred Reichheld, *it is a question of transitioning from zero defects to zero defections.*

Additionally, enterprises must ensure seamless and real-time integration between

- Customer-facing demand generating
- Back-end demand fulfilling intra- or inter enterprise supply chain processes

An effective CRM strategy aims at achieving the following:

- Continuously attract new customers
- Gain customer insight and manage intimacy
- Retain profitable customers and phase-out nonprofitable customers
- Establish long-term relationships with current customers
- Increase the customer spend and profits by cross selling and up-selling

This book takes a stance that customers are not the exclusive preserve of the marketing function, but are the key to an enterprise's enduring and compounding competitiveness and success.

1.1 SAP: Company and Its CRM Product

SAP is the world's leading provider of business software solutions with a sales of more than $14 billion. With more than 75,000+ employees who operate in more than 34 countries, SAP has more than 25,000 customers with more than 100,000 installations of SAP across the world. And, worldwide, more than 15 million users in 120+ countries work on SAP systems. Through SAP™ Business Suite, people in enterprises across the globe are improving relationships with customers and partners, streamlining operations, and achieving significant efficiencies throughout their supply chains. The unique core processes of various industries, ranging from Aerospace to Utilities, are effectively supported by SAP's portfolio of 23 industry solutions.

Throughout this book, we will sometimes refer to SAP as a company as well its products by the same term *SAP*. This should not lead to any confusion because we believe that, at any point, the context would make it clear as to which meaning is intended.

The phenomenal success of SAP comes from the fact that SAP systems are comprehensive but at the same time configurable to the specific needs of any company. Companies prefer off-the-shelf packages like SAP CRM because they are flexible and can be configured to satisfy most requirements of any company in any industry. SAP CRM can be deployed on various hardware platforms providing the same comprehensive and integrated functionality and flexibility for addressing individual company's requirements. SAP CRM implements a process-oriented view of the extended enterprise.

There is a substantial difference between the concept of Customer Relationship Management (CRM) and Customer Relationship Management Systems (CRM Systems). CRM is a concept of much broader scope than the CRM Systems that implement a subset of the tenets of CRM. The reason for maintaining this distinction becomes clear when we consider latest extensions to the traditional CRM like Big Data Analytics and Social CRM (see Chapter 14, Section 14.10 "Big Data Analytics" and Section 14.11 "Social CRM via Social Networks"). In the next section, we take an overview of the concept of CRM, whereas Chapter 2 "Customer Relationship Management (CRM) System" looks at the basic characteristics of CRM Systems of which SAP CRM is a prime example. Notwithstanding all this, in the next few chapters, we first familiarize ourselves with the background and significance of CRM before we introduce SAP CRM in Chapter 5. Figure 1.1 presents the underlying Customer Relationship Framework for the whole book.

1.2 Concept of Customer Relationship Management (CRM)

Customer Relationship Management (CRM) is a customer-centric business strategy that encompasses all business models, processes, methodologies, and techniques for closing the gap between an organization's current and potential performance in acquisition, growth, and retention of valuable customers for mutual benefit.

In an era where the advantages based only on product features and add-on services are shortened to a *click of a customer* (see Chapter 2, Section 2.6 "Customer-Triggered Company"), the key to success is to forge long-term, profitable relationships with valuable customers. This involves two major aspects: customer centricity and customer responsiveness. CRM aims to identify the customers that are most profitable to the company and optimizes relationships with those customers.

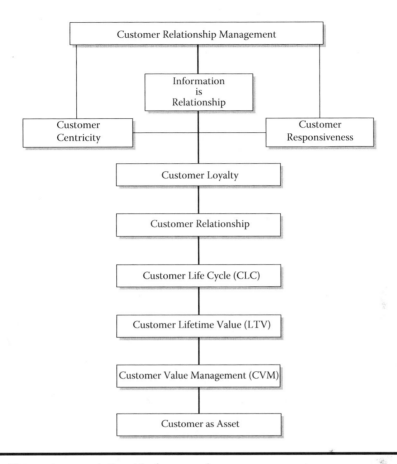

Figure 1.1 The customer relationship framework.

Whereas this view may lead to increased services and incentives for customers that provide the greatest returns to the company, on the other hand, it may also result in reduced services or even strong disincentives for nonprofitable customers. If a company or organization was to put more of its efforts into its existing customers, it would make sense that it did this with customers that had the greatest potential. This means that at some point, it has to start to lose those customers that are not ones that offer long-term future value—this might be because of transaction spend, the value of a customer, or the cost of transacting or dealing with that customer or customer group. All customers aren't created equal! Consequently, the traditional customer-centric slogan should be transformed to

Valuable (i.e., Profitable) customers are always right.

Thus, even customers compete for bestowing their custom! Customer retention is extremely important for companies because it is more efficient and effective to retain a current customer than gain a new one. Companies can generate additional revenue and profits without incurring the costs for acquiring new customers. In light of this, the management is really concerned with having the right product in the right place, at the right price, at the right time, in the right condition *for the right customer.*

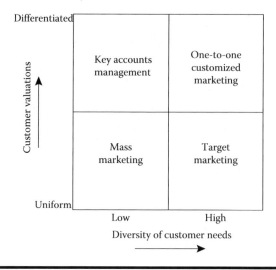

Figure 1.2 Marketing techniques for different types of customers.

Don Peppers and Martha Rogers pioneered the concept of one-to-one marketing made possible by the advent of computer-assisted database marketing. Figure 1.2 represents the entire spectrum of customers and the corresponding marketing techniques. The horizontal axis measures the diversity of customer needs, and the vertical axis measures the differentiation in *customer valuations*. The representative businesses for each of the quadrants are as follows: Gas Station, bookstore, airlines, and a computer systems company.

According to Don Peppers and Martha Rogers, the following patterns have been observed:

1. Businesses with relatively undiversified customer needs and relatively uniform customer valuations will do best with mass marketing techniques (refer to Section 1.2.7.1 "Customer Value")
2. Businesses with diversified customer needs but uniform valuations can benefit from target marketing
3. Businesses with relatively undiversified customer needs but with highly differentiated customer valuations will benefit immensely with a key account management approach
4. Businesses with highly diversified customer needs and highly differentiated customer valuations will benefit from one-to-one customized marketing

How does one handle a set of highly differentiated customers having a large diversity of needs? It is through customer responsiveness that is discussed later. In Chapter 2, Section 2.6 "Customer-Triggered Company," we describe the latest variation of the traditional CRM geared to handle such customers. Section 1.3 "Management by Collaboration" introduces a unifying framework for the various aspects of the CRM-enabled *extended collaborative enterprise* (ECE) and sets the tone for the rest of the book as well. We end the next chapter with a discussion of how CRM systems such as SAP CRM provide the new organizational architecture essential for the extended enterprise of the twenty-first century.

The enterprises' business model governs both its business strategy and its use of IT. Figure 1.3 shows the product–process change matrix that illustrates the four distinct business models based on

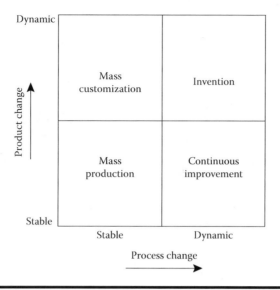

Figure 1.3   Business models.

- ■ The dimensions of change (product or process change)
- ■ The fundamental nature of change (dynamic or stable)

On the vertical axis, product change reflects changes in the demand for goods or services because of competitor moves, shifting customer preferences or entering new geographical or national markets. On the horizontal axis, process change means altering the procedures or technologies used to generate, produce, or deliver the corresponding products or services. Taken together, these factors result in four distinct business models, as follows:

1. *Mass Production*: In these enterprises, the primary use of technology is to automate tasks.
2. *Invention*: In these enterprises, technology must support collaborative efforts among teams or a set of individuals.
3. *Continuous Improvement*: In these enterprises, technology must augment tasks by enhancing people's deep process knowledge and skills. It can also link people and processes across functions to provide customer-focused, horizontal, informational flows enabling them to continuously improve the processes they execute.
4. *Mass Customization*: In these enterprises, technology not only must automate tasks and augment knowledge and skills but most significantly must also automate relationships between processes and people.

The advent of the Total Quality Management (TQM) movement in the United States led to the emergence of customer satisfaction measures, and efforts aimed at improving and sustaining them led to greater emphasis on customer centricity. The total quality management turned attention to customer needs and forced a rethinking of traditional management methods.

One of the keys to mass customization is the use of dynamic business networks within and among enterprises. These are formed out of a set of loosely coupled autonomous business process capabilities with a linkage system that allows them to be reconfigured instantly for any particular customer order. By engineering the flexibility of the processing units and coordinating the flow of resources (materials or services) between these units, the mass customizer can produce an almost infinite variety of base products or service, at a cost that is competitive when compared even with a mass producer. Whereas labor in the mass production design is organized to perform repetitive tasks according to a singular command-and-control system, the mass customizer organizes labor to routinely respond to an ever-changing set of rules and commands. The mass customizer organizes labor to work effectively in a dynamic network of relationships and to respond to work requirements defined by the dynamically changing customer needs. Although there is apparently a great degree of centralization in both of these models, there is a fundamental difference in the nature of centralization: in case of mass production, all decision making is centralized, whereas in the case of mass customizer, it is only the coordination and control that is centralized. The mass customizing organizations centralizes *the allocation of work* to different processing units to produce the customer's product or service order (see Sections 1.3.8 "Agile Enterprise" and 1.2.2.2.2 "Business Webs").

1.2.1 Customer Centricity

CRM is a different approach to business that involves relationship marketing, customer retention, and cross selling leading to customer extension (see Section 1.2.7 "Customer Life Cycle (CLC)"). CRM represents a culmination of a long-evolutionary shift in the traditional thinking of business. Until the last few decades, the business of the global economy was, essentially, manufacturing. The focus on goods rather than services led to a product-focused, mass-market marketing strategy resulting in a high cost of acquiring new customers and a low cost for customers switching to other brands.

LOGICS OF BUSINESS

The fundamental logics of business that have been identified are as follows:

1. *Product-centric business*: These types of business believe that customers primarily choose products with the best quality, performance, design, or features. These are characteristically highly innovative and entrepreneurial firms usually driven by the founders' vision but with marked descent on market research or hearing the *voice of the customer*. Their managements usually make assumptions regarding what the customers want, resulting in over specified or over engineered products that are normally costly for the majority of the customers. They actually target a relatively small segment of price-insensitive customers called innovators.

2. *Production-centric business*: These types of business believe that customers primarily choose low-price products. Consequently, they strive to keep operating costs low.

3. *Sales-centric business*: These types of business believe that if they invest enough in advertising, selling, public relations (PR), and sales promotion, customers will be persuaded to buy their products or services.

4. *Customer-centric business*: These types of business believe in the primacy of the customers and their specific wants at a particular moment. Based on customer and competitive information, they develop better value propositions that are attractive for the customers. Customer-centric businesses are learning organizations that constantly adapt to customer requirements and competitive conditions.

Table 1.1 Traditional Mass Marketing versus Customized Relationship Marketing

	Traditional Mass Marketing	*Customized Relationship Marketing*
Objective	Mass Marketing	Customer as an Individual
Focus	Customer Acquisition	Throughout Customer Life
Timetable	Transaction term	Medium to Long Term
Performance Indicators	Market share, Product Profitability	Wallet share of the Valuable (i.e., profitable) customers
Customer Knowledge	Segment-based Habits, Behavior Modeling, Occasional Market Research	Individual-based Habits, Behavior Modeling and Prediction
Product	Stand-alone Product	Product and Service
Price	General Price Reductions	Customer Loyalty-based Differential Pricing
Channels	Traditional Channels	New Technology Channels
Sales	Salesman as the *lone hunter*	Team Sales
		Sales Automation
Communication	One way	Two way
	Brand oriented	Interactive Personalized

CRM and CRM systems like SAP CRM enable customer-centric business, though they also support the other logics of business that may become essential at a certain stage of the market development, products, or services.

Table 1.1 compares the traditional mass marketing approach with that of the relationship-oriented customized marketing.

There has always been a focus on the customer needs, but with the advent of computers, there has been a shift away from producing goods or providing services, toward discovering and meeting the needs of the individual customer. The challenge to the company's future is not necessarily from the competitors, but from its own complacency toward its customers. Product differentiation is eroding. The change is driven by intensified compensation, deregulation, globalization, and saturation of market segments. Internal business processes are being reengineered as never before, but process changes are initiated, designed, implemented, and evaluated in terms of meeting the needs of the customer (see Chapter 7 "SAP CRM and Enterprise Business Process Re-Engineering"). These businesses are organized for customer centricity and responsiveness, not for the routine performance of standardized predefined tasks.

The customer needs and values can itself be defined in terms of the following:

- *The need for relationship*: Customers with a high *need for relationship* place a high value on the supplier's ability to understand their needs; their organization, strategy, and challenges; and their future plans.

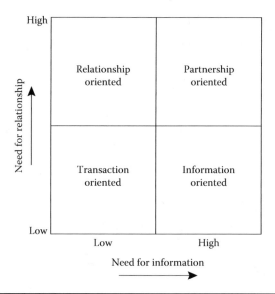

Figure 1.4   Type of customer relationships.

■ *The need for information*: Customers with a high *need for information* place a high value on the supplier's ability to provide all relevant information on the company, its products, and services enabling them to make an informed decision regarding using the company's products and services.

Accordingly, Figure 1.4 presents a map that classifies customer relationships depending on what customers value most:

■ Transaction oriented
■ Relationship oriented
■ Information oriented
■ Partnership oriented

For a successful CRM program that can produce bottom-line financial results, the customer centricity needs to pervade the whole of the demand and supply chain. A process view, as embodied in SAP CRM, assists in achieving this by integrating the downstream customer-facing processes with upstream supply chain processes. As emphasized throughout this book, the process view cuts through the impeding organizational boundaries to focus on business results for the satisfaction of the end customer.

1.2.1.1 From Products to Services to Experiences

By the middle of the last Century, the products, goods, and property came to increasingly mean an individual's exclusive right to possess, use, and, most importantly, dispose as he or she wished in the market. By the 1980s, the production of goods had been eclipsed by the performance of services. These are economic activities that are not products or construction, but are transitory, are consumed at the time they are produced (and, thus, cannot be inventoried), and primarily provide intangible value. In a service economy, it is the time that is being commoditized, not prices or places or things—this also leads to a transition from P&L to market cap as the base metric of success (see Chapter 15, Section 15.4.1 "Time Value of Customers and Shareholder Value"); what the customer is really purchasing is the *access for use* rather than *ownership* of a material good. Since the 1990s, goods are becoming more information intensive and interactive, are continually upgraded, and are essentially evolving into services. Products are rapidly being equated as cost of doing business rather than as sales items; they are becoming more in the nature of *containers* or *platforms* for all sorts of upgrades and value-added services (see Section 1.2.2.1.6 "Customer Service Management"). Giving away products is increasingly being used as a marketing strategy to capture the attention of the potential customers. But with the advent of electronic commerce, feedback, and workflow mechanisms, services are being further transformed into multifaceted relationships between the service providers and customers, and technology is becoming more of a medium of relationships. In the *servicized* economy, defined by shortened product life cycles and an ever-expanding flow of competitive goods and services, it is the customer's attention rather than the resources that is becoming scarce.

> The true significance of a customer's attention can be understood the moment one realizes that time is often used as a proxy for attention. Like time, attention is limited and cannot be inventoried or reused. In the current economy, attention is the real currency of business, and, to be successful, enterprises must be adept in getting significant and sustained mindshare or attention of their prospects or customers. As with any other scarce and valuable resource, markets for attention exist both within and outside the enterprise. For extracting optimum value, the real-time and intelligent enterprises must impart optimal attention to the wealth of operational and management information available within the enterprise. This fact alone should automatically put a bar on overzealous re-engineering and downsizing efforts (although re-engineering and other cost-cutting tactics are necessary, it is essential to ascertain if undertaking such tactics will contribute to the delivery of superior or at least *on par* value to the customers). This is the fundamental vision underlying the emergence of outsourcing strategies (see Section 1.3.7 "The Virtual Enterprise", Chapter 2, Section 2.5 "Electronic CRM", Chapter 14, Section 14.7 "Applications Outsourcing", and Chapter 4, Section 4.5.1.2.2, "Applications as Web Services").

One major result of this trend toward the importance of experience has been the blurring of lines between the content (the message) and container (the medium) in the market, which we describe in the next section (see Figure 1.5).

1.2.1.2 Convergence: From Marketplaces to Market Spaces

Traditional capitalism considered market share as the prime determinant of profits. Market share was a classic example of the zero sum game, where increase of market share by one company was typically at the expense of corresponding loss by other(s). Market share, which is a lagging indicator, does not distinguish in favor of valuable, satisfied, or repeat customers. On the other hand, market spaces are defined with reference to a customer's perception of the delivered value, and the resulting market size may be essentially limitless. Market spaces typically emerge because of the convergence across disparate or differing industries. For instance, the convergence of computers,

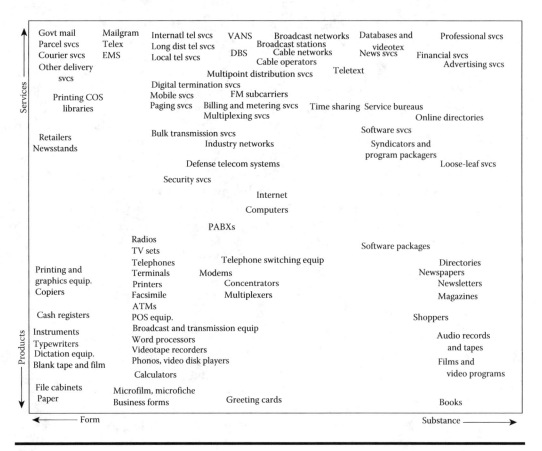

Figure 1.5 Spectrum of offerings (product/service) versus medium (or form or container)/ message (or substance or content).

data communication, telecommunications, and media industries has resulted in the emergence of one of the biggest market spaces with possibly the largest growth opportunities in recent times.

Convergence describes the phenomenon in which two or more existing technologies, markets, producers, boundaries, or value chains combine to create a new force that is more powerful and more efficient than the sum of its constituting technologies. The value chain migration alludes to the development of real-term systems that integrate supply chain systems and customer-facing systems, resulting in a single and unified integrated process.

This convergence is primarily because of three factors:

1. The digitization of information to enable the preparation, processing, storage, and transmission of information regardless of its form (data, graphics, sound and video, or any combination of these).
2. The rapidly declining cost of computing that has enabled computing to become ubiquitous and available with sufficient power (see note "Moore's Law").
3. The availability of broadband communications is critical to convergence because multimedia is both storage intensive and time sensitive.

Figure 1.6 presents the hardware trends in the 1990s and the current decade.

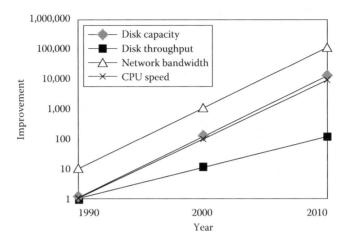

Figure 1.6 **Hardware trends in the 1990s and the last decade.**

Table 1.2 **Comparison of Communications Technologies**

Communications Technology	Bandwidth	Time for Sending 1 MB File
Modem using analog signal over phone line	28.8 kB/s	5 min
ISDN using digital signal over phone line	128 kB/s	1 min
T1 using digital signal over private phone line	1.5 MB/s	16 s
Cable using Modem digital signal over Ethernet	10 MB/s	0.80 s
T3 using digital signal over private phone line	45 MB/s	0.53 s
ATM using digital signal over ATM-switched network	155 MB/s	0.05 s
ATM using digital signal over ATM-switched network	1 GB/s	0.008 s

Table 1.2 gives a comparison of communications technologies in terms of the approx. time required to send file with a size of 1 MB.

The merging of previously disparate technologies, products, and information to give rise to compelling new products and services also underscores the concept of the merging of the container and content that we referred to earlier. Convergence increasingly means that products in the experience economy (see Section 1.2.1.1 "From Products to Services to Experiences") combine the attributes of both content and container in novel ways to create new value chains.

1.2.1.3 Customer Relationships as a Strategy

Customer relationship strategy is emerging as one of the most important components of corporate strategy. A well-executed customer relationship strategy can result in a number of quantitative benefits including greater ability to up-sell and cross sell, improved customer retention, and reduced cost of service and support.

Customer relationship management has emerged as a corporate strategy driven by the following factors:

- *Implosion of product life cycles*: This has robbed companies from enjoying the sustained financial benefits of being product innovators for sustained periods. Competitors introduce alternative, substitute, and even improved products much more rapidly.
- *Explosion of new technologies*: They are enabling even nascent players to compete effectively with established players not only in terms of superior technology but in terms of flexibility, reliability, maintainability, costs, and so on.
- *Explosion of new distribution channels*: Companies need to effectively integrate interactions through newer technology-driven channels like the Internet, wireless, telephone, mobile sales, kiosks, and ATMs.
- *Explosion of competitors*: The convergence of industries like computers, networking and data communications, TV and print media, and publishing has radically redefined the traditional boundaries between industries resulting in an explosion of the number and kinds of competitors (see Section 1.2.1.2 "Convergence: From Marketplaces to Market Spaces").

Ongoing changes rule the marketplace. The only permanent factor is the customer, and abiding relationships with the customer alone can buffer the impact of change. Thus, only those organizations that nurture customer relationships can survive product obsolescence and overcome the onslaught of superior competitors and still manage to maintain profitability.

Traditionally, competitive advantage came from strategies based on following value determinants:

Cost	Ownership, use, training support, maintenance, and so on
Time	Cycle time, lead time, and so on
Response time	Lead time, number of hand-offs, number of queues, and so on
Flexibility	Customization, options, composition, and so on
Quality	Rework, rejects, yield, and so on
Innovation	New needs, interfaces, add-ons, and so on

Most enterprises have squeezed (and continue to do so) as much as they can from these value determinants in the last few decades. Now, one of the sources for competitive strategy of substantial value that remains to be exploited in a major way is from the enterprise relationships, especially customer relationships, which are truly the real source of revenue.

For instance, in a B2B environment, a leading supplier of aggregates and industrial materials harnessed its CRM systems to help build loyalty and retain customers. However, the company faced the challenge of rapid growth through acquisition of synergetic businesses. The company grew from $140 million in revenues and 7 locations in 1997 to $360 million in revenues and 21 locations in 2000. Now, it was distributing throughout the United States. With the addition of many new products to its product portfolio (through the acquisitions), the company wanted to be sure that it was maximizing its cross selling opportunities and that the salesman had as much information about the different products and each of the customers as possible. This was because the company could no longer depend on the sales representatives *knowing it all* at any instance of time.

1.2.1.3.1 Information Is Relationship

Companies cannot have relationships with the customers unless they *know* them, that is, unless they have detailed information on them. Companies have a wealth of knowledge in the files and records that customer-facing employees have on customer interactions. The best way to leverage this knowledge is to free it from the shackles of experience, institutionalize it, and transfer it in real time to all employees, so that they are empowered to build relationships with customers.

As stated earlier, companies are finding it harder and harder to differentiate on factors that prevailed in the 1980s—product quality, operations, logistics, and business processes. Across the last decade, the quality of products has improved, many companies have undertaken business process re-engineering (BPR) with reference to the enterprise processes, and many businesses have also streamlined their supply and distribution channels. In this environment, it has become essential for companies to identify new ways to attract new customers, to maximize the value from each existing customer, and to retain the most profitable ones. Studies show that maintaining loyalty can increase customer profitability between 25% and 85%. Knowing who your customers are and what they are buying is a major step toward ensuring their loyalty without necessarily increasing the costs.

The approximate value of a customer can also be estimated easily based on the information on the defection rate and the profitability of customers by year. Since

$$\text{Average life of customer} = \frac{1}{\text{Attrition rate}}$$

it is evident that profits are determined not by sales but by the retention rate.

A major step in this direction would be to realize that whereas customer relationships are not all about information, all customer-related information is certainly about customer relationships. And everything else being the same, there is a huge potential in leveraging on the totality of information that is gathered from all the interactions that the company has with each customer. This is achievable by

1. Knowing the customer better than the competition does
2. Employing that knowledge to create better and more personalized interactions in future
3. Incorporating or embedding the costs of switching to competing solutions into the current customer relationships

It is interesting to realize that as much as 80% of the sales process may be controlled by specific knowledge of a customer's business. Information as relationships can help in enhancing the effectiveness of the various functions within the company:

■ In sales, it helps companies to make the offers that are most likely to be accepted and to focus sales efforts on the highest lifetime-value customers.
■ In after market service, it reduces customer hassles, lowers costs, and streamlines repair and return processes.
■ In marketing, it is key to planning, executing, and evaluating campaigns.
■ In manufacturing and distribution, it helps to forecast optimally delivered solution.
■ In design, it guides in the development of product features and style.
■ In finance, it helps in managing credit risks and opportunities.

Customer information bases within CRMs like SAP CRM consist mainly of two components, namely, a customer database and an enterprise-level statistical database. Customer database typically contains

■ Descriptive data such as the customers' name, address, and phone number
■ The customer's status data, such as outstanding balance, line of credit, and preexisting conditions
■ The customer's lifestyle preference dàta, such as meals, meals, clothes, cars, housing, and allergies
■ The customer's history, such as search history, purchase history, returns, failed deliveries, complaints, recommendations, and any other data that could affect the customer's relationship with the firm

1.2.1.4 Customer Capital: Customer Knowledge as the New Capital

Adam Smith helped start the industrial revolution by identifying labor and capital as the economic determinants of the wealth of a nation. In this century, however, the size of the land, mass of labor, and materials that you may possess might be worthless if you do not control the related know-how including customer know-how.

 The information about an asset is more important than the asset itself. This stance also opens up possibilities ranging from co-ownership, options on ownership, etc., to ownership for access/use or even ownership by consumption.

In the twenty-first century, know-how will reside and flourish in people's minds; what might matter more are how many enterprising and innovative people you have and the freedom that they have in realizing their dreams. It will be the century of information economics and, in particular, customer economics. Traditional capitalism made companies more efficient by the classical means of cutting costs of producing and distributing volumes of offerings, rather than giving customers the value they were after. This is why more than two-thirds of the companies identified in *In Search of Excellence* in 1980 fell from grace within 5 years. Similarly, this is also why so many companies in the Fortune 1000 improved their margins between the mid-1980s and 1990s, but fewer than 40 companies actually grew their total shareholder value by more than 25% (see also Chapter 15, Section 15.1.1 "From Built-to-Last to Built-to-Perform Organizations"). In contrast to the traditional capitalism where it was the scarce offerings (and, thus, resources) that produced wealth, in customer capitalism, it is the intangible customer relationships that are driving growth and prosperity in the networked economy (see Section 1.2.2.2.1 "Networks of Resources" and Chapter 14, Section 14.11 "Social CRM via Social Networks").

CRM systems like SAP CRM also act as transformers of the knowledge that resides in the heads of the operational and subject experts into a more explicit and accessible form. This corresponds exactly to the *tacit knowledge* talked about by I. Nonaka and H. Takeuchi in their book titled *The Knowledge Creating Company*. These could be learning experiences, ideas, insights, rules of thumb, business cases, and so on. They exhort companies to convert the illusive, unsystematized, uncodified, and *can-be-lost* knowledge of the corporation and its customers into *explicit knowledge* that can be codified, collated, and managed like any other capital investment. This could be in the form of documents, case studies, analysis reports, evaluations, concept papers, internal proposals, and so on. Most importantly, it is available for scrutiny and can be improved on an ongoing basis. SAP CRM performs the invaluable service of transforming the implicit customer-related knowledge into the explicit form (see Section 1.2.2.1.2 "Best-Practice Guidelines Management").

Customer capital has gained importance because of the following trends:

■ Information-based targeted marketing is becoming more efficient and effective than unfocused mass marketing because of factors like affordable information technology, sophisticated statistical modeling, low-cost communications, and flexible fulfillment.

■ Enterprises are no longer dependent solely on the vertical channel systems to control customers' buying behaviors.

■ Enterprises utilizing all the data on customer purchase behavior are not only acquiring new customers, retaining existing ones, and cross selling more effectively, but they are also linking these data with the corresponding cost data much more efficiently as well.

■ Customers have access to comprehensive comparative data on competing solutions resulting in barriers to switch to competing solutions dropping dramatically.

■ Competitors' targeted acquisition efforts to wean away more attractive customers are undermining enterprise's mass marketing strategies entailing more-profitable customers subsidizing less-profitable ones to achieve targeted profits.

INFORMATION AS THE NEW RESOURCE

All computerized systems and solutions in the past were using past-facing information merely for the purpose of referring and reporting only. As pointed out in my earlier book *Implementing SAP*, for the first time in history of the computerized system, ERP, began treating information as a resource for the operational requirements of the enterprise. Furthermore, unlike the traditional resources, information resources as made available by ERPs can be reused and shared multiply without dissipation or degradation. Among all resources, this is one resource, which in practical terms almost defies the universal law of increase of Entropy as understood in the physical sciences. The impressive productivity gains resulting from the ERPs truthfully arise out of this unique characteristic of ERPs to use information as an inexhaustible resource.

It was emphasized there that the importance of packages such as SAP is not due to the total integration of various modules, single-point data entry, data integrity, ad hoc reporting, instant access to information, end-user computing, and so on. The importance of ERP and CRM packages arises primarily from the fact that information is by now the fifth resource (the first four being manpower, materials, money, and time). And, unlike other resources, information is inexhaustible. It can be shared infinitely without any reduction. Thus, if we can use information as a substitute for other resources (which we can; see the following discussion), we can use it many times over without any appreciable further cost.

For instance, Just-in-Time (JIT) inventory permits us to order for just the right kind of material at the right time at the right place. Therefore, it reduces inputs of manpower in ordering, handling, storing, and so on. It also results in reduced materials inventory and, hence, cost of storage mechanisms, cost of locked capital, and so on. The availability of detailed and up-to-the-minute information on, for example, production runs can result in up-to-the-minute information on

■ Production plans for the next run
■ Material requirements for the next run
■ Issue of materials from the main stores for the next run
■ Stock on hand in the stores for the next run
■ Material to be ordered for the next run

It is not difficult to see that this ultimately results in drastically increased throughputs and reduced business cycle times, which is equivalent to improved production or technological processes through the use of improved resources. Traditionally, appreciably higher throughputs and lower production/business cycles were possible only through innovation in technology or production methods or processes. How information provided by CRM systems and ERPs is a resource of an organization can be seen from the analogy with fuel that drives automobiles: information made available by SAP greatly increases the velocity of business processes within the organization. These gains are a class apart from what is achievable with the manual or even fragmented legacy computerized systems. Enterprise-wide JIT (Just-in-Time), and not just the one confined primarily to the production department, is impossible without integrated computerized systems like CRM/ERP packages for correct, current, consistent, and complete information.

It should be specially noted that only a CRM/ERP implemented within an enterprise enables the optimal utilization and efficient conversion of such a seemingly intangible resource as information into a tangible commercial product, which is also a highly perishable resource!

Enterprises that use customer capital as the defining component of the marketing systems benefit because of the following:

■ They address the customer as a whole who uses myriad services and products.
■ They utilize customer interactions to reinforce relationships and attain customer extensions.

- They adjust marketing investment levels as customer relationships move through their dynamic life cycles.
- They organize processes and structures around acquisition, retention, and add-on selling to maximize the profitability of each over the customer life cycle.

1.2.1.5 Increasing Returns and Customer Capitalism

Traditional capitalism encourages managers to focus on short-term rewards that eventually lead to diminishing returns. In contrast, customer capitalism focuses on becoming the customer's preferred choice to ensure an enduring and compounding competitive advantage and sustainable growth, eventually leading to increasing returns, that is, positive, disproportionate gains over time. With customer capitalism, customers *lock on* to a corporation, and such customers become the most effective barrier to competitive entry. However, this *lock in* is very different from the product *lock in* envisaged in the traditional offering-based mass marketing approach. The latter is primarily based more on the product architectures and standards that once established give the customer little or no option and give the corporation quasi-monopolistic powers for as long as that particular technology wave lasts.

Increasing returns are the consequence of a combination of network effects (see note "Metcalfe's Law and Network Effects") and minimal marginal costs. This situation typically occurs when enterprises have very large start-up costs but very low marginal costs; this effect becomes pronounced with incidence of network effects. Network effects is manifested as a change in the benefit, or surplus, which a customer derives from goods when the number of other customers using similar kind of goods changes. The classic example of this case is the use of fax machines, whose value rises rapidly dependent on the number of other people using similar machines.

 Please note that while the positive loops of increasing returns reinforce successes, in reverse, they will also aggravate losses. If an enterprise falters in delivering value to its customers, the *value gap* will get amplified rapidly to pull the enterprise down a descending spiral of ever-decreasing customer values and number of customers.

1.2.1.6 Leveraging the Customer Capital

Each piece of information in the enterprise, including that residing in the company's information systems, has a value. This value is primarily associated with manner in which this piece of information is utilized by the enterprise for remaining competitive, providing good customer service and optimizing e-business operations. If SAP CRM is not to be used as a past-facing system merely for recording and reporting purposes but more as a future-facing handler of strategic information and relationships, implementation of all the *basic components* corresponding to the businesses of the enterprise is essential. As recommended in the last chapter, the organization should consider a *big bang* implementation of SAP CRM, wherein all the base components of SAP CRM (relevant to the enterprise's area of business) are implemented and put in production together. By implementing only certain components of the system, the company cannot hope to reap more significant benefits than those accruing from the traditional systems. A piecemeal approach of progressive implementation should be abandoned because delaying the implementations of all basic components together only delays the benefits of a fully functional SAP CRM and, therefore, incurs opportunity costs.

In analogy with the Metcalfe's Law for networks (see note on "Metcalfe's Law and Network Effects"), the value of customer information can be assessed to be proportional to

$$n^m \times d$$

where

n is the average number of active users

m is the average number of employees involved in any business process from different departments

d is the number of interacting departments involved in the primary business processes of the enterprise

One of the major users of CRM is database marketers whose objective is to automate the process of interacting with the customers to

■ Identify the customers or prospects with high-profit potential using mountains of data about prospective customers and their buying behavior

■ Build and execute campaigns that impact this behavior favorably to the benefit of the enterprise's business

Data mining applications automate the process of searching the mountains of data to find patterns that are good predictors of purchasing behaviors based on analyses of past activity. Data mining uses well-established statistical and machine learning techniques to build models that predict customer behavior.

Table 1.3 lists the various mechanisms that an enterprise can employ to retain, leverage, and enhance its customer capital.

1.2.2 Customer Responsiveness

It comes as a revelation that customers are neither necessarily looking for more products and services nor are they looking for a wider range of choices. Customers simply want solutions to their individual needs—when, where, and how they want it. The goal of a responsive enterprise is the cost-effective delivery of an interactively defined need of a customer.

In the traditional mass marketing, the primary focus is on the offering, and the goal is the sales transaction. It is the offering (whether tangible or intangible) that must be defined, produced, and distributed. All measures of activity, namely, cost, revenue, and profits, are based on the offering. Mass marketing organizations emphasize deterministic planning, for example, the best offering, the best way to produce and deliver the offering, and the best way to inform potential customers about the offering. The *best* method is typically based on the anticipated need of a prototypical customer who represents the needs of the target market. And success depends on how many customers buy the offering. In customized marketing, the focus is on flexibility—the flexibility to obtain the capability and capacity needed to respond quickly to a wide variety of individual customer requests. Customer-responsive activities are used to find the best way to solve the individual

Table 1.3   Loyalty Models

Name	Description
Personal profile/data	Customers are averse to furnish or confirm the same information again. This model involves maintaining and sharing existing customer databases to obviate the need to demand the same information again across related functions or corresponding Call Centers, Service Centers, Websites, etc.
Lethargy	Customers are averse to negotiate the interaction or dialog mechanisms with the enterprise again and prefer to stick to the familiar experiences including searching, assessing, evaluating, configuring, ordering, and paying. Loyalty through lethargy is a very powerful mechanism for loyalty.
Customized service	Customers vote for identified and customized service that creates personalized experience of excellence attributable to the enterprise. The customized service can get configured over time through either user-selected options or a customer profile maintained current.
Making it easier to do business with the enterprise	Customers appreciate informed and nonintrusive assistance while doing business with the enterprise. The information and assistance gets calibrated dynamically suitable to the available customer profile and the current flow of the interaction or dialog.
Personal involvement	In later stages of customer bonding, customers have a great desire to be involved and identify with the specific product design, development, and production support activities or with the brand or even the enterprise as a whole. User groups, vendor-sponsored development communities, sponsored case studies, etc., are manifestations of the customers wanting to share a sense of ownership with the enterprise.
Free services, discounts, and promotional incentives	All customers get reassured with occasional reward for continued relationship with the enterprise—even if, in real terms, these only have a notional value.
Payments	Customers are gratified if they are rewarded, even with small monies or points, for specific actions or activities, be that satisfaction surveys, suggestions on promotional slogans, etc.
Sole supplier	This is akin to attaining the Everest of loyalty whereby customers return again and again despite of numerous other hardships.

customer needs. In customized relationship marketing (or, in short, customized marketing), the emphasis is on delivered solution effectiveness (i.e., how well are the individual problems communicated, diagnosed, and solved) and delivered solution efficiency (how few resources are required to solve the problems).

While mass marketing enterprises try to sell a single product to as many customers as possible, customized marketing enterprises try to sell to a single customer as many products across as many different product lines over as long period of time as possible. CRM Systems like SAP CRM give enterprises the ability to interact *One to One* with individual customers and the ability to produce in response to individual customer requests.

The mass marketing and customized marketing approaches are organized very differently. The mass marketing approach anticipates customer needs and defines solutions before interacting with the customers, while the customized marketing approach involves developing a process that allows interaction with each individual customer One to One to define his or her need and then to customize the delivered solution in response to that need. Each type of marketing requires a different type of organization.

When the inflexibilities are because of natural causes beyond control of the enterprise, competitors will not be able to gain a responsive edge and, hence, competitive advantage. However, to the degree that inflexibilities are institutionally caused by organizational structure, processes, or strategies, the inflexibility is self-inflicted, and the enterprise should definitely be liberated from such inflexibilities to make it customer responsive. True customer centricity is reflected in the enterprise transitioning from providing customers a range of choice offerings to providing solutions to the specific needs of the customers; until the organization becomes customer centric, the emphasis will be on the offering, not on the responsiveness. In the offering-based approach, when the range of offerings is small and demand is relatively stable, enterprises can focus on producing and mass marketing more new offerings and rely on the customer attending to the best of these offerings. As against this, in the customer-responsiveness-based or customized marketing approach, rather than merely proliferating the number of offerings, enterprises focus on meeting individual needs of the customers.

Whereas offering-based enterprises are characterized by *top-down management*, customer-responsive organizations are *bottom-up management* oriented. As the response is guided by prior organizational experience that is embodied in the best-practice guidelines that are readily available to all the frontline workers, the delivery is necessarily effective and efficient. Customer-responsive enterprises are knowledge based rather than plan based. This knowledge base consists of knowing how to divide the envisaged work into tasks, identifying individual delivery units capable of performing it, assigning the work/tasks, and monitoring activities to ensure that the tasks are completed as per agreed requirements. Unless the knowledge is captured, it will only be available to those who have experienced it or learned about it. Because it is modifiable, rather than a plan, the captured knowledge becomes a list of *best practices* to guide responses to requests in the future. Conditional best-practice guidelines specify the processes required for diagnosing needs and developing customized delivery plans. We discuss the development of best practices in Section 1.2.2.1.2 "Best-Practice Guidelines Management".

1. *Advantages of customer responsiveness*: The various advantages of customer responsiveness are
   a. Improving the fit between the customer's need and what the enterprise delivers
   b. Increasing profits through customer retention
   c. Increasing profits by reducing costs
   d. Making the enterprise more change capable
   Responsiveness reduces costs for the providers by reducing capital costs, making planning activities more efficient and effective, and increasing capacity utilization. Section 1.2.2.2.3 "Economics of Customer Responsiveness" looks at several aspects of costs associated with customer responsiveness.
2. *Responsiveness reduces costs*: But can an enterprise be more responsive at reduced cost? Yes! In a career spanning about four decades, Taiichi Ohno spent years fine-tuning the principles for controlling costs that became the foundations of the world famous Toyota Production

System. He surprisingly discovered that not only the best way for increasing revenue but also the best way to reduce cost of automobile production was to make the system more flexible and responsive! This is akin to the situation in the 1960s and 1970s when manufacturing quality and costs were mistakenly believed to be in the opposition to each other; however, by the early 1990s, it was clearly established that not only can an enterprise achieve excellent quality *at reduced costs* but it was also imperative for its success.

Ohno discovered that the best way to reduce cost was also the best way to make the enterprise more responsive: customer-responsive management was the most cost-effective way to solve customer needs. Toyota found that to control costs, they had to *separate* capacity scheduling (capacity management) from the work dispatching (task assignments): the responsiveness was not necessarily limited because of the constraints or inflexibilities or limitations of the infrastructure but primarily because of the inflexible way the deliveries are scheduled and assigned (i.e., coordinated, monitored, and, if delayed, expedited).

3. *Customer responsiveness is activity based*: Customer responsiveness is activity based, where every activity is constituted of four parts:
   a. The first is an event (whether internal, external, regular, or dramatic) that triggers the response.
   b. The second defines the actions or tasks (guided by existing or customized best-practice guidelines) that need to be taken in response to the event.
   c. Third is the assignment (i.e., JIT coordination) of the identified actions to resources with appropriate capability and capacity, in response to the event. Assignment minimizes lead time and thus contributes in enhancing the flexibility.
   d. Lastly, the desired benefits are delivered to the customer.

1.2.2.1 Salient Aspects of Customer Responsiveness

A major part of the following sections has been inspired by the insightful book entitled *Customer-Responsive Management: The Flexible Advantage* authored by Frank W. Davis and Karl B. Manrodt. The literature on enterprise responsiveness is rather limited, but this book is an exception and had a lasting impression on the author in that it ignited an abiding interest into the nature of responsiveness and characteristics of responsive enterprises.

Salient aspects involved with the Customer Relationship Management are as follows.

1.2.2.1.1 Needs Diagnosis Management

This involves activities related to identifying, discovering, or understanding the needs of prospects or newer needs of existing customers. Traditional offering-based or mass marketing organizations typically achieve this through product catalogs, demonstrations, or even product datasheets. However, responsive organizations achieve this through dialog with the customer regarding their operational or design issues problems, inefficiencies, and so on.

1.2.2.1.2 Best-Practice Guidelines Management

Best-practice guidelines management is to response-based enterprises what strategic and tactical planning is to the offering-based or mass marketing enterprises. It is the management of the enterprise's knowledge base by collecting newer needs encountered and solutions proposed and delivered by the frontline workers and disseminating to all frontline workforce on a continual basis. It involves activities like the development of new guidelines when new resources become available, the dynamic modification of existing guidelines when new situations are encountered, and the periodic review of existing guidelines for continuous improvement.

There are two major categories of best-practice guidelines:

1. Needs diagnosis
2. Defining work, identifying resources/capacity, assigning work, and coordinating deliveries

The guideline should identify each task required, the skill needed to perform that task, the timing of the task, the conditions under which the task needs to be performed, and the capacity required to perform the task.

Processes are under continual review to verify the result and assess the delivered solution effectiveness and efficiency of adopting the best-practice guidelines.

1.2.2.1.3 Responsive Task Management

Responsive task management is not unlike project management except that

- Customer requirements are often more similar than different, but never completely identical
- Instead of a single big project, it is a series of smaller projects or tasks
- Lead time is typically shorter

It deals with the prioritized assignment list that is used to determine, plan, assign, and coordinate the work steps composing the deliveries to the individual customers. It also deals with the best-practice guidelines that must be developed to oversee the assigning, tracking, and delivery process.

1.2.2.1.4 Responsive Capacity Management

Responsive capacity management is the process of maximizing capacity utilization to deliver benefits to their customers. It is the process of minimizing unutilized capacity because whereas delivered capacity generates revenue, unutilized capacity creates only additional cost as this wasted capacity cannot be inventoried. As discussed in the following, capacity is scheduled in the short term but sold only in the real term.

The various methods utilized to maintain high utilization are as follows:

- Forecasting needs so that access capacity is not scheduled in the short term—the ideal situation being the matching of capacity scheduling to the capacity utilization.
- Cross-training of employees so that the same capacity can be used for a wider variety of tasks; this is counter to the tendency of specialization in mass production or offering-based enterprises.
- Developing cooperative networks for real-term flexibility; the main driver for this method is the fact that cost of transactions coupled with the cost of interfacing, collaboration, coordination, and communication between enterprises may be lower than the cost of those

transactions being undertaken by a vertically integrated enterprise. Mass production or offering-based enterprises are more amenable to *cooperative partnerships* that are oriented toward long-term, steady-state, and continuous relationships. Typically, a customer will have a limited number of cooperative partnerships because while it ensures the customer a consistent and reliable supply of know-how and offerings, it also ensures a steady business for the provider. However, customer-responsive enterprises, rather than limiting the number of partners, lay more emphasis on developing a large network of providers (each having their own special core competency) to increase the range of capabilities that they can access to meet their customer's needs. Instead of emphasizing steady-state relationships, customer-responsive enterprises focus more on obtaining a greater diversity of capabilities by enabling ready access to a broader network of solution-delivering units (i.e., resources) that are available for assigning on as-needed basis at any instant, at a lower cost, seamlessly, and with minimal friction.

Please also see Section 1.2.2.2.3 "Economics of Customer Responsiveness."

1.2.2.1.5 Resource Interface Management

Interface management is not unlike channel management whose prime objective is to minimize the number of interfaces and to continuously optimize the performance of the existing interfaces in line with the business objectives and strategies of the enterprise. The more diverse are the final customer needs, the broader is the network necessary to provide access to more core competencies (i.e., capabilities); the greater is the variation in capacity needs, the greater is the depth of the network required to ensure the capacity required for each core competency. For enterprises to be flexible, they need access and the ability to integrate, assign, and coordinate the delivered solution at a very low cost. Whereas efficient network interface management enables network members to actually become additional solution-delivering units for the response-based enterprise just as in-house delivery units do, inefficient interface management forces the enterprises to integrate vertically, thus limiting its options for access solely to the capabilities (i.e., core competencies) of its in-house delivery units.

With successful interface management, an enterprise has advantages

- Virtually, all enterprises can become part of the delivery network
- Thus, the enterprise has virtually unlimited capability and capacity at its disposal to serve the needs of its customers
- Thus, the enterprise can focus on meeting the needs of the customer unfettered by the need to find a revenue-generating use of the existing unused in-house capacity

1.2.2.1.6 Customer Service Management

As discussed in Section 1.2.1.1 "From Products to Services to Experiences," products are rapidly being equated as cost of doing business rather than as sales items; they are becoming more in the nature of *containers* or *platforms* for all sorts of upgrades and value-added services. This allows the enterprise to initiate and maintain a long-term relationship with the customer. By this reason, platforms are often sold at cost, or even being given away free, in the expectation of selling even more lucrative services to the customer over the lifetime of the product or, rather, more correctly, the lifetime of the customer!

In these times of rapid product obsolescence and continual onslaught of superior competitors, a sustainable competitive advantage can only be obtained through services, such as

- Tailor-made designs
- Just-in-time logistics
- Installation of the equipment
- Customer training
- Documentation of goods
- Maintenance and spare part service
- Service recovery and complaints management
- Handling of inquiries
- Customer-oriented invoicing
- Pricing below the market standard

In the *servicized* economy, defined by shortening product life cycles and ever-expanding flow of competitive goods and services, it is the customer's attention rather than the resources that is becoming scarce. Giving away products is increasingly being used as a marketing strategy to capture the attention of the potential customers. A growing number of enterprises are giving away their products *for free* to attract customers and then charging them for managing, upgrading, and servicing for uninterrupted availability and usage of the products. Microsoft, after initially missing the Internet wave, invested massively to come up with a reasonably competitive Internet Explorer (IE) Web browser, but decided to give away this web browser *for free* to its customers.

Especially in the case of software companies, the cost of producing and delivering individual product orders is almost zero; hence, if enough number of customers *hook* on to the company's product and if the enterprise can set its product as an industry standard, it can sell upgrades and services at significant margins. The more are the number of customers linked together through an enterprise's program (see note "Metcalfe's Law and Network Effects"), the more are the benefits to each of the participating customer and, consequently, the more valuable are

- The services provided by the enterprise (at much lower cost, because the costs are spread across much larger installed base of customers)
- The attendant long-term relationships with the customer

1.2.2.2 Customer-Responsive Management

The traditional philosophy of management focused on mass production was developed during the twentieth century. The foundation of mass production is based on

- Eli Whitney's concept of interchangeable parts
- Ford's development of the production line
- Frederick W. Taylor's scientific management
- GM and Dupont's cost accounting methods

Mass production management focused on large-scale production and mass marketing of standardized, low-cost products produced for homogenous markets. Customers are researched so that the right product is offered to the marketplace. This approach results in centralized product planning, process planning, production scheduling, and market planning that is separated from the daily operations. When the change is gradual and incremental, the traditional make-and-sell enterprises focus on optimizing the efficiency of execution in terms of the following:

- Predicting or forecasting or projecting the market demand
- Minimizing the cost of making and selling the corresponding offering

In contrast, when the customer-driven change becomes rapid and essentially unpredictable, adaptiveness takes precedence over efficiency: the enterprises need to sense early the need of the customer and respond in real term, individual customer by individual customer. The sense-and-respond enterprise becomes a pool of modular capabilities that can be dynamically configured and reconfigured to respond to the customer's latest requirements. Therefore, in make-and-sell enterprises, the plan comes first, while in the sense-and-respond enterprises, the customer comes first; *make-and-sell enterprises primarily focus on what is common among many customers rather than what is different about individual ones* (see Section 1.2.6.4 "One-to-One Marketing"). The customer commitment rather than the command-and-control structure defines the dynamic interactions between the modular capabilities.

Customer-responsive management (CRM) enables enterprises to be more adaptable to changing conditions and responsive to smaller markets. The responsiveness could be in terms of

1. Timeliness (e.g., a schedule)
2. Time window (i.e., by a specified time range)
3. Priority (e.g., a dynamic dispatch list)

It recognizes that forecasting and planning become more difficult as the marketplace and environment become more turbulent. The detailed planning of work is done at the front line. The purpose of flexible planning is not to plan all the details of the work but to plan the infrastructure that is necessary to enable and facilitate individual-level changes. *CRM* emphasizes taking steps that minimize the time and cost required to recognize and respond to changes. Whereas mass production was based on defining a product and designing the most efficient means of producing large quantities of a product, *CRM* designs flexible processes that could make it easier to respond to changing conditions.

Thus, *CRM* consists of two major relationships: one relationship is with the customers to identify and diagnose needs, and the second relationship is with the network of suppliers who make the delivery. For offering-based enterprises, the former corresponds to the marketing function (e.g., market research, product planning, advertising, sales, and customer service) and the latter corresponds to the operations function (e.g., purchasing, production, supply chain logistics, and human resources). For traditional offering-based enterprises, logistics is generally understood as the process of managing the efficient flow and storage of raw materials, in-process inventory, finished goods, and information for conformance with the customer requirements. But within the *CRM* framework, this logistics concept transforms to the coordination of deliveries that are responsive to individual customer requests using a network of resources and integrated by flexible processes and communications.

As emphasized brilliantly by Frank Davis (see Davis and Manrodt 1996), for achieving responsiveness, the separation of assignment and delivery is critical. It is the frontline worker that interacts with the individual customer to determine individual needs. These individual needs are then used in conjunction with the conditional best-practice guidelines to develop the individual delivery plan. The individual delivery plan, which itemizes each task, schedule, and the responsible person, becomes the prioritized assignment list or Kanban. This list is used to assign each task dynamically to the resource network as also for recording the results.

The offering-based deterministic enterprise uses highly structured systems or channels to develop a plan that includes not only the product design but also the channels that will be used to deliver the product to the customer. When enterprises do not have the flexibility to respond to a wide variety of needs, a different system must be established to meet each type of need. This makes it very expensive to respond to new markets. In contrast, the customer-responsive enterprise tends to build and use networks of resources that it can call upon to respond to a wide range of needs. The customer-responsive enterprise is able to put together a large combination of resources to respond according to initial-condition-determined best-practice guidelines to a wide range of needs.

The role of the responsive enterprise is to develop an infrastructure that facilitates the integration of the provider network into the solution process and the assigning and monitoring of each delivery. When the infrastructure works, the relationship is effective and hassle-free; otherwise, it is frustrating and unresponsive. Similarly, when the infrastructure works, the delivery is efficient and coordination cost is low; otherwise, the delivery is late and ineffective, and special recovery mechanisms such as expediting, inspection, sign-offs, and approvals must be implemented to work around these shortcomings of the infrastructure. These recovery mechanisms unduly increase expense, slow delivery, and make the enterprise inflexible and unresponsive.

Thus, to be able to respond, the enterprise must create an organization infrastructure that includes

■ Best-practice guideline development to maintain a repertoire of delivery practices
■ Resource network development that identifies resources and interfaces and builds relationships to ensure that the resources are available when needed
■ Information infrastructure development that integrates and coordinates individual deliveries

 Surely, the Internet is the classic illustration of a *neural network* on a large scale that displays a *top-down* oversight combined with a *bottom-up* cooperative delivery of digital content.
    It displays characteristic features of

■ Network Effects
■ Small-World Networks (SWNs)
■ Cooperative Patterns

We touch upon these topics briefly in the following sections

1.2.2.2.1 Networks of Resources

The customer-responsive enterprise is not aware of the exact needs of the customer until the customer calls them. Therefore, the enterprise cannot ever be more responsive to its customers than its delivery units are to it. The enterprise's ability to respond is determined by the capability and capacity available for assignment. Consequently, customer-responsive enterprises constantly seek to expand the core competencies, that is, capabilities and capacity for assignment to serve customers. The more capability and capacity that is available, the more customers can be served.

Because responsive enterprises typically deliver benefits to customers in the form of products, information, or even money, an enterprise utilizes a wide range of resources. Resources typically provide functions (or services) such as transport, storage, security, or processing. The range of resources includes

- Transportation network resources like satellites (for communication movement), datacom (for data movement), truck lines (for products movement), and airlines (for people movement)
- Storage resources like computer hard disk storage banks (for e-data or e-content), voice mails (for messages), e-mails (for information messages), warehouses (for products), and hotels (for people)
- Security resources like PINs and e-passports (for computer authentication), vaults or refrigeration units (for products), and escort services or smart cards or identity cards (for people)
- Processing resources like data processing centers (for data and information), fulfillment centers (for products), janitorial services (for facilities), and health-care providers (for people)

Each of these resources would have a core competency. An enterprise cannot be more responsive than their resources enable them to be. To make responsive deliveries, the enterprise must be able to build a network of resources and develop guidelines that allow the integration of the resources into the delivery task and information systems (ISs) that allow the coordination and assigning of work to these resources. The resource units either may be owned by the responsive enterprise or may have a relationship with the responsive enterprise. Notwithstanding the legal nature of these collaborative relationships, which could either be collaborative exclusive partnership or intermittently used network, these resources have to be *always on*, that is, available when needed and have the capability and capacity needed to respond to the responsive enterprise's dynamic assigning and monitoring requirements.

Infrastructure development is not a one-time effort but must evolve continually to allow the organization to stay ahead of competition and keep pace with technology and environmental changes. For instance,

- As new customer needs evolve, the infrastructure must enable these needs to be satisfied
- As new resources become available, the infrastructure integrates the new resource into the delivery process readily
- As new technology becomes available, the infrastructure must allow newer options for communicating, coordinating deliveries, and relating with customers
- As new measurement technique becomes available, the infrastructure must incorporate them to enhance delivery coordination and monitoring

The network of resources achieves two apparently contradictory goals: a greater ability to respond to customer needs and a reduction in the cost of the response.

In fact, in analogy with Sun Microsystems's vision of *Network is Computer*, one can say that *Network is Resource Provider*! (see Kale 2014)

1.2.2.2.2 Business Webs

Don Tapscott introduced the concept of a Business Web (B-Web) as a cluster of businesses coming together particularly over the Internet. B-Webs are the mechanisms for accumulation of digital capital consisting of three parts:

1. *Human capital*: Is the sum of the capabilities of individuals in the enterprise including skills, knowledge, intellect, creativity, and know-how.
2. *Customer capital*: Is the wealth contained in an enterprise's relationships with its customers.
3. *Structural capital*: Is the knowledge embodied in enterprise procedures and processes.

The rise in affiliate marketing and the existence of Internet-based extranets or exchanges are examples of the rise of B-Webs.

MOORE'S LAW

Gordon Moore, one of the Intel founders, observed that computer processor performance for transport, storage, and processing of data doubled roughly every 18 months at constant cost. This law has held true for the last few decades and has potential to hold valid in future as well. The true significance of this law is its indication of the rapidly shrinking footprint of the computing devices.

METCALFE'S LAW AND NETWORK EFFECTS

Robert Metcalfe, the inventor of the Ethernet and founder of 3Com, evaluated that the value of a network increases as the square of the number of users; consequently, additional users are attracted to connect to the network resulting in a virtuous cycle of positive feedback. Considering that the original observation was inspired by telephonic systems that are typically bilateral, the value associated with computer networks that admit multilateralism is manyfold. Thus, for computer networks with n number of nodes allowing conversations of m users simultaneously, the value of the computer network may increase as n^m! This phenomenon has important implications for corporations competing in network markets. While in the traditional economy, value is derived from scarcity, in the network economy, critical mass supercedes scarcity as a source of value. Positive feedback works to the advantage of big networks and to the detriment of smaller networks. Consequently, the bigger networks continue to grow bigger, while the smaller networks are sucked into a vortex of negative feedback and shrink to insignificance. The classic examples of this phenomenon are Microsoft Windows rapid ascendancy to market domination against other alternatives like Apple or UNIX operating systems or the VHS versus Betamax standard battle.

GILDER'S LAW

The technologist George Gilder conjectured that the communication capacity triples every 12 months at constant cost (see Figure 1.6).

POWER LAW AND SMALL-WORLD NETWORKS (SWNs)

The phenomenon of networks is pervasive, and they deeply affect all aspects of human life and relationships. Networks matter because local actions have global consequences, and the relationship between local and global dynamics depends on the network structure. The idea of small worlds is applicable to diverse problems—community of prospects or customers, organizations, national markets, global economy, flying routes, postal services, food chains, electrical power grids, disease propagation, ecosystems, language, or firing of neurons. In 1998, Cornell mathematician Duncan Watts with his advisor, Steve Strogatz, recognized the structural similarity between graph problems describing any collection of dots connected by lines and

- The coordinated lightning of fireflies
- The 1967 idea of sociologist Stanley Milgram that the world's six billion people are all connected by six degrees of separation, that is, the average number of steps needed to get from one selected person to another is six

They showed that when networks of connected dots have a degree of order to their clustering, the degree of separation is correspondingly high, but adding random links shrinks the degree of separation rapidly. Real-world networks are far from being a bunch of nodes randomly linked to each other; instead, a few well-connected hubs keep most of the networks together. They showed that networks operate on the Power Law, the notion that *a few large interactions carry the most action* or *the rich get richer*! This explains why the Internet is dominated by a few highly connected nodes or large hubs such as Yahoo! or Amazon.com as also the dominance of Microsoft Windows on desktops. Similarly, in a separate context, a few individuals with extraordinary ability to make friendships keep the society together.

Thus, networks combine order and randomness to reveal two defining characteristics of the *small worlds networks*: local robustness and global accessibility. Local robustness results from the fact that excepting the hubs, malfunctioning at other smaller nodes does not disrupt or paralyze the network; it continues to function normally. However, paradoxically, the elegance and efficiency of these structures also make them vulnerable to infiltration, failures, sabotage, and, in case of the Internet, virus attacks.

Infosphere

The implications of Moore's Law and Metcalfe's Law lead me to conceive of the concept of *Infosphere* along with the other factors like

- Pervasiveness and convergence of information technology (see Section 1.2.1.2 "Convergence: From Marketplaces to Market Spaces")
- Ubiquity of the Internet (see Chapter 9's note "The Significance of the Internet")
- Application Service Providers (ASPs) (see Chapter 14, Section 14.7 "Applications Outsourcing" and also Kale 2014)

Infosphere is a highly dense network of apparently invisible intelligent computing nodes permeating across the world that could be tapped into dynamically for supplementing existing computing capabilities with additional resources for processing power, Random Access memory (RAM), data storage, peripherals, etc. Infosphere is the expanded concept of Cloud Computing (for "Internet of Things (IoT)" see Vivek Kale 2014).

1.2.2.2.3 Economics of Customer Responsiveness

Unlike the case of mass production enterprise that defines average cost per unit in terms of the constituent fixed and variable costs, customer-responsive enterprise classifies costs into three components, namely,

1. *Fixed capacity costs*: Are incurred to acquire or develop facilities, tools, and skills
2. *Scheduled capacity costs*: Are incurred when the acquired facilities, tools, and skills are scheduled so that they become available to serve customers
3. *Service delivery costs*: Are the costs incurred when the benefits are actually delivered to the individual customer

Consequently,

1. The total capacity costs are the combination of both fixed capacity and scheduled capacity costs
2. Total service delivery costs are the sum of total capacity costs and service delivery costs

While fixed capacity costs remain unchanged even in the long term, scheduled capacity costs are variable costs in the short term, and the service delivery costs are variable costs even in the real term.

For the responsive enterprises, revenues are determined in real time when the organization interacts with the customer. Therefore, for responsive activities, capacity acquisitions, modifications, or abdications are decided on a long-term basis, capacity is scheduled on a short-term basis, and capacity is committed on a real-term (or real time or immediate term) basis. While the capacity acquisition costs are based on the long-term trends analysis, the capacity is usually scheduled on a periodic basis like accounting periods because of the availability of the relevant information on sales, production, costs, revenue, and inventory on which the schedule is based. As against this, the capacity is committed on the basis of real-term operational data available in CRM systems like SAP CRM.

Moreover, the role of inventory changes radically in the process of the enterprise becoming more customer responsive. In the mass production (i.e., mass marketing) approach, inventory greatly simplifies the task of managing an offering-based enterprise because it allows the enterprise to manufacture products and ship finished goods to the marketplace in anticipation of market demand. It is the key for enabling various functions like purchasing, production, distribution, and sales to function independently and also seek optimal performance independently. There is no major emphasis on extensive coordination, planning, and scheduling, as inventory is used to buffer purchasing, planning, and scheduling. In times of market uncertainty and turbulence, inventory

- Desensitizes decision making
- Enables longer lead times
- Reduces flexibility
- Reduces complexity of coordination

Thus, in offering-based enterprise, the local functional efficiencies and strategies are truly at the cost of increased inventory and inventory-carrying costs at the enterprise level. However, in the mass customization (i.e., customized marketing) approach, enterprises seek minimization of inventory because this not only reduces the costs but also enhances the organization's flexibility, that is, the ability to respond to changing conditions. But an increase in flexibility also increases the complexity of coordination; the enterprise has to shift from the deterministic planning and scheduling management approach to the protocol and assignment method of coordination.

> However, inventory could change from a large user of capital (because inventory turns slower than payment terms) to a source of capital for financing retail outlets by dramatically increasing the normal inventory turns to much more rapid inventory churns. An inventory churning 24 times per year generates cash flow fast enough to provide its value in working capital to help finance the building of a new store. One can conceive the concept of *Chart of Inventory* in analogy with *Chart of Accounts* that involves the use of a hierarchy of actual and virtual stores to segregate and aggregate inventory of various types like nature (aging, damaged, returns, rejects, in-transit, etc.) and usage (moving or nonmoving). This has many advantages like independent valuation, stock taking, effective inventory control, and stock analysis. Normal transactions can be performed at either of these storage locations—actual or virtual.

As pointed out by Frank Davis, a customer-responsive enterprise does not have the luxury of inventory to buffer real-term variations and reduce management complexity. Although capacity has to be scheduled in anticipation of customer requests, the *use* of capacity can only be scheduled after receiving such a customer request. If the provider scheduled too much capacity, the excess capacity gets wasted because capacity cannot be preserved in an inventory. But, on the other hand, if inadequate capacity is scheduled, some users are likely to go unserved. As the service delivery costs are typically less than 10% of the total delivery costs explained earlier, the profitability of the enterprise depends on reducing the fixed and scheduled capacity costs and maximizing the percent utilization.

For minimizing wasted capacity, responsive enterprises have to enable more flexible scheduling in the short term and higher utilization in the real term. This can be achieved through the following:

- *Economies of scope*: Approach that allows the provider to increase capacity utilization (e.g., percentage billable hours, load factors, occupancy rates) through cross-training of the workforce.
- *Economies of use*: Approach that seeks to utilize every unit of scheduled capacity to generate revenue to minimize the amount of non-revenue-generating and wasted capacity.
- *Economies of modularity*: Approach that seeks greater flexibility to schedule capacity by developing modules so that less capacity can be scheduled when the demand is expected to be low. The more modular the organizational structure is, the more efficiently the enterprise can respond to variation in expected capacity utilization. One way of increasing modularity is through networking.
- *Economies of networking*: Approach that seeks to allow enterprises the flexibility to focus on the changing customer needs rather than to be burdened with finding a revenue-generating

use for the inflexible resources. Resources can either be acquired or networked: responsive enterprises will typically acquire resources where expected demand is continual and stable, whereas if there is a greater variation in the expected capability and capacity needs, the enterprise will network with resources on as-needed basis. Acquired resources become fixed capacity costs, whereas networked resources become variable service delivery costs because they are paid on a per-use basis. It may be more efficient to have the resource in-house on a per-hour basis, but on a per-use basis, it is more efficient to network for the resources. Thus, the network approach does not only enhances the flexibility to respond to the customer needs, but it also makes this possible at a much lower cost!

The purpose of a network is to provide the enterprise with the range of capabilities and capacities it needs to serve its customers' diverse needs while at the same time maintaining the cost of the resource as a service delivery cost (which is a variable cost in the real term) rather than as a capacity cost (which is a fixed cost in the real term).

1.2.2.3 Activity-Based Customer Responsiveness

The customer responsiveness of an enterprise is really dependent on the corresponding business processes or activities. As explained in Section 1.2.2.2 earlier, in *CRM*, the focus is on flexibility—the flexibility to obtain the capability and capacity needed to respond to a wide variety of individual customer requests. Customer-responsive activities are used to find the best way to solve the individual customer needs. In customer-responsive activities, the emphasis is on delivered solution effectiveness (i.e., how well are the individual problems communicated, diagnosed, and solved) and delivered solution efficiency (how few resources are required to solve the problems).

Enterprises that deploy customer-responsive activities have the following objectives:

■ Building relationships so that customers become *conditioned* to contact the enterprise first whenever they have a need
■ Establishing the enterprise to provide effective diagnoses and response whenever customers make such a contact with the enterprise
■ Creating the capability and processes to enable customer-facing members to cultivate deep and long-term relationships with the customers and cost-effectively coordinate each individual delivery of benefits

Traditional mass marketing or mass production approach considered a process to be a way to produce a product; it focuses on limitations (e.g., setup time, resource availability, capability of the existing workforce) and develops the most efficient process that can function within the constraints. The focus is on coping with internal limitations (often self-inflicted) instead of becoming more responsive to customers and the changing business climate. The emphasis is on control rather than performance. As against this, mass customization obtains its flexibility by viewing the process as a way of converting resources into products so that a single process can be used to produce many different products. The balance of control and power has shifted from producers to the customers. Mass customization develops processes to minimize or eliminate limitations (e.g., reduce setup time, locate alternative resources, expand capabilities of current workforce, develop a network of resources). Customer-responsiveness management develops numerous best-practice guidelines to guide frontline workers as they interact with customers to plan deliveries and enable them to modify them, if necessary, to improve the customer fit.

Therefore, for an enterprise to be totally flexible in responding to individual customers, the enterprise must develop three things:

1. Process(es) for interacting with individual customers and defining their individual needs
2. Conditional best-practice guidelines for defining how the organization will respond to various types of customer requests
3. A dynamic assigning system that allows Just-in-Time (JIT) assignment of work for delivery to resources with appropriate capability and capacity

1.2.2.3.1 Activity-Based Costing (ABC)

ABC is a way of linking an enterprise's market positioning to its internal cost structure, that is, capability. The basic premise is that activities, which are realized via the processes, consume resources and convert them into products and services that are usable by the customers. Thus, costs are the consequence of resource decisions and income the consequence of the business processes that deliver value to the customers. In other words, the requirement is to improve resourcing decisions as a means of managing costs and to improve processes as the means of improving business effectiveness leading to improved customer loyalty and, therefore, revenue.

The ABC data are useful as a source to support

- Profitability management, such as costing and profitability analysis, customer and product mix decisions, and support for marketing decisions
- Revenue and performance management, such as resource to volume and service-level changes, activity budgeting, and cost driver analysis

The principle of ABC is based on knowledge of activities, the reason of their existence, and the factors that drive them. The BPM effort helps in identifying a list of cost drivers that are allocated to the various activities. These could include

- Volume of materials used, labor hours consumed, and parts produced
- Number of new parts, new suppliers, and new prototypes
- Number of customers, orders raised, and invoices sent
- Number of design modifications and customer warranty claims

The database of activities can then be aggregated into *pools* of activities that have common cost drivers. By assigning such pools of activities to *objects* (such as products, distribution channels, customer groups), a proper allocation of product and customer costs is then derived.

To build up activity-based product costs, the total for any one product (or a group) would be the sum of

$$\sum_{l=1}^{M}\{\text{Activity-based product costs}\}_l = \sum_{l=1}^{M}\left\{\begin{array}{l}\text{Direct material and labor +}\\[4pt]\text{volume-dependent overheads +}\\[4pt]\text{variable cost driver-dependent overheads}\end{array}\right\}_l$$

Similarly, to build up activity-based customer costs, the total for a customer (or a group) would be the sum of

$$\sum_{l=1}^{M}\left\{\text{Activity-based customer costs}\right\}_{l} = \sum_{l=1}^{M}\left\{\begin{array}{l}\text{Activity-based product costs} + \\[6pt] \text{volume-dependent customer costs (e.g.,} \\[6pt] \text{packaging materials or cost of delivery)} + \\[6pt] \text{variable cost driver-dependent overheads}\end{array}\right\}_{l}$$

ABC provides the basis to understand product and customer profitability and allows the management to make decisions both on positioning and capability—the twin pillars of BPM. The understanding of product and customer costs that comes from using ABC provides its real value when the revenue resulting from the total activity within a business area is related to the costs of achieving that revenue.

It is usually possible to trace revenue to customers only if the enterprise operates a billing system requiring customer details or if there is in place a membership scheme like a store card or loyalty program. Costs vary from customer to customer on account of

- *Customer acquisition costs*: Sales calls and visits, free samples, engineering advice, and so on
- *Terms of trade or transaction*: Price discounts, advertising and promotion support, extended invoice due dates, and so on
- *Customer service costs*: Handling queries, claims and complaints, demands on sales person and contact center, and so on
- *Working capital costs*: Cost of carrying inventory for the customer, cost of credit, and so on

If an enterprise wants to assess which of its customers are profitable, it has to be able to trace costs as well as revenues to the customers (see Chapter 15, Section 15.7 "Customer-Centric Activity-Based Revenue Accounting (ABRA)"). In Chapter 15, Section 15.3 "Economic Value Added," we look at the EVA concept for assessing performance of responsive enterprises.

1.2.2.3.2 Time-Driven Activity-Based Costing (TDABC)

The conventional ABC systems had many drawbacks in that they were expensive to build, complex to sustain, and difficult to modify. Their reliability was highly suspect as the cost assignments were based on individuals' subjective estimates of the percentage of time spent on various activities. It also made unrealistic assumptions like

- Identified activities (e.g., processing customer's orders or inquiries) take about the same amount of time without any variations for particular circumstances
- Resources work at full capacity without discounting for idle or unused time

Moreover, implementing an ABC system for realistic enterprise scenarios (a few hundred activities, few hundred thousand cost objects, and time duration of a couple of years) quickly ended up confronting computational challenges of gargantuan proportions requiring huge computational resources that were beyond the capabilities of normal enterprises. Because of the subjectivity, time-consuming surveying, and data processing costs of ABC systems, many enterprises either abandoned ABC entirely or localized it in isolated units or ceased updating their systems, which left them with out-of-date and highly inaccurate estimates of the business process, product, and customer costs.

Time-driven activity-based costing (TDABC) gives enterprises an elegant and practical option for determining the cost and capacity utilization of their processes and the profitability of orders, products, and customers. Based on this accurate and timely information, enterprises can prioritize for business process improvements, rationalize their offering variety and mix, price customer orders, and manage customer relationships.

TDABC avoids the costly, time-consuming, error-prone, and subjective activity surveying task of the conventional ABC by skipping the activity definition stage and, therefore, the very need to estimate allocations of the departments' costs to the multiple activities performed by the department (Robert Kaplan and Steven Anderson).

TDABC defines activity costs with only two parameters:

1. Capacity cost rate for the department executing the activity or transaction
2. Capacity usage time by each activity or transaction processed in the department

Thus,

$$\text{Activity-based cost} = \text{Capacity cost rate} * \text{Capacity usage time}$$

where

$$\text{Capacity cost rate} = \frac{\text{Cost of capacity supplied}}{\text{Practical capacity of resources supplied}}$$

and

Cost of capacity supplied is the total cost of the department executing the activity or transaction

Practical capacity of resources supplied is the actual time employees, machines, and equipments perform productive work

Capacity usage time is observed or estimated time for performing the activity or transaction

Both of these parameters can be estimated and validated easily and objectively. These estimates are not required to be precise; a rough accuracy is adequate. The cost of capacity includes the cost of all the resources like personnel, supervision, equipment, and maintenance and technology that are supplied to this department or business process. However, the practical capacity of resources supplied is usually lower as compared to the rated capacity because it excludes the cost of unused resources on account of scheduled breaks, training, meetings, setting time, maintenance, and so on.

Table 1.4 compares the conventional activity-based costing (ABC) and time-driven activity-based costing (TDABC).

TDABC does not require the simplifying assumption, unlike that for the conventional ABC, which all customer orders or transactions are the same and require the same amount of time for the processing. TDABC is not only more accurate but also granular enough to capture the variety and complexity of actual operations. For example, it allows time estimates to vary on the basis of particular requirements of individual customers or orders such as manual or automated orders, orders for fragile or hazardous goods, expedited orders, international orders, or orders from a new

Table 1.4 Conventional ABC versus Time-Driven ABC

Conventional Activity-Based Costing	Time-Driven Activity-Based Costing
Tedious, costly, and time consuming to build a model that is error prone, difficult to validate, and localized model.	Easier, inexpensive, and faster to build an accurate and enterprise-wide model
Drives cost first to the activities performed by a department and then assigns the activity costs down to orders, products, and customers on the basis of subjective estimates (based on interviewing and surveying process) of the quantity of departmental resources consumed by various activities.	Drives costs directly to the transactions or orders using specific characteristics of particular business processes, products, and customers
Complexity and variations are incorporated by adding more activities to the model increasing its complexity and subjectivity, resulting in lower accuracy, and creates an exploding demand for estimates data, storage, and processing capabilities.	Incorporates complexity and variations that add accuracy at little additional cost and effort without creating and exploding demand for estimates data, storage, and processing capabilities
Calculates cost driver rates by taking into account the full-rated capacity of resources without discounting for idle or unused resources.	Calculates cost driver rates by taking into account only the practical capacity of resources supplied by discounting for idle or unused resources, rather than the full-rated capacity of the resources
As most of the data are estimates furnished by employees in respective areas, it has to be fed separately into systems for further processing; data being localized, this model cannot provide integrated view of enterprise-wide profitability opportunities.	Integrates well with order and transaction-specific data already available from ERP/CRMs like SAP CRM, thus providing integrated view of enterprise-wide profitability opportunities
Cannot be easily updated to accommodate changing or anticipated circumstances.	Can be easily updated by simply estimating the unit times required or by adding additional terms in the time equation for each changed or anticipated activity
Being based primarily on users' insights and conjectures, cannot provide visibility into process efficiencies; since it ignores idle or unused capacity, capacity utilization is at 100% by definition.	Provides transparent visibility to process efficiencies and capacity utilization
Being already based primarily on users' insight and conjectures, cannot guide user with identifying the root cause of problems.	Furnishes granular information to assist users with identifying the root cause of problems

(*Continued*)

Table 1.4 (*Continued*)   Conventional ABC versus Time-Driven ABC

Conventional Activity-Based Costing	Time-Driven Activity-Based Costing
Not a universal model; cannot be applied to other companies even within the same industries.	Can easily be applied to other companies in the same or even industries with similar business processes; hence, useful in M&A
Being based primarily on users' insights and conjectures cannot act as a correct or consistent basis for initiatives like business process re-engineering, benchmarking, lean management, and enterprise performance management.	Potentially usable in initiatives like business process re-engineering, benchmarking, lean management, enterprise performance management, balance scorecard, and supply chain management

customer without an existing credit record. It achieves this through the simple mechanism of altering the unit time estimates or adding extra terms to the departmental time equation on the basis of the order's activity characteristics. Thus, TDABC can readily incorporate many more variations and complexities (in business process efficiencies, product volume and mix, customer order patterns, and channel mix), which adds accuracy at little additional cost and effort and with fewer number of equations compared (i.e., without creating an exploding demand for estimates data, storage, or processing capabilities) than the conventional ABC. TDABC models expand only linearly with variation and complexity by merely adding terms in the time equation, but a department is still modeled as one process with one-time equation.

Consequently, the expressions for the total costs presented in the previous section get modified to

$$\sum_{l=1}^{M}\{\text{Activity-based product costs}\}_l = \left\{(\text{capacity cost rate})*\left(\sum_{l=1}^{M}\text{capacity usage time}\right)\right\}_l$$

and

$$\sum_{l=1}^{M}\{\text{Activity-based customer costs}\}_l = \left\{(\text{capacity cost rate})*\left(\sum_{l=1}^{M}\text{capacity usage time}\right)\right\}_l$$

 SIGNIFICANCE OF TIME-DRIVEN ACTIVITY-BASED COSTING (TDABC)

TDABC plays an increasingly significant role in strategy and operations of an enterprise because of reasons like the following:

1. Time is a decisive factor in all efforts for process improvements, business process re-engineering (BPR), enterprise performance management (EPM), balanced scorecard (BSC), and so on, because of the criticality of wait times, lead times, cycle times,

handover processes across department boundaries, etc. By contributing through increased accuracy at dramatically reduced complexity, efforts, resources, costs, etc., TDABC plays a determining role in enabling all such exercises.

2. Along the critical path of departmental business processes, any drastic imbalances in the capacity usage times of the various processes or subprocesses will highlight the potential for dramatic improvements in terms of complexity, efforts, resources, materials, technology, costs, and so on and will become obvious candidates for detailed scrutiny. This will usually result either in a BPR initiative or even in restructuring or reconfiguration of the department(s).

3. Based on the analysis of capacity cost rate, TDABC plays a crucial role in deciding the boundaries of an enterprise, that is, in bifurcation of core activities (that get executed in-house) from noncore activities (that can get outsourced). TDABC is critical for addressing the issues of dramatically reduced response times, turnaround times, high throughputs, increased accuracy, etc. Hence, the reason that all customer-facing processes like call centers or contact centers, customer service or customer response desks, and help desks is usually outsourced.

The TDABC model simulates the actual business processes deployed across the enterprise. In addition to addressing the improvement of inefficient processes and transforming nonprofitable products and customers, an enterprise can also use TDABC to tackle the issue of excess capacity revealed by the application of this model. An enterprise can use the TDABC model as the core of its budgeting process to link its strategic plan and sales and production forecasts to the specific demands for capacity required to implement the plan and realize the forecast. Thus, TDABC can assist in deciding on the capacity the company needs to provision in the future.

1.2.2.3.3 Responsive Activity Pricing

For the sake of completeness, we will touch briefly on the issues related to the pricing of responsive activities for BPR.

Some of the relevant characteristics of customer-responsive activities are as follows:

- There is no standardized product for which there is a market price. As the delivered solution is customized to each individual customer's need, the value of the delivered solution is determined by how well the solution solves the customer's need and must be priced separately.
- There are no products that are tradable; delivery services are not tradable. Therefore, there is no market price for the delivery service.
- There are no products to inventory, only capacity that continuously perishes if it is not utilized to deliver benefits.
- Commitments to the customers are made on the real-time basis.

Thus, the emphasis must be on pricing in the immediate run to maximize the yield that can be obtained from the capacity scheduled in the short run, that is, minimizing wasted capacity (or maximize capacity utilization) and maximizing the customer value of capacity. The objective must be not only to collectively cover the fixed capacity costs but also to profit through contributions from customers, or in other words, the objective is to maximize contribution to fixed capacity and to profit from each sale. The price will range between the customer value at the upper limit and the larger of the cost of delivery or the competitor's price at the lower limit.

However, the final price is determined by the customer's perception of a reasonable price in light of the corresponding hassles (to identify the right solution) and the risks (see Section 1.2.6 "Customer Relationships"). Evidently, the customer will pay a premium for response commitments like guaranteed response, time of day, lead time, and response level.

The frontline worker can make the pricing decision based on information like customer value, cost of delivery, competitor's charges, and alternative use of capacity.

1.2.3 Compelling Customer Experiences

For an enterprise, to get the positive reinforcing loops that produce the increasing returns of customer capitalism depends on its ability to link benefits and deliver a totally integrated experience to its customers over time. The pervasiveness and convergence of information technology is transforming the traditional feature-benefit-oriented marketing to experiential marketing. As recognized by B. Joseph Pine II and James Gilmore, experiences have emerged as the latest step in the *progression of economic value*. However, the experience economy envisaged by them is only another manifestation of the overarching customer economy whereby customers are now demanding not only the quality of the enterprise solutions and services but also the quality of the experience of *using* these solutions and services. While solutions and services are external to the customer, experiences are inherently individualistic, involving and engaging the customer's attention directly. The competitive edge in the future would lie in staging engaging, compelling, and memorable experiences. Thus, the same product delivered with the same portfolio of surround services may still be perceived to generate varying levels of value depending on the final rendering or performance for individual customers.

Customer-responsive enterprises recognize that customers may not be aware of what they really need unless they experience it and, hence, realize the importance of anticipating rather than reacting to expressed need after it is too late.

1.2.3.1 Personalization

Relationships evolve and grow through trust, responsibility, and the mutually beneficial exchange of value. Personalization is a combination of technology and prior information to tailor customer interactions with the enterprise. Using information previously obtained or provided in real time about these and other customers, the conversation between the parties is altered dynamically to fit the customers' interests, preferences, and needs so that the interaction/transaction locates the best suited product or service with minimal expenditure of time and cost. Deliveries are personalized to suit the evolving, unique, and multiple needs of individuals, as opposed to only providing the standard offering in that range that the company makes or has in stock at that moment of time. This strengthens the bonding that enables the corporation to be proactive and the deliveries to be more customized—this is what gets customers to *lock in* (see Section 1.2.1.5 "Increasing Returns and Customer Capitalism").

Delivering content, products or services, and pricing specific to a unique customer's interests and needs is based on collection of information about individual customer preferences, interests, and buying behavior by employing the following techniques:

- Customer profiling aggregates data from allied Websites based on the identification (ID) made available when the customer arrives on an event venue or a Website.
- Collective filtering involves utilizing the prior experiences of a customer or similar customers to devise responses to individual customers.

Advantages of personalization are as follows:

- Higher degrees of customer service to the customer by anticipating their needs delivering content, products, services, or pricing information that meets their needs
- Improving the efficiency of the interaction and, thus, enhancing the likelihood of a purchase being made during the current visit
- Increasing the level of knowledge about customers and understanding why and how they prefer to do business with your organization
- Establishing a relationship that encourages customer relationship and enhanced customer
- Improving the performance with customer site by using tracking to provide insight into factors that have salutary effect on the performance of the application

1.2.4 Customer Loyalty

Traditionally, companies have focused on winning customers, rather than retaining them. The conventional wisdom was that a dominating market share typically translated into production economies of scale and the ability to become a low-cost producer. The goal was to continually add customers to replace those customers that defected to the competitors and also to grow the market share.

However, lately, financial analysis of the cost of customer acquisition versus the cost of retention has shown that, for most organizations where the cost of acquisition is high, keeping customers can be a more profitable strategy. It is estimated that it can cost four to seven times more to replace a current customer than it does to retain one. On the average, US companies lose half of their customers every 5 years. It is easier to get existing customers to try new capabilities than to engage and acquire new ones. The cost of contacting existing customers, researching their needs, and getting them to begin using new services is minimal compared with either acquiring new customers. It is easy to see how effective this approach of *customer loyalty* can be if we recognize that the revenue accruing from customers follows the Pareto's Law: 20% of the customer base accounts for 80% of the revenues and more than 110% of the profits generated by a company. A study published in *Harvard Business Review* by Reichheld and Sasser concluded that some companies could boost profits by almost 100% by retaining just 5% more of their customers. Mass unfocused marketing is a thing of the past. As stated earlier, as much as 80% of the sales process may be controlled by specific knowledge of a customer's business. As the marketing spend needs to show a higher return on investment, a longer-term relationship becomes essential.

The relative costs for acquiring, retaining, and winning back a lost customer are as follows:

Cost of retaining a current customer	1×
Cost of acquiring a new customer	5× to 10×
Cost of winning back lost customer	3× to 8×

Customized Relationship Marketing recommends that companies identify their most valuable customers (MVCs) and then have a close relationship with them. Many companies may use ABC analysis (e.g., identify the top 20% of customers who account for 80% of sales) to identify their MVCs. However, this maybe a misguided effort because, this being a lag measure, this would lead to concentration of efforts on customers, who although are currently contributing to the profitability of the company may not necessarily have a long-term profit potential. The best way of assessing the long-term profit potential of customers is through their Lifetime Value (LTV), which we discuss in Section 1.2.7.2 "Customer Lifetime Value."

While most companies measure some form of customer satisfaction, that measure does not determine customer loyalty: reasonably satisfied customers often defect to the competition. Customer loyalty is different from customer satisfaction per se. For instance, higher levels of customer satisfaction do not necessarily translate into repeat purchases and, therefore, increased sales and profits. A related problem is that even enterprises such as department stores, which are critically dependent on access to data on *loyalty schemes*, may possibly be using only about 2% of the data to which they have access to. One of the primary reasons for this is the sheer volume of data that is being captured inside these organizations. For instance, a regular shopper may buy 50–100 items during a monthly visit. Many of these stores have 10–20 checkout points operating at any moment in time. These can process on an average about 12 customers an hour for 10 h a day. So, each and every day, they are open, and they are gathering between 60,000 and 240,000 data points per store. Even for a midsized supermarket chain with about 200 stores, working 7 days a week, this would result in something like 65–340 million data points per working week!

Table 1.5 compares the traditional customer satisfaction-oriented approach with that of the value orientation of relationship marketing.

Customer loyalty is characterized by repeat purchases and a willingness to continue the relationship. Loyal customers

- Stay longer
- Cost less to service
- Buy more
- Provide higher margins
- Purchase across product lines
- Demonstrate immunity to the lure of competition
- Demonstrate less price sensitivity

There are various ways to represent progress up the ladder of customer loyalty. Customer Pyramid is one such approach that assists in planning for enhanced relationship with the company's prospects and customers and is also helpful in visualizing the progress toward higher-value relationships. Figure 1.7 presents the Customer Pyramid consisting of the following:

1. *Top* that are the top 1% revenue customers
2. *Big* that are the next 4% revenue customers
3. *Medium* that are the next 15% revenue customers
4. *Small* that are the next 70% revenue customers
5. *Inactive* that are the remaining 10% revenue customers

Table 1.5   Customer Satisfaction Orientation of Traditional Mass Marketing versus Value Orientation of Customized Relationship Marketing

Traditional Mass Marketing's Customer Satisfaction Orientation	Customized Relationship Marketing's Customer Value Orientation
Focuses on the product—emphasizes the firm's offering or tactical solution.	Focuses on the customer/product interaction—emphasizes fundamental needs of customer
Emphasizes product attributes and features.	Considers all aspects of the customer/product interaction, viz., attributes, values, and consequences
This is inherently more short term and unstable, leads to incremental or marginal product/service change and improvement, and results in historical orientation.	Is inherently more long term and stable, leads to innovation and radical improvements, and has a future orientation
Typically fails to measure trade-offs that determine customer value.	Measures the trade-offs that determine customer value
Often difficult to assess in the absence of consequence-level information.	Helpful to assess because of available interaction-level information and actionability

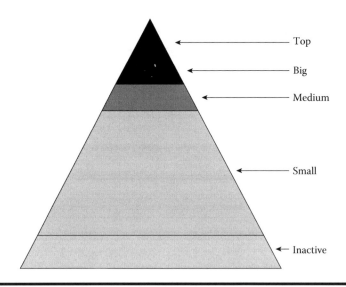

Figure 1.7   Customer Pyramid.

The objective of enhanced customer loyalty then translates into the movement of customers in, up, and out of this pyramid. It helps in getting new customers into the pyramid, getting a larger share of the business of the existing customers, and prevents losing those who are most profitable. A 2% upward migration in the customer pyramid can mean 10% more revenues and 50% more profit. Hence, the reason that CRM initiatives that are targeted at getting, growing, and keeping valuable customers resulting in revenue and profit increases represent very high returns on the company's CRM investments.

1.2.5 Customer Relationships

In today's world of decreasing margins, increasing competition, and ever-changing business environment, corporate success depends on an enterprise's ability to build and maintain loyal and valued customer relationships.

In a market where loyalty has plummeted and the cost of acquiring new customers is prohibitive, companies have turned to their current customers in an attempt to retain and maximize the business potential from them.

The value of relationship can be expressed as follows:

$$\text{Value of Relationship} = \text{future value} \sum_{I=1}^{M} \left(\text{expected benefits}_I - \text{cost of obtaining the benefits}_I \right)$$

where

Expected benefits = *economic cost* + *hassle* + *risk*

Cost of obtaining the benefits = solution value = (customer value × customer *fit*)

economic cost is typically the cost of delivered solution

hassle includes all noneconomic costs, such as effort required to place orders and locate potential providers

risk includes all of the uncertainties about the delivered solution and the cost of protecting against risk such as insurance, inspections, and contracting

fit is delivered solution effectiveness of the customized individual deliveries

The customer-responsive enterprise adds value for the customer even by eliminating the hassle required to research the product and to learn how to use it. When relationships exist uninterruptedly for extended periods of time, they improve need diagnosis and delivered solution effectiveness as well as establish procedures that minimize the hassle of communicating needs and responses.

1.2.5.1 Why Cultivate Customer Relationship?

The relationship-oriented organization sees the customer not as a single sale but as a long-term relationship in which the value of future solutions will always be greater than the value of any existing transactions. Relationships not only define and determine expectations but also minimize transaction costs. Good relationships obtain substantial outcomes with a minimum of effort (i.e., cost and hassle). When relationships are positive, solutions are more effective, and the effort expended for making these solutions also gets reduced (e.g., the hassles, risks, or transactions).

Such a relationship results in several benefits because of the following:

1. The parties understand and trust each other:
   a. Parties have shared values.
   b. Have confidence in each other.
   c. Rely on each other.
   d. Communicate clearly.
   e. Work easier.

2. The parties are more committed and responsive:
   a. The parties are willing to pay premium for the mutual commitment.
   b. The parties are mutually persuasive rather than coercive.
   c. The parties resolve delivered solution errors or other differences amicably.
3. The parties are predictable to each other.
4. It not only reduces the time to diagnose the needs of the customer but also reduces diagnosis errors.
5. The parties develop the solutions jointly.
6. The parties integrate schedules mutually.

Relationships based purely on contracts may not be long lasting because no contract can be comprehensive enough to cover all possible future eventualities. The purpose of a contract is primarily to eliminate uncertainties regarding delivered solution commitments in terms of scope, functionality, schedule, costs, etc. Consequently, especially in these times of market change and turbulence, contracts tend to restrict responsiveness of the relationships and, hence, eventually the responsiveness of the respective organizations.

Customer relationships are important because it establishes customer expectations. When expectations are realistically high, customers call to seek solutions for their needs. Once the customer does call, the provider needs to respond and reassure the customer. Customers empower people and organizations they trust. Each time their needs are met, the customer's trust is increased. Even if the delivered solution is below expectations, trust levels get restored if the provider accepts responsibility for the problems and makes a good recovery. Few managers realize that more than 80% of customers return if their complaints are resolved quickly.

1.2.5.2 Customer Interaction Channels

To strengthen customer relationships, companies draw on and integrate information from a wide range of resources to develop insights into customer wants, needs, and values. These sources may include direct contacts, customer information systems, sales reports, call center data, market surveys, focus groups, billing data, and demographic studies. This may also include prior records and analysis of interactions of the customer with the enterprise. The customer may interact with different units of the business through different channels, but the enterprise must have a coordinated, consistent, and complete picture of the customer available throughout the enterprise. All these impart a greater degree of stability, continuity, and predictability to the customer base, which eases the planning and operations all along the supply chain.

Customers are demanding more access and interaction points with their suppliers. In addition to getting more information from the companies with which they do business, customers are demanding more ways of interacting with those companies—including phone, fax, e-mail, Web, mail, and on-site. Most companies practicing CRM set up call centers, which are able to provide customized services to individual customers. This further enhances the enterprise's organizational memory about the customers' interactions with the company. While these interactions are momentary and could be across many interaction channels, the organizational memory about these interactions (and, therefore, the customer) can be made persistent by incorporating them within the growing customer knowledge base.

Accessibility creates responsiveness. In terms of sales, responsiveness depends upon how easy it is for the prospect or the customer to reach the company through multiple modes of communication and how fast the enterprise can respond. On the other hand, responsiveness in service also depends upon the speed of reply and action (which in turn is dependent upon the speed of executing the corresponding business processes). More than the product itself, many a times, it is the degree of responsive support and service received by a customer that decides between a loyal customer and a lost customer.

1.2.5.2.1 Internet: The Web of Relationships

The Web is a key factor in the emergence of CRM as an important technology. The emergence of Web, like only printing and telegraph earlier, has caused a fundamental change in the ease with which people communicate with each other. The Web has enhanced by a quantum measure, the ability of much more people to produce information and disseminate it to a much larger audience and that too at much lesser costs, much more easily. In some cases, the Web simply offers a new and better way to perform existing services, such as checking an account balance. But other Web applications offer novel products and services that are possible only through Web technology. Customer self-service is the best example of the Web's enablement of customer relationships. It is estimated that a typical banking transaction at a local branch costs about 50% by telephone, 30% at an ATM, and only 1% on the web! (See Chapter 9's note "Significance of the Internet")

1.2.5.2.2 Customer Channel Integration

Once we have a proliferation of channels, the objective is to make the sales and marketing as efficient and effective as possible while also delivering rapid growth, reduced sales expenses, and seamless services. Figure 1.8 illustrates how the strategy of channel integration

	Engage	Transaction	Fulfill	Service	
Face to face			●	●	$400
Partners				●	$250
Call center		●		●	$40
Electronic	●	●		●	$1

	Transaction costs ($)
In-branch teller	3.00
ATM	0.80
Telephone	0.60
PC banking	0.50
Internet banking	0.05

Figure 1.8   Channel costs and channel integration.

can be effective in reducing the costs while also providing the complete functional coverage demanded by the customers.

1.2.5.3 360-Degree View of Customer

In the customer-centric approach, the goal is to provide personal service—recreating the individual attention, flexibility, and understanding that the best neighborhood stores have always provided to their most valued customers—on a mass scale. Meeting this goal involves solving the *many-to-many* problem, that is, many people within different departments of the enterprise interacting with many different customers. None of the information on interactions is shared across these different departments, leaving all employees involved with only partial information. Each employee has at the most only a fragmentary view of the customer resulting in possibly below-par service, inappropriate product offering and pricing, and ineffective branding. To address this effectively and inefficiently, each of the company's representatives who interacts with the customer needs to have a clear and complete picture of that customer's activity. This holistic picture is what is termed as the *360-degree view.*

Achieving a 360-degree View of the customer is critical to

- Interact with a customer in a fully informed way
- Assess the customer's potential value correctly
- Determine the programs that could realize this potential value from each customer

The key is to integrate in a single environment the related data that come from all points of interaction with the customer. This can be achieved effectively by a CRM system like SAP CRM (see Chapter 2 "Customer Relationship Management (CRM) Systems") that will give each employee at each customer touch point a *360-degree view of Customer.* SAP NetWeaver, which is a critical enabler of enterprise-wide integration of diverse applications across various products and divisions, affords the enterprise a 360-degree view of its customer relationships across multiple channels of interaction. It enables every customer to perceive the enterprise as a whole and also expect to be recognized and valued by the enterprise as a whole. By tracking and managing interactions with individual customers and making the customer history available across the enterprise, such a system provides companies with the data they need to improve relationship across the board.

1.2.5.4 One-to-One Marketing

In traditional mass marketing approach, companies use demographic segments—segments based on standard demographic measures, like age, income, geography, gender, and marital status—to divide up their customer base and define marketing program. While this is a step in the direction of recognizing the fact that not all customers are the same, this does not address the problem adequately. The problem is that demographic segments tend to be very large or coarsely grained because of which major differences among individual members of such segments, and the corresponding marketing opportunities, are overlooked. This is also the primary reason that standard response rates for direct marketing, such as direct mail, are only about 2%.

Don Peppers and Martha Rogers introduced the notion of one-to-one marketing in their hit book, *The One to One Future* (1997). This advocates the move toward more fine-grained segments, with the ultimate goal of reaching the segment of *one.* One-to-one marketing treats each customer as an individual, based on a holistic view, with consistent actions across all touch points and to think in terms of wallet share of each customer rather than that of market share.

1.2.5.5 Permission Marketing

It is estimated that, by 2004, e-business marketers will take advantage of the e-mail channel by sending more than 200 billion e-mails to reach customers, increase their brand visibility, and jump-start sales. This is primarily because e-mail marketing has been assessed to achieve purchase rates as high as four times those achievable using the traditional direct mail methods. But with the increasing use of the Internet and other digital channels as vehicles for marketing or selling, the need to manage customer data more effectively in line with government rulings has become very important (see Chapter 14, Section 14.6 "Privacy and Security").

The Distance Selling Directive implemented from June 4, 2000, requires the following:

- The consumer to be provided with information in a clear and comprehensible manner and in good time before concluding any distance contract.
- The consumer has the right to cancel a distance contract within a specified *cooling off* period.
- The consumer cannot be targeted for unsolicited e-mails, faxes, and automatic calling systems for distance selling purposes, unless the consumer has consented to be contacted by the vendor enterprise in that way.

Permission marketing is an approach to selling goods and services in which a prospect explicitly agrees in advance to receive marketing information. Conceived by Seth Godin, Yahoo!'s Internet marketing pioneer, permission-based marketing seeks to build trust and involve the customers by putting them in control of asking the enterprise to keep them informed on information and offers that they are of specific interest to them. The objective is to gain permission from customers to keep them informed by e-mail, SMS, and WAP or through official channels, on a regular basis of things that are of interest to them.

1.2.6 Customer Life Cycle (CLC)

Customer relationships evolve over time along with their needs and expectations from the companies at various stages. The concept of a customer life cycle provides a framework for understanding and managing these differences at various stages of relationship with the company. Supporting for the existence of CLC comes from the various studies and research undertaken on new product acceptance and Recency, Frequency, and Monetary (RFM) analyses.

The different types of customers are as follows:

- *Prospects*: This is the precustomer stage, where the prospects are not customers yet, but they represent potential value for the enterprise. In fact, managing prospects is much more difficult than managing even the disgruntled customers at a later stage. This is because all customers have predefined thresholds of cost, quality, and price for making the *buy* decision. If the company's offerings are not perceived to exceed such thresholds, it may not result in a purchase. But, on the other hand, exceeding them overly also may prove to be counterproductive as such very high expectations are likely to be unmet resulting in difficulty in retaining such customers later.
- *First-time buyers*: A company's customer capital is heavily dependent upon the potential value of the first-time buyers. Customers achieve this stage upon making their first purchase. At this stage, the customer is highly vulnerable for defections due to even minor disappointments or lure of the competitor's offerings.

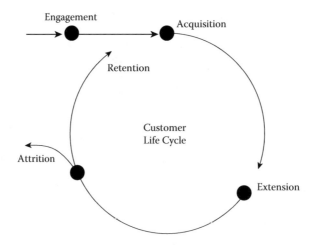

Figure 1.9   The various stages during the customer Life Cycle (CLC).

■ *Core customers*: Customers advance to this stage when they begin to make repeat purchases regularly. At this stage, the relationship has stabilized, the expectations have stabilized as well, and, finally, there are no major changes in the customer's needs or product specifications. An occasional product failure does not trigger defection or even a reevaluation of the firm's offerings. Core customers have the highest and most stable retention rates, and they also account for the highest sales per customer.

■ *Defectors*: Customers may reach this stage either because of a massive, though rarely occurring, failure on part of the company or a compelling alternative offering from a competitor or, in a few cases, frequently recurring failure that goes unaddressed by the company for an extended period of time despite repeated reporting by the customer (Figure 1.9).

The focus of the activities during the various phases is as follows:

1. *Customer engagement*: To contact a new customer through marketing, advertisement, telemarketing, personal selling, direct mail, promotions, and publicity.

2. *Customer acquisition*: To increase customer involvement through collection of as much information about the customer as possible, understand the buying context, purchase conditions and associated costs, offer post purchase reassurance, promote the price–value relationship, and, finally, develop the foundation for a long-term relationship.

3. *Customer retention*: To create long-term, committed, and loyal customers, develop a service philosophy, identify and close service gaps, manage your retention-related costs, increase responsiveness to customers, measure customer satisfaction, and reward positive customer behavior.

4. *Customer extension*: To extend your customer's loyalty through first defining loyalty parameters and discover customer lifetime, determine customer lifetime value (see Section 1.2.7.2, "Customer Lifetime Value"), learn customer needs and extended needs (e.g., up-sell), search and communicate solutions (e.g., cross sell), counter defection rates and patterns, bond closely with your customers, manage your loyalty costs, and reward loyal behavior. Initially, Amazon only sold books, then it added CDs, and now it also sells DVDs, toys, electronics,

computer peripherals, and much more. The customer capital model leads to greater customer value once the firm understands how to apply it as a business model.

5. *Customer attrition*: To reduce defection rates and patterns through identification of defection parameters (both controllable and uncontrollable); focus on *at-risk* customers; arrange loyalty schemes, programs, and events; felicitate and reward loyal customers; improve customer satisfaction ratings; extend customer lifetime; discover customer *wish lists* to propose effective customized solutions; and improve customer spend. Despite questionable on-time reliability and poor customer service, the airline industry has been able to foster high loyalty by instituting barriers to the customer's exit including increasing customer's cost of switching to the competitors. For instance, frequent-flyer programs pitch the customer's status in the next year dependent upon the mileage clocked in the current year.

To grow, an enterprise needs to acquire customers at a rate greater than its defection or attrition rate. Unlike customer satisfaction, the attrition rate being unambiguous is an excellent predictor of long-term (non)profitability. To increase its profits, an enterprise must place as much emphasis on reducing customer defections as it does on new customer acquisitions.

1.2.6.1 Customer Value (CV)

Customer Value (CV) is the long-term financial value that a customer delivers to a business and, therefore, is a result of the following factors:

- All income streams, right from the initial purchase through all the subsequent purchases
- All directly variable costs associated with managing the customer
- The envisaged length of the customer's relationship with the enterprise
- The customer's propensity to recommend the company to other prospective customers
- The resulting final value discounted, at an appropriate rate, to calculate the net present value

Customer value could be of different kinds:

1. *Historic value*: What has been the total CV till date?
2. *Current value*: Assuming the current customer behavior to remain the same, what will be the CV in the future?
3. *Potential value*: What could the customer be worth if we cost-effectively cross sell, increase their useful life with the company, and encourage them to recommend us?
4. *Influence value*: What is the value of the sales that the customer indirectly influences through reference, referrals, and the like (see note "Power Law and Small Worlds Networks [SWN]")?

> **CO-CREATION OF CUSTOMER VALUE**
>
> Co-creation or co-production of customer value occurs when enterprise delivers the value desired by the customer with the active participation of the customer. This is such a significant concept that it would need another book in itself to explore it to its full potential and depth. In the co-creation of value, the customer contributes time, effort, or resources essential for the selection, production, packaging, and delivery of the offering or

services. Because of the co-participation of the customer in the production and delivery of the offering and services, inherently, there is an assured minimum level of customer satisfaction. ATM systems, Self-Service Restaurants, etc., are typical examples of value co-creating systems, but the best exemplars of the value co-creating systems are the Internet-based applications (also see earlier Sections 1.2.6 "Customer Relationships" and 15.2 "Aspects of Enterprise Value").

1.2.6.2 Customer Lifetime Value

As mentioned earlier, the Customer Lifetime Value (LTV) is measured typically on an individual customer basis by tracking all transaction and expense details. This information is used to project the Net Present Value of the future revenue streams from this customer throughout the envisaged lifetime of this customer.

The kinds of data that are essential for calculating LTV include

1. Customer Transaction History
   a. What was the revenue generated from the purchase?
   b. What was purchased?
   c. How much was purchased?
   d. When was it purchased?
   e. Where was it purchased?
   f. What were the special offers/promotions?
   g. What was returned/canceled?
2. Revenue History
   a. Initial revenue
   b. Incremental revenue
   c. Service and support revenue
3. Promotion History
4. Costs
   a. Acquisition costs
   b. Product costs
   c. Incremental sales costs
   d. Incremental product costs
   e. Ongoing service and support costs

A general formula for LTV can be defined as follows:

$$\text{Customer LTV} = \text{Value}\left(\text{Initial Revenue} - \text{Costs}\right)$$

$$+ \text{Net Present Value}\left(\text{Loyalty} * \left(\text{Future Revenue} - \text{Costs}\right)\right)$$

$$+ \text{Net Present Value}\left(\text{Loyalty} * \text{Influence Value}\right)$$

The LTV for various customers may also be helpful in identifying several groups of customers who have similar patterns of behavior, which in turn could be helpful in tailoring value propositions to such identified groups of customers.

The Customer Lifetime Value (LTV) is easier to predict if it incorporates recurring number of the corresponding product's use cycle(s). For instance, if the average use cycle of a vehicle costing $20,000 is 5 years, the CV for a single vehicle–owning customer with the relevant *customer lifetime* of about 40 years may range between $140,000 and $200,000. The LTV of this customer will be much larger because of additional values representing warranty, maintenance, repair, and other services during the use cycle of a vehicle.

> This is based on the powerful idea of the *business cycles* or the constituent product *use cycles*. A database of the ownership and use history of product(s) can be used to perform sales projection, at any moment of time, for a specific period for a named prospective customer. It is possible to predict the requirements of a company with a reasonable accuracy based on
>
> ■ The average use life cycle of a product
> ■ The average innovation cycle of the underlying technology
> ■ The business cycle of the particular company as well as the concerned industry
> ■ The purchase history of company for the relevant product
>
> This kind of information on enterprises used strategically for sales and marketing could help in improving
>
> ■ Efficiency of the sales by reducing the time to sell
> ■ Effectiveness of the sales by entering the natural procurement cycle at an appropriate time as predicted by this analysis

1.2.7 Customer Value Management (CVM)

In the process of reorienting the business around the customer, companies are increasingly realizing that not all customers are equal. Different customers provide different revenues to the companies, they choose its products and services for different reasons, and, finally, they also defect for different reasons. This range of customer behavior results in widely differing values across the customer base, in terms of customers' future revenue to the business. To maximize profitability, it is important for companies to determine the future value of prospects and customers, so that they can differentiate their marketing activity and business processes to optimize future revenues and return on investment.

Customer Value Management (CVM) is the management of processes and communications designed to maximize Customer Lifetime Value (LTV) by closing the gap between the current and potential Customer Value (CV). CVM provides a way of measuring and improving the value delivered by the customer to the business and using this as the basis for decision making. It identifies those customers that really count: identifying what it is that they want as individuals (or as groups) and determining how to deliver it profitably.

CVM improves profitability and delivers greater Return on Investment (ROI) by assisting in the following:

■ Target acquisition efforts and activities at those prospects with the greatest CV.
■ Develop stronger and more profitable relationships with existing customers.

- Observe shifts in CV that reflect changes in customer behavior.
- Identify the gap between the current value and potential value, that is, the value gap to drive targeted cross sell/up-sell campaigns as well as measure improvements in CV.
- Ensure that the scarce financial and staff resources are allocated to interactions with those customers with the largest proven CV or potential CV.

Any business initiative can be assessed in terms of how much it contributes in increasing the CV versus the costs involved. But CVM is more than just a new method for calculating the value of customer relationship or a new way that a business allocates marketing resources and efforts. It is a total marketing system that entails the need to build organizations, processes, and performance measures that work together to maximize the value of the customer capital. In contrast with the traditional brand management approaches that focus primarily on the brand equity, CVM treats customer capital as the primary marketing asset. Figure 1.9 compares the features of these two approaches. Whereas the traditional mass marketing and tactics revolve around segmentation, targeting, and positioning, CVM is driven by acquisition, retention, and add-on selling model. In the case of CVM, the marketing mix is determined by the stage of the customer life cycle (CLC) (Figure 1.10).

Mass customization of products and services enables companies to market *off-the-shelf* products and services as tailored to the individual customers. This reduces the need for standard offerings and their associated carrying costs. However, this is possible only if the vendor has an accurate profile of the individual customer; a good CRM program will generate and maintain this kind of information. Building such a profile also facilitates cross selling of products and services through the different delivery channels available, adding incremental revenues. It can also reduce time to market new products as potential latent demand can be quickly identified and addressed.

	Customer Capital Approach	Brand Equity Approach
Product and service quality	Create strong customer preference	Create high customer retention
Advertising	Create brand image and position	Create customer affinity
Promotions	Deplete brand equity	Generate repeat buying and enhance customer lifetime value
Product development	Use brand extensions to sell related products	Use relationships to sell other products
Segmentation	Based on customer characteristics and benefits	Based on observed customer buying behavior
Channels of distribution	Multistage distribution system	Direct distribution to customer
Customer service	Enhance brand image	Enhance customer affinity

Figure 1.10 Comparative features of the customer capital and brand equity approaches.

1.2.8 Customers as Lifelong Investments

Relationship-based enterprises view customers as lifelong investments, and, therefore, their primary objective is to maximize the sum total of the time value of current and envisaged future customers. Relationship-based enterprises (RBEs) focus on accomplishing the intricate and long-term goal of *owning* the customer.

Traditional offering-based organizations are focused on maximizing the ROI on customers as early on in the relationship as possible because once the competition sets in, the margins and pay-off would invariably go down leading to the regime of rapidly diminishing returns. Figure 1.11 shows the classic product life cycle or the *S* curve for offering-based enterprises. On the other hand, customer-responsive organizations are more focused on maximizing the sum of the area under the curve, that is, the sum total of time value of the current and envisaged future customers. Figure 1.12 shows the characteristic exponential curve for the relationship-based enterprise.

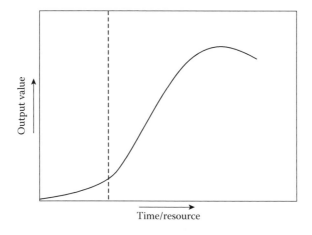

Figure 1.11   Value curve for offering-based enterprises.

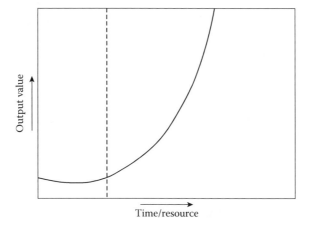

Figure 1.12   Value curve for relationship-based enterprises.

Initially, the returns are minimal or even reducing; thereafter, with increasing inputs of resources, the returns increase exponentially.

1.2.8.1 Customer as an Asset

In the framework being proposed here, the customer is akin to a financial asset that enterprises can measure, manage, and maximize like any other asset. Enterprises can use financial valuation techniques and information about the customers to optimize the acquisition, retention, and cross- and up-selling of additional products to an enterprise's customers, and that maximizes the value of the customer relationship throughout its life cycle.

Enterprises that take a customer asset approach differ significantly from those that treat brand equity as the primary marketing asset. Brand approach focuses on activities that maximize a brand's total revenues and the greatest possible returns on the brand investment. Rather than confining attention to singular brands, the customer asset approach focuses on the sum total of net income stream across all brands and services. Table 1.6 compares the characteristic features of the marketing mix for the customer equity and brand equity approaches.

Chapter 15, Section 15.4.1 "Time Value of Customers and Shareholder Value" elaborates on the concept that a company's market valuation/capitalization is truly dependent on the sum total of the envisaged lifetime value of its current and future customers. The market valuation in turn determines the company's share price on the stock markets. Patricia Seybold was the first one to point out that the success in the customer economy will depend on companies managing their enterprises by and for customer value—they will have to use customer lifetime value as a strategic

Table 1.6   Marketing Mix for Customer Equity and Brand Equity Approaches

Element of the Marketing Mix	Customer Equity Approach	Brand Equity Approach
Segmentation	Behavioral segmentation based on the customer base.	Customer characteristics and benefit segmentation.
Product and service quality	Creates high customer retention rate.	Create strong customer preference.
Product development	Acquire products to sell to the installed customer base.	Use brand name to create line extensions into new areas.
Advertising	Create customer bonding and affinity.	Create brand image and position.
Promotions	Create repeat buying and enhance customer lifetime value.	Momentarily enhance perceived value for money; but this depletes brand equity.
Customer service	Enhance customer bonding and affinity.	Enhance brand image.
Channels of distribution	Direct distribution to customer.	Multistage distribution system.

management tool. Company's source of investor value will increasingly be based on the value of their customer franchise, the lifetime customer value of their present and future customers (see Chapter 9, Section 9.1.1 "Basic E-Business Strategy Patterns").

1.3 Management by Collaboration (MBC)

The business environment has been witnessing tremendous and rapid changes in the 1990s. There is an increasing emphasis on being customer focused and on leveraging and strengthening the company's core competencies. This has forced enterprises to learn and develop abilities to change and respond rapidly to the competitive dynamics of the global market.

Companies have learned to effectively reengineer themselves into flatter organizations, with closer integration across the traditional functional boundaries of the organization. There is increasing focus on employee empowerment and cross functional teams. In this book, we are proposing that what we are witnessing is a fundamental transformation in the manner that businesses have been operating for the last century.

This change, which is primarily driven by the information revolution of the past few decades, is characterized by the dominant tendency to integrate across transaction boundaries, both internally and externally. The dominant theme of this new system of management with significant implications on organizational development is *collaboration*. We will refer to this emerging and maturing constellation of concepts and practices as Management by Collaboration (MBC). CRM packages such as SAP CRM are major instruments for realizing MBC-driven organizations.

MBC is an approach to management primarily focused on relationships; relationships by their very nature are not static and are constantly in evolution. As organizational and environmental conditions become more complex, globalized, and therefore competitive, MBC provides a framework for dealing effectively with the issues of performance improvement, capability development, and adaptation to the changing environment. MBC, as embodied by CRM packages such as SAP CRM, has had a major impact on the strategy, structure, and culture of the customer-centric organization.

The beauty and essence of MBC are that it incorporates in its very fabric the basic urge of humans for a purpose in life, for mutually beneficial relationships, for mutual commitment, and for being helpful to other beings, that is, for collaborating. These relationships could be at the level of individual, division, enterprise, or even between enterprises. Every relationship has a purpose and manifests itself through various processes as embodied mainly in the form of teams; thus, the relationships are geared toward attainment of these purposes through the concerned processes optimally.

Because of the enhanced role played by the individual members of an enterprise in any relationship or process, MBC not only promotes their motivation and competence but also develops the competitiveness and capability of the organizations as a whole. MBC emphasizes the roles of both the top management and the individual member. Thus, the MBC approach covers the whole organization through the means of basic binding concepts such as relationships, processes, and teams. MBC addresses readily all issues of management, including organization development. The issues range from organizational design and structure, role definition and job design, output quality and productivity, interaction and communication channels, and company culture to employee issues such as attitudes, perception, values, and motivation.

The basic idea of collaboration has been gaining tremendous ground with the increasing importance of business processes and dynamically constituted teams in the operations of companies. The traditional bureaucratic structures, which are highly formalized, centralized, and functionally specialized, have proven too slow, too expensive, and too unresponsive to be competitive. These structures are based on the basic assumption that all the individual activities and task elements in a job are independent and separable. Organizations were structured hierarchically in a *command-and-control* structure, and it was taken as an accepted fact that the output of the organization as a whole could be maximized by maximizing the output of each constituent organizational unit.

On the other hand, by their very nature, teams are flexible, adaptable, dynamic, and collaborative. They encourage flexibility, innovation, entrepreneurship, and responsiveness. For the last few decades, even in traditionally bureaucratic-oriented manufacturing companies, teams have manifested themselves and flourished successfully in various forms such as superteams, self-directed work teams (SDWT), and quality circles. The dynamic changes in the market and global competition being confronted by companies necessarily lead to flatter and more flexible organizations with a dominance of more dynamic structures like teams.

People in teams, representing different functional units, are motivated to work within constraints of time and resources to achieve a defined goal. The goals might range from incremental improvements in responsiveness, efficiency, quality, and productivity to quantum leaps in new product development. Even in traditional businesses, the number and variety of teams instituted for various functions, projects, tasks, and activities has been on the increase.

Increasingly, companies are populated with worker teams that have special skills, operate semi-autonomously, and are answerable directly to peers and to the end customers. Members not only must have higher level of skills than before but must also be more flexible and capable of doing more jobs. The empowered workforce with considerably enhanced managerial responsibilities (pertaining to information, resources, authority, and accountability) has resulted in an increase in worker commitment and flexibility. Whereas workers have witnessed gains in the quality of their work life, corporations have obtained returns in terms of increased interactivity, responsiveness, quality, productivity, and cost improvements.

Consequently, in the past few years, a new type of nonhierarchical network organization with distributed intelligence and decentralized decision-making powers has been evolving. This entails a demand for constant and frequent communication and feedback among the various teams or functional groups. A CRM package such as SAP CRM essentially provides such an enabling environment through modules like WebFlow, SAP Business Intelligence, and SAP Product Lifecycle Management (PLM).

 The significance of Management by Collaboration (MBC) becomes clear when we consider latest extensions to the traditional CRM like Social CRM (see Chapter 14, Section 14.11 "Social CRM via Social Networks").

1.3.1 The Relationship-Based Enterprise (RBE)

A Relationship-Based Enterprise (RBE) builds customer relationships to sustain business growth and to increase the profitability of the business. A relationship is a series of dialog each consisting of numerous instantaneous interactions with the customer. The Relationship-Based Enterprise

(RBE) has the ability to recognize and interact with different types of customers. The Enterprise uses these dynamic interactions to discover its customers through customer-related and customer's need-related information and create value by organizing itself to serve those customers. Customers and their corresponding needs are changing constantly depending on the market environment and, therefore, it is only because of these dynamic interactions that it can continue to discover the current needs of its customers.

1.3.2 The Information-Driven Enterprise

The combined impact on companies of increasing product complexity together with increased variety has been to create a massive problem of information management and coordination. Information-based activities now constitute a major fraction of all activities within an enterprise. Information-based organizations alone can enable companies to survive in the dynamically changing global competitive market. Only integrated, computer-based information systems such as SAP CRM are (and can be) enablers for this kind of enterprise-level collaboration.

The information-based organization as proposed by management theorist Peter Drucker is a reality today; correspondingly, companies are compelled to install both end user and work–group-oriented enterprise-level integrated computing environments. Only information-based extended organizations can possibly store, retrieve, analyze, and present colossal amount of information at the enterprise level that is also up to date, timely, accurate, collated, processed, and packaged dynamically for both external and internal customers. It should be noted that this subsection title uses the phrase *information driven* rather than *information based*. The primary reason for that is technology in the 1990s permits us to use information as a resource that is a legitimate substitute for conventional resources.

1.3.3 The Process-Oriented Enterprise

CRM packages like SAP CRM enable an organization to truly function as an integrated organization—integration across all functions or segments of the traditional value chain: sales order, production, inventory, purchasing, finance and accounting, personnel and administration, and so on. They do this by modeling primarily the business processes as the basic business entities of the enterprise, rather than by modeling data handled by the enterprise (as done by the traditional IT systems). Every CRM might not be completely successful in this; however, in a break with the legacy enterprise-wide solutions, SAP CRM treats business processes as more fundamental than data items.

Collaborations or relationships manifest themselves through the various organizational and interorganizational processes. A *process* may be generally defined as the set of resources and activities necessary and sufficient to convert some form of input into some form of output. Processes are internal, external, or a combination of both; they are cross functional boundaries; they have starting and ending points; and they exist at all levels within the organization.

The significance of a process to the success of the enterprise's business is dependent on the value, with reference to the customer, of the collaboration that it addresses and represents. Or, in other words, the nature and extent of the value addition by a process to a product or services delivered to a customer is the best index of the contribution of that process to the company's overall customer satisfaction or *customer collaboration*. Customer knowledge by itself is not adequate; it is only when the organization has effective processes for sharing this information and integrating the activities of frontline workers and has the ability to coordinate the assignment and tracking of work that organizations can become effective.

Thus, MBC not only recognizes inherently the significance of various process-related techniques and methodologies such as Process Innovation (PI), Business Process Improvement (BPI), Business Process Redesign (BPRD), Business Process Re-Engineering (BPR), and Business Process Management (BPM) but also treats them as fundamental, continuous, and integral functions of the management of a company itself. A collaborative enterprise enabled by the implementation of a CRM is inherently amenable to business process improvement, which is also the essence of any Total Quality Management (TQM)-oriented effort undertaken within an enterprise. We will deal with such process improvement related issues in Chapter 7 "SAP CRM and Enterprise Business Process Re-Engineering."

1.3.4 The Value-Add Driven Enterprise

Business processes can be seen as the very basis of the value addition within an organization that was traditionally attributed to various functions or divisions in an organization. As organizational and environmental conditions become more complex, globalized, and competitive, processes provide a framework for dealing effectively with the issues of performance improvement, capability development, and adaptation to the changing environment.

Along a value stream (i.e., a business process), the analysis of the absence or creation of added value or (worse) destruction of value critically determines the necessity and effectiveness of a process step. The understanding of value-adding and non-value-adding processes (or process steps) is a significant factor in the analysis, design, benchmarking, and optimization of business processes in companies leading to BPR. As will be discussed in Chapter 7 "SAP CRM and Enterprise Business Process Re-Engineering," SAP CRM provides an environment for analyzing and optimizing business processes.

Values are characterized by both value determinants such as time (cycle time and so on), flexibility (options, customization, composition, and so on), responsiveness (lead time, number of hand-offs, and so on), quality (rework, rejects, yield, and so on), and price (discounts, rebates, coupons, incentives, and so on). We must hasten to add that we are not disregarding cost (materials, labor, overhead, and so forth) as a value determinant. However, the effect of cost is truly a result of a host of value determinants such as time, flexibility, responsiveness, and so on.

Consequently, in this formulation, one can understand completely the company's competitive gap in the market in terms of such process-based, customer-expected value and the value delivered by the enterprise's processes for the concerned product or service. We will refer to such customer-defined characteristics of value as Critical Value Determinants (CVDs). Therefore, we can perform market segmentation for a particular (group of) product or service in terms of the most significant of the customer values and the corresponding CVDs.

1.3.5 Enterprise Change Management

Strategic planning exercises can be understood readily in terms of devising strategies for improving on these process-oriented CVDs based on the competitive benchmarking of these values. The strategies resulting from analysis, design, and optimization of especially the customer-facing processes would in turn result in a focus on the redesign of all relevant business process at all levels. This could result in the modification or deletion of the concerned processes or even the creation of new process.

Initiating change and confronting change are the two most important issues facing the enterprises of today. The ability to change business processes contributes directly to the *innovation* bottom line. The traditional concept of change management is usually understood as a one-time event. But if an organization is looking for the capability to handle not only change management but also management of changes on a continual basis, then CRM, like SAP CRM, is a must!

SAP CRM enables the essential changing of customer-facing processes that are so critical to the success of the enterprise. Business processes that *reside* or are internalized within an organization's employees are difficult to change simply because human beings naturally find it more difficult to change. However, processes that reside within any computerized systems are much more easy to change. The consequences of using information technology/information systems (IT/IS) can itself be managed by using more IT! The abstraction and electronic manipulation that have increased the speed of change can itself be used to manage (transparently to the end users) these changes. It is reported that in the mid-1980s, managers at the Australian bank Westpac concluded that the bank's adaptability to change could be enhanced by first modularizing and then codifying core functions, policies, and knowledge in a computerized system. Linking this separate system to the regular operational systems, the bank was able to reduce their time to market with new products; thus, the bank was able to enhance their ability to meet changed market conditions in weeks or months instead of months or years.

1.3.6 The Learning Enterprise

RBE builds customer relationships based on customer-related information. Evidently, all this information is necessarily finite in nature and also keeps on changing with changes in the customer environment. RBE recognizes that perfect information at any instance and especially on an ongoing basis is impossible and, therefore, incorporates them incrementally. Customer-responsive management enables enterprises to be more adaptable to changing conditions and responsive to smaller markets. It recognizes that forecasting and planning become more difficult as the marketplace and environment become more turbulent. It gives frontline workers more responsibility and authority so that they can innovate. The delivered solution may be expensive, but it is probably less expensive than the traditional deterministic planning and approval process. The solution may not be optimal, but the customer gets served (called *single-loop* learning), and the first delivered solution occurrence serves as a learning process for new guidelines that will need to be developed (called *second-loop* learning). Thus, the detailed planning of work is done at the front line. Customer-Responsive Management develops numerous best-practice guidelines to guide frontline workers as they interact with customers to plan solutions and also enables them to modify these if necessary, to improve the customer fit. After the problem has been identified and resolved, it is added dynamically to the best-practice guidelines. Thus, CRM not only would assist in the immediate problem-solving efforts in the present but would also define the problem in a new way. The essential difference between the two types of learning is between being adaptive and having adaptability. CRM provides and increases the adaptability of the enterprise. It is the dynamic development of best-practice guidelines that keeps the organization flexible in responding to new needs and in making continual improvements to the process as new techniques and technologies develop. CRM also automatically transforms the tacit knowledge within the enterprise to its explicit form for everyone to know it, feel it, analyze it, and, if possible, improve it further.

MBC also underlies the contemporary notion of the learning organization. To compete in an ever-changing environment, an organization must learn and adapt. Because organizations cannot think and learn themselves, it is truly the individuals constituting the organization who have to do this learning. The amount of information in an organization is colossal. A single individual, however intelligent and motivated, cannot learn and apply all the knowledge required for operating a company. Moreover, even this colossal amount of information does not remain constant, but keeps changing and growing.

The only effective solution is collaborative learning, that is, sharing this learning experience among a team of people. This not only caters to differences in the aptitudes and backgrounds of people, they all can also do this learning simultaneously, thus drastically shortening the turnaround time on the learning process itself. If organizational learning is seen in terms of the creation and management of knowledge, it is very easy for us to see the essential need to share the learning experience among the various member teams at the enterprise level and, within each team, among the members of the teams. Thus, we see another reason for collaboration among and within teams for contributing effectively in the learning process of the organization as a whole.

 What distinguishes learning from mere training is the transformation that results from the former. This, again, can be implemented successfully only by collaborations between various teams as it becomes apparent when such collaborations are embodied in the form of a CRM package, such as SAP CRM.

1.3.7 The Virtual Enterprise

Along with the general economic growth and globalization of markets, personal disposable incomes have increased, so the demand for product variety and customization has increased appreciably. Additionally, technological progress driven by the search for superior performance is already increasing the complexity of both the products and especially customer-facing processes. Because volume, complexity, and variety are mutually exclusive, this has invariably led to collaborative endeavors for achieving this with greater flexibility in terms of enhancing of capabilities, minimization of risks, lower costs of investments, shortened product life cycles, and so on.

These collaborative endeavors, which have been known variously as partnering, value-added partnering, partnership sourcing, outsourcing, alliances, virtual corporations, and so on (see Chapter 2, Section 2.4.1 "Collaborative Enterprise"), recognize the fact that optimization of the system as a whole is not achievable by maximization of the output at the constituting subsystem levels alone. Only CRMs with mature partner relationship management (PRM) packages such as SAP CRM can provide a backbone for holding together the virtual value chain across all these collaborative relationships. In Chapter 14, Section 14.7 "Applications Outsourcing (AO)," we look at such issues that are beyond the borders of the conventional enterprise.

Outsourcing will become a dominant trend in the millennium enterprise, whereby the enterprise concentrates only on being competitive in its core business activities and outsources the responsibility of competitiveness in noncore products and functions to third parties for mutual benefit. The development and maintenance of its core competencies are critical to the success of its main business; an enterprise cannot outsource these because it is these core functions that give it an identity. On the other hand, competitiveness in noncore functions, which is also essential for overall efficiencies, is outsourced to enterprises that are themselves in business of providing these very products or services; the outsourced products and services offerings are *their* core competencies.

It is important to realize the significance of another extension of the Sun Microsoft's vision of *Network is Computer*, namely, *Network is Customer*; to explore the profound implications of this statement is worth a book in itself.

Most of the major manufacturers over the world have become to a large extent *systems integrators*, providing only some of the specialized parts and final assembly of subsystems from a network of suppliers (see Section 1.2.2.2.1 "Networks of Resources"). Their economic role has transformed mainly into the basic planning, coordination, design, marketing, and service, but not complete production per se. For the existence and growth of such virtual organizations, it is important that the company be able to manage the complexities of managing such relationship on day-to-day basis. A PRM system provides all the functionality and processes for managing and accounting for such outsourced jobs. But, more significantly, only a PRM can make it possible for such a collaborative enterprise to exist and grow to scales unimaginable with traditional organizational architectures.

ENTERPRISE NETWORKS

It must be emphasized that contrary to the common perception, customer centricity and responsiveness as an alternative logic of business (or management) has applications not only for services but also for production activities. The achievement of CRM objectives like customer acquisition, retention, and value delivery requires enterprises to develop and manage a business network comprising suppliers, partners, distributors, investors, and employees. An enterprise network is a coalition of enterprises that works collectively and collaboratively to create value for the customers of a focal enterprise. Sometimes, the coalition is loosely connected; at other times, it is tightly defined, as in the relationship between Dell and its component suppliers. An enterprise network consists of a wide range of companies—suppliers, joint venture (JV) partners, contractors, distributors, franchisees, licensees, and so on—that contribute to the focal enterprise's creation and delivery of value to its customers. Each of these enterprises in turn will have their own enterprise networks focused around themselves. Thus, relationships between enterprises in the network both enable and constrain focal companies in the achievement of their goals. Therefore, liberating the potential value in customer relationships hinges on enterprises effectively managing their noncustomer network relationships.

CRM performance is more assured when the resources of the network are aligned and coordinated to contribute to the responsive creation and delivery of value to the focal company's customers. Consequently, CRM now includes applications for the extended enterprise encompassing relationships with the partners, suppliers, investors, employees, and, of course, the ERP systems (see Chapter 2, Section 2.4.2 "Extended Collaborative Enterprise").

1.3.8 The Agile Enterprise

Agile companies produce the right product, at the right place, at the right time, at the right price for the right customer. In an agile enterprise, products will be built quickly and at a lower cost for a customer because of the detailed data received at the point of sale.

The organizational requirements of an agile enterprise include

- A flat, fast, flexible organization, with continuous interaction, support, and communications among various functions
- Highly decentralized management that recognizes its knowledge base and manages it effectively
- A multi skilled, flexible workforce that is proactive and responsible
- Extremely flexible strategies and relationships with suppliers
- Complete control of lean production and concurrent engineering
- Flexible tooling and automation
- Deep understanding of the customer based on operating integration and real-time market data collection and analysis

Though they appear similar, there are fundamental differences between the *agile* and *lean* approaches for running a business. Lean production is at heart simply an enhancement of mass-production methods, whereas agility implies breaking out of the mass production mold and into mass customization. Agility focuses on economies of scope, rather than economies of scale, ideally serving ever-smaller niche markets, even quantities of one, without the high cost traditionally associated with customization. A key element of agility is an enterprise-wide view, whereas lean production is usually associated with the efficient use of resources on the operations floor.

As pointed out by Jagdish Sheth in these times of market change and turbulence, the *half-life* (i.e., the time within which it loses currency by 50%) of customer knowledge is getting shorter and shorter. The difficult challenges facing businesses today require organizations to be transitioned into flexible, agile structures that can respond to new market opportunities quickly with a minimum of new investment and risk. As enterprises have experienced the need to be simultaneously efficient, flexible, responsive, and adaptive, they have turned increasingly to the network form of organization with the following characteristics:

- Networks rely more on market mechanisms rather than on administrative processes to manage resource flows. These mechanisms are not simple *arm's length* relationships usually associated with independently owned economic entities. Instead, to maintain the position within the network, members recognize their interdependence and are willing to share information, cooperate with each other, and customize their product or service.
- While a network of subcontractors have been common for many years, recently formed networks expect members to play much more proactive role in improving the final product or service.
- Instead of holding in-house all assets required to produce a given product or service, networks use the collective assets of several firms located along the value chain.

The agile organization is composed of small, autonomous teams or subcontractors who work concurrently and reconfigure quickly to thrive in an unpredictable and rapidly changing customer environment. Each constituent has the full resources of the company or the value chain at its disposal and has a seamless information exchange between the lead organization and the virtual partners. Sections 1.2.1 and 1.2.2 earlier discussed aspects of the customer-centric and customer-responsive enterprises.

The rationale for establishing elaborate relationship-based enterprise architecture and the framework of Management by Collaboration (MBC) can only be understood in context of the future potential of, for instance, social networks-based Social CRM. Chapter 14, Section 14.11 "Social CRM via Social Networks" discusses the phenomenally important concept of Social CRM. Throughout human history, a social turn has always led to tremendous spurt in human's enterprise. So we are in for an explosive surge in next few decades that will leave even the information revolution/economy of the 1990's far behind.

1.4 Summary

Customer relationship strategy is emerging as one of the most important components of corporate strategy for competitive differentiation and shareholder value. The concept of CRM aims at identifying the customers that are more profitable to the company and helps in optimizing relationships with those customers. In today's world of decreasing margins, increasing competition, and ever-changing business environment, corporate success depends on an enterprise's ability to build and maintain loyal and valued customer relationships. The key to forge long-term, profitable relationships with valuable customers involves two major aspects: customer centricity and customer responsiveness. The importance of customer relationships is based on a simple fact: *it can cost four to seven times more to replace a current customer than it does to retain one.* A major step in this direction is to realize that whereas customer relationships are not all about information, all customer-related information is certainly about customer relationships.

This chapter looked at the concept of Customer relationship management (CRM). We presented a definition of CRM and the importance of customer centricity and customer responsiveness. Following this, we positioned customer relationship as the core strategy to achieve the objective of delivering value to customers at a profit. After explaining the concept of *information is relationship* as the underlying theme of CRM, we discussed related topics such as customer capital, customer responsiveness, customer loyalty, and measures to cultivate it. With a view to judging the profitability of customers, we then looked at the concept of customer value and customer lifetime value. Finally, we introduced the concept of management by collaboration (MBC) as a unifying framework in the context of the customer-centric enterprise.

 It must be highlighted that this chapter discussed major concepts, factors, and issues in the CRM space without major references to the Internet whose operating characteristics are natural manifestations of many of these concepts.

Chapter 2

Customer Relationship Management (CRM) System

What is a Customer Relationship Management (CRM) system? Not only is there little agreement on what it really stands for, there is even less agreement on what constitutes a CRM system, how it should be used, the potential of profitability gain, the impact on customer loyalty, the costs involved, the personnel needed, and the training needed for the CRM personnel. CRM system characteristics are not limited to the CRM products and tools that are currently available in the market, and CRM is certainly not a technique or methodology. There is every reason to believe that the boundaries described for CRM in this book will be constantly enlarging in the coming years (see Section 2.2 "Anatomy of a CRM System").

2.1 Introduction to Customer Relationship Management (CRM) Systems

Notwithstanding all these caveats, a CRM system could be defined reasonably as follows: *A Customer Relationship Management (CRM) System is a suite of pre-engineered, ready-to-implement, integrated application modules that focus on automating and optimizing all customer-centric and customer-responsive functions—sales, marketing, service, and support—of an enterprise and possessing the flexibility for configuring, customizing, and personalizing dynamically the delivered functionality of the package, through any channel of interaction, to suit even the specific requirements of an individual customer. CRM enables an enterprise to operate as a relationship-based, information-driven, integrated, enterprise-wide, process-oriented, real-time, and intelligent customer-centric and customer-responsive enterprise.*

CRM System applications provide the framework for executing the best practices in customer-facing activities; it provides a common platform for customer communication and interaction. The use of CRM System applications helps in improving customer responsiveness and also provides a comprehensive view of the entire Customer Life Cycle. With reference to Figure 1.2, one can state that CRM Systems, like CRM, are useful to companies that have customers with large variability both in their needs and their value to the company's business.

A CRM System like SAP CRM can provide this comprehensiveness and flexibility because at the heart of the system resides a CASE-like repository that stores all details of these predeveloped applications. These details include every single data objects, business objects, and user-interface (UI) programs that are used by the complete system. It also has additional support subsystems that help it to manage, secure, and maintain the operations of this package on a day-to-day basis.

Off-the-shelf packages, and especially enterprise-wide solutions such as CRM systems, are considered as the best approach for confronting the software crisis of the 1980s (see the following note on customized vs. packaged solutions). This was because

1. CRM Systems ensure better validation of user requirements directly by the user.
2. CRM Systems ensure consistent quality of delivered functionality.
3. CRM Systems provide a cohesive and integrated information system architecture.
4. CRM Systems ensure a fair degree of standardization.
5. CRM Systems provide a consistent and accurate documentation of the system.
6. CRM Systems provide outstanding quality and productivity in the development and maintenance of the system.

Half a decade later, as companies are reporting their experiences in implementing a CRM System, a base of experience seems to support the fact that companies that plan and manage the use of CRM System are usually successful. Today, the recognized management decision is not *whether* to use CRM System, but rather *when* to use CRM System and *which* CRM System to use. As we go through this book, it will become evident that SAP CRM is the best-of-breed product in this genre.

The success of CRM Systems is based on the principle of reusability. The origin of reusability goes back almost to the beginning of the computer era, when it was recognized that far too much program code was being written and rewritten repeatedly and uneconomically. Very soon, most of the programming languages provided for routines or packets of logic that could be reused multiple times within individual programs or even by a group of programs. Databases enabled the reuse of data, resulting in a tremendous surge in programmer productivity. Similarly, networks permitted reuse of the same programs on different terminals or workstations at different locations.

CRM Systems, like ERPs, extended the concept of reusability to the functionality provided by a system. For instance, SAP CRM was based on the essential commonality observed in the functioning of companies within an industry. SAP built a reusable library of normally required processes in a particular industry, and all that implementing SAP CRM customers had to do was to select from this library all those processes that were required by their company. From the project effort and cost that were essential for the development and implementation using the traditional software development life cycle (SDLC), CRM reduced the project effort and cost to that associated only with the implementation phase of the SDLC. Even though the cost of implementing a CRM System like SAP CRM might seem higher than that of traditional system, the CRM system gets implemented sooner and therefore starts delivering all of its benefits much earlier than the traditional systems.

Although there have not been any published results as yet, it has become an accepted fact that enterprises that implemented CRM systems for only a part of their organizations, or for only a few select functions within their organizations, did not benefit greatly. CRM Systems, like ERPs earlier, recognize the fact that business processes of an organization were much more fundamental than data characterizing various aspects of the organization. Most importantly, CRM systems elevated information systems from a mere enabler of the business strategy of an organization to a significant part of the business strategy itself.

Thus, CRM Systems brought to an end the subsidiary and support role that IT had played throughout the last few decades. But in turn, the very nature of IS has also undergone a complete transformation. Implementing a CRM System within an enterprise is no longer a problem of technology; it is a business problem. CRM Systems have been the harbingers of a paradigm shift in the role of the IS/IT function within an enterprise. This book was motivated by the need to address these fundamental changes in the very nature of IS/IT activity within an enterprise.

The distinguishing characteristics of a CRM system are

- CRM System transforms an enterprise into an information-driven enterprise.
- CRM System fundamentally perceives an enterprise as a global enterprise.
- CRM System reflects and mimics the integrated nature of an enterprise.
- CRM System fundamentally models a process-oriented enterprise.
- CRM System enables the real-time enterprise.
- CRM System enables the intelligent enterprise.
- CRM System elevates IT strategy as a part of the business strategy.
- CRM System represents Advance on the approaches to Manufacturing Performance Improvement.
- CRM System represents the new Department Store model of implementing computerized systems.
- CRM System is a mass-user-oriented application environment.

> We have differentiated between the concepts of Customer Relationship Management (CRM) and Customer Relationship Management Systems (CRM Systems) that implement possibly a part of this holistic concept. This book mainly relates to SAP CRM as a system to realize the CRM programs of a company; hereafter, for the sake of convenience, by CRM, we will usually refer to aspects of a comprehensive CRM Program that are embodied into a CRM System like SAP CRM implemented within the enterprise.

2.1.1 CRM Transforms an Enterprise into an Information-Driven Enterprise

All computerized systems and solutions in the past used past-facing information merely for the purpose of referrals and reporting only. ERP, for the first time in the history of computerized systems, began treating information as a resource for the operational requirements of the enterprise. But unlike the traditional resources, information resource as made available by CRMs (and ERPs) can be reused and shared multiply without dissipation or degradation. The impressive productivity gains resulting from the CRMs truthfully arise from the unique characteristic of CRMs (and, earlier, ERPs) to use information as an inexhaustible resource.

Customer interactions, which are the mainstay of CRMs, create real-time organizational knowledge providing insights into the customer behavior. CRMs enable an organization to use the real-time knowledge and information gained at any touch point to manage and synchronize the communications and marketing messages it delivers to its customers in all its touch point applications.

This is also the root of one of the major problems leading to failures of SAP CRM implementations. Sales persons, sales consultants, and sales managers are extremely possessive of their customers and related interaction information; such withholding of critical customer information prevents the information stored in CRMs to be treated fully as customer relationships and to be leveraged for maximum benefit.

2.1.2 CRM Perceives an Enterprise as a Global Enterprise

In these times of divestitures, mergers, and acquisitions, this is an important requirement. Unlike some of the earlier enterprise-wide solutions available on mainframes, CRM packages like SAP CRM cater to corporation-wide requirements even if an organization is involved in disparate businesses such as discrete industries (manufacturing, engineering, and so on), process industries (chemicals, paints, and so on), and service industries (banking, media, and so on). CRM packages enable the management to plan, operate, and manage such conglomerates without the impediment of mismatching systems for different divisions.

Although it might seem a minor point, CRM packages also permit the important functionality of enabling seamless integration of distributed or multilocation operations; we consider this aspect in the next subsection.

2.1.3 CRM Reflects and Mimics the Integrated Nature of an Enterprise

By promoting cross functional processes and work teams, CRM, like SAP CRM, provides a powerful medium for supporting, reconciling, and optimizing the conflicting goals of different functions within an organization. For instance, marketing may want production of more customized products to cater to the requirements in the market, whereas production function will want to standardize products for reducing setup times and related costs. The tussle between these two functions may result in releasing products that incur (say) five times the normal failure rates, the brunt of which is borne by the service function. Thus, marketing and to a large extent manufacturing obtain their short-term sales forecasts at the expense of the service function. The longer-term adverse effect on customer retention and loyalty may not even become evident until after many months have elapsed.

Companies interact with their customers across a variety of channels: offline channels such as branch stores and direct mail, as well as online channel as call centers, e-mail, and the Internet. In any CVM strategy, all of these interactions are part of an integrated communications strategy to realize the full value-creation potential of these interactions. In fact, as customers continue to use more channels to interact with the enterprise, the company must ensure that it has the infrastructure to provide consistent and optimal marketing messages across each of its touch point applications.

CRM provides an integrated view of an enterprise's customers to everyone in the organization so that the customer can be serviced effectively throughout the customer life cycle. For instance, if marketing runs an outbound campaign, all the information about the customers and the program should be retained for

- The salespeople to follow up
- The customer service people to answer any queries
- Technical support to provide any field support

Similarly, CRM enables even the customer to experience that they are dealing with the different functions of the same enterprise rather than independent departments that force them to run from pillar to post when trying to meet their demands.

2.1.4 CRM Fundamentally Models a Process-Oriented Enterprise

As organizational and environmental conditions become more complex, globalized, and competitive, processes provide a framework for dealing effectively with the issues of performance improvement, capability development, and adaptation to the changing environment. Process modeling permits the true nature of the characteristic structure and dynamics of the business.

Conventional systems primarily store only snapshots of customer interactions in terms of discrete groups of data at predefined or configured instants of time, along a business process within an organization. *This predominating data-oriented view of the enterprise as implemented by traditional IT systems is a most unnatural and alien way of looking at any area of human activity.* The stability of the data models, as canonized in the conventional IT paradigm, might have been advantageous for the systems personnel, but for the same reason, it would have been unusable (and unacceptable) to the business stakeholders within the organizations. Traditional systems could never really resolve this simple dichotomy of the fact that systems based on leveraging the unchanging data models, although easy to maintain, can never describe the essentially dynamic nature of businesses. This is the postmodern version of C. P. Snow's *Two Cultures*, which he had initially mooted to talk meaningfully about the worlds of humanities and sciences in the middle of the last century. Business processes are the most important portions of the reality that had been ignored by the traditional information systems. The traditional IT process modeling techniques, methodologies, and environments are a misnomer, for they truly model only the procedures for operating on the data associated at various points of the business subprocesses—which themselves are never mirrored within the system.

CRM packages recognized the fundamental error that was perpetuated all these past decades. Although many CRM packages still carry the legacy of the data-oriented view, the parallel view of business process and business rules is gaining prominence rapidly. This is the reason for the rapidly maturing groupware and workflow subsystems within the core architecture of current CRM systems.

2.1.5 CRM Enables the Real-Time Enterprise

The real-time responsiveness of the enterprise coupled with the enterprise-wide integration mentioned earlier also enables enterprises the powerful capability of *concurrent processing*, which would be impossible without systems like SAP CRM. Enterprises can obtain tremendous efficiencies and throughputs because of this ability to administer in parallel many processes that are related but independent of each other. In non-ERP enterprises, such closely related processes are typically done sequentially because they are usually handled by the same set of personnel, who may obviously be constrained to address them only in a sequence.

Customer responsiveness is an outcome of real-time sharing of current, complete, and consistent information on interactions with individual customers. Furthermore, it implies instantaneous, transparent connectivity and visibility between customer-facing processes with the corresponding order fulfilling processes. This visibility not only permits the salesman to give accurate available-to-promise (ATP) information to the customer but also enables him to assess for himself the latest capable-to-promise (CTP) status for a particular order prior to making any commitments. In turn, the various members of the supply chain also have a better visibility and understanding of the customer requirements and commitments made to the customer, thus ensuring *on-time delivery* (OTD). The tight integration with the fulfillment processes enables coordination, monitoring, and managing of goods across the ECE; it also provides instant notifications and alerts on exceptions and problem that may delay the on-time delivery of the order.

Furthermore, this integration also helps in matching the growing trend of customers postponing the buying decision closer to the purchasing decision with the corresponding ability of the enterprise to postpone the point of product differentiation as close as possible to the point of demand by the customer. Every action of the customer needs to be met by a highly automated and tightly integrated response across the supply chain to fulfill the need. More succinctly, one can say that *sell one, make one* has become the manufacturing watchword and corresponds closely to the current marketing watchword of *the market of one.*

2.1.6 CRM Enables the Intelligent Enterprise

The ability to access, collect, and analyze information in real term is an essential prerequisite of a customer-responsive enterprise. For remaining competitive, providing good customer service, and optimizing e-business operations, enterprises have to enable a *zero latency enterprise* (*ZLE*) that supports real-term decision processing providing rapid access to information and analyses from any place at any time for making real-term business decisions. Such decision processing systems are also required to integrate with the corresponding business processes to attain a closed-loop system whereby the output of the decision processing applications is delivered as inputs to influence favorably the business operations of the enterprise.

A real-term decision processing system typically consists of

- An event-driven hub that (via messaging and EAI) captures, transforms, and loads operational data into a data warehouse
- An analysis engine that generates business analyses from any place at any time
- A rule-driven decision engine that generates recommendations or e-business action messages in the real term

Business Intelligence (BI) applications are decision support tools that enable real-time, interactive access, analysis, and manipulation of mission-critical corporate information to provide users with valuable insights into key indicators to identify business problems and opportunities. BI enables users to access and leverage vast amount of information to analyze relationships and trends to support real-term business decisions. BI systems enable enterprises to become proactive and *information agile* (see Chapter 1, Sections 1.3.8 "Agile Enterprise" and 7.1.3 "Enterprise Agility") by delivering information to

- Empower enterprise users in the assessment, enhancement, and optimization of organizational operations and performance
- Deliver real-term business information to users about customer and partners

2.1.7 CRM Elevates IT Strategy as a Part of the Business Strategy

The coming of CRM heralded an enhanced role for IT systems. They are no longer the support functions of the earlier years. If someone is under that illusion, he or she will pay a very high price. Today, the real focus of IS/IT systems is no longer its alignment with the business strategy of the enterprise, but with that of the customer.

1690	Division of Labor	Adam Smith
1890	Scientific Measurement	Frederick Taylor
1900	Mass Production	Henry Ford
1920	Industrial Engineering	F. Gilbreth and Frederick Taylor
1930	Human Relations Movement	Elton Mayo
1950	Japanese Quality Revolution	J. M. Juran and W. E. Deming
1960	Material Requirement Planning	William Orlicky
1970	Manufacturing Resource Planning	Oliver Wright
1970	Focused Factory	Wickham Skinner
1980	Total Quality Management	Philip Crosby
1980	Just-in-Time	Taiichi Ohno
1980	Computer Integrated Manufacturing	
1980	Optimized Production Technology	Eliyahu Goldratt
1980	ISO 9000	NASI
1980	World Class Manufacturing	Richard Schonberger
1990	Mass Customization	Stan Davis and B. Joseph Pine II
1990	Lean Manufacturing	Jones and Roos
1990	Business Process Re-Engineering	Michael Hammer
1990	Enterprise Resource Planning	
1990	Customer Relationship Management	Frederick Reichheld

Figure 2.1   Timeline of performance improvement movements in the twentieth century.

2.1.8 CRM Advances on the Earlier Approaches to Performance Improvement

CRM is the latest in the succession of approaches that have been adopted throughout the history of enterprises for the improvement of enterprise-level performances. CRMs have realized the failed dream of improvements that were expected from the MRP-II-based Manufacturing Resource Planning systems of the 1970s. CRMs have enabled combining the *hard* approach of Quality Function Deployment (QFD) with the much broad-scoped *soft* approaches to customer satisfaction like support and services that were widely adopted during the 1980s in the last century. Figure 2.1 gives a list of major enterprise performance improvement movements during the last century. CRMs like SAP CRM provide the basic platform for devising techniques and tools for better implementations of the earlier approaches.

2.1.9 CRM Represents the New Department Store Model of Implementing Computerized Systems

The coming of packaged solutions like CRM (like the ERP before them) has been the death knell of the development model of IS systems. Along with it went the concept of requirements capture, modeling languages, development of software programs, testing, and so on that have usually been associated with the conventional developmental model. In its place, for the first time, is the end-user friendly model of what one could call the Department Store model of computerized systems: you pick and choose the functionality you require from the array of functional goodies on display!

Today, an organization solves critical information management need by purchasing the best-of-class application software package available in the relevant domain. This package is then configured, customized, and integrated to its specific requirements. The benefits of such an approach over the traditional full custom development project include

- Immediate access to the best technologies and industry practices, that is, typical package represents the synthesis of many years of business analysis and software engineering
- Quick return on investment (ROI) because the organization can begin to implement and deploy a packaged application immediately
- Lower software application life-cycle costs in every aspect: business and technical expertise, initial configuration and customization, maintenance, and future enhancements
- Mitigation of financial and delivery risks
- Much higher probability of overall success due to the use of a proven solution

A comprehensive CRM, like SAP CRM, is the analog of the great Department Store of functionalities or processes required within an organization. CRM makes the transition from the world of carefully engineered and running systems to the world of consumers, in which the value of the delivered functionality is based not on its pedigree, but only on what, how, where, and when it can be used gainfully.

This then is the final commoditization of the IS/IT products and services!

In the past few decades, all of us have witnessed a procession of different methodologies, tools, and techniques emanating from this industry that have had tremendous impact on the very nature and operations of business enterprises. But in the midst of all this turmoil, one fact has remained constant, and that has been the lack of productivity improvements, irrespective of the extent and nature of computerization.

But right from the start, there was an even more basic problem in terms of the number of software applications that were actually completed and implemented successfully. Much has been written on the software crisis that was engulfing information service groups in the 1980s. The reasons were multifold:

- With the advent of PC-like functionalities, users were becoming more aware and demanding.
- Consequently, applications were becoming more bigger and complex.
- Correspondingly, productivity was reducing rather than increasing.
- Software development times were increasing, and cost and time overruns were fairly routine.
- Quality, trained professionals were always in short supply, resulting in increased costs for programmers; hence, systems development costs were ever increasing.
- Mortality of systems was very high.

On average, out of the total number of IT systems under development, more than half used to be canceled; out of the remaining half, only about two-thirds were delivered. Half of the delivered systems never got implemented, whereas another quarter was abandoned midway through the implementation. Out of the residual quarter of the delivered systems, half failed to deliver the functionality required by the management and, therefore, were scrapped. Only the remaining half of the systems were used after great modifications, which entailed further delays and costs in an almost never-ending process.

One of the root causes identified for these problems was the inherent weakness of the phase in which requirements were captured and analyzed. This phase never seemed to get the correct and complete requirements. As a result, completed projects never seemed to deliver on the promised functionality and had to be recycled for more analysis and development. Maintenance and enhancements were called for indefinitely and became harder to undertake as time passed by. Because individuals often changed midway, both on the development and user sides, system requirements changed frequently, and the whole process continued indefinitely. This is primarily because there is a fundamental disconnect between the business and the IT/IS people. Notwithstanding how much both the parties try to bridge the gap, there is a fundamental chasm between the perception of a business user and what is understood by the systems staff; both classes of people speak different languages. Even if the systems personnel tried to increase precision by using methodologies and specification tools, because users were unfamiliar with these tools, they were never able to ratify the documented requirements completely.

Typically, surveys found that 50%–80% of the IT/IS resources were dedicated to application maintenance. The return on investments in IT were abysmally low by any standard of measurement and expectations. With IT/IS budgets stretching beyond the capabilities of most organizations, there was a compelling need for a radically new approach that could result in actual usable functionality that was professionally developed, under control, and on time.

The traditional software implementation involving the development of applications was characterized by

- Requirement-driven functional decomposition
- Late risk resolution
- Late error detection
- Use of different languages or artifacts at different phases of the project
- Large proportion of scrap and rework
- Adversarial Stakeholder Relationship with non-IT users
- Priority of techniques over tools
- Priority of quality of developed software rather than functionality per se
- Great emphasis on current, correct, complete, and consistent Documentation
- Great emphasis on testing and reviews
- Major effort on change control and management
- Large and diverse resource requirements
- Schedules that are always under pressure
- Great effort on projected or estimated target performance
- Inherent limitations on scalability
- Protracted integration between systems

Many alternate strategies were devised like CASE and prototyping; however, none were able to cross this basic hurdle. CASE provided more rigorous environment for requirement analysis and design and automated to a large extent the subsequent development of code, testing, and documentation efforts. The increased time spent on requirement definition with the users was envisaged to lead to systems that were closer to the users' actual requirements. On the other hand, prototyping was designed to address the requirement capture issue by making the users directly participate in the process of defining the requirements. This was mainly focused on the screen and reports design because these were the elements that could be visualized directly by the user. But none of these strategies really resolved the problem. Packages like ERP and CRM adopted a totally different approach by providing the most comprehensive functionality within the package. Company personnel were only expected to pick and choose whatever was required by the company actually using the package. Thus, ERP/CRM packages effectively short-circuited the whole issue of capturing requirements. The traditional project life cycle consisting of analysis, design, development, testing, and implementation was transformed to the ERP/CRM implementation life cycle consisting merely of requirement mapping, gap analysis, configuring and customizing, testing, and implementation. Figure 2.2 shows a comparison of efforts expended during ERP/CRM and the traditional Software Development life cycle.

This ultimately led to the ERP revolution that we are witnessing today.

Unlike the traditional systems, the CRM software implementations, involving the implementations of preengineered ready-to-implement application modules, are characterized by

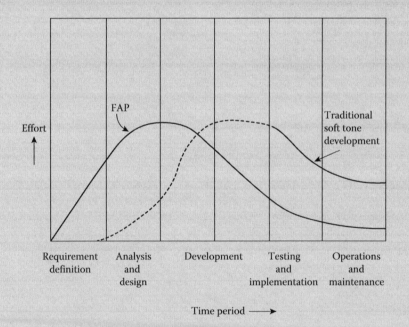

Figure 2.2 Comparison of efforts expended during ERP and the traditional software development life cycle.

- Primacy of the architecture; process-oriented configurability
- Primacy and direct participation of the business user
- Early risk resolution
- Early error and gap detection
- Iterative life-cycle process; negligible proportion of scrap and rework
- Changeable and configurable functionality
- Participatory and cohesive stakeholder relationship with non-IT users
- Priority of functionality over tools followed by techniques
- Quality of the functional variability and flexibility of the available functionality
- Great emphasis on current, correct, complete, and consistent documentation of customizations
- Great emphasis on integration testing
- Actual demonstration of functionality at all phases of the project
- Twin categories of resource requirements: functional and technical
- Schedules devoid of long-term cascading impact
- Demonstrated performance
- Larger span of scalability
- Efficient integration between systems

2.1.10 CRM Is an End-User-Oriented Application Environment

Compared to the degree of involvement of functional managers and end users in traditional software project implementations, their participation as recommended here in SAP CRM implementations might seem unusual. CRM brings computerization and decisions to the desktops and in this sense is an end-user-oriented environment in the true sense of the word (see Table 2.1). Unlike traditional systems in which users accessed the system directly only in well-defined pockets within the enterprise, in CRM, end users are truly the personnel actually involved with the

Table 2.1 Back-Office Automation Technology versus Relationship Building Technology

	Traditional Back-Office Automation Technology	*Relationship Building Technology*
1. Strategic focus	Internal: Operational efficiency	External: Customer relationship
2. Key business benefit	Control Cost	Drive corporate performance
3. Expertise required to develop applications	Algorithmic optimization	Business knowledge (e.g., sales, marketing, customer service)
4. Industry focus	Manufacturing	Services
5. Nature of process flows	Structured, deterministic	Unstructured, spontaneous
6. Process focus	Transactional	Relationship Building
7. Number of internal users	10s–100s	1000s to millions
8. Number of external users	10s–100s	Millions

operations of the business. Because of the intense involvement of a sizable portion of the work-force of the company with the CRM implementation from the beginning, the probability of users embracing the system (and not struggling against it) is much higher. Users also act as the advocates and facilitators during and after the implementation phase.

2.2 Anatomy of a CRM System

A comprehensive CRM system is massively complex. As mentioned in Section 2.1 "Introduction to Customer Relationship Management (CRM) System," CRM essentially treats an application development environment as an application *in itself*. The integrated application repository holds a full set of correlated information regarding the application as well as the data that will reside in the system when it's in production, which also greatly facilitates documentation, testing, and maintenance. In this section, we briefly give an overview of the various systems that constitute a comprehensive CRM like SAP CRM. Every system described in the following has two simultaneous aspects: managing the application data and also the metadata related to the very nature and configuration of the implemented CRM itself.

The exhaustive list provided as follows illustrates the complexities of modern off-the-shelf packages. It can also act as a reference list when we look at the issues related to the evaluation and selection of CRM packages in later sections of this chapter.

2.2.1 Application Maintenance–Related Systems

2.2.1.1 Application Repository System

The application repository system forms the core of the CRM system. It provides the essential information on the structure and design of the whole application to all other modules or systems. It records the information regarding the information model of the system in terms of the entities, attributes, relations, processes, views, user scenarios, and so on. It also promotes a methodology that is native to the development and maintenance of the CRM system. It contains information on every single program, file, and data item in the system. This includes information on the various components and elements: identity, purpose, type and nature, defining attributes, *where-used* list, tables accessed, processing cycles and times, and sizing.

This module provides facilities to check the consistencies and integrity of definitions for all system components and elements within the CRM.

The application repository needs analysis and design modeling subsystems. It also needs a graphics environment to represent the processing requirements of the company operations. The graphic module provides a diagram representation of the processes that enable rapid changes whenever necessary. Detailed requirements can be defined and stored in a related database that can be analyzed for dependencies, consistencies, impact analysis, and so on. This is usually called the *data dictionary* and provides support for the database and data tables or file design (including forming data tables, normalization, indices, and referential integrity).

2.2.1.2 Fourth-Generation Language Development Environment

This environment provides facilities to customize or extend the CRM system's functionality to meet the specific requirements of an enterprise. This has the standard tools set for the development, testing, debugging, and documentation of the programs, especially data entry programs.

2.2.1.3 Query Management System

This system provides extensive querying facilities on the system details stored in the application repository (and data dictionary). These details include process information, entities, data tables, programs, and also the data stored in the tables of the application database. This query management system enables the painting of query screens; the specification of tables to be accessed, fields to be displayed, and their sequences; the selection of a set of records to be displayed; and so on.

2.2.1.4 Report Management System

This report management system is similar to the query management system, except that it permits the queried information to be printed for reference. It defines customized reports for specific requirements of the company related to preprinted documents like purchase orders and invoices. It provides advanced features for rapidly programming break totals, page breaks, line details, and so on within a report.

2.2.1.5 Configuration Management System

This permits the CRM to be configured to the specific organizational structure of a company. This may include the physical locations, operational divisions, profit/loss (P/L) entities and accounts, the fiscal period, the taxation and discount structures, and the categories of customers, suppliers, and products. All subsequent reporting and analyses are based on the details of configuration defined at the time of inception. This system also customizes the CRM system to embody the various functions and processes specific to an enterprise.

2.2.1.6 Change Management System

This system provides the facility to register, release, and control all changes introduced into the system. This permits control over system components being changed or tested and those that are released in the production environment for access and use by all. It also enables gathering and monitoring details on dates, persons, and the duration required for affecting changes. This helps both in the security and in the productivity of the CRM operations.

2.2.1.7 Version Management System

This system provides facilities to keep track of the current versions of the various systems constituting the CRM. This enables prompt diagnosis of any malfunction that may arise because of incompatible systems, wrong interfaces, noncompliant systems, and so on.

2.2.1.8 Application Programming Interface (API) System

This system provides facilities for a standardized interface of the CRM to upload or download data from legacy systems; specific application systems like supply chain management (SCM), customer relationship management (CRM), and electronic data interchange (EDI); high-end project management systems; or scientific and industrial application systems. These interfaces could be in batch or asynchronous modes or, for ongoing operations, in synchronous mode. Even multiple installations of the same CRM at different sites for the organization will need such interfaces. These may also be needed as basic enablers for such sophisticated facilities like data replication and database mirroring.

2.2.2 User-Interface-Related Systems

2.2.2.1 Graphical User-Interface (GUI) Management System

This module provides the standard facilities of any presentation manager in terms of layouts, navigation among and within screens, help features, error recoveries, and so on. The graphical user-interface (GUI) management system controls the design and functioning of the dialog flow on the screen, validations and table lookups, default values, lists of values, and so on. This system will usually be one of the standard Relational Database Management Systems (RDBMS) like Oracle and DB2.

2.2.2.2 Menu Management System

This system presents the various choices that are available in various areas of functionality. It also lets you dynamically define the choices that are available to a particular user, depending on his level of access and authorization in different areas within the CRM.

2.2.2.3 Help Management System

This system provides the specific or contextual help at every field or processing step within the system. At any moment, it provides information on programs, screens, or particular fields of interest. This system also incorporates the architecture to report on errors and warnings, as well as give more specific diagnosis or suggestions on resolving problems encountered during the usage of the system.

2.2.3 Application Management–Related Systems

2.2.3.1 Database Management System

This module is responsible for the storage of information required or supplied by all other modules of the CRM product. This will usually be one of the standard RDBMSs like Oracle and DB2.

2.2.3.2 Application Administration and Management System

This provides facilities to guide and assist in installation, upgrades, system maintenance, printer/spool management, and so on. This application administration and management system interfaces with other related systems for managing software distribution, configuration and change releases, versions, security and authorization, disaster recovery, archival, and so on. It also provides facilities for operational requirements of performance monitoring, backups, background processing, creating and managing jobs, and so on.

2.2.3.3 Software Distribution Management System

This system enables the facility to upgrade the client-based software automatically from a centralized place. The system can enforce the access and authorization profiles at the various users' PCs.

2.2.3.4 Security and Authorization Management System

In an integrated environment of CRM, this system provides the architecture for the security and hence the access and usage available to the system. This enables maintaining the profiles of authorized access, assigning such profiles to specific user accounts, authenticating the users in the production environment, logging user access and usage, tracking attempts to breach the system security, changing access profiles and passwords, and so on.

2.2.3.5 Audit Management System

This system provides monitoring for user access and usage, system processing and updates, system and data changes management, error logs, and so on.

2.2.3.6 Disaster Recovery Management System

This provides the facility to define the alternate disaster recovery servers and systems, triggering or initial response procedures, databases' recoveries, activating backup resources, full recovery procedures, and so on.

2.2.3.7 Archival Management System

This provides the facility to archive system and application data that have been identified as essential for future reference. This defines details on data, the data sources, duration, frequency, the target archival system, and so on.

2.2.3.8 Communications Management System

This provides the communication layer for the CRM system. It provides features like distributed processing, distributed databases, and security.

2.2.4 Application Support–Related Systems

2.2.4.1 Online Documentation System

This provides the ability to make system documentation available on the system while one uses it and, more importantly, in the context of the particular functionality being used at any moment. This system provides links to related issues as well as the facility to pursue individual topics in full detail.

2.2.4.2 Print Documentation System

This provides facilities for printing the full technical details and the application design of the system for offline reference. Moreover, it enables updates to this documentation depending on upgrades, enhancements, and new releases of functionality in any of the aforementioned systems.

2.2.4.3 Online Tutorial, Training, and Demonstration Management System

This system provides an online tutorial carefully designed to highlight the comprehensiveness of the application and also advanced features that are available within the system. This training and demonstration system provides a path to be followed during the learning phase on the CRM. The system also provides the ability to measure and assess the progress made by the trainees during such exercises.

2.2.4.4 Implementation Project Management System

This system provides integrated capabilities for monitoring and managing the progress during the implementation of the CRM. It provides the capability to define the work steps, dependencies, schedules, estimates on duration and effort, work in progress, work completed, work under testing, and so on.

2.2.5 Miscellaneous

2.2.5.1 Office Automation System

This system provides the functionalities provided by word processors, document formatters, spreadsheets, and so on. This office automation system is used for recording annotations on the system or for project management, defining preformatted letters generated by the systems, and so on.

2.2.5.2 Groupware and Workflow System

This system provides extensive communication between users of the CRM system. More significantly, it provides direct interfaces between itself and the mail system in order to inform and alert concerned personnel about predefined events occurring during processing, like released purchase orders, dunning notices, and alarms on exceeding credit limits.

This system also provides for broadcasting mail to multiple persons, routing mail in the operating sequence, triggering reminders at various stages along the workflow, soliciting approvals or authorizations, and so on.

2.2.5.3 Data Warehouse and Data Analysis System

This system provides for mapping and populating operational data from the CRM tables into the multidimensional tables of the data warehouse for manipulation and analysis. It provides advanced tools for detecting data patterns, trends, correlations, and so on within the available data and prospecting for any significant relationship between data across the organization.

2.3 Types of CRM Systems

The CRM ecosystem is comprised of three categories of applications:

1. *Operational CRM*: These applications help the salespeople in becoming more productive and effective. These include automation software for sales, marketing, and services. These systems hold transactional level data on individual products, customers, and transactions. They provide support for customer-facing processes done by direct mail, phone, the Internet, third-party agents, and field sales. These applications are also referred as the front-office applications.

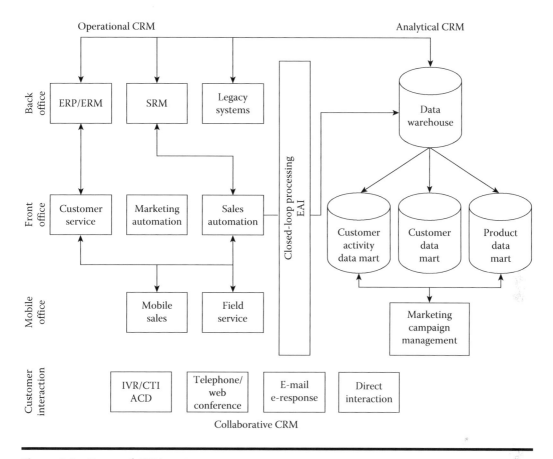

Figure 2.3 Types of CRM systems.

2. *Analytical CRM*: These applications support the *one-to-one* customized marketing programs. These systems hold aggregated data where the unit of analysis is the campaign, market segment, key account, and market or product group. These applications provide support for the strategic planning processes.

3. *Collaboration CRM*: These applications help in smoothing the dialogs with the customers. These constitute the traditional and new groupware/web technologies to facilitate customer, staff, and business partner communications, coordinations, and collaborations.

Figure 2.3 shows the relationships between the three categories of applications.

2.3.1 Closed-Loop CRM

Closed-loop CRM systems not only enable execution of customized marketing campaigns but also measure their effectiveness, which in turn is used to improve their performance even further (the next time around).

Closed-loop marketing consists of three basic steps that lead to an ever-improving marketing performance:

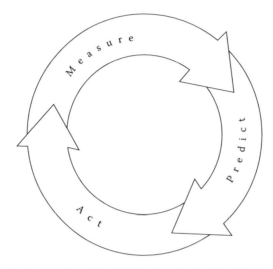

Figure 2.4   Basic schema of the closed-loop CRM system.

1. *Measure*: The effectiveness of the marketing effort in terms of the resulting customer profitability.
2. *Predict*: Analyze the available data for modeling the consumer behavior and predict consumer behavior close to the actual observations. These models are then used to focus and refine the design and configuration of the future marketing campaigns.
3. *Act*: The CRM systems then assist in executing the modified marketing campaigns along with the corresponding changes in measurements for ascertaining the success of the new campaign.

Figure 2.4 presents the basic schema of the closed-loop CRM system.

2.3.2 Why Use CRM?

The implementation of CRM engenders the following business and technical advantages:

■ Reconciles and optimizes the conflicting goals of different divisions or departments for consistent and coordinated customer interactions and fulfilling experience at all customer touch points.
■ Standardizes business processes across all constituent companies and sites, thus increasing their efficiencies.
■ Provides the ability to know and implement global best practices and provides the best means for benchmarking the organization's customer-centric competitiveness.
■ Alters the function-oriented organization toward a more team-based, cross functional, process-oriented organization, thus leading to a more flexible, flatter, tightly integrated, and customer-responsive organization.
■ Provides a responsive medium for undertaking all variants of process improvement programs and methodologies, including process innovation, process improvement, and interaction channels.

- Provides a responsive medium for quality improvement and standardization efforts including QC, QA, TQM, and QFD.
- Is process oriented and therefore is a fertile ground for implementing Activity-Based Management (ABM) efforts, be they for budgeting, costing, efficiency, or quality.
- Provides the best conduit for measuring the benefits accruing to an organization by monitoring the Return on Investment (ROI) of not only money but also manpower, materials, time, and information. This could be in terms of various parameters like cost, quality, responsiveness, and cycle time. Thus, CRM could assist in the implementation of, for instance, the balanced scorecard within the enterprise.
- Enables an enterprise to scale up its level of operations drastically or even enter into different businesses altogether, without any disruption or performance degradation.
- Enables real-time creation of data directly during the actual physical transaction or processes by the persons who are actually responsible for it.
- Pushes latest data and status to the actual operational-level persons for better and faster decisions, at least on routine issues; empowers and gives ownership to the customer-facing operational personnel at the customer touch points (this automatically goes away with problems associated with the collection of voluminous data, preparation, entry, corrections of inaccuracies, backups, and so on).
- Integrates data of the organization into a single comprehensive database.
- Provides online availability of correct, current, consistent, complete, clear, and authentic operational data across multiple channels and touch points that could be populated into the enterprise data warehouse for analysis and mining.
- Greatly reduces the cost of maintaining systems.

As mentioned in the introduction to this chapter, all these characteristics of CRM implemented in organizations arise primarily from the fact that what they handle is not merely organizational data, but relationships that are of strategic importance to the customer-centric enterprise.

In the next section, we turn to this aspect of the relationship-based organizations.

2.3.3 ERP versus CRM

There are two primary chains within an enterprise:

1. The supply chain covers the back-of-office to external suppliers and distributors. This includes functions and processes associated with finance, accounting, inventory, human resources, manufacturing, shipping, and logistics.
2. The demand chain covers the front-of-office to external customers and the channel. This includes functions and processes associated with sales, marketing, service, and support.

The ERP and CRM approaches differ in their focus and tactical objectives. The ERP orientation, for example, views business as a set of rigid back-office processes, and customers are modeled as *resources* that fall under the control of internally focused, command-and-control systems. Because domain expertise in ERP and other back-office applications focuses on algorithmic optimization of structured and deterministic processes, the ERP perspective does not accommodate the random, unstructured, and highly dynamic nature of customer behavior.

Table 2.1 compares the traditional back-office automation technology like ERPs with that of the Relationship Building Technology like CRM.

ERP vendors have been acquiring or building new modules for Sales Force Automation (SFA) and CRM to front-end traditional Sales Order, Billing, and Accounts Receivable (AR) application modules. This streamlines the information flow from the initiating sales forecasting activity to servicing an established customer. While this extends the business functions and activities supported by information processing, it also extends the reach of the traditional back-of-office ERP products. However, this does not necessarily deliver functionality of a true CRM. Extended ERP is seldom more than a vendor's best-of-breed and piecemeal application add-on functionality intended simply to extend the market share of their ERP product. Front-of-office applications grafted on an ERP may not be as functionally rich as SAP CRM but may have a certain advantage in terms of the in-built provisions for integration with back-of-office modules. A judicious balance needs to be struck between these aspects to evaluate and select the most appropriate vehicle for delivery of CRM functionality for the enterprise. These issues are the focus of Chapters 3 "CRM Evaluation" and 4 "CRM Selection."

2.4 CRMs as Keepers of Customer Knowledge Assets

CRM implementations must ultimately be business driven and not dictated and driven by technology issues. The survival and success of an enterprise depend on how it differentiates itself and its products and services from those of its competitors. In this era of mass customization, what organizations need is not more standardization and generic processes, but the ability to be more dynamic, more flexible, more proprietary, and more customized. Because the CRM strategy basically embodies the *theory of business* of a company (a la Peter Drucker), it must also mirror these differences in strategies and processes. To leverage their competencies, distinct advantages, edges, or competitive advantages, companies cannot abandon the corresponding differentiating processes and will have to incorporate such fundamental variants in their CRM implementations or interface with such systems. SAP's Industry-Specific (IS) solutions are primarily efforts driven by recognition of this fundamental need of its customer organizations.

All of these unique value propositions and differentiating factors are information assets of an organization and are captured and configured into the CRM system. These information assets include the business rules and procedures or methods of operations, customer analytics, parameters of analysis, ranges for defining credit limits, credit periods, discounting structures, and ratings. Like any other assets, CRM packages like SAP CRM register, maintain, monitor, and report on these informational assets. This helps in maintaining these assets current and useful.

2.4.1 Collaborative Enterprise

CRM provides the design and architecture for the collaborative enterprise as has been discussed in this chapter. It provides the basic platform for enabling the enterprise-wide, integrated, information-based, process-driven, real-time intelligent enterprise. This has a direct impact on many aspects that traditionally have been more relevant to issues of organizational development:

- *Vision*: CRM enables the realization of an organization that has a customer-centric vision to be competitive by raising the level of skills and competencies of its personnel so that they can respond better, faster, and at the optimal cost to the changing customer expectations every day.
- *Strategic goals*: CRM enables access to customer-sensitive data to all customer-related personnel to keep track of the organization's overall performance, with reference to the company's

customer-centric goals as well as their own contribution to the same on a daily basis. This engenders a sense of involvement and transparency that was not been achievable earlier.

- *Culture*: CRM truly makes it possible to operate a collaborative, value-add driven, and customer-centric organization in a real-time mode. CRM permits learning happening in any part of the enterprise to be incorporated into the system, even on a daily basis.
- *Structure*: CRM system provides visibility to the responsibility-oriented organization structure rather than the designation-oriented structure of earlier times. It provides instant communication and interaction with all customer-facing members irrespective of their reporting department or designation.
- *Systems*: CRM provides for adequate control without encumbering the work that directly contributes in the value-add delivered to the external or internal customers.
- *Processes*: CRM enables the process-oriented enterprise that might not always be feasible to realize physically, for instance, by locating all concerned members of a team in one place. It makes it possible for members to participate in multiple customer interactions efficiently and effectively.

2.4.2 Extended Collaborative Enterprise

The future of CRM is closely related with the efforts to reengineer such interenterprise interfaces and foster closer collaborations across multiple enterprises, that is, the extended collaborative enterprise (ECE). This is in quite contrast to the traditional adversarial relationships that have been known to exist among the suppliers, manufacturers, distributors, and retailers. The true economies of production can only be gained by the economies of cooperation. The virtual organization that we referred to in Chapter 1 spans all such members of the traditional supply and demand chain.

In the 1990s, the enterprise resource planning systems or ERPs focused attention on enhancing performance within the enterprise, yet more than 50% of the variable costs that affect the performance of an organization are mainly driven by decisions outside the boundaries of the organization. After benefiting from streamlining and re-engineering the internal processes, enterprises will address the potential for major gains obtainable from these cross company processes. But why is this extended value chain considered important for the next quantum leap in organization performances? Enormous opportunities for enhanced efficiencies exist at the interfaces between contributing value chain partners, as also the potential for a greater level of customer satisfaction.

Like the non-value-adding hand-offs within an organization, many of the interfaces and hand-offs between partners are non-value-adding, efficiency depleting, and time consuming. The customer ends up paying for all these inefficiencies, regardless of how far removed or hidden he or she may be from the source. Similar to the inefficiencies associated with typical internal processes (before the implementation of enterprise-wide solutions like SAP CRM), value chain inefficiencies can easily account up to 25% of the company's operating costs.

Thus, an ECE differs from a traditional supply chain in the extent to which a company can integrate with its partners.

2.4.3 Extended Relationship Management (ERM)

ERM provides a unique global view that consolidates all information about stakeholders, their interactions, and activities into a centralized repository for both real-time and analytical use. The objective of Extended Relationship Management (ERM) is to build and maintain profitable business relationships with all key stakeholders of the company, namely, customers, suppliers, partners, and employees. Relationships that continually engage, satisfy, sustain, and enhance these relationships across all channels and touch points result in greater loyalty, revenues, and profitability. ERM enables an integrated business experience that spans service, marketing, and commerce and extends outside the enterprise to incorporate customers, partners, and suppliers in collaborative business processes. By integrating and sharing information and processes across various constituents, the enterprise enables precisely targeted marketing campaigns, increases up-sell and cross sell opportunities, and ensures consistent and personalized treatment of every customer throughout this extended value chain. Such an extended dialog between its stakeholders creates collaborative relationships that yield greater customer loyalty.

Unlike the problems that confronted the traditional supply chain, today the issues extend beyond the conventional static and predefined individual supply chains. This is because of the dynamic reconfigurations that are possible by the Internet. The Internet enables the formation and dissolution of momentary supply chains even for individual customer transactions depending on the optimal combination of collaborations to deliver a product and/or service triggered by the customer. More than supply chains, these will be a network of suppliers and partners. The extended collaborative enterprise will be more like a community of enterprises guided by the major value-adding players within the communities. Instead of the competitive advantage of individual enterprises, the competition today will exist among different communities of enterprises, that is, ECEs. The success of an enterprise will depend on the *collaborative advantage* of the corresponding supply chain or, more correctly, the supply network to which it belongs. Since the threat of substitution is available not only to the end customers but also to the other constituents of the ECE, it may become vital to become a valued member of a successful supply chain.

2.5 Electronic Customer Relationship Management (eCRM)

The Internet has altered forever the ways in which enterprises interact and work with their customers, suppliers, and even their own members. The Internet has enabled a dramatic reduction in the cost of transactions and interactions between the enterprise and its customers. Online customers expect shorter sales cycles, personalized information, quicker resolution of issues, and added value at each stage of the transaction. Internet-supported Customer Relationship Management (eCRM) is rapidly emerging as the *killer app* of the Web of the 2000s.

eCRM provides a standard-based Web architecture for information, process, and application integration so that the enterprise can integrate information and processes across marketing, commerce, and service. The enterprise can integrate existing databases, legacy applications, and systems to create a virtual centralized information repository so that the company can market, sell, and service its offerings more effectively. And the Web's architecture scalability and flexibility enable it to be more responsive leading to rapid growth.

2.5.1 Data Warehouse and Customer Analytics (ERM)

Many enterprises find it necessary to complement their CRM systems, as well as their ERP systems, with Business Intelligence (BI) tools that support decision making. BI includes a range of tools such as query and reporting, business graphics, online analytical processing (OLAP), statistical analysis, forecasting, and data mining. Data Warehouse, OLAP, and Data Mining are the *killer apps* for CRM. CRM tries to capture information from each customer touch point and store it in a single repository so that all customer-facing personnel have a complete understanding of the company's relationship with each customer.

More than merely gathering of the information, it's the accurate analysis of the information that gives businesses the opportunity to improve their customer relationship and maximize their bottom lines. OLAP software helps an enterprise to maximize the profits from its customer base by focusing on

1. What is done, when, and how (processes, activities, and communications)
2. To whom (i.e., to which specific segment of the customer base)
3. Its effect on the behavior, loyalty, and value of the targeted customers

Being able to monitor the effect that various actions have on the customer base will allow a company to make sure that they retain the *best* customers and that the candidates with the best growth potential are identified and appropriately targeted.

Chapter 15 describes SAP Business Intelligence and Business Warehouse (BW) solutions from SAP.

2.5.2 Data Mining

Data mining is of great interest because it is imperative for enterprises to realize the competitive value of the information residing within their data repositories. The goal of data mining is to provide the capability to convert high-volume data into high-value information. This involves discovering patterns of information within large repositories of enterprise data. Enterprises that are most likely to benefit from data mining

- Exist in competitive markets
- Have large volumes of data
- Have communities of information consumers who are not trained as statisticians
- Have enterprise data that are complex in nature

More traditional Business Intelligence (BI) tools enable users to generate ad hoc reports, business graphics, and test *hunches*. This is useful for analyzing profitability, product line performance, and so on. Data mining techniques can be applied when users don't already know what they are looking for: data mining provides an automatic method for discovering patterns in data (see Delmater and Hancock 2001).

Data mining accomplishes two different things:

1. It gleans enterprise information from historical data.
2. It combines historic enterprise information with current conditions and goals to reduce uncertainty about enterprise outcomes.

Customer-centric data mining techniques can be used to build models of past business experience that can be applied to predict customer behavior and achieve benefits in the future. Data mining provides the following insights:

- Learning patterns that allow rapid, proper routing of customer inquiries
- Learning customer buying habits to suggest likely products of interest

■ Categorizing customers for focused attention (e.g., churn prediction, prevention)
■ Providing predictive models to reduce cost and allow more competitive pricing (e.g., fraud/waste control)
■ Assisting purchasers in the selection of inventory of customer-preferred products

2.6 Customer-Triggered Company

The Internet has engendered a dramatic shift in the business environment from a production-centric model to a customer-centric one. It has led to a tidal wave that has swept the market beyond the model of a customer-driven company to the more recently witnessed phenomenon of what I term as the customer-triggered company. The outstanding potential for the survival and success of customer-triggered companies is amply demonstrated by the ubiquity of customer-centric e-commerce services companies.

Currently, more than computers and computing, it is the customer that is all pervasive. The pervasive customer wants

1. Personalized attention
2. To buy in smaller quantities
3. Customized products
4. To postpone the buying decision closer to the purchasing decision
5. To enjoy the buying experience at any convenient time or place with any convenient mode of payment
6. Easy access to the status of the order
7. Instant gratification
8. Increased excellent service and support at a lower cost

In the Internet-based economy, success hinges on establishing a *pull*. In this century, instead of the four Ps of marketing (product, price, place, and promotion), the four Cs (content, cost, convenience, and communications) would reign, all centered on the individual customers, rather than the products earlier. Figure 2.5 shows the old and the new marketing mix. The content includes the information on the products and services as well as the direct context of the presentation.

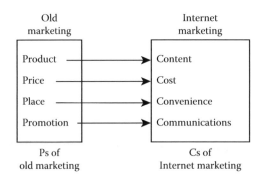

Figure 2.5   Internet marketing mix.

Never before has it been so easy for a customer to find a desired product or service along with contextual data necessary to make an informed purchase decision. Companies need to truly focus on sensing, feeling, thinking, relating, and acting to each individual customer. This is the best example of a *high-tech and high-touch* organization. Customers are no more than a click away from a world of comparative information about products, prices, and alternatives that are resulting in heightened competition among the suppliers. Companies need to respond rapidly and profitably to this generation of net-savvy and opportunistic customers who are perpetually on the verge of switching or clicking to alternate suppliers.

The power of the customer will continue to grow to unprecedented levels with the ever-increasing ability to shop and buy anything from any one at any price at any time anywhere.

2.6.1 Event-Driven Business Systems

Unlike the make-to-stock strategy that has dominated since the 1980s, the millennium enterprises must adopt the strategy of make-to-order, or even beyond to a *sense and respond* to the customized requirements of individual customers. In fact, the JIT philosophy for increasing the efficiencies and effective responsiveness of the supply chains would have to surpass itself to become synchronized with the actual event of an order being placed by the customer, which will truly become the universal point of purchase (POP). It is in this sense that the market is moving rapidly toward the event-driven enterprise where all actions are actually triggered by the click of the customer on the personalized WUIs of enterprises.

All actions of procurement, production, dispatch, and collection will result from the subsequent cascade of events triggered within the enterprise and the extended enterprise. The lines among the CRM, eCRM, ERM, and back-of-office systems like ERP and SCM are blurring. This will lead organizations to shed the monolithic, vertically integrated infrastructures of the past and embrace loosely coupled, independent, and Internet-agile organizations that engage collectively to address a momentary customer transaction.

2.7 Summary

The real power of this concept can be seen when we go beyond the boundaries of an enterprise. In the last chapter of this book, we look beyond the physical confines of an enterprise to include its partners like vendors and customers into an extension of the enterprise to the next higher level of what we term as the Extended Collaborative Enterprise (ECE). We also introduced the powerful notion of the *Customer-Triggered Company* as an event-driven enterprise where all actions are triggered by the *click of the customer* on the personalized Web user-interfaces WUIs of the enterprises. SAP has adopted a symbiotic strategy to go beyond simple integration to collaboration between the customer-centric enterprises.

Chapter 3

CRM Evaluation

This chapter outlines the concepts and criteria for evaluating the CRM package most suitable to the requirements of a company. Managers must initially make a careful decision on the functional requirements that are desired and the characteristic features and facilities expected of the CRM system as a whole. Managers can then make an objective selection of the best CRM to deploy, considering the various factors described in this chapter.

3.1 Capital Budgeting Models

The business case of the cloud computing project should contain the cost–benefit analysis. The evaluation point is to justify that the benefits have outweighed the costs. In this subsection, six capital budgeting models will be examined briefly. These models are

- The Payback method
- The Accounting Rate of Return on Investment (ROI)
- The Net Present Value (NPV)
- The Cost–Benefit Ratio
- The Profitability Index
- The Internal Rate of Return (IRR)
- The Economic Value Added (EVA)

3.1.1 Payback Method

The payback method calculates the number of years it will take before the initial investment of the project is paid back. The shorter the payback time, the more attractive a project is as it reduces the risk of longer-term payouts. The method is quite popular due to its simplicity; the weakness of the method is it ignores the time value of money:

$$\text{Number of Years to Pay Back} = \frac{\text{Original Investment}}{\text{Annual Net Cash Flow}}$$

Although a popular investment appraisal method, payback period only qualifies as a first screening technique to initially appraise a project. Its scope is limited to the period the investment is recovered; hence, it ignores potential benefits as a result of investment gains or shortfalls thereafter.

3.1.2 Accounting Rate of Return on Investment (ROI)

This method calculates the return of investment (ROI) by calculating the resulting cash inflows (produced by the investment) for depreciation. The investment inflows are totaled and the investment costs are subtracted to derive the profit. The profit is divided by the number of years invested, and then by the investment cost, to estimate the annual rate of return.

An ROI analysis calculates the difference between the stream of benefits and the stream of costs over the lifetime of the system discounted by the applicable interest rate. In order to find the ROI, the average net benefit has to be calculated:

$$\text{Net Benefits} = \frac{\text{Total Benefits} - \text{Total Costs} - \text{Depreciation}}{\text{Useful Life}}$$

leading to

$$\text{ROI} = \frac{\text{Net Benefits}}{\text{Initial Investment}}$$

3.1.3 Net Present Value (NPV)

The Net Present Value (NPV) approach calculates the amount of money that an investment is worth, taking into account its costs, earnings, and time value of money (inflation). Thus, it compares the economic value of a project today with the value of the same project in the future, taking inflation and returns into account. If the NPV of a prospective project is positive, it should be accepted. If the NPV is negative, the project should probably be rejected because the resulting cash flows will also be negative.

First, the present value is calculated as

$$\text{Payment} = \frac{1(1 + \text{interest}) - n}{\text{Interest}}$$

Leading to

$$\text{Net present value}(\text{NPV}) = \text{Present Value of Expected Cash Value} - \text{Initial Investment Costs}$$

3.1.4 Cost–Benefit Ratio

This calculation method views the total benefits of an investment over the costs consumed to deliver these benefits:

$$\text{Cost–Benefit Ratio} = \frac{\text{Total Benefits}}{\text{Total Costs}}$$

3.1.5 Profitability Index

The profitability index attempts to identify the relationship between the costs and benefits of the project through the ration calculated as

$$\text{Profitability Index} = \frac{\text{Present Value of Cash Flows}}{\text{Investment}}$$

The lowest acceptable value of Profitability Index is 1.0; any value lower than 1.0 would indicate that the project's present value is less than the initial investment. As values of the profitability index increase, so does the financial attractiveness of the proposed project.

3.1.6 Internal Rate of Return (IRR)

The IRR calculates the rate of return that an investment is expected to earn, taking into consideration the time value of money. The higher is the project's IRR, the more desirable it is to carry out the project.

Internal rate of return (IRR) is a capital investment measure that indicates how efficient an investment is (yield), using a compounded return rate. If the cost of capital used to discount future cash flows is increased, the NPV of the project will fall. As the cost of capital continues to increase, the net present value will become zero before it becomes negative. The IRR is the cost of the capital (or a required rate of return) that produces an NPV of zero.

> For the NPV method, we assume that the generated cash flows over the life of the project can be invested elsewhere, at a rate equal to the cost of capital, as the cost of capital represents an opportunity cost. The IRR, on the other hand, assumes that generated cash flows can be reinvested elsewhere at the internal rate of return. The larger the IRR in relation to the cost of capital, the less likely that the alternative returns can be realized; hence, the underlying investment assumption in the IRR method is a doubtful one, whereas for NPV, the reinvestment assumption seems more realistic. In the same way, the NPV can accommodate conventional cash flows, whereas in comparison, we may get multiple results through the IRR method.

If a company has several competing cloud computing projects, the IRR can be used in selecting which project to prioritize.

3.1.7 Economic Value Added (EVA™)

Economic Value Added (EVA), also known as economic profit, is a measure used to determine the company's financial performance based on the residual wealth created. It depicts the investor or shareholder value creation above the required return or the opportunity cost of the capital. It measures the economic profit created when the return on the capital employed exceeds the cost of the capital. Reducing costs increases profits and economic value added. Unlike ROI, economic value added takes into account the residual values for an investment.

3.1.8 Total Cost of Ownership (TCO)

Total cost of ownership (TCO) is simply the sum total of all associated costs relating to the purchase, ownership, usage, and maintenance of a particular product. As with any consumer product—let us say an automobile—there is the end-user cost or the purchase price, and then there are the costs associated with tires, oil, fuel, batteries, and so on over the useful life of the automobile. Similarly with investments in IT infrastructure (hardware, networking, data center, etc.) and applications (enterprise packages, databases, data warehouses, office productivity applications, etc.), there are costs associated with ownership that are over and above the initial purchase price. There are costs for hardware and software maintenance (the costs paid to the vendor for ongoing support, bug fixes, upgrades, and case escalations.) There are costs for power to run and cool servers, storage, and network hardware in the data center. There are also the costs associated with internal support and break-fix activities (also known as moves, adds, and changes [MAC]).

Depending on the type of investment, it may be either be expensed or capitalized. Small tools and noncapital expenditures under a certain threshold (usually $3,000–$5,000) are typically expensed and are not depreciated over their useful life. Items such as fiber and copper cables often fall into this category. Larger, more expensive items—such as disk storage, servers, tape libraries, switches, routers, computer room air chillers, and so on—are considered fixed assets (FA), and are capitalized, and thus depreciated over their useful life. If an asset is depreciated, the depreciation expense should be included in the TCO analysis.

 Generally accepted accounting principles (GAAP) recognize multiple methods of depreciation, including straight-line, declining, sum of the years' digits, and double-declining. For the purposes of our examples, we use straight-line depreciation only, purely for ease of use.

For a basic example of TCO analysis, consider a disk storage unit that costs $1,000,000 and has a useful life of three years. Using the straight-line depreciation method, the depreciation charge for this unit would be $333,333.33 per year. Additionally, there is a maintenance contract with the vendor for $100,000 annually. The physical footprint of the device equals four tiles in the data center (which we know from our facilities management firm costs $10,000 a year, including power and cooling charges). Finally, the MAC associated with provisioning storage for our clients requires one full-time equivalent (FTE) storage engineer at $150,000 annually.

Item	Annual Charge	Three-Year Charge
Disk storage	$333,333.333	$1,000,000.00
Maintenance	$100,000.00	$300,000.00
Facilities	$10,000.00	$30,000.00
FTE labor	$150,000.00	$450,000.00
Total	$593,333.33	$1,780,000.00

Thus, for this simplified example, the TCO is $593,333.33 annually and that the TCO over the lifetime of the product is $1,780,000.00.

3.2 Preparing a Business Case for CRM

Before proceeding with the evaluation, selection, and implementation of a CRM, it is essential to prove that its introduction will have demonstrable benefits for the organization. Each application has a different purpose, nature, certainty, and risks. This is achieved by preparing a business case for the implementation of a CRM. The basic premise of a business case is that an investment will have an impact and payback that spans a timeline spreading across a few months or years. However, to be relevant, it is essential that the input costs and the resulting outcomes must be directly related to the specific investment decision. This is difficult because

- There are no baseline data available prior to the implementation of the CRM, making before and after comparisons impossible.
- There are too many independent variables to be accounted for.
- Many of the resulting benefits are soft (or intangible) and hard to quantify.

There are several approaches for assessing the payback potential and period of any investment. Here are some of these approaches.

3.2.1 Financial Approach

The financial approaches use techniques like Return on Investments (ROI) based on the calculations of the Net Present Value (NPV) or the Internal Rate of Return (IRR). But one of the simplest methods is to compute the *breakeven/payback* period, when the cumulative flow of income or benefits exceeds the cumulative flow of the costs. Clearly, the shorter is the payback, better is the opportunity. However, this is not very reliable beyond a period of couple of years, as it does not take into account the time value of money.

Financial benefits from the implementation of CRM can be assessed in terms of the increased revenues. This increase could result either from the generation of new revenue or because of more efficient production of erstwhile revenue.

Revenue growth envisaged from the implementation of CRM systems could result from

1. Increased sales through
   a. Gaining new customers
   b. Retaining the customers longer
   c. Realizing higher price for existing products or from new sales (up-sell and cross sell)
   d. Drastic reduction in the costs of closing the first sale through reduced no. of calls, accelerated search, and evaluation
2. Better sales mix or customer mix:
   a. Increasing sales of higher-margin products or platform products (see Section 3.2.3 "Strategic Approach")
   b. Bonding strongly with higher-value customers and at the same time motivating other customers to exit from the company's customer base
3. Enhanced customer benefits resulting in improved retention through
   a. Improved response time to customer requests
   b. Easy access to current order status
   c. Reduced costs of searching, evaluating, and buying the product/solution or service
   d. Reduced costs of using and supporting the product/solution or service
   e. Delivered product/solution or service, which meets or exceeds customer expectations
   f. Greater range of products/solutions or services addressing varying needs of the customer

3.2.2 Cost Reduction Approach

This is one of the most direct ways of justifying an investment for the introduction of information systems. Assuming that the benefits from the new systems are equal to or greater than the existing system, one simply compares the costs of the proposed system with the existing system. A variation on this approach is the value-added analysis of the related business processes within the organization. In this approach, that is, the essence of the BPM approach presented in Chapter 7, the organization essentially identifies the non-value-added tasks and either eliminates them or substitutes for them more efficient processes via automated systems like CRM:

1. *Sales support*: The Major factors that contribute in reducing sales costs are
   a. Automation of proposals, configuration, and quotations
   b. Referencing and reviewing notes and files before calls
   c. Managing samples, demo stock, sales literature, etc.
   d. Preparing sales forecasts and customer call reports
   e. Providing better-quality leads in usable format
   f. Reducing the number of customer calls necessary to close a sale by enabling capture of critical information at the point of sale, better customer information, and on-the-spot reports on different configurations and costs
   g. Finding and providing product or technical information to the customers
   h. Information and learning about new product/solutions and services, best-practice templates, domain knowledge guides, etc.
2. *Direct marketing*: Cost savings can result from better targeting, personalization, and elimination of duplicates and blank calls. In fact, better targeting and validated data should enable the volume of direct mail to be reduced while simultaneously increasing the response rates.
3. *Call centers/customer contact centers*: Staff is the most expensive element in setting up and running a contact center. By automating as many processes as possible—no. of calls, call routing, and assisted call answering—companies can save up to 70% on the staff costs.
4. *More accurate sales forecasts*: For some organizations, better sales forecasting will enable
   a. Reductions in inventory resulting in savings on stockholding costs
   b. More efficient production schedules resulting in reduced per unit costs
5. *Staff motivation and loyalty*: Like customer loyalty, employee loyalty also has a positive effect on profitability. High sales staff turnover has an adverse effect on the sales relationship and the potential of subsequent up-sell and cross sell opportunities.

3.2.3 Strategic Approach

Unlike the earlier approaches, the strategic approach takes a view on the future. CRM systems provide support for organizational change as also for rapid delivery of strategic changes to product, pricing, and customer information. For a better payback, it is important that the CRM strategies should be linked to the company's business and market strategies.

 While CRM strategies are based on the fundamental premise of enhancing customer relationships, this does not necessarily imply that CRM systems require a single view of the customer across all channels and customer touch points. As noted in Chapter 1, Section 1.2 "Concept of Customer Relationship Management (CRM)," all customers are not equal and may prefer certain specific channels or touch points over the others.

Thus, it is critical to identify and develop models for managing different types of profitable customer relationships. For adoption, each of these models may need a different business and market strategy and, therefore, a different approach to implement the CRM systems. The following are some of these profitability models relevant to CRM systems projects:

3.2.3.1 Solutions Profit

This strategy demands up-front investment commitment to understand customers' economics and identify ways to make them more favorable. This demands working closely with the customer to discover how they search, evaluate, test, buy, and use their products and then find ways to help the customers in improving the difficult, time-consuming, or expensive areas of their functions and processes. This strategy is characterized by

- Early negative cash flow
- Customized products that are finely integrated with customer's operations
- Midterm to long-term payback horizon
- High customer retention

For this model, the CRM systems have to provide a unified view of key customers across all channels and touch points.

3.2.3.2 Time Profit

This strategy enables exploitation of the early mover advantages for innovative solutions; being first allows innovators to generate excess returns, but only until imitators begin to erode margins. Price premiums exist, but the opportunity window is for a short period of times. This strategy is characterized by

- Sporadic but large investments
- Constant innovation as value migrates away from the current innovation
- Ability to bring new products and services to market quickly
- High prices and abundant profits but for short period of times
- Immediate-term to short-term payback horizon
- High customer satisfaction resulting from acquiring unique products or solutions

For this model, the CRM systems require rapid development and quick deployment.

3.2.3.3 Multiplier Profit

This strategy churns out gains from the same product, character, trademark, capability, or service, over and over again. Technologically, this corresponds to the economics of *increasing returns* that is characteristic of network effect phenomenon as witnessed in media, software, and related industries. Business-wise, this is allied closely to the brand-building strategy. This strategy is characterized by

- Large and even huge investments in building brands
- Unified brand across a broad array of products

- Risk of brand erosion or dissipation if extended to unrelated areas
- Payback horizon highly dependent on the rapidity of buildup of the installed base
- Brands, which are valuable but intangible assets like customer relationships

For this model, the CRM systems must support international brand management as also localization for identifying and developing opportunities in specific markets:

3.2.3.4 Platform Profit

This strategy demands maintenance and management of a user base of high-value customers focused around its product platform. Such a group of committed customers can then be promoted through up-selling and cross selling to higher-margin add-on solutions and services. The More proprietary is the base product platform, the more powerful is this strategy as a profit-generating mechanism. This strategy is characterized by

- Comprehensive platform architecture and design standards
- Established conformance programs for qualifying third-party coproducts
- Comprehensive interface design preferably proprietary standards
- A product/service portfolio that meets the needs throughout the Customer Life Cycle (CLC)
- Efforts to establish the standard industry-wide and achieve ubiquity

For this model, the CRM systems must cater to the company's standardized architecture and interfaces for integrating best-of-breed solutions.

3.2.3.5 Innovation Profit

This strategy demands that companies remain in direct contact with the customers to dynamically solicit feedback and also remain lean and agile to quickly reconfigure their business operations and processes more suitable to the altered requirements or expectations. Successful companies tend to become more risk averse, more formalized, more bureaucratic, more insulated from the customers, and, finally, more lethargic in their responses to demanding circumstances. However, the most damaging factor is the widening gap from the actual customers: direct feedback from customers is reduced, filtered, and often ignored. The twin forces of direct customer contact and agile operations create potential for enormous profits. This strategy is characterized by

- Organizational design that emphasizes direct customer contact and agile responsiveness
- Smaller autonomous and agile strategic business units (SBUs)
- Early positive cash flow, but volatile P/L scenarios
- Unalloyed direct feedback from the customers
- High-performance-based rewards and compensation resulting in highly responsive sales operations

For this model, the CRM systems have to focus on becoming highly responsive to the top 20% of the customer including customized requirements, rapid implementations, and deployments.

3.2.3.6 Exchange Profit

This strategy brings multiple sellers and buyers together and enables them to place offers, match offers, and, finally, execute the deals. The exchange reduces the costs for both the buyers and sellers coupled with assured throughputs, security, and integrity of the system. This strategy is characterized by

- Increasing profits with increasing transaction or business volumes
- Easy access to accredited customers
- Control of the information flow through the exchange
- Myriad value-added services for payments, settlements, account maintenance, and so on

For this model, the CRM systems must enable robust and high-performing systems.

3.3 CRM Acquisition Decision Process

The evaluation and selection of the CRM packages for implementation within organizations is a major exercise. A Specific effort needs to be taken for the evaluation of highly complex CRM packages, like SAP CRM, in terms of their functionality and technology. The package needs to be selected by judiciously balancing on both the dimensions of functionality and technology and the mutually contradictory requirements for complexity and flexibility of the CRM packages. Companies have processes ranging from make-to-order to continuous flows. For certain short-comings in functionality, they may also have to decide to build, rather than buy, some of the applications.

In the following section, we discuss the various aspects to be considered when evaluating the CRM packages suitable for an organization. The actual process of selecting a CRM is the topic of the next chapter.

3.3.1 General Considerations of CRM Evaluation

The general characteristics of CRM packages to be reviewed include

- Comprehensive functionality
- Ease of use
- Capability for customizing
- Controls and reliability
- Ease of installation
- Efficiency of operation
- Ease of user management
- Open system architecture
- Open system interfaces; legacy system and third-legacy products
- Data synchronization
- Internationalization and Euro currency
- Online documentation and contextual help
- Future upgrades and enhancements
- Skill transfer and training programs
- User group activity

3.3.2 Checklists for CRM Evaluation

The exercise of evaluating CRMs becomes easier if detailed checklists of major points of interest are prepared beforehand. These checklists can be used to gather relevant information that can be analyzed and used as the basis for the selection process.

Tables 3.1 through 3.8 are included for reference:

1. CRM vendor issues are illustrated in Table 3.1.
2. CRM product issues are illustrated in Table 3.2.
3. CRM technical issues are illustrated in Table 3.3.
4. CRM installation and operation issues are illustrated in Table 3.4.
5. CRM integration and interface issues are illustrated in Table 3.5.
6. CRM modification and maintenance issues are illustrated in Table 3.6.
7. CRM audit and control issues are illustrated in Table 3.7.
8. CRM standards and documentation issues are illustrated in Table 3.8.

The meaning of the column headings is as follows:

■ *Available*: Indicates that the functionality is currently available as standard functionality in the CRM system
■ *Configured*: Indicates that the functionality is not available as the standard functionality, but the CRM system can be configured easily to deliver the required functionality
■ *Upgraded*: Indicates the functionality is planned and would become available in future named upgrades or release versions of the CRM system
■ *Third party*: Indicates that the functionality is not available but is available with third-party packages that have been specifically qualified for the CRM system
■ *Absent*: Not available at the time of the evaluation

3.3.3 Checklists for CRM Functional Requirements

When evaluating the suitability of a CRM package, the detailed functional requirements of an enterprise need to be analyzed and enlisted for detailed scrutiny later. This also acts as the baseline for the comparative evaluation of the various CRM packages.

CRM applications are subdivided into three segments—marketing automation software, sales automation software, and customer support and call center software. Sales software is designed to manage functions, from high-end processes like account/contact management and list management to low-end processes like simple content management. Marketing software assists with such things as campaign management and execution and list management and telemarketing. Customer support and call center applications are designed to enhance the management of relationship with existing customers.

In the CRM space, Sales Force Automation (SFA) represents the oldest set of functionality that has been addressed by IT solutions in the past but is also the most difficult because of the inherent relationship orientation of the processes involved. SFA applications focus on functionalities like lead distribution and tracking, pipeline management, contact centralization, and management and group collaboration. The advent of the Internet has also altered the fundamental premise of SFA by attempting to make the sales process devoid of the salesman by providing RFP/RFI type of capabilities through an automated interface.

Table 3.1 CRM Evaluation: Vendor Issues

Item No.	Description	Available	Configured	Upgraded	Third Party	Absent
1.	How long has the CRM under consideration been sold by the vendor in the market?					
2.	Has it been developed in-house or acquired? Is the core development team still with them?					
3.	What is the gross annual turnover and profit of the company? What is the ratio of sales to support revenue?					
4.	How long has the vendor been in the packaged solution market?					
5.	What is the installed base of this CRM?					
6.	What are the hardware and operating systems that it is currently available on?					
7.	How are they distributed: industry-wise or location-wise?					
8.	What is the geographical spread of the vendor's development, sales, and support offices?					
9.	How many employees does the company have in technical and support functions?					
10.	What are the vendor's support and service policies?					
11.	Does the vendor provide online modem-based support?					
12.	What are vendor's training programs and facilities?					
13.	How many employees does the company have in development, technical support, training, and commercial areas?					
14.	Do the company's products have user groups? How are they organized?					
15.	Who are the technical and business partners of the vendor?					
16.	What is the company's strategy for industry-specific solutions?					
17.	Is the vendor itself ready to implement the CRM package within the company?					

Table 3.2 CRM Evaluation: Product Issues

Item No.	Description	Available	Configured	Upgraded	Third Party	Absent
1.	How many actual package users are there?					
2.	How many years have they been using the package? How many locations has the package been operational?					
3.	Have the users been satisfied with the package?					
4.	Can the vendor provide references of companies where the CRM under consideration is in operation?					
5.	Can the vendor provide details of installations at these customer sites?					
6.	Can the vendor provide professional references who can be contacted in these companies?					
7.	Can the vendor arrange a visit to one or two sites where the package has been operational? Can this visit include detailed demos and a review of experiences, operations, and problems?					
8.	Is the package user friendly?					
9.	What is the product map? Is it comprehensive?					
10.	Does it cover all functions of a CRM?					
11.	How scalable is the CRM in terms of the number of users that can be supported as well as its ability to be deployed as a company-wide solution?					
12.	Does it follow the principle of one-point data entry?					
13.	Does it have a centralized database for enterprise data?					
14.	Are the transactions updates done in batch or online mode?					
15.	Can it be integrated? Can its modules work in a stand-alone mode?					
16.	How easy is it to integrate with third-party systems and solutions?					

17.	Does it have an open architecture with adherence to worldwide standards?					
18.	Is it based on nonproprietary technology? Can it work on standard hardware and operating system platforms?					
19.	Does it follow standard protocols and interfaces? Can it interface with legacy and other systems like ERP, SCM, CRM, EDI, and CTI?					
20.	Does the source code made available along with the system?					
21.	Is it accessible for making modifications? How will modifications and corrections be made?					
22.	Will modifications of the CRM be necessary to obtain efficient and effective operations?					
23.	Will the CRM markedly affect other user services?					
24.	How easy is it to configure the CRM to the specific requirements of a company quickly and simply?					
25.	Does the system enable the uploading of data from the legacy systems used by the enterprise?					
26.	Does the system have utilities for doing the data conversion? What is the cost of such utilities?					
27.	What is the development status of the product? Is it slated to go through a major revamping or major additions?					
28.	Does the package contain current technological features?					
29.	What is the enhancement and upgrade strategy of the product?					
30.	How many releases or upgrades have been introduced in the last 2 years?					
31.	How often are the new releases introduced?					
32.	Did the releases meet the customers' schedule?					

(Continued)

Table 3.2 (*Continued*)   CRM Evaluation: Product Issues

Item No.	Description	Available	Configured	Upgraded	Third Party	Absent
33.	What is the design strategy for addressing Euro currency and international languages?					
34.	What is the product strategy to make it Web enabled?					
35.	Does the system have e-commerce functionality, or does it have third-party e-commerce solutions?					
36.	What is the product strategy to introduce and enhance country-specific functionality?					
37.	What is the product strategy to introduce industry-specific functionality?					
38.	What is the market view of the product? Has it been analyzed, compared, and benchmarked?					
39.	Does the package rate well in surveys?					
40.	What is the cost of the package?					
41.	Is the cost based on the envisaged number of users?					
42.	What are the licensing policies of the product?					
43.	What is the cost of additional features and modules required by the enterprise?					
44.	What are the annual recurring costs?					
45.	What is the cost of periodically purchasing updated versions?					
46.	What is the cost of installation?					
47.	What is the cost of training?					
48.	What is the cost of system documentation?					
49.	What is the cost of vendor support and services?					

Table 3.3 CRM Evaluation: Technical Issues

Item No.	Item Description	Available	Configured	Upgraded	Third Party	Absent
1.	Does the CRM run on the target platform identified by the enterprise including Windows NT/2000, UNIX (AIX, HP-UX, Solaris), and OS/390?					
2.	Does the CRM support a variety of architectures like three tiers, multitier, and n-tier?					
3.	What is the minimum configuration required for the target computer for installing the CRM including the Application Server, Database Server, Connected Client, Thin Client, and Mobile/Handheld Client?					
4.	Does the package support the following mail servers: MS Exchange, MS Outlook, MS Mail, cc:Mail, and Lotus Notes?					
5.	Does the package support the Web scripting languages like Hyper Text Markup Language (HTML), Dynamic Hyper Text Markup Language (DHTML), Extended Markup Language (XML), JavaServer Pages (JSP), JavaScript, and Visual Basic VBScript?					
6.	Does the package need any optional features from the OS?					
7.	Does the CRM have an application repository system?					
8.	Does it have a GUI system?					
9.	Does the system provide for defining default screen characteristics, function keys, fonts, and so on?					
10.	Does the menu have pictures or icons? Is the status information displayed on the screen for reference?					
11.	Does it have a menu management system?					
12.	Is the system start-up satisfactory, including date, time, operator identification, control numbers, and security controls?					

(Continued)

Table 3.3 (*Continued*) CRM Evaluation: Technical Issues

Item No.	Item Description	Available	Configured	Upgraded	Third Party	Absent
13.	Are there clear, brief, and well-documented instructions to guide the user through the system?					
14.	Are error messages well formatted, clear, and well documented?					
15.	Are the error correction options and instructions satisfactory?					
16.	Are single-key action commands used to speed the interaction of the user?					
17.	Does it have a help management system? Is contextual help available on a field or a program?					
18.	Does it have a database management system or utilize a variety of standard RDBMSs like Oracle 8, IBM DB2, MS SQl Server, Sybase, and Informix?					
19.	Does the package provide ability to record e-mails, voice files, multimedia files (including compression mechanisms), etc.?					
20.	Does it have a facility for database reorganization?					
21.	Does the system provide direct access to the data within the database outside of the system?					
22.	Are the record sizes, key structures, and other elements relatively independent of the target environment?					
23.	Are the detailed layouts available for all data tables?					
24.	Do the data tables contain sufficient audit trails including date changed, by whom, and the type of change?					
25.	Does the system test for the existence of numbers such as account numbers, document numbers, and code numbers?					

26.	Does the package have adequate input and output edits and controls?					
27.	Does the package have adequate controls for maintaining the integrity of tables and data?					
28.	Does it have a 4GL development system?					
29.	Does it have a query management system?					
30.	Does it have a report management system?					
31.	Can the user select documents, formats, and fields and control the output on the screen to the printer?					
32.	Administration system?					
33.	Does the system provide mirroring or data replication?					
34.	Does it have facility for data replication and synchronization?					
35.	Can the system tolerate errors and difficulties at the terminals and continue operating?					
36.	Does the system save the data needed for recovery in case of power failure, entry of improper data, and so on?					
37.	Are terminal users prevented from stopping, disrupting, or destroying the operation of the system?					
38.	Are there simple nondestructive methods for EXIT or GO BACK or PREVIOUS SCREEN?					
39.	Does it have a software distribution system?					
40.	Does the system provide for defining an access profile at specific terminals?					
41.	Does it have a configuration management system?					

(*Continued*)

Table 3.3 (Continued)   CRM Evaluation: Technical Issues

Item No.	Item Description	Available	Configured	Upgraded	Third Party	Absent
42.	Does the system help in guiding through the configuration system?					
43.	Does it have a change management system?					
44.	Does the system have facilities to control the release of new or changed programs into production?					
45.	Does it have a version management system?					
46.	Does it have a security and administration system?					
47.	Does the system provide for defining and maintaining access profiles and passwords?					
48.	Does it have an audit management system?					
49.	Does it have a disaster recovery system?					
50.	Does the system provide automatic recovery procedures?					
51.	Does it have an archival management system?					
52.	Does it have a communications management system?					
53.	Does the package support the following communications channel: telephone, Web, Fax, E-mail, Dial-up Modem, Interactive Voice Response (IVR), Wireless/PDA, and so on?					
54.	Does the package have the capability to handle and route inbound and outbound faxes to selected destinations/groups/users?					
55.	Does the system have a Computer Telephony Integration (CTI) architecture based on Telephony Application Programming Interface (TAPI), Java Technology Application Programming Interface (JTAPI), and CallPath Services and Telephony Architecture (CSTA)?					

56.	Does the package support intelligent responses to callers by identifying them via Automatic Number Identification (ANI), Dialed Number Identification Services (DNIS), Calling Line ID (CLID), or caller information given via IVR?				
57.	Does the system provide facilities for Automatic Call Distribution (ACD) depending on the type of the routing to be employed based on skill, predefined rules, or customer information?				
58.	Does the system provide facilities or real-time monitoring of ACD queues and outbound call activity?				
59.	Does the CRM provide facilities for recording phone conversations?				
60.	Does the system provide softphone support for functions such as Dial, Answer, Transfer, Conference, Hold, and Speed Dial?				
61.	Does the system support call scripting?				
62.	Does the system support Web callback facility?				
63.	Does it have an API system?				
64.	Does it have an online documentation system?				
65.	Does it have a powerful search facility as well as suggestions on related topics?				
66.	Does it have a print documentation system?				
67.	Does it have an online tutorial, training, and demonstration system?				
68.	Does it have an office automation system?				
69.	Does it have a GroupWare and Workflow system?				
70.	Does the system have a built-in system for the following: workflow/routing capabilities, escalation, and flexible query system?				

(Continued)

Table 3.3 (Continued) CRM Evaluation: Technical Issues

Item No.	Item Description	Available	Configured	Upgraded	Third Party	Absent
71.	Does the Workflow system interface with the e-mail system?					
72.	Does it have a data warehouse and data analysis system?					
73.	Does the CRM have an integrated knowledge engine and built-in knowledge bases (especially for industry-specific functionality) and/or support third-party knowledge engines and knowledge bases?					
74.	Does the system have the ability to support and access multiple knowledge engines and knowledge bases concurrently?					
75.	Does the system provide capability for a group to build and populate knowledge bases as needed (including any attached files such as text, binary, and multimedia files)?					
76.	Does the knowledge engine support capabilities like Boolean logic processing, rule-based representation, explanatory facility, pattern matching, rule performance/efficiency algorithms, and case-based matching algorithms?					
77.	Does the system enable the knowledge engine and knowledge bases to support databases, the Internet, hyperlink/hypertext, Web pages, reporting software, batch import/export of data, customization/upgrades/updates/new releases of knowledge engine and knowledge source databases, APIs (for IVR, ACD, and MS Exchange/Lotus Notes), and testing and validation of the knowledge engine and knowledge base?					
78.	Does it have an implementation project management system?					
79.	Does the system report on missed milestones, schedules, and so on?					

Table 3.4 CRM Evaluation: Installation and Operation Issues

Item No.	Description	Available	Configured	Upgraded	Third Party	Absent
1.	Are the vendor's and purchaser's installation responsibilities clearly defined?					
2.	Are installation specifications defined clearly?					
3.	Does the vendor have a manual or computer-assisted installation procedure?					
4.	Does the configuration of the installation depend on the specifics of the enterprise, and is there enough assistance available via documentation or vendor personnel?					
5.	Are the acceptance criteria clearly defined?					
6.	Does the operation of the system need extensive training for computer operators and system programmers?					
7.	Does the vendor provide sample operating standards and procedures that can be adapted and used?					
8.	Does the system documentation conform to the installation's documentation standards?					
9.	Can the system be installed in the operating system environment, database, LAN, and so on without major modifications?					
10.	Are the system's performance criteria for acceptance clearly stated?					
11.	Does the system have guidelines for maximization of performance of the software for the following: network bandwidth requirements, database sizing threshold, number of concurrent users, and synchronization of remote clients?					
12.	Does the system provide for audit trails for the following activities: backups, failures in the system, and recovery in case of failures?					
13.	Does the vendor promise full support until the system is installed satisfactorily?					
14.	Will the vendor be available for the data conversion effort?					

Table 3.5   CRM Evaluation: Integration and Interface Issues

Item No.	Description	Available	Configured	Upgraded	Third Party	Absent
1.	Does the CRM support Application Program Interfaces (APIs) for interfacing to customized modules or third-party applications?					
2.	Does the package have APIs developed in any of the common standards like Component Object Model (COM) or Distributed Component Object Model (DCOM), Common Object Request Broker Architecture (CORBA), and Enterprise JavaBeans (EJB)?					
3.	Does the package provide facilities to access these APIs through 4GL environments like Microsoft VB, Visual C++, PowerBuilder (PB), and Java?					
4.	Does the package support APIs or specific connectors to other packages like ERPs, CRMs, and SCMs?					
5.	Does the CRM system provide an interface to its database?					
6.	Does the CRM system provide an interface to other databases and systems?					
7.	Does the CRM system conform to known communications protocols and standards?					
8.	Does it conform to known standards of encryption?					
9.	Does the system provide online or batch interfaces?					

10.	Does the system provide for controlling the upload of data into the system?					
11.	Does it provide facilities for quickly mapping the external data into the system tables and vice versa?					
12.	Does the system provide for defining and scheduling the upload or download of data in an online mode?					
13.	Does the system provide a report or audit trail on the transfer of data?					
14.	Does the package provide e-mail integration through various interfaces such as Simple Mail Transfer Protocol (SMTP) and Microsoft Windows Messaging Application Programming Interface (MAPI)?					
15.	Does the system provide an interface with the workflow system?					
16.	Does the system provide an automatic interface for loading data into a data warehouse system?					

Table 3.6 CRM Evaluation: Modification and Maintenance Issues

Item No.	Description	Available	Configured	Upgraded	Third Party	Absent
1.	Can the system function on an as-is basis without modification?					
2.	Can the users change the administrative procedures to suit their requirements?					
3.	Are all the system requirements defined through parameters and tables, making modifications easy to accomplish?					
4.	Does the vendor inform about other customers that have made similar modifications that may be available rapidly?					
5.	Are customers advised of outstanding problems that other users have discovered?					
6.	Are new releases available regularly and automatically to all the purchasers?					
7.	Can a system dump be sent to the vendor for review?					
8.	Does the vendor provide on-site support and maintenance?					
9.	Will the vendor support an installation that has the package modified by a customer?					

Table 3.7 CRM Evaluation: Security, Audit, and Control Issues

Item No.	Description	Available	Configured	Upgraded	Third Party	Absent
1.	Does the system have adequate backup if the operational version of the system is destroyed? Are all transactions properly recorded at the point of origin?					
2.	Does the system have controls to ensure that all data recorded enter the computer for processing?					
3.	Does the system provide for determining the proper authorization of transactions?					
4.	Does the system provide facilities to ensure that all data received by the system are accurate and complete?					
5.	Can the system ensure the complete and accurate processing of data through the system?					
6.	Does the system provide controls to detect the loss of data or nonprocessing of data?					
7.	Does the system ensure that all transactions are recorded in the proper accounting period and also posted to the proper records?					
8.	Can the system ensure that the organization's procedures and processing rules have been followed?					
9.	Can the system ensure that the data in the tables are accurate and complete?					
10.	Does the system have information on when the file was created and modified, by whom, and for what purpose?					

(Continued)

Table 3.7 (Continued)   CRM Evaluation: Security, Audit, and Control Issues

Item No.	Description	Available	Configured	Upgraded	Third Party	Absent
11.	Does the system provide audit trails for varied activities such as security breaches, user log-ins, profile log-ins, group log-ins, and report format modifications and generation?					
12.	Does the system provide capabilities to maintain audit trails for varied activities like database structure modifications, data field modifications, database entry, and query generation.					
13.	Does the system provide safeguards such as passwords or authorized terminals to protect the tables from unauthorized access?					
14.	Does the system provide for varied access rights for activities related to systems configuration, systems administration, systems development, MIS activities, Data Field modifications, Files/Database viewing, Files/Database editing, Report Format Modifications, Report Generation, Printing, Viewing Screens, etc.?					
15.	Does the system ensure that the processed data do not include unauthorized alterations?					
16.	Does the system have controls to ensure that all the errors detected by the system get corrected?					
17.	Do the transmitted messages include sufficient identification including the message number, terminal, date, and transaction type?					
18.	Does the system maintain logs to ensure that lost or garbled messages can be recreated?					
19.	Does the system retain information to permit the reconstruction of transactions to prove the accuracy and completeness of the processing?					

Table 3.8   CRM Evaluation: Standards and Documentation

Item No.	Description	Available	Configured	Upgraded	Third Party	Absent
1.	Does the package have standard documentation that is available online and in printed form?					
2.	Does the package provide documentation on the system's functionality, technical design, and operating environment?					
3.	Is the documentation easily referenced?					
4.	Does the system provide extensive cross-referencing facilities?					
5.	Does the system provide the capability to automatically change the relevant documentation when making modifications in the system, such as tables, fields, screen formats, and report layouts?					
6.	Does the user documentation have clear representations of menus, screens, and so on?					
7.	Does the system provide the ability to prepare relevant training material on the modified system?					
8.	Does the system describe the programming standards and procedures in sufficient detail to establish conformity and make documentation easy?					
9.	Does the system enable easy maintenance of the modifications in the system as well as the corresponding documentation?					

Applications that offer marketing automation primarily provide two major functions, namely, campaign management and demographics analysis. Campaign revolves around marketing budget management, ad management and placement, targeting campaigns, response management, and the like. While these activities have always involved a degree of statistical analysis, the variety and the colossal amount of data that are captured on the websites have led to a quantum jump in the level of such analysis.

In the past, typical customer service automation and management consisted of setting up a contact center with access to a customer database. With the advent of the Internet, the norm is a totally integrated contact center, where customer agents respond to e-mails, phone calls, and chat requests using a fully integrated customer database connected to various subsystems like the ERPs, sales and procurement portals, and supply chain applications.

The following is a detailed checklist of functional requirement needs to be compiled for the various functional areas within the company:

1. Sales Function:
    a. Field/Mobile, Indirect (resellers, brokers, and distributors) and Retail Sales
    b. Opportunity Management and Pipeline Analysis
    c. Forecasting
    d. Sales Cycle Analysis
    e. Sales Metrics
    f. Activity Reporting and Management
    g. Mapping Tools and Territory Alignment
    h. Time and Expense Reporting
    i. Quotas and Incentive Designer and Compensation Management
    j. Sales Training
    k. A sample checklist of Sales requirements shown in Table 3.9
2. Contact and Account Management Function:
    a. Contact Profile
    b. Activity Management and History
    c. Organization Chart
    d. Correspondence
    e. Business Relationships
    f. Order Entry, History, and Tracking
    g. Presentations, Proposal, and Sales Contract Generation
    h. Internet Account Maintenance
    i. E-mail System and CTI Integration and Process
    j. Wireless
    k. Sales Calendar
    l. Multiplatform Data Synchronization
3. Telemarketing/Telesales:
    a. Call Planning
    b. Call List Assembly
    c. Dynamic Branch Scripting
    d. Call History and Statistics
    e. Autodialing
    f. Productivity and Performance Analysis
    g. Literature Fulfillment

Table 3.9   CRM Functional Requirements: Sales

Item No.	Description	Available	Configured	Upgraded	Third Party	Absent
(a) Sales channel management						
1.	Does the CRM support territory management?					
2.	Does the system provide support for territory realignment or reassignment?					
3.	Does the CRM provide the ability to identify Channel Partners?					
4.	Does the system support/help in developing profile of the desired channel?					
5.	Does it help in identifying channel requirements by matching the desired with the existing channel coverages?					
6.	Does it help in identifying channel resource requirements (by matching the desired with the existing channel resources) and the enablers to bridge these gaps?					
7.	Does the system provide for Geographical Information System (GIS) for mapping out the existing channels?					
8.	Does the CRM provide facilities for management of a distribution policy, strategic partnering guidelines, Channel Partner review policy, and other information generated by internal sources?					
9.	Does it provide facility to create joint agreements/programs in conformance with the predefined agreement standards, methods, and procedures and furnish the requisite information for the same?					
10.	Does it provide the capability to (or interface with another application to) set up contracts, manage a contract against objectives, monitor/manage contract consumption, set up payment schedules, and manage terms?					
11.	Does it provide support for project planning and administration to ensure timely fulfillment of these requirements?					

(*Continued*)

Table 3.9 (Continued) CRM Functional Requirements: Sales

Item No.	Description	Available	Configured	Upgraded	Third Party	Absent
12.	Does the CRM enable evaluating performances of individual channels on selected measurement criteria?					
13.	Does it provide maintaining a repository for performance objectives against these Channel Partner agreements and provide performance analysis?					
14.	Does the CRM provide for ready read-only access to a Channel Partner and write access to the enterprise Product Catalogs and related information?					
15.	Does the system provide for management of external information from external sources such as governmental regulations, service bulletins, documents, and spreadsheets?					
16.	Does it provide for electronic distribution of collateral materials (including product and pricing information) through fax on demand or automated voice response?					
17.	Does the system enable online product-related information accessible to employees and channel partners in the form of their choice, viz., audio, video, or multimedia?					
18.	Does the CRM support forecasting of sales by product, customer segment, and promotional campaign and track the actual sales results against the forecast by sales region, sales manager, sales person, or any other user-defined criteria?					
19.	Does it trend actual, campaign management, advertising, and sales events and identify potential future shortfalls?					
20.	Does it track variance on sales discounts, margins, etc., as well as identify any correlation between compatible and/or mutually exclusive products and services?					
21.	Does the system predict the most effective sales method for a particular market, product, and/or promotion?					

22.	Does it provide the capability to evaluate, on a continuous basis, the relative success of the sales channel by tracking the conversion leads/prospects into customers and the associated sales events?						
23.	Does the CRM provide the capability to assign and track sales quotas and sales performance by region, by sales person, by channel, or by product/service?						
24.	Does the system provide for numerous details on rebates, such as special price agreement costs, rebate amounts, and volume discounts?						
25.	Does it provide support for supplier sponsored bonus/special supplier incentives to a singular or multiple recipients?						
26.	Does the system provide for calculating commissions, gross margins, and related rebates at sales person level and region or enterprise level?						
27.	Does it support payment and reporting on commissions paid over a predetermined period (weekly, monthly, and quarterly) to sales people or distribution channels/agents?						
28.	Does the system support in-depth reporting on amount and timeliness of bills collected in respect to actual and estimated sales?						
29.	Does it track receivables versus sales to monitor the quality of sales?						
30.	Does the system provide sales performance measurement by commission with number of sales, revenue per customer, margin per customer, customer service, etc.?						
31.	Does the CRM analyze channel data for fraud detection and reduce commissions for bad debt, returns, etc.?						
32.	Does it track and store historical data to help in devising of future commission plans for different market segments, products, and services?						
33.	Does it produce an accounts payable (A/P) transaction file with data on commissions, bonus/special supplier incentives, rebates, etc., for interfacing with the accounting system.						

(Continued)

Table 3.9 (*Continued*)   CRM Functional Requirements: Sales

Item No.	Description	Available	Configured	Upgraded	Third Party	Absent
(b) Sales campaign management						
1.	Does the CRM support the collection and analysis of standard and segment-specific information to assist in the selection and evaluation of marketing, materials, and media selection and placement?					
2.	Does the system help in identifying campaigns by matching the desired objectives with the results of earlier campaigns?					
3.	Does it assist in planning, monitoring, assessing, and analyzing the effectiveness of a campaign?					
4.	Does it provide facilities to define the type of campaign plan, the eligibility rules, campaign conditions, and the campaign components for both the customer and the sales person or agent?					
5.	Does it analyze competitive pricing options in support of the objectives of a campaign plan by utilizing internal and external data?					
6.	Does the system provide facilities for automatic selection of the channel to be used (face to face, phone, IVR, fax, or the Internet)?					
7.	Does the CRM provide for detection of customers ineligible for specific campaigns and discounts (depending on prior discounts being availed by the customer) and determine alternative options?					
8.	Does the CRM provide the ability to track total revenue from customers over monthly, yearly, and customer lifetime periods, awards, and bonus point programs?					
9.	Does the system have the facilities to identify *at-risk* customers through *early warning* signs such as returns, customer service inquiries, and/or significant decreases in purchasing?					

10.	Does it provide facilities to assess the desirability of maintaining an *at-risk* customer based on the corresponding payment history, profitability, and projected lifetime value (LTV) of the customer?				
11.	Does the system identify customers who have stopped purchasing products and services for *win-back* considerations?				
12.	Does it generate a retention call and/or survey distribution to valuable but *at-risk* customers to gauge the degree and reasons for dissatisfaction?				
13.	Does the system provide for undertaking win-back programs and special campaigns for selected valuable customers?				
(c) Opportunity management					
1.	Does the CRM provide for capturing all sales leads and all associated criteria?				
2.	Does the CRM provide facilities for opportunity management using a variety of methods including logging in a lead, generating a lead from customer history, or validating the lead from third-party sources?				
3.	Does the system provide for qualifying, profiling, categorizing, and prioritizing of leads for effective and efficient opportunity management?				
4.	Does the CRM support the selection and evaluation of direct marketing material as well as the corresponding target customers?				
5.	Does the system provide automated generation and distribution of product information to target customer segments?				
6.	Does it provide support for numerous methods of selling to customers including Direct Sales, Telemarketing, the Internet, and IVR?				
7.	Does it provide facilities for integrated team selling including Head office Sales Managers, Area Office Sales Officers, and Channel Partner Sales Manager?				

(*Continued*)

Table 3.9 (*Continued*) CRM Functional Requirements: Sales

Item No.	Description	Available	Configured	Upgraded	Third Party	Absent
8.	Does it support territory assignment to various members of the sales team including Area Manager, Territory Manager, and Channel Partner Sales Person?					
9.	Does the CRM provide the ability to search for customers within proximity of a Channel Partner of the enterprise?					
10.	Does the system predict potential customers for an existing product/new product or service?					
11.	Does the system provide facilities for automatically assigning leads to appropriate sales persons based on geographical location, type of customer, vendor, etc.?					
12.	Does the system support contact profiles (public addresses, phone numbers, information sent or received, calls, sales visits) for all contacts including leads, prospects, existing customers, and previous customers?					
13.	Does the CRM provide the facility to capture opportunity profiles (including status), summarize opportunity status, and view pipeline across the territory?					
14.	Does the system provide the ability to prioritize opportunities?					
15.	Does it provide the ability to track and display a customer's contact history across all channels?					
16.	Does the CRM have the ability to generate a *to-do* list from the contact history and also have the activities assigned automatically or manually?					
17.	Does it provide the ability to automatically notify the sales persons of expected future activity?					

(d) Sales management							
1.	Does the CRM assist in identifying the offering (products and services) to fit the customer's needs on the basis of captured information?						
2.	Does the system provide *offering configurator* to fit the customer's need based on captured information?						
3.	Does it provide for the development of requirements for selling compatible products and services, that is, up-sell/cross sell offerings?						
4.	Does the system provide templates for proposals/quotes, opportunity/call allocation report, call report for sales person, route plan report for sales person, expense report for sales person, etc.?						
5.	Does it provide for customizations of these templates?						
6.	Does the system provide for the generation of proposal/quotation incorporating the relevant customer, product, pricing, commercial, and statutory information?						
7.	Does it provide for automatic transposition of the proposal information to the order (in case of receiving a confirmation on the proposal)?						
8.	Does the system provide facilities for the generation of proforma invoice or invoice incorporating the relevant customer, product, pricing, commercial, and statutory information?						
9.	Does the CRM provide for tracking order completion and provide automated notifications of orders that are not completed within a specified due date or within a predefined period?						
10.	Does it provide the ability for notifying a customer of the order status?						
11.	Does the system provide prompts/alerts for campaign management, opportunity management, proposal/quote generation, product configuration, proforma invoice/invoice generation, expected future activities for sales personnel, development of offerings, etc.?						

4. Lead Management Function:
   a. Internet Lead Generation
   b. Lead Enhancement
   c. Routing to Partners
5. Marketing Function:
   a. Campaign Planning and Budgeting
   b. Marketing Event Management
   c. Marketing Encyclopedia
   d. Content Management and Literature Material
   e. Database Marketing
   f. Campaign ROI Analysis
   g. Customer Retention
   h. Word Processor Integration
6. Service Function:
   a. Service Call Management
   b. Incident Analysis
   c. Incident Assignment and Escalation
   d. Incident Tracking
   e. Multiple Issues per Incident
   f. Self-Service
   g. Warranty and Contract Management
   h. Order Tracking
   i. Solutions Repository
   j. Service Calendar
   k. Quality Management
   l. Customer feedback system and satisfaction survey
   m. Cross sell and Up-sell
7. E-Commerce:
   a. Order Catalog
   b. Interactive Advisor
   c. Auction Management
   d. Order Configurator
   e. Shopping Cart
   f. Online Ordering
   g. E-mailed Order Confirmation
8. Business intelligence:
   a. Reporting—Standard and Ad hoc
   b. List Management
   c. Dashboard
   d. Alerts and Alarms Scheduling
   e. Real-time Productivity Monitoring

3.4 Significant Issues to Be Considered while Evaluating CRM

In this section, we describe a set of issues that need to be considered while evaluating a CRM.

3.4.1 CRM Product Functionality and Features

Just as a vendor company, a similar exercise would have to be taken for the company's suite of CRM products. Product evaluation criteria would involve queries as illustrated in Table 3.2.

Unlike the traditional computerized systems, which take a data-oriented view of the operations of the company, the enterprise-wide systems primarily emphasize the process-oriented view of the organization. Hence, special attention needs to be paid to ascertain whether the CRM package can configure, support, and maintain business process of the organization.

3.4.1.1 Support for Standard Processes and Best Practices

Companies that are multidivisional and multilocated develop differently at different sites and acquire a character of their own at each site that may not fit into a uniform mold across the organization. A CRM package must have an ability to provide a comprehensive functionality to implement such deeply ingrained, differing ways of operations at different locations. It should be able to provide ready-to-use, best-practice processes that incorporate such varying ways of executing any business transaction or process.

A standardization of processes usually leads to tremendous gains in terms of maintenance, future upgrades, documentation, training, and even routine operations and the administration of the CRM applications system.

3.4.1.2 Support for Customizing the Processes

This custom support is counter to the general emphasis on standardizing the processes and implementing generic ones. It's a business truism that the survival and success of a company depends on how it differentiates itself and its products or services from those of its competitors. To leverage on their competencies or advantages, companies cannot abandon the corresponding differentiating processes and will have to incorporate such fundamental variants in their CRM implementations.

Therefore, in addition to the best-of-class processes, a CRM package must provide a basic framework and philosophy for the customization of processes for a company or even for a different division of the company. As is suggested in Chapter 6 "SAP CRM Implementation Project Cycle", a company should rationalize, standardize, and, as much as possible, use the process configurations that have been made available in SAP CRM.

Customization requirements could arise because of

■ Country-specific rules and regulations
■ State-specific differences, if any
■ Country-specific business requirements
■ Company-specific business strategy and tactics
■ Division- and location-specific business and operational requirements

3.4.1.3 Support for Cinderella Process

These processes are also known as *exception* processes or *strange* processes. Process scenarios occur in an organization that may result from particular or peculiar circumstances at any moment of time. Such exceptions could either be treated as erroneous scenarios or be handled as specifically identified exception processes. For instance, occasionally, every organization makes or is required to make an exception in the procedures for selection of suppliers, proposals submitted to prospective customers, delivering supplies to defaulting but otherwise loyal customers, releasing of delayed payments, partial payments against unverified invoices, and so on.

Exception processes are major targets for customizations. However, as discussed in relation with the preceding customizations, decisions on customizations need to be taken after assessing the resulting complexity in terms of use, training, and maintenance of these dependent processes.

3.4.1.4 Support for Application Users

A CRM package must be able to support and enable access to different kinds of users of the corporate database:

- *Connected Users*: Telesales Call Center Agents connected via LAN and WAN
- *Mobile Users*: Field Sales Executives with a local database on their laptops who synchronize with central database
- *Thin Client Users*: Channel partners/dealers who log on to the corporate database via the Internet
- *Handheld Device Users*: Typically field service engineers with a Palm device to manage their field activities
- *WAP Users*: Customers accessing critical information by logging on to the corporate database via mobiles or WAP-enabled devices

3.4.2 Vendor Credibility

An organization may select a CRM primarily on the basis of the product credibility to be discussed in the next section. However, the credibility of the vendor company to upgrade and continuously improve its suite of offerings is important because of the rapid changes in the technology and market requirements. The relevant issues are listed in Table 3.1 for reference.

3.4.3 CRM Architecture and Technology

The CRM system should be implemented using the latest technology, architecture, and methodology. As technology keeps on undergoing rapid change, the product architecture becomes very important, because this enables relevant portions of the monolithic packages like SAP CRM to be upgraded modularly without disrupting the function of the full package.

3.4.3.1 Graphical User Interface (GUI)

It may seem strange that we are talking about the importance of GUIs, but what are generally accepted standards of GUI functionality today are not available even a few years back. This was more so for CRM-like solutions, where the emphasis tended to be on comprehensive functionality and flexibility to make changes. The GUIs basically enable the systems to become more user friendly by providing and controlling the features like

- Structuring and nesting of menus
- Facilitating cursor movement on the screen

- Navigating between different screens
- Providing context-sensitive help
- Flashing of error messages

With the advent of the Internet, the importance of a separable GUI has become even more pronounced.

3.4.3.2 Open System Interfaces and APIs

The information technology (IT) developments in the past decade have amply demonstrated the importance of open systems, that is, the need for nonproprietary systems, protocols, and interfaces. CRM systems are conceptually easy to understand but very difficult to deliver. Developing such monolithic products at one instance is simply inconceivable. Therefore, CRM architecture and interfaces must permit the evolutionary development of the various components of the CRM system without disrupting its integrated functionality.

The CRM systems should permit easy interfacing with legacy systems and other specialized systems like SCM, CRM, product development management (PDM), automatic data recording (ADR), data capturing like bar codes, EDI, and computerized telephony. It is impossible for any vendor to develop a suite of products to address all these functionalities provided by all these systems with the same panache as its core product.

3.4.3.3 Web-Based Functionality

With the growing importance of the Web as a primary medium of interaction and executing transactions, CRMs have to be flexible by design to enable not only business-to-business commerce but also personalized interactions with end customers. The architecture of CRM should permit easy conversions to Web-enabled functionality. In this regard, a CRM-like SAP CRM with a user-interface layer, which is separate from the underlying business logic, just as the corresponding database layer, is ready for its functionality to be seen on an Internet browser.

3.4.4 CRM Implementation and Use

In CRMs, which are end-user-oriented systems, there is a major emphasis on the ease of implementation and use. This refers especially to the ease of operations and management of the end users:

1. *Ease of installation*: Although the installation of packages like CRMs is not envisaged to be simple, a systematic and menu-driven facility for installation of the various components of the system is in vogue. But more importantly, the installation application component should make the installation process independent of (say) the operating system.
2. *Ease of configuration*: After the installation, facilities for configuring the system for the existing or envisaged IT infrastructure of the company are very important. The system should have an easily understandable path and method for gathering the company-specific details of the IT infrastructure. Using present empirical models or theoretical models and the information furnished at the various stages, the system should be able to suggest various default values that would define the configuration of the installation for a particular company.

3. *Ease of operations*: The CRM system should provide sample procedures and documentation for routine operations of the system. The system should also provide for automated backup and recovery procedures.

4. *Ease of user management*: CRM, being an enterprise-wide and end-user-oriented system, must enforce a complete control on the access and authorization profiles of its users. Unlike the traditional computerized systems, the number and categories of people who operate the CRM system on a routine basis have undergone a change. CRM is now operated directly by the end-user operational persons. They create all the business transactions and functions directly on the system or with the help of the CRM system.

The CRM system must provide a judicious mixture of role-oriented and individual-oriented access profiles. This is necessary to cater to the needs of personnel working in rotation on different production shifts during a month.

3.4.5 Investments and Budgets

The ratio of the implementation expenses is broadly as follows:

1. Hardware infrastructure	×
2. SAP CRM license and other software infrastructure	×
3. SAP CRM implementation project	2–3×

The breakup of the SAP CRM implementation project cost could be as follows:

External consultants	35%
In-house consultants	25%
Travel and local expenses	15%
Training	7%
Miscellaneous	13%
Contingency	5%

For capital equipment, the operating costs that are not directly related to the implementation effort are as follows:

Annual maintenance contracts	10%
Depreciation	20%

A full CRM package from a vendor like SAP, Oracle, or Clarify can cost more than $1 million and as much as $3 million; the necessary integration and consulting work can then double that amount.

3.4.6 CRM Infrastructure

An important element that must be considered while evaluating the CRM for an organization is the type and size of the envisaged hardware infrastructure essential for the enterprise-wide operations.

3.4.6.1 Hardware

This is the central horsepower that is required to drive the functioning of the CRM throughout the enterprise. The nature of CRM will dictate this to be either a monolithic server or a cluster of servers, each focusing on a part of the envisaged load. The number of computers within the cluster can be based on either the particular functional areas or the sublocations that are to be served by the cluster as a whole. The sizes of the individual computers may be dependent upon

- The envisaged processing load of the system
- The number of terminals through which the system will be accessed

3.4.6.2 System Software

Usually, deciding on the system software is coupled with the selection of the hardware boxes. The operating system environment should have the capability to provide fault-tolerant operations with facilities for automatic backup, mirroring, and replication across sites and automatic failure recovery features.

3.4.6.3 Networking

Since CRMs are end-user-oriented systems, the usage and load expected on the terminals will be substantial. The network should be able to provide enough throughput so as not to impair the performance of access at these terminals.

3.4.7 CRM Implementation Time

The time required for implementing a whole suite of CRM applications within an organization is important. As will be discussed later, this book recommends that for real payoffs from a CRM implementation, an organization should adopt the big-bang strategy of implementing all the SAP CRM modules that cater to the company's sales and marketing operations. This includes basic modules like sales, contact and account management, telesales/call centers, marketing, campaign management, service, and support.

The CRM project duration is dependent upon the characteristics of the company, such as its cultural, organizational, and technical readiness, as well as on the innate complexity of the CRM product. The cultural readiness of an organization is dependent upon its vision of its future as well as its willingness to embrace change toward that end. The organizational readiness has to do with the management's commitment, empowerment of the employees, streamlined systems and procedures, standardized processes, and so on. Technical readiness deals with the maturity of the infrastructure for hardware and communications, training, help desks, office automation, groupware, and so on.

The complexity of CRM products arises because of the multiple demands for comprehensiveness as well as flexibility of customization. When implementing CRM, it becomes critical to have prior familiarity with the functionality provided by the CRM system. In an integrated system, any wrongly configured process may have adverse and unforeseen effects on processing in some other related functions. And this may not get detected until a rigorous integration-testing phase of the implementation or, worse, when the system is in actual production! Consequently, the effort to identify the all-functional gaps between the required and available functionalities, coupled with the effort required to configure the resulting processes in an integrated CRM package, leads to comparatively longer implementation times.

3.5 Summary

In this chapter, we introduced the concept and criteria for evaluating a CRM package that is suitable for the requirements of a company. After considering the basic characteristics of a full-featured CRM system, we considered in detail various checklists for ascertaining the technical and functional requirements expected of the envisaged CRM system. In the later part of this chapter, we discussed several dimensions of a CRM that are essential for any enterprise-wide customer-centric solution.

Chapter 4

CRM Selection

4.1 SAP CRM for Small and Medium Enterprises (SME)

The majority of companies that will be implementing customer relationship management (CRM) systems in the millennium will be small and medium enterprises (SMEs). SMEs are usually defined as companies that have revenues ranging from $250 million up to $1 billion. These companies have modest IT/IS resources and budgets and are expected to benefit the most from implementing off-the-shelf application products like CRMs. This is because they do not have the depth of experience and a constant availability of adequate expertise to be able to handle the in-house development of an enterprise-wide system.

Like the large enterprises within their markets, SMEs are impacted by the rapidly changing marketplace and their own ability to respond to these changes. CRMs provide the platform for SMEs to address the competitive demands of the rapidly changing marketplace and be successful in terms of the following:

- Improve customer responses and experience.
  - Increase customer satisfaction.
  - Improve communications.
- Improve customer relations and management.
  - Consolidate critical information about each customer.
  - Target the most profitable customers and develop programs to increase their loyalty to your company.
  - Virtually eliminate the possibility of prospects or customers *falling through the cracks* of an obsolete or overloaded system.
  - Yield faster and more accurate follow-up on sales leads, referrals, and customer inquiries.
  - Personalize the service and product offerings to each customer.
  - Boost the revenue-per-salesperson and territory performance while reducing both cost-per-lead and cost-of-closed-business expenses.
  - Give top managers a detailed and accurate picture of all sales and marketing activities.
  - Instantly react to changing market conditions.

■ Improve quality sales.
 – Improve sales effectiveness.
 – Improve sales management.
 – Support team selling.
■ Improve margins and reduce buying and using costs.
 – Reduce sales costs.
 – Improve forecasts.
 – Increase revenues.
 – Effective Channel Management.
■ Reduce product development time.
■ Reduce manpower for routine operations.

CRM implementations in SMEs also need a completely different type of skills set as compared to the implementation of the same system in a Fortune 500 company. We will touch upon this aspect again in Appendix A.

4.2 CRM Selection Process

The objective of a systematic selection of CRM is to optimize the benefits for the organization. Careful selection to acquire the most acceptable enterprise-wide system is important, as it has a salutary effect on the overall acceptability, usefulness, cross functionality, and collaboration within the customer-centric enterprise.

An enterprise must select the most suitable CRM system based on the predefined, predetermined, and preagreed criteria of evaluation. The process should follow the organizational policies and procedures in reaching the final decision.

The use of checklists for such purposes has proved especially valuable. We discussed a handful of checklists in Chapter 3, to evaluate the different characteristics of the CRM systems. These checklists should be supplemented or altered depending on the requirements of the organizations. It is important, however, to use such checklists because it helps in focusing discussions on issues that matter objectively. Later in this chapter, we discuss using metrics to compare CRMs.

The process of selecting a CRM system for a customer-centric enterprise involves the following steps:

1. Establish the CRM selection team (discussed in Section 4.3 "Selection Team").
2. Establish the functional requirements of the envisaged customer-centric enterprise-wide system (discussed in detail in Section 4.4 "CRM Core Selection Methodology").
3. Search and screen for prospective CRM systems.
4. Prepare detailed checklists of different class characteristics in order of priority, such as necessary, desirable, good to have, and great to have. This can be cued from the list of features available from the CRM vendors (see Table 4.1).
5. Screen the available CRM products that most nearly meet the agreed criteria against the necessary requirements that have been established. The company can also partner with the vendor companies in this stage by issuing an RFP based on the finalized checklists.
6. Evaluate the resulting shortlist of CRM products against the detailed desirable requirements like those presented in Chapter 3.

Table 4.1 Sample List of Features for Architecture

Description	Characteristics
1. General Architecture Characteristics	Extensible
	Multitiered
	Object oriented
	Component Architecture
	Multiple-Language Support
	Rapid Application Development
	Internet enabled
	Multiple deployment technologies
	Global Enterprise Support
	Compliance with important standards
	Graphical configuration
	Open application programming interfaces
	Enterprise-class scalability and performance
2. Global Enterprise Support	Multiple-language support
	Externalized message strings
	Bidirectional character display support
	Euro currency support
	Multilingual list of values
3. Standards Compliance	Microsoft COM
	CORBA
	Microsoft IE4
	Netscape 4
	Crypto-2 security
4. Rapid Application Customization	Powerful, extensible object classes
	Graphical development tool
	Base-of-class functionality provided in repository
	Metadata repository
	Integrated scripting language
	Multideveloper tools
	Object versioning and modification control
5. Component Architecture	In-process objects
	Lightweight, Server or Client based
	Support reusability
	Published application program interfaces
	Accessible from Web page editors

(Continued)

Table 4.1 (*Continued*)   Sample List of Features for Architecture

Description	Characteristics
6. Open Application Programming Interface COM compliant	CORBA Compliant Intuitive methods Common events exposed
7. Automatic Object Upgrader	Automatic repository upgrade Three-way object definition evaluation Retains user customizations Business rules used to define upgrade behavior Upgrade behavior that can be overridden
8. Web-based N-tiered Architecture	Well-defined layers Applet layer for user-interface control Applets reusable in multiple views Applet Manager that supports multiple applet technologies simultaneously Support Java, ActiveX, HTML, Netscape plug-in Configurable business object support Data manager abstraction from physical database Ability to deploy without persistent software

7. Select the few remaining CRM systems for demonstrations, site visits, and hands-on trials.
8. Direct and help the vendors to conduct script tests and stress tests and report on the results of these tests using the same test data provided by the company to all of the CRM vendors.
9. Conduct a comparison and rating of the various CRMs using metrics by compiling, collating, and analyzing the submitted information.
10. Compile the findings of the product ratings and test reports with special emphasis on the cost of installing and operating the CRM, the time frame for implementing the package, the experience and strength of the vendor, and the risks associated with each of the alternative CRMs.
11. Prepare the recommendation report to the management.

A systematic and metrics-based approach would not render the decision process as foolproof, but it would help in making the decision clearer. The recommendation report will give clear descriptions of how the CRM systems were rated, for what reasons, and how the selection decision was reached. At a later stage, others can know the principal points that were considered and why certain CRM systems were rejected, while others were considered more suitable. This approach leaves a clear *audit trail* of the route taken in the decision process used for the final selection of the CRM for the organization.

4.3 Selection Team

Implementation of enterprise-wide systems like SAP can be successful only when all stakeholders are willing participants in such an effort. It is necessary for ensuring the future interest and involvement of all concerned that all stakeholders and their views should be properly represented and incorporated during the planning, organizing, executing, and managing the implementation of the CRM system. In the SME enterprise, the mistakes committed while implementing computerized systems in the last century should be avoided. In the remaining part of this section, we discuss the important constituents of the selection team.

4.3.1 Functional Team

This team is the major constituent of the selection team. Its members should consist of senior officers who are knowledgeable of the company's business operations, manufacturing technology, competencies, and the competitive gaps. Since the CRM implementation projects are user driven, involving the functional team members in the evaluation and selection phase is the best prescription for ownership during the implementation of the selected package. They should preferably be members who have participated in similar customer-centric enterprise-wide performance improvement efforts like TQM, BPR, and BPM.

4.3.2 Technical Team

The members of this team should be members who have extensive experience at least in the traditional application development and implementation projects. They should be familiar with conventional development environments and the traditional methodologies employed during the software development life cycle (SDLC). They should be perceptive of the rationale for deploying CRM solutions in the organization and the reasons for the implementation project to be driven and led by the functional users.

4.3.3 Technology Team

The members of this team should be conversant with the latest hardware, networking issues, and solutions. They should be familiar with issues of portability, scalability, and interoperability. They need to be aware of the latest standards and protocols to make an informed judgment on the infrastructure issues for the CRM implementation within the organization. They must be comfortable with issues of compatibility, upgrade paths, network traffic on LANs and WANs, and estimating system loads and system responses.

Technology team members should also be familiar with solutions for backup, archival, and disaster recovery systems. The members of this team need to be conversant with site preparation, cabling, installation, maintenance, and support requirements for the CRM system installation.

4.3.4 Commercial Team

The members of this team need to be conversant with the issues of negotiating with vendors, signing commercial contracts, defining deliverables and milestones, laying out acceptance criteria and approval procedures, performance guarantees, payment terms, legal liabilities, licensing procedures, upgrades and releases, regulatory issues and taxes, and so on.

4.4 CRM Core Selection Methodology

As CRM fundamentally implements a process-driven customer-centric enterprise, the selection of processes for implementation is of primary significance. The selection team will make its choice depending on how easily the CRM can implement the process considered critical for the company operations. It will depend upon how flexibly the system implements the business processes of interest to the organization.

4.4.1 Process Selection

This involves systematically compiling all processes and variants that are prevalent within the organization. These could be processes at every level within the organization, irrespective of whether it has been computerized or not. Compared with the financial systems (generally defined by FASB) and manufacturing systems (generally defined by MRP II), the processes used in sales, marketing, customer service, and other parts of the customer life cycle are not very well established.

4.4.2 Enterprise Process Mapping

This involves painstakingly mapping a selection of processes that are considered critical for the business operations of the company. This entails detailing each process in terms of its name, purpose, responsible owner, process description (including inputs and outputs), quality and efficiency, subprocesses, interfaces with other functions and systems, exceptional conditions, areas for improvement, impact analysis of suggested scenarios, and so on. This compilation of process mapping is helpful in preparing the script tests. The topic of process mapping is discussed in detail in Chapter 7.

4.4.3 Script Tests

Script tests are process scenarios that have to be demonstrated by the vendor in the product licenses. These tests are a handful of process scenarios that are considered especially critical for the business operations and are not easily configurable within the standard functionality provided by the CRM systems.

The approach recommended for handling these specifically identified processes indicates the robustness, depth, and inherent flexibility of the CRM systems. CRM systems may have the following approaches for mapping a process within the package:

- Provide it as a basic or standard functionality.
- Suggest a work-around for achieving the same functionality and configure it accordingly.
- Indicate if this functionality is to be introduced in the next scheduled release of the system.
- Suggest third-party add-ons or plug-ins that provide the desired functionality and have been qualified for compatibility with the concerned CRM.
- Program the required functionality in CRM system by developing the same in the 3GL/4GL native to the CRM system.

CRMs that can accommodate such processes, even if these are achieved only by resorting to work-arounds, are preferable to others where the only options are to wait either for these functionalities to be addressed, possibly in the next released version of the system, or for the company to customize the package itself by programming such functionality directly into the system.

4.4.4 Stress Test

This is similar to the stress test administered for traditional systems. This involves estimating the load anticipated in the production environment and simulating the same in the test environment to ascertain whether the suggested configuration can handle the expected load. This test can involve predictable volumes of data in the database, transaction throughputs on the LAN/WAN, or interactive sessions on the terminals serviced by the central servers. Industry-level benchmarks for the relevant areas should be used for reporting on the observed performances. This could be a full-scale test conducted on the company site or at the technology demonstration centers of the concerned vendor.

4.5 CRM Vendors and Products

CRM is a customer-focused business strategy designed to optimize profitability, revenue, and customer satisfaction. To improve business processes associated with selling, servicing, and marketing, enterprises across a number of industries are launching CRM initiatives. To realize CRM, enterprises must implement collaborative processes and technologies that support customer interactions throughout all channels. The problem is that many of those software vendors provide only single-function-focused or single-channel-focused offerings and are often not strong in each of the three domains relevant to CRM.

Most CRM packages are targeted at three types of companies:

1. Enterprise or those with more than 500 employees
2. Midmarket, with between 100 and 500 employees
3. Small businesses with less than 100 employees

By about 1994, CRM had clearly been identified as the emerging market with a great potential. Siebel and Pivotal emphasized sales management aspects; Vantive, Clarify, Onyx, and Remedy developed customer service applications. Newer entrants such as BroadVision and Silknet concentrated on e-commerce. Since then, all of the leading vendors have undergone significant consolidation by moving toward a model of all-encompassing system that covers all functional areas and all customer interaction channels and touch points.

The major players like SAP, Oracle (Siebel), and Salesforce have been targeting the enterprise and are moving slowly into the midmarket area by reason of its great growth potential.

Other vendors such as Aptean (Onyx, Pivotal) and Microsoft who are typically associated with the midmarket, are trying to capture some of the enterprise market. Finally, vendors such as FrontRange (GoldMine) and Sage (SalesLogix) are targeting the small enterprises by providing one-stop shop for a spectrum of functionalities.

4.5.1 Application Suites or Best in Class

4.5.1.1 Suite of Applications

An integrated application suite is a set of applications that employ a common architecture, referencing a common logical database with a single schema. Some suites are more of an interfaced application bundle, that is, a set of interfaced applications from a single vendor containing more than one technical architecture or more than one logical database—frequently assembled by the vendor through the process of acquisition or partnership. This approach attempts to standardize on a single vendor's application suite and compromise on functionality that is good enough for minimum requirements but engenders the disadvantageous of vendor lock-in.

Adherents of the single-vendor suite approach are primarily motivated by cost and risk avoidance, believing that delivered integration and the requirement of a single set of IT skills outweigh trade-offs in the timing and breadth and depth of the business process functionality. But application suites turn out to be quite difficult and expensive to implement or upgrade. The engineered complexities of suites can lessen the benefits of delivered integration in many cases. In a few extreme cases, when implementation and upgrades are not planned properly or when companies lack adequately trained resources in vendor-specific IT skills, such projects can potentially destabilize a company.

Finally, suite vendors are even more challenged while addressing the requirements of inter- or cross customer–centric enterprise collaborative activities that are becoming pervasive with the advent of the Internet. Getting a customer-centric enterprise to standardize on a single vendor's application suite is fairly difficult, but to get an entire value chain to adopt and standardize on a proprietary set of applications and interfaces is highly impossible.

4.5.1.2 Integrated Best-in-Class Applications

An alternative approach to suites is an interfaced best-in-class or best-of-breed solution—an approach whereby an enterprise selects from multiple vendors a set of applications that must be interfaced to work together, either by the enterprise, one of the selected vendors, or a third-party integrator. Customer-centric enterprises select the applications because they best meet the particular needs. Such process-specific applications generally lead in the areas of time to market and the breadth and depth of functionality—especially for industry-specific processes. The benefits of this approach are

- Streamlining operating cycles on high-volume business processes
- Reducing processing and inventory costs
- Improving compliance with contracts
- Enhancing collaboration while strengthening long-term relationships with strategic trading partners

The downside of this approach is the higher efforts and costs of integration. The challenge with this approach is that, in some cases, the enterprise fails to complete the necessary interfaces to get the individual applications working together; consequently, the applications remain stovepipes.

Thus, this approach attempts to deploy state-of-the-art application functionality from multiple vendors at markedly increased cost of integration. A variation on this theme, called *the Best of cluster*, is similar to best of class, except that instead of individual applications, suites or bundles are interfaced.

4.5.1.2.1 Component-Based Architectures

A component-based architecture can eliminate the customary trade-off between best-practice functionality and large integration and ongoing support costs. A standards-based architecture provides a unified framework on which componentized applications from multiple vendors can be easily and cost-effectively

- Deployed and distributed across servers on heterogeneous networks
- Integrated directly with the logic layer of other component-based applications
- Extended to support customer-specific business processes
- Upgraded individually

Because the business components share and open common programming standards, they can communicate with other similar components by exchanging messages, whether located on the same memory space or distributed across a network. Each component is self-identifying and is self-contained and is wrapped with communications, event handling, relationship management, and data validation services. Functions, objects, or data located within one component can be accessed and reused by another. This also enables it to be better positioned to take advantage of the shift to Web Services.

Component-based solutions rely on application servers to deliver robust scalability and apportion the functionality into several self-contained units of business process. Encapsulating business logic in components and delivering it through an open interface allows companies to deploy and integrate functionality very systematically. Such rolling deployments speed time to payback and minimize upgrade expense by shortening both the planning cycles and extended implementations that are usually associated with traditional upgrades. Componentization also enhances the company's ability to extend or modify particular business functionality without disrupting the other applications' data structures and process flows. By eliminating direct exposure or interaction with data elements of a component, component-based solutions like SAP CRM make it easier for companies to link with not only their other internal process but also those of their partners. Such flexibility facilitates easy access to market-leading functionality and process and can make the entire value chain more responsive to the market conditions. Moreover, such flexibility can better position a company to meet the challenges of rapidly changing business requirements resulting from rapid growth, process re-engineering, and M&As (Mergers and Acquisitions).

4.5.1.2.2 Applications as Web Services

Web services are new standards for creating and delivering co-operative applications over the Internet. Web services allow applications to communicate irrespective of the platform or the operating system. By using Web services, developers can eliminate major porting and quality testing efforts, potentially saving millions of dollars. They will radically change the way that applications are built and deployed in future.

As explained in Chapter 10, Section 10.1.3 "Enterprise Architecture," a developer can create an application out of reusable components. But what good is it to have a large library of reusable components if nobody can find out that they exist, where they are located, and, how to link to and communicate with such programmatic components? Web services are standards for finding and integrating object components over the Internet. They enable a development environment where it is no longer necessary to build complete and monolithic applications for every project. Instead, the core components can be combined from other standard components available on the Web to build the complete applications that run as services to the core applications.

Major hardware vendors and certain key software vendors are looking at these new Web standards for providing solutions for program-to-program communication. IBM's WebSphere Server environment, Sun Microsystems's Open Network Environment (ONE) constituting of various Sun technologies and third party products, and, Microsoft's .NET initiatives deliver Web Services based solutions.

4.5.2 Industry-Specific Functionality

Every industry has characteristic requirements that are specific (or even unique) to the companies operating in that industry. As CRM implementations become more prevalent, industry-specific functionality is becoming more and more important. Some examples of industry-specific functionality are

- Promotion management for consumer goods
- Available-to-promise capabilities for manufactures
- Merchandising for retailers

No CRM system provides the full spectrum of features associated with the CRM strategy. Even the most comprehensive of the packages will still require extensive customization (if it implements a suit of applications) or integration (if it implements a best-of-breed solution).

SAP Industry Applications deliver comprehensive, out-of-the-box e-Business functionality that is uniquely tailored to the specific business practices across a broad range of industries. Developed in close collaboration with customers and partners, SAP Industry Applications enable organizations to manage, coordinate, and synchronize all customer touch points, including the Web, call center, field, retail, and distribution channels.

With SAP Industry Applications, organizations can lower customization and maintenance costs, shorten implementation time frames, and seamlessly access information residing in diverse back office and legacy systems (Table 4.2).

4.5.3 Large Enterprises*

This category comprises vendor solutions primarily targeted toward organizations with revenues of more than $1 billion per year and/ or more than 1000 employees. CRM vendors focused on the enterprise-class organizations typically offer a full range of functionalities, can scale to serve large user populations, and offer support for multiple languages and countries. They offer their products primarily through the traditional on-premise license model. However, hosted and SaaS (software-as-a-service) deployment options are now offered by several of the leading players. Oracle offers Siebel On Demand and SAP Business ByDesign. The typical cost paid by large enterprises for products from such vendors as Oracle's Siebel and PeopleSoft CRM, and SAP CRM is about $2500 and higher per user.

SAP CRM strategy is closely linked to the success of its enterprise applications portfolio; SAP CRM customers benefit from the enormous depth of industry expertise accumulated in the past in its products and the group as a whole. Oracle's CRM product lines, specifically its Siebel CRM, are market leading solutions in almost every aspect of the CRM technology. Oracle strategically positions Siebel CRM as the most fully featured solution with a breadth and depth of functionality for many industry verticals. Both products offer strong capabilities across most of the CRM functionalities including marketing, sales, service, field service, and partner channel management. However, both SAP CRM and Oracle Siebel CRM implementations are characterized by comparatively lengthy time-to-value, relative inflexibility for changing business processes and higher costs.

---

* These are only representative profiles; please update the same for the latest features and functionalities with the respective vendors.

Table 4.2   Industry-Specific CRM Requirements

Industry	Applications/Functionality
Commercial Banking	Contact center, profitability analysis, integrated target marketing, data mining
High Technology	Full-field sales, e-sales, reseller extranets, contract management, blended sales and service contact center, integrated field service, sales commission management, bottom-up/top-down forecasting
Insurance	Blended sales and service contact center with Web integration, consumer credit checking, and lease underwriting process
Telecom	Blended sales and service contact center, competitive pricing analysis, integration with billing system, churn management
Utilities	Integrated customer service and support call center and field service, integration with billing system
Consumer Goods	Category management, trade promotions, demand planning, interactive selling
Manufacturing	Bottom-up/top-down forecasting, available and capable to promise sales data, supply chain integration
Pharmaceuticals	Contract management, portable marketing analysis, regulatory compliance
Retail	*E-tailing*, space planning, merchandising, integration with point-of-sale systems

This is only a representative comparison; please update the same for the latest features and functionalities with the respective vendors.

4.5.3.1 SAP

SAP has steadily built up comprehensive functionality in the SAP CRM product. Most recently, the company has focused on improving usability and deepening support for strategic business processes as part of the SAP business suite. SAP CRM is particularly strong in sales, marketing, partner channel management, and analytics but offers less support for customer data management requirements. The product can scale to support global deployments and offers many industry-specific process solutions. The SAP CRM SaaS offering provides more deployment flexibility, while cost, complexity, and lengthy implementations schedules remain drawbacks of the on-premise product. SAP CRM is best suited for global buyers committed to SAP and its ERP platform who need to support end-to-end industry processes.

The SAP customer relationship management (SAP CRM) application provides best-in-class functionality for marketing, sales, and service. By supporting customer-facing business processes across multiple interaction channels, SAP CRM enables organizations to focus on strategies for customer-driven growth and to differentiate themselves in the market by providing a superior customer experience.

Since its latest release in December 2007, SAP has evolved CRM beyond traditional task automation to a flexible, user-driven, and end-to-end business process execution platform. SAP CRM is architected to help companies achieve a complete 360-degree view of customers, which is one of the most critical factors in enabling a successful CRM strategy.

4.5.3.2 Oracle Siebel CRM

Siebel remains the key market shareholder in technology-enabled selling and is a leader in large enterprise customer service and support, making it the only front office suite vendor with a dominant position in two of the three front office domains. Siebel also provides solutions tailored to the following verticals—Automotive, Public Sector, Communications, Consumer Goods, Apparel and Footwear, Energy, Finance, Insurance, Healthcare, Pharma, and Retail.

In addition to Oracle Siebel CRM for enterprise customers, the product family also includes Oracle's Siebel On Demand and Oracle's Siebel Professional Edition for the mid-market. The Siebel product for enterprise-class customers has achieved best-of-breed status for most CRM functionalities, with the exception of customer service and e-commerce. It also boasts good industry vertical adaptations. However, it faces the challenges arising out of application complexity, high cost, and lengthy implementation. The product is best suited for buyers who value advanced functionality tailored for specific industries, customer insight through strong analytics and customer data management, and the ability to support global organizations. For instance, Siebel CRM's superior analytics enable closed-loop analysis delivering marketing management metrics that can optimize the customer's marketing strategy.

4.5.3.3 Salesforce

This company is growing quickly by making CRM solutions available through the Software as a Service (SaaS deployment model. As with other SaaS vendors, the value proposition has found success in the SMB market, which values quick time-to-value, usability, and lower upfront costs compared with traditional on-premise solutions. Enterprise-class customers seeking these benefits are increasingly turning to salesforce.com to understand whether SaaS deployment can meet their more complex CRM requirements. As indicated by its name, it is very strong in supporting SFA requirements and recently moved to expand its partner channel management offerings.

4.5.4 Small and Mid-Market Enterprises

Mid-size enterprises are defined as those with annual revenues between $200 million and $1 billion, and an overall staff strength of fewer than 1000. CRM vendors in this group also offer a breadth of CRM functionalities, but these often have more limited capabilities in specific areas and are simpler to use than solutions built for the enterprise market. These vendors are less suitable for large-scale global deployments. Vendors in this group also offer a variety of deployment options, including on-premise license, hosted, and SaaS. Some vendors in this category have upgraded their solutions to be more suitable to enterprise-class buyers and are gaining acceptance in that segment as well. The typical cost of a front office application from a vendor targeting the mid-size enterprise is $600 to $1700 per user.

This is only a representative comparison; please update the same for the latest features and functionalities with the respective vendors.

4.5.4.1 Aptean

4.5.4.1.1 Onyx

Onyx is a leader in mid-market customer service and support solutions. Onyx was one of the first vendors to determine portals as the focus of the various components of their CRM offerings. The portals act as the information aggregators and toolboxes to maximize the efficiency of their target groups, which include internal users, external customers, and external partners. All portals employ a common engine that serves to provide data, workflow, and integration capabilities. The Onyx CRM solution was one of the first enterprise CRM solutions to adopt a flexible, three-tier architecture, with tight alignment to Microsoft technologies. Onyx is best suited for customers who want a flexible CRM solution incorporating a BPM capability that also leverages Microsoft infrastructure technologies.

4.5.4.1.2 Pivotal

Pivotal is the leading visionary in mid-market sales solutions. It is Microsoft based; it executes well in field sales opportunity management systems and has expanded its solution to include support for multiple selling channels, as well as enterprises with basic servicing and marketing requirements.

4.5.4.2 Microsoft Dynamics CRM

Microsoft leverages its desktop applications strength in large enterprises and promotes its now more robust business applications to this sector. Customer interest in Microsoft Dynamics 4.0 solutions is high in the SMB market and is growing in the enterprise segment. Enterprise customers that have made a commitment to a Microsoft infrastructure to lower their TCO (total cost of ownership) are attracted to Microsoft Dynamics CRM. Customers also like Microsoft Dynamics CRM usability and its quick time-to-value compared with traditional CRM applications. The product provides basic capabilities in sales, customer service, and field service adequately but is weaker in marketing and customer data management. On the other hand, sales force automation, integration, and interoperability across the whole suite of products are very strong. But partner channel management and e-commerce capabilities are not very strong, and there are no industry-specific solution sets.

4.5.4.3 FrontRange Solutions (GoldMine)

GoldMine is a leading provider of sales force automation, internal helpdesk, and CRM software for small- to medium-sized business. Its products provide powerful solutions for managing customer life cycles. GoldMine provides affordable, easily deployable solutions to organizations that do not need expensive and complex systems.

4.5.4.4 Sage (SalesLogix)

SalesLogix provides CRM and e-commerce software that enables business to sell more—faster and easier. It enables organizations to create interactive selling networks that connect mobile sales, internal telesales, marketing, and support organizations as well as third party resellers and other partners. Its pricing is effective.

4.5.5 CRM Products Comparison*

Table 4.3 presents a comparison of current CRM systems, namely, Oracle, SAP, Salesforce, Aptean (Onyx, Pivotal), FrontRange Solutions (GoldMine), Infor, KANA, Maximizer, Microsoft, NetSuite, Pegasystems, Sage (SalesLogix), and SugarCRM.

4.6 CRM Selection Report

When reporting on a selection of systems like CRM, which are large, complex, and integrated, functionalities are not very easy to compare. Moreover, the participation of members from different functional areas into the selection team also brings forth widely differing views on every aspect of the envisaged customer-centric enterprise-wide system.

As noted in Section 4.2 "CRM Selection Process," it is best to state the variables involved as objectively as possible and to apply some sort of measuring scale for each of these variables. A metrics approach is the best way to assign values and resolve disputes. Although the assigned numbers are only comparisons on a relative scale and not actual costs, they help in focusing the discussions more on the specific numbers assigned to definable points. The relative scale or the weighty factors assigned to various aspects could always be reworked until most participants are satisfied with the scale. The resulting conclusions will arise from all such smaller agreements made along the way.

In the next subsection, we discuss a metrics approach for comparison of the CRM systems.

4.6.1 CRM Systems Comparative Chart

Table 4.4 presents a form that can be used for comparison of CRM systems.

The steps to be used by the selection team for using this form are as follows:

1. Using the information gathered in response to the various criteria for evaluation, as suggested in Chapter 3, prepare a list of characteristics that are mutually acceptable as important for the envisaged customer-centric enterprise-wide systems.
2. Place these characteristics in the order of importance as agreed by all the members of the selection team.
3. Decide on which of these characteristics are necessary.
4. Decide on which of these characteristics are desirable.

---

* These are only representative profiles; please update the same for the latest features and functionalities with the respective vendors.

Table 4.3 Comparison of CRM Systems[a]

	SAP *SAP CRM, SAP Jam, SAP Web Channel Experience Management, SAP Social Media Analytics*	*Oracle* *Oracle Siebel CRM, Oracle CRM On Demand, Oracle WebCenter Sites, and others*	*Salesforce* *Salesforce. com, Chatter, Work.com, Ideas, and more*	*Aptean* *Onyx CRM, Pivotal CRM, and others*
Functionality				
Sales Force Automation (SFA)				
Account and contact management	x	x	x	x
Opportunity management	x	x	x	x
Social sales[b]	x	x	x	x
Sales analytics	x	x	x	x
Marketing Automation				
Campaign management	x	x	x	x
Lead management	x	x	x	x
Social marketing[c]	x	x	x	x
Marketing analytics	x	x	x	x
Customer Service and Support (CSS)				
Issue/case management	x	x	x	x
Feedback management	x	x	x	x
Social customer support[d]	x	x	x	x
CSS analytics	x	x	x	x
Customer Experience Management				
Personalization	x	x	x	x
Social and real-time communication	x	x	x	x
Rich media support	x	x	x	
Customer experience profile[e]	x	x	x	x
Field Service Management	x	x		
E-commerce	x	x		
Partner Relationship Management	x	x	x	x
Global Business Management[f]	x	x	x	x
Social Business Platforms	x	x	x	
Product Technology				
Mobility				
HTML5	x	x	x	x
Native apps	x	x	x	x
Delivery Model				
Cloud	x	x	x	x
On premises	x	x		x
Hybrid	x	x		x

(Continued)

Table 4.3 (*Continued*)   Comparison of CRM Systems[a]

	Microsoft *Microsoft Dynamics CRM, Yammer, Skype*	NetSuite *NetSuite CRM, SuiteCommerce, Retail Anywhere*	Pegasystems *Pega CRM*	Sage *Sage CRM, SalesLogix*	SugarCRM *Sugar Enterprise*
Functionality					
Sales Force Automation (SFA)					
Account and contact management	x	x	x	x	x
Opportunity management	x	x	x	x	x
Social sales[b]	x	x	x	x	x
Sales analytics	x	x	x	x	x
Marketing Automation					
Campaign management	x	x	x	x	x
Lead management	x	x	x	x	x
Social marketing[c]	x	x	x		x
Marketing analytics	x	x	x	x	
Customer Service and Support (CSS)					
Issue/case management	x	x	x	x	x
Feedback management	x	x	x		x
Social customer support[d]	x	x		x	x
CSS analytics	x	x	x	x	x
Customer Experience Management					
Personalization		x		x	
Social and real-time communication	x	x	x	x	x
Rich media support				x	
Customer experience profile[e]		x	x	x	x
Field Service Management					
E-commerce		x			
Partner Relationship Management	x	x			x
Global Business Management[f]	x	x	x	x	x
Social Business Platforms	x				
Product Technology					
Mobility					
HTML5		x	x	x	x
Native apps	x		x	x	x
Delivery Model					
Cloud	x	x	x	x	x
On premises	x		x	x	x
Hybrid	x			x	

(Continued)

Table 4.3 (*Continued*) Comparison of CRM Systems[a]

	FrontRange Solutions GoldMine Premium Edition CRM	Infor Epiphany, Inforce	KANA KANA Enterprise, KANA Express, Lagan Enterprise, Lagan Express	Maximizer Maximizer CRM
Functionality				
Sales Force Automation (SFA)				
Account and contact management	x	x	x	x
Opportunity management	x	x		x
Social sales[b]	x			
Sales analytics	x	x		x
Marketing Automation				
Campaign management	x	x	x	x
Lead management	x	x		x
Social marketing[c]			x	
Marketing analytics	x	x		x
Customer Service and Support (CSS)				
Issue/case management	x	x	x	x
Feedback management		x	x	
Social customer support[d]			x	
CSS analytics			x	x
Customer Experience Management				
Personalization	x	x	x	
Social and real-time communication	x		x	x
Rich media support	x		x	
Customer experience profile[e]		x	x	
Field Service Management				
E-commerce				
Partner Relationship Management				
Global Business Management[f]	x		x	x
Social Business Platforms			x	
Product Technology				
Mobility				
HTML5	x		x	x
Native apps		x	x	x
Delivery Model				
Cloud			x	x
On premises	x	x	x	x
Hybrid			x	

(Continued)

Table 4.3 (*Continued*) Comparison of CRM Systems[a]

[a] These are only representative profiles; please update the same for the latest features and functionalities with the respective vendors.
[b] Social sales functionality includes blended customer profile, collaboration and content exchange, and collaborative proposal generation.
[c] Social marketing functionality includes cross-channel campaigns, social segmentation, and social sharing.
[d] Social customer support functionality includes social communities, a customer co-created solutions knowledge base, and a multi-channel contact center.
[e] Customer experience profile includes purchasing history; visits to e-commerce, Web sites, and social media sites; time spent on different sites; marketing response to campaigns; customer service requests; and reports.
[f] Global business management functionality includes multi-language or multi-currency support.

5. Assign factors on a scale of 1–10 for each of the characteristics; the higher the factor is, the more important the characteristic for the envisaged CRM. Characteristics that are considered necessary should definitely be assigned a factor closer to 10, using a scale like the following:
   a. Vital = 10
   b. Critical = 9
   c. Essential = 8
   d. Significant = 7
   e. Important = 6
   f. Mandatory = 5
   g. Required = 4
   h. Useful = 3
   i. Desirable = 2
   j. Optional = 1
   The actual weights should be decided by consensus.

6. Next, rate the various CRM systems for each of these characteristics on a scale of 1–5. Five indicates excellent, while 1 denotes poor or unacceptable. A good rule of thumb is to agree on the best package for a particular characteristic and give only that package a rating of 5:
   a. Excellent/best = 5
   b. Remarkable = 4
   c. Moderate = 3
   d. Acceptable = 2
   e. Poor/worst = 1
   Then agree on ratings for other packages by consensus.

7. Compute the score for each CRM system by each characteristic by multiplying the weighting factor by the corresponding rating as follows:

$$\text{Score} = \text{Weighting factor} \times \text{Rating}$$

8. Total all the scores for each CRM system.

Table 4.4   Evaluative Comparison of CRM Systems

CRM System Characteristics	Weighting Factor	SAP CRM Rating Score	Oracle Siebel CRM Rating Score	Salesforce Rating Score	Aptean Rating Score
Technical					
Comprehensive functionality					
Ease of use					
Extendibility, flexibility, and configurability					
Ability of customization and modification					
Open systems architecture and interfaces					
One-point data entry					
Data synchronization					
Centralized database					
Interfacing of other devices, bar codes, EDI, CTI, and so on					
Integration with Legacy and ERP, SCM, DW, and other Third-party Products					
Internationalization and Euro compliance					
Online documentation and contextual help					
Future upgrades and enhancements					
Skill transfer and training programs					
User group activity					
Total score					
Operational					
Controls and reliability					
Ease of installation					
Efficiency of operations					

(*Continued*)

Table 4.4 (*Continued*) Evaluative Comparison of CRM Systems

CRM System Characteristics	Weighting Factor	SAP CRM Rating Score	Oracle Siebel CRM Rating Score	Salesforce Rating Score	Aptean Rating Score
Ease of performance tuning					
Ease of user management					
Security and authorization					
Backup and disaster recovery					
Availability					
Resource requirements					
Total score					
Financial					
System costs					
Hardware, system software, and networking					
Base license					
Enhancements					
Third-party solutions					
Site preparation					
Installation					
Services					
Staffing					
Training					
Implementation consultancy					
Documentation					
Travel					
Communications					
Maintenance					
Spread of investment					
Total score					
Grand total					

4.6.2 Script and Stress Test Reports

The results of the script test and stress test reports could also be included as one of the characteristics for comparing the CRM systems. This should be considered if the test results vary widely among the various CRM systems.

4.6.3 Recommendation Report

The report on the recommendations for the CRM submitted to the company's management should include the following:

- The advantages and disadvantages of the selected CRM system. This would be based on the information collected on evaluation criteria presented in the earlier chapter.
- A detailed profile of SAP CRM is presented in the next chapter; by the end of this chapter, it will be clear as to why SAP CRM is a clear winner among all other CRM systems available on the market today.
- The CRM systems comparative chart.
- The estimate of cost and benefits for the implementation of the CRM. This would be based on the information collected in Table 4.4 for costs of the requisite hardware, system software, CRM software, networking software, installation, training, yearly maintenance, implementation consultancy services, travel, communications, and so on.
- The implementation project schedule with dates of key milestones. An overview of a SAP CRM implementation project is discussed in Chapter 6.
- A recommendation for the approval by the management.

4.7 Summary

In this chapter, we saw the methodology for selecting the CRM package most suitable to the requirements of a company. In the later part of the chapter, we discussed the preparation of the CRM systems comparative chart and the final recommendation report. In the following chapters, we talk about SAP CRM and its Enterprise and e-Business Applications products. We will talk in sufficient detail about the architecture, structure, and design of SAP CRM to understand the comprehensiveness and complexity of this system. Chapters 5 through 11 will amply demonstrate why SAP is now the leading CRM product on the market. It will also substantiate to a great extent our claim that SAP CRM will be the CRM system of choice for any customer-centric enterprise of the twenty-first century.

Chapter 5

SAP CRM Solution

In this chapter, and in the remaining part of the book, we talk in detail about SAP AG's product SAP CRM. We present the architecture and salient features of the system in sufficient detail to highlight its overwhelming superiority. It will become evident by perusing this chapter and the following ones that SAP CRM is indeed the best CRM system on the market today. With its N-tiered distributed architecture, excellent repository-driven development environment, and comprehensive componentized business functionality covering all customer-facing functions across several industries, SAP represents perhaps one of the best software development efforts in recent times.

5.1 SAP the Company

SAP Systems, Inc. was founded in 1993 to address the growing need of organizations of all sizes to acquire, retain, and better serve their customers. Today, SAP with sales revenue of $14 billion is the world's leading provider of business application software. As reported by SAP, there are more than 25,000 plus customers with more than 100,000 installations of SAP across the world, and more than 15 million users work on SAP systems worldwide. By any standards, these are impressive numbers coming from a company that has a great vision and is destined to play a significant role in the Internet-driven markets of this century as well.

SAP CRM system is the world leader in Web-based front-office solutions for sales, marketing, and customer service. The phenomenal success of SAP comes from the fact that SAP CRM systems are comprehensive but at the same time configurable to the specific needs of any company. Companies prefer off-the-shelf packages like SAP because it is flexible and can be configured to satisfy most requirements of any company in any industry. SAP can be deployed on various hardware platforms providing the same comprehensive and integrated functionality, flexibility for addressing individual company-specific requirements, as well as ensuring independence from specific technologies deployed in the company. SAP implements a process-oriented view of the extended enterprise.

SAP CRM ensures success in a number of ways. The closed-loop sales, marketing, and customer service solution available from SAP is one of the most functionally complete solutions in the market. The company also aligns with world-class partners that provide certified system integration and hardware and software solutions. SAP solutions are designed to enable rapid implementation and customization to unique business requirements; provide for fast application upgrades; provide upwardly compatible enterprise application interfaces; allow for automatic software distribution to mobile, handheld, connected, and thin client users; and be easy to administer and support. SAP also provides a systematic and responsive service and support infrastructure that contributes to the success of each of the SAP implementation projects.

This chapter understandably banks heavily on the SAP's product messages and documentation. At this level, it is not very easy to make objective assessments of SAP's architecture, strategies, and products vis-à-vis other CRM products on the market. And, therefore, hereafter this book assumes that SAP is the preeminent CRM solution on the market—which it is! Scores of SAP features and characteristics are par excellence and need to be applauded. These include SAP Architecture, SAP Tools, SAP Application Customization and Upgrades, and SAP's lowest Total Cost of Ownership (TCO).

In 1972, five former IBM employees, Hasso Plattner, Dietmar Hopp, Claus Wellenreuther, Klaus Tschira, and Hans-Werner Hektor, launch a company called SAP (Systems Analysis and Program Development). Their vision was to develop standard application software for real-time business processing. These been involved in the provisional design of a software program that would allow information about cross functional and cross divisional financial transactions in a company's value chain to be coordinated and processed centrally—resulting in enormous savings in time and expense. They observed that other software companies were also developing software designed to integrate across value chain activities and subunits. Using borrowed money and equipment, the five analysts worked day and night to create an accounting software platform that could integrate across all the parts of an entire corporation.

5.1.1 SAP R/1

In 1973, SAP unveiled an instantaneous accounting transaction processing program called R/1, one of the earliest examples of what is now called an enterprise resource planning (ERP) system.

Today, ERP is an industry term for the multimodule application software that allows a company to manage the set of activities and transactions necessary to manage the business processes for moving a product from the input stage, along the value chain, to the final customer. As such, ERP system can recognize, monitor, measure, and evaluate all the transactions involved in business processes such as product planning, the purchasing of inputs from suppliers, the manufacturing process, inventory and order processing, and customer service itself. Essentially, a fully developed ERP system provides a company with a standardized information technology (IT) platform that gives complete information about all aspects of its business processes and cost structure across functions and divisions. Right from the beginning, SAP's goal has been to create the global industry standard for ERP by providing the best business application software infrastructure.

In its first years, SAP not only developed ERP software, but it also used its own internal consultants to install it physically on-site at its customers' corporate IT centers, manufacturing operations, and so on. Determined to increase its customer base quickly, however, SAP switched strategies in the 1980s. It decided to focus primarily on the development of its ERP software and to outsource, to external consultants, more and more of the implementation services needed to install and service its software on-site in a particular company. It formed a series of strategic alliances with major global consulting companies such as IBM, Accenture, and Cap Gemini to install its R/1 system in its growing base of global customers.

To some degree, its decision to focus on software development and outsource at least 80% of installation was a consequence of its German founders' *engineering* mindset. Founded by computer program engineers, SAP's culture was built on values and norms that emphasized technical innovation, and the development of leading-edge ERP software was the key success factor in the industry. SAP poured most of its money into research and development (R&D) to fund projects that would add to its platform's capabilities; consequently, it had much less desire and money to spend on consulting and building consulting expertise. Essentially, SAP was a product-focused company and believed R&D would produce the technical advances that would be the source of its competitive advantage and allow it to charge its customers a premium price for its ERP platform. By 1988, SAP was spending more than 27% of gross sales on R&D.

5.1.2 SAP R/2

In 1981, SAP introduced its second-generation ERP software, R/2. Not only did it contain many more value chain/business process software modules, but it also linked its ERP software to the databases and communication systems used on mainframe computers, thus permitting greater connectivity and ease of use of ERP throughout a company. The R/1 platform had been largely a cross organizational accounting/financial software module; the new software modules could handle procurement, product development, and inventory and order tracking. Of course, these additional components had to be compatible with each other so that they could be seamlessly integrated together at a customer's operations on-site. SAP's system was made compatible with Oracle's database management system (DBMS) software; this was to have repercussions later, when Oracle began to develop its own ERP software.

As part of its push to make its R/2 software the industry standard, SAP had also been in the process of customizing its basic ERP platform to accommodate the needs of companies in different kinds of industries. The way value chain activities and business processes are performed differs from industry to industry because of differences in the manufacturing processes and other factors. ERP software solutions must be customized by industry to perform most effectively. Its push to become the ERP leader across industries, across all large global companies, and across all value chain business processes required a huge R&D investment. In 1988, the company went public on the Frankfurt stock exchange to raise the necessary cash.

By 1990, with its well-received multilingual software, SAP had emerged as one of the leading providers of business application software, and its market capitalization was soaring. SAP began to dominate ERP software sales in high tech and electronics, engineering and construction, consumer products, and chemical and retail industries. Its product was increasingly being recognized as superior to other ERP softwares being developed by companies such as PeopleSoft, JD Edwards, and Oracle. One reason for SAP's increasing competitive advantage was that it could offer a broad, standardized, state-of-the-art solution to many companies' business process problems, one that spanned a wide variety of value chain activities spread around the globe. By contrast, its competitors, like PeopleSoft, offered more focused solutions aimed at one business process, such as human resource management.

ERP installation is a long and complicated process. A company cannot simply adapt its information systems to fit SAP's software; it must use consultants to rework the way it performs its value chain activities so that its business processes, and the information systems that measure these business processes, became compatible with SAP's software. SAP's ERP system provides a company with the information needed to achieve best industry practices across its operations. The more a particular company wishes to customize the SAP platform to its particular business processes, the more difficult and expensive the implementation process and the harder it becomes to realize the potential gains from cost savings and value added to the product.

SAP's outsourcing consulting strategy allowed it to penetrate global markets quickly and eliminated the huge capital investment needed to provide this service on a global basis. For consulting companies, however, the installation of SAP's software became a major money spinner, and SAP did not enjoy as much of the huge revenue streams associated with providing computer services, such as the design, installation, and maintenance of an ERP platform on an ongoing basis. It did earn some revenue by training consultants in the intricacies of installing and maintaining SAP's ERP system.

5.1.3 SAP R/3

In 1991, SAP had presented its R/3 or third-generation solution for the first time at the CeBIT in Hannover and was released to the general market in 1992. The product met with an overwhelming approval due to its client/server concept, uniform appearance of graphical interfaces, consistent use of relational databases, and the ability to run on computers from different providers. Essentially, expanding on its previous solutions, R/3 offered seamless, real-time integration for over 80% of a company's business processes. It had also embedded in the platform hundreds and then thousands of industry best-practice solutions, or templates, that customers could use to improve their operations and processes. The R/3 system was initially composed of seven different modules corresponding to the most common business processes. Those modules are production planning, materials management, financial accounting, asset management, human resources management, project systems, and sales and distribution.

R/3 was designed to meet the diverse demands of its previous global clients. It could operate in multiple languages and convert exchange rates, and so on, on a real-time basis. SAP, recognizing the huge potential revenues to be earned from smaller business customers, ensured that R/3 could now also be configured for smaller customers and be customized to suit the needs of a broader range of industries. Furthermore, R/3 was designed to be *open architectured*, meaning that it could operate with whatever kind of computer hardware or software (the legacy system) that a particular company was presently using. Finally, in response to customer concerns that SAP's standardized system meant huge implementation problems in changing their business processes to match SAP's standardized solution, SAP introduced customization opportunity into its software. However, the costs of doing this were extremely high and became a huge generator of fees for consulting companies.

SAP used a variable-fee licensing system for its R/3 system depending upon

- The cost to the customer, which was based on the number of users within a company
- The number of different R/3 modules that were installed
- The degree to which users utilized these modules in the business planning process

SAP's R/3 far outperformed its competitors' products in a technical sense and once again allowed it to charge a premium price for its new software. It was seeking to establish R/3 as the new ERP market standard and lock in customers before competitors could offer viable alternatives. This strategy was vital to its future success because, given the way an ERP system changes the nature of a customer's business processes once it is installed and running, there are high switching costs involved in moving to another ERP product—costs that customers want to avoid.

Although the United States had become SAP's biggest market, the explosive growth in demand for SAP's software had begun to slacken by 1995. Competitors such as Oracle, Baan, PeopleSoft, and Marcum were catching up technically, often because they were focusing their resources on the needs of one or a few industries or on a particular kind of ERP module (e.g., PeopleSoft's focus on the human resources management module). Indeed, SAP had to play catch-up in the HRM area and develop its own to offer a full suite of integrated business solutions. Oracle, the second largest software maker after Microsoft, was becoming a particular threat as it expanded its ERP offerings outward from its leading database systems and began to offer more and more of an Internet-based ERP platform.

With the advent of the Internet, newer companies like SAP Systems, Commerce One, Ariba, and Marcum, which began as niche players in some software applications such as SCM, CRM, intranet, or website development and hosting, also began to build and expand their product offerings so that they now possessed ERP modules that competed with some of SAP's most lucrative R/3 modules. Commerce One and Ariba, for example, emerged as the main players in the rapidly expanding B2B industry SCM market. B2B is an industry-level ERP solution that creates an organized market and thus brings together industry buyers and suppliers together electronically and provides the software to write and enforce contracts between them. Although these niche players could not provide the full range of services that SAP could provide, they became increasingly able to offer attractive alternatives to customers seeking specific aspects of an ERP system. Also, companies like SAP, Marcum, and i2 claimed that they had the ability to customize their low-price systems, and, consequently, prices for ERP systems began to fall rapidly.

In the new software environment, SAP's large customers started to purchase software on a *best-of-breed* basis, meaning that customers purchased the best software applications for their specific needs from different, leading-edge companies rather than purchasing all of their software products from one company with a monolithic package—such as SAP offered. Sun began to promote a free Java computer language as the industry *open architecture* standard, which meant that as long as each company used Java to craft their specific web-based software programs, they would all work seamlessly together and there would no longer be a need or an advantage to using a single dominant platform like Microsoft Windows or SAP's R/3. Sun was and is trying to break Microsoft's hold over the operating system industry standard, Windows.

5.1.4 mySAP.com

In 1997, SAP sought a quick fix to its problems by releasing new R/3 solutions for ERP Internet-enabled SCM and CRM solutions, which converted its internal ERP system into an externally based network platform. SCM, identified as the *back end* of the business, integrates the business processes necessary to manage the flow of goods, from the raw material stage to the finished product. SCM programs forecast future needs and plan and manage a company's operations, especially its manufacturing operations. CRM, identified as the *front end* of the business, provides companies with solutions and support for business processes directed at improving sales, marketing, customer service, and field service operations. CRM programs are rapidly growing in popularity because they lead to better customer retention and satisfaction and higher revenues. In 1998, SAP followed with industry solution maps, business technology maps, and service maps, all of which were aimed at making its R/3 system dynamic and responsive to changes in industry conditions. In 1998, recognizing that its future rested on its ability to protect its share of the US market, it listed itself on the New York Stock Exchange fueled its expansion in the US market.

In May 1999, Cochairman and CEO Hasso Plattner announced the mySAP.com strategy, heralding the beginning of a new direction for the company and its product range. mySAP.com connects e-commerce solutions with existing ERP applications using up-to-date Web technology. In the same year, numerous mySAP.com customers are won, among them Hewlett-Packard and the pharmaceutical company Hoechst Marion Roussel. The mySAP initiative was a comprehensive e-business platform designed to help companies collaborate and succeed, regardless of their industry or network environments.

To meet its customers' needs in the new electronic environment, SAP used the mySAP platform to change itself from a vendor of ERP components to a provider of e-business solutions. The platform was to be the online portal (SAP Enterprise Portal) through which customers could view and understand the way its Internet-enabled R/3 modules could address their evolving needs. SAP recognized that its customers were increasingly demanding access to networked environments with global connectivity, where decisions could be executed in real time through the Internet. Customers wanted to be able to leverage new e-business technologies to improve basic business goals like increasing profitability, improving customer satisfaction, and lowering overhead costs. In addition, customers wanted total solutions that could help them manage their relationships and supply chains.

SAP realized that cost was becoming a more important issue because competition from low-cost rivals demonstrated that customers could be persuaded to shift vendors if they were offered good commercial deals. Indeed, major companies like Oracle often offered their software at discount prices or even gave it away free to well-known companies to generate interest and demand for their product (and wean them away from SAP). SAP focused on making mySAP more affordable by *unbundling* its modules and business solutions into smaller, separate products. Customers could now choose which particular solutions best met their specific needs; they no longer had to buy the whole package. All mySAP offerings were fully compatible with the base R/3 system so that customers could easily expand their use of SAP's products. SAP was working across its whole product range to make its system easier and cheaper to use.

mySAP was aimed at a wider range of potential customers. By providing a simpler and cheaper version of its application software coupled with the introduction of the many mySAP e-business solution packages, SAP broadened its offerings targeted not only to large corporations but also to small- and medium-sized companies. mySAP enabled SAP to provide a low-cost ERP system that could be scaled down for smaller firms. For example, for small- to medium-sized companies that lack the internal resources to maintain their own business applications on-site, mySAP offered hosting for data centers, networks, and applications.

SAP's number of software installations and customers increased steadily between 1998 and 2002. The number of software installations grew at a faster pace than the number of customers, a characteristic of the lock-in feature of investment in one ERP platform. In 2002, SAP was still the number one vendor of standard business application software, with a worldwide market share of over 30%. Oracle was next with a 16% share of the market. SAP claimed that it had 10 million users and 50,000 SAP installations in 18,000 companies in 120 countries in 2002 and that half of the world's top 500 companies used its software.

5.1.5 R/3 Enterprise

In April 2002, SAP announced that its revenues had climbed 9.2%, but its first-quarter profit fell steeply because of a larger-than-expected drop in license revenue from the sale of new softwares. Many customers had been reluctant to invest in the huge cost of moving to the mySAP system given the recession and continuing market uncertainty. Accordingly, SAP announced it would introduce a product called R/3 Enterprise; it was an interim product, which would be targeted at customers not yet ready to make the leap to mySAP. R/3 Enterprise is a collection of web software that can be added easily to the R/3 platform to provide a company with the ability to network with other companies and perform many e-commerce operations. SAP hopes this new software will show its R/3 customers what mySAP can accomplish for them once it is running in their companies.

5.1.6 SAP NetWeaver

SAP's managers believed these initiatives would allow the company to jump from being the third largest global software company to being the second, ahead of main competitor Oracle. They also wondered if they could use its mySAP open system architecture to overcome Microsoft's stranglehold on the software market and bypass the powerful Windows standard. Pursuing this idea, SAP put considerable resources into developing a new business platform called SAP NetWeaver that is a web-based open integration and application platform that serves as the foundation for enterprise service-oriented architecture (SOA) and allows the integration and alignment of people, information, and business processes across business and technology boundaries. Enterprise SOA utilizes open standards to enable integration with information and applications from almost any source or technology and is the technology of the future. SAP NetWeaver is now the foundation for all enterprise SOA SAP applications and mySAP Business Suite solutions; it also powers SAP's partner solutions and a customer custom-built applications. Also, NetWeaver integrates business processes across various systems, databases, and sources—from any business software supplier—and is marketed to large companies as a service-oriented application and integration platform. NetWeaver's development was a major strategic move by SAP for driving enterprises to run their business software on a single SAP platform.

5.1.7 mySAP Business Suite

In 2003, SAP changed the name of its software from mySAP.com to mySAP Business Suite because more and more customers were now using a suite licensing arrangement to obtain its software rather than buying it outright. Part of the change in purchasing was because of the constant upgrades SAP was rolling out; in a licensing arrangement, its clients could expect to be continually upgraded as it improved its ERP modules. This also had the effect of locking its customers into its software platform for its raised switching costs. However, while SAP continued to attract new large business customers, the market was becoming increasingly saturated as its market share continued to grow—it already had around 50% of the global large business market by 2003. So, to promote growth and increase sales revenues, SAP began a major push to increase its share of the small and medium business enterprise (SME) market segment of the ERP industry.

5.1.8 Small and Medium Business Enterprise

The small size of these companies, and so the limited amount of money they had to spend on business software, was a major challenge for SAP, which was used to dealing with multinational companies that had huge IT budgets. Also, there were major competitors in this market segment that had specialized in meeting the needs of SMEs to avoid direct competition with SAP, and they had locked up a significant share of business in this ERP segment. By focusing primarily on large companies, SAP had left a gap in the market that large software companies like Oracle, Microsoft, and IBM took advantage to develop their own SME ERP products and services to compete for customers and revenues in this market segment—one also worth billions of dollars in the years ahead and the main growth segment in the future ERP market. So, to reach this growing market segment as quickly as possible, SAP decided to develop two main product offerings for SMEs: SAP All-in-One and SAP Business One.

SAP is facing competition in the SME market especially from CRM companies such as salesforce.com that specializes in on-demand software downloaded directly from the Internet. Complementing SAP's existing portfolio for medium-sized companies, a new solution Business ByDesign was introduced to leverage on-demand and hosted delivery at a significantly lower cost, and that will allow them to *try–run–adapt* the software to meet their needs.

5.1.8.1 SAP All-in-One

SAP All-in-One is a streamlined version of its R/3 mySAP Business Suite; it is much easier to install and maintain and much more affordable for SMEs. To develop All-in-One, SAP's software engineers took its mySAP Business Suite modules designed for large companies and scaled them down for users of small companies. All-in-One is a cutdown version of SAP's total range of products like SAP Customer Relationship Management, SAP ERP modules, SAP Product Life-Cycle Management, SAP Supply Chain Management, and SAP Supplier Relationship Management. Despite its reduced size, it is still a complex business solution and one that requires a major commitment of IT resources for an SME.

5.1.8.2 Business One

So, recognizing the need to provide a much simpler and more limited and affordable ERP solution for smaller companies, SAP decided to also pursue a second SME ERP solution. To speed the development of a new suite of programs, SAP decided not to develop a new software package from scratch based on its leading R/3 product, as it did with its All-in-One solution. Rather, it took a new path and bought an Israeli software company called Top Manage Financial Solutions in 2002 and rebranded its system as SAP Business One. SAP Business One is a much more limited ERP software package that integrates CRM with financial and logistic modules to meet a specific customer's basic needs. However, it still provides a powerful, flexible solution and is designed to be easy to work and affordable for SMEs. Business One software works in real time; no longer does an SME need to wait until the end of the month to do the accounts. The system manages and records the ongoing transactions involved in a business such as cost of goods received, through inventory, processing and sale, and delivery to customers and automatically records transactions in a debit and credit account.

5.1.9 SAP HANA

SAP is also working to be able to offer all of its customers the advantage of cloud computing as it matures and becomes a more reliable and secure option. SAP BusinessObjects solutions are continually being upgraded and developed to help companies optimize business processes on premise, on demand, and on device.

More recently, SAP was the first company to introduce in-memory technology to enable both online transaction processing (OLTP) and online analytical processing (OLAP) with full enterprise data loaded in memory through its product SAP HANA. High-Performance Analytic Appliance (HANA) is designed to speed up analysis of business data. Post the 2008 recession, SAP expects HANA to be a game changer solution in light of the increasing focus of enterprises *to do more with less* entailing focus on enterprise performance management and analytics (see Chapter 14, Section 14.9.4 "SAP HANA").

5.2 Significance of SAP

In the remaining part of this chapter, we provide an overview of the salient features and advantages of SAP CRM system. Although not patterned on our discussions in Chapters 3 "CRM Evaluation" and 4 "CRM Selection," for the evaluation and selection of a CRM system, it will become evident that SAP CRM excels in all of those dimensions compared to any other competing product on the market today. This chapter covers the most significant characteristics of the SAP CRM product and the related services provided by SAP.

SAP CRM is a fully integrated suite of application for customer relationship management (CRM) and related applications for partner relationship management (PRM) and HRM, all based on a common web-enabled SAP NetWeaver architecture. SAP helps organizations by providing three key functional areas that together enable organizations to fully align their partners, employees, and customer touch points, processes, and channels around the goal of maximizing the value of customer relationships. These three key areas are as follows.

5.2.1 Customer Relationship Management (CRM)

SAP enables organizations to more effectively identify, select, acquire, and retain customers. By providing a centralized repository of customer data captured from all customer interactions across all channels and touch points, SAP enables organizations to maintain an ongoing and seamless dialog with its customers regardless of when, where, or how the interactions occur. Companies are able to understand, anticipate, and respond to customer needs and are able to do so more effectively and efficiently over time. SAP gives managers better visibility into market dynamics and customer demand by providing real-time views of customer activity.

5.2.2 Employee Relationship Management (ERM)

Organizations also face the problems of their employees not being fully aligned with the organization's focus on customers. SAP ERM helps organizations to rapidly communicate the corporate policies and decisions to the entire workforce, mobilize employees to execute those decisions, and monitor workforce performance in real time. As employees are able to perform their job more effectively, organizations benefit from increased employee satisfaction and, hence, increased customer satisfaction (as happier and better-informed employees provide better customer service).

5.2.3 Partner Relationship Management (PRM)

SAP e-Business Applications for PRM allow organizations to manage their business partner's ecosystem as a virtual extension of their sales or Commercial, marketing, and service organizations.

Organizations can maximize their channel partners' efficiency and productivity by ensuring that their partners' incentives, resources, and objectives are fully aligned with those of the organization.

By providing organizations with real-time analytical ability to track and understand both customer behavior and key performance indicators of corporate performance, SAP enables organizations to be *digitally wired* to their customers, channel partners, and employees. The result is a total solution enabling organizations to fully focus the resources of their entire company on maximizing the value of their customer relationships. SAP enables organizations to overcome the five major obstacles that typically thwart its way toward becoming a customer-centric organization:

■ *Information silos*: Organizations have a tendency to get fragmented into silos based on product or line of businesses; this results in the customer data being scattered throughout the organization in a disjointed fashion, which gives a highly fragmented and incomplete view of their customers.

■ *Disconnected channels*: The organization lacks the ability to maintain a unified and coordinated interface with the customer across different interactions through different channels; this lack of synchronization invariably leads to a disjointed customer experience.

■ *Business processes that do not reflect best practices*: The organizational processes may not be aligned with the customer-centric focus of the organization; for instance, instead of being customer focused, many a time, business processes are optimized with reference to the back-office functions of the organizations. Though this may not be without some advantages in terms of back-office efficiencies, this may deny the organization the opportunity to achieve increased revenues while reducing the costs.

■ *Poorly coordinated business or channel partners*: Organizational partners are not aligned with the organizational objectives of delivering value to its customers; thus, though organizations increasingly rely on partners to deliver value to its customers, they may not be able to monitor and manage the performance of its partners.

■ *Unaligned employees*: Organization lacks systems to keep its employees informed and resources to enable its employees to do their jobs effectively; managers do not have a means to optimize workforce performance.

In addition to enhanced customer loyalty and retention, SAP's customer-focused e-business technology also delivers other measurable benefits that directly enhance an organization's effectiveness, productivity, and revenue. All these collectively have a positive impact on the company's performance in terms of

1. E-business applications improving the organization's effectiveness in sales, marketing, and customer service, resulting in increased revenue because of factors such as more selling time for salesman, higher-order sizes, and improved close rates for new leads
2. E-business applications increasing the productivity of the organization's sales, marketing, and service operations, thus effectively reducing the costs of the revenue-producing resources and increasing the availability of productive resources substantially (Table 5.1)

5.2.4 N-Tier Principle

N-Tier computing is a style of computing where the computer processing load is distributed across several synchronously or asynchronously cooperating computer programs running on a single computer or on a group. During the last decade of development, this has become one of the

Table 5.1   Benefits Achieved from SAP E-Business Technology

Achieved Area	Benefits Activity
Sales	Increased selling time per sales representative
	Increased revenue per sales
	Shorter sales cycle
	Improved prospect targeting
	Increased close rate
	Increased prospect-to-customer conversion rate
	Increased order size
	Increased revenue per customer (*wallet share*)
	Incremental revenue gains from new channel capabilities
	Reduced training costs
	Reduced sales overhead
	Improved team selling effectiveness
	Reduced costs for collateral distribution
	Increased order accuracy
	Decreased cost to manage partner/channel interactions
	Increased partner/reseller satisfaction
	Increased salesperson satisfaction
	More accurate sales forecasting
	More accurate and complete information to support sales managers
	Improved visibility into sales pipeline
Marketing	Reduced marketing campaign overhead
	Increased marketing campaign response rate
	Decreased cost to generate new leads
	Decreased cost to acquire new customers
	Decreased cost to identify potential customers
	Better, more detailed information on lifetime value of customers
	Faster cycle time to create, execute, and analyze marketing campaigns
	Faster lead generation
	Improved ability to test campaigns (offers, lists, etc.)
Service	Increased customer retention
	Decreased cost to retain existing customers
	Reduced customer service costs
	Faster response times to service requests

(*Continued*)

Table 5.1 (*Continued*)   Benefits Achieved from SAP E-Business Technology

Achieved Area	Benefits Activity
Service	Shorter wait times for callers requiring customer service
	Decreased time to resolve service requests
	Higher rate of service issues resolved on first call
	Increased productivity of customer service representatives
	Higher rate of service issues resolved on first field service visit
	Decreased rate of service issue escalation
	Extended customer service through 24 × 7 self-service options
	Increased customer service representative satisfaction
	More accurate information concerning customer service operations

architectures of choice for computerized systems because of the tremendous flexibility permitted by this approach. Applications can be installed, configured, and run on a central computer or distributed across several numbers, depending on the type and load of the applications. Moreover, as the processing requirements and loads change, the corresponding systems can be upgraded selectively. This approach provides a path for the companies to achieve greatly enhanced performance at only incremental costs while preserving the investments made in the earlier hardware.

In SAP, N-Tier computing forms the basis of cooperative processing of disparate software components that could reside on either a centralized or distributed configuration on many servers that are networked to each other. The communication between the servers could be based on

■ Synchronous program-to-program communication
■ Asynchronous message exchange
■ Remote SQL

These disparate software components could be meant for graphical presentation, for processing applications, or even for the storage of data. Special application servers can also be installed for individual work areas as well. Allocating separate servers not only helps in balancing loads but also enables allocating individual server configurations that are appropriate for the concerned tasks. This not only helps in improving the throughput and response times but also optimizes costs.

The N-layer approach, with its distribution of presentation, applications, and database functions on separate computers, truly provides a viable foundation for extended enterprise solutions. However, for integrated systems like SAP, the real achievement is to implement the multilayer concept without losing the integration of data and the processes across the entire system.

5.2.5 *Comprehensive World-Class Functionality*

SAP provides a suite of prepackaged, best-in-class applications to manage customer, partner, and employee relationships on a global basis, delivering the broadest and deepest set of features in the marketplace. The prebuilt features and business processes are designed to satisfy the majority of an organization's business requirements out of the box. SAP covers most of the significant business processes within several industries and businesses. Organizations can utilize divisional operations that are discrete or continuous in nature, or both. Similarly, a company can also have operations in service industries like banking and financial services. Such organizations (and many such enterprises exist now) need a uniform enterprise-wide system that can span customer-related functions across all such disparate business activities and help in controlling and managing them on a day-to-day basis. It's understandable that organizations that have interests in heterogeneous business activities across different regions of the world can be handicapped when managing day-to-day operations if different, incompatible, and nonintegrated systems are functioning at all these locations.

5.2.5.1 Application Components

SAP's standard application components address functionality that is commonly used across a broad spectrum of industries. They are mainly divided into three major groups: Sales, Marketing, and Service. SAP Sales consists of standard components like Opportunity Management and Pipeline Management, Account Management, Contact Management, Activity Management, and Quotas and Incentives. SAP Marketing consists of major components like Marketing Analysis, Customer Management, Marketing Communications, Content Management and Literature Material, and Database Marketing. SAP Services consist of components like Service Request Management, Self-Service, Account Management, Activity Tracking, Service Calendar, and Customer Feedback System and Satisfaction Survey.

We will be discussing more details of these modules in Chapter 8 "SAP CRM Enterprise Applications".

5.2.5.2 Industry-Specific Applications (IAs)

Almost every industry has characteristic requirements that are specific to companies operating in that industry. Each industry has different needs—different competitive challenges, customer requirements, business processes, and so on. SAP provides a wide array of industry-specific vertical solutions that address such unique requirements through industry applications (IAs) that are complementary to the base solution. SAP Systems have invested extensively in developing these industry-specific applications with deep out-of-the-box functionality and embed the industry best practices for customer-facing processes such as sales, marketing, and customer service (Table 5.2).

5.2.6 Lowest Total Cost of Ownership (TCO)

SAP enables rapid implementation and customization to unique business requirements; provides for fast application upgrades; provides upwardly compatible enterprise application interfaces; allows for automatic software distribution to mobile, handheld, connected, and thin client users; and is easy to administer and support.

SAP is built on a scalable Web architecture that prepackages several important core technologies critical to E-Business deployments. These include a full-featured rule-based personalization engine, a content management platform, a business rule, or workflow engine, among others. The N-tier architecture increases portability and allows business objects and logic to be built in a modular fashion. This allows for business logic to be shared among multiple applications and multiple client devices, including connected and offline browser clients, personal digital assistants (PDAs), phones that are enabled with Web Application Protocol (WAP), and voice.

SAP allows organizations to leverage industry best practices embedded in the software while enabling them to easily make modifications and provide business edge. The prebuilt features and

Table 5.2   SAP Industry-Specific Applications

Industry	Industry-Specific Applications
Financial Services	Retail Banking and Brokerage
	Institutional Finance
	Insurance
Communications	Wireless
	Media
Energy	Energy
	Oil and Gas
Life Sciences	Pharmaceutical
	Clinical
	Medical Products
Industrial	Automotive
	Chemicals
	High Technology
Consumer Sector	Consumer Goods
	Retail
	Apparel and Footwear
Public Sector	Public Sector
Travel and Transportation	Travel and Transportation

business processes are designed to satisfy the majority of an organization's business requirements out of a box. These features are upgradable from one version to the next, which allows customers to leverage a steady stream of new features and enhancements.

5.2.7 Customization and Upgrades

Organizations increasingly rely upon the strategic value of their customer, partner, and employee relationships to achieve higher revenues, greater loyalty, and increased competitive advantage. Cultivating those relationships requires sound business processes that are dynamic and require frequent modifications. For example, business frequently changes marketing campaigns, realigns territory assignments, and alters escalation procedures in a call center to deal with changing market conditions or because of constraints on internal resources. Consequently, E-Business applications need to provide industry-specific functionality that can be easily modified to fit the needs of an ever-changing business. SAP provides the tools for a company to tailor SAP to its specific requirements by configuring the parameters at the time of implementation. This custom support is counter to the general emphasis on standardizing the processes and implementing generic ones. It's a business truism that the survival and success of a company depend on how it differentiates itself and its products or services from those of its competitors.

To leverage on their competencies or advantages, companies cannot abandon the corresponding differentiating processes and will have to incorporate such fundamental variants in their CRM implementations.

Traditional client/server applications, typically developed using 4GL tools, used to be customized by changing the source code of the application to customize the screens, business logic, triggers, or even the database schema of the application. This approach led to problems in the ability to upgrade and support the applications, thereby dramatically inflating the full life-cycle costs of application maintenance.

Because of the way SAP applications are designed, they are highly configurable and easy to upgrade. SAP e-Business Applications are *declaratively configured*: that is, they are defined as metadata in the SAP Repository. The customizations are implemented by configuring or setting properties of business objects using the graphical toolset of SAP Tools rather than traditional programming (see Section 5.2.9 "Internationalization and Localization"). Furthermore, because the customizations are defined in terms of metadata, configurations and integrations can be upgraded to the next release of software without additional effort. Not only does this obviate the need for expending additional time and effort, it also provides a smooth upgrade path that accelerates the deployment of the new version of applications. Overall, this strategy helps to preserve the organization's investment in custom configurations and integrations.

Competing solutions do not allow for a high level of configurability to tailor the application to unique requirements of businesses. Generally, such applications are developed using a fourth-generation language (4GL) against a relational database management system (DBMS). The customer's ability to tailor the application revolves around changing the source code of the application by changing the business logic using the 4GL or the database schemas. Such changes not only render supporting and upgrading such customized applications extremely difficult, if not impossible, but they also make them costlier. Compared to SAP, competing solutions have much higher TCOs. Some packaged applications permit a certain degree of configuration, like being able to turn on or off various switches or being able to set parameters that affect the behavior of programs constituting the application. However, when this is inadequate to meet the needs of the business, the customer is forced to change its business to suit the needs of the application—this is not BPR! (See Chapter 7.)

5.2.8 Highly Interactive Browser Interface

SAPGUI was the standard GUI of the SAP system. SAPGUI's design logic and element definitions are independent of the presentation system, and hence, the SAP user interfaces have the same look and feel, irrespective of the presentation software used at any installation. The graphical systems could be from any platform, including MS Windows, OS/2 Presentation Manager, OSF/Motif, and Apple Macintosh. SAPGUI includes all the graphical capabilities of modern Windows interfaces, with menu bars, toolbars, push buttons, radio buttons, online help, value lists, and so on.

Moreover, because SAP does not transmit fully prepared screen images between R/3 application servers and presentation systems, the volume of data transmitted for every screen is very low, approximately 1–2 kb. This results in minimal network traffic, which is another major contributing factor toward the overall scalability of the SAP system.

5.2.9 Internationalization and Localization

As noted while relating the history of SAP in Section 5.1 "SAP the Company," SAP has always had as a part of its core strategy a plan to support multiple languages and related aspects of currencies, taxation, legal practices, and import/export regulations within its systems. The same logic of presentation mentioned previously also has enabled SAP to provide multilingualism as an innate capability of the system. All onscreen text is maintained separately in several languages, and the presentation screens are assembled only at the time of display, depending on the language version chosen by the user at the time of logging into the system.

SAP also maintains programs for the development and enhancement of country-specific functionalities in different parts of the world. As more and more companies have facilities operating in different parts of the world, such country-specific functionalities are becoming critical for obtaining the promised benefits of implementing solutions like SAP CRM worldwide.

5.2.10 SAP Architecture

Figure 5.1 shows SAP components from a functional as well as an infrastructural point of view. From a functional point of view, the topmost layer is the presentation layer that is made of the GUI system. The middle layer is the application layer that handles not only business applications but also the middleware layer called NetWeaver. Integration of all business applications relies on the NetWeaver system. This system includes components such as the ABAP Development Workbench, system administration tools, system management tools, authorization and security systems, and cross application systems. The lowest layer is made up of the network, the database, and the operating system.

The presentation layer deals with the following services: SAPGUI, SAP Logon, and the SAP Session Manager. The Application layer deals with business applications and is grouped into the following services: Marketing, Sales, Service, Interaction Center, and Channel Management. The Application Middleware layer deals with the following services: dialog, update, enqueue (lock management), background processing, message server, gateway, and spool. The database

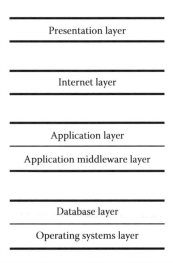

Figure 5.1 SAP architecture.

layer deals with native and open SQL services. The application layer will be tackled in Chapters 8 "SAP CRM Enterprise Applications" and 9 "SAP E-Business Applications", while the middleware layer is described in Chapters 10 "SAP CRM Application Environment" and 11 "SAP Tools and Programming".

5.2.10.1 Scalability

SAP's scalability on the technical front is easy to grasp. The multilayer client/server architecture enables SAP to easily scale the operations from a configuration for few hundred users to a few thousand. On particular sites, this scaling might also be dictated by the implementation of additional modules or third-party specialized applications that are interfaced with SAP. SAP, however, also provides scalability on the business front as well, where an SME might commence using only a subset of the functionality provided by the SAP system. As a result of business successes, an organization might witness rapid growth and expansion in terms of volume, type, and the complexities of business activities. SAP can keep pace with such positive developments in the nature and structure of a company's business by customizing its delivered functionality on an ongoing basis suitable to the increased scale and complexity of its business. This is the genesis of SAP's configure-to-order strategy for SMEs.

5.2.11 SAP Repository

As mentioned in Chapter 2, Section 2.2, "Anatomy of a CRM System" the SAP Repository is the central collection area for access or information on every kind of development object in the SAP system. These development objects include the data and process models, the ABAP Dictionary, function libraries, user exits, and Workbench Organizer objects. The Repository Information System also provides a comprehensive cross-reference facility that delivers information on all of the points of use for a specified object.

5.2.12 Comprehensive Application Development Environment

SAP has a centralized, integrated, full-featured development environment for custom development or enhancement of SAP standard functionality.

5.2.12.1 ABAP Development Workbench

The Advanced Business Applications Programming (ABAP) language is a full-featured 4GL available for custom development in the SAP environment (see Chapter 11 "SAP Tools and Programming"). The ABAP Development Workbench provides all the necessary facilities, tools, and aids for the design, development, and testing of application data tables, screens, programs, inquiries, reports, and so on. At the heart of the Workbench is the ABAP Data Dictionary. The data dictionary stores the descriptions of the table structures used throughout the system. It is the central metadata repository that we talked about in Chapter 2, Section 2.2 "Anatomy of a CRM System." In addition, the Workbench has an object repository that stores all objects under development, be they programs, dynpros (dynamic programs), documentation, and so on. This controls the actual development and testing of programs directly. On successful completion of the development, another component called the Workbench Organizer handles the transfer of new developments and customizations into productive systems or to other SAP systems. The Workbench Organizer maintains facilities for version control.

5.2.12.2 SAP System Controls

Every user has a valid user identity and password that is authenticated when logging in to the system. The SAP authorization concept is implemented on the basis of the authorization objects. This ranges from general access down to the level of access to individual tables, fields, and values. Authorization could be for access to particular set of enterprise data or for a set of operations or both.

An authorization object consists of several system elements that need to be protected like parametric or configuration data, master data, transactions, and processing tasks. For efficient authorization, authorization objects are packaged into predefined authorization profiles. SAP supports an array of standard profiles for a wide range of applications and activities. These profiles can be maintained independently and can be assigned to the appropriate users on demand. Users can also be given authorizations to create, change, or view objects. Authorization profiles are further combined into composite profiles for personnel who are required to work in areas that are not covered by one profile.

More importantly, SAP's transport and release system controls and manages all programs that are released into production as well as changes that are to be made from time to time on the system. This transfer can only be done under the strict control of the transport and release system. The transport system has a strict version control on all development objects that are transferred to the production system. The transport system is subject to the SAP authorization concept.

All activities occurring in a SAP system get recorded in the system logs and can be listed according to the user or transaction. Similarly, every change to the SAP startup profile, the customizations, database parameters, and the operating system parameters is also recorded and is available for analysis. To ensure protection from unauthorized tampering, the SAP system as a whole is stored in separate directory structures of the operating system with exclusive access authorizations.

5.2.13 Open Architecture

SAP enables the cooperation and portability of applications, data, and interfaces across different computers, because they use internationally accepted standards for definitions of interfaces, services, and data formats.

Because of the open architecture, SAP can work flexibly with multiple solution options at all levels:

- Graphical interface level
- Desktop level
- Application level
- Database level
- External interface level
- Communication protocol level
- Hardware and O/S level

Figure 5.2 gives the various platforms supported by SAP.

5.2.13.1 Portability

The SAP system can be used on a variety of systems. In fact, its platform independence permits the use of different hardware or O/S platforms for presentation, application, and database servers with

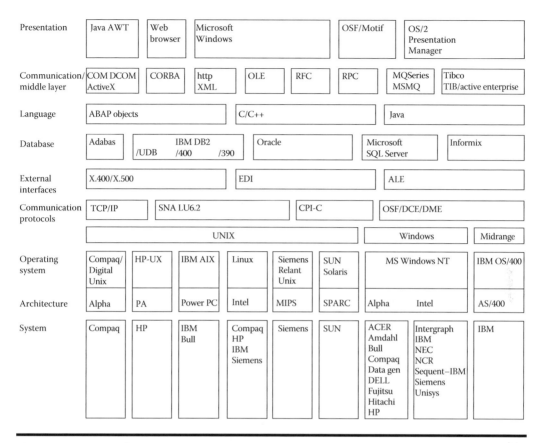

Presentation	Java AWT	Web browser	Microsoft Windows				OSF/Motif	OS/2 Presentation Manager	
Communication/ middle layer	COM DCOM ActiveX	CORBA	http XML	OLE	RFC	RPC		MQSeries MSMQ	Tibco TIB/active enterprise
Language	ABAP objects			C/C++				Java	
Database	Adabas	/UDB	IBM DB2 /400	/390	Oracle		Microsoft SQL Server		Informix
External interfaces	X.400/X.500			EDI			ALE		
Communication protocols	TCP/IP	SNA LU6.2			CPI-C		OSF/DCE/DME		
		UNIX					Windows		Midrange
Operating system	Compaq/ Digital Unix	HP-UX	IBM AIX	Linux	Siemens Relant Unix	SUN Solaris	MS Windows NT		IBM OS/400
Architecture	Alpha	PA	Power PC	Intel	MIPS	SPARC	Alpha	Intel	AS/400
System	Compaq	HP	IBM Bull	Compaq HP IBM Siemens	Siemens	SUN	ACER Amdahl Bull Compaq Data gen DELL Fujitsu Hitachi HP	Intergraph IBM NEC NCR Sequent–IBM Siemens Unisys	IBM

Figure 5.2   Some of the platforms supported by SAP.

tremendous advantages in terms of performance and costs. This also enables any installations to benefit from the latest developments in infrastructure technologies (hardware, O/S, networking, DBMS, and so on) without disrupting the SAP system in production.

5.2.13.2 Interoperability

Open system interfaces permit SAP to be integrated with other applications using earlier-noted industry standard interfaces like Object Linking Enabling (OLE) and Remote Function Call (RFC).

Figure 5.3 shows the standard protocols used by SAP with reference to the OSI-layered model for networks.

5.2.14 SAP Worldwide Services

SAP provides companies with a comprehensive set of services during the implementation and support phases of their implementations. SAP delivers support services mainly on remote connections between customer SAP installations and the network of SAP support servers spread throughout the world.

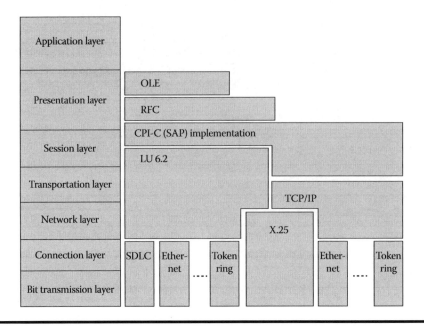

Figure 5.3   Some of the protocols supported by SAP.

5.2.14.1 Online Service System (OSS)

This OSS service is provided by SAP via customers logging into the nearest SAP support servers. This is basically a service for registering problems as well as accessing information, including solutions to registered problems. It is also the forum for disseminating up-to-date release, installation, and upgrade information. OSS provides 24 h Hotline support to assist users in determining solutions to problems faced in the system. A problem is logged with all the relevant information. When logging a problem, the customer states how important the problem is and how quickly a solution is required (low, medium, high, or very high). When a customer is in a live-production environment and a resolution to the problem is critical, SAP will respond immediately, resolving most issues in less than an hour. SAP support staff can be given access to log directly into a customer's system and assist in resolving issues for the customer. Using OSS, customers have access to download patches and code corrections to known errors in the release of SAP that is being implemented.

5.2.14.2 EarlyWatch

EarlyWatch is a service offered by SAP, wherein SAP experts from SAP support centers connect to your SAP systems. They access customers' SAP installations and gather numerous data on various aspects of system performance data and system operations. This information is analyzed and processed for diagnosing problems or detecting potential problems and bottlenecks. This is largely useful at the time of initial installation or whenever major changes occur in the infrastructure or configuration of a SAP installation. The EarlyWatch specialists analyze customer installations and provide a written report on the optimal parameterization of the system, on performance improvement, and on bottlenecks that might appear in the future.

5.2.15 Partnering for Growth

Partnering has been one of the driving forces in the growth of SAP. SAP has adopted partnering as a growth strategy not only with its business and technology partners but also with its customers. This partnership with customers has led to the success of its ISs. SAP combines the horizontal functionality of its base solution with focused, vertical functionality provided by ISs that are developed along with specific, best-in-class SAP customers in each industry.

Until the past decade, SAP did not consider itself to be in the implementation business per se. Most of the SAP implementations have been undertaken by SAP implementation partners that range from the erstwhile Big Six accounting firms and Big IT firms to national-level consulting companies. Most of them have built exclusive practices for providing SAP implementation and support services.

Technology partners are the leading software vendors of products that form the standard components of the multitier client/server architecture of SAP implementations. These include vendors of operating systems, databases, and networking products.

SAP has the following types of partners: hardware, consulting, technology, development, and the traditional value-added resellers. Development partners are companies that participate along with SAP's personnel in the development and enhancement of SAP. Additionally, SAP also has partnerships with third-party product developers called Complementary Software Program (CSP) partners. These are parties with specialized solutions like CAD, plant data collection systems, process control systems, identification and access control systems, mobile data collection systems, and geographical information systems (GIS).

5.3 Other Significant Aspects of SAP

This section will mention briefly some aspects of SAP system operations that might not get highlighted in SAP literature yet are nonetheless, in my opinion, of great value in terms of their potential for leading to major gains in productivity. They are also indicative of the exactness of the research done by SAP in the usability engineering of their system.

5.3.1 SAP Document

In analogy with the integrity of an accounting transaction document in accounting systems, SAP has defined the concept of a SAP Document. A SAP Document contains all information pertaining to a transaction and is always retained in its complete form. This enables tremendous advantages in traceability, audit, and maintenance of document history.

5.3.2 Recording by Example (RBE)

SAP by design is oriented toward screen-based interactions. It religiously follows the principle of recording any data only once. The system recognizes that this data entry effort is substantial, however, and goes further to help in expediting this data entry effort by providing a facility that I would term as Recording by Example (RBE).

Across the entire system, while doing data entry of any master or transaction record, SAP provides a facility to essentially provide a copy of relevant data from similar data items created earlier. For instance, when creating a new vendor, the system prompts you to optionally give a reference of an existing vendor whose details are similar to the new one being created. After providing an existing vendor number, the system provides a copy of all relevant details from the referred vendor record for you to accept or override for the new vendor record being created. This is a novel application of software engineering's basic guiding principle of reusability to as mundane an issue as that of data entry. It reduces keystrokes, minimizes individually keyed errors, automatically inputs standard information, and assures that none of the mandatory items are missed by an oversight. All this leads to tremendous gains in productivity, even in routine operations of data entry.

5.3.3 Variants

Here is another variation on the concept of reusability. A group of data items that may be required, often even in differing contexts, is packaged and identified uniquely as variants. This can then be retrieved and employed quickly at the required stages of processing, without having to specify all the minute details again and again free of errors. Variants are useful for situations like printing using specified format layouts and posting in a predefined manner to a set of accounts. It is amazing to witness how a little amount of reusability enlivens the drudgery and tediousness of routine operations.

5.3.4 Drill-Down Reporting

Drill-down reporting is another facility that makes the inquiry and reporting functions in SAP very powerful. Any inquiry or report in SAP can be chosen at any point with a mouse click to access the supporting details of the source transaction. One can continue doing the same further, or, in other words, drill down to a level where the relevant supporting information is located. For instance, in a statement of accounts for a customer, a user can click on any outstanding amount to immediately scrutinize the corresponding invoice and then go on to the customer order, the specific line item detail, and so on. After finishing, the user can return to the initiating program screen. This is of great value, especially for finance and accounting reports where an audit trail becomes available almost instantaneously without leaving the report or enquiry program of immediate interest.

5.4 SAP Strategic Initiatives

In the past couple of years, SAP has taken the initiative to address the concerns reported by their customers. These initiatives have also been based on the experiences gained from thousands of SAP implementation projects that have been undertaken by SAP and its partners in the last few years. The thrust of all these initiatives has been to increase the efficiency of project efforts, decrease project completion times, and make SAP easy to use and operate.

5.4.1 AcceleratedSAP (ASAP) Implementation Methodology

The ASAP implementation methodology represents the process component of TeamSAP. ASAP is a comprehensive solution to achieve successful SAP implementations with optimal resources, costs, and time periods. It is based on the experiences obtained from thousands of SAP implementations in the past few years. It includes technical guides for expediting all stages of the ASAP methodology, especially the business blueprint and realization phases. It contains detailed project plans that guide you through project management in order to optimize time, ensure quality, and make efficient use of resources throughout the duration of a project.

5.5 Summary

In this chapter, we looked at several aspects of SAP to substantiate the fact that SAP is the leading CRM solution there is on the market. Even though it is not directly patterned on various evaluation criteria discussed in Chapter 3 "CRM Evaluation", this chapter clearly demonstrates the overwhelming superiority of SAP in all those criteria.

The intelligent use of Internet technology for business operations has already become a critical success factor for many enterprises. The sudden explosion in e-business implies that beyond-the-enterprise issues such as customer relationship management (CRM) have become crucial for the competitiveness of many companies. SAP has always worked with the tremendous foresight and vision that have powered its growth to its present position as the number one business application software company. With the advent of the Internet, SAP truly stands challenged not only to provide competitive solutions but also to keep on changing and upgrading them continuously on Internet time.

Chapter 6

SAP CRM Implementation Project Cycle

In this chapter, we consider an overview of the SAP CRM implementation project life cycle. First, we consider the context of launching such a project, which includes the objectives of the project, implementation strategies, and the resource requirements for a company. We also provide an overview of the pre-implementation, implementation, and post-implementation phases of the project. The chapter ends by identifying some of the aspects involved with the deployment of SAP CRM at remaining sites, as well as the issues of supporting a SAP CRM production environment.

It is assumed that after the evaluation and selection of the CRM system for the company, the company has decided to implement SAP CRM as the core solution throughout the company. All other systems, whether they are legacy or that might be implemented in the future, have to interface with the SAP backbone that will be implemented within the company. We will also assume that the company has evaluated, selected, and contracted for the hardware and networking infrastructure and the SAP CRM implementation partners, as well as any other vendors for training, testing, system and network management support and services, and so forth.

> It must be noted that the approach being presented here is based on the author's experience and perception of SAP CRM projects. The situations in particular projects might certainly be different, and the measures presented here might not be applicable. SAP CRM projects should still be considered recent phenomena, and no one is in a position to take a definitive stance on various aspects of such projects. We urge readers to modify the prescriptive message, particularly of this and subsequent chapters, to suit the particular circumstances of individual companies. This might also be true by reason of the fact that SAP CRM implementations for SME enterprises might differ qualitatively from implementations for the earlier Fortune 500 enterprises.

6.1 Mission and Objectives of the SAP CRM Project

The mission of the SAP CRM project should dovetail into the mission and objectives set forth by the company for the following 3–5 years.

The SAP CRM implementation project itself could have a mission similar to the following:

> To prepare, implement, and support SAP CRM throughout the organization in the planned period of 1 year, with the full participation of all stakeholders of the company and to the satisfaction of all of these stakeholders.

Project objectives set for the SAP CRM effort are quantifiable items such as

- Reducing by 3% the percentage of customers that deliver 80% of revenues (in total, by product category, by specific product, etc.)
- Reducing by 5% the percentage of customers that deliver more than 100% of profits
- Increasing the marketing spend on existing customers by 15%
- Increasing customer retention by 5%
- Increasing process throughputs by 30%
- Reducing transaction turnaround times by 50%, which could be related to collecting or making payments, responding to internal requisitions or external queries, and so forth

The success of the CRM strategy, which is directly related to engaging, acquiring, retaining, and growing customers, can be assessed using various CRM metrics like

- Customer Value Metrics
- Customer Behavior Metrics
- Customer Loyalty Metrics

6.1.1 Examples of Cited Reasons for Implementing SAP CRM

By now, there are more than 5000 SAP CRM installations throughout the world. The reasons cited for undertaking SAP CRM vary markedly from company to company. Some of the cited reasons are as follows:

- Limitations in expanding on the existing applications.
- Application should be able to function on heterogeneous hardware and infrastructure.
- Application should provide a company-wide uniform user interface across incompatible front-end hardware.
- Application should provide all business events online.
- Application should provide access to real-time information.
- Application should provide support for cross functional processes.
- Application should enable flexible adjustment of business processes to market demands.
- Application should provide integration of customer-facing systems with back-office systems.
- Application should ensure that business processes should not be hampered by system or national boundaries.
- Application must support country-specific functionality.
- Application should lead to reduction in lead time.

6.2 Guiding Principles for CRM's Best Practices

CRM is the sum of the people, processes, and technologies working together to

■ Attract target customers
■ Grow the value of the existing customers
■ Retain profitable customers for as long as possible

The guiding principles to create CRM's best practices are as follows:

1. Define the Customer Relationship strategies required to
   a. Acquire new customers by creating awareness of your differentiated product and service offering
   b. Retain your best customers by better responding to their needs
   c. Grow the value of the relationship with your customers
2. Design and implement the CRM processes and programs that will allow you to
   a. Create a closed-loop relationship with the customer
   b. Manage the customer throughout their relationship and life cycle with the company and its employees
   c. Respond in real time to customer needs, inquiries, problems, and opportunities across all channels and touch points
   d. Anticipate customer needs and expectations in order to differentiate the experience you deliver to the customer
3. Select, develop, and integrate the applications, tools, and technology infrastructure needed to
   a. Capture all relevant transactions and relationship information about the customer's behavior, requirements, attitudes, and expectations
   b. Analyze the information and data in order to create a meaningful relationship experience regardless of the marketing, sales, service, or communication objective
   c. Plan the programs, initiatives, and tactics for interacting with the customer based on anticipated customer needs and corporate objectives
   d. Execute the process, programs, and initiatives in real time, providing the necessary decision-making support for people within the company who are called upon to flawlessly execute the specific customer interactions

6.3 Project Initiation and Planning

For business-driven projects such as SAP CRM, it is vital that the top management should not only be involved but should also be driving the project at every stage. Therefore, the project initiation would start with the appointment of an executive sponsor for the project. Usually, the executive sponsor should be the CEO of the company. That appointment should be followed by the formation of a project executive committee and a steering committee. These should be followed by the appointment of a Chief Project Officer (CPO) and also the finalization of the scope of the project.

The CPO, under the guidance of the executive and steering committees, should assemble the implementation team, including the identification of module and site managers. The project management policies and guidelines should be finalized. The central project office should be established, including the critical support staff such as the training manager, the resource manager, and the project administrative staff. This team will have to prepare a plan and schedule for the implementation project, including the various activities, the manpower required, the duration, and the schedule for completing each of these activities.

The CPO will have to form another team to look after the procurement, installation, and productive operation of the basic infrastructure, including the hardware servers and clients, networking hardware and software, operating systems, databases, and office automation software.

6.4 Critical Success Factors

Various factors are considered critical for the success of the SAP CRM projects. We'll look at each of them in this section.

6.4.1 Direct Involvement of Top Management

SAP CRM implementation is not an IT project but a business strategy project. As with any other business strategy project for new product development, new marketing strategy, BPM project, and so on, a SAP CRM project should get the direct attention and involvement of the senior management. If this involvement is confined only to the initial stages of the project, the project is certain to falter later.

One of the issues in which top management is required to demonstrate and encourage full commitment to the SAP CRM project is the deputation of key managers from different departments. Particularly in consumer goods industries, participating in IT-oriented projects might be considered a non-value-adding activity in terms of its ability to further managers' career goals. This perception must be corrected because SAP CRM implementation is not an IT-driven effort. Furthermore, for employees who would use SAP CRM for their routine operations, their full participation in the project is very critical. This can be ensured only by deputing the key managers of the company for this effort.

6.4.2 Clear Project Scope

It is very important for a project to have a well-defined scope. Any ambiguities lead only to diffusion of focus and dissipation of effort. There are always adherents especially for increased scope, and a series of such increments in scope would render any project unsuccessful. This is also referred as *scope creep*. Hence, the CPO must be vigilant on any creep in the scope of the project.

6.4.3 Covering as Many Functions as Possible within the Scope of the SAP CRM Implementation

Companies that are multidivisional and multilocated develop differently at different sites and acquire a character of their own at each site that may not fit into a uniform mold across the organization. A CRM package must have an ability to provide a comprehensive functionality to implement such deeply ingrained differing ways of operations at different locations. It should be able to provide ready-to-use, best-practice processes that incorporate such varying ways of executing any business transaction or process. We have mentioned that the more functions are integrated and performed in real time, the more competitive the organization would be. For this, it is essential that as many functions as possible should go productive together on SAP CRM. This *big-bang* strategy will have to be adopted in the beginning stage of the projects, such as the Discovery and Design Stage. Hence, it is critical that at least all the basic components of SAP CRM, like Sales, Services, Marketing, Interaction Center, Partner Channel Management, and E-Business, should be implemented at the pilot site.

6.4.4 Standardizing Business Processes

Every office or customer service center of a company develops its own character and culture, which are the results of the company's recommended corporate environment blending with the local situations. Such local practices have strong adherents and generate fierce loyalty and pride. These factors often harm the progress of a system implementation across the organization at all of its sites and offices, even if it is a computerized system such as SAP CRM. As a prerequisite, it's important to streamline and standardize a business process.

6.4.5 Proper Visibility and Communication on the SAP CRM Project at All Stages

It is important to give proper visibility to the SAP CRM project. This might entail communicating about the strategic direction of the company, the relevance of SAP CRM, the SAP CRM implementation project and team, and the implementation plan and schedule. Either there could be a bulletin exclusively focused on the SAP CRM project or the company's in-house newsletter must have regular features and articles on SAP CRM project–related issues and milestones.

6.4.6 Allocation of Appropriate Budget and Resources

After the company has made the strategic decision to undertake the SAP CRM implementation effort, it must also prepare and approve the budget plan and estimates for the complete SAP CRM project. Because the project schedules are dependent nonlinearly on the prerequisite at all stages, any changes or deferment of release of funds, and therefore resources, will always have an adverse effect on the successful commencement of the project.

Many times, the controllers or decision makers will withhold sanction for the resources at a particular stage at a pilot site or for other sites for optimization of costs. It must be noted that when any business project is launched, and SAP CRM implementation is no exception, any deferment of such strategic programs only *increases the opportunity cost* for the period that the project is delayed. Moreover, for an integrated project such as SAP CRM, that opportunity cost is not confined only to the local activity or site that contributes to the delay but at the level of the whole company. Thus, for a company with a turnover of $500 million, after launch of the SAP CRM project, that company would effectively be incurring an opportunity cost of $25–$50 million for every delayed month in the schedule.

6.4.7 Full-Time Deputation of Key Managers from All Departments

In traditional IS/IT projects, the personnel normally allocated to such efforts are either members who were young and newly joined or older members who could be spared from their respective departments. In either case, this will not help in a large way to lead the projects to success. SAP CRM, being a strategic project, should get allocation of the key personnel of different departments because only if the inputs are accurate and functionally correct will the SAP CRM system truly deliver when it goes in production. SMEs, whose staff strength is small unlike the large enterprise, must allocate their best people with the conviction that after SAP CRM is in production correctly, it will give better returns not only in terms of money but also in other dimensions like relationships, satisfaction surveys, and improved brand.

6.4.8 Completing Infrastructural Activities on Time and with High Availability

Consistent with the approach being taken in this book, the infrastructure for a SAP CRM project whether it's the computers and networking infrastructure or human infrastructure in terms of skills acquisition and training must not be treated as an IS/IT infrastructure. It must be monitored like any other non-IS/IT infrastructure. Any mismatch between the readiness of the infrastructure and the overlaying SAP CRM system will only lead to delays in the project and, hence, incur opportunity costs.

6.4.9 Instituting a Company-Wide Change Management Plan

Like any other strategy implementation plan, SAP CRM implementation is a prime case of an organizational change. It should be recognized and planned as such. In parallel with the SAP CRM implementation effort, it makes sense to undertake a change management program to address the disorientation and lost sense of direction that might be experienced by a large number of members. If not managed properly, this could jeopardize the success of the whole project.

Top management should note that unlike traditional IS/IT projects, most SAP CRM implementations do not have *parallel runs* in which incumbent systems are run along with the older ones for a predetermined time period until the new systems are declared operational and the company switches over to the new regime. This happens because after SAP CRM goes productive, the transactions and the actual operational tasks are done on the SAP CRM system itself; any major error could turn fatal for the company. The situation might seem alarming based on the past experiences of the traditional IT systems going productive; however, that is the exact point that we are trying to make in this book. SAP CRM is not like a traditional IT/IS project; it represents a totally different model of computerization (see Chapter 2, Section 2.1.9 "CRM Represents the New Departmental Store Model of Implementing Computerized Systems").

6.4.10 Training of SAP CRM Team Members

All training needs for all the members of the team should be identified, and either corporate training programs should be arranged on-site or members should be nominated for external training programs. For the SME, in which project schedules are shorter and the manpower base in the organization is smaller, it is essential that training of the team members is initiated and completed before the scheduled start of the program. Members should be encouraged to take certification tests in their concerned area of activity.

6.4.11 Training of User Members

Awareness, as well as familiarity training for all users who might use the SAP CRM productive system, is important. Training plans should not only have training programs but should also budget refresher courses for all members. Sometimes, when the SAP CRM project is reaching critical mass, the user community as a whole might be disadvantaged because of a time lag between the actual training and the commencement of SAP CRM going into production. In such cases, refresher courses might have to be undertaken either very close to the actual commencement of implementation or, if all sites and offices go live on SAP CRM, on a staggered schedule. Again, top management should allocate a good contingency training budget in light of the fact that when SAP CRM goes into production, there is no fallback arrangement; once launched, it has to reach *critical mass*.

6.4.12 Scheduling and Managing Interface of SAP CRM with Other Systems

There are many legacy systems, non-SAP systems, external systems, and even manual functions that might be considered out of the scope of the SAP CRM project. SAP CRM does not address all the functional requirements of a company. This might be involved with solutions for security and access, e-mail, CTI, digitizing system, and so on. SAP CRM has a complete program of interfacing with, and qualifying, third-party products to leverage on companies with special expertise and products (see Chapter 5, Section 5.2.12 "Comprehensive Application Development Environment"). Interfacing these systems should be scheduled in such a way that the interfaces are operational when SAP CRM goes into production.

In cases in which a peripheral or support system could be replaced by some functionality provided by SAP CRM, the steering committee must make the judgment as to the schedule of that functionality's implementation in SAP CRM. Considering the onerous agenda of the SAP CRM project itself, the committee could decide to continue using the earlier system and transit to the functionality in SAP CRM at a more appropriate time.

6.4.13 Transition Plan for Cutover to SAP CRM

The company must have a subsidiary project plan for transitioning from the earlier systems, whether they are computerized or manual, to the SAP CRM system. This might entail uploading data in a timely fashion into the SAP CRM system. The timeliness of the data might be dictated by whether it is master unchangeable data or transaction data, or it might be like opening balances for general ledger (GL) accounts and party ledger accounts. It could also be processing jobs that are done on a periodic basis, which might have to be transferred to the SAP CRM production system. Because everything cannot just be transferred automatically to SAP CRM, a phased approach starting with uploading of data, to transactions, to posting statuses and subsequent processing steps might have to be designed and executed.

6.5 Implementation Strategy

In this section, we consider strategies that should be adopted by an SME for its SAP CRM implementation projects.

6.5.1 Big-Bang Implementation of SAP CRM Components

The organization should consider a *big-bang* implementation of SAP CRM, wherein all the base components of SAP CRM (relevant to the enterprise's area of business) are implemented and put in production together. By implementing only certain components of the system, the company should not hope to reap more significant benefits than those accruing from the traditional systems. If SAP CRM is not to be used as a past-facing system merely for recording and reporting purposes but more as a future-facing handler of strategic information and relationships, implementation of all the *basic components* corresponding to the businesses of the company is essential. SAP CRM system is componentized and, thus, allows component-wise implementations. However, this is one feature that we recommend that should be ignored unless it is unavoidable because of extreme circumstances. A piecemeal approach of progressive implementation should be abandoned because delaying the implementations of all basic components together only delays the benefits of a fully functional SAP CRM and, therefore, incurs opportunity costs.

There have been strong suggestions sometimes that the 'big bang' approach of implementation was not suitable for implementation of CRM and it was better to adopt a piecemeal approach while implementing CRM. While not underestimating the challenges of implementing enterprise-wide CRM, it should be highlighted that the experience of implementing enterprise resources planning (ERP) systems was not better. In spite of the hundreds and thousands of SAP ERP implementations completed across the world and the corresponding accumulated experience, every single SAP implementation project is quite a challenge and takes extended duration of time for completion (see Kale 2000).

6.5.2 Base Components Implemented First

This strategy clearly dictates that the base components should be implemented with highest priority, though the definition of base component may vary from industry to industry. But, in contrast, other components or interfaces to other systems could be handled more appropriately after the base components as a whole have stabilized.

6.5.3 Implementation of SAP CRM Standard Functionality

A standardization of processes usually leads to tremendous gains in terms of maintenance, future upgrades, documentation, training, and even routine operations and the administration of the CRM applications. Custom support is counter to the general emphasis on standardizing the processes and implementing generic ones. It's a business truism that the survival and success of a company depends on how it differentiates itself and its products or services from those of its competitors. To leverage on their competencies or advantages, companies cannot abandon the corresponding differentiating processes and will have to incorporate such fundamental variants in their CRM implementations. But, as far as possible, avoid the bugbear of customization by altering and additional programming in ABAP. Additional programming should be evaluated and adopted only as a last resort. SAP keeps upgrading its suite of products, and if custom software is built for a particular version, it will have to be upgraded every time SAP releases new upgrades. Like any other product, SAP goes through oscillating cycles between major functional upgrades followed by technical upgrades and vice versa.

The best solution is to

- Use SAP CRM standard functionality
- Accommodate the variation of the business process by using SAP CRM's flexibility for configuring variant processes
- Adopt a workaround that indirectly takes care of the required functionality, for example, in the absence of the HR module, some accounts interfacing HR functions can be managed by treating employees as customers
- Use third-party products that are properly certified and qualified by SAP

6.5.4 Pilot Site Deployment Followed by Rollouts at Other Sites

This strategy entails deploying as comprehensive functionality as possible at the pilot site and preparing the base reference SAP configuration at the first site. This configuration is merely rolled out rapidly, with minimal changes at other sites. These changes might have to do, for instance, with loading separate master data for a different portfolio of products or services or marketing programs that may be sold or promoted at different sites. Thus, subsequent to the implementation at the pilot site, the project effort at the other sites will mainly involve

1. Installing SAP CRM
2. Functional training of super users and end users
3. Training technical personnel in SAP CRM system administration and management functions
4. Uploading corresponding data
5. Integration testing

6.5.5 Utilize External Consultants to Primarily Train In-House Functional and Technical Consultants

No external consultant can match the know-how of the functional and operational requirements of the company better than its own members who have the requisite expertise and experience working in various capacities and on different functions in the company. External consultants should be used as facilitators for getting their own key members familiarized with the functionality and navigation of the SAP CRM system (see Appendix A, "Selecting SAP CRM Implementation Partners").

Considering the tight schedules, external consultants would have to shoulder the main effort and deliverables during the business Design and Configure stages of the ASAP methodology. But the focus of their participation should be in transferring the SAP CRM product know-how to the key members of the implementation team. The key members of the implementation team will have the key responsibility of not only rolling out SAP CRM to other sites but also providing the necessary support for the SAP CRM effort in the future. As may be noted, it is not as simple as it might sound because after gaining expertise on SAP CRM product know-how, such key members have a marked tendency to quit their jobs and join the growing number of independent SAP CRM consultants or join one of the SAP CRM Consultancy firms.

Because of their backgrounds, the IS/IT professionals have a critical role in acting as facilitators for non-IS/IT-savvy functional members to clarify, define, and decide on their business requirements and in assisting the functional members in configuring the system to obtain the desired functionality.

6.5.6 Centralized or Decentralized SAP CRM Configuration

SAP CRM installations have had centralized database servers. The enterprises with distributed database servers might need to use the decentralized configuration. As we have noted in Chapter 5 "SAP CRM Solution", SAP CRM's distributed architecture enables the integration of data and processes across the entire system.

6.5.7 User-Driven Functionality

In marked contrast to traditional IS/IT projects, SAP CRM projects are user driven. The key members on the implementation team from the functional and business departments play the critical role of documenting and mapping the *AS-IS* (or existing) processes and deciding on the *TO-BE* processes. The mapping and configuration of the desired functionality proceed by an approach closer to the Joint Application Development and prototyping methodology of the 1980s.

6.6 SAP CRM Implementation Project Bill of Resources (BOR)

Taking a cue from the Bill of Materials (BOM) employed in Production Planning and Control (PPC) functions, we can define a generalized version of the same for the SAP CRM implementation project called the Bill of Resources (BOR). It enables one to define the hierarchy of the inputs, resources, and costs in the same structure. In this section, we provide an overview of what resources are needed for a SAP CRM implementation project.

SAP recommends the ASAP methodology as the primary implementation methodology for SMEs (which will be discussed in detail in Section IV, "Implementation Stage").

6.6.1 Money

Although it is obviously dangerous to make any kind of generalization, an average SAP CRM project for SMEs might range from $3 to $5 million.

In a typical CRM implementation, 28% of the total cost goes to buying software, while 38% of the cost goes to services such as software customizations, application integration, and training. Hardware makes up 23% of the cost, while telecommunications expenses make up the remaining 11%.

 Companies may spend about $10,000 per user per year on hardware, software, customization, support, and training.

6.6.2 Materials

The material inputs needed would be

1. *Hardware*: Servers (database, application, data warehouse, communications, network, e-mail, and so on) and client PCs
2. *Networking*: Hardware and software
3. *Software*: CRM, front-end GUI software, data warehouse, DBMS, operating system, office automation systems, and so on
4. Project Office and SAP CRM Center infrastructure

6.6.3 Manpower

The manpower resources essential are

1. Executive management
2. Senior officers
3. Technical personnel
4. System administrative and support personnel
5. Office administrative and support personnel
6. Super users
7. End users

6.6.4 Time Period

The duration of a SAP CRM project for SMEs might range from 4 to 9 months.

6.6.5 Information

The significant input is the documentation of the business process for the whole of the enterprise. This includes documentation on each process, including inputs, outputs, duration, labor, frequency, processing, purpose, interfaces, initiator, and supervisor.

6.7 Implementation Environment

The implementation environment consists of several components as listed:

- SAP CRM Applications
- SAP NetWeaver
- SAP Tools and Programming
  - ABAP Custom Development
  - Java Custom Development

We discuss these in Chapters 8 through 11.

6.8 Implementation Methodology

Under ideal conditions, projects can be completed in the most efficient manner in time and on budget. However, what is essential is to have a standardized approach of systems and procedures that could guide a company, which is new to SAP CRM, to implement SAP CRM successfully without any major risk of failure. Such an approach is called a *methodology*. A methodological approach may not be the *most* efficient one, but it ensures success under *optimal conditions*. Companies survive and grow not by planning for the most ideal or adverse conditions but by planning for optimal conditions. In the case of a SAP CRM implementation project, the implementation methodology must ensure success given the usual complexity of businesses, resources, organizational structures, time schedules, and so on.

An enterprise implementation methodology broadly covers the following:

1. *Modeling Business Processes*: Where the company defines the envisaged or *TO-BE* business processes
2. *Mapping Business Processes onto the Processes supported by SAP CRM*: Where the company discovers the SAP standard processes and functionality that address the requirements of the modeled process
3. *Performing the Gap Analysis*: Where the company assesses the difference or gap between the SAP standard and functionality and the requirements of the modeled processes
4. *Finalizing the scope of the SAP CRM implementation project*: Where the company decides on the scope of the SAP CRM implementation in terms of the processes that would be implemented in the SAP system
5. *Configuring the SAP CRM system*: Where the company configures the basic parameters in the SAP CRM
6. *Validating the customized SAP CRM system*: Where the configured system is tested for delivered functionality with actual data

The identified gaps in functionality can be rectified by any of these measures:

■ Devise a workaround for achieving the same functionality and configure it accordingly.
■ Program the required functionality in CRM system via user exits.
■ Suggest third-party SAP add-ons or plug-ins that provide the desired functionality and that have been certified for compatibility through SAP's Complementary Software Program (CSP).
■ Defer its implementation to the next wave of implementation or defer it until the SAP's release update (that will introduce this functionality) becomes available.
■ Change the business process radically so that it is suitable to the functionality available in SAP CRM to achieve the same objectives.
■ Modify SAP CRM software directly, although modified software may lead to incompatibility with future releases of SAP.

6.8.1 Accelerated SAP (ASAP) Methodology

SAP provides a process-oriented, clear, and concise implementation roadmap for individual implementation projects. This Roadmap acts as a project guide that specifies steps, identifies milestones, and generally sets the pace for the entire project to deliver a live system at top speed and quality utilizing the optimal budget and resources. The ASAP Roadmap consists of the following phases: project preparation, business blueprint, realization, final preparation, and go live and support:

1. *Project Preparation*: The project preparation phase deals with setting up the project organization, including the teams, roles, and responsibilities. In this phase, the aims and objectives of the implementation are decided. The strategy and draft project plan is prepared. The project infrastructure, including the hardware and networking issues, is determined and finalized. Sizing and benchmarking the envisaged installation are performed, and the acquisition of the SAP system is initiated. The project starts officially with a kickoff meeting attended by members of the executive and steering committees, project team members, and SAP consultants.

2. *Business Blueprint*: The business blueprint phase deals mainly with the documentation and finalization of the requirements. The team members and consultants conduct interviews and workshops in different activity areas to ascertain the requirements of various business processes. The functionality provided by SAP is demonstrated using the Information and Design Education (IDES) and is supported by questionnaires and process diagrams from Business Engineer. Any gap in addressing functional requirements is identified, and appropriate solutions are explored and devised. The final outcome of this phase is the Business Blueprint document, which details the *TO-BE* processes, including written and pictorial representations of the company's structure and business processes. Once this has been approved, the blueprint is the basis for all subsequent phases.

3. *Realization*: The goal of realization is to configure the baseline system using the IMG based on the Business Blueprint document. To do so, the business processes are divided into cycles of related business processes. The system is documented using the Business Engineer. The baseline system prepared here is the basis for the production system. The SAP team undergoes advanced training. The system is presented to a team of power users who also undergo requisite training in their respective areas of operations. The baseline system is fine-tuned by the validation done by the power users who employ an iterative approach. The technical team sets up the system administration and plans interfaces and data transfers. The interfaces, conversion programs, enhancements, reports, end-user documentation, testing scenarios, and user security profiles are defined and tested for effectiveness. The final deliverable is a fully configured and tested SAP system that meets the company's requirements.

4. *Final Preparation*: The final preparation phase is aimed at readying the system and the company for the SAP implementation. It consolidates all the activities of the previous phases. Any exceptions and out-of-turn situations are addressed and resolved. The super users under the supervision of the SAP team members conduct end-user training. The conversion and interface programs are all checked, volume and stress tests are performed, and user acceptance tests are conducted. This is followed with the migration of data to the new system.

5. *Go Live and Support*: The go live and support phase addresses the issues of putting the SAP system in production. The Going Live check is also performed and completed. This involves solving issues of day-to-day operations including problems and security-related issues reported by end users. SAP is also monitored for possible optimizations. This phase also involves verifying that milestones like day-end processing, first-month end, first-quarter end, and first-year end processes work correctly. It also involves completing any processes or parameters left uncompleted or undefined by oversight. Lastly, the business benefits of the new system are measured to monitor the return on investment (ROI) for the project, which may trigger further iterations of the implementation cycle in order to improve the business processes. A formal close of the implementation project is also performed.

We discuss ASAP methodology in detail in Chapter 13 of Section IV "Implementation Stage" of this book.

6.9 Project Management

The purpose of project management is to help define the tasks that are necessary to complete a project, control the progress of the activities, and account for the resources expended through the project.

6.9.1 Project Organization

Project organization consists of constitution of the various teams that are assigned to different tasks of the project. It entails nominating the various members of all teams, appointing team leaders, and reporting structures for compiling the progress reports of each team, which are consolidated progressively into higher-level progress reports. Usually, the team will consist of the technical team, the ABAP programming team, and many teams corresponding to major components within SAP CRM. Each of these later will contain subteams for performing analysis and design, as well as undertaking documentation and testing of the various components.

6.9.2 Project Control

It is essential that the work of all teams and groups of teams in different areas be controlled for gauging the progress, or lack of it, in the corresponding tasks. For this, the effort and time expended will have to be recorded and monitored on a daily basis. This would be helpful in detecting delays and slippage, reconstituting the teams, and reinforcing any team with additional resources wherever necessary:

1. *Time Recording*: Time recording involves recording the time expended under various categories of activities by every member of the team. This is essential not only for the external consultants but also for company members. An analysis of the time expended in various activities could be helpful in identifying the effort and cost expended in identifying gaps, resolving gap issues, talking with end users, configuration, documentation, functional and technical testing, debugging functional and technical errors, and so forth.
2. *Meetings*: Project meetings could be for all project-related issues, such as
   a. Scope of the project
   b. Project strategy
   c. Constitution of teams
   d. Project schedule and milestones
   e. Requirements and business processes
   f. Gap issues and their Resolution
   g. Issues that have not been resolved
   h. Decisions on standardizing processes
   i. Preparation of test plans and data
   j. Test reports
   k. Debugging and candidate solutions
   l. Documentation and updates

    m. Software upgrades
    n. Scheduling training programs
    o. Nominating team members for training
    p. Resource availability and utilization
    q. Conflicts and resolutions
    r. User accounts, access, and authorizations
    s. Performance and availability
    t. Hardware and networking vendors
    u. Providers of implementation services and consultancy
    v. Bill payments
    w. Leave and resignations

3. *Project Monitoring*: The actual effort and time expended need to be compared to the planned effort and schedule on a frequent basis. Any observed deviations, or pattern of deviations, are corrected immediately. Any rescheduling of the project plan is addressed only in the project reviews.

4. *Project Reviews*: The main objective of project reviews is to ascertain the progress made with reference to the planned schedule. Progress on the action points of the last review is reassessed. Any shortfalls in achieving milestones or delays are diagnosed for the reasons, and corrective measures taken are endorsed or changed. Any suggestions for changing strategies are considered during the reviews. Any unforeseen problems cropping up during the project are analyzed here.

6.10 SAP CRM Implementation

Unlike the traditional software development project, this involves three main phases: pre-implementation, implementation, and post-implementation. The pre-implementation issues have been discussed in Chapters 12 and 13. Implementation by using ASAP methodology is presented in Chapter 14. The post-implementation phase is discussed in Chapter 15.

6.10.1 Pre-Implementation

Pre-implementation involves the formation of the project and steering committees, the constitution of the implementation project team, and the installation of hardware and SAP CRM software. The latter involves readying the hardware and infrastructure and installing the operating systems, database software, client software, and SAP CRM software. The SAP CRM administration function entails system administration, application administration, ISS transaction server administration, communications server administration, network administration, database administration, printer administration, client administration, user's authentication and access security administration, and so forth. Another major activity during this phase is training for the implementation team and other users, which is very critical to the success of the project:

1. *Training*: Considering the short time frames of the SAP CRM implementation projects, SAP CRM has identified training as an important determinant in the success of any project. SAP CRM offers a broad spectrum of training courses covering all stakeholders of a SAP CRM project. These courses cover a range of topics from a general overview to in-depth coverage of individual topics.

SAP Partner Academy's technical and Functional courses provide comprehensive training for the entire implementation team. SAP's courses are designed to get a team up to speed quickly and efficiently, some of which are

a. Using SAP CRM
b. SAP NetWeaver
c. SAP Tools and Programming
d. SAP Enterprise Applications:
   i. SAP CRM Marketing
   ii. SAP CRM Sales
   iii. SAP CRM Service
   iv. SAP CRM Interaction Center

2. *SAP CRM Installation*: This basically involves installing the base license and designing the system landscape including the SAP NetWeaver Server, the SAP CRM Enterprise Applications, and the SAP development environment for ABAP and Java.

3. *Implementation*: For the SMEs, SAP CRM recommends the Accelerated SAP (ASAP) Methodology (see Section 6.8.1 "Accelerated SAP (ASAP) Methodology" and Chapter 13 "SAP ASAP Methodology"). It consists of the following five stages:

a. Project preparation
b. Business blueprint
c. Realization
d. Final preparation
e. Go live and support

6.10.2 Post-Implementation

The post-implementation phase involves instituting support and services such as the SAP CRM Interaction Center. Following the implementation of the base components, other components such as SAP BI and SAP HANA Workflow can be implemented.

For effective SAP CRM operations, training of implementation team and user personnel is essential.

6.11 SAP CRM Support

Support includes various measures or activities that are undertaken to ensure availability in terms of the application functionality or continued functioning of the system.

It deals with design, organization, and operation of a help desk or a call center for the SAP users within the company. Users can register their complaints and queries and get specific responses that can be implemented by the end users with the help of the super users in their respective departments.

Hardware availability is ensured by various measures, such as disaster recovery systems and archival of data.

6.12 SAP CRM Deployment

After SAP CRM goes into production at the pilot site, it is important to have scheduled the focus to immediately shift to the other sites. In fact, at those other sites, certain activities, including training of super users and preparation of data for uploading into the SAP CRM system, should be undertaken in parallel with the last stages of implementation at the pilot site. It is advised to immediately commence implementation at other sites because doing so enables the company to leverage the momentum generated by the implementation at the pilot site. Moreover, any breaks between the implementations might cause members of the core team to look for other challenging opportunities.

If training super users and data loading are done in parallel with the finishing stages of the deployment at the pilot site(s), what remains during the actual SAP CRM project at the sites is

1. Deploying the base configuration prepared at the pilot site
2. Conducting the integration test
3. Conducting the training of the end users at the concerned site
4. Going live

6.13 Why Some SAP CRM Implementations May Sometimes Be Less than Successful

There are various reasons why SAP CRM projects might be less than successful. CRM is a complex endeavor requiring significant change management expertise, business process experience, and domain knowledge. Failure in CRM projects might be because of the following reasons:

■ Top management involvement and interest falters or is perceived as faltering.
■ Lack of clear project scope and strategies; project is too narrowly focused.
■ Implementation of nonoptimized processes in SAP CRM.
■ Decisions regarding changes in processes and procedures may not be effected; they might be ignored or subverted.
■ Lack of proper visibility and communication on the SAP CRM project at all stages.
■ Lack of adequate budget and resources such as for training of large group of envisaged end users.
■ Not deputing the key managers on the implementation team.
■ Support infrastructure and systems are delayed inordinately.
■ Disputes and conflicts in the team are not resolved quickly.
■ Company members of the team might not get along with the external consultants.
■ External consultants might have differences with end users or user managers.
■ Core team members might have differences with user departments.
■ A company-wide change management plan is not implemented.
■ Too much time between the implementation at the deployment/pilot site and rollout sites.
■ Members of the company do not participate actively because
  – Sales persons, sales consultants, and sales managers are extremely possessive of their customers and related interaction information and such withholding of critical customer information prevents the information stored in CRMs to be treated fully as customer relationships and to be leveraged for the maximum benefit of the enterprise as a whole.
  – Members feel the system has been implemented in haste and that it does not address their requirements and they feel they have not been taken in confidence.

- Members feel they have not been given adequate training.
- Members of the company are apprehensive of their future roles.
- Members of the company are afraid that they might not be able to learn the new system and perform satisfactorily.
- Members of the company feel unsettled by the lack of hierarchy in the system.
- Members feel they have been reduced to data entry operators.
■ Members of the core implementation team might resign and leave the company.
■ Members of the core team might be averse to moving on projects at rollout sites.
■ Inexperienced consulting resources.
■ Slow decision-making process.
■ Scope creep.

The solutions for tackling these problems will vary from company to company. The approach to be adopted will depend upon the industry, culture, and history of the company. An approach for handling these kinds of issues is referred in Section 6.4 "Critical Success Factors."

6.14 Summary

This chapter gave an overview of the complete implementation cycle of a typical SAP CRM project. Chapter 12 discusses the prerequisites to undertaking a SAP CRM implementation project. Chapter 13 of Section IV "Implementation Stage" discusses the various phases of the ASAP methodology for implementing SAP CRM. The post-implementation issues are dealt with in Chapter 14 of Section V "Post-Implementation Stage."

Chapter 7

SAP CRM and Enterprise Business Process Re-Engineering

This chapter clarifies the role played by SAP CRM in re-engineering an enterprise, while implementing SAP CRM in the organization. After introducing the concept of business process management (BPM), we look at the full cycle of an enterprise BPM methodology. The relevance and the role that SAP CRM can play at every stage in the re-engineering effort within an enterprise are considered in Section 7.3 "BPR and SAP CRM Implementation."

SAP CRM implementation can result in BPR (or top-down dramatic improvements through redesigned or completely new processes); however, it all depends on the approach taken by the enterprise. Some companies implement SAP CRM trying to duplicate their existing business practices. Although implementing SAP CRM will result in some improvements in such case, BPR will not result. For achieving BPR, top-down management focus on BPR during the implementation of SAP CRM is required; the time frame and project plan must also reflect the goal of BPR.

7.1 Background of Business Process Re-Engineering (BPR)

BPR addresses the following two important issues for an enterprise:

1. The strategic long-term *positioning* of the business with respect to the current and envisaged customers that would ensure that the enterprise would be competitively and financially successful, locally and globally
2. The enterprise's *capability/capacity* that is the totality of all the internal processes that dynamically realize this positioning of the business

Traditionally, positioning has been considered as an independent set of functional tasks split within the marketing, finance, and strategic planning functions. Similarly, capability/capacity has usually been considered the preserve of the individual operational departments that may have mutually conflicting priorities and measures of performances (see Chapter 2, Section 2.1.3 "CRM Reflects and Mimics the Integrated Nature of an Enterprise").

The problem for many enterprises lies in the fact that there is a fundamental flaw in the organizational structures: organizational structures are *hierarchical*, while the transactions and workflows that deliver the solutions (i.e., products and services) to the customers are *horizontal*. Quite simply, the *structure* determines who really is the customer. The traditional management structures condition managers to put functional needs above those of the multifunctional processes to which their functions contribute. This results in

- Various departments competing for resources
- Collective failure in meeting or exceeding the customers' expectations
- Inability to coordinate and collaborate on multifunctional customer-centric processes that would truly provide the competitive differentiation in future markets

The traditional mass marketing type of organization works well for researching market opportunities, planning the offering, and scheduling all of the steps required to produce and distribute the offering to the marketplace (where it is selected or rejected by the customer). It takes a very different kind of organization, namely, the customized marketing-type organization, to build long-term relationships with customers so that they call such organizations first when they have a need because they trust that such enterprises will be able to respond with an effective solution. This is customer-responsive management that we discussed in the Chapter 1, Section 1.2.2 "Customer Responsiveness".

BPM is the very process that manages and optimizes the inextricable linkage between the positioning and the capability/capacity of an enterprise.

7.1.1 Value-Added View of Business Processes

Business processes can very easily be seen as the basis of the value addition within an enterprise that has been traditionally attributed to various functions or divisions. As organizational and environmental conditions become more complex, globalized, and therefore competitive, processes provide a framework for dealing effectively with the issues of performance improvement, capability development, and adaptation to the changing environment. Along a value stream (i.e., a business process), the analysis of the absence, creation, addition of value, or (worse) destruction of value critically determines the necessity and effectiveness of a process step. The understanding of value-adding and non-value-adding processes (or process steps) is a significant factor in the analysis, design, benchmarking, and optimization of business processes in the companies leading to BPM.

Values are characterized by value determinants like time (such as the cycle time), flexibility (options, customization, and composition), responsiveness (lead time, number of hand-offs, and duration), quality (rework, rejects, and yield), and price (discounts, rebates, coupons, and incentives). We must note that we are not disregarding cost (such as materials, labor, and overheads) as a value determinant, but the effect of cost is truly a result of other value determinants like time, flexibility, and responsiveness.

The nature and extent of a value addition to a product or service is the best measure of that addition's contribution to the company's overall goal for competitiveness. Such value expectations are dependent upon

- The customer's experience of similar product(s) and/or service(s)
- The value delivered by the competitors
- The capabilities and limitations of the base technological platform (see Chapter 1, Section 1.2.1.5 "Increasing Returns and Customer Capitalism")

However, value, as originally defined by Michael Porter in the context of introducing the concept of the value chain, is meant more in the nature of the cost at various stages. Rather than a value chain, it is more of a cost chain! Porter's value chain is also a structure-oriented and hence a static concept. Here, we mean value as the satisfaction of not only external but also internal customers' requirements as defined, and continuously redefined, as the least total cost of acquisition, ownership, and use.

Consequently, in this formulation, one can understand the company's competitive gap in the market in terms of such process-based, customer-expected levels of value and the value delivered by the company's process for the concerned products or services. Customer responsiveness focuses on costs in terms of the yield (see Chapter 1, Section 1.2.2.3.1 "Activity-Based Costing (ABC)"). Therefore, we can perform market segmentation for a particular product or services in terms of the most significant customer values and the corresponding value determinants, or what we term as critical value determinants (CVDs) (see Chapter 1, Section 1.3.4 "Value-Add Driven Enterprise").

Strategic planning exercises can then be understood readily in terms of devising strategies for improving on these process-based CVDs, based on the competitive benchmarking of these *collaborative* values and processes between the enterprise and customers. These strategies and the tactics resulting from analysis, design, and optimization of the process would in turn focus on the restrategizing of all relevant business processes at all levels. This can result in the modification or deletion of the process or creation of a new one.

7.1.2 Business Process Re-Engineering (BPR)

Although BPR has its roots in information technology (IT) management, it is basically a business initiative that has a major impact on the satisfaction of both the internal and external customer. Michael Hammer, who triggered the BPR revolution in 1990, considers BPR as a *radical change* for which IT is the key enabler. BPR can be broadly termed as *the rethinking and change of business processes to achieve dramatic improvements in the measures of performances such as cost, quality, service, and speed.*

Some of the principals advocated by Hammer are as follows:

- Organize around outputs, not tasks.
- Put the decisions and control, and hence all relevant information, into the hands of the performer.
- Have those who use the outputs of a process to perform the process, including the creation and processing of the relevant information.
- The location of user, data, and process information should be immaterial; it should function as if all were in a centralized place.

As will become evident when perusing the aforementioned points, the implementation of SAP CRM possesses most of the characteristics mentioned earlier.

The most important outcome of BPR has been viewing business activities as more than a collection of individual or even functional tasks; it has engendered the process-oriented view of business. However, BPR is different from quality management efforts like TQM and ISO 9000, which refer to programs and initiatives that emphasize bottom-up incremental improvements in existing work processes and outputs on a continuous basis. In contrast, BPR usually refers to top-down dramatic improvements through redesigned or completely new processes on a discrete basis. In the continuum of methodologies ranging from ISO 9000, TQM, ABM, and so on, on one end and BPR on the other, SAP CRM implementation definitely lies on the BPR side of the spectrum when it comes to corporate change management efforts.

BPR is based on the principle that there is an inextricable link between positioning *and* capability/capacity. A company cannot position the organization to meet a customer need that it cannot fulfill without an unprofitable level of resources nor can it allocate enhanced resources to provide a cost-effective service that no customer wants!

BPR in practice has developed a focus on changing capability/capacity in the short term to address current issues. This short-term change in capability/capacity is usually driven by the need to

- Reduce the cycle time to process customer orders
- Improve quotation times
- Lower variable overhead costs
- Increase product range to meet an immediate competitor threat
- Rebalance resources to meet current market needs
- Reduce work-in-progress stocks
- Meet changed legislation requirements
- Introduce short-term measures to increase market share (e.g., increased credit limit from customers hit by recessionary trends)

THEORY OF CONSTRAINTS

One factor that drives down customer loyalty is the primary focus on cost and the waves of downsizing, with the resulting adverse impact on the customers. Dr. Eliyahu M. Goldratt's conceived the Theory of Constraints (TOC) by focusing on the concept of throughput as a panacea for the disastrous decisions resulting from misguided overhead cost allocations to different products, services, facilities, and other entities. With unfailing regularity, companies end up treating these wrongful allocations as the actual costs that lead to disastrous results like termination of *apparently* unprofitable product lines, manpower layoffs, and plummeting employee morale and customer confidence.

Dr. Goldratt first introduced TOC in the 1980s, with its application to manufacturing planning and scheduling. He later expanded the theory to systematically and holistically address the problems of complex organizations with many interrelationships and dependencies.

Within TOC,

$$\text{Throughput}(T) = \text{Sales} - \text{Direct variable costs}$$

where Direct variable costs are usually raw materials.

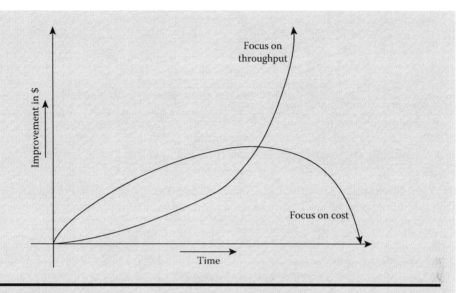

Figure 7.1   Throughput-oriented versus cost-oriented Enterprises.

In terms of TOC, enterprises can be considered to be focused either on cost or throughput. The enterprise's focus is directly related to

- Measurements focused either on reducing cost or building throughput
- Policies that dictate enterprise's responsive behavior
- Training that dictates improvement in the efficiency and effectiveness in executing identified job responsibilities

A primary focus on throughput includes dealing with issues of customer loyalty and value and how to increase throughput through employee initiative and productivity. In contrast, a primary focus on cost only deals with decreasing the operating expenses (plant labor, administrative costs, utilities, corporate overheads, depreciation, sales and marketing expenses, and so on) and investments (assets like buildings, equipment, fixtures, as well as cost of the inventory). Figure 7.1 contrasts the characteristics of a throughput-oriented versus a cost-oriented enterprise. Cost-focused enterprises via cost-cutting efforts initially experience quick and dramatic improvements that are followed eventually by stagnation, financial losses, and loss of competitiveness. In contrast, the throughput-focused enterprises show a slower start to improvement that reflects time expended on analysis, understanding and confirming customer needs, researching offerings, gaining buy-in from employees and partners for the proposed offering, devising the offering, launching and testing the offering, and, finally, installing, servicing, and supporting the offering. But, this is usually followed by a phase of exponential improvement.

Costs cannot be ignored, and cost cutting may seem to work in the short term, but this cannot create the kind of return of investment (ROI) that keeps shareholders around for the long term.

Positioning leads to higher levels of revenue through increasing the size of the market, retaining the first-time customers, increasing the size of the wallet share, and so on. Positioning has to do with factors such as

- Understanding customer needs
- Understanding competitor initiatives
- Determining the businesses' financial needs
- Conforming with legal and regulatory requirements
- Conforming with environmental constraints

The capability/capacity has to be aligned with the positioning or else it has to be changed to deliver the positioning. Capability/capacity has to do with internal factors such as

- Key business processes
- Procedures and systems
- Competencies, skills, training, and education

The key is to have a perceived differentiation of being better than the competition in whatever terms the customers choose to evaluate or measure and to deliver this at the lowest unit cost.

7.1.3 Enterprise Agility

The difficult challenges facing businesses today require organizations to be transitioned into flexible, agile structures that can respond to new market opportunities quickly with a minimum of new investment and risk. As enterprises have experienced the need to be simultaneously efficient, flexible, responsive, and adaptive, they have transitioned themselves into an agile enterprise with small, autonomous teams that work concurrently and reconfigure quickly and adopt highly decentralized management that recognizes its knowledge base and manages it effectively.

Enterprise agility is the ability to be the following:

1. *Responsive*: Adaptability is enabled by the concept of loosely coupled interacting components reconfigurable within a unified framework. This is essential for ensuring opportunity management to sustain viability.

   The ability to be responsive involves the following aspects:
   a. An organizational structure that enables change is based on reusable elements that are reconfigurable in a scalable framework. Reusability and reconfigurability are generic concepts that are applicable to work procedures, manufacturing cells, production teams, or information automation systems.
   b. An organizational culture that facilitates change and focuses on change proficiency.
2. *Intelligence intensive*: That manages and applies knowledge effectively whether it is knowledge of a customer, a market opportunity, a competitor's threat, a production process, a business practice, a product technology, or an individual's competency. This is essential for ensuring innovation management to sustain leadership.

The ability to be intelligence intensive involves the following aspects:
a. Enterprise Knowledge management
b. Enterprise collaborative learning

 When confronted with a competitive opportunity, whereas a smaller company is able to act more quickly, a larger company has access to more comprehensive knowledge and can decide to act sooner and more thoroughly.

7.1.3.1 Patterns of Enterprise Agility

Christopher Alexander introduced the concept of patterns in the late 1970s in the field of architecture: a *pattern* describes a commonly occurring solution that generates decidedly successful outcomes.

A list of success patterns for agile enterprises (and systems), in terms of their constituting elements or functions or *components*, is as follows:

1. Reusable

   Agility Pattern 1: The components of agile enterprises are autonomous units cooperating toward a shared goal.

   Agility Pattern 2: The components of agile enterprises are reusable and multiply replicable, that is, depending on requirements, multiple instances of the same component can be invoked concurrently.

   Agility Pattern 3: The components of agile enterprises share well-defined interaction and interface standards and can be inserted, removed, and replaced easily and noninvasively.

2. Reconfigurable

   Agility Pattern 4: The components of agile enterprises communicate, coordinate, and cooperate with other components concurrently and in real term sharing of current, complete, and consistent information on interactions with individual customers.

   Agility Pattern 5: The components of agile enterprises establish relationships with other components in the real term to enable deferment of customer commitment to as late a stage as possible within the sales cycle coupled with the corresponding ability to postpone the point of product differentiation as close as possible to the point of purchase by the customer.

   Agility Pattern 6: The components of agile enterprises are defined declaratively rather than procedurally; the network of components displays the defining characteristics of any *small-world* network, namely, local robustness and global accessibility.

   Agility Pattern 7: The components of agile enterprises are self-aware, and they interact with other components via on-the-fly integration, adjustment, or negotiation.

3. Scalable

   Agility Pattern 8: The components of agile enterprises operate enterprises within predefined frameworks that standardize intercomponent communication and interaction, determine component compatibility, and evolve to accommodate old, current, and new components.

Agility Pattern 9: The components of agile enterprises replicate components to provide the desired capacity, load balancing and performance, fault tolerance, and variations on the basic component functionality and behavior.

Agility Pattern 10: The components of agile enterprises enable dynamic utilization of additional or reduced number of resources depending on the requirements.

Chapter 10, Section 10.1.3 "Enterprise Architecture" presents the current approaches to enterprise agility and architecture that is embodied in post-Internet packaged applications like SAP CRM.

7.1.4 Enterprise Change Management with SAP

Initiating change and confronting change are the two most important issues facing the enterprises of today. The ability to change business processes contributes directly to the *innovation* bottom line. The traditional concept of change management is usually understood as a one-time event. But if an organization is looking for the capability not only to handle change management but also management of changes on a continual basis, then CRM, like SAP, is a must!

SAP enables the essential changing of processes that are so critical to the success of the enterprise. Business processes that *reside* or are internalized within an organization's employees are difficult to change simply because human beings naturally find it more difficult to change. However, processes that reside within any computerized systems are easy to change (see Chapter 1, Section 1.3.5 "Enterprise Change Management").

7.2 Enterprise BPR Methodology

In this section, we look at the full life cycle of an enterprise's BPM methodology. We will indicate opportunities where SAP CRM can be of assistance in an ongoing BPM effort within the enterprise:

Outsourcing is distancing the company from noncore but critical functions; as against this re-engineering, which is associated with BPM, it is exclusively about the core.

We present an overview of the seven steps in a BPM methodology. These steps are as follows:

1. Develop the context for undertaking the BPM and in particular re-engineer the enterprise's business processes. Then identify the reason behind redesigning the process to represent the value perceived by the customer.
2. Select the business processes for the re-engineering effort.
3. Map the selected processes.
4. Analyze the process maps to discover opportunities for re-engineering.
5. Redesign the selected processes for increased performance.
6. Implement the re-engineered processes.
7. Measure the implementation of the re-engineered processes.

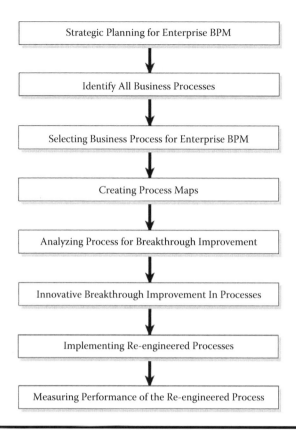

Figure 7.2   A Cycle of Enterprise BPR Methodology.

The eight steps of the enterprise BPR methodology are shown in Figure 7.2.

The BPR effort within an enterprise is not a one-time exercise but an ongoing one. One could also have multiple BPR projects in operation simultaneously in different areas within the enterprise. The BPR effort involves business visioning, identifying the value gaps, and, hence, selection of the corresponding business processes for the BPR effort. The re-engineering of the business processes might open newer opportunities and challenges, which in turn triggers another cycle of business visioning followed by BPR of the concerned business processes. Figure 7.3 shows the iteration across the alternating activities without end.

7.2.1 Strategic Planning for Enterprise BPR

All markets are fluid to some degree, and these dynamic forces and shifting customer values necessitate changes in a company's strategic plans. The significance of a process to the success of a company's business is dependent on the nature and extent of the value addition to a product or service. Consequently, as stated earlier, one can understand the competitive value gap in terms of the customer-expected level of value and the value delivered by the enterprise for the concerned product or service.

The competitive gap can be defined as the gap between the customer's minimum acceptance value (MAV) and the customer value delivered by the enterprise. Companies that consistently

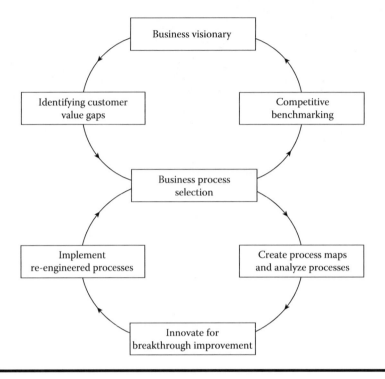

Figure 7.3   The alternate activities of Business Visioning and BPR.

surpass MAVs are destined to thrive, those that only meet the MAVs will survive, and those that fall short of the MAVs may fail.

CVDs are those business imperatives that must happen if the enterprise wants to close the competitive gap and are similar to the critical success factors (CSFs) at the enterprise level. CVDs are in terms of factors like

- Time (lead time, cycle time, and so on)
- Flexibility (customization, options, composition, resource network interfaces, and so on)
- Responsiveness (lead time, duration, number of hand-offs, priority, number of queues, and so on)
- Quality of work (rework, rejects, yield, and so on)

Market segmentation is performed based on the customer value and the corresponding CVDs. Such a market segmentation helps in suggesting corrective strategic and tactical actions that may be required, such as in devising a process-oriented strategic business plan. The strategic plan can in turn help identify the major processes that support these critical value determinants that must be innovatively improved and re-engineered.

7.2.1.1 Identifying the Business Processes in the Company

All business processes in an enterprise are identified and recorded. A process can be defined as a set of resources and activities necessary and sufficient to convert some forms of input into some forms of output. Processes can be internal or external, or a combination of both. They have cross functional boundaries, they have starting and ending points, and they exist at all levels within the organization, including section, department, division, and enterprise levels. In fact, processes exist across enterprise boundaries as well. Processes evolve and degrade in terms of their efficiency and effectiveness.

A process itself can consist of various substeps. The substeps in a process could be

- Value-added steps
- Non-value-added steps
- Legal and regulatory steps (which are treated as value-added steps)

7.2.2 Selecting Business Processes for BPR

Selecting the right processes for an innovative process re-engineering effort is critical. The processes should be selected for their high visibility, relative ease of accomplishing goals, and, at the same time, their potential for great impact on the value determinants.

Customers will take their business to the company that can deliver the most value for their money. Hence, the MAVs have to be charted in detail. MAV is dependent upon several factors, such as

- The customer's prior general and particular experience base with an industry, product, and/ or service
- What competition is doing in the concerned industry, product, or service
- What effect technological limitations have on setting the upper limit

As mentioned earlier, MAVs can be characterized in terms of the CVDs; only four to six value determinants may be necessary to profile a market segment. CVDs can be defined by obtaining data through

1. The customer value survey
2. Leaders in noncompeting areas
3. The best-in-class performance levels
4. Internal customers

A detailed Customer Value Analysis analyzes the value gaps and helps in further refining the goals of the process re-engineering exercise. The value gaps are as follows:

- Gaps that result from different value perceptions in different customer groups
- Gaps between what the company provides and what the customer has established as the minimum performance level
- Gaps between what the company provides and what the competition provides
- Gaps between what the organization perceives as the MAV for the identified customer groups and what the customer says are the corresponding MAVs

It must be noted that analyzing the value gaps is not a one-time exercise; neither is it confined to the duration of a cycle of the breakthrough improvement exercise. Like the BPM exercise itself, it is an activity that must be done on an ongoing basis.

As a goal for the improvement effort, a clear, competitive advantage can be gained if best-in-class performance levels can be achieved in some key customer value areas and at least some MAVs can be achieved in all others.

7.2.3 Creating Process Maps

A process map documents the flow of one unit of work (the unit may be one item, one batch, or a particular service that is the smallest unit possible to follow separately) or what actually happens to the work going through the process. A process map is developed at several process levels, starting at the highest level of the enterprise. It documents both value-added and non-value-added steps. A process map could be either sequential or concurrent in nature.

Process could be mapped in two forms:

1. Workflow chart form
2. Work breakdown structure form

Process Workflows fall into three categories: continuous Workflows, balanced Workflows, and synchronized Workflows.

Workflow becomes nonsynchronized because of

1. Steps or tasks produced at different rates, that is, an imbalanced workflow
2. Physical separation of operations causing work to move in batches, that is, a noncontinuous workflow
3. Working in batches, causing intermittent flow
4. Long setup or changeover times resulting in batched work along with its problems
5. Variations in process inputs in terms of quality availability on time

All these add time and costs to the process and reduce flexibility and responsiveness.

Using the value-added Workflow analysis of the process map, we can

1. Identify and measure significant re-engineering opportunities
2. Establish a baseline of performance against which to measure improvement
3. Determine which tools may be most useful in the re-engineering effort

Evidently, the major goal in re-engineering the process is to eliminate non-value-added steps and wait times within processes. A good rule of thumb is to remove 60%–80% of the non-value-added steps, resulting in the total number of remaining steps to be no more than one to three times the number of value-added steps. Even this would be a credible goal for the first iteration of the BPR effort.

7.2.4 Analyzing Processes for Breakthrough Improvements

An enterprise's competitive strength lies in eliminating as many costly non-value-added steps and wait times as possible. The key to eliminating any non-value-added steps is to understand what causes them and then eliminate the cause.

For breakthrough improvements, the process maps are analyzed for the following:

- *Organization complexity*: Commonly, organizational issues are a major deterrent to efficiency of the processes.
- Number of hand-offs, especially, other than those associated with resource network interfaces.
- *Work movement*: Workflow charts are utilized to highlight move distances, that is, work movements.
- *Process problems*: Several factors may have a severe effect on the continuity, balance, or synchronicity of the workflow. Examples are loops of non-value-added steps designed to address rework, errors, scraps, and so on. These may be on account of
    - Long changeover times
    - Process input/output imbalances
    - Process variabilities
    - Process yields

These problems need to be identified, measured, analyzed, and resolved through innovative problem-solving methodology.

7.2.5 Innovative Breakthrough Improvement in Processes

The steps involved in innovative problem-solving methods are as follows:

1. Define a problem.
2. Find alternate solutions.
3. Evaluate the solutions.
4. Implement the best solution.
5. Measure and monitor the success.

The responsive process consists of the following components:

- Diagnosing customer need
- Developing customized solutions specific to organizational interfaces
- Dynamically assigning work to the appropriate delivery unit
- Tracking performance as each task is completed

Business problems fall into three basic categories:

1. System problems (methods, procedures, and so on).
2. Technical problems (engineering, operational, and so on).
3. *People problems* (*skills, training, hiring, and so on*): These problems arise because "if you change what a person does, you change what he or she is."

7.2.6 Implementing Re-engineered Processes

This involves the following:

- Re-engineered vision and policies
- Re-engineered strategies and tactics

- Re-engineered systems and procedures
- Re-engineered communication environment
- Re-engineered organization architecture
- Re-engineered training environment

7.2.7 Measuring the Performance of Re-engineered Processes

Measuring the performance of any process is very important, because the lack of measurement would make it impossible to distinguish such a breakthrough effort from an incremental improvement effort of a Total Quality Management (TQM) program.

Measurements are essential because they are

- Useful as baselines or benchmarks
- A motivation for further breakthrough improvements, which are important for future competitiveness

The measures for innovative process re-engineering should be

- Visible
- Meaningful
- Small in number
- Applied consistently and regularly
- Quantitative
- Involving personnel closest to the process

Table 7.1 enlists tools and techniques for continuous improvement, and Table 7.2 lists some of the advanced techniques.

7.3 BPR and SAP CRM Implementation

While perusing the various steps of a BPM methodology presented earlier, it becomes evident that SAP CRM can play a critical role in enabling and assisting any BPM effort in an enterprise in a major way.

7.3.1 Reference CRM Processes

There are different degrees of process automation:

- Time-out processing on external interactions is the ability to time out and take action upon noncompletion of an asynchronous interaction.
- Internal activity is automatically triggered upon successful completion of an asynchronous interaction with an external application.
- Workflow automation across applications; multiple automated activities distributed across applications are coordinated through the exchange of events and monitored for exception conditions.

A world-class application like SAP includes the tools to achieve process integration and also integrate with third-party middleware as appropriate. The SAP CRM architecture includes several mechanisms for supporting automation across a wide range of business processes:

Table 7.1   Benefits Tools and Techniques for Continuous Improvement

Tools or Technique	Use
External customer survey	To understand the needs of the external customers
Internal customer survey	To understand the perceptions of internal Services
Staff survey	To obtain employee feedback on work environment
Brainstorming	To generate ideas for improvements
Cause and effect diagrams	To prompt ideas during brainstorming
Benchmarking	To compare similar processes to find the best practice
Service Performance	To quantify the importance/performance of services
Activity data	To understand the allocation of time in processes
Activity categories	To obtain the level of core/support/diversionary activities
Activity drivers	To relate volumes of activity to causes
High–low diagram	To group objects using two variables
Force-field analysis	To show the forces acting for/against a variable
Histogram	To show frequency of a variable in a range
Scatter diagram	To view the correlation between two variables
Affinity analysis	To measure the strength of functional relationships
Bar chart	To plot the frequency of an event
Run chart	To show how a variable changes over time
Pie chart	To show frequency of a variable in a range

Table 7.2   Advanced Techniques for Continuous Improvement

Tools or Technique	Use
Statistical process Control (SPC)	SPC is a means to understand if a process is producing and is likely to produce an output that meets the specifications within limits.
Failure mode and effects Analysis (FMEA)	FMEA is a means to understand the nature of potential failure of components and effect this will have on the complete systems.
Quality function deployment (QFD)	QFD is a structured process to build.
Taguchi methods	The design of experiments to create robust processes/products where final quality is subject to many variables.

- Assignment Manager for apportioning and sharing critical information such as leads, customers, and service requests across members of an enterprise
- Rule-based data synchronization for the coordination of a mobile force
- A workflow manager for workforce collaboration in reacting to business events
- An assignment engine to automate the assigning of resources to asset of planned activities
- Call scripting to support call center agents in their interactions with customers

The SAP CRM strategy is to integrate all business operations in an overall system for planning, controlling, optimizing, and monitoring all customer-related activities of a given business. SAP CRM has included hundreds of best-business practices or scenarios that can help an enterprise to restructure its processes. These scenarios provide logical models for the optimization of the specific business processes and can be modeled around primary and support business activities. SAP guides an enterprise to automatically integrate all primary and support functions of logistics like customer orders, production, procurement, packaging, delivery, service, and accounting. Companies can simply print out the relevant data models and analyze the most critical processes quickly and efficiently. The customizing features of SAP CRM can then help in implementing the required changes.

7.3.2 Changeability of SAP-Driven Enterprises

SAP-driven enterprises are fundamentally enabled for managing changes in the operations of the business. There changes could be driven by external market conditions or they could also be planned and generated internally. You have already seen many aspects of this in the beginning of this chapter. In this section, we highlight two characteristics of SAP-driven enterprises that achieve a measure of BPR simply by implementing SAP in the first place.

7.3.2.1 Real-Time SAP Operations Make Processes Transparent

SAP transactions are immediately updated into the concerned functional areas, be they inventory, party ledgers, accounting, and so on. SAP re-engineers the business immediately to eliminate all wait times and minimize time period required for communication between various functions. And all of these postings are done simultaneously so that a consistent view is always available for any transactions—there is no lag between material, management, or financial accounting of any transactions. All this adds up to tremendous transparency and visibility in the functioning of the SAP system and hence the organization.

With traditional systems, which were not integrated and had batch-oriented processing cycles, a consistent picture was available only for a short period of time near the close of a month or a year. It also permitted different functions certain latitude in exercising a manner of ownership and degree of authority even to the detriment of the overall functioning of the company's operations.

By effecting all transaction in real time, SAP also enables the organization to minimize reaction time to changing situations in the market and take immediate corrective action. This automatically also makes the organization more efficient, which is discussed in the following subsection.

7.3.2.2 Integrated SAP Operations Eliminate Hand-Offs

The integration of all organization functions and processes engendered by SAP eliminates various kinds of hand-offs between departments, wherein tasks and copies of related documents are handed over to the next department for further processing. At every stage, this generates the need for inwarding, reconciliation, negotiations, and follow-up with upstream and downstream activities along the process path, and so forth. All this merely adds more overheads, elapsed time, manpower effort, information overload, and, therefore, costs. The inherent integration provided by SAP eliminates all such overheads and non-valued-added activities. Reduced time cycles encourage various operational decision makers not to pad heavily plans, projections, estimates, requisitions, material and purchase orders, production orders, etc., to accommodate contingencies. Overall, implementing SAP makes companies to become more lean and efficient. However, one cannot discount the possibility of an organization under some misguided zeal for accountability may enforce highly restrictive authorization and access profiles that may essentially negate the advantages arising out of basic transparency, real-time interfaces, and integration provided by SAP.

7.3.3 Changeability Embedded in SAP

While perusing the various steps of a BPR methodology presented earlier, it becomes evident that SAP can play a critical role in enabling and assisting any BPR effort in an organization in a major way.

7.3.3.1 SAP Reference Model

SAP's Business Blueprints that are available in the SAP reference model successfully integrate business re-engineering with information technology. The reference model can help companies define their needs and develop solutions; business solutions are already built into the reference model eliminating the need for organizations to start from scratch. The components of the reference model not only cover the functional model but also process model, data model, organization model, information flow model, and communication and distribution model. SAP strategy is to integrate all business operations in an overall system for planning, controlling, optimizing, and monitoring a given business. SAP has included over 800 best-business practices or scenarios that could help a company to restructure its processes. These scenarios provide logical models for the optimization of the specific business processes and can be modeled around primary and support business activities. SAP guides a company to automatically integrate all primary and support functions of logistics like customer order, production, procurement, packaging, warehousing, delivery, service, and accounting. Companies can simply print out the relevant process models and analyze the most critical processes quickly and efficiently. The customizing features of SAP can then help in implementing the required changes.

7.3.3.2 Relevant Significant Concepts of SAP

Three significant components that concern the basic functions and applications of SAP NetWeaver as well as the SAP Business Suite are

1. The client concept
2. The ability to establish organizations
3. The adaptation of the systems to customer-specific business processes (called Customizing using the Implementation Guide (IMG) in the SAP system)

The client in a SAP system is a concept for the comprehensive logical separation of various work areas within the system. Technically speaking, a client is the first key field of every application database table. When a user logs into a SAP system, he or she always enters a client number (000–999). For this, the user has to be defined in that particular client. After a successful log-in, the user only has access to the data and processes present in that client. Data of other clients are not accessible (they can be neither displayed nor edited). This enables separately operating organizations to work parallel to one another in their own client areas within a single SAP system without influencing one another (but a maximum of 150 clients per system is recommended for performance reasons). Via integration processes, data transfer can also take place between clients. Thus, the client is a strict, organizational separating criterion for users working independently on a SAP system. Figure 7.4 displays the organizational layers of a SAP system.

For users working in separate organizations within the same company, further organizational layers are available that are developed in the applications:

1. *Separate systems for corporate subsidiaries and/or regions*: Such a case is characterized by complete logical and technical system separation, uniform usage, data integration via SAP NetWeaver PI, and common or separate technical financial processing.
2. *Separate system-internal clients for corporate subsidiaries and/or regions*: This case is characterized by complete logical separation with common usage of technical system resources,

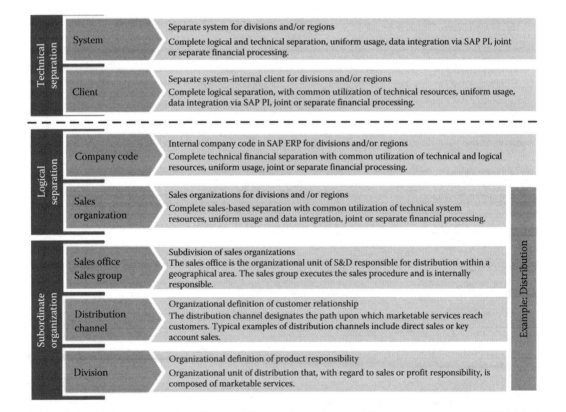

Figure 7.4 Organizational Layers of a SAP system.

uniform usage, data integration via SAP NetWeaver PI, and common or separate financial processing.

3. *Internal company code for corporate subsidiaries and/or regions*: This case is characterized by complete technical financial separation with a common use of technical system and logistic resources, uniform usage, and common or separate financial processing.

4. *Sales organization for divisions and/or regions*: This case is characterized by complete technical sales separation with common usage of technical system resources, uniform usage and data integration, and common or separate financial processing.

5. *Subdivision of sales organizations*: The sales office is the organizational unit of the sales and distribution department, responsible for distribution within a geographical area. The sales group executes the sales procedure and is internally responsible.

6. *Organizational definition of customer relationship*: The distribution channel designates the path upon which marketable services reach customers. Typical examples of distribution channels include direct sales or key account sales.

7. *Organizational definition of product responsibility*: This case is characterized by the distribution department forming an organizational unit that, with regard to sales or profit responsibility, is composed of marketable services.

There are further specific organizational hierarchies within the individual applications. For instance, in purchasing, there are purchasing organizations and purchasing groups. In distribution, there are sales organizations, distribution channels, etc. These organizational layers enable users to work together within a single client of the SAP system, while on the other hand being limited to their respective organizational areas.

7.3.3.3 Implementation Guide (IMG)

SAP Implementation Guide (IMG) plays a critical role in the customization of SAP delivered to a customer to the specific requirements of the customer. This is achieved through configuration of the SAP software without modifying the base SAP software. SAP provides the implementation environment called Business Engineer, which manages and assists this effort for the configuration of SAP. This contains tools like the Business Navigator, Implementation Guide (IMG), Business Workflow, and IDES.

IMG tool is similar to the initialization modules of the traditional systems except that, in comparison, the number of parameters that are definable here are very large. In fact, it is the most vital tool for successful configuration of SAP for specific requirements of different companies. Over a course of time, the IMG exists in the following versions:

1. Reference IMG
2. Enterprise IMG
3. Project(s) IMG

The Reference IMG is the initial IMG that has the base set of configuration options from which all SAP functionality can be derived as per specific requirements. It is the most generic version of the system available. All other IMGs are derived from this basic version.

In contrast, the Enterprise IMG is a subset of the Reference IMG, which represents only the functionality that is needed by a particular enterprise implementing the system. Configuration options related to these excluded modules get filtered out at the time of generation of the Enterprise IMG.

Further down, since SAP implementations could be undertaken in waves or phases, the Enterprise IMG is specified for each of these projects separately resulting in the corresponding Project IMG for each of these projects. All configurations for a particular project are executed on the corresponding Project IMG. The access to Reference IMG and Enterprise IMG is restricted so as to avoid inadvertent changes being effected on them. Whenever required, the scope of the Project IMG can be increased at any time, and, hence, such architecture rather than being a hindrance is very helpful in the management of the customization effort. We will refer only to the Project IMG for the rest of this section.

7.3.3.4 Features of Project IMG

A Project IMG contains multiple configuration transactions. Configuration transactions are the means for configuring the various processes or functionality delivered by the SAP system. A particular business process could be configured in terms of more than one configuration transaction. In conventional terms, each configuration transaction is one of 8000 parameter tables existing within SAP. They could be parameters like company code, type of G/L accounts, ranges of account numbers, A/P and A/R control account codes, posting codes, location codes, vendor or customer categories, tax codes, fiscal calendar, currencies and conversion factors to the base currency, and accounting transaction number ranges.

For each configuration transaction, the configuration help text provides explanation on a particular configuration transaction, why it is needed, and how it affects the functionality for a particular process.

The configuration status can be maintained at every level of the Project IMG hierarchy. It helps in the visual tracking of the customizing effort. The status flag can be configured to represent user-defined statuses. SAP provides standard status values like complete and In Process. Statuses have to be maintained manually.

The configuration Documentation provides facility for recording annotations, notes, issues, problems, etc., on the various configuration settings for each configuration transaction. It is usually in the freeform text but could be standardized based on the requirements of different projects.

7.3.3.5 Using Project IMG for Customizing SAP

The basic structure of Project IMG is hierarchical. The various configuration transactions are grouped in a hierarchy of folders that are broadly arranged in the order that the customizations are undertaken within a SAP module. Among the various SAP modules, the IMG folders are arranged in the order that the modules get implemented in real life. However, there are some parameters or configuration transactions that are independent of any specific modules and are relevant to all modules and functionality of the system. All such configuration transactions are arranged within the topmost IMG folder termed as Global Settings. Obviously, further down the hierarchy, it becomes fairly difficult to maintain strictly the order in which the transactions may be required to be configured. And, therefore, this ordering is only a general guidance; otherwise, it could degenerate into a huge list of configuration transactions at a single level that would certainly become unmanageable.

For a typical SAP implementation, a small selection of the initial parameters or configuration transactions that need to be defined is as follows:

- *Client*: The highest organizational level in SAP, not to be confused with a customer or client as defined in SAP Basis environment.
- *Company Code*: The lowest legal entity for external reporting purposes of balance sheet, P/L statement, etc. There can be multiple company codes for a Client but not the other way around.
- *Chart of Accounts*: This is useful for legal reporting. Every client has only one chart of account; all company codes within one client must use only this chart of account.
- *Credit Control Area*: This is useful for credit control management and reporting.
- *Business Areas*: It is useful for flexible financial reporting.
- *Controlling Area*: The highest entity for internal reporting and accounting purposes. A controlling area can have multiple company codes.
- *Operating Concern*: There is only one operating concern for each controlling area. It is used if the profitability analysis module is implemented (this module may not be implemented by all customers). Controlling area is assigned to an operating concern.
- *Valuation Area*
- *Plant*: A unit where inventories are stored, accounted, processed, or manufactured. There can be multiple plants for a company code as well as a purchasing organization.
- *Sales Organization*: The highest level for managing and reporting sales.
- *Sales Distribution Channel*: This characterizes different modes of supplying to end customers (retail sales, distribution agents, factory outlets, Internet sales, and so on). There can be multiple distribution channels for a sales organization.
- *Sales Division*: This is useful for management and reporting of a group of products. There can be multiple product divisions for multiple sales organization as well as a distribution channels.
- *Sales Area*: It is useful for flexible management and reporting. It is a combination of a sales organization, distribution channel, and division.
- *Purchasing Organization*: This is an organizational unit for purchasing activities and generation of purchase orders.
- *Storage Locations*: The physical location where a company's inventory is stored. There can be multiple storage locations for multiple plants.
- *General Ledger (G/L) Account*: G/L accounts are used for legal, external reporting through the chart of accounts.
- *Housing Bank and Bank Account*: These organization structures reflect a company's banking institutions and their individual bank accounts.
- *Vendor Master*: This contains important information on the company's vendors. For example, a vendor's name, address, telephone number, fax number, contact person, purchasing information, bank information, and accounting information are stored in the vendor master data. This information saves on transaction entries; when a transaction is made with the vendor, the vendor master data can automatically be used by default in the transaction.
- *Customer Master*: Similar to the vendor master data, the customer data contain important information on the company's customers. Information such as customer's name address, buying habits, marketing information, and accounting information are stored here. When a transaction is made with a customer, the customer master data can automatically be used by default in the transaction.

As may have been noted, some of the IMG transactions actually correspond to the programs for creation of master data like General Ledger Account, Vendor master data, and Customer master data. Programs or the functionality for the creation and maintenance of master data and transaction data is also available through the respective modules.

7.3.3.6 Implementation of SAP Standard Functionality

As far as possible, avoid the bugbear of customization by altering and additional programming in ABAP. Additional programming should be evaluated and adopted only as a last resort. SAP keeps upgrading its suite of products and if custom software is built for a particular version, it will have to be upgraded every time SAP releases new upgrades. Like any other product, SAP goes through oscillating cycles between major functional upgrades followed by technical upgrades and vice versa. The best solution is to

- Use SAP standard functionality
- Accommodate the variation of the business process by using SAP's flexibility for configuring variant processes
- Adopt a work-around that indirectly takes care of the required functionality, for example, in the absence of the HR module, some account-interfacing HR functions can be managed by treating employees as customers
- Use third-party products that are properly certified and qualified by SAP

7.3.3.7 Selecting the Most Critical Processes

A company should evaluate and select the processes that are critical to its business and focus on implementing them effectively to add maximum value for optimal effort:

1. *Implementing Best-of-Business Processes*: SAP has a library of 800 of the best-of-business processes derived from companies throughout the world. The success of SAP in providing comprehensive functionality within a shorter time frame compared with traditional implementations is based on the strategy of leveraging the commonality that is found in similar processes prevalent in companies within an industry.

   Reusability has been a powerful concept in enhancing productivity and the quality of delivered software in the areas of traditional software development. SAP, in particular, extends this concept of reusability to the design of mission-critical systems. It packages such universal commonalities of functionality for rapid and successful implementations.

   Before adding reusability to the library of the best-of-business processes, however, the company should document, rationalize, and standardize the company's select group of processes that are to be implemented using SAP:

   a. *Documentation of Processes*: Documenting the various business processes permits the true comprehension of the characteristic structure and dynamics of the business environment within a company. This involves recording various details on the business processes like name; purpose; responsible function; process description, including inputs and outputs; and subprocesses. This also includes interfaces with other functions and systems, exceptional conditions, areas for improvement, and impact analysis of suggested scenarios.

   b. *Rationalization of Processes*: Many of the systems and procedures adopted by traditional systems were influenced by the architecture of the systems themselves. For instance, these earlier systems were designed to be used by IT-literate personnel managed and supported by a centralized IT function. In contrast, because of the end-user orientation of ERP packages like SAP as well as the online availability of data on all aspects of company operations, SAP permits the rationalizing of many processes. This could be in terms of eliminating sequential wait periods for approvals, acknowledgements prior to further processing, collating status updates from various departments before compiling the latest positions on inventory, and so on.

In enterprise-wide integrated packages like SAP, many of these facilities and features become available automatically as a part of the architecture of the system. Thus, such process steps could be eliminated entirely from the business processes.

c. *Standardization of Processes*: Every plant or office site *of* a company develops its own character and culture, which is a result of the company's recommended corporate environment blending with the local situations. Such local practices have strong adherents and generate loyalty and pride. These factors often harm the progress of implementing a fairly uniform system, even if it's a computerized system like SAP, across the organization at all of its sites and offices.

The Chief Project Officer (CPO) must take ample measures to ensure the broad acceptance within the organization of standardized implementation. This can be ensured by

i. The rapid implementation at the pilot site
ii. The rapid rollout of SAP at other company sites and offices
iii. The deputation of key personnel from all sites for the teams at the pilot sites, even at the risk of overstaffing these teams
iv. The judicious selection and documentation of functionalities for implementation at the pilot sites
v. The democratic and transparent process of standardization based on the predefined criteria of value addition in terms of customer friendliness, quality, timeliness, costs, and so on
vi. Configuring and customizing the maximum possible functionality at the pilot site, keeping in view the businesses and practices prevalent at all other sites and offices

2. *Centralized Base Reference Configuration*: A company can experience the real payoff of implementing an ERP like SAP only when it has implemented SAP at all of its plants, facilities, and offices. Traditional computerized systems have a much more difficult time implementing standardized processes across all locations of their organizations. Since a SAP project entails implementing both best-of-business and standardized processes, it leads to fairly standard implementation solutions across all of its sites.

A company should plan to implement a fairly comprehensive functionality at its pilot site. This is termed as the centralized base reference configuration (CBRC). This can simply be transplanted at each of the rollout sites in the subsequent stages of the project. Such an approach engenders faster customization, training, integration testing, and, finally, go-live stages.

7.3.4 Converting Changed Business Processes into SAP Functionality

Implementing SAP solutions to meet business requirements is always a daunting task. It gets even more challenging when the business processes within an organization are complex and the standard functionality provided within the SAP solution is not enough to meet even 80% of the business requirements.

Changed functional development with regard to SAP solutions can be broadly categorized as follows:

- *Configuration*: This involves setting up the SAP solution by adding, selecting, and configuring a certain set of available parameters for the business processes to be executed in SAP without making any programming updates.
- *Customization*: This involves making programming changes to the standard software solution provided by SAP so that the standard business processes will not behave in a manner different from what is expected, primarily to meet the customer requirements.

During the Business Blueprint phase of the SAP Implementation methodology, business processes are converted into a SAP-specific functional plan—a blueprint. One of the first steps in this process is to understand the current business processes existing within an enterprise. The functional specialist spends the next few days diving deeply into each functional area, understanding all the current business processes, and describing any additional processes identified as part of the visioning exercise described in the previous section. Existing business process documentation is analyzed and discussed with the project team members. Business process flowcharts are developed as a means to capture the information shared by the business process owners and subject matter experts (SMEs). Each process flow diagram contains its subprocesses and decision trees depicted together in a visual format where each row of activity is described as a swim lane. The flowchart depicts not only the business process in detail but also links to other functional areas, such as Inventory Management, MRP, and Finance. Additionally, it shows the processes that will be executed in SAP ERP, those that are carried out manually, and those being executed in a non-SAP system. Effectively, the flowchart depicts the business process mapping to the SAP ERP solution and clearly identifies any gaps that might exist within the business process.

The corresponding Business Blueprint (BBP) consists of the following:

- Policies and procedures
- Instructions
- Exclusions, if any
- Decisions
- Change management items
- Business process description including business process flow diagrams
- Business process mapping to the SAP ERP solution
- Local business process requirements (if different from above for legal reasons)
- Gap analysis
- RICEFS (Reports, Interfaces, Conversions, Enhancements, Forms, and SAPscripts)
- Authorization
- Data volume per site
- Archiving details
- BBP acceptance of results—Sign-off by leads

Gaps are processes or functionality that does not exist within the standard SAP solution. These gaps are categorized as either critical or *nice to have*. A gap can be mitigated with a work-around within the SAP solution or through the process of customization in which the actual SAP programs are changed to accommodate these gaps in business processes or functionality. A cost–benefit analysis is carried out to conclude whether this gap can be mitigated with a work-around or through customization. In some cases, even if a work-around exists, it might not be beneficial because it might be time consuming and/or might result in human errors that an organization cannot afford to make. If the decision is made to add new functionality into the standard SAP solution, then the solution is designed and a detailed design document for this new functionality is developed. This detail design will also include functional specifications of the new functionality to be developed:

1. *SAP Configuration*: SAP configuration is a two-step process. The first step is to develop the baseline configuration, which involves configuring SAP ECC based on the information provided during the Business Blueprint phase. The second step is to fine-tune the configuration further based on the outcome of each unit and integration test scenario. As noted earlier, this is achieved through SAP Implementation Guide (IMG).
2. *SAP Customization*: The term customization refers to developing programs not available within the SAP standard functionality to cater to an organization's business requirements. Such customized programs could be used to create the following:
   a. Enhancements to the standard SAP programs for additional business requirements
   b. Reports required to run the business and not available within the SAP solution
   c. Interfaces between SAP and non-SAP systems
   d. Conversion programs to transfer data from the legacy to the SAP solution

7.3.4.1 Advanced Business Application Programming (ABAP)

SAP solutions have primarily been developed using ABAP, which dates back to the 1980s. ABAP programs communicate with the database management system of the central relational database and with the presentation layer, which could be a SAP-specific GUI (such as the fat client SAPGUI) or, in the case of web-based SAP applications, a web browser.

The ABAP programming tools can be accessed via the ABAP Development Workbench.

The ABAP Development Workbench provides the following primary functions:

- Package Builder
- Object Navigator
- Web Application Builder for ITS (Internet Transaction Server) Services
- Web Application Builder for BSPs (Business Server Pages)
- Web Dynpro
- Web Services
- ABAP Dictionary
- ABAP Editor
- Class Builder and Function Builder
- Screen Painter and Menu Painter
- Testing tools such as ABAP Debugger for runtime analysis and performance trace
- Transport Organizer

7.3.4.2 Legacy System Migration Workbench

LSMW is a tool that supports data migration from legacy systems, such as non-SAP systems, to SAP systems. Instead of using individual tables or field contents, this tool migrates user-defined datasets or objects, combined according to business criteria. The following primary features and functions are available:

- Read data from an input file.
- Display the data (for review purposes).
- Convert these data to make them compatible to the target system (SAP) requirements.
- Display the converted data (again, for review).
- Create a batch input session for data transfer.
- Execute the data transfer into SAP.

Log files are created for every step executed during the data migration process, and each step can be controlled by authorization so that only the appropriate person having access to a step can execute that step.

To transfer data (master data as well as transactions) between clients in a SAP system or from a non-SAP system into a SAP system or to set up these data automatically, other tools may be used, such as Application Link Enabling (ALE), Computer-Aided Test Tool (CATT), or the application interfaces provided in the Business Object Repository (BOR).

7.3.4.3 Java and the SAP NetWeaver Development Studio

SAP offers the SAP NetWeaver Developer Studio to create, build, and deploy applications that are compliant with the Java Platform, Enterprise Edition 5 (Java EE 5). Through this toolset, developers have the flexibility to design user interfaces, use Web services, and handle XML-based messages across heterogeneous environments based on the new Java EE 5 standard. The following features and functions are available:

- The use of the latest Java standards makes development of business applications easier.
- Service Data Objects (SDO) 2.1 standards make data programming easier.
- Architecture provides scalability and robustness.
- Connectivity capabilities make it possible to interface with all SAP systems adherent to the latest open standards.

7.3.4.4 SAP NetWeaver Composition Environment (CE)

The SAP NetWeaver Composition Environment (SAP NetWeaver CE) provides a service-oriented and standards-based development environment in which developers can easily model and develop composite applications. These applications, commonly known as *composites* (because they combine previously available functions and datasets in a new way), accelerate business process innovation. Composite applications provide data and functions as services. The developer accesses and combines these from the underlying repository to combine them into a new solution for a business process, to add functionality to an already existing application, and so on.

As an example of a composite application, consider a typical end-to-end process within a manufacturing organization starts with demand creation, wherein a sales order is created for a product ordered by a customer. Based on this demand signal, material requirement planning is executed. Here, the bill of materials (BOMs) for this product is exploded; the stock at each level of the BOM is checked for its material availability and, if there are shortages, a purchase and a production plan is created. This plan consists of purchase requisitions created for raw materials and planned orders created for manufacturing parts, namely, the semifinished and finished parts. Purchase orders are created from these requisitions and sent to the supplier. The suppliers will fulfill the purchase order requirements, and the raw materials will be received into inventory at the manufacturing plant.

The manufacturing process will start with the receipt for the raw materials from stock. The raw materials will be processed to subassemblies or semifinished parts and then will be manufactured further to get the final finished product ordered by the customer. The finished product is then picked, packed, and shipped to the customer. The suppliers are paid for their raw materials, and the customer is billed for the product they ordered. The customer then pays the manufacturer of the product.

This end-to-end process consists of sales, planning, procurement, manufacturing, and financial processes. All of these processes are executed in one or more online transaction systems. The product executive wants to monitor the progress of this product through all these processes and needs one view. A developer can develop a composite application using tools and technologies such as the SAP NetWeaver Visual Composer or SAP's Composite Application Framework (CAF) Guided Procedures (CAF GP). A good example is a dashboard-type application residing on the portal. The data extracted from the OLTP systems like SAP CRM will be formatted to provide the view, as per the product executive's requirements, where he or she can monitor this end-to-end process from the desktop.

The SAP NetWeaver CE is a key innovation enabler; SAP NetWeaver CE allows an organization to take its SAP business application to the next level and adopt real-world SOA principles. Its model-driven development tools enable developers to create custom services as well as custom user interfaces. And by combining these, a custom workflow or complex business process can be assembled not only quickly but in a manner that enables it to be decomposed and changed again later as business changes dictate. It's this innate flexibility of SAP NetWeaver CE—combined with access to a robust set of existing services and the capability to create new services—that makes this tool an indispensable asset for any contemporary SAP developer tasked with quickly standing up new business solutions.

This section described how SAP enables customary changes required of companies as part of their routine operations. However, it must be highlighted that SAP enables even disruptive changes in the enterprise's business processes and logic via the service-oriented architecture (SOA) nature of SAP NetWeaver, but the requisite rationale and supporting details are too technical to be tackled here and out of scope for the objective of this book, which is essentially focused on CRM program and SAP CRM implementation project management.

7.4 SAP CRM and Change Management

In the last chapter, which gave an overview of a SAP CRM implementation project, we identified the fact that a SAP CRM implementation project is like any other business performance improvement program. Because of the enterprise-wide character of these projects, the issues arising out of SAP CRM project necessitate that a formal change management program be undertaken within the enterprise.

7.4.1 Change Champions: Core Team

The key members from the various functional departments of the SAP CRM team are the ideal *change champions* for the SAP CRM project. They can best communicate to the end users of their department, with whom the key members already have a good standing. After mapping and configuring the processes in SAP suitable for their requirements, the key members are also in the best position to talk to the other members of their respective departments and quickly address their particular common requirements and apprehensions. The change process is furthered by the core team members being directly involved in training the super users from their respective departments.

7.4.2 Change Facilitators: Super Users

Super users are the key to a full-scale implementation and subsequently the productive operation of SAP CRM. The super users are trained by the key members of their respective departments. Their training consists of an overview of their module (and related modules) and all the critical processes of interest within their departments.

Under the guidance of the key users, the super users participate in the full-scale validation and integration testing with other departments. This will help them to see the power and potential of SAP CRM through actual experience with the system. It will also help them understand the practical implications of the tight integration, immediate updates, and transparency available in the SAP CRM system. The super users can then convey the real power of the system as experienced by them, especially during the integration-testing phase, to the end users in their respective departments. The super users would be the messengers who would not only advocate changes in the processes but would also demonstrate its actual functioning and its benefits.

7.4.3 Change Agents: End Users

The super users train the end users in their respective departments, covering an overview of the processes in their area of operation, the details of the process, and programs of direct relevance to their daily operations.

The transparent and instant access to relevant information that SAP CRM provides from other departments is always a great motivator, but the implications of instantaneous updates and integration also make all members conscious of the enhanced responsibility and discipline that the system demands from all the concerned participants. Although new systems are always viewed with suspicion, the sense of involvement and ownership inherited from contacts and interaction far outweighs all misgivings about using a SAP CRM system in production.

7.5 Summary

This chapter introduced the concept of BPR especially for customer-centric and customer-responsive enterprises. It details the full cycle of the enterprise BPR methodology. We saw the relevance and role that SAP can play at various stages in the re-engineering effort within an organization. In the later part of the chapter, we looked into the change management aspects enabled by implementation of SAP CRM within an enterprise. The valuation of processes and measurement of performances (MOPs) has been tackled in greater details in Chapter 15.

SAP CRM APPLICATIONS | II

This part has four chapters, which cover respectively the four main components of the SAP CRM. Chapters 8 and 9 are on the heart of the SAP CRM system—the various application modules catering to the customer-facing or front-office-related functional requirements of different areas of the enterprise. Chapter 10 is on SAP CRM's operating environment and related products. Chapter 11 is on SAP NetWeaver, which is the complete development and operating environment within SAP.

Chapter 8: SAP CRM Enterprise Applications
Chapter 9: SAP E-Business Applications
Chapter 10: SAP CRM Application Environment
Chapter 11: SAP Tools and Programming

SAP CRM did not develop in isolation from the IT industry in general. The design and architecture of SAP CRM picks on the best of development in IS/IT in the latter half of the twentieth century. At relevant stages, we have taken the opportunity to highlight the connections with parallel development in software development technologies and methodologies to make the context of several outstanding features available in SAP more meaningful.

Chapter 8

SAP CRM Enterprise Applications

In this chapter, we discuss the main functional modules of SAP CRM covering Marketing, Sales, Service, Interaction Center, Partner Channel Management, and Mobile applications.

The importance of referring to the original SAP ECC 6.x, SAP NetWeaver and SAP CRM 200x documentation corresponding to the version of your installation cannot be over emphasized. What we have presented in this chapter are the essential details of the various functional modules of SAP. However, this chapter is not intended as a replacement for the colossal amount of instructive documentation, guidelines, checklists, templates, samples, questionnaires, and so forth provided and recommended for use by SAP. Those are well-proven instruments, and for an actual project, it is highly recommended that you procure the version of the documentation corresponding to the version of your installation and use it in conjunction with the implementation project.

8.1 SAP CRM Marketing

Every enterprise needs to market its products, services, and concepts to its customers. The SAP CRM Marketing provides a central marketing platform that helps business analyze, plan, develop, and execute all marketing activities through all customer touch points. The marketing component supports important marketing processes, including marketing resource management, trade promotion management, telemarketing, e-marketing, lead management, and marketing analytics. An integrated solution like SAP CRM gives the marketing team detailed business insights that help them to make smart business decisions and drive end-to-end marketing processes.

8.1.1 Salient Features

- *Marketing resource management*: Enables marketing manager to design a marketing plan with budget and requisite resources
- *Segment management*: Enables defining the context of a complete marketing campaigns, including planning, content development, audience definition, market segmentation, and communication
- *Campaign management*: Enables delivery of complete marketing campaigns, including planning, content development, audience definition, market segmentation, and communications
- *Trade promotion management*: Enables brand managers to optimize trade funds to optimize brand awareness and maximize sales volumes
- *Lead management*: Enables development of new leads through lead qualification, routing, tracking, and finally handing sales leads to opportunity management
- *Marketing analytics*: Enables marketing managers to assess the effectiveness of marketing activities based on the impact and resulting outcomes to improve the marketing plans, campaigns, and efforts

8.1.2 Feature Details

SAP CRM Marketing enables the company in planning, budgeting, executing, analyzing, and optimizing all aspects of marketing and campaign execution. In the following, we look at each component of SAP CRM Marketing.

8.1.2.1 Marketing Resource Management

SAP CRM Marketing Resource Management (MRM) provides the tools to enhance the effectiveness of your marketing resources. MRM manages all of the resources that businesses need to run successful marketing campaigns. It enables the planning and forecasting, managing costs and budgets, and control of digital assets (brands, logos, collaterals, and so on). The marketing calendar tool is used as the central entry for marketing personnel. The tool can be used to view, edit, and interlink campaigns and promotions.

8.1.2.2 Market Planning

Large complex enterprises must plan and organize their marketing initiatives on different levels, namely, company level, area level, product level, brand level, and regional level. Global companies can use this functionality to coordinate and optimize the use of internal and external marketing resources. The rationalized planning process offers the flexibility needed to deal with ever-changing market conditions; it enables to deal with complex and ever-changing requirements by enabling companies to react quickly to demand changes with access to centralized marketing plan.

A company's marketing plans depend on the allocated budgets that, in turn, drive your planning options. You can run budget scenarios with each of the marketing planning scenarios under consideration. SAP CRM's integration with SAP NetWeaver BI helps analyze past budgets and create a budget forecast based on historical data. The SAP CRM Marketing comes integrated to SAP Project Systems (PS); thus, marketing planning can be managed in either Microsoft Project or SAP PS module.

The marketing planning of SAP CRM allows companies to plan marketing activities centrally and transparently across all levels involving all personnel concerned, including external partners. Since SAP CRM is integrated, it uses all relevant customer, financial, product, and market data for its marketing planning. Thus, SAP CRM bridges the gap between the supply and demand chains, improves the customer service at the front office, and optimizes the cost-effectiveness at the back office.

> SAP CRM offers companies all the market analysis functions they need to be able to analyze and report on customer-related information, which is necessary to give a better understanding of customer behavior and value. Companies can use this information to plan campaigns, promotions, and events, make their customers effective product proposals, increase customer satisfaction, enhance the use and profitability of products, and retain customers in the long run.

Important functions of marketing planning are

- Collaborative planning functions with embedded marketing workflows and approval processes for faster planning cycles and reduced planning and execution costs
- Interactive and personalized marketing calendar functions to manage campaigns, marketing planning, and trade promotions
- Integration in supply and demand chains for higher efficiency and accuracy (it enables simulation of different supply chain scenarios)
- Proper ROI reporting functions based on current financial data and not on estimates
- The possibility to formulate and communicate marketing strategies across the company; enables the flexibility in distributing and coordinating plans, which allows companies to perform top-down and bottom-up planning
- The possibility to coordinate and optimize the use of internal and external marketing resources and initiatives across the company
- The availability of snapshots—versions of modified marketing plans—which offer detailed budgeting functions as well as better understanding of plan modifications over a particular period
- Individualized planning of key performance indicators to enable planning on a financial, supply logistics, and product level

8.1.2.3 Segment Management

The SAP CRM Marketing includes a tool called the Segment Builder that can be used to build large groups for marketing campaigns based on marketing attributes such as age, income, geographical location, hobbies, buying behavior, and RFM (recency, frequency, monetary) values. Groups of customers who possess similar attributes and needs fall into what are termed as *customer segments*. Customer segmentation, which is the basis of marketing campaigns, can be performed using various attributes or other criteria. To help marketing fine-tune its selection of target groups, SAP CRM offers all the tools required for analytical and ad hoc segmentation. Business users can create target segments for customers, partners, organizations, prospects, and groups and integrate them separately with market campaigns.

The Segment Builder can access customer data from a variety of sources, including SAP NetWeaver BI, SAP ERP, or even purchased customer lists. To speed up the process of searching for and retrieving customer data, it uses the TREX high-speed engine; additionally, it offers a number of other advanced features such as predictive modeling, dynamic filtering, segment duplication, target group optimization, clustering, data mining, decision trees, and ABC analysis based on profitability and retention scores.

While creating the marketing segments, SAP CRM provides support for

- Embedded functions for optimizing response rates
- Random selection of smaller customer groups that are representative of the entire customer base but can be analyzed faster for sampling
- Control group functions
- Simplified operation through personalized attribute lists for each user and access to partial quantities of customer and consumer data to enable a personalized view on the data
- Analytical segmentation functions, including clustering, decision trees, and other data mining technologies
- Real-time determination of the number of business partners that correspond to the selection criteria for the purpose of more precise planning and segmentation

8.1.2.4 List Management

List management enables generation, operation, and maintenance of both internally and externally purchased customer and prospect list as also effective tracking of their responses and follow-up.

8.1.2.5 Campaign Management

SAP CRM provides companies with complete control over the campaign process, from conception to execution, coordination, optimization, and monitoring. Companies can create goal-oriented, personalized campaigns via all communication channels, including the field, call center, e-mail, fax, the Internet, and mobile devices.

SAP CRM campaign management provides tools for setting up and tuning a campaign from start to finish, beginning with market analysis, continuing with the execution of the campaign, and ending with analytics. The results of the campaign can then be used for planning future campaigns to enable closed-loop SAP CRM (see Chapter 2, Section 2.3.1 "Closed-Loop CRM"). Using SAP CRM campaign automation tools, you can graphically model a campaign and conduct campaign simulation. An easy-to-use graphical interface provides a clear overview of the campaign process flow, including support for multichannel and multiwave campaigns.

Integrated campaign management that is linked with the financial and supply chain systems helps marketing organizations to optimize resources and coordinate activities across the organization. It is also possible to monitor the company-wide profitability at program, product, customer, and partner levels. In addition, the company can plan, execute, and assess the success of direct and indirect communication (through print media and television) with the consumers.

The marketing calendar functionality offers a comprehensive overview of all marketing activities. Companies can view their plans, trade promotions, and campaigns from several perspectives (like by brand, customer, or product groups) and can use aggregation, drill-up or drill-down methods, and print functions. Marketing plans can be visualized on daily, weekly, or monthly basis and can be color coded to make them easily recognizable.

For marketing campaigns, SAP CRM provides support for

- Campaign manager portal that provides a personalized, role-based point of entry that can be used by all users to gain access to all relevant information, applications, and services
- Embedded functions for campaign planning, which enabled optimized processes with low implementation costs and short-planning and development cycles and also promote trouble-free campaign execution
- Calendar functions that offer a complete view of marketing activities
- User-friendly design that enables common users to create sequential campaigns and activities that promote dialog with customer and make communications more effective
- Complete multichannel functions, including letter, e-mail, the Web, telephone, SMS, fax, face to face, and mobile devices
- Efficient reading of external lead data for use in all marketing campaigns and initiatives
- Analytical functions that companies can use to determine the value of their customers
- Tight integration with financial, supply chain, and logistics data, as well as analytical data warehouse systems

8.1.2.6 Trade Promotion Management (TPM)

TPM helps organizations increase the effectiveness of their in-store retail promotions. Many manufacturers spend a significant percentage of their sales revenue on trade promotions—refunds or discounts given by manufacturers to the retailers to enable the retailer in turn to lower the price of the product and pass the savings on to the consumers—for generating more demand for the manufacturer's product. SAP TPM provides manufacturers the tools to ensure that retailers sold the required quantity of product in the appropriate retail location.

TPM begins by enabling the decision on how to use allocated funds, based on sales targets and budgets, across various possible promotions to optimize sales revenue and brand awareness. After the trade promotions are created, a company can use the forecasting tools to preanalyze the planned trade promotion spending, after which the promotions can be released. SAP CRM TPM provides trade funds management, trade spend budgeting, account/product allocation, deductions management, and payment processing.

SAP TPM is fully integrated with SAP ERP, SAP SCM, and Business Process Simulation (SEM-BPS). The integrated TPM system handles the creation, execution, monitoring, and optimization of the TPM programs at key account level as well as for individual in-store promotions.

8.1.2.7 Lead Management

Lead management provides capabilities to generate leads on the Webs as well as automatically qualify leads or to qualify leads by dispatching leads for qualifications using workflow or business rules. The lead management function of SAP CRM is used by marketing personnel to collect, qualify, and distribute leads and to give sales employees the opportunities to capitalize on the best leads. Before a lead becomes an opportunity, it needs to be qualified. Only leads that lead to turnover contribute to company profits. Lead management in marketing empowers companies to quickly convert qualified leads into paying customers and simultaneously avoid wasted time and efforts on unproductive leads.

Lead management paves the way for sales; leads are potential customers of tomorrow or today's customers that companies would like to interest in a different product range.

For lead management, SAP CRM provides support for

- Lead manager portal, which offers a single, personalized, and role-based point of entry that provides the lead manager and lead qualifier with access to relevant information, applications, and services
- Functionality for managing external lists, including reading potential leads and the execution of corresponding follow-up activities
- Lead qualification to enhance conversion rate and realized revenue
- Lead forwarding to bring the right leads to the right employees or business partners

8.1.2.8 Marketing Analytics

SAP CRM offers comprehensive Web cockpits and evaluation tools that present all information relating to campaign success and response rates. Campaign managers receive all information relevant for decision making, especially the actual financial campaign success in terms of the realized value. This is enabled by back-office integration of the SAP solution. SAP provides a special account assignment object for the systematic cost and revenue monitoring of marketing campaigns made available in the SAP BI.

SAP CRM is integrated with both SAP ERP and SAP NetWeaver BI, providing closed-loop marketing analytics that measure, predict, plan, and optimize marketing plans. Analytics help you to understand the effectiveness of your marketing activities, allowing you to convert data into actionable intelligence.

Various types of marketing analytics are available, including campaign analytics, lead analytics, and trade promotion analytics. Based on this, a company can accurately predict customer behavior, anticipate customer needs, and generate appropriate marketing messages.

8.2 SAP CRM Sales

8.2.1 Salient Features

- *Sales planning*: Plans and forecasts accurately across all sales channels
- *Territory management*: Accounts coverage with clear territory definition, assignment, and scheduling and has complete visibility into team distribution
- *Account and contact management*: Manages all relevant information regarding the customer
- *Activity management*: Records all interactions with the customer
- *Opportunity management*: Provides visibility into the opportunity pipeline, improves team communication, and routes leads to the right salespeople
- *Quotation and order management*: Generates accurate quotes and configurations, places orders, confirms product availability in real time, and tracks order status
- *Product configuration and pricing*: Guides through the product configuration process, enforcing business rules to ensure that correct product combinations are recommended to customers and that pricing is tailored to each sales channel or customer
- *Billing and contract management*: Develops and manages long-term customer contracts, monitors the sales process from inquiry to completion and billing, and seamlessly integrates these activities with back-end financial and accounts receivable process

- *Incentive and commission management*: Provides the sales force with easy and accurate visibility into possible commissions and managing actual commissions
- *Time and travel management*: Records working times, expenses, and managing travel costs
- *Sales analysis*: Reports on the complete sales process ranging from territory management to billing and provides analysis by region, area, territory, and key account level

8.2.2 Feature Details

SAP CRM Sales helps sales personnel to build trusted and long-term relationship with their customers by providing the functionality they need to turn insight into action and acquire, grow, and retain profitable relationship; companies can plan and analyze the entire sales life cycle, find newer ways to speed up the sales cycle, uncover new areas of revenue potential, and determine new methods for enhancing sales productivity.

8.2.2.1 Sales Planning

SAP CRM helps a company to plan and forecast accurately across all sales channels, manage budgets and opportunities, and allocate resources effectively; it proactively enables companies to handle trends, shortfalls, and opportunities, optimizes supply chain planning and execution, performs strategic planning and account planning, and monitors the planning cycle.

SAP CRM is integrated with SAP NetWeaver BI and SAP ERP to provide sales planning and forecasting functionality. Sales planning is constituted of strategic planning and operational planning; the former is about what, where, and to whom to sell and, consequently, about market share, profit, revenue, market leadership, and penetration. Operational planning provides demand forecasting based on historic and real-time data coming from pipeline analysis and sales booking. SAP CRM with SAP NetWeaver BI and SEM-BPS enables enhanced sales planning and forecasting.

Sales planning is supported by sales analysis figures; planning can take place top-down or bottom-up. With top-down planning, requirements are specified right down to the smallest sales unit; in contrast, bottom-up planning consolidates plan figures upward along the sales organization hierarchy (available from Territory Management component). Bottom-up and top-down plannings, together with planning for individual customer contacts and related activities, constitute the best prerequisites for lasting sales success. For example, it is possible to determine which products were successful in which regions and which customers contributed the most to profitability—on the basis of this information, a company can forecast sales figures and make decisions regarding the assignment of individual sales employees.

For sales planning, SAP CRM provides support for

- Multidimensional planning with flexibly designed planning levels for strategic and operative sales targets
- Planning tasks personalized according to the area of responsibility for individual sales employees
- Comprehensive toolbox with planning methods for modifying and restructuring plans, such as top-down distribution, evaluations, simulations, and copying functions
- Integrated account planning as part of the Account Management and integrated opportunity planning as part of Opportunity Management

8.2.2.2 Territory Management

Territory management enables companies to optimize customer accounts coverage with clear territory definition, assignment, and scheduling as well as have complete visibility into team distribution. The company can recognize and rapidly respond to shifting market demands by placing the right resources in the right locations to optimize team performance.

Territory management is a tool that can be used to structure and organize the market into individual territories according to different criteria like postal codes, products, customer groups, and customers. Territory hierarchy describes the structure of territories. Using territory management, a company can define sales territories and territory hierarchies and assign people (and managers) to the territories, generate sales performance reports by territory, and update the sales territories in sync with changing market sales.

While the organizational model represents the structure of sales, Territory Management mirrors the market. The connecting link between the two is the sales employee, who (from the point of view of the organizational structure) belongs to the sales office and, from the point of view of Territory Management, is responsible for a particular sales territory.

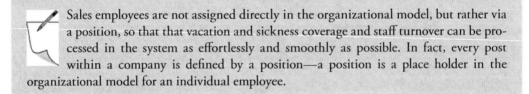

Sales employees are not assigned directly in the organizational model, but rather via a position, so that that vacation and sickness coverage and staff turnover can be processed in the system as effortlessly and smoothly as possible. In fact, every post within a company is defined by a position—a position is a place holder in the organizational model for an individual employee.

8.2.2.3 Account and Contact Management

SAP CRM manages all relevant information regarding the customer, especially in the context of cross company cooperation. Using SAP CRM Sales, the sales manager or salesperson can break sales planning down to the account level. The salesperson can also create, edit, update, and delete the customer contacts. All of the interactions with the customer, such as phone calls and visits, can be recorded in the system as activities and follow-ups. And the activities and follow-ups are visible to all salespeople and sales managers who have access to the customer information.

Information about different people involved in the sales process can be managed in Account Management, including

1. Customers
2. Sales prospects
3. Sales partners
4. Competitors
5. Employees

Account management equips sales managers with portal-based access to an abundance of information on business partners. The information presented in Account Management can be adapted to meet the information needs of a variety of employee groups. In this way, agents in the Interaction Center receive information that is important when addressing problems or processing questions raised by customers during a call.

For Account Management, SAP CRM provides support for

- Search for and list of important business partners
- Contact history with all business partner–specific documents over the last *n* number of days (orders, quotations, activities, opportunities, complaints, etc.)
- Fast entry of activities and opportunities in Account Management and fast entry of contact persons in Account Management
- Important financial and logistical information
- Business partner–specific analysis

8.2.2.4 Activity Management

Interactions between companies and customers are recorded as business activities. Activity Management is not only available in sales; it is a general component of SAP CRM that supports employees in organizing their daily work. They can be created at any time in order to document an interaction with a customer. Activities can also be created as follow-up documents for a large number of business transactions that are related to opportunities, leads, sales orders, or contracts. Each of these activities also provides a quick link to Account Management. Activities appear automatically in the calendars of all employees who are entered as partners in activity. Consequently, all employees involved are always kept up to date on discussions, visits, and results.

Together with other documents, activities offer a reliable history of the results achieved as well as the possibility of forecasting future tasks. SAP CRM has the following categories of reports for following up on individual activities:

1. Operative report that informs on all open business activities for a particular business partner or a set of business partners that have been contacted in a certain period
2. Analytical report that informs regarding the amount of time it took to win a customer and the results that were achieved

For Activity Management, SAP CRM provides support for the following:

- *Calendar*: Activities are saved as appointments in the calendars of all people involved in a given business transaction.
- *Documents for business activities*: Documents contain information on business partner address, times, and dates as well as related documents such as product information, letters to customers, and marketing brochures.
- *Results and reasons for activities*: For the purpose of analysis, it is important to know what happened with an activity and why. Therefore, the reasons for carrying out an activity, its status, and whether it was successful can all be recorded and evaluated in that activity.
- *Activity journal*: Using an activity journal, any number of key figures can be generated with product reference and later evaluated.
- *Surveys*: It is possible to create surveys centrally and to assign corresponding activities. This enables suitable customer surveys to be managed in parallel with a marketing campaign; consequently, the appropriate survey is assigned to all activities (like customer visits or calls) that are created (say) as a result of a campaign. Any number of surveys can be assigned to an individual activity; all information that is gathered in a survey or using the Activity Journal can be analyzed in detail and can be drawn upon for defining target groups in a marketing campaign.

8.2.2.5 Opportunity Management

Using SAP CRM Sales, a company can manage its sales cycle more effectively, predictably, and at a lower cost. The sales employees can obtain full visibility into the opportunity pipeline, improve team communication, and route leads to the right salespeople. SAP CRM can improve opportunity planning, team selling, opportunity hierarchies, and sales and selling methodologies. SAP CRM provides an SAP-proprietary methodology (based on guided selling) that helps in maintaining high-quality sales process throughout the sales engagement.

Opportunity management as part of SAP CRM Sales is linked directly with the SAP CRM Marketing functionality, allowing marketing leads to be converted into sales opportunities. The salesperson responsible for the account will be automatically notified about the opportunity.

An opportunity is a qualified sales chance or a verified chance of a company to sell a product or service. Opportunities can be created either from leads or directly by a sales employee as a result of (say) a trade show discussion, a sales promotion, or a bid invitation.

Salespeople create documents called opportunities in SAP CRM to capture sales-relevant data, including

1. Description of the sales project
2. Description of the products and services inquired
3. Budget of the sales prospect
4. Potential sales volume
5. Estimated sales probability

> It is possible to set up opportunity hierarchies so that sales projects can be mapped out even more effectively. In other words, for every product belonging to a sales project, a separate opportunity is created and linked to the higher-level opportunity; the structure of the opportunity hierarchy can be as deep as required. In contrast, for sales projects with large companies, it is also possible to divide up the entire sales project, for example, according to individual products.

The salespeople also record the names of the members of the sales team working on the opportunity as well as the members of the customer's buying center—the group of customer's employees who are decision makers for the current opportunity.

Fundamental elements of the sales methodology of SAP CRM are

- Project goal description
- Buying center
- Analysis of competition
- Opportunity assessment
- Opportunity plan
- Analysis and reporting

This results in an opportunity plan that pulls together all key information related with each opportunity. The opportunity plan provides a comprehensive overview of the stage a project is at any moment. It serves as a basis for presentations and discussions in internal sales project meetings and is available to be displayed, printed, or e-mailed at any time. An opportunity plan consists of

- *Project overview*: Expected sales volume, customer budget, chance of success, current phase in the sales cycle, closing date, sales team, project goals of the customer, and sales goal
- *Product overview*: Products, quantities, and expected product value
- *Buying center*: Customer's organizational chart with key people and definitive attributes for influence, opinion, and decision criteria
- *Analysis of competitors*: Strengths, weaknesses, and strategies of competitors
- *Opportunity assessment*: Evaluation of the chance of success as per sales employees and the chance of success as per the system
- *Activity plan*: Overview of all activities, employees responsible, and the degree of completion

Opportunity management is also integrated with real-time monitoring, reporting, and analytical tools. For instance, opportunity management provides real-time updates to the pipeline analysis by transferring the data to SAP NetWeaver BI after the opportunity is saved. Also, data about opportunities and their results can be exported to SAP NetWeaver BI for detailed analysis. As a result, ready-made queries are available that make it possible to gain a comprehensive overview of all opportunities, thus forming the basis of detailed sales planning and simulation. For instance, the opportunity pipeline delivers information about the current status of all opportunities and allows you to monitor short- and long-term sales volume possibilities.

8.2.2.6 Quotation and Order Management

Using SAP CRM Sales, a company can generate accurate quotes and configurations, place orders, confirm product availability in real time, and track order status. It can also provide order information to the supply chain for planning and fulfillment and help synchronize billing and fulfillment.

The created orders can be used as an inquiry, quotation, or firm order by setting the line-item status as the discriminator at the item level:

1. *Header*: The document header contains all important data relating to the entire document, for instance, type (inquiry, quotation, or sales order), number, and status of the transaction. Furthermore, information on shipping, payment, and delivery conditions as well as tax data and organizational, administrative, and partner information and texts can all be stored here. It can also contain information on the campaign through which the business transaction was originally triggered. It is possible to determine campaign-specific pricing conditions (e.g., discounts or other price reductions) or to evaluate at a later stage, the number of sales orders that were won using a certain campaign.
2. *Items*: This contains each individual document item, including schedules, prices, conditions, texts, order information, and partner, delivery, payment, and organizational data. Products can be configured at item level.

8.2.2.7 Product Configuration and Pricing

SAP CRM guides the salesperson through the product configuration process, enforcing business rules to ensure that correct product combinations are recommended to customers and that pricing is tailored to each sales channel or customer. It also gives up-to-date information based on centrally maintained pricing rules and conditions to enable contractual pricing, discounting, promotional pricing, and customer-specific pricing.

SAP CRM leverages the SAP Internet Pricing and Configurator (IPC) tool for pricing; the IPC consists of the Sales Pricing Engine (SPE), Configuration Engine (SCE), and product-modeling environment (PME). The SPE manages pricing, including variant pricing; the SCE supports configurable products and variant configuration; and the PME is used for master data maintenance of product configuration–related data.

For product configuration, SAP CRM provides for the following:

■ During the first phase of the customer contract, the configurator records a description of the customer problem (for which a solutions is required) in a standardized format and uses it to determine the optimal product or solution.

■ The product configurator helps the user to find the most suitable product; it supports adaptation of a product by presenting the end user with the range of available product options in a dialog and then checks the selected product configuration against a predefined set of rules for completeness and consistency.

■ The integrated pricing functionality calculates the price for the requested product variant. The total price of the product is always kept up to date, depending on the chosen options and on the basis of other established pricing rules.

■ The result of a configuration can be forwarded to downstream systems through standardized interfaces so that downstream processes receive the necessary data entries for order processing.

■ The configurator enables an availability check so that the customer can know immediately when the requested product configuration can be delivered.

■ SAP IPC ensures the integration between the sale itself and order processing to that exactly what was ordered is also delivered and billed for.

8.2.2.8 Billing and Contract Management

SAP CRM supports two types of billing scenarios: transaction-related billing and delivery-related billing. Transaction-related billing includes billing options such as usage-based billing and transaction-related billing after completion. External billing and nonbilling (for nonbilling-related transactions) are also supported. In contrast, delivery-based billing generates a billing document in SAP CRM only after a delivery is created in SAP ERP based on a goods issue. With this billing option, the billing documents are always created in reference to specific deliveries.

Using the SAP CRM contract management functionality, a company can create long-term purchasing agreements and sales contracts with customers that allow customers to buy products and services at special prices and with favorable delivery terms over a predetermined period. A contract typically specifies the exact terms and conditions, pricing agreements, specific releasable products, authorized customer companies, and completion rules.

SAP CRM allows companies to develop and manage long-term customer contracts, incorporate customer agreements into ongoing process, monitor the sales process from inquiry to completion, and seamlessly integrate these activities with back-end financial and accounts receivable process. It allows companies to manage value-based and quantity-based contracts, sales agreements, collaborative contract negotiation, release-order handling, cancelation processing, credit management, invoicing, and payment processing.

For contract management, SAP CRM provides for

■ Creating long-term agreement with price and product agreements for a customer
■ Monitoring the sales process from inquiry through the contract completion

- Capturing the touch points with the customer during contract negotiation
- Guiding the salesperson through the follow-up with the customer and recording the follow-up in the system
- Preventing the salespeople from giving discounts or price reductions beyond a specified threshold price
- Tracking whether the customer has been buying products as agreed in the contract
- Tracking the competitors' pricing for the same products and their sales strategies
- Analyzing customer satisfaction during the contract period

8.2.2.9 Incentive and Commission Management

SAP CRM incentive and commission management provides the sales force with easy and accurate visibility into possible commissions if a sales deal is closed. Sales personnel can perform *what-if* analysis to see how much their commission would increase if they closed a particular deal; with the expected incentives and commissions information, the sales force is in position to focus exclusively in closing the deal; as employees can project commissions amounts at any time, they are able to recognize the opportunities that will guarantee that not only their personal goals, but also those of the enterprise, are achieved.

ICM supports many different commission scenarios, for instance, sales commission, channel-specific incentives, and remuneration of internal employees. The scope of functionality covers the complete management of commissions and incentives.

SAP CRM provides the following tools that are also available:

- A tool to automatically and precisely calculate remuneration
- Tools for flexible modeling, cost simulation, and plan individualization
- Administrative functions for processing routine tasks
- Accurate cost and activity reporting

8.2.2.10 Time and Travel Management

SAP CRM provides an integrated solution that helps companies to keep travel costs under control. The time and travel solutions provide off-line access to the time and travel component to record working times and expenses and later synchronize up with the enterprise system at a convenient time. The solution helps in enforcing corporate travel policies and monitoring and controling the costs associated with the activities of the sales force; consequently, it enables improving time tracking, expense reporting, and assignment of costs to sales activities.

8.2.2.11 Sales Analytics

SAP CRM Sales analytics provide standard out-of-the-box business content to enable reporting on the complete sales process ranging from territory management to billing. It provides sets of analytical data targeted for both sales managers and salespeople; easy slice-and-dice functionality enables them to view sales statistics by region, area, territory, and key account level. Using SAP NetWeaver BI and SEM-BPS, sales analytics also provide comparison of planned and actual sales. Thus, this component enables sales to respond to the requirements in real time, forecast accurately, maintain budget, optimize resource alignment, and enable the team to achieve the revenue goals.

Supported sales performance analysis include pipeline analysis, sales volume analysis, Top *N* opportunities, order and contract analysis, sales funnel analysis, and customer profitability and customer lifetime value (CLTV) analysis.

Sales performance analysis is divided into the following areas:

- *Finances*: Pipeline analysis for opportunities and open contracts provide an overview of current and expected development. Using sales order analysis, open and incoming order value as well as the potential sales volumes can be analyzed.
- *Customers*: ABC analysis can be used to compare and categorize different customers according to the degree of importance. Analyses can also be conducted on customer value and profitability.
- *Sales process*: The Follow-up on business transactions such as opportunity quantities, success rates, profit and loss comparisons, quotation analysis, and the connection between quotations and contracts or sales orders that are actually won.
- *Employee development*: Satisfaction surveys can be used to analyze staff turnover, the number and costs of courses and the number of participants, sick leave and overtime figures, and employee satisfaction.

8.3 SAP Service

Service plays a key role in retaining customers for the long term. SAP recognizes the importance of customer service through a wide range of applied functionality within the integrated solution of SAP CRM. The SAP CRM service components support the entire service cycle right from the initial contact with the customer, to the carrying out of services or the shipment of parts, to billing.

8.3.1 Salient Features

- *Installed base management*: Management of installed equipment at customer sites
- *Warranty management*: Management of warranty, claims, and services rendered to customers
- *Knowledge management*: Compilation and access to issues and solutions reported in the field updated with analyses back home
- *Contract and entitlement management*: Management of service contracts, SLAs, and service rendered against these contracts
- *Resource planning*: Management of schedule and dispatches of field service professionals
- *Service order and service ticket*: Recording and follow-up on service orders and delivery
- *Complaints and returns*: Registration of complaints and returns processing
- *Service analytics*: Performance reporting of the services delivered

8.3.2 Feature Details

8.3.2.1 Installed Base Management

The management of existing customer installations refers to all of the different equipments installed at the company sites. Individual pieces of equipment are termed as *objects*; when an individual piece of equipment belongs to a larger group of installed equipment, the object is termed as *component* of that particular installed base.

Installed base information is useful internally to the customer to keep track of their equipment and to determine when any particular equipment was last updated or serviced; it is also useful for a service technician who needs to locate a specific piece of equipment that requires specific repair. Installed base information also makes it very easy to manage customer service requests.

8.3.2.2 Warranty Management

Warranties play an important role in service; usually, warranties are the starting point of service work. Warranties can be assigned flexibly to the individual components of the installed base; it is also possible to assign more than one warranty to each component.

A warranty is a guarantee from a manufacturer or supplier or vendor that a product is free from defects and will remain operational for a specified period of time. For instance, a warranty will specify the length of time during which the product will be serviced or repaired by the manufacturer or supplier or vendor free of cost; warranties define the terms and conditions of how repairs, replacement, and exchange of defective products are handled.

SAP CRM Service also supports the warranty claim process, including the generation of return materials authorization as well as receipt and inspection. A warranty claim is a request from the warranty holder for service, replacement, or exchange of a defective product as specified in the terms and conditions of the warranty.

8.3.2.3 Knowledge Management

SAP CRM provides users like interaction center agents, service engineers, and E-Service customers, with access to solutions and other knowledge gained from various interactions with all customers in the past. For instance, when a new, previously undetected issue is reported by a customer, the company's engineers will come up with a solution or fix and then register the solution in the company's knowledge base called the Solution Database.

All known problem descriptions are saved in the Solution Database; they are entered as free text or by using defined codes that describe a problem or damage that occurred. The Solution Database uses a variety of information sources to document, save, and map solution options to known problems that are weighted by statistical data preparation (which is based on success-case user reports). This kind of support enables the content of the Solution Database and the search quality to be continuously refined and improved. The list of FAQs and answers is a collection point for the organizational knowledge bank saved in the database and represents an important source of information for both the customer and company employees alike.

SAP provides a search engine tool known as the Text Retrieval and Extraction (TREX) engine, which works in conjunction with Software Agent Framework (SAF) that is responsible for continually updating, indexing, and compiling the knowledge base.

SAP case management provides a central repository for consolidating and keeping track of all of the different documents and information related to a single issue or case. Case management gives everyone involved in the case access to the most updated information.

8.3.2.4 Contract and Entitlement Management

Service contracts are long-term agreements between companies and their customers in which the company offers to provide a certain level of service in exchange for a fixed fee. Service contracts are extremely profitable with profit margins as high as 50%–60% depending on the industry, and hence, it is important for companies to be able to sell and manage service contracts and entitlement successfully. Service contract management provides tools for managing service agreements, service contract quotations, and service contracts.

Service contracts typically include a Service Level Agreement (SLA) in which the company specifies the response time and an availability time to which the customer is entitled; additional company-specific parameters can also be defined freely and integrated to support specific business processes. Service agreements can be created for certain customer groups, specifying general parameters of service contracts such as pricing and discounts. SLAs and automatic entitlement both are supported, which enables service employees to ascertain if a customer is entitled to a service.

8.3.2.5 Resource Planning

The SAP CRM resource planning application (RPA) is used for scheduling and dispatching field service technicians to service-related customer appointments. When a customer contacts a company's interaction center to request installation of a new product, or maintenance or repair of an existing product, the interaction center agent will schedule an appointment for the customer based on the response and availability time specified in the customer's service contract or SLA. At this point, no service technician is actually assigned to the job; the actual assignment is done later by a dispatcher. After a service task has been assigned to a service technician, who in turn has accepted the assignment, the service order is transferred down to the mobile device of the technician; the service order contains all of the information that is required to serve the customer.

In addition to installations and repairs of equipment, resource planning can also be used for any type of industry or business that needs to schedule on-site customer visits, including insurance companies that do damage inspection, health-care professionals who conduct on-site evaluations, and physical therapists.

8.3.2.6 Service Order and Service Ticket

SAP CRM service order management provides two types of service requests, namely, the service order and the service ticket; while both of these have the same underlying business transaction, they differ in the corresponding screens. The service order view was originally designed for repair, maintenance, or installation situations; in contrast, the service ticket was introduced in response customer's need for a leaner and easier-to-use screen that better supported the interaction center service desk scenario. While the service order is available across all SAP CRM communication channels (including the Web), the service ticket is available only in the interaction center.

8.3.2.7 Complaints and Returns

SAP CRM provides complaints and returns functionality for managing the entire customer complaint process; a complaint is filed by customer when the customer is dissatisfied or has an issue with a product or service, or shipment, or invoice: if the customer received a damaged or wrong product or an incorrect quantity or if the customer was over billed.

The entire complaint and return process is fully automated and integrated with back-end SAP ERP functionality for all the financial and quality management (QM) process, such as generating Credit/Debit Notes, billing docs, and QM notification.

8.3.2.8 Service Analytics

Service analytics monitor the operative performance of a company's service business, helping them to respond effectively to emergencies while maintaining the normal business health. Analytics are available for each of the service components, including installed base management, warranty management, service contract and entitlement management, resource planning, case management, service order management, and complaints and returns. For instance, installed base analytics detail the amount of money generated by orders for a particular product installation, enabling an analysis of cost, revenue, and profit by product installation. Similarly, service contract analysis enables the company to look at billing information and planned versus actual contract usage to determine which service contracts are most profitable and which are unprofitable.

8.4 SAP Interaction Center

Existing SAP ERP customers, who want to start leveraging CRM, will often begin their SAP CRM project with the interaction center. These SAP customers will typically start with a help desk for providing customer-facing service and support. As the company becomes more focused on maximizing the benefits from CRM, it will expand into its interaction center footprint to include telemarketing and telesales. Many companies eventually leverage the CRM platform to set up IT help desk and employee interaction centers to provide internal IT and support.

Interaction centers enable two-way communication between customers and companies that are mutually beneficial. Customers benefit from being able to contact the company any time they want through the communication channel that they are comfortable with, and companies benefit from actually being able to speak directly with their customers (who can otherwise be hard to contact due to stringent privacy laws and do-not-call lists). Such interactions give companies a chance to

- Reinforce its brand image and marketing messages
- Increase customer satisfaction and loyalty through excellent service
- Drive revenue and profitability via postservice cross selling efforts

Interaction Centers enable customers to interact with companies through communication channel of their choice, namely, telephone, e-mail, the Web chat, fax, and postal letter. Companies typically use the interaction center to provide product support and address queries from customers, whereas some companies also use the interaction center for outbound marketing and sales.

The challenge of companies that have deployed individual stand-alone solutions is to convert their legacy call center, e-mail, and chat point solutions into a consolidated multichannel interaction center. The capabilities of an integrated SAP CRM Interaction Center are discussed as follows.

8.4.1 Core Business Processes

The central processes in the interaction center are related to telemarketing, telesales, and teleservice. The main elements of these processes are discussed in the following sections.

8.4.1.1 Telemarketing

One of the core tasks of marketing is to generate sufficient contacts for the sales organization. Campaign management is an important tool in this context. Personalized, customer-specific offers originate on the basis of the target group selection, the identification of appropriate communication channels, and the available products and services. If the marketing management decides on a telephone campaign, call lists are drawn up and passed onto to the interaction center organization together with predefined scripts. The scripts are used by the agents as personalized templates for their calls and often contain relevant customer data, for example, about preferences, previously bought products, or preferred contact times. The call center manager assigns the call lists to the individual agents or agent groups. The progress of the active campaign can be monitored any time using the interaction center portal.

8.4.1.2 Telesales

Selling products and services by telephone has been popular both in the business-to-business (B2B) environment and in the business-to-consumer (B2C) environment. Within order receipt, the agent has access to all instruments that provide information about availability (available to promise [ATP]), pricing, alternative products (up-selling or down-selling), and product accessories (cross selling). Longer sales cycles for higher-quality goods require that the agent has access to the entire interaction history. All customer-related data and functions for managing contacts and follow-up activities, creating quotations, and converting the quotations to orders can be reached using a single interaction step. By accessing the incentive and Commission Management, agents can see how their sales success affects their salaries.

8.4.1.3 Teleservice

The majority of the interaction centers are in the service environment. They often take the form of help desks that deal with internal and external complaints or problem messages. The quality of the service processes can have a major influence on customer and employee satisfaction.

Depending on the complexity of the requests, the service processes are supported by the following functions:

- *Activity management*: Confirmations to customers are documented and monitored for acknowledgment (from the customer).
- *Case management*: Increased focus on activity management, with the option of combining different activities into a *case*.
- *Service orders*: Monitoring of agreements incorporating services and spare parts.

Many companies in industrial maintenance integrate the SAP CRM service application with logistics processes in the back-end system. This means that immediate check can be made to determine whether specific spare parts are available in the store. Similarly, the integration with the human resource systems enables query on the skills inventory of the service technicians—which can be useful while allocating resources or manning the shifts at the interaction center.

8.4.1.4 Interactive Center Analytics

Companies that have already been using CRM systems for years are oftentimes confronted with a peculiar problem wherein they have phenomenal amount of data on various customers, and yet they do not have better insights into the nature of their customers or customer segments. The problem is often that there are not enough analytical instruments for evaluating the collated data and incorporating the insights gained regarding the customers.

SAP CRM Interaction Center has numerous analytical tools that are incorporated with the interaction center manager portal. The interaction center can find all evaluations regarding channel statistics, capacity of agent groups, and progress of campaigns on the manager portal.

8.4.2 Capabilities of SAP CRM Interaction Center

The SAP CRM Interaction Center is an integrated solution providing access to all customer-facing SAP CRM Marketing, Sales, and Service functionality as well as access to the back office SAP ERP functionality. The interaction center can be integrated with other SAP and stand-alone non-SAP systems such as contact center software (like SAP Business Communications Management [BCM] or SAP-certified products from partners such as Genesys, Avaya, Cisco), knowledge management, and trouble ticketing systems, ATP systems, pricing engines, and even legacy billing systems. The interaction center provides a complete 360-degree overview of your customers, allowing you to strengthen relationships and increase loyalty and profitability.

8.4.2.1 Interaction Center Agent Desktop Productivity Tools

SAP CRM provides a set of agent desktop productivity tools designed to enhance the efficiency and effectiveness of the interaction center agents. For instance, templates are available for agents when creating e-mails or chat responses, allowing the agent to reuse standard greetings, signatures, and frequently asked questions (FAQs) instead of manually typing every e-mail. Agents have access to a knowledge base, including automatically suggested solutions that can be inserted into an e-mail or chat. Similarly, text alerts can be used to remind agents of important customer-relevant information, such as the fact that a customer is a Gold customer. Interactive scripts can be provided to agents to step through difficult or complex procedures.

The goal is to free agents from repetitive mundane tasks and to let them focus on value-added activities. Agents should spend their time helping customers or selling products, not cutting and pasting or constantly searching for the same documents all day long.

8.4.2.2 Multichannel Integration

Many interaction centers do not have multichannel integration that enables them to integrate inbound queries or outbound responses across all possible channels to provide a seamless responsiveness to the customer. For instance, an incoming caller will get routed to an available agent by the company's telephone PBX switch, but the agent would not get any visual indicator of the incoming call or details on the incoming caller.

SAP CRM supports marketing efforts both to the existing and new customers. The interaction center supports marketing efforts directed at inbound customers who contact the interaction center for service or support. After resolving the customer's issue, the system can propose relevant accessories or cross sell items that complement the customer's existing products. Telephone campaigns and outbound telemarketing lists can be set up to target new prospects. Additionally, the interaction center can also be used to qualify sales leads collected from websites, trade shows, and conferences or external lists. The interaction center is also integrated with SAP Real-Time Offer

Management allowing real-time, intelligent cross sell recommendations, retention effort, and targeted marketing messages.

SAP CRM Interaction Center supports all scenarios of customer interactions for order and follow-up through any of the interaction channels like service center, interaction center, and the Web chat. Interaction center agents can create new sales orders or pull up existing sales orders to provide customers with up-to-date shipping and delivery information or even make a change to the order. Agents can also create quotations or convert an existing quotation into an order. The SAP CRM processes are also integrated with SAP ERP allowing orders and quotations to flow freely between the two systems. Agents can create orders in SAP CRM using the interaction center and then replicate the orders to SAP ERP. Alternatively, they can manage leads, opportunities, and questions in SAP CRM but then create the actual orders in back-end SAP ERP applications (obviating the need to use the sales order capabilities of SAP CRM). Thus, the entire order management process, including pricing, could be handled using SAP ERP logic, but accessed by the agents through the interaction center.

SAP CRM Interaction Center can help companies to provide world-class customer service via customer-preferred interaction channel. Interaction center agents have access to a customer's complete information and history and can quickly pull up an order or trouble ticket to provide the customer with the most up-to-date status. Agents can also search for product information to answer customer questions. For technical issues or troubleshooting, agents can reach a knowledge base of solutions and knowledge articles and white papers; solutions can also be automatically recommended to the agent based on the problem classification or product information. Agents can provide customers with the information they need (product information, solutions, and other documents) through customer-preferred communication channel like e-mail or the Web chat. In case the customer has an issue with the shipment or an invoice, the agent can create a complaint on customer's behalf and generate follow-on tasks such as return, credit memos, or free-of-charge replacement deliveries. Finally, regarding service issues that require installation, maintenance, or repair, agents can schedule appointments for the customer based on the customer's service contract and preferred dates and times.

8.4.2.3 Shared Service Centers

Instead of having, for example, several regional IT help desks and employee interaction centers, a company can consolidate its operations to a single (operationally low cost) location and provide centralized HR and IT services. The resulting efficiency gains and cost savings are not only on account of economies of scale but also because of the business process re-engineering and elimination of redundancies. These companies centralize their back office functions such as HR, IT management, finance and accounting, facilities management, and travel management to save money and optimize resources.

SAP CRM Interaction Center provides an out-of-the-box solution for both IT help desks and employee interaction centers (EIC). The IT help desk solution leverages several features of the service ticket business transaction that were designed specifically for IT help desk scenarios, including multilevel categorization of trouble tickets, automatic suggestion of solutions based on categorization, an auto-complete feature for easy-to-resolve but frequently occurring issues such as password resets and an escalate feature for unresolved tickets. SAP also provides out-of-the-box solution for EIC that allows HR professionals to provide consistent and personalized services.

8.4.2.4 Operations and Administration

SAP CRM Interaction Center provides managers with real-time reports and dashboards to monitor things such as queue levels and agent behavior as well as historic reports to analyze information such as service ticket volume and resolution times. Managers can pull a report to see how many high-priority service tickets were reported the previous month and how many of them were still open. Companies can create their own reports and analytics using tools provided with SAP NetWeaver BI.

8.5 SAP CRM Partner Channel Management

SAP CRM provides companies a comprehensive channel management solution that enables them to efficiently build relationships with partners and supports them in selling more successfully and servicing the end customers better. SAP's strengths in the areas of classic CRM with marketing, sales, and service (see sections earlier) and e-business (see Chapter 9 "SAP E-Business Applications") have been expanded to enable partner collaborations.

Not all companies sell directly to their customers; many businesses rely on their partners to sell their products. The partners take over responsibility for selling to the end customers and often provide a range of additional services; this is generally termed as indirect or multitier channel sales. The partnership spectrum ranges from independent sales agents, dealers, value-added resellers, distributors, wholesalers, or retailers to importers, exporters, and service providers, all of whom play a critical role in the sales efforts of the brand owner. The relationships with customers depend to a large extent on the partners and are generally formed and maintained outside the reach of the brand manager's area of influence. When customers buy the company's products from channel partners, the customer's impression of the company is based solely on the customer's interaction with the channel partner. Therefore, it is crucial for the brand manager not only how the sales can be ensured or increased through the multitier sales channel but also how the indirect sales channel is managed. For instance, what must a brand owner do to ensure that the partners correctly represent the brand, identify potential customers early, process leads and opportunities precisely, sell the products competently, provide high-quality customer service, and guarantee a high level of customer satisfaction while simultaneously also realizing a high resale rate?

SAP CRM Channel Management covers the following areas:

1. Partner management includes functions for managing partner relationships throughout the partner life cycle:
    a. Partner recruitment
    b. Partner profiling and segmentation
    c. Partner training and certification
    d. Partner compensation
    e. Partner planning and forecasting
2. Channel marketing is for gaining customers and increasing sales through indirect channel:
    a. Partner communication
    b. Catalog management
    c. Campaign management
    d. Lead management
    e. Channel marketing funds

3. Channel Sales helps partners to increase the quantity of their sales and to sell more effectively:
   a. Account and Control Management
   b. Activity management
   c. Opportunity management
   d. Channel sales analytics
4. Channel Service ensures a constantly high level of service by providing partners with access to service functions, expert knowledge, and problem-solving help:
   a. Knowledge management
   b. Live support
   c. Service order management
   d. Complaints and Return management
5. Channel Commerce or Partner Order Management:
   a. Quotation and order management
   b. Interactive selling and configuration
   c. POS and channel inventory
   d. Distributed order management
6. Partner and Channel Analytics

In the following section, we describe partner management as the other areas have been covered earlier for the classic CRM.

8.5.1 Partner Management

SAP CRM enables companies to manage channel partner relationships more efficiently throughout the partner life cycle and increase profitability:

8.5.1.1 Partner Recruitment

SAP CRM provides tools for locating and recruiting channel partners. Once the company has short-listed potential partners, the partner recruitment functionalities allow interested prospective partners to fill out an online application on the company's website. The completed form is then forwarded via automated e-mail workflow to the concerned channel manager. The channel manager can scrutinize the application and then communicate the decision to the prospective partner.

8.5.1.2 Partner Profiling and Segmentation

SAP CRM enables brand owners to segment partners based on partner type, industry focus, and competencies so that they can customize and target communications, training, marketing efforts, and so on. Brand owners or channel managers can dispatch sales leads and opportunities to the best-suited channel partner based on factors such as geographic region, industry, size, and sales conversion success rates.

8.5.1.3 Partner Training and Certification

Companies need a way to ensure that partners are effectively educated and prepared to represent their product and services. SAP CRM enables brand owners to provide partners with online access to training courses, curriculum, and registration. They can target courses and content that is most relevant to the right type of partners. They can track course enrollment, participation, and completion rates for the various partners.

Furthermore, brand owners can create, target, and manage certification programs for channel partners and track status and completion at employee level. The number of employees certified for products and services can be linked to the partner profile for use in partner analysis, partner segmentation, and lead distribution.

8.5.1.4 Partner Compensation

SAP CRM enables the setup of partner compensation planning for different partner types and individual partners. It also calculates compensation based on posted sales data and also provides a compensation simulator to demonstrate how much compensation partners can earn, if the deal is closed. This simulator also provides a look at compensation settlements in which partners can view the earned compensation as also the payment dates.

8.5.1.5 Partner Planning and Forecasting

SAP CRM provides tools that enable companies to plan and manage their sales and channel strategy. Brand owners can set annual goals, targets, and measurements as well as track and measure partner progress against those goals. This supports both collaborative channel forecasting and pipeline channel forecasting. With collaborative channel forecasting, the brand owner can plan and forecast sales by partner segment or product line, including *what-if* analysis. Pipeline forecasting can be done by region, product, partner type, and so on, including forecasting channel revenues and funnel analysis.

8.6 Industry-Specific Solutions

SAP CRM supports more than 25 different vertical industries. SAP offers industry-specific solutions for a variety of manufacturing industries (such as automotive, chemical, consumer goods, high tech, oil and gas, pharmaceuticals, and engineering, construction, and operation) and service industries (such as banking, financial services, insurance, leasing, retail, media professional services, telecommunications, and utilities).

Deregulation, privatization, and technological innovation have dramatically altered the global business landscape. In this evolving marketplace, companies are competing to find and manage a sustainable competitive position. The winners will recognize that their only lasting competitive advantage is knowledge about their customers, leveraged throughout the enterprise. SAP is committed to delivering software solutions that allows its customers to build and exploit this competitive advantage. SAP provides unrivaled breadth and depth of sales, marketing, and customer service functionality. SAP industry-specific solutions provide comprehensive front-office functionality, customized to address the business requirements of various industries.

In most industries, vast amounts of valuable customer information remain isolated in back-office systems, largely inaccessible to potential users. SAP's vision has been to provide sales, marketing, and customer service professionals with immediate access to customer information residing in diverse back-office systems and to enable them to leverage this information into increased profitability and customer satisfaction. SAP's flexible architecture and standard-based integration tools, which facilitate rapid, seamless integration with the back office, make this vision a reality.

SAP industry-specific solutions are the result of a collaborative effort with customers and integration partners to address-specific business challenges using SAP's state-of-the-art information technology. Each industry solution leverages SAP's unparalleled front-office functionality, preconfigured to reflect industry-specific terminology, required functionality, and process flows. In contrast to the generic point solutions offered by competitive software providers that require extensive customization, SAP's industry-specific solutions deliver comprehensive out-of-the-box functionality tailored to unique industry requirements.

1. Discrete industries
   a. SAP for Aerospace and Defense
   b. SAP for Automotive
   c. SAP for Engineering, Construction, and Operation
   d. SAP for Industrial Machinery and Components
   e. SAP for High Tech
2. Process industries
   a. SAP for Chemicals
   b. SAP for Mill Products
   c. SAP for Pharmaceuticals
   d. SAP for Oil and Gas
   e. SAP for mining
3. Financial services
   a. SAP for Banking
   b. SAP for Insurance
4. Consumer industries
   a. SAP for Consumer Products
   b. SAP for Retail
5. Service industries
   a. SAP for Professional Services
   b. SAP for Media
   c. SAP for Service Providers
   d. SAP for Telecommunications
   e. SAP for Utilities
6. Public services
   a. SAP for Health Care
   b. SAP for Higher Education and Research
   c. SAP for Public Sector

8.7 SAP CRM Mobile Applications

SAP CRM Mobile options allow field sales professionals and service technicians to access the latest customer information. Sales professionals can check the sales pipeline and forecasts from airport, hotel, or customer site. Field service professionals can view appointments and schedules, check availability of service parts, and perform technical analysis and troubleshooting from an off-line mobile device in the field.

Mobile applications can add value in the following manner:

- *Direct availability of current information*: Sales professionals in the field require current information on products, prices, offers, and conditions. Similarly, central sales and marketing departments are focused on current customers and buying behavior. Mobile applications enable a communication channel for automatically providing all relevant information to both parties.
- *More flexible work process and working conditions*: Mobile applications enable sales professional to access commercial applications independent of the time and location.
- *Fewer interruptions and delays to work processes*: Mobile applications enable eliminating many steps in the manual processes, rendering the processes to become faster and more efficient.
- *Increased return on investment (ROI) due to better use of existing systems*: In addition to the usage in the office, the latest information can also be accessed by additional professionals in the field rendering more effective use of available information without incurring additional costs (other than those of the access devices).

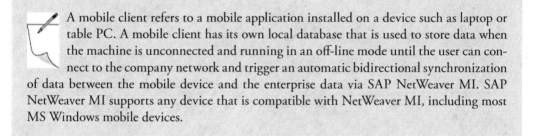

A mobile client refers to a mobile application installed on a device such as laptop or table PC. A mobile client has its own local database that is used to store data when the machine is unconnected and running in an off-line mode until the user can connect to the company network and trigger an automatic bidirectional synchronization of data between the mobile device and the enterprise data via SAP NetWeaver MI. SAP NetWeaver MI supports any device that is compatible with NetWeaver MI, including most MS Windows mobile devices.

SAP CRM Mobile applications allow field sales and service professionals to access SAP applications and customer data from a variety of devices and operational modes, including connected (off-line) mode for laptop or tablet PC or connected (off-line) mode for handheld devices such as PDAs and smartphones or a real-time online version for select laptops and handheld devices such as Blackberry.

8.7.1 SAP CRM Mobile Sales

8.7.1.1 Mobile Sales Laptop

The Mobile Sales Laptop solution provides the most comprehensive functionality of the three alternatives including contact management and activity management. It provides a full-feature, off-line solution for notebooks or tablet PCs that are only occasionally connected to a network.

The Mobile Sales Laptop solution offers

- Account management
  - Account planning
- Activity management
  - Calendar and task management

- Product search and display
- Opportunity management
- Contract management
- Sales order management
- Service order management
- Complaint management
- Campaign and trade promotion management
- Shelf management
- Territory management
- Time and travel management
- Sales analytics

8.7.1.2 Mobile Sales Handheld

Mobile Sales Handheld provides the necessary tools to retrieve customer account information, access product and pricing information, manage customer visits and calls, manage opportunities, and create quotations and orders. However, due to limited screen real estate, memory, and processing power, handheld devices support relatively light sales applications and do not offer the data processing functionalities of a laptop or tablet PC solution. While sales professionals can perform basic sales-related tasks, there is no support for (say) contract management or analytics.

The Mobile Sales Handheld solution offers

- Account management
  - Account planning
  - Search for, display, and retrieve customer data
- Activity management
  - Calendar and task management
- Product search and display
  - Search for and display products from a product catalog
- Opportunity management
- Sales order management
- Service order management
- Complaint management

8.7.1.3 Mobile Sales Online

SAP CRM Mobile Sales Online solution provides sales professionals with direct, real-time online access to SAP CRM functionality via smartphones such as RIM BlackBerry, Microsoft Pocket PC, Nokia Series 80, and Siemens SK65 (with built-in BlackBerry).

The Mobile Sales Handheld solution offers

- Account management
- Activity management
- Opportunity management (header data only)
- Contract management (header data only)
- Sales order management (header data only)
- Analytics

8.7.2 SAP CRM Mobile Service

Service technicians have a need for immediate access to the SAP CRM system from the field. Engineers need to record the time and costs spent on an issue; lacking access to SAP CRM may necessitate writing it down and entering it into the system when they are back in the office—which increases the possibility of omissions, errors, and incomplete entries. Similarly, if service technicians don't have access to the SAP CRM system from the field, delivery of spare parts is delayed because the technicians must wait until he or she is back in the office to place the order. Even the most basic tasks, such as rescheduling a repair or updating an appointment in the calendar, are not achievable without access to the SAP CRM system.

SAP CRM Mobile Service is primarily available via an occasionally connected (off-line) version for handheld device (i.e., available with SAP CRM release 4.0); however, this offering is not available or supported in the subsequent releases:

1. *Mobile service laptop*: The Mobile Service Laptop solution provides service technicians with all of the information and tools they need to resolve a customer's on-site service issues and accurately record their work in the field using an off-line laptop or tablet PC.
   The service technicians can perform various tasks directly on the laptop computer:
   a. Technicians have access to their calendar and inbox to view appointments, e-mails, and pending work orders.
   b. Technicians can pull up service contracts and service orders.
   c. Technicians can view a structured overview of all the equipment and products installed at the customer site.
   d. Technicians can search for product documentation, installation/repair guides, or technical procedures via the knowledge management tool.
2. *Mobile service handheld*: SAP CRM Service Handheld enables service technicians perform various tasks like
   a. Search for, display, and update customer data
   b. Search for and display products from a product catalog
   c. Manage personal tasks and calendar
   d. Create e-mails
   e. Display and create service orders
   f. Access service confirmation
   g. Create complaints

8.8 Summary

In this chapter, we familiarized ourselves with the main components of SAP CRM Applications including Marketing, Sales, Service, Interaction Center, Partner Channel Management, and Mobile Applications.

In the next chapter, we look at SAP's e-Business Applications and the corresponding functionality.

Chapter 9

SAP E-Business Applications

E-Business is the relocation of internal and external business processes to the Internet. Customer-led E-Business has been highly publicized due to the astronomical market valuations attained by hundreds of dot-com companies as well as the unprecedented amounts of venture capital attracted by them during the period of Internet boom. Research studies suggest that the business-to-business (B2B) segment will prove to be much more significant in terms of the overall E-business impact by an order of magnitude. However, there is no denying of the fact that the Internet revolution was launched in the business-to-consumer (B2C) arena. SAP's E-Business suit of products, called SAP eBusiness Applications, fully addresses the requirements of the entire market spanning the entire spectrum of B2C, B2B, and B2E scenarios. In this chapter, we discuss the functionality and features of the SAP eBusiness Applications.

9.1 What Is E-Business?

E-Business refers to an enterprise that has reengineered itself to conduct its business via the Internet and Web. Successful enterprises need to reconceptualize the very nature of their business.

As customers begin to buy via the Internet and enterprises rush to use the Internet to create new operational efficiencies, most enterprises seek to update their business strategies. Enterprises survey the changing environment and then modify their company strategies to accommodate these changes. This involves major changes in the way companies do business, including changes in marketing, sales, service, product delivery, and even manufacturing and inventory. Changed strategies will entail changed business processes that, in turn, imply changed software systems or, better still, software systems that are changeable!

Table 9.1 lists the various business models that an enterprise can employ to retain, leverage, and enhance its customer capital. Table 9.2 lists the various pricing mechanisms that an enterprise can employ to retain, leverage, and enhance its customer capital.

Table 9.1 Business Models

Name	Description	Benefits to Customer	Benefits to Enterprise	Source of Value
Collaboration platform	Collaboration, cooperation, and coordination between enterprises	Collaboration on specific functions, design, and engineering Virtual team of consultants	Low-cost high-value activities.	Membership fee Fee per use Charging for specialist tools for design, workflow, and document management
Information brokers, trust, and other services	Adding value to the colossal amount of information on the Internet	Up-to-date, quality information available whenever and wherever it is needed Information management services for ascertaining authenticity and accuracy	Selling information search results. Selling customer profiling information. Selling business opportunities. Providing Investment advice. Providing trust certificates.	Subscription fee Service fee Software sales Consultancy fee
Virtual communities	Medium of communication between members	Communities of common interests Sharing of issues, solutions, work-arounds, future requirements	Establish customer loyalty. Receive customer feedback. Join third-party marketplaces.	Membership fee Advertisement fee
E-shop	Seeking orders Commonly for regular goods, groceries, and consumables	Lower price Wider choice of products and services Better comparative information Easy selection Buying and delivery 24 × 7 availability Personalized and customized	Low-cost option. Increased sales. Advertisement. Global presence.	Lower cost Newer sales channel

E-procurement	Seeking vendors Electronic tendering Electronic procurement of goods and services	Wider choice of vendors Reduced cost of procurement Reduced price Better quality Improved delivery Electronic negotiation and contracting Collaborative work on specification Convenience Faster turnaround	More tendering opportunities. Global reach/presence. Lower cost of tendering. Small companies can share/apportion tender work. Collaborating tendering work.	Reduction of procurement cost More cost-effective offers
E-auction	Electronic bidding	Multimedia presentation Integration of bidding with contracting, payment, and delivery Increased efficiency and faster turnaround Bid on smaller quantities and lower value Reduced purchasing overhead	Increased efficiency and faster turnaround. New channel for global presence.	Selling technology solution Transaction fee Advertising Reduced surplus stock Better utilization of the production capacity Lower sales overhead
E-mall	Collection of E-shops with common functionalities such as common customer database, common target customer segments, combined marketing campaigns, and promotions	Common guaranteed payment method Value added via establishment of a virtual community Convenience of inquiring on related e-shops	Opportunities for sale of supporting technologies. Cross sales of other e-shops. Advertising space. Brand reinforcement. Ease of setting up Web front ends. Provide sophisticated payment methods. Benefits from up-selling of competing brands. Ease of outsourcing Web-based operations.	

(*Continued*)

Table 9.1 (*Continued*) Business Models

Name	Description	Benefits to Customer	Benefits to Enterprise	Source of Value
Internet Service Provider (ISP)	Providers of infrastructure and attendant services for management, operations, and support	Easy access to Internet services	Advertising space. Collaboration with related companies. Direct access to customers for direct marketing.	Subscription fees Surround services like telephony
Portal	Integrated collection of services providing a seamless and compelling customer experience	A one-stop shop A unified experience bound by a common purpose	Provision of common services. Portal as a distinct brand.	Membership fee Advertisement Transaction fee Service fee
Third-party marketplace	Third-party marketing Uniform transaction support to multiple businesses	Automatic benefits of branding, ordering, secure transactions, payments, logistics, delivery, etc.	ISP can offer Web application building services. Bank can offer transaction services.	Joining fee Service fee Transaction fee
Value chain service provider	Specific services spanning across the value chain such as e-payment and logistics	Indirect benefits via efficiencies gained in the enterprises' cost and processes	Beneficial especially to the Banks. Management of inventory, stock, production, etc.	Service fee Percentage of transaction value
Value chain integrator	Integrating across the complete value chain	Beneficial to customers of third-party marketplaces	A dynamic marketplace with continually changing constituent partners.	Consultancy fee Percentage of the transaction value

Table 9.2   Pricing Models

Name	Description
E-Commerce	The sale of real and electronic merchandise through the medium of an electronic shop via browsable catalog.
Subscription	The customer pays for a predetermined amount of money for use of the service; the ownership of the merchandise is not transferred to the customer.
Charges on per use basis	The customers pay each time they use the service such as video on demand; ownership of the merchandise is not transferred to the customer.
Charges on usage basis	The customer pays based on the duration of usage as in the case of playing interactive games; ownership of the merchandise is not transferred to the customer.
Advertisement	The customer indirectly pays via interested vendor companies purchasing advertising space on the Website to target the visiting customers.
Sponsorship	This is akin to the advertisement model except that the space is purchased only by the sponsor companies and advertises only their messages.
Public support	The public interest Websites are typically supported by donations from general public and social and government institutions.
Indirect	The customer pays indirectly not for use of the website but indirectly via the use of telephony, search, survey response, etc.

SIGNIFICANCE OF THE INTERNET

It is not easy to speculate on the reasons that the Internet is begetting the revolutionary changes that we have witnessed in the past few years. What gives it the power to drive the massive changes that have been witnessed in the last 5 years, while similar changes in the past have taken ages to sweep across the globe?

In the earlier book *Implementing SAP*, I had proposed that the fundamental reason is that a medium is always more powerful than a message. It may be that, at certain stages in history, messages (and their messengers) have had a determining effect on the course of history, but these passages have been few and far between. The impact of the medium has always been more powerful and long lasting than any message. Throughout history, the powerful have always recognized this truth and have concentrated on controlling a medium as the most powerful facet of governance, rather than becoming martyrs as revolutionaries with a new message to tell to the world. The print medium has outlasted all ideological and technological revolutions seen in the past centuries since the dawn of civilization. In one form or another, this has been a known fact in all fields of human endeavor, but Marshall McLuhan brought this out much more forcefully for the electronic media in the middle of the last century.

Computers were always positioned as both the message and media of the new era, but it is clear that right from the beginning, the Internet was a medium. Considering that the Internet is not governed or dictated by any specific authority and is one of the most democratic of institutions, one can be absolutely sure that the Internet is destined to herald the next major cultural revolution in human history.

Additionally, underlying all human endeavors lies the quest for immortality, the desire to transcend space and time forever. It may seem that this is only the concern of spiritualists and philosophers or mathematicians, relativists, and other scientists. Similarly, it may seem that all commercial endeavors are driven by the pursuit of money, but that could be wrong! At the base of all commercial transactions lie the fundamental concerns for transcending space and time!

All major technological advances, be they discoveries or inventions, which had lasting impact on the future course of human development, had to do with one of the following:

■ Sliding space and/or time in a direction that satisfied the basic urge to transcend space and time in practical terms and in a direction that was convenient.
■ Altering space and/or time, that is, expanding or contracting space and/or time, to satisfy the basic urge to transcend space and time again in practical terms and in a direction that was convenient. Although such effects are not unknown in physical sciences, here we are referring to effects that are psychological and experiential in nature.

Table 9.3 shows the technological advancements witnessed in the last century interpreted in this new light. In the table, the legend used is given as follows:

Sliding Space
    +ve Bringing Near
    –ve Taking afar
Sliding Time
    +ve Bringing Near
    –ve Taking afar
Altering Space
    +ve Compressing Space
    –ve Expanding Space
Altering time
    +ve Compressing Time
    –ve Expanding Time

For instance, telephones permit you to converse with a person as if he or she were close (Sliding Space +ve and Altering Space +ve) and without waiting for a time in the future when you can meet him or her in person (Sliding Time +ve). It is a simple grid, but it enables us to understand in a powerful way the essential unity behind the technological advances in the last couple of centuries. It also gives rationale for the difference in the degree of impact that these technological inventions have had on human life and thought. It is evident that Internet's power on the consumer's mind comes from its unprecedented facility to slide and

Table 9.3 Technological Advances in the Last Century

Description	Space Sliding +ve	Space Sliding –ve	Space Altering +ve	Space Altering –ve	Time Sliding +ve	Time Sliding –ve	Time Altering +ve	Time Altering –ve
Paper	X	X	X	X	X	X	X	X
Vehicles		X						X
Telephones	X		X		X			
Voice Mail	X	X	X		X	X		X
Photographs	X	X	X			X		
Transmitted Pictures	X	X	X	X	X	X	X	
Motion Pictures		X	X		X	X		
Audio/Video CDs	X	X	X		X			X
Audio/Video CD Players	X	X		X	X			X
Deepfreezers					X			
Microwaves					X		X	
Credit Card Payments	X	X			X			
Telephone Charge Cards	X				X			
Computers			X	X	X	X	X	
Networks	X	X		X	X			X
Internet	X	X	X	X	X	X	X	X

alter both space and time to a degree that is unlikely to be surpassed for quite some time in the future and is matched only by that of printed paper.

Frances Cairncross coined the phrase "the death of distance" to describe the way in which the Internet helps in eliminating geographical constraints. In a 1995 article on telecommunications, she had predicted that "the death of distance as a determinant of the cost of communications will probably be the single most important economic force shaping society in the first half of the next century."

9.1.1 Basic E-Business Strategy Patterns

Patricia Seybold was the first person to point out that the Internet economy was first and foremost a *customer* economy because of the power that it gave to customers in terms of the information on competitive products and real-term pricing that it made available to them via any channel of interaction of their immediate choice.

The customer economy heralded the following:

- Significance of the customer relationships in a way that they had never done before
- Fundamental strategy of making it easy for customers to do business with the enterprise

Success in the customer economy will demand that companies manage their enterprises by and for customer value—they will have to use customer lifetime value (CLV) as a strategic management tool. Company's source of investor value will increasingly be based on the value of their customer franchise, the lifetime customer value of their present and future customers (discussed in Chapter 15, Section 15.4.1 "Time Value of Customers and Shareholder Value").

Companies will have to focus on the branded customer experience whenever they interact with the company's products via any touch point (Web, e-mail, phone, or face to face) and across any channel (retail, dealer, agent, or broker). To win in the customer economy, companies will have to build and sustain an exquisite branded experience and to measure and monitor what matters to customers in the real term that may get tracked not unlike financial information and share price information at present. Just as customer satisfaction indexes are by now well established as good indicators of profitability, in the future, investment decisions may get made based on the changing values of the customer metrics and value indexes.

In the customer economy, the employees' performance-linked pay may be based on such customer metrics that assess achievement of customer satisfaction and customer loyalty goals like

- Growth in active number of customers
- Customers' commitment to the company's products, strategy, and vision
- Customers' propensity to defect
- Customer retention
- Customer referrals
- Customer acquisition costs

The concept of pattern was introduced by Christopher Alexander in the late 1970s in the field of architecture. A pattern describes a commonly occurring solution that generates decidedly successful outcomes (see Chapter 7, Section 7.1.3.1 "Patterns of Enterprise Agility").

Listed in the following are the patterns learned from e-business efforts in the past few years:

9.1.1.1 Target the Right Customers

Some of the steps involved with this strategy pattern are as follows:

- *Know customers and prospects*: This involves identifying the customers and then knowing as much about them as possible.
- *Identify profitable customers*: This involves looking not only at the revenue but also at the costs to service particular customers or customer segments.

- *Decide on which customers to attract*: This involves deciding on which existing customers should be prevented from defecting and the new customers that should be attracted and engaged.
- *Locate customers influencing the key purchases in any home or enterprise*: This involves identifying, communicating, and engaging them directly, for instance, inviting into community forums discussed later.
- *Discover which customers generate referrals*: This involves identifying especially their wants, delivering solutions, and measuring their levels of satisfaction. Repeat customers that are profitable are the best barometers of *getting it right*.
- *Differentiate clearly between customers, partners, and stakeholders*: This involves focusing and caring about the actual consumers:

9.1.1.1.1 Know the Customer

The following are some of the steps involved with this strategy pattern:

- Know the customer's business context.
- Know the customer's needs and wants.
- Know the customer's preferences.
- Know the customer's prior interactions and history.

9.1.1.1.2 Care about the Customer's Wants

Here are some of the steps involved with this strategy pattern:

- Nurture deep commitment to customers and their outcomes.
- Enhance mindshare and market space as against market share.
- Create a customer-centric culture.
- Move from the earlier product-centric approach to a customer-centric approach.

9.1.1.1.3 Value the Customer's Time

Some of the steps involved with this strategy pattern are as follows:

- Streamline decision making.
- Offer ubiquitous and convenient access.
- Design using customer scenarios.

9.1.1.1.4 Measure What Matters to Customers

Some of the steps involved with this strategy pattern are listed here:

- Determine customer's outcomes.
- Understand the customer's context.
- Identify key customer scenarios within customer life-cycle stages.
- Determine what tasks matter the most to customers.
- Monitor customer scenarios in real term and take effective action.

9.1.1.2 Own the Customer's Total Experience

The following are some of the steps involved with this strategy pattern:

■ *Deliver a consistent, high-value, and enriching experience*: The company's branding should include not only the product or the service but also the actual *experience* of using them.

■ *Value customer's time and convenience*: This involves focusing on the customer's convenience for locating, selecting, evaluating, and ordering for the company's offerings, rather than the convenience of the company or its partners for manufacturing, distributing, and delivering them.

■ *Partner for delivering consistent quality and service*: The customer, especially repeat customers, should be assured of and be able to avail of the same seamless experience whenever or wherever they chose to opt for the company's offerings.

■ *Personalize and celebrate the customer's individuality*: This involves leveraging on the information from the customer directly or from the customer's profile to tailor the customers experience to suit their preferences and expectations. This may be related with the look and feel, navigation, types of products, range of prices, special options, and so on.

■ *Give customers control over their experience*: This involves enabling customers the flexibility to customize even the personalization factors dynamically:

9.1.1.2.1 Deliver Personalized Service

Some of the steps involved with this strategy pattern are to

■ Enable customers to specify and modify their profiles
■ Customize information presentation and offers based on customer's profiles
■ Provide appropriate service and information based on customer's needs
■ Give access to their transaction histories

9.1.1.2.2 Deliver a Seamless Customer Experience across Channels and Touch Points

Some of the steps involved with this strategy pattern are to

■ Create a multi–touch point strategy
■ Deal with channel conflict
■ Integrate channel partners
■ Share customer information

9.1.1.2.3 Provide a 360-Degree View of the Customer Relationship

Some of the steps involved with this strategy pattern are the following:

■ Provide one-stop shopping for the customer to enable them to access information, perform transactions, and request service across all the product lines from your organizations.

■ Improve the company's *memory* about the customer's interactions with the company by consolidating all the information about each customer's account and relationship in one single, easily accessible place. The company must support and encourage sharing of information.

- Ensure that everyone in the company dealing with the customer has access to the complete picture of the customer.
- Put the technical infrastructure essential to provide a 360-degree view of the customer.

9.1.1.2.4 Streamline Business Processes That Impact the Customer

Here are some of the steps involved with this strategy pattern:

- Identify the actual end customer.
- Streamline processes from the end customer's point of view.
- Streamline the processes for the other key stakeholders.
- Continuously improve the processes based on the customer feedback.
- Give everyone involved a clear view of the process.

9.1.1.2.5 Establish a Customer-Centric E-Business Architecture

Enumerated here are some of the steps involved with this strategy pattern:

- Enable multiple touch points.
- Enable multiple channels for interaction.
- Integrate or interoperate multiple applications.
- Integrate or interface multiple customer and transaction databases.
- Integrate or interoperate with multiple partners.
- Make it easy for customers to do business with you anytime, anywhere, and via any device.

9.1.1.3 Foster Customer Loyalty

The following are some of the steps involved with this strategy pattern:

- Increase the customer base.
- Increase the tenure, within the total customer life cycle, with the company.
- Measure the retention power.
- Measure the customer revenue.
- Measure customer costs.
- Measure customer profitability.
- Evaluate defection and loyalty.

9.1.1.3.1 Help Customers Do Their Jobs

Given here are some of the steps involved with this strategy pattern:

- Establish an understanding of how the customers do their jobs.
- Continuously refine the enterprise business processes to make it easier for the customers to do their jobs.

- Give customers the tools to assist in making the purchasing decision.
- Prepare the bills as desired by the customer.
- Enable customers to satisfy their own customer or target entities.

9.1.1.3.2 Let Customers Help Themselves

Listed here are some of the steps involved with this strategy pattern:

- Let customers help themselves to access information and perform transactions online.
- Let customers check on the status of orders, pay or adjust bills, and access related services.
- Let customers interact using whatever channel or media of communication they like: telephone, voice response, fax, mail, and so on.
- Give customers the ability to customize the company's offerings to their requirements and preferences.

9.1.1.3.3 Foster Community

Some of the steps involved with this strategy pattern are specified:

- Attract and encourage customers to become valuable members of customer communities focused on specific areas of interest.
- Facilitate introduction of the customer to others with common interests.
- Reinforce the understanding and commitment on common standards, terminology, and values.
- Enable members of customers to share the issues, resolutions, and experiences of using the company's offerings.

9.1.2 E-Business Challenges

The challenges of E-Business are as follows:

1. *Business fit*: Most systems are designed as point solutions for intraenterprise needs. But as we have seen in Chapter 7, the processes are not necessarily confined to an enterprise alone but can extend to incorporate the business partners as well as the customers. This fundamental shift from enterprise-focused to primarily customer-focused multienterprise spanning business processes is the most fundamental challenge faced by any E-Business.
2. *Time to market*: Because of the rapid changes in the market, it is essential that the E-Business systems are able to adopt themselves quickly to the changes in the market environment and respond with competitive offerings and solutions.
3. *Cost-effectiveness*: However, this ability to change should be achievable in a cost-effective manner without compromising on the quality of the design, maintainability, and upgradability of the E-Business solutions.
4. *Quality*: Since E-Business solutions are targeted at thousands of anonymous users, its design, at both the user-interface and architecture levels, needs to be usable, intuitive, reliable, robust, and consistent for enhancing the quality of the customer' experience.
5. *Adaptability*: E-Business solutions must enable business innovation and respond to strategic opportunities while at the same time being able to interface or integrate readily with the existing systems and databases.

6. *Scalability*: E-Business should be able to address the basic E-Business paradox—the more visitors that you have, the more successful you are; but the more successful you are, the more venerable you are! A crashed Website at a critical juncture and the resulting customer ire can jeopardize the very existence of your business. The success of E-Business Websites hinges on their ability to attract customers and prospects, but if the deluge of customers does materialize, woe the Website that cannot service them.

7. *Integration*: E-Business solutions need to interface or integrate with existing systems both Web applications and back-end enterprise systems across heterogeneous architectures and protocols to enable continual returns on earlier investments.

9.1.3 E-Business Applications for a Customer-Centric World

Internet-supported Customer Relationship Management is rapidly emerging as the *killer app* of the Web of the 2000s. The Internet has enabled a dramatic reduction in the cost of transactions and interactions between the enterprise and its customers. Online customers expect shorter sale cycles, personalized information, quicker resolution of issues, and added value at each stage of the transaction.

E-Business applications like SAP CRM provide a standard-based Web architecture for information, process, and application integration so that the enterprise can integrate information and processes across marketing, commerce, and service. The enterprise can integrate existing databases, legacy applications, and systems to create a virtual centralized information repository so that the company can market, sell, and service its offerings more effectively. And the Web architecture's scalability and flexibility enable it to be more responsive leading to rapid growth. E-Business applications, like SAP CRM, are a fully integrated suite of applications for customer relationship management (CRM) and closely related applications for partnership relationship management (PRM) and employee relationship management (ERM), all based on a common web architecture. They help enterprises by providing all these three key functionalities to fully align their partners, employees, and customer touch points, processes, and channels around the goal of maximizing the value of customer relationships:

9.1.3.1 Business-to-Customer (B2C) Applications

Historically, it was the B2C applications that launched the Internet revolution by extending the reach of the organization directly to the consumer market. B2C applications were typically referred to as e-Commerce applications and involved credit or debit payments. Over time, B2C applications have matured to enable organizations to identify, select, acquire, and retain customers more effectively. By providing a centralized repository of customer data captured from all customer interactions across all channels and touch points, B2C applications enable organizations to maintain an ongoing and seamless dialog with its customers regardless of when, where, or how the interactions occur. Companies are able to understand, anticipate, and respond to customer needs and are able to do so more effectively and efficiently over time. CRMs like SAP CRM give managers better visibility into market dynamics and customer demand by providing real-time views of the customer activity.

9.1.3.2 Business-to-Business (B2B) Applications

These applications employ Internet technologies to link one enterprise with another, many of whom are traditional brick-and-mortar companies that have been doing business together for a time, using direct connection technologies like Electronic Data Interchange (EDI) to trade with each other. B2B or related Partnership Relation Management (PRM) applications allow enterprises to manage their business partner's ecosystem as a virtual extension of their sales, marketing, and service organizations. Enterprises can maximize their partners' efficiency and productivity by ensuring that their partners' incentives, resources, and objectives are fully aligned with those of the enterprise. We discuss channel enablement solution in the next section.

9.1.3.3 Business-to-Employee (B2E) Applications

These applications typically involve internal business processes that are moved to the Internet specifically for the benefit of employees that are remotely located. Enterprises face the problems of their employees not being fully aligned with the organization's focus on customers. B2E or the related Enterprise Relationship Management applications help organizations to rapidly communicate the corporate policies and decisions to the entire workforce, mobilize employees to execute those decisions, and monitor workforce performance in real time. As employees are able to perform their job more effectively, organizations benefit from increased employee satisfaction and, hence, increased customer satisfaction (as happier and better-informed employees provide better customer service).

The importance of referring to the original SAP ECC 6.x, SAP NetWeaverand SAP CRM 200x documentation corresponding to the version of your installation cannot be overemphasized. What we have presented in this chapter are the essential details of the various components of SAP E-Business applications. However, this chapter is not intended as a replacement for the colossal amount of instructive documentation, guidelines, checklists, templates, samples, questionnaires, and so forth provided and recommended for use by SAP. Those are well-proven instruments, and for an actual project, it is highly recommended that you procure the version of the documentation corresponding to the version of your installation and use it in conjunction with the implementation project.

9.2 SAP CRM Web Channel Enablement Solution

SAP E-Business is a comprehensive suite of Web-based products that allow enterprises to leverage the Web as the basic communication channel to acquire new customers and enhance relationships with the existing ones.

SAP E-Business includes the following components:

- SAP E-Marketing
- SAP E-Commerce
- SAP E-Service
- SAP Web Channel Analytics

SAP E-Business enables enterprises to accrue all the benefits entailed in the usage of packaged applications, including profitability, lower software applications, maintenance costs, ongoing enhancements, and technical support. SAP E-Business provides a comprehensive out-of-the-box functionality, scalable Web-based product architecture, flexible application customization capabilities, and a solution that is built on current and emerging Internet and Web computing standards.

9.2.1 Salient Features

SAP E-Business Applications are a leading example of comprehensive and world-class prebuilt applications that are scalable, configurable, integrable, readily customizable, and easily upgradable. With SAP CRM applications, customers, field sales, service professionals, call center agents, and channel partners can use a uniform customer management architecture that delivers a consistent, integrated store of business-related information and a compelling interface that meets the needs of all of these constituencies.

SAP eBusiness Applications have the following outstanding characteristics:

1. *Web-based architecture*: Enables geographically dispersed users to access comprehensive functionality through their web browser with no software installed on the client.
2. *Rapid development and deployment*: Enables complete application versioning for maintenance revisions and automated deployment strategies for rapid and continuous E-Business site customization.
3. *Support for all channels*: Enables enterprises to coordinate and deploy sophisticated multi-tiered distribution and support strategies across all channels simultaneously. SAP E-Business delivers a suite of applications built on a singular set of objects and a common set of business logic valid across multiple interaction channels. Thus, it provides support across the entire spectrum of front office including Web-based sales, marketing, and service, field sales and service, indirect sales, and traditional marketing, call centers, and customer service.
4. *Support for multiple platforms*: Enables users to select the platform of choice among Web browser–based thin clients, connected clients, mobile clients, and handheld computer clients.
5. *Comprehensive interfaces*: Enables transaction to process in real term and reliably across systems by supporting functional, high-performance, and maintainable integration with intra- and interenterprise applications including those of channel partners and third-party service providers.
6. *Robust middle tier*: Enables flexible and scalable support for large numbers of concurrent users, workflow and process automation, data visibility and security, data synchronization, application integration, and other key server processes.
7. *Customizable yet automatically upgradable software*: Enables enterprises to customize the E-Business applications to conform to their specific business practices, yet benefit from the technological advances and functional enhancements of the corresponding software upgrades.
8. *High performances, scalability, and availability of functionality*: Enables support of high-volume transaction E-Business sites accessed by thousands to even millions of users on a 24 × 7 basis.
9. *Global support*: Enables satisfying the demanding multilingual, multiple currency, and localization requirements of particular E-Business implementations.

9.2.2 E-Business Applications

SAP CRM Web Channel Enablement solution enables companies to increase their revenues and market reach by extending their sales process to the Web. It also allows them to reduce their Total Cost of Ownership (TCO) and cost of sales and support by providing customers with convenient and personalized tools for buying products and requesting service online.

9.2.2.1 SAP E-Marketing

E-Marketing allows companies to target customers and prospects with personalized, relevant offers. E-Marketing supports demand generation through targeted marketing campaigns, catalog management for products, and personalized offers and recommendations. Doing business on the Internet still requires companies to follow the standard business processes of marketing, selling, providing service, and analyzing data. To sell something, companies typically have to generate demand and inform potential customers about their product or services. After a customer or prospect is interested, the company needs to provide the customer with an organized catalog of products and services so that the customer can find what he or she is looking for. To keep customers coming back to their Website for repeat business, rather than abandoning them in favor of a lower-cost competitor, a company needs to provide the customer with a personalized, value-adding shipping experience:

1. *Demand generation*: A customer who has been targeted as part of a marketing campaign might receive an e-mail containing a campaign-specific code, for instance, entitling the customer with a discounted price. When the customer clicks on the link, the customer is navigated to the Web shop where the appropriate product catalog and pricing are displayed.
2. *Catalog management*: Gives customers the tools they need to find the product and information that is of interest to them. The company can include customer-specific catalog views, provide personalized product recommendations, and allow customers to do comparisons of different products. They can maintain and publish multiple catalogs for different customer groups, regions, seasons, holidays, and so on. They can also create multimedia product catalog hierarchies with detailed product information, image files, customer-specific pricing, and product availability information.
3. *Personalization*: Using information about the customer, including preferences and marketing attributes, the SAP CRM Web Channel allows companies to dynamically personalize the customer's Web experience. For instance, product recommendations can be made based on customer analysis and customer segmentation, including personalized cross sell and up-sell offers as well as recommendations of accessories and related or complementary products.

9.2.2.2 SAP E-Commerce

E-commerce helps a company model and run a complete end-to-end order-to-cash sales process on the Internet. It includes support for interactive selling process, such as configurable products and guided selling (on a project basis). E-commerce also supports pricing and contract management, enabling companies to provide pricing tailored to each customer based on items, such as product, contracts, or quotes. Standard Web shop features such as shopping cart management are also available; E-commerce also enables selling through auctions:

1. *Interactive selling*: SAP CRM supports variant product configuration and variant pricing through the SAP Internet Pricing and Configurator (IPC). Although configurable products afford the consumer greater choice and flexibility, they also present a challenge in terms of pricing; rather than having one set of pricing for a product, pricing needs to be determined

dynamically dependent upon customer's selections for product configuration. For instance, when ordering a computer online, a customer can generally choose options such as memory size, CPU power, sound and video cards, monitor size, and color.

SAP CRM also supports guided selling by posing a series of questions to customers to determine which product (or product configuration) best suits the customer's needs. This obviates the need for the customer to manually navigate through a large product catalog or click through product configuration options.

2. *Pricing*: SAP CRM supports both B2C and B2B scenarios. In a B2C scenario, companies generally do not have customer-specific pricing or contract-based pricing like in B2B scenarios.

3. *Order to cash*: Once an order has captured, payment has been processed via the credit card information created, and order dispatch has been initiated to the shipping address; the order-to-cash process wraps up with billing, accounting, and settlement with external financial institutions. All of this handled through the back-end SAP ERP application.

4. *Web auctions*: SAP CRM also provides support for selling through Web auctions. Companies are increasingly turning to Web auction as a way to get rid of surplus goods, excess inventory, and used assets in a timely fashion. It supports both auctioning through eBay and auctioning through the company's own Web store.

9.2.2.3 SAP E-Service

SAP CRM provides robust E-Service functionality, but it also provides knowledge management and service management capabilities. Customers can view answers to frequently asked questions (FAQs) and search solutions to problems. They can request services such as installation or maintenance of a product as well as track open service requests through to completion. Customers can create complaints and returns for problems with orders or deliveries. Above all, customers can view their account balances and pay their bills online:

1. *Knowledge management*: SAP CRM provides on customer portals answers to Frequently asked questions (FAQs) about products either by doing a search by keyword or by model number or by browsing through a list of products. Customers can also search for knowledge-based articles or solutions to technical problems. Furthermore, the Web portal might also provide product fixes and downloads that the customer could access.

2. *Service management*: SAP CRM provides customer to request for service and track the status of a service request through completion. The customer can monitor the processing status of the service request online without having to call the interaction center every day to find out about the status.

9.2.2.4 Web Channel Analytics

SAP CRM provides out-of-the-box Web Channel Analytics, including sales analyses, technical analyses, and customer behavior analyses. Sales analyses indicate what the company's top 10 products are, top 10 customers are, and the percentage of quotations that are converted to sales orders and the total number of sales orders. Technical analyses show how many hits the company's website is getting and who its top referrers are. Customer behavior shows the number of viewed products, the number of ordered products, and the percentage of visitors who placed orders.

9.3 Summary

SAP E-Business applications provide a standard-based Web architecture for information, process, and application integration so that the enterprise can integrate information and processes across marketing, commerce, and service. They empower enterprises by aligning their partners, employees, and customer touch points, processes, and channels around the goal of maximizing the value of customer relationships.

Chapter 10

SAP CRM Application Environment

SAP introduced SAP NetWeaver in 2003. Driven by the vision of Enterprise Services Architecture (ESA) and revolving around the concept of integration, SAP NetWeaver was targeted to reduce the Total Cost of Ownership (TCO) dramatically by building innately integration capabilities into each and every component of SAP NetWeaver.

The vision of the responsive integrated enterprise is not that of a singular monolithic enterprise-wide application but that of a real-time integrated constellation of distributed applications (see Chapter 2, Section 2.1.3 "CRM Reflects and Mimics the Integrated Nature of the Enterprise"). SAP NetWeaver, which is motivated by this overarching vision of a responsive integrated enterprise, is embodied in the all-encompassing vision of Enterprise Application Integration (EAI), distributed systems, Component-Based Development (CBD), Web Services, Service-Oriented Architecture (SOA), Enterprise Services, and SAP Enterprise Services Architecture (ESA).

As highlighted in Chapters 1 and 3, integration is a major determinant of enterprise success. This is necessitated by the occurrence of

- Frequent mergers and acquisitions
- Innovative applications such as CRM and SRM maintaining local databases
- Business process that spans across multiple companies

The advantages of a service-oriented architecture for enterprise applications are obvious. A new generation of applications can be built on the basis of enterprise services: composite applications. Composite applications use services from several underlying systems, thus generating additional value. Composite applications can combine the services of SAP solutions and partner solutions. This effectively transforms the technology platform into an application platform.

The growth and development of the IT industry in the twenty-first century is primarily driven by the need to provide more and more domain-specific flexible and innovative functionality at more and more commoditized, low-cost, distributed, multilayered, heterogeneous, and interoperable architectural infrastructures.

10.1 Distributed Applications

Distributed applications are constituted of a collection of heterogeneous but fully autonomous components that can execute on different computers. While each of these components has full control over their constituent subparts, there is no master component that possesses control over all the components of a distributed system. Thus, for the system to appear as a single and integrated whole, the various components need to be able to interact with each other via predefined interfaces through a computer network.

The characteristic global features of a successful distributed application are as follows:

1. *Distributed systems are heterogeneous* arising from the need to (say) integrate components on a legacy IBM mainframe, with the components newly created to operate on a UNIX workstation or Windows NT machine.
2. *Distributed systems are scalable* in that when a component becomes overloaded with too many requests or users, another replica of the same component can be instantiated and added to the distributed system to share the load among them. Moreover, these instantiated components can be located closer to the local users and other interacting components to improve the performance of the overall distributed system.
3. *Distributed systems execute components concurrently* in a multithreaded mode via multiple invoked components corresponding to the number of simultaneously invoked processes.
4. *Distributed systems are fault tolerant* in that they duplicate components on different computers as that if one computer fails, another can take over without affecting the availability of the overall system.
5. *Distributed systems are more resilient* in that whereas distributed systems have multiple points of failure, the unaffected components are fully operational even though some of the components are not functional or are malfunctioning; moreover, the distributed system could invoke another instance of the failed components along with the corresponding state of the process (characterized by the program counter of the process, the register variable contents, and the state of the virtual memory used by the process) to continue with the process.
6. *Distributed systems demonstrate invariance or transparency* with reference to characteristics like
   a. Access locally or across networks to the components
   b. Physical location of the components
   c. Migration of components from one host to another
   d. Replication of components including their states
   e. Concurrency of components requesting services from shared components
   f. Scalability in terms of the actual number of requests or users at any instance
   g. Performance in terms of the number and type of available resources
   h. Points of failure, be it a failure of the component, network, or response

Performance transparency is achievable through the technique of load balancing that is based on the replication transparency; the middleware layer transparently decides on the balancing decision to select the replica with the least load to provide the requested service. Furthermore, the performance can also be prevented from degrading by continuously monitoring the patterns of access to components and migrating the components appropriately to minimize remote access.

10.1.1 Distributed Application Requirements

As described earlier, an application is made up of three main constituents, namely, data, servers, and clients. A large-scale system is one that is capable of supporting simultaneously hundreds of thousands of components that run in a server, dozens or hundreds of servers, and tens of thousands of clients. The key to building large-scale applications is optimum resource utilization involving two aspects:

■ Determining the critical resources in a system
■ Devising a mechanism to not only use the resources efficiently but to also enable selective addition of more resources as required

10.1.1.1 Resource Management

SAP CRM Enterprise Server manages a pool of SAP CRM Servers, mediates the coordination between them, and balances the workload among them. The modularity of the enterprise component architecture enhances scalability by adding, as required, more resources to the system configuration.

The SAP CRM Server itself uses several different resource pools to manage critical resources:

1. *Data connection*: Links the server to the database; each server has one or more connections to the database. For applications to scale well, a server employs a database connection pool to reuse connections among the component/client rather than using one connection for each component/client.
2. *Components' process threads*: Is effectively the flow of control corresponding to the component in using processing resources on the server. A component has two aspects: behavior as demonstrated via executing threads and the state of the business entity being processed upon. Each component uses several additional resources such as memory, database connections, and locks. The server apparently supports many components concurrently by maintaining a pool of threads that are shared among the many components that need to be executed. When needed, the server creates the instance of (or restores the state of) the component for use in any application; subsequently, the server saves the component's state, flushes the component from the server, and redeploys those resources for other components. This process of saving and restoring a component's state is termed as *state management*.

   The state-management trade-off is between
   a. Cost of keeping a set of related objects concurrently in memory in terms of tying down of requisite resources like memory, database connections, and locks on various database and systems resources

  b. Saving and restoring the object in terms of the resources required for writing the same set of object's states to a persistence storage and reading them back into the memory.

 3. *Client connection*: Links the client to the application via a server; for each client, there is an associated connection on the server, and the corresponding information regarding the client and connection is also stored on the server. For the application to support tens of thousands of clients, the number of such client connections in the pool should be minimized.

10.1.1.2 State Management

State management enables optimal utilization of the memory for active components while supporting a much larger number of inactive components that can be made active when needed. State management is the action of saving and restoring the state of components. Servers have to guarantee the availability and consistency of a component as and when needed by any application.

A Server achieves this by apparently supporting a much larger number of components than can be accommodated by the limitations of its memory. Whenever an object or a component is needed, the server creates an instance of the object or component to make it available to the concerned application. When the component is no longer needed, the server saves the *state* of the component and flushes the component from the server to enable reuse of its resources for another component.

10.1.1.3 Application Management

Application management refers to the tasks necessary to set up the application and to keep the application running successfully including

- *Configuration*: Is the ability to set up the system and assign resources, including specifications of the number of servers, the number of clients supported concurrently, assignment of servers to particular machines, and assignment of components to servers. For high availability, the configuration is changeable dynamically while the system is in operation.
- *Monitoring*: Is the ability to get statistics about the system's configuration and operation including the number of connected users, the status of the servers, resources utilization of the servers, and throughput and response times. For high availability, tracing and troubleshooting, systems automatically monitor information such as server status and also respond to detected errors or predefined events.
- *Controlling*: Is the ability to effect system configuration and operations including the ability to start and stop servers or components and modify parameters.

10.1.1.4 Application Deployment

Application deployment relates to the issues of initial deployment, securing the application, and upgrading the application. The ideal deployment scenario involves no special software on the client at all, as is the case with browser-based thin clients.

The application architecture must support application versions and the ability for multiple versions of the same application to operate simultaneously. Security is also a critical requirement for the deployment of an application (see Chapter 14, Section 14.6 "Privacy and Security").

10.1.2 N-Tier Application Architecture

In the 1980s, the prior monolithic architecture began to be replaced by the client/server architecture that split applications into two pieces in an attempt to leverage new inexpensive desktop machines. Distributing the processing loads across many inexpensive clients allowed client/server applications to scale much more linearly than single host/single process applications could, and the use of off-the-shelf software like Relational Database Management Systems (RDBMSs) greatly reduced application development time. While the client could handle the user interface and data display tasks of the application and the server could handle all the data management tasks, there was no clear solution for storing the logic corresponding to the business processes being automated. Consequently, the business logic tends to split between the client and the server: typically, the rules for displaying data became embedded inside the user interface, and the rules for integrating several different data sources became stored procedures inside the database. Whereas this division of logic made it difficult to reuse the user interface code with a different data source, it also made it equally difficult to use the logic stored in the database with a different front-end UI (like ATM, mobile) without being required to redevelop the logic implemented in the earlier interface. Thus, a customer service system developed for a particular client system (like a 3270 terminal, a PC, or a workstation) would have great difficulty in providing telephony and Internet interfaces within the same business functionality.

The client/server architecture failed to recognize the importance of managing the business rules applicable to an enterprise independent of both the user interface and the storage and management of enterprise data. The three-layered application architecture of the 1990s resolved this problem by subdividing the application into three distinct layers:

- *Presentation*: Which formats and displays the data independent of the way it is interpreted or processed and stored by the other two layers
- *Business logic*: Which implements the business logic to process data independent of how it is stored or displayed by the other two layers
- *Data management*: Which stores and manages data independent of how it is processed and displayed by the other layers

With the advent of the Internet, in the past few years, the three layers were split even further to accommodate the heterogeneity and differing priorities of different parts of the enterprise in terms of the functionality and performance of user interfaces, processing systems, or databases.

 The power of the N-tier architecture derives from the fact that instead of treating components as integral parts of applications, components are treated as stand-alone entities that can provide services for applications. Applications exist only as cooperating constellation of components, and each component in turn can simultaneously be part of many different applications.

10.1.2.1 N-Tier Architecture Advantage

The N-tier architecture has many advantages over the more traditional client/server architecture:

1. *Agile software*: The N-tier architecture is useful in creating more flexible and easily modifiable software; by treating software components as stand-alone data providers, middleware service providers, business service providers, and service consumers, the N-tier architecture creates software infrastructure of reusable parts.

2. *Maintainable software*: The N-tier architecture is useful in creating more maintainable and easily upgradable software; because software components are stand-alone reusable parts of business logic, they are used from the same place without need for multiplication or replication and are, therefore, easier to change and upgrade rendering the application as a whole more easily maintainable.

3. *Reliable software*: The N-tier architecture is useful in creating more testable, more easily debuggable, and thus more reliable software; flexible and maintainable software does not automatically imply reliable software, but because software components are stand-alone packets of business logic, bugs can be localized more easily and their functionality can be calibrated more accurately rendering the application as a whole more reliable.

4. *Reduced complexity*: The N-tier architecture is useful in creating more streamlined, simplified, and standardized software, because the software component's paradigm eliminates the need for custom interconnections between disparate constituents of a composite application (which includes existing and legacy systems) that increases in complexity rapidly with the increase in the number of disparate constituents. For instance, for a composite application constituted of n applications and m data sources, the problem of corresponding $n \times m$ interconnections is barely manageable even for small values of n and m. However, in the N-tier architecture, this problem is resolved to a great extent by interfacing all components to (say) a single standardized data bus: this reduces the problem of $m \times n$ interconnections to that of only $n + m$ interconnections! All components can connect with each other via connections to this singular data bus without the need for multiple customized single-purpose interconnects between each pair of components.

The interfacing approach of point-to-point interfaces between two applications would be prohibitively expensive for EAIs that may involve tens and hundreds of such interfaces. EAIs also adopt the alternate approach of instituting an information broker whereby all systems communicate with the information broker by uploading data into the same while simultaneously translating it into a single format and protocols native to this central broker. Because information is routed through the information broker, rather than going directly among different systems, this simplifies the problem considerably and it becomes easy to connect disparate systems via their respective adapters for this broker that use the singular format and protocols of this central broker. Any future systems have only to devise one *adapter* to integrate with the central broker to start communicating transparently with all other systems. The exchange of data between the various systems interconnected by EAI is governed by the business rules determined by the user; and the message broker routes the messages according to these rules. However, the data in the messages is translated en route into whatever format is required by the concerned application.

5. *Simplified systems management*: The N-tier architecture is useful in reducing the effort of systems management especially of the software on client machines, particularly for large enterprises that may have tens of thousands of client machines or even for enterprises that have multilocated and decentralized IT/IS operations. For instance, for conventional client/ server systems, the plan for deploying a new version of any application would immediately run into a difficulty of choosing between

   a. Changing the entire installed base of clients in a single massive effort, during which the normal operations come to a complete standstill

   b. Undergoing a long and expensive but more regulated phase-in of the new software, during which IT/IS is required to support multiple and mutually incompatible versions of the server and client codes; and, above all, the new application is available to only a part of the target user base

N-tier architecture by reason of its software-on-demand paradigm reduces the need for physical updates of the client machines considerably; in many of these cases, the updates can be distributed through the HTTP and a Web browser or through separately available automatic application distribution systems. But in the case of applications with zero-footprint clients, like SAP, this need is completely eliminated. Moreover, as the majority of the code resides in the business logic, middleware, and data layers that are typically deployed on centralized, back-end servers supported by professional staff, the updates and enhancements to these layers are relatively painless.

10.1.2.2 Limits of the N-Tier Architecture

While the N-tier architectures deliver all the advantages associated with distributed systems, they also have a downside. The N-tier systems are workable only because of a network-based data bus for communications between the various tiers.

Such a communications layer will have the following adverse effects:

■ Add to the latency of the system and degrade overall performance.
■ Libraries of software components (and classes) required for interfacing with the data bus will typically increase the size of the application.

However, the system architects usually take these problems into account at the time of planning and designing the overall enterprise infrastructure and architecture. And in the event that these problems become noticeable (because of dramatic increase in business and transaction volumes) or foreseeable (because of envisaged M&A activities, split or divesting activities, etc.), the enterprise architecture is revisited in its entirety.

10.1.3 Enterprise Architecture

Large corporations that have already invested vast sums of money in the existing enterprise applications, in infrastructure, in hardware, and employees cannot change overnight. Moreover, the software skills and techniques that are essential for Web-based applications development are different from those prevalent in most of the companies. In this subsection, we will briefly examine why a successful enterprises should be based on enterprise component architecture as embodied in Enterprises Services Architecture starting with the mySAP ERP applications.

The ultimate promise of component-based development (CBD) is that adaptive enterprise systems can be composed from components. Unpredictable and discontinuous changes in the market trigger technological changes and innovation. Enterprises need to be agile to enable timely responses to business change as also for adopting to new technologies necessitated by this change. Strategically, enterprise architecture provides overall structure and set of rules for managing growth and complexity while simultaneously providing ability to be flexible and agile to meet the existing and new challenges facing the enterprise. Tactically, it provides a framework for reuse and integration of preexisting internal and external components as well as newly developed components to deliver a complete enterprise solution.

Table 10.1 lists the advantages of a CBD approach to Internet-enabled enterprise applications.

10.1.3.1 Enterprise Components

Flexible applications can be constructed by assembling a variety of components (functional modules) to create newer products and services. CBD involves a range of provisioning technologies that includes development, reusing legacy systems, and even buying off-the-shelf components. Although the initial components would have to be developed from scratch, over time, with accumulation of basic components, applications will be assembled more and more from increasing reuse of the existing components. The process is more of evolution and loosely coupled integration rather than pure development from scratch every time. However, to accomplish this, the software would have to be designed as component-based applications, and an infrastructure needs to exist to support the component-oriented development of applications.

 Component-based applications affect a clear-cut segregation between system development, deployment, and execution, thus enabling independent development, integration, and upgrade of components. A component is different from an object in that, unlike an object, a component is both a unit of functionality and also a unit of deployment.

An organizational structure that enables change is based on reusable elements that are reconfigurable in a scalable framework. In the componentized architecture, an enterprise application is considered as a group of enterprise components sharing a common interaction framework and serving a common purpose. A Framework is a set of standards constraining and enabling the interactions of compatible system components, where the component itself is an autonomous system subunit with a self-contained identity, purpose, and capability and is capable of interacting with other components. To publish and subscribe function is the ability of a component to handle events, that is, to notify automatically other components or be notified when something of interest occurs. A component can notify or publish an event to those components that have registered interest in that event or class of events; conversely, components can register to be notified or subscribe when a given event or class of events occurs.

Enterprise components are self-contained packets or units of defining data and processing logic. By definition, a component has predetermined hooks or connection points for integration with a component framework and prespecified interfaces for other components and applications to access its functions. A precisely defined interface provides a contract between the supplier of the services and the consumer of these services through this interface; an interface essentially is a collection of related functions that can be invoked on a component. The interface of a component

Table 10.1   Advantages of a Component-Based Development (CBD) Approach

Determining Factor	Enterprise Challenge	Characteristics of the Component-Based Development (CBD) Approach
Quality	Consequences of software application errors are often catastrophic for enterprise systems.	Specification guidelines provide rigor, assisted by a provisioning process for engineering of quality enterprise systems.
Cost savings	There is a need to reduce costs, be competitive in providing functionality, and exploit niche markets with specialized requirements.	Component reuse results in long-term cost savings.
Scalability	The requirements of responsiveness vary across a group of users of the enterprise systems.	Components can be implemented and deployed in technology corresponding to the envisaged operational constraints and requirements.
Consistency	The enterprise systems need to adhere to a consistent architecture that also enables flexibility and innovation.	The enterprise system is organized and developed based on the consistency and constancy of the components' interfaces.
Integration	There is a need to leverage on existing investments in technology and legacy applications.	This is enabled by *wrapping* of legacy systems into components, with consistent interfaces, which are organized into an enterprise system.
Adaptability	Business processes change dramatically especially because of mergers and acquisitions (M&As).	This is enabled by loosely coupled components with consistent interfaces, which are organized into an enterprise system.
Time to market	There are rapidly reducing windows of opportunity that need to be exploited quickly.	An assembly, integration, and implementation process is more effective than redevelopment.
Business Fit	There is a need to constantly improve, repurpose, and fine-tune the business processes.	Components can be altered or exchanged, while maintaining consistent interfaces, which are organized into an enterprise system.

is separated from its implementation; an implementation of a component may change, but as long as its interface does not change, other components can continue to interact with this component without experiencing any changes. Interfaces are mechanisms that enable enterprise applications to be built as a constellation of cooperating components.

Enterprise components are classified according to where they reside, namely, client or server. JavaBeans and ActiveX provide technologies for building reusable user interface client components. The major advantage of client components is that they are downloadable to a client desktop or other devices as part of the normal usage of the applications, rather than having to be installed or deployed to each client device. This leads to tremendous optimization of TCO by obviating the need for deployment or upgrade of the client devices whose total number across the enterprise could run into hundreds or thousands. Unlike client components that are mainly focused on the GUI, server components exist primarily to provide business functionality. Examples of server component models are Microsoft COM, Sun's Enterprise JavaBeans, and OMG's CORBA component model.

Enterprise components run within the contexts of supporting frameworks called *containers*. Containers provide standard infrastructural services to running components such as state management, persistence management, security, and transaction management. This reduces the burden on the application developers and enables them to focus on implementing business logic rather than intricate code that supports basic application support infrastructure. Again, containers are also classified into client and server containers. Web browsers are examples of client containers as are the traditional Web servers that worked with CGI-BIN, HTTP, HTML, servlets, and so on. Application servers are examples of server containers as are object-oriented databases or object stores with their object/relational mapping tools, object request brokers (ORBs), and transaction monitors.

In addition to the requirements of the distributed applications stated earlier, application servers may also variously provide

- Openness
- Interoperability
- Scalability
- Availability
- Configuration control
- Management (administration, configuration, deployment, etc.)

10.1.3.2 Enterprise Component Architecture

Enterprise component architecture is a high-level description of the major components of an enterprise and the relationship between them. Enterprise component architecture defines the enterprise's design (patterns and constraints) and infrastructure for components as well as defines how compliant components are built and how they interact, how components are stored and cataloged, and how components are located and reused.

Enterprise architecture is subdivided into two parts, namely, functional layers and distribution tiers; they can also be seen as the specification and implementation architectures, respectively. Functional layers specify application-level responsibilities and address specific application requirements with specific solutions, while distribution tiers address more general set of requirements or services that are mapped to a distributed computing system or infrastructure.

Here are characteristic features of enterprise component architecture:

1. *Separation of perspectives*: The development of distributed component architectures entails many separate perspectives ranging from design, development, deployment, and execution. Each of these perspectives highlights select aspects of the required architecture. Separation of perspectives entails dividing the enterprise into a set of related but quasi-independent subarchitectures that focus on a set of related aspects of distributed, N-tier, technology-independent, and changeable architecture.

2. *Technology independence*: The development of enterprise applications as interface-dependent but implementation-independent cooperating constellation of N-tier components enables applications to be continuously upgraded in terms of the technology that is most suitable for the specialized requirements of different units of the applications. This enables the application to employ the most suitable technologies currently available while also accommodating new technologies as and when they become available in the future.

3. *Phased implementations*: This is a very significant architectural characteristics for large enterprise applications like mySAP ERP. Enterprise applications like mySAP ERP not only have to continuously enhance and upgrade its functionality and performance to meet the relentless expectations of new customers, but they also have to achieve this without disrupting the ongoing operations of the ever-increasing installed base of its existing customers. In context of a specific enterprise, this characteristic implies the ability to implement or upgrade various functionalities or modules of the enterprise solution as and when required across an extended period of *time regardless of the versions, upgrades, and even changed landscapes of this solution or, for that matter, even other applications.* We discuss below the basic service-oriented strategy for the enterprise component architecture (see Section 10.1.3.4 "Enterprise Component Architecture as a Strategy: Service-Oriented View").

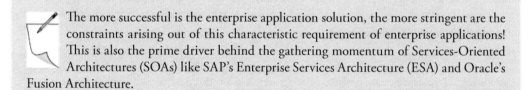

The more successful is the enterprise application solution, the more stringent are the constraints arising out of this characteristic requirement of enterprise applications! This is also the prime driver behind the gathering momentum of Services-Oriented Architectures (SOAs) like SAP's Enterprise Services Architecture (ESA) and Oracle's Fusion Architecture.

4. *Accommodation of changes*: The enterprise component architecture enables accommodation of changes in a unit of the applications without affecting the actual functioning and performance of the other units. This characteristic and the advantages accruing from it are directly related to the partitioning or layering of the enterprise applications. For example, enterprise architecture conceives of a database abstraction layer to access a database rather than writing directly to a specific database. This layer presents a constant interface to user components of the database while taking care of the specificities of communicating with a particular database(s). As and when required, merely by changing the database abstraction layer enables changing the existing database without disrupting any other parts of the system.

10.1.3.3 Enterprise Component Model

The component model maps the business processes and entities identified by the business model onto a platform-independent IT model. The component model takes into account various aspects like the distributed nature of the application, interface design, relationships and dependencies within the components, and locality of data. A component model can be described as an architecture and a set of Application Programming Interfaces (APIs) that enables developers to define and create software components that also have an ability of be connected dynamically together and interoperate with other components. Most components operate within a possible nested hierarchy of containers.

Typically, an architecture is a more abstract description, while a model is a more concrete description—similar to the distinction between classes and instances in object-oriented development environments (see Chapter 11, Section 11.1.4.1 "Object-Oriented Paradigm").

Component models provide an array of mechanisms and services for interoperation of components:

- Self-discovery of components enables rendering of information on supported interfaces and methods to other components. This enables components to publish its capabilities as well as interact with other components dynamically.
- Properties of components determine the state, behavior, or appearance of the component.
- Customization of components enables the properties of a component to be set or modified from within a component or externally by another component/container.
- Persistence of components involves the process of saving and restoring a component's current state.
- Event control of components enables a component to create (or generate) an event for another component or to respond to an event. Predefining various kinds of events can also differentiate the occurrence of different kinds of events.

The principles of distributed system design are quite different from the traditional concepts of object-oriented design. For instance, not every object is required to be a distributed object.

An enterprise application is constituted of three types of objects:

1. Distributed component that has a well-defined interface and is network addressable so that it can be searched and invoked over a network
2. Value object that is essentially a data holder and can be passed as a parameter, but cannot be invoked over a network
3. Local object that is neither passed nor invoked over a network

10.1.3.4 Enterprise Component Architecture as a Strategy: Service-Oriented View

The component architecture provides an integration framework to help identify and design the interfaces between business processes and the diverse software assets or components of the enterprise. As mentioned earlier, the interface of a component is separated from its implementation; the interface guarantees the services specified by the component. The consumer of these services can exclusively focus on the overall solution via a constellation of such interfaces rather than how these interfaces have themselves been rendered in terms of the specific programming language(s) or the technology platform(s). As long as the *ensemble* of the interfaces is maintained, the overall solution is transparent to their implementations or their changes. However, whenever the processes change, the component architecture should be able to handle the change by unplugging unwanted interfaces and plugging in the new ones.

A set of services that work cooperatively for a defined business objective is termed as a business or enterprise capability. Thus, an enterprise component provides interfaces that offer enterprise capability. Enterprise capability helps in moving from a functional view of a predetermined core competency-driven enterprise to a *service-oriented view* of a flexible and innovation-driven open-ended Web-based enterprise.

The decoupling of the enterprise process and enterprise capability provides the enterprise with the flexibility to adapt processes to business changes while simultaneously making them immune to changes in the implementation platforms or technologies. Consequently, we move from applications that are designed as tightly coupled and inflexible software islands to those that are loosely coupled flexible ensemble of interfaces enabling the leveraging of enterprise capabilities.

Enterprise component architecture provides a framework for reuse and integration of preexisting internal legacy components and external off-the-shelf components as well as newly developed components to deliver an effective enterprise solution. The most successful component strategy would be the one that enables reconfigurations or integration of components to best leverage their capabilities to achieve the most effective response to the changes in the business environment. This is what we turn to in the following section.

10.2 Enterprise Application Integration (EAI)

In these times of market change and turbulence, enterprises are confronted with the increasing need to interconnect disparate systems to satisfy the need of the business. It is estimated that 35%–60% of an organization's IT resources are spent on integration (see Chapter 2, Section 2.4.2 "Extended Collaborative Enterprise"). E-business application integration is the creation, maintenance, and enhancement of leading-edge competitive functionality of the enterprises' business solutions by combining the functionality of the existing legacy applications, Commercial Off-The-Shelf (COTS) software packages, and newly developed custom applications via a common middleware.

Enterprise Application Integration (EAI) provides components for integrating SAP eBusiness Applications with external applications and technologies within the enterprise and is designed to work with third-party products.

By employing EAI effectively, an enterprise can leverage its existing enterprise-wide information assets, that is, customer relationships,

- ■ To provide new products and services easily and quickly
- ■ To streamline its internal process and operations
- ■ To strengthen supply relationships
- ■ To enhance customer relationships

Figure 10.1 shows the N-tier architecture of current applications like SAP CRM.

As EAI enables enterprise-wide integration of diverse applications across various products and divisions, EAI affords the enterprise a 360-degree view of its customer relationships across multiple channels of interaction. Every customer perceives the enterprise as a whole and also expects to be recognized and valued by the enterprise as a whole. As we have seen in Chapter 1, familiarity with customer's earlier interactions and purchases helps frontline members of the enterprise to create opportunities for selling other products or additional add-ons and services to the earlier purchases.

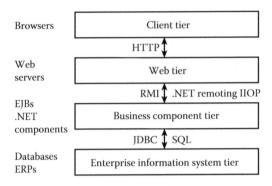

Figure 10.1   N-tier architecture.

   One of the important objectives of application integration is to achieve the integration between applications with as reduced level of coupling or interdependency as possible, so that the impact of changes in one application does not affect the other application(s).

10.2.1 Basic Concepts

The basic concepts related with EAI are described below. A robust and flexible EAI provides a combination of the methods of integration and modes of communication that are embodied into the various models of integration that are deployed within the EAI architecture as discussed later.

10.2.1.1 Methods of Integration

Methods of integration are the approaches used to guide a request from a sender to a receiver. The two primary methods of integration are described:

1. *Messaging*: In this approach, the sender constructs a message that contains the information on the actions desired as well as the data required to perform these actions: the message contains both the control information and data. Messages provide a lot of flexibility because the control information can be easily changed and extended; they are independent of any of the applications. However, to function correctly, the integration messages must be predefined precisely so that the messages can be coded and decoded exactly the same way by all senders and receivers.
2. *Interface*: In this approach, the sender communicates through an interface, which defines explicitly the actions that can be invoked by an application: the interface is self-describing in terms of the actions that can be taken. Interfaces make the application look like a procedure or a method or an object. Interfaces are difficult to change and extend; they are associated with a particular application.

10.2.1.2 Modes of Communication

The flexibility of systems is critically dependent on the modes of communications that are utilized by the systems. Assuming that a *request* refers to a communication from a sender to a receiver, the two basic options for communications are as follows:

1. *Synchronous communication*: Requires the sender of a request to wait until a reply—which is the result of the request—is received before continuing the processing. Synchronous communication between systems implies a high degree of coupling and requires the sender and the receiver to coordinate the communications with their internal processing. A reliable network infrastructure is essential for this kind of communication. It is used when the sender requires a notification of the receipt or needs the result of the processing from the receiver. For instance, interactive systems need a synchronous type of communication.

   There are three popular types of synchronous communications:
   a. Request/response
   b. Transmit
   c. Polling

2. *Asynchronous communication*: Allows the sender to continue processing after sending the request, without waiting for a reply to this request. The sender does not concern itself with whether or when the request has been received, how it is processed, or the results returned from the receiver. Asynchronous communications does not demand a high degree of coupling and also does not require the sender to coordinate the communications with their internal processing. It is used when the communication of information is required without the need to coordinate activities or responses.

   There are three popular types of asynchronous communications:
   a. *Message passing*: This is used in situations where information needs to be transmitted but a reply is not required. This needs a reliable network for guaranteed delivery.
   b. *Publish/subscribe*: This is used in situations where a reply is not required, but unlike all other cases, the recipient is determined based on the content of the request and the predeclared interest of the receiver application. This type of communication is useful for STP type of functional integration (see Section 10.2.2.2.3 "Straight-Through Processing (STP)").
   c. *Broadcast*: This is used in situations where again a reply is not needed, but the request is sent to all of the applications and each of the receiver decides if it is interested in the request/message and accordingly processes that request/message in accordance with the business and functional logic programmed into each of the receiver system.

10.2.1.3 Middleware Options

Middleware is a software that enables disparate applications to interact with each other: it facilitates the communication of requests between software components through the use of predefined interfaces or messages. The five basic types of middleware are as follows:

- *Remote Procedure Calls (RPCs)*: Is based on the notion of developing distributed applications that integrate at the procedure level but across a network.
- *Database Access Middleware*: Is based on the notion of developing distributed applications that integrate at the distributed data level whether in files or databases but across the network.

■ *Message-Oriented Middleware (MOM)*: Is based on the notion of developing distributed applications that integrate at the message level but across the network.
■ *Distributed Object Technology (DOT)*: Is based on the notion of developing distributed applications that integrate at the interface level but those that make the application look like an object.
■ *Transaction Processing Monitors (TPMs)*: Is based on the notion of developing distributed applications that integrate at the distributed transaction level but across the network.

10.2.2 Models of Integration

An integration model defines the approach and configurations used to integrate software applications depending on the nature and methods of the envisaged integration. There are three possible points of integration, namely, presentation, functional, and data integration.

10.2.2.1 Presentation Integration

In this model, the integration is accomplished by deploying a new and uniform application user interface: the new application appears to be a single application although it may be accessing several legacy and other applications at the back end. The integration logic, the instructions on where to direct the user interactions, communicates the interaction of the user to the corresponding application using their existing presentations as a point of integration. It then integrates back any results generated from the various constituent applications. Thus, a single presentation could replace a set of terminal-based interfaces and might incorporate additional features, functions, and workflow for the user. For instance, a mainframe application can be integrated into a new Microsoft Windows application at the front end using the screen-scraping technology that effectively copies, maps, and imports data from specific locations on character-based screens of the mainframe application onto the new schemas and data structures of the new system.

Presentation integration is the easiest to achieve and can be automated almost 100%; however, it is also the most limiting of the three models.

10.2.2.2 Functional Integration

In this model, the integration is accomplished by invoking from other applications functionality or business logic of the existing applications by using code-level interfaces to the existing applications. This might be achieved at the level of an object or a procedure or via application programming interface (API) if it exists for each of the corresponding applications. The business logic includes the processes and workflow as well as the data manipulation and rules of interpretation. For instance, for changing the customer's address in an enterprise application, the functionality of the existing customer order and billing application can be accessed if it is functionally integrated with these later applications. Rather than re-create the logic in the new application, it is more efficient and less error prone to reuse the existing logic.

Traditionally, Remote Procedure Calls (RPCs), which have been employed for this kind of integration, have provided the definitions for access and basic communications facilities. However, lately distributed processing middleware has become the preferred method of integration as it not only provides a more robust approach to the interface definitions and communications but also enables runtime support for intercomponent requests. The three categories of distributed processing are as follows:

- *Message-Oriented Middleware (MOM)*: Achieves integration by providing for the communication of messages between applications by means of the messages placed in MOM, which itself is implemented in a variety of configurations, including message queuing and message passing. The MOM is then responsible for delivering to the target system. Microsoft's MSMQ, BizTalk, IBM's MQSeries, and Talarian's Smart Sockets are examples of MOM.
- *Distributed Object Technology (DOT)*: Achieves integration by providing object interfaces that make applications look like objects; the application can then be accessed by other applications across a network through the object interfaces. OMG's CORBA, Microsoft's COM+, and Sun's Java 2 Enterprise Edition (J2EE) are examples of DOT.
- *Transaction Processing Monitors (TPMs)*: Achieves integration by providing critical support for integrity of distributed resources such as databases, files, and message queues across distributed architectures by allowing various types of transactions to be managed using a variety of concepts including two-phase commit. BEA's Tuxedo is an example of TPM.

Functional integration, which is more flexible than the other two integration models, can be applied in three different forms described below.

10.2.2.2.1 Synchronization

This corresponds to the coordination of data updates from multiple sources across integrated applications that may have been developed and enhanced across a long period of time. It provides integration that is loosely coupled and predominantly asynchronous. These applications may represent various relationships that a customer may have had with the enterprise or manage employees or products related information. When an update is made into anyone of the systems, the update needs to be propagated across all of these systems. Typically, synchronization is implemented by propagating a request that describes the intended action and the corresponding data to each of the relevant systems.

10.2.2.2.2 Component Integration

Component integration is the integration of applications where a well-defined interface exists that allows a component to be accessed via requests from other components without modifications. The interfaces for each component must identify the specific functions that the component supports. It provides integration that is tightly coupled and predominantly synchronous.

10.2.2.2.3 Straight-Through Processing (STP)

This corresponds to a coordinated set of automated actions executed across all relevant applications in the correct order of precedence automatically, that is, without human intervention. It provides integration that is tightly coupled and can be both synchronous and asynchronous. This kind of process is commonly associated with workflow though it does not involve decision making or complicated scheduling. For instance, if an order for a product is placed on a website, the order processing system (OPS) creates the order and notifies the logistics and shipping system to ship the product. When the order is completed, the OPS is notified of the change of status and the billing system triggers a bill for payment. Once the payment is received, the OPS is notified to close the order.

10.2.2.3 Data Integration

In this model, integration is accomplished by bypassing the existing application business logic and accessing directly the data created, processed, and stored by each of the corresponding applications. For instance, an Oracle-based billing system can be integrated with an IBM-based customer order system using the database gateway technology that integrates the DB2 database with the Oracle database.

This has been one of the earliest models applied for accessing information from databases including

- Batch file transfer
- Open Database Connectivity (ODBC)
- Database access middleware
- Data transformation

The data integration model provides greater flexibility than the presentation integration model: it simplifies access to data from multiple sources and also allows the data to be reused across other applications. However, integrating at the data level necessitates rewriting of any functionality required by each of the applications that imply much larger effort for avoiding inconsistencies, standardizing, testing, and debugging for each of the applications on an ongoing basis. Since this model is highly sensitive to changes in the data models for each of the applications, this integration model is not very amenable for change and maintenance.

10.3 Service-Oriented Architecture (SOA)

An SOA focuses on the message-based interactions of components in a network rather than the details of individual component implementation. An SOA (see Figure 10.2) relates three component roles and three operations between the roles in support of dynamic, automated discovery and use of services:

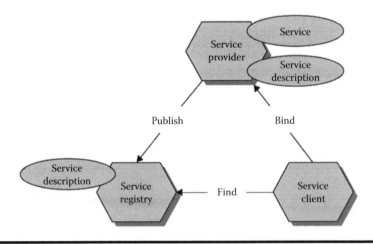

Figure 10.2 Web service roles and operations.

1. A service provider can publish the availability of its service(s) and respond to requests to use, or alternatively, it can bind to its service(s). A *service provider* is a Network node that provides a service interface for a software asset that manages a specific set of tasks. A service provider node can represent the service interface for a reusable subsystem.

2. A service broker allows service providers to publish (register and categorize) themselves and their services; a service broker also offers find mechanisms for business entities attempting to locate appropriate services for use in a solution. A *service requestor* is a Network node that discovers and invokes other software services to provide a business solution. Service requestor nodes will often represent a business application component that performs remote procedure calls to a distributed object, the service provider. In some cases, the provider node may reside locally within an intranet, or in other cases, it could reside remotely over the Internet. The conceptual nature of SOA leaves the networking, transport protocol, and security details to the specific implementation.

3. A service requestor uses service brokers to find the services needed to construct a solution, or part of a solution, and then invokes (bind to) those services offered by service providers. The third SOA participant is that of the *service broker*; it is a Network node that acts as a repository, yellow pages, or clearing house for software interfaces that are published by service providers. A business entity or independent operator can represent a service broker.

These three SOA participants interact using three basic operations *publish*, *find*, and *bind*. Service providers publish service to a service broker. Service requestors *find* required services using a service broker and bind to them.

An SOA is an abstract concept. To support the use of Web Services in e-business, IBM, Microsoft, and others are working to create a concrete Web Service *stack* that defines how to construct Web-Service-based solutions. It is populated with existing and emerging standards to foster widespread interoperability and availability:

■ The Web Service transport layer provides the basis for communicating between Web Services; many different transport standards can be used, all leveraging existing Internet protocol standards; the specific transport used for an interaction can be negotiated at the higher layers in the stack.

■ The service description layer, using an emerging XML-based standard protocol called Web Services Description Language (WSDL), supplies descriptions of Web Service interfaces, that is, the message and parameters that flow between interacting Web Services.

■ The Web Service messaging layer provides a lightweight protocol for the exchange of messages between Web Services in a decentralized, distributed environment; the layer uses the XML-based Simple Object Access Protocol (SOAP) for interactions between all service requesters and service providers.

■ The publication and discovery layer enables the service broker role for Web Services, and the layer leverages the Universal Description, Discovery, and Integration (UDDI) specifications that define XML-based service and business description format and a SOAP-based API for a service broker.

In addition to the layers, the Web Service stack offers some *verticals* that apply across all the layers. These verticals represent the fact that some aspects of a solution permeate all layers of the stack and thus may impact existing formats, protocols, and APIs or require new ones:

■ The security vertical denotes the serious commitment to security in Web Services while not complete; work is well underway to enhance SOAP and UDDI with security mechanisms; examples include authentication and nonrepudiation.

■ The management vertical denotes the absolute need for building solutions that can be easily deployed, monitored, and upgraded. At this time, the impact on the stack layers is unclear.

■ The quality of service vertical denotes the increasing importance of guarantees regarding response time, cost, transactional characteristics, and other aspects of e-business interactions; work is just starting in this vertical.

Service-oriented architecture has the following characteristics:

■ *Distributed service-oriented architectures*: These are distributed functional elements of the application that are deployed on multiple systems and across local and even remote networks.

■ *Loosely coupled interfaces*: These require a much simpler level of coordination and also allow for more flexible configuration compared to the traditional applications that depend upon a tight interconnections of all subsidiary elements.

■ *Standards*: All these connections are based upon vendor-independent standards.

■ *Process centric*: All services are designed with a task orientation; they function as discrete steps in a larger workflow or business process.

10.3.1 Web Services

Web Services emerged from the initial efforts to achieve integration and interoperability between distributed software applications. The last decade was dominated by the client/server-and-database approach to systems, an innovation that was pioneered by SAP for enterprise applications with the introduction of SAP R/3 in 1993. Client/server applications are designed with a dedicated client and server, each server used by a single application and with integration performed by expensive point-to-point data connections that quite often use proprietary communication protocols. Because of the huge number of required interfacing connections, this resulted in large escalations in costs for the development and maintenance of applications. As mentioned earlier, this approach to application integration resulted in integration costs that were reported to be between 30% and 60% of the total IT budget of companies. EAI solutions thus led to a very dense network of applications and interfaces, which were difficult to maintain and that too at very high costs. As an intermediate solution, to obviate the need for developing customer-specific interfaces, the communication between applications was abstracted by using XML messages to enable different applications to interact by using a standardized format. However, this still leaves unaddressed the fundamental issue of integrating the business processes themselves.

Web Services are the interface technology of the future. They are the new standards for creating and delivering cooperative applications over the Internet. Web Services allow applications to communicate irrespective of the platform or the operating system. By using Web Services, developers can eliminate major porting and quality testing efforts, potentially saving millions of dollars. They will radically change the way that applications are built and deployed in the future.

As explained in Section 10.1.3 "Enterprise Component Architecture," a developer can create an application out of reusable components. But what good is it to have a large library of reusable components if nobody can find out that they exist, where they are located, and how to link to and communicate with such programmatic components? Web Services are standards for finding and integrating object components over the Internet. They enable a development environment where it is no longer necessary to build complete and monolithic applications for every project. Instead, the core components can be combined from other standard components available on the Web to build the complete applications that run as services to the core applications.

Some of the past approaches for enabling program-to-program communications included combinations of program-to-program protocols such as Remote Procedure Call (RPC) and Application Program Interfaces (APIs) coupled with the architecture such as Common Object Model (COM), the Distributed Common Object Model (DCOM), and the Common Object Request Broker Architecture (CORBA). But without a common underlying network, common protocols for program-to-program communication, and a common architecture to help applications to declare their availability and services, it has proven difficult to implement cross platform program-to-program communication between application modules. These previous attempts to set up standards for accomplishing these objectives were not very successful because

- They were not functionally rich enough and are difficult to maintain as *best of breed*.
- They were vendor specific as opposed to using open and cross vendor standards.
- They were too complex to deploy and use.

The use of Web Service standards holds the potential of correcting each of these deficiencies. This new approach presents applications as services to each other and enables applications to be rapidly assembled by linking application objects together.

With the advent of the Internet and its protocols, most vendors and enterprises have graduated to a common communication and network protocol—the Internet's TCP/IP. And with the availability of web standards such as Extended Markup Language (XML), Simple Object Access Protocol (SOAP), Universal Description, Discovery and Integration (UDDI), and Web Services Definition Language (WSDL), vendors enable customers to

1. Publish specifications about application modules via WSDL
2. Discover those modules (either on the internal intranet or on the Internet) via the UDDI
3. Bind the applications together to work seamlessly and cooperatively and deliver the holistic functionality of composite application via SOAP and XML

Figure 10.2 shows the schematic of the interaction between the Web Service Provider, Discovery Service Provider (Service Registry), and Web Service Consumer (Service Client).

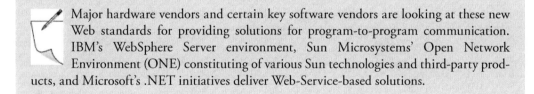

Major hardware vendors and certain key software vendors are looking at these new Web standards for providing solutions for program-to-program communication. IBM's WebSphere Server environment, Sun Microsystems' Open Network Environment (ONE) constituting of various Sun technologies and third-party products, and Microsoft's .NET initiatives deliver Web-Service-based solutions.

The significance of Web Services for the future is by reason of the following:

- Web Services will enable enterprises to reduce development costs and expand application functionality at the fraction of costs per traditional application development and deployment methods.

- Web Services will enable independent Software Vendors (ISVs) to bring products to market more quickly and respond to competitive threats with more flexibility.
- Web Services will enable enterprises to reuse existing legacy application functionality with the latest applications and technologies.
- Web Services will obviate the need of porting applications to different hardware platforms and operating systems at great expense.
- Web Services enable applications to communicate irrespective of platform or operating system.
- Web Services will have the effect of leveling the playing field because it will enable even specialized boutique application firms to compete easily with well-established and resourceful Original Equipment Manufacturers (OEMs).
- Web Services will enable only those OEMs to flourish that focus on providing comprehensive implementations and highly productive application development environments for Web Services.
- Web Services will enable applications to be packaged not only as licenses but also as services; this would give a big fillip to ASP services (as discussed in the earlier section) that would consequently expand the overall market size tremendously.
- Web Services will enable value-added resellers (VARs) to rapidly add new functionality to current product offerings or to customize existing applications of customers.
- Web Services will enable enterprises to adopt better to the changing market conditions or competitive threats.

Though Web Services may seem just another component model, they differ in the following important ways:

1. *Granularity*: Refers to the complexity of the description of a service. A simple UNIX call has a very fine level of granularity, but a Purchase Order (PO) has a very coarse level of granularity.
2. *Coupling*: Refers to the nature of the interface between the producer of the service and the consumer of the service. It is concerned with the impact on the consumer of the service, in case the implementation changes.

While components are very good at doing tightly coupled and fine-grained things, Web Services are very good at doing loosely coupled and coarse-grained kind of things. For instance, while components are capable of interoperating only with other components designed using the same APIs or object model, Web Services are designed to interact with any other component, irrespective of its origin, as long as it is encapsulated in a self-describing wrapper.

10.3.1.1 Describing Web Services: Web Services Description Language (WSDL)

The Web Services Description Language is an XML-based language used to describe the goods and services that an organization offers and provides a way to access those services electronically.

WSDL is an XML vocabulary that provides a standard way of describing service IDLs. WSDL is the resulting artifact of a convergence of activities between NASSL (IBM) and SDL (Microsoft). It provides a simple way for service providers to describe the format of requests and response Messages for Remote Method Invocations (RMIs). WSDL addresses this topic of service IDLs independent of the underlying protocol and encoding requirements. In general, WSDL provides an abstract language for defining the published operations of a service with their respective parameters and data types. The language also addresses the definition of the locations and binding details of the service.

10.3.1.2 Accessing Web Services: Simple Object Access Protocol (SOAP)

Simple Object Access Protocol is an XML-based lightweight protocol for the exchange of information in a decentralized distributed environment. SOAP is a means by which different systems can communicate, based on the HTTP Web standard. It specifies how to encode an hypertext transfer protocol (HTTP) header and XML file so that different applications, running on different systems, can share data. SOAP defines a messaging protocol between requestor and provider objects, such that the requesting objects can perform a remote method invocation on the providing objects in an object-oriented programming fashion. The SOAP specification was coauthored by Microsoft, IBM, Lotus, UserLand, and DevelopMentor. The specification subsequently spawned the creation of W3C XML Protocol Workgroup, which is constituted of over 30 participating companies.

In most vendor implementations of SOA, SOAP forms the basis for distributed object communication. Although SOA does not define a messaging protocol, SOAP has recently been referred to as the Service-Oriented Architecture protocol due to its common use in SOA implementations. The beauty of SOAP is that it is completely vendor neutral, allowing for independent implementations relative to platform, operating system, object model, and programming language. Additionally, transport and language bindings as well as data-encoding preferences are all implementation dependent.

10.3.1.3 Finding Web Services: Universal Description, Discovery, and Integration (UDDI)

The Universal Description, Discovery and Integration is an XML-based registry that enables organizations in a global business-to-business (B2B) environment to locate each other. UDDI specification provides a common set of SOAP APIs that enable the implementation of a service broker. The UDDI specification was outlined by IBM, Microsoft, and Ariba to help facilitate the creation, description, discovery, and integration of Web-based services.

UDDI is like a telephone directory that additionally also

- Indicates the suitability of a potential partner
- Describes the access mechanism by which an enterprise can be interfaced with

The motivation behind UDDI.org, a partnership and cooperation between more than 70 industry and business leaders, is to define a standard for B2B interoperability.

10.3.2 Enterprise Services

Enterprise Services are based on the same technology as Web Services. SAP recognized early the potential of Web Services as the basic theme to enable provisioning of flexible and innovative functionality on an ongoing basis in a fast, flexible, and efficient manner. SAP enlarged the concept of Web Services to Embrace Enterprise Services.

ESA applications are designed with shared application systems (or components) that are combined together to form composite applications. The components expose a standard set of services that are usable by various enterprise business processes. These standard services such as *create Purchase Requisition* or *Issue goods from Inventory* are called enterprise services.

10.3.3 Enterprise Services Architecture (ESA)

In 2003, SAP introduced a revolutionary vision for the future of business applications called Enterprise Services Architecture (ESA). ESA is a radical departure in technology architecture. The ESA platform offers Web Services as a way to make IT environments more flexible with interoperability and deployment of cross system functions. Simultaneously, it builds on existing solutions to protect legacy investment while still providing innovative solutions. ESA is based on a service-oriented approach to applications; ESA-based applications are designed with shared application systems (or components) that are combined together to form composite applications. By eliminating much of the *impedance mismatch* between systems and business processes, ESA can yield much greater agility while simultaneously achieving substantial reduction in TCO.

As discussed in Chapter 4, Section 4.5.1.2 "Integrated Best-in-Class Applications," enterprises are driven to select a composite of applications that best meet the specific needs of the enterprise in different areas. The downside of this approach is the higher efforts and costs of integration. Also, enterprises face increasing and ever-changing competition. To survive long term in the market, they have to adopt themselves flexibly and quickly to the market conditions and to continually develop innovative business solutions. Enterprises are also under tremendous pressure to reduce costs; hence, replacing functioning systems with totally new solutions is not cost efficient (if not impossible). The existing systems and infrastructures are incapable of supporting fast, flexible, and cost-effective adoption to the changed or novel business processes or operational strategies. The key to continuing success in such an environment is the capability with flexibility to use existing infrastructures, capabilities, and processes within the context of new applications, that is, composite applications in the context of ESA.

An ESA platform provides flexible and unified access to the integrated functionality of heterogeneous system landscapes within enterprises and can be realized by using SAP NetWeaver.

The ESA application stack consists of the following layers:

- *User interface layer*: This layer provides and manages the interaction with the user.
- *Process layer*: This layer manages the sequence of steps carried out during runtime of the application.
- *Service layer*: This layer consists of all services that provide analysis and processing to business objects.
- *Object layer*: This layer combines data from different sources and basic access methods and maps them to target business objects.
- *Persistence layer*: This layer is responsible for the physical storage of data.

ESA platform is constituted of the data, the relevant services to work with these data, and processes that span the sequence of access and processing of these data. The ESA model does not maintain its own copies of business objects. Identified objects are mapped to their original sources in order to ensure the currency and consistency of data as also to avoid redundant data. In case of the business processes, ESA affects a clear separation between the process and the application logic, which enables mapping of the complete processes. Extracting the application logic of the underlying systems and providing it in the form of a service wrapper enables the description and configuration of the processes in a central instance that is valid across all applications within the enterprise. This separation also enables the changeability of business processes because the process can be optimized or reoriented with changing the actual implementation of the processes. Consequently, continual and incremental improvements can also be made depending on the changing requirements of the business environment.

> The importance of referring to the original SAP NetWeaver documentation corresponding to the version of your installation cannot be overemphasized. What we have presented in this chapter are the essential details of the various components of SAP NetWeaver. However, this chapter is not intended as a replacement for the colossal amount of instructive documentation, guidelines, checklists, templates, samples, questionnaires, and so forth provided and recommended for use by SAP. Those are well-proven instruments, and for an actual project, it is highly recommended that you procure the version of the documentation corresponding to the version of your installation and use it in conjunction with the implementation project.

10.4 SAP NetWeaver Overview

SAP NetWeaver is the most comprehensive integration and application development, deployment, and management platform available on the market today. Enterprises face the challenge of supporting the growth of the enterprise and at the same time protecting IT investments in the past. SAP NetWeaver supports the integration and applications in a multiplicity of environments and thus reduces the Total Cost of Ownership (TCO) of the IT landscape.

The real proof and power of the SAP NetWeaver's all-encompassing vision can be seen in the seamless combination of distributed systems, Enterprise Application Integration (EAI), Component-Based Development (CBD), Web Services, Service-Oriented Architecture (SOA), and Enterprise Services Architecture (ESA).

> SAP NetWeaver provides a complete interoperability with IBM WebSphere and Microsoft's .NET.

As discussed earlier, SAP NetWeaver connects people, information, and processes beyond the organizational and technological boundaries of the enterprise.

SAP NetWeaver, which is based on open standards, consists of four layers:

1. People integration
2. Information integration
3. Process integration
4. Application platform

Figure 10.3 presents the SAP NetWeaver components.

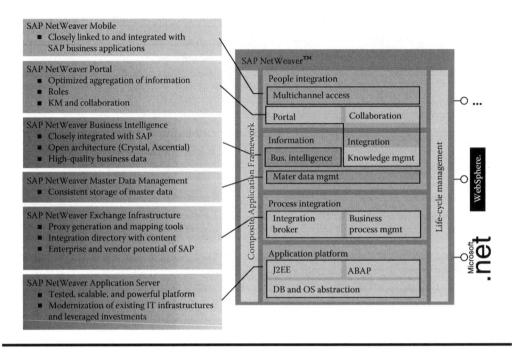

Figure 10.3   SAP NetWeaver components.

10.4.1 People Integration

People integration ensures that users are empowered to the following:

10.4.1.1 Multichannel Access

Customers are demanding more access and interaction points with their suppliers. In addition to getting more information from the companies with which they do business, customers are demanding more ways of interacting with those companies—including mobile phone, e-mail, Web, and regular mail. SAP Mobile Infrastructure enables members of the enterprise to work remotely independent of the networks and be able to conduct time-critical business processes in an offline mode.

SAP Mobile Client, which is installed locally on the client devices, consists of Web server, a database server along with native business logic. It features a Java Virtual Machine (JVM) and provides an open programming model that developers can use to create mobile applications. The SAP Mobile Client is used as a runtime environment for mobile applications providing a host of requisite services like

- Data persistence
- Data synchronization
- Application management
- Tracing for monitoring purposes
- Configuration (administration of system and user attributes)
- Programming models for user interfaces (UIs)
- User management

SAP Mobile Infrastructure provides tools for data synchronization and replication for synchronizing between the client devices and back-end servers.

SAP Mobile Server has J2EE and Advanced Business Application Programming (ABAP) server components that run, respectively, on the J2EE and ABAP stacks of the SAP NetWeaver Application Server (AS). The J2EE server component receives compressed data from the mobile client device via HTTPS and forwards it to the ABAP server component. The ABAP server component carries out relevant tasks such as managing data containers and identifying and then calling the relevant back-end applications for processing the data received from the mobile client devices. The ABAP server components are also responsible for the major part of the synchronization process.

10.4.1.2 Enterprise Portal

In the course of his or her daily routine, a user may have to access the Internet, intranet, or several incompatible operational, business, and decision-support applications. Users may find themselves overwhelmed with information and technology options that may have to be exercised to move across these various resources. Users may dissipate enormous amounts of time and effort in switching between applications and entering passwords and other identification information every time. SAP Enterprise Portal (EP) solves these problems by devising a single gateway to all such resources. Users have the convenience of a single sign-on accessible from anywhere using only a single password.

SAP EP allows for a consistent and role-based access to SAP and non-SAP applications, external applications, repositories, databases, and services within and outside of enterprises—all integrated in a uniform user experience. It includes tools that enable management, analysis, and correlation of this information with each other as well as for exchanging it to work more effectively as teams.

SAP EP solves the problem of information logistics caused by the use of diverse applications. This enables users to focus more on the content, context, and relevance of corporate information, rather than on the complexities of accessing from diverse, autonomous, and often proprietary sources, which leads to better decisions. Inevitably, these later factors restrict the access of valuable information and hence deprive a majority of personnel from playing a more effective role in the organization. EP enables all users to subscribe, create, design, value add, publish, collaborate, reuse, and share information using tools and formats with which they are more familiar and comfortable.

EP has the following efficiency and productivity-multiplying features:

■ Interactive and secure access from anywhere
■ Explicit and implicit subscribe and publish facilities that enables users to schedule receipts when sending of just-in-time (JIT) information from or to identified resources
■ A single point of interactive access via a Web browser to both internal and external industry-specific and company-specific applications, content, and services
■ A wide variety of information formats, including relational database tables, multidimensional databases, and decision-processing objects like queries, reports, word-processing documents, spreadsheets, images, video, audio, HTML and XML pages, and e-mail messages
■ Personalized, easy, uniform, role-specific, company-specific, industry-specific user interfaces (with options for multiple roles)

SAP EP at its central core has a *portal framework* consisting of

■ Portal Runtime (PRT) running iViews
■ Portal Content Directory (PCD) that is shared between the portal and the SAP NetWeaver AS and provides an interface to the database
■ Database that centrally manages all portal-specific data

The portal framework supports common standard technologies and standards like HTTPS, JDBC, SOAP, SAP Java Connector (JCo), and SAP P4 that is analogous to RMI for synchronous and asynchronous communications and Hyperrelational Navigation Protocol (HRNP). The last protocol is essential for providing Drag & Relate functionality within iViews. Additionally, it supports protocols and services for authentication like the Lightweight Directory Access Protocol (LDAP), Active Directory Services (ADS), and digital certificates. Via interfaces, the portal framework uses the security mechanisms provided by the J2EE Engine of the SAP NetWeaver AS including user authentication, Single Sign-on (SSO), authorization management, and secure communication. The portal framework establishes an SSO mechanism that uses encrypted cookies to safely select and use user-specific authorizations and authentication across disparate systems.

10.4.1.3 Collaboration

As discussed in Chapter 1, Section 1.3 "Management by Collaboration," the business environment has been witnessing tremendous and rapid changes in the 1990s. There is an increasing emphasis on being customer focused and on leveraging and strengthening the company's core competencies. This has forced companies to learn and develop abilities to change and respond rapidly to the competitive dynamics of the global market. Companies have learned to effectively reengineer themselves into flatter organizations, with closer integration across the traditional functional boundaries of the organization. There is increasing focus on employee empowerment and cross functional teams.

The basic idea of collaboration has been gaining tremendous ground with the increasing importance of business processes and dynamically constituted teams in the operations of companies. By their very nature, teams are flexible, adaptable, dynamic, and collaborative. They encourage flexibility, innovation, entrepreneurship, and responsiveness. Increasingly, companies are populated with worker teams that have special skills, operate semiautonomously, and are answerable directly to peers and to the end customers. Members must not only have higher level of skills than before but must also be more flexible and capable of doing more jobs. The empowered workforce with considerably enhanced managerial responsibilities (pertaining to information, resources, authority, and accountability) has resulted in an increase in worker commitment and flexibility. Whereas workers have witnessed gains in the quality of their work life, corporations have obtained returns in terms of increased quality, productivity, and cost-reduction improvements. Consequently, in the past few years, a new type of nonhierarchical network organization with distributed intelligence and decentralized decision-making powers has been evolving. This entails a demand for constant and frequent communication and feedback among the various teams or functional groups.

The collaboration component of SAP NetWeaver includes services that support communication and collaboration in enterprise-specific business processes. It provides facilities for virtual rooms in which users can organize their tasks and share documents, applications, and ideas. It enables virtual teams and project group members to work together across time zones and geographical distances to access common data and services. Collaboration services can be configured in the collaboration launch pad or the user detail iView.

The collaboration component is tightly integrated with SAP EP, KM, and BI components. It provides many features for real-time collaboration via the SAP EP including

- Interactive online access to applications
- Interactive online exchange of information
- Integration of third-party services

10.4.2 *Information Integration*

Information integration enables continuous, consistent, and transparent access to both structured and unstructured information of the enterprise.

Information integration consists of the following three components:

1. Business Intelligence
2. Knowledge Management
3. Master Data Management

10.4.2.1 *Business Intelligence (BI)*

As we have seen in Chapter 1, Section 1.2.1.4 "Customer Capital: Customer Knowledge as the New Capital," real-time information that is collated and analyzed in the proper context is the most important asset of the organizations in this century; it is also a tremendous competitive advantage to a company. A company can enhance its effectiveness and the efficiency of its management processes by gaining the ability to quickly extract mission-critical actionable information from a flood of data made available by its operational systems. For achieving this, on one hand, companies need solutions that can provide immediate access to information that is relevant for making decisions as well as the ability to analyze it flexibly. On the other hand, these solutions also need to be integrated with the existing operational systems for easy and fast access and action on this essential information.

SAP Business Intelligence (BI) provides a data warehousing functionality, a business intelligence platform, as well as a suite of business intelligence tools for enterprises to achieve these objectives. With the toolset provided, relevant historical or up-to-date business information from SAP, non-SAP, and even external systems can be integrated, transformed, and consolidated in SAP BI.

The traditional solution for meeting such divergent goals is known as *data warehousing*. A data warehouse is a separate application environment with a dedicated database that draws on diverse data sources and is designed to support sophisticated query and analysis. Data warehousing with SAP BI is the basis for a comprehensive solution for converting data into valuable information and, finally, knowledge regarding the enterprise that can be used for goal-oriented actions. It is a comprehensive solution that includes a relational online analytical processing (OLAP) engine, automated data extractor and population tools, a preconfigured metadata repository, a user-friendly, front-end tool with powerful reporting and analysis facilities, and an administrator's workbench to manage this whole environment. Additionally, SAP, being a highly secure and auditable environment, is also a source of correct, clean, and reliable data, all of which are major concerns for normal data warehousing projects.

Compared to the traditional data warehousing solutions, the SAP BI has a tremendous advantage, because it can benefit from the simple fact that mySAP ERP itself is a repository-based application environment. BI includes a number of components that permit it to perform many of its tasks with a high degree of automation and to complete a fast implementation with minimal ongoing maintenance. Usual data warehouse solutions are designed to extract and map at the level of the individual database fields, because they do not recognize the context of the data. This information on the context and meaning of data has to be established as a separate exercise. SAP BI is based on the SAP business processes. Making use of SAP's integration and metadata concepts, SAP BI extracts, loads, and aggregates data in accordance with the enterprise-wide business processes and presents them in a flexible and user-friendly manner customized to the needs of the user.

Also, because of the fundamental integration of BI with mySAP ERP, the results of the BI analysis can also be immediately integrated back into the SAP system, which is the powerful *second loop* learning that we spoke about in Chapter 1's "The Learning Organization." It represents the capability of institutional learning that gives a tremendous advantage to companies in these times of rapidly changing markets.

Business Explorer (BEx) is the component of SAP BI consisting of flexible reporting and analysis tools for providing strategic, tactical, and operational analysis and decision support. These tools include functionality for query, reporting, and analysis. Information can be disseminated via SAP Enterprise Portal, an intranet (Web Application Design), or mobile presentation devices including WAP or Personal Digital Assistants (PDAs). Web Application Design provides the option of implementing the generic OLAP navigation in both Web applications and BI cockpits for simple or even highly customized scenarios (by using standard Web technologies or SAP BI technologies like BI Java SDK, Open Analysis Interfaces, or Web Design APIs). BEx Web Analyzer provides an independent Web application for data analysis that can be called via a URL or as an iView in the SAP Enterprise Portal (EP). BEx Information Broadcasting allows precalculated documents with historical data or links with live data to be disseminated via e-mail or published in the SAP EP.

SAP BI provides related analytical functions, technologies, and infrastructures like

- *Metadata Repository* that enables maintenance and access to the metadata objects of the BI system
- *Online Analytical Processing (OLAP)* that enables multidimensional analyses according to several different perspectives
- BI Business Planning and Simulation (BI-BPS) that enables planning applications
- *Analysis Process Designer* (*APD*) that enables special analysis like data mining

 SAP BI includes preconfigured role- and task-oriented information models based on consistent metadata. These models include roles, workbooks, queries, InfoSources, InfoCubes, ODS objects, key performance indicators, attributes, update rules, and extractors for SAP and other selected applications.

10.4.2.2 Knowledge Management (KM)

SAP KM provides a generic framework for integrating and accessing unstructured information via iViews of SAP Enterprise Portal (EP). SAP KM consists of two main components: SAP Content Management (CM) and search, retrieval, and classification (TREX). Normally, information is stored in several repositories like file servers, groupware system, or document management systems. SAP KM uses several preconfigured repository managers to integrate these repositories and serves as the central role-specific point of entry for all unstructured information irrespective of the nature of the data (text documents, presentation, or HTML files) or data sources (file servers, intranet, or the World Wide Web). Content management services enable the usage of various KM functions across all these varieties in a uniform manner.

The search functions finds documents in all repositories that are integrated in SAP KM, but in the results list, the system displays only those documents for which the user has read authorization. Using a web crawler, the contents of websites can also be added to indexes in order to make them available for the search function in SAP EP. Documents and other objects stored in the repositories have properties that can also be assigned values. This can be used to achieve a higher hit rate during the search process, thus enhancing the effectiveness and efficiency of leveraging the existing knowledge base within the enterprise.

Taxonomy is a hierarchical structure of categories in which documents are classified according to content, organization, or other criteria. Documents stored physically in several different repositories can still be assigned to a single category. Taxonomy enables the users of a portal to navigate through an enterprise-wide consistent hierarchical structure even though the data storage environment itself may be heterogeneous. Once set, the system automatically refreshes the classification for new or changed documents.

SAP KM enables dissemination of information to the target groups entailing features like search, classification, or subscription of information. SAP KM also enables joint work on documents irrespective of roles and departments. As mentioned earlier, business information from SAP BI (using BEx Information Broadcasting) can be disseminated to a broad range of users via the SAP KM folders that include objects like

- Documents with precalculated reports
- Links to BEx Web Applications and queries with live data

10.4.2.3 Master Data Management (MDM)

SAP Master Data Management (MDM) provides a central and consistent framework for the maintenance, management, and installation of master data integrated across different system, locations, and service providers or partners. SAP MDM enables storage, update, and consolidation of master data as also its dissemination across all applications in the enterprise. Thus, any member from any function of the enterprise (engineering, procurement, manufacturing, marketing, sales, service, etc.) always receives the current and correct information about products, product catalogs, business partners, or documentation. SAP MDM is based on an open and Web-based architecture designed for collaboration within enterprises. Collaborative e-business scenarios in heterogeneous IT environments become viable primarily because of the data harmonization enabled by SAP MDM. Similarly, provisioning of real-time mission-critical actionable information seamlessly across disparate systems across the enterprise accelerates the decision-making process while reducing the costs of maintaining master data. This effectively contributes to lower the TCO of the IT landscape.

SAP MDM entails use of master data objects independently of each other. This is essential because individual applications invariably have disparate data models. Additionally, this is dictated by the reality of business process and especially the analytical applications spanning heterogeneous environments across the enterprise.

To obtain data from the corresponding systems, SAP MDM supplies specific adapters for different Master Data Client (MDC) systems like SAP Enterprise, SAP CRM, or SAP SRM.

SAP MDM supports the following scenarios:

- MDM Consolidation entails the process of consolidating master data used across different application systems and transferring the information regarding identical data objects to SAP BI to enable an accurate evaluation of operational status of the enterprise. MDM Consolidation enables identification of identical or similar master data objects across different systems, so that a cleanup can be affected whenever necessary.
- MDM Harmonization extends the consolidation process to include accurate (i.e., correct, consistent, current, and complete) maintenance and dissemination of the master data objects across all systems within the enterprise. This ensures that all client systems are provided with accurate master data and that all business processes are carried out accurately. However, MDM Harmonization also allows client applications to supplement the global attributes of the disseminated data objects with additional local attributes.
- MDM Centralization is similar to the harmonization process except that the maintenance and dissemination of master data objects is allowed only from a central server. Unlike harmonization, it does not permit direct maintenance or extension with local attributes in local systems.

> **GOLDEN SOURCES OF DATA**
>
> MDM Harmonization enables what is termed as *golden sources* of enterprise data. Data entities are duplicated in various tables across multiple systems. However, for each of these entities, there is one place where they are primarily created and updated; this is termed as the golden source for those data. Using the golden source of data obviates the need for ensuring consolidation, consistency, currency, correctness, or completeness of the data items, which is of enormous advantage especially in the case of analytical applications. Thus, the golden source of data functions as the primary source of those data across all the tables and systems in the enterprise.

10.4.3 Process Integration

Process integration supports seamless business processes in a heterogeneous environment enabling definition, control, and monitoring of cross system business processes.

10.4.3.1 Integration Broker: SAP NetWeaverExchange Infrastructure (XI)

SAP NetWeaverExchange Infrastructure (XI), which is now known as SAP NetWeaver Process Integration (PI), is the primary enabler of the cross system business processes. It offers services that are critical in a heterogeneous environment like runtime infrastructure for exchanging messages (with facility for transforming messages between sender and recipient), configuration options for controlling collaborative processes and message flow, design and execution of cross system business processes, and B2B support.

SAP XI is based on an open architecture and primarily uses open standards (associated with XML and Java) to interface with non-SAP systems to and from the *Integration Server* between the sender and recipient using XML-based communication via HTTP by employing either of these approaches:

■ Direct communication via proxies that are generated into the application system based on descriptions in the corresponding WSDL
■ Communication via adapters enabled by creating exchange interfaces in the application system

The combination of disparate system is primarily enabled by the fact that the sender and recipient exchanging messages via the Integration Server are effectively decoupled from each other. Moreover, consequently, every system that can exchange messages with the Integration Server can automatically exchange messages with all other systems connected to the Integration Server (see note on page 280 of this chapter).

The normal processing on the Integration Server is *stateless*, which means that the Integration Server is usually not aware of the semantic correlation between different messages, that is, the context of the messages. But one can describe the logical dependencies between the messages as well as additional conditions for defining the message flow, thus enabling the modeling and maintenance of cross system business process with SAP XI. Business processes are objects stored in the Integration Repository or Integration Directory along with other objects like message interfaces. During the design phase, the business process can be defined using the graphical process editor within the Integration Builder (in the Integration Repository). During the configuration phase, the recipient determination for the business process can be set using the Integration Directory of the Integration Builder. At runtime, the business processes can be run using the Business Process Engine.

Similarly, in the case of collaborative processes, all the integration-related information in its entirety is stored and accessible centrally in SAP XI:

■ Objects during the design phase are stored in the Integration Repository.
■ Objects during the configuration phase are stored in the Integration Directory.

The costs of development and maintenance of distributed systems are effectively reduced by the centralized storage and access to knowledge on business processes.

10.4.3.2 SAP Business Process Management (BPM)

SAP BPM extends SAP XI to include *stateful* processing of messages by enabling persistence of business processes on the Integration Server. As a result, business processes can be made to wait indefinitely or according to a schedule of messages or send the messages after grouping them in a specific manner or process the messages within a business process further recursively or so on.

10.4.4 Application Platform

The SAP NetWeaver Application Server (AS) provides a complete development environment for developing, deploying, and running platform-independent, resilient, and scalable applications.

SAP NetWeaver AS enables a homogenous infrastructure for both ABAP and J2EE-based applications. The development environments of ABAP Workbench and SAP NetWeaver

Developer Studio coupled with the Java Development Infrastructure (JDI) are completely integrated in the server. These include

- Sources code editors
- Version control
- Structuring of development objects
- Development tools and editors for interfaces
- Support of multilingual text elements and messages
- Debugging functionality
- Various text and analysis tools
- Support for modification
- Direct access to all data definitions via the ABAP and Java dictionaries, respectively
- Connection to corresponding transport system via Transport Organizer in ABAP and Change Management System in JDI, respectively

All business objects and interfaces can be used in the same way in both ABAP and Java environments.

10.4.4.1 ABAP Application Platform

ABAP development is managed natively in the system; metadata and source code are stored in the database. The ABAP programming language combines the benefits of an object-oriented language with those of an integrated 4GL language. It provides the typical language constructs like classes, interfaces, and inheritance. Many server-based services, which in other languages are embedded as libraries and have to be accessed via APIs, are integrated directly into the language—like the direct usage of data types in the ABAP Dictionary as well as the integration of the database access. ABAP objects include Open SQL as a part of the language.

While the interfaces of the classic SAP applications were based on SAP GUI, Dynpro technology enabled programming dialogs in SAP GUI at runtime via a proprietary protocol.

A Business Server Pages (BSP) employs the server-side scripting approach (much like the JSP) enabling the creation of HTML-based Web applications with ABAP code.

10.4.4.2 Java Applications

The SAP J2EE Engine supports component-based enterprise technologies and enables quick development and installation of portable, resilient, and scalable applications. The portability of these applications is guaranteed by the support of many operating systems and database platforms.

The J2EE Engine complies with the current JMX and J2EE standards and implements Enterprise JavaBeans, servlets, JSPs, JNDI, JMS, and Java mail according to the standards specified. It provides scalability, availability, and reliability, support for current security standards, caching, dynamic load balancing, options for data replication, and clustering of Web pages and components as well as a wide range of functionalities for configuration, monitoring, and administration.

SAP AS provides the following enhancements:

- SAP NetWeaver Developer Studio (NWDS) coupled with SAP Java Development Infrastructure (JDI)
- SAP Java Connector (JCo) for connecting the ABAP and Java components
- Web Dynpro for creating professional, high-quality, cross platform Web user interfaces

SAP NWDS along with JDI provides consistent access to all Java development tools and serves as the central point of entry for all SAP infrastructure components irrespective of whether SAP technologies like Web Dynpro Java Dictionary or standard technologies like J2EE or XML are being used. The JDI consists of tightly connected central services for design, implementation, building, and testing purposes that can be used either in the localized or centralized mode of operations.

SAP NetWeaver JDI includes the following components:

- Design Time Repository (DTR) for central storage, versioning, and management of Java source code and other resources. It provides an automatic mechanism for conflict detection and resolution.
- Component Build Service (CBS) creates the corresponding runtime objects like Java archives that are installable on the central J2EE server. The CBS creates incremental build and updates them automatically with the dependent components via DTR.
- Change Management Service (CMS) takes the results of the build process from CBS and accordingly initializes the distribution and installation in the J2EE server environment.
- Software Deployment Manager (SDM) manages the installation and update of the software components on the J2EE server.
- Java Dictionary, like the ABAP Dictionary, maintains the global definition of tables and data types.
- Java Test Tools enable starting, stopping, debugging, and testing of Java components irrespective of whether they reside on local or remote AS server.

10.4.5 SAP Solution Manager

SAP Solution Manager (SM) plays a critical role in providing the tools required for the entire life cycle of the solution, from implementation to the productive operation, including continuous changes and upgrades that are unavoidable in any implementation. SM provides a wide range of tools and functionalities such as implementation and upgrade documentation, tools for managing SAP licenses, tools for solution monitoring and systems management, comprehensive statistics regarding system performance and load, high availability concepts, the application log, and tools for customizing, testing, and data archiving. It also provides facilities for managing and monitoring systems and business process of the enterprise.

10.5 Summary

This chapter discussed SAP CRM application environment with special focus on SAP NetWeaver, which is SAP's implementation of the Service-Oriented Architecture. SAP NetWeaver enables integration at various levels with myriad of heterogeneous systems that populate most of the enterprises.

Chapter 11

SAP Tools and Programming

SAP's ABAP Development Workbench and SAP NWDS are the integrated and full-featured development environments for custom development or enhancement of SAP standard functionality in ABAP and Java/J2EE respectively. SAP customers can use either of these environments to rapidly configure the various aspects of SAP applications like the look and feel, behavior, and workflow. They are examples of interactive enterprise application builder that enable definition, creation, and modification via visual manipulation of all of its application components and their services.

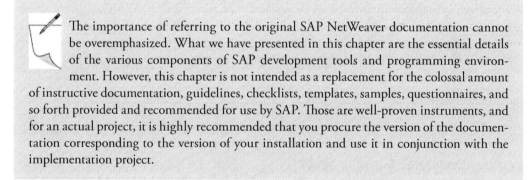

The importance of referring to the original SAP NetWeaver documentation cannot be overemphasized. What we have presented in this chapter are the essential details of the various components of SAP development tools and programming environment. However, this chapter is not intended as a replacement for the colossal amount of instructive documentation, guidelines, checklists, templates, samples, questionnaires, and so forth provided and recommended for use by SAP. Those are well-proven instruments, and for an actual project, it is highly recommended that you procure the version of the documentation corresponding to the version of your installation and use it in conjunction with the implementation project.

11.1 ABAP Custom Development

11.1.1 ABAP Genesis

The programming language ABAP originated in the 1980s and continues to be enhanced and developed with every release of SAP R/3. All R/3 business applications are developed in ABAP. ABAP has its origin in the report generation programming language developed for R/2 that enabled the creation of simple print lists. That language has expanded over time into a full-fledged development environment called the Advanced Business Application Programming (ABAP) language, which originally stood for Allgemeine Businessprozess Aufbereitungsprogramme.

ABAP is highly reminiscent of the programming languages COBOL and Pascal, especially in its reporting aspects. However, ABAP is quite different from typical third-generation languages (3GLs) and fourth-generation languages (4GLs) in that it is a language, as well as a full-featured client/server development environment, consisting of the ABAP Development Workbench and R/3 Basis functionality (now taken over by NetWeaver).

The essential characteristics of the ABAP environment are

- It is a fourth-generation language based on structured programming methodologies; especially in its reporting aspects, it has a COBOL-like flavor.
- It is an event-driven language, especially in its dialog programming aspects, which are central to the SAP system.
- It is an interpretative language; this makes possible prototyping of applications.
- It is an integrated, full-featured development environment including a data dictionary, data modeling tools, program editors, screen and menu painters, and testing and debugging tools and provides ready navigation between all these objects.
- It is open and portable because of the portability and open programming interfaces provided by the SAP system.
- It provides modularization by using reusable subroutines and function modules from a centrally managed library.
- It provides extensive data manipulation functions such as dates, strings, and floating-point numbers.
- It supports multilingual text elements including labels and messages.
- It contains a set of standard SQL statements for transparent access to any of the underlying standard databases such as Oracle, DB2, and Informix.

The programs developed in ABAP can run without customization effort on any operating system, graphical user interface, database management system, network interface, and so forth, in both centralized and decentralized client/server environments.

Especially with the introduction of ABAP Objects, ABAP is no longer a fourth-generation language alone. In a later section, we get familiarized with the concept of object orientation and its significance for the future of all software application environments.

11.1.2 ABAP Development Workbench

ABAP Development Workbench is a full-fledged development environment for developing enterprise-wide client/server applications. It supports the entire software development life cycle (SDLC) from data definition, user interface design, processing logic, reporting, testing and debugging, and documentation to management of the work-in-process (WIP) programming effort. It provides a sophisticated metadata-management environment called ABAP data dictionary, as well as a library of reusable executable functions. It is the centralized place for development and organization of all components required for a software project. All Workbench objects must be generated to become active in the runtime system.

All development objects of the ABAP Development Workbench, such as data and process models, ABAP dictionary, reports, dynpro, function module libraries, and authorization objects, are stored in the ABAP repository. The Repository Information System is fully integrated with the entire Development Workbench. The Repository Information System allows searching and sorting of various objects using various criteria. It also provides an extensive *where-used* list, giving all the points of use for a specified object. By default, it displays the different object types that are defined in the SAP system in hierarchical form.

As its name suggests, the application hierarchy contains the structure of the complete SAP standard business applications. For the customized version, SAP permits maintenance of the customer application hierarchy along with a development class defined for each node on the hierarchy.

11.1.2.1 ABAP Dictionary

The ABAP dictionary is the logical representation of the data stored in the underlying physical standard databases, such as Oracle, DB2, and Informix.

The dictionary contains metadata about data that are stored in the application tables in the database. The metadata description in the dictionary involves two different levels: a syntactical or technical level and a semantic level. The first level corresponds to the domain object and the second level to the data element object.

Tables, structures, and composite objects are defined in terms of the data element objects, which in turn are modeled on the domain objects. This systemic hierarchy of domain, data element, field, and structure renders them reusable at all levels. This builds up tremendous flexibility and maintainability in the system. For instance, an increase in the size of the amount domain CDO instantly propagates the change to all data elements and fields and therefore to the tables, structures, and ultimately database tables.

Because of the interpretive nature of the runtime environment for ABAP programs and dictionary, any changes made in the ABAP dictionary are immediately propagated to all relevant application programs.

11.1.2.2 Data Browser

The data browser allows navigation through and display of the ABAP dictionary tables. It displays the table content along with the key fields, and it can also display foreign key relationships. It also permits new entries in case the specific table is set with the Maintenance Allowed check box within the dictionary.

11.1.2.3 Object Browser

This is the main navigation tool in the ABAP Development Workbench. The object browser groups objects by development class.

11.1.2.4 Program Editor

The ABAP program editor enables you to edit programs, performs checking of syntax, provides online help, and so forth.

This can be used to edit the source code of different development objects, such as

- ABAP program source code for reports, interactive reports, and module pools
- Flow logic for the screen painter
- Logical databases
- Function modules
- Maintenance of documentation and text elements

As a Workbench tool, the program editor also enables you to specify the attributes for ABAP programs.

11.1.2.5 Screen Painter

The screen painter enables you to define and design the screen, as well as the flow logic for dynamic programs (dynpros). Supplementary control information includes the language used and the number of the follow-on dynpro. The screen is interpreted not by the ABAP interpreter but by a separate DYNPRO interpreter. It should be noted that DYNPRO is a full-fledged 4GL environment that enables you to develop prototypes quickly and then flesh out the full logic.

The screen painter specifies the following:

- Screen program attributes such as screen number and screen type (normal, subscreen, dialog)
- Screen layout, including field locations, labels, radio buttons, icons, check boxes, and element group
- Fields, including database field and cross validations
- Flow logic

For screen design, the screen painter has a graphical as well as an alphanumeric editor. In the former, the field labels, positions, and so on can be changed or arranged directly on the screen. All text on the screen can also be represented by graphical icons. However, with the alphanumeric editor, screen design has to proceed only by selections from the menus of the screen painter.

11.1.2.6 Menu Painter

This is the ABAP Development Workbench tool for developing user interfaces or more correctly presentation interfaces.

It must be noted that these are not the customary user screens or menus but only user interface standard frames that are used as a template for all SAP screens. They are not related to any screen generated by the screen painter. But they could become associated through the menu object called *GUI status*, which groups together the menu bar, standard toolbar, application toolbar, and the function keys that are usable in the presentation interfaces.

The control elements provided by the front-end O/S are employed mainly for movement of the screen itself or for the movement of the display screen. A dialog program consists of several variants of the user interfaces, called the statuses. A status is defined by the following editable elements:

- Menu
- Push-button identifications
- Function key assignments
- Title bar

A main menu can consist of up to three levels, and each level can consist of up to 15 entries. By using the menu painter, every menu item is mapped to a SAP transaction code. Important function codes are assigned to function keys for immediate access; this avoids the need to search through the menus for relevant functionality. Similarly, function codes can also be assigned to push buttons located below the toolbar. Again, it should be noted that these push buttons are not the same as those created by the screen painter; these push buttons can be defined only by the menu painter and can be mapped to SAP transactions (i.e., ABAP programs), but are not part of ABAP applications directly.

This separation of the user interface and access—that is, the presentation interface and the SAP system—has been fortuitous because it enables SAP to use the latest Web browsers as front ends without a major rehaul of their application architecture! In fact, SAP has adopted the strategy of replacing the front-end O/S, such as Microsoft Windows, with Microsoft Explorer. It is not only a change of presentation interface. The system that supports Web browsers has also helped SAP to launch a slew of services in the rapidly developing Internet-based service market.

11.1.2.7 Function Library

The Function Library, which is now called Function Builder, is a tool for maintenance and testing of function modules, which are usable from any program.

11.1.2.8 Testing and Performance Analysis

In this section, we look at some of the tools available in the Workbench for testing and performance analysis.

11.1.2.8.1 ABAP Debugger

This is a tool available for testing ABAP programs. It has facilities for setting breakpoints as well as step-by-step executions. Every time the program is stopped within a debugging session, the system has a provision for displaying or modifying the contents of the tables and fields. Breakpoints themselves can be static, dynamic, or watch points and specific to a keyword or an event.

The debugger can work in different display modes in terms of the program-related information that the modes display. The default or preferred mode is V in which the contents of all data fields are displayed. The various display modes are as follows:

- V mode: Displays content of fields
- T mode: Displays content of internal tables
- F mode: Displays detailed information on a particular field, including content, every time a value is signed to that field
- S mode: Displays the call sequence of various subroutines, function calls, and events
- P mode: Displays all programs that are required to execute the current program

In later versions, these display views do still exist, but without the modes (V, T, and so on).

11.1.2.8.2 Extended Computer-Aided Test Tool (eCATT)

This tool permits automated testing of business processes. It has facilities to describe and automate the testing of business processes, for example, by simulating the input screen dialogs. Because the test is automated, it can be repeated whenever required; the results of the test run and messages can be logged by CATT.

11.1.2.8.3 Runtime Analysis

This is a tool to aid diagnosis of performance problems in ABAP transactions or programs. It provides information on the following:

- Executed instructions
- Chronological sequence of executed instructions
- Tables accessed and type of access
- Execution time

11.1.2.8.4 SQL Trace

This tool enables the analysis and display of the database calls made by reports and transactions written in ABAP. This assists in performance analysis, especially for batch programs.

11.1.2.9 Workbench Organizer

The Workbench organizer provides an environment and tools for the ABAP development.

11.1.3 Programming in ABAP

ABAP is a full-featured 4GL that originated as a reporting language. Like any traditional computer language, ABAP's features can be described by broadly dividing them as follows:

■ *Data definition statements*: These describe the data processed in an ABAP program, for example, DATA, TYPES, and TABLES.
■ *Data query statements*: These specify the attributes of the data record that must be retrieved and processed, for example, SELECT.
■ *Data manipulation statements*: These render standard manipulation of data, for example, ADD, SUBTRACT, MOVE, and COMPUTE.
■ *Data control statements*: These signal control structures such as loops, decisions, and subroutines, for example, DO, WHILE, IF, CASE, and PERFORM.
■ *Data event statements*: These trigger the execution of certain routines depending on the occurrence of certain predefined events, for example, Pfnn, GET/SET, END-OF-PAGE, AT USER-COMMAND, and AT LINE-SELECTION.

11.1.3.1 Data Types and Operations

ABAP supports most of the standard data types. Based on those basic data types, ABAP also enables you to develop complex data types or structures. It is in this area that the influence of languages such as COBOL is striking.

ABAP also has all the standard language elements for manipulation of data such as assignment, comparison, computation, and complex computation involving data of different types. It also provides extensive functions for processing textual data, including assignment, truncating or adding blank spaces, searching for a specific string, matching strings, concatenating strings, and comparing strings. ABAP also provides various operations for date calculations, such as calculating time periods in days, future dates, and comparison of dates.

11.1.3.2 Data Table Processing

ABAP permits access to data tables defined in the ABAP dictionary as well as those in the underlying database. The former is achieved through SAP's Open SQL and the latter through the native SQL specific to any of the standard databases, such as Oracle, DB2, and Informix. To retain the independence of the SAP system from the underlying databases, Open SQL implements the barest set of SQL commands and features. The relational join operation, although not available in Open SQL, can be used through views defined by ABAP dictionary.

11.1.3.3 Internal Tables

These tables are temporary and exist only during the run of an ABAP program. ABAP provides various operations for processing internal tables such as sorting, searching, and sequential access.

When a similar processing has to be done on a subset of records from the database tables, defining internal tables helps to simplify the programming effort by using control statements such as DO loops and CASE.

11.1.3.4 SAP Transactions

A transaction in SAP is like a program in normal computer languages and is identified by a four-character transaction code. A transaction can be initiated directly from the command field on the presentation interface or from the corresponding menu option. There are two kinds of transactions: report and dialog transactions:

1. *Report Transactions*: Report transactions are SAP programs that collect selection parameters from the selection screen followed by the output called the lists.
2. *Dialog Transactions*: Dialog programs consist of more than one interactive screen called a dynpro. These transactions sometimes also need preselected information for triggering them, not unlike the explicit selection screens in report programs; these are called parameter transactions:
   a. *Subroutines*: As in any other programming language, ABAP allows subroutines for modularization of programs. This helps in reusability and, therefore, in increased quality, productivity, maintainability, and documentation of the developed system. ABAP provides for definition of subroutines using the FORM language element. Subroutines can be called by using PERFORM statements, and they can be called from within programs or from external programs.
      Here are other characteristics of subroutines:
      i. Parameters of any type can be passed to subroutines.
      ii. Calls can be generated dynamically during the processing.
      iii. Calls can be nested, recursive, and so on.
   b. *Functions*: Functions, which are a special kind of subroutine, are very important for the modularization of ABAP programs and applications. Function modules are available in a central library and can be called from there by any ABAP program. Function modules are encapsulated objects and have clearly defined interfaces with parameters such as import, export, and table parameters. Function modules have facilities for programming the handling of exceptional situations that occur during the processing of these functions.

11.1.3.5 Reporting

Reports access one or more tables and display their contents in the form of a list, which can be viewed either on the screen or on a printout. Report programs are very similar to the report programs in other languages, such as COBOL:

- *Logical Databases*: For reporting data, reports might have to access several logically dependent tables. Consequently, the report program has to establish a connection with the concerned tables every time. Because many reports refer to the same set of tables, such requirements might be common across various reports. SAP provides a special category of program, called a logical database, which reads data from several databases and makes one data set available that can then be used by several reports at once. Each report then has to read only a single data set, analyze, and display it per specifications. This increases programming productivity, maintainability of the programs, and so on.

■ *Selection Screens*: Selection screens are presented before the execution of a report. Selection screens work as filters to limit the number of records included for analysis within a report. A selection screen is an automatically generated screen for every report. Selection screens can collect either a range of values or parameters for a field in a table.

■ *Interactive Reporting*: Interactive processing involves providing inputs or additional processing on report lists displayed on-screen. Additional processing, transactions, or reports can be triggered during the display of the report with the function keys. The latter case refers to the drill-down reporting that was mentioned in Chapter 4.

11.1.3.6 Dialog Programming

Dialog programming deals with the development of interactive applications in SAP. Dialog programming is based on the concept of a *dynamic program (dynpro)*, which is a combination of input screen and corresponding processing code. A dialog program consists of more than one dynpro.

A dialog program includes the following elements:

■ One or more presentation interfaces
■ One or more dynpro screens
■ Flow logic

11.1.3.7 ABAP Query

End users can define simple reports through ABAP query. Through a user-friendly interface, a user can specify the subject area of interest, the tables concerned, the desired fields, and also the list layout. The system automatically generates a selection screen, not unlike that produced in report programming, and asks for required inputs immediately.

Thereafter, the report is produced automatically. The output can also be routed optionally either to file storage or to a Microsoft Excel file or another file type.

11.1.3.8 SAPscripts

SAPscript is SAP's word processing program. A typical output produced by ABAP programs is devoid of any special fonts, size variations, etc. SAPscripts enable SAP to produce professionally printed reports. It can also cater to the requirements for producing multilingual reports. SAPscripts define the layout set as well as other components like paragraphs and text elements. Using the SAPscript function modules, layout sets can be called from ABAP programs; in reverse, ABAP subroutines can also be called from the layout sets.

11.1.3.9 Batch Data Communication and Interfaces

Before going live, a large amount of data needs to be uploaded into the system before it can be released into production. R/3 release 4.0 introduced a utility to accomplish this, called Legacy

System Migration Workbench (LSM Workbench). This primarily works by mapping the source data structure onto the target data structures in SAP.

However, in the earlier systems, there were three different methods for achieving the same:

1. Batch Input
2. Direct Input
3. Fast Input

11.1.4 ABAP Objects

Before delving into the aspects of object orientation of SAP, we need to elaborate briefly on what object orientation means. The object-oriented paradigm is based on a new way of looking at the old dichotomy of data and computational procedures.

11.1.4.1 Object-Oriented Paradigm

A *paradigm* is the totality of techniques, tools, attributes, and patterns of thinking or exemplars that constitute a world view. The 1960s were characterized by the *algorithmic view*, wherein the primary concern was to design and implement correct and efficient algorithms, which were related mostly to the performance issues of the numeric computations within the hardware constraints of main memory and offline storage memory. Subsequently, attendant problems of programming such as writing, debugging, and modifying led to the progressive crystallization of the *procedural view*. In the procedural view, algorithms were packaged into subprograms or procedures and handled independently of the programs using them. This gradually led further to the *structural view* of the functional paradigm. In the functional paradigm, the focus is on the various functions and subfunctions that a system has to perform and the manner in which those functions have to be performed. The object-oriented view extends and couples this trend of abstractions not only to operations (such as subprograms and procedures) but also to the data.

The principal building blocks of the object-oriented paradigm are four in number: object, class, message, and method. They broadly correspond to the record, record type, procedure, and procedure call in traditional language systems. A set of methods is sometimes referred as an interface.

An *object* is a thing that exists and has identity (i.e., it occupies memory and is addressable). An object consists of data that are tightly coupled with all the operations that can act against it. The operations are referred to as *methods*, and the communication to the object triggering some method is the *message*. A collection of such messages defines the public interface of the object, and an object may be inspected or altered only through this predefined protocol of messages.

Because there is a considerable amount of commonality between the methods of several objects, objects with the same internal structure and methods are grouped into a class called the Class Defining Object (CDO) and are themselves called instances of this class. A class may have multiple instance classes; however, each instance has only one CDO and keeps reference to its CDO. Thus, a computation is performed by sending messages to an object, which inherits or invokes a method of its CDO. This method in turn might invoke other objects by addressing to them and so on. This chain might terminate when a primitive object is invoked that either changes the instance variable or affects external entities such as the printer and hard disk. For instance, gasoline and diesel cars can be seen as the instance (sub)classes of the four-wheeled vehicle object, which itself is an instance (sub)class of the automobile class.

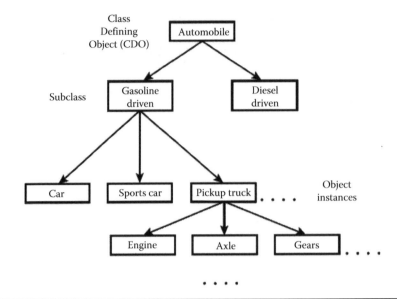

Figure 11.1 Subclasses and instance classes of the Class Defining Object (CDO) *Automobile.*

11.1.4.1.1 Inheritance and Encapsulation

A class is also a template from which newer objects can be quickly generated and used. This logically leads to many important characteristics of object-oriented environments, such as *inheritance* and *encapsulation*. We will illustrate these with reference to Figure 11.1 that shows the various subclasses and instance classes of the Class Defining Object (CDO) called *automobile*.

In the automobile illustration, inheritance can be understood in terms of certain standard characteristics and components, such as the fuel, fuel tank, wheels, gears, axle, and engine, which can be presumed to be constituents of gasoline and diesel cars. These are properties as inherited from the four-wheeler class and as inherited, in turn, from the automobile class. It is not difficult to imagine that this phenomenon of objectification can be carried out in either direction, from locomotion objects, down to the combustion engine parts, through the Bill of Materials (BOM). In fact, BOM itself is an example of a legitimate object! This results in a hierarchy or ladder at each level or step of classes and objects, not unlike the classification hierarchies of species in biology.

The second important characteristic of encapsulation refers to the transparency of any object within such a hierarchy of objects. That is, each object (for instance, X) merely performs a service, and queries as to how that service is accomplished, or for that matter queries regarding the constituting objects of X, are immaterial. If one persists in getting answers to these queries, one might have to ascend or descend the ladder of inheriting objects for an appropriate answer.

11.1.4.2 Advantages of Object Orientation

Object orientation has gradually matured, and now it also subsumes activities of planning, analysis, and design of not only information systems but also of enterprise modeling and engineering. Uses of the object model produce systems that are built upon stable intermediate forms and thus are more resilient to change. Object-oriented methodologies, when fully developed, can also provide a smooth and seamless transition across the various stages in the SDLC, such as the requirement definition, detailed specification, detailed design, and code generation stages. This also implies that such a system can be allowed to evolve over time, rather than being abandoned or completely redesigned when the first major change in requirements comes along.

Therefore, the basic advantages of the object-oriented paradigm are drastically increased opportunities for reuse of software components, the development methodology of rapid prototyping and incremental redesigning, and increased maintainability and environmental portability of finished applications. I am tempted to refer to the object-oriented approach as the reengineered version of the traditional software engineering process!

11.1.4.3 Object Orientation and SAP

This completes the introductory framework necessary for us to tackle an object-orientated environment. Although there is a host of other related complex issues, such as composite objects, multiple inheritance, polymorphism, concurrency, and persistence, this is sufficient for us to appreciate the object orientation of the SAP environment as a whole.

SAP is not an object-oriented environment per se, but SAP's architecture and design are highly influenced by that approach. The basic framework of SAP, including the ABAP dictionary, event-driven programming, and event-driven business process chains, already implements a host of these concepts and may be reengineered into a full-featured object-oriented environment in the future. With SAP 3.0 was introduced SAP Workflow that was based completely on object-oriented architecture of business objects, methods, events, subclasses, and so forth. In SAP R/3 4.0, ABAP Objects was a full-featured object extension to ABAP that is useful for providing and programming SAP on the Internet, which is discussed in the later part of this book. However, for reaching the full potential of object orientation, SAP basic architecture would have to be implemented in object-oriented fashion, and all SAP functional modules themselves would need to be developed, maintained, documented, etc., in such an object-oriented environment. This is the underlying agenda of the roadmap to SAP NetWeaver. You can see the advantages of such an approach during our discussions on SAP NetWeaver in Chapter 10 and in subsequent chapters.

11.1.5 Web Application Builder

This enables the creation of Web development objects within the ABAP Workbench. Existing SAP transactions need Web objects in the context of running the Web transactions in the Web browser. Web Application Builder is fully integrated with the ABAP Workbench. Various Web development objects like service files, HTML templates, and MIME objects are created in the SAP repository and integrated with the Transport Organizer.

Web Application Builder addresses functions like

- Creating Web-based transactions corresponding to the existing SAP transactions
- Creating MiniApps
- Generating and editing HTML templates for screens of transactions
- Including as additional layout design objects, MIME objects (icons, graphics, animation, Java Applets, etc.)
- Creating language-specific text and MIME objects

■ Running the complete Web application
■ Connecting to the Transport Organizer

Web Application Builder was introduced as a development tool for BSP applications, which we discuss next.

11.1.5.1 Business Server Pages (BSP) Application Development

BSP, which was introduced with SAP Basis version 6.10, is similar to the other server-side tag languages like JSP, ASP, and PHP, except that it uses ABAP as the integrated programming language.

BSP applications use two state models, namely, stateful and stateless provided by the Internet Communication Framework (ICF) of the SAP Web Application Server. A stateful BSP application is executed in a single context across all user interactions. An active BSP application is referred to as a *BSP session*; data entered by a user or calculated by the application over the course of the process can be held over the entire life cycle of the session. Consequently, this leads to lower network load but higher load on the Web Application Server. On the other hand, in the case of the stateless model, as soon as a request is processed, all assigned resources are released immediately.

11.1.5.2 BSP Development Tools

Web Application Builder is integrated with the Repository Navigator. Consequently, BSP applications can access Repository objects such as function modules, classes, BAPIs, or database objects and are also embedded in the SAP Correction and Transport System.

BSP application consists of several components:

■ Object Navigator
■ Web Application Builder (WAB) Tools
■ WebDAV Interface
■ BAPI browser
■ Online Test Repository (OTR)
■ The XSLT Editor

11.1.5.3 BSP Application Components

The BSP application consists of several components:

■ *Application class*: Application class is a regular ABAP Objects class with characteristic methods, attributes, and events. Multiple BSP applications can reuse the same application class to create a single BSP application with multiple user interfaces without having to replicate the business or application logic.
■ *Controller*: As we will see later, the controller is a component of the MVC design and the connector between model and view. The controller manages and transfers data and directs the data to the various views.
■ *Business Server Pages (BSP)*: BSPs are the basis of the content displayed in Web pages. BSPs consist of static HTML code and dynamic server scripts, which permit the dynamic creation of Web content. It implements the complete life cycle of a web page in a single component including event handling, data retrieval, and data display.

- *Views*: Views are responsible for only the layout of the application data. A view's life cycle is determined by its corresponding controller, which also routes the view's calls and communicates with a model.
- *Event Handler*: The event handler is part of the flow control, which determines the temporal and logical flow of an application. Event handlers are executed at predefined times in a predefined sequence during the life cycle of a BSP page. The event handler is implemented in ABAP Objects and allows access to certain objects at the runtime.
- *Navigation*: The navigation structure consists of the beginning and end of a request. This makes it possible to change the flow control of a BSP application without changing any code.
- *Multipurpose Internet Mail Extensions (MIME) objects*: MIMEs are outcome of the original Internet e-mail protocol that enabled exchange of a variety of data on the Internet. MIMEs include audio, video, and image data, cascading style sheets (CSSs), and ASCII files.

Each new BSP application creates an identically named MIME directory that stores all the application-specific MIME objects.

11.2 Java Custom Development

Java programming language is responsible for the success of J2EE. Though Sun developed the J2EE specification, it is a cross vendor standard. In fact, this ensures that the software components can be reused, and ERP systems from different vendors can integrate with each other easily. Support from other vendors like IBM and Sun has ensured that J2EE continues to evolve and adopt to meet the latest challenges and requirements of the market. The J2EE platform is suitable for a wide range of distributed Web-enabled applications and Web-based applications.

SAP Java Development Infrastructure (JDI) and SAP NetWeaver Developer Studio (NWDS) enable more efficient software development while addressing the challenges of global development and delivery scenarios, namely, support for the entire life cycle of the software application, multi-located distributed development by numerous teams, and customizations at partner and customer sites.

A software application or product life cycle is spread across an extended period of time as it includes the maintenance of the application involving periodic upgrades and releases. This leads to the need for modularization, encapsulation, reusability, maintainability, and so on. Current approach to address these requirements is to develop software in components that encapsulate functions accessible only via the predefined interfaces. Such an approach reduces coupling between the software components rendering them easily maintainable because of their mutual independence while also making them accessible via predefined interfaces. This dilemma is solved by the SAP Component Model.

Similarly, during the development phase, when the development teams are spread across different locations, the software development effort is confronted with many problems related to currency and correctness of versions, automatic synchronizations of code developed by different teams at different locations at different times, and so on. These problems are related to the issues of using libraries of different versions, preparing source files and runtime object consistently, and simultaneously accessing and changing of files or objects at different locations. The complexities of the synchronization arise from the fact that these sources and objects are used in different versions in the development and consolidation systems and again in different versions in the customizations, support packages, and new releases. This dilemma is solved by using an integrated SAP Java Development Environment (JDI) that consists of a central source file storage location (DTR) and executing the build for the entire software via a central build service (CBS).

SAP JDI environment consists of

- System Landscape Directory (SLD) that defines the products and its software components
- Design Time Repository (DTR) that administers the source files
- Central Build Service (CBS) that administers the archives (runtime objects)
- Change Management Service (CMS) that arranges the access to the source and object files via DTR and CMS

The issues cited previously get further exacerbated when customers customize delivered products to suit the specific requirements of their enterprise, business units, or operational sites. This dilemma is solved by the DTR, which has inherent facilities to detect such version conflicts even after the files have been transported into production.

All these problems are addressed and handled adequately by the SAP NetWeaver JDI through the very architecture and structure of the product coupled with the engendered development process enabled by the various development tools of the SAP JDI environment.

11.2.1 SAP Java Development Infrastructure (JDI)

As collaborated development is very critical for large teams of developers and since existing Java development environments did not provide an equivalent centralized development environment like the ABAP Workbench, SAP embarked on an effort to build a reliable and efficient equivalent environment in Java called the SAP Java Development Infrastructure (JDI). It consists of tools like DTR, CBS, and CMS that support team-based software development in Java within the SAP world and are directly integrated with the Integrated Development Environment (IDE), the NetWeaver Developer Studio (NWDS). The development follows the SAP component model. The JDI environment is available in SAP Web AS 6.40 and later versions and includes comprehensive features for version management, change management, and automated deployment of components.

NWDS is the centralized place for developing presentation logic accompanied by the corresponding business logic including data persistence and retrieval. NWDS has evolved into a comprehensive SAP development environment that spans across the whole cycle of a Java project including configuration and transport management. It provides full support for developing large-scale Java projects as well as standard technologies like J2SE, J2EE, XML, and Web Services and SAP technologies like Web Dynpro and Java Dictionary. Large projects are apportioned into a number of projects sharing clearly defined dependencies. These projects can be undertaken by a large number of teams distributed across geographical distances.

JDI represents the main difference of the NWDS from other Java IDEs. It makes it easy for developers to collaborate and enables NWDS to support hundreds of programmers within a project. JDI links the central and local development environments. A simple file import makes the project development objects available centrally. These objects can be transferred into the local environment, creating a flexible development environment wherein Java developers can continue to work locally, while the central development environment provides the necessary synchronization for teamwork.

NWDS also supports a local development process that does not utilize the JDI, refrains from external referencing, and, in the absence of a central repository, also stores all the project resources locally.

JDI environment consists of two parts: local and central. The local part consists of the NWDS as the IDE, the local system as the temporary storage for all new development objects, and usually a local installation of the J2EE as a testing environment. The NDWS connects the developer to the other part, the central JDI. The SLD is used to load the development of the corresponding configuration of the CMS into the NWDS. This enables access to both the source file storage in the DTR workspace for regular work and the buildspace in CBS. Created objects are checked by the name service for the uniqueness of the name. The CMS is used for deployment to the central system. The development cycle within JDI starts with the import of a development configuration file into the NWDS. The local system is synchronized with the centralized DTR and the CBS. This is followed by the usual development process involving local application development, build process, and automatic deployment to the test environment. After a successful test, the objects are checked into the DTR. Once the central build of the archives is run, they are automatically loaded into the CBS that initiates the build process. Once the central build is successful, the elements are released automatically.

NWDS provides an optimum infrastructure and tools to access a centralized deployment and test environment. The facilities of JDI enable easy implementation of reusability and maintenance. Control of distributed versions coupled with access to the corresponding development objects enables efficient management of large geographically distributed projects.

11.2.1.1 Overview of the Development Process in SAP JDI Using SAP NWDS

We present an overview of the release cycle using SAP NetWeaver Developer Studio (NWDS) and Java Development Infrastructure (JDI).

The development process is given as follows:

1. A product release is defined in the SLD with details of name, release, and used Software Components (SCs) along with the constituting development components (DCs) and the corresponding use dependencies.
2. The corresponding *track* is created for this release in the CMS consisting of logical development systems that define the access to the source files and archives (runtime objects) required for the project.
3. Central Development Environment:
   a. SLD is used to import the development configuration using the name and URL of the configuration into every local development environment NWDS of the developer group.
   b. Download into local NWDS by synchronizing the source files from DTR.
   c. Download into NWDS by synchronizing the archives (runtime objects) from CBS.
4. NWDS Local Development Environment:
   a. Create new objects (DCs or packages) or check out the existing ones and change them.
   b. Call Name Service to ensure uniqueness of names while creating new objects.

5. NWDS Local Build Environment:
   a. Start the local build in NWDS.
   b. Build new archives.
   c. Store archives locally subsequent to a successful build.
6. Deploy the archives for testing into the local J2EE Engine.
7. Check in new versions (stored in activities) into the DTR, subsequent to a successful test.
8. Central Build Environment:
   a. Activate the activity.
   b. Retrieve new objects from the inactive workspace and prebuilt source files from the active workspace.
   c. Start the build with source files from DTR (i.e., in sync with the global version history) and archives from CBS, which ascertains that only the latest versions of all objects have been used in the build.
   d. Activate the source files subsequent to a successful build.
9. Change Management Environment:
   a. Deploy new activities into test systems.
   b. Release activities for the next step in the CMS, subsequent to a successful central test.
   c. Import objects into the consolidation system.
   d. Assemble subsequent to successful test of the objects.
   e. Approve for release subsequent to successful assembly.
10. Repeat the release cycle with the definition of next release in SLD.

11.2.1.2 SAP Component Model

SAP Component Model helps to structure the applications and their architecture. It makes applications easy to reuse and maintain by breaking them down into components that can be changed independent of each another. This entails, on one hand, the individual components to be uncoupled, and, on the other hand, paradoxically they need to have well-defined interfaces to enable the essential interaction between components. This is also the basis for the success of the build process described later.

SAP Component Model structure applications at four levels, namely, product, software components, development components, and development objects. *Products* are the solutions in the business environment and are defined in the Software Landscape Directory (SLD) in terms of the information on name, owner, constituting software components, etc. Each product is defined in the Software Landscape Directory.

Software components (SCs) are group of related functions and are implemented in development components. General and specific software components are the basis for the reusability demonstrated by this model. SCs developed specifically for a product can be changed for this product, whereas general SCs used by the product usually cannot be changed in this context by the product directly. An SC is a structure of folders and files. All folders are stored in one common folder that also contains a folder *TopLevelDCs* with all top-level DCs that are not contained in other DCs along with the corresponding .dcref files. The build result of an SC is a deployable Software Component Archive (SCA).

Software components (SCs) are constituted of the development components that are the basis for the independence demonstrated by this model. Development component (DC) contains and encapsulates the development objects that are actually programmed by the developers;

these include the Java classes and interfaces, image files for icons, or SAP-specific metadata or Web Dynpro files. All development components can be stored as versioned resources in DTR (see Section 11.2.1.2.1 "Design Time Repository (DTR)"). DCs can be nested, that is, one DC can contain other DCs, just as software components can also be nested. But, for a product, a development object can occur only within one development component, just as a development component can occur only within one software component. DCs are containers for the corresponding development objects, which are invisible outside of this DC. This achieves perfect decoupling of the all DCs; however, to enable DCs to use one another, they define interfaces called *public* parts that publish the development objects termed as *public part entities* that can be accessed and used by the other DCs. There are two types of public parts: compilation types can be used for the development of other DCs and are used accordingly during a compilation, and assembly types provide a build result that can be wrapped by other DCs. The later types are required when DC type does not produce a deployable build result, like in the case of Java DC mentioned in the following; part of such a DC is wrapped in an assembly-type public part to be uploaded to the server in the form of (say) a J2EE Java library file.

SAP Component Model supports the important concept of *use dependency* between DCs, whereby for using development objects of another DC, their usage has to be declared in the metadata of the concerned DC and must also be included in its public parts. The new build process in the CBS checks this information on dependencies to enable build of individual DCs. Thus, the use of external DCs is limited by the attachment to the SC and nesting of DCs. Access Control Lists (ACLs) explicitly list the DCs that are enabled unrestricted but exclusive access to a particular DC. ACLs consist of Access Control Entities (ACEs) that assign one or more privileges to a user or a group. Cyclic dependencies are detected and disallowed.

The DC type controls the build process required to create the corresponding DC structure along with the relevant settings. The various DCs are listed as follows:

1. Composite Application Service DC contains all of the corresponding elements required, namely, Dictionary objects, metadata, and Java classes. Each Composite Application Service DC is associated with Dictionary, Metadata, EJB Module, and enterprise projects. Build outcome is a combination of Software Deployment Archive (SDA) and Enterprise Archive (EAR) files.
2. Dictionary DCs define the global structures. Build outcome is an SDA file.
3. J2EE DCs correspond to various DCs like the following:
   a. Java Enterprise Application DC, which is a combination of Web Module DCs and EJB Module DCs. Build outcome is an EAR file.
   b. EJB Module DC contains the Message-Driven Bean, Container-Managed Persistence (CMP) Bean, Bean-Managed Persistence (BMP) Bean, Stateful Session Bean, and Stateless Session Bean for an Enterprise Application DC. The build outcome is a set of compiled classes.
   c. Web Module DC contains JSPs, Servlets, and Proxy classes for beans defined in an EJB project. The build outcome is a Web Archive file.
   d. J2EE Server Component Library DC is an add-on for the SAP's J2EE Engine; the build outcome is an SDA file.
   e. Java DC contains Java code. The build outcome is a JAR file.
   f. Web Dynpro DC: The build outcome is an EAR file containing a Web Dynpro Archive (WDA) file.

Every DC is a structure of folders and files; all DCs contain a folder named as *_comp* that contains folders for binaries and public parts that are stored as XML files. For every DC, there exists a folder called *DC Meta Data* that contains the DC properties that go beyond those defined in an Eclipse project. A subfolder called *DC Definition* enlists folders, child DCs, used DCs, and public parts. Other folders depend upon the type of the DC. The *gen* folder contains generated data. In the NWDS, DCs are represented in the DC-specific views as folders and files.

11.2.1.2.1 Design Time Repository (DTR)

Design Time Repository (DTR), which is the central source file management system of the JDI, is a database-supported J2EE application that runs as a service on the J2EE Engine of the SAP NetWeaver. DTR manages centrally versions of all development objects including tables, Java classes, Web Dynpros, and project files. It provides for versioning of all project components and synchronization among all members of the development team guaranteeing that all programmers are working on the same code base.

DTR has a client and server architecture; the central DTR server saves and manages all the files as versioned resources in the form of BLOBs (Binary Large OBjects) in a database, which is shared with CBS, CMS, etc., but presents them to the DTR client UIs in the form of files and folders. Developers use the local NWDS, which contains the DTR client and communicates with the DTR server to provide access via DTR workspaces to files, making it possible to check in and out, compare version, and so on. This also makes it possible to synchronize project components and other related project data between the repository and the local file system.

 DTR workspace should not be confused with the Eclipse workspace in NWDS. Eclipse workspace is a folder in the local system controlled by the development system. Eclipse workspaces can be used for the local management of the versions that can be accessed only via DTR workspaces.

All changes related to creating a new file or changing an existing file are organized via *activities*. Activities are akin to transport requests in ABAP and are always created in the context of a particular workspace. A new version of a file is contained in an activity that can be changed locally. Deletion of a file is affected by creating a deletion version of a file that is also stored in an activity. Activity is open as long as it has not been checked in. In contrast, for changing files on the DTR server, they are first synchronized into the local file system and checked out to make them changeable. On completing the changes and upon checking onto the server automatically set the new version as the active version of the DTR workspace in which the activity was created and checked in. As the name of the activity contains an ID and a time stamp, this enables in rendering the latest version of a source file as the active version. An activity is closed as soon as it is checked in and can no longer be changed. A central build can activate or transport closed activities like in the case of a transport into the consolidation workspace after a file has been released in the development workspace. Such copying of files into a workspace is called integration. Thus, constituting activities characterizes the state of a workspace as also the corresponding SC. The integration of activities changes the sate of a workspace.

Using DTR to move objects like this helps in resolving conflicts that are unavoidable in large multilocated long-lasting development projects.

In the DTR, while authentication determines only the access to a DTR, authorization determines further if that DTR can be changed by an authenticated developer.

In summation, DTR addresses the following tasks:

- Ensures availability of all versions of files.
- Restricts access to only those objects required by the project.
- Maintains versioning information even after they have been transported to other instances of DTR at other development locations or at customer locations.

11.2.1.2.2 Component Build Service (CBS)

Component Build Service (CBS), which is the central build environment of the SAP JDI, is also a database-supported J2EE application based on the SAP component model. CBS saves Java archives (runtime objects) and builds packages based on relevant information available in the DTR; it creates a *buildspace* for each software component. For each configuration, CBS maintains the build environment (libraries, generators, and build scripts) and corresponding results in a central archive pool in the CBS that ensures that only the latest version will be used by all concerned. The centralized storage in DTR makes centralized build processes possible. Older versions are not overwritten; rather a global version history is created. For the communication, the HTTP is used. CBS build process is based on the SAP Component Model with development components (DCs) as the build units; during the build, all dependent DCs are checked. Cyclic dependencies are detected and disallowed.

Buildspace is the logical storage locations used to access the archives and serves as logical build servers. Every product release creates one development and consolidation state, both of which are represented by one buildspace. As mentioned earlier, for every buildspace, there is a pair of DTR workspaces in the DTR, namely, inactive and active workspaces that are closely connected with the build process in the CBS. New objects are always created in the inactive workspace; after these objects within an activity have been built successfully, the source files are automatically integrated into the active DTR workspace. Using source files exclusively from this workspace ensures that the state is consistent with the latest version of the entire software. This achieves synchronization of all development efforts encompassing both the source and archive files.

11.2.1.2.3 System Landscape Directory (SLD)

System Landscape Directory (SLD) stores information on the system landscape and the System Catalog, which contains the list of all products and software components available. Each product release of a product is defined separately in the SLD; different products can share SCs. The development environment is created for a product based on the information in the SLD.

11.2.1.2.4 Software Logistics

Software Logistics (SL) enables handling of tasks like application deployment, corrections, and hand-off to the customer or maintenance. SL component consists primarily of two components: Change Management Service (CMS) and Software Delivery Manager (SDM).

CMS manages the software versioning and the transportation of the software changes within the development landscape. SDM is responsible for the deployment of the Java applications. All requisite descriptions of the system landscape are maintained centrally in the SAP System Landscape Directory (SLD).

11.2.1.2.4.1 Change Management Service (CMS) — CMS, which is the central administration and quality management environment of the SAP JDI, is also a database-supported J2EE application that runs in the J2EE Engine of the SAP NetWeaver. CMS Web UI and the Transport View in NWDS are available as User Interfaces (UIs).

Transport Studio uses the definition of the logical development systems to enable central availability of all objects used by a particular release to the team of developers. This process involves the following steps:

- Check in all used SCs as archives.
- Import the archives into the development system.
- Import the archives into the consolidation system.
- Assemble the deployable SCA file from the imported and new archives and optionally also from the source files.
- Test and approve the SCA file.

11.2.2 SAP NetWeaver Developer Studio (NWDS)

SAP NetWeaver Developer Studio (NWDS) is the primary environment for developing Java-based multitiered business applications. SAP NWDS is based on IBM's open source Eclipse Integrated Development Environment (IDE). Eclipse is an open and extensible development environment that focuses primarily on Java. Eclipse consists of extremely lean core that hosts a comprehensive plug-in architecture. This process is controlled by the Java API that is provided, which plug-in vendors can use to develop IDE extensions in any direction. The freely available standard distribution of Eclipse already includes plug-ins for the workspace (to display project trees) and Workbench (which provides the basis for the GUI). In addition, there is both free and third-party commercially available plug-ins for designing software using UML, for designing Web interfaces using Drag-and-Drop functionality, editors for programming interfaces, RDBMS, and so on. Thus, based on Eclipse, NWDS enables working seamlessly with J2EE, Web Dynpro, and Java Dictionary projects that are not included in the standard distribution of Eclipse. Apart from the standard plug-ins, NWDS contains additional plug-ins from SAP like Design Time Repository (DTR), Web Dynpro, Java Dictionary, and EJB development.

NWDS enables collaborative development by a geographically distributed team by providing support for project types and object types as well as logical views of these projects along with their development objects. NWDS workspace is the centralized location for managing all resources, metadata, as well as user-specific IDE settings. A workplace is largely constituted of one or more projects, which are displayed in the navigator view. A project is basically a structuring element for a part of an application that contains as a logical unit all the relevant objects of that part: the related development objects are controlled together at the design time. All SAP-specific projects offer a logical view of the resources that are also displayed hierarchically in the form of a tree structure. Starting with the project structure, developers can start different context-specific actions, such as creating a new object and opening the editor. However, projects cannot be nested, that is, a project cannot contain other projects. For instance, EJBs cannot be created in the Web module project including Web resources such as Servlets or Java Server Pages (JSPs) and vice versa.

NWDS user interface comprises of perspectives, views, and editors. A perspective has a toolbar and a set of views and editors that are grouped together to address specific tasks. Views are used to represent a tree of structured data and, hence, are suitable for displaying structures of projects or XML files. Views and editors are closely linked: editors are often launched from a view to open an object from the tree structure for processing. Editors enable users to open, process, and save development objects. In addition to editors for texts and Java source code, NWDS is equipped with editors for processing special development objects like Enterprise JavaBeans (EJBs) entailing the bean class along with the corresponding components and the home interfaces.

An overview of the user interface of the NWDS is described in the following:

- *File Bar and Toolbars*: This enlists the familiar tools for saving, printing, and so on. It also provides options for saving metadata, which are required to generate automatically the Java class model and also update simultaneously the corresponding metadata projects like Java Dictionary and Web Dynpro. The program section provides facilities for debugging and test runs.
- *Perspectives*: This enlists projects of a particular type. Apart from the standard view for class trees, special views are available for J2EE, Web Dynpro, and Java Dictionary projects.
- *Project Tree/Workplace*: This enlists projects of particular type along with their constituting development objects. The project tree structure displayed here depends on the corresponding perspective selected earlier.
- *Different Workplace Views*: This indicates the extended view when they are applicable.
- *Characteristics and Excerpt Views*: This displays the characteristics of the selected project or development object along with its current values. Alternatively, in case of Java classes, this extends the navigation to the methods and variables of the classes.
- *Characteristics/Excerpt View Selection*: This toggles between the characteristic and excerpt view.
- *Open Documents*: This displays all currently open documents, with an asterisk (*) to indicate changed documents.
- *Work Area of Current Document*: This displays one document in the regular development view, which also provides for syntax highlighting and error detection. This also provides for the visual design or layout environment for Web Dynpro and JSP previews.
- *Warning and Error Display*: This displays the warnings and errors on account of syntax errors, structure violations, etc., adjacent to the concerned line of code on the left-hand side of the work area. Clicking on the respective icon, it automatically displays a potential solution that is implemented via a user dialog.
- *Warning and Error Navigation Bar*: This provides navigation to the individual error locations within the active document: clicking on the bar, the work area automatically scrolls to the error and its surrounding coding.
- *Task List*: This enlists warning and error messages across all documents and projects; double-clicking on a particular error opens the corresponding document with the cursor positioned on the error.

11.2.2.1 NWDS Tools and Perspectives

NWDS provides a range of tools for various aspects and tasks in developing applications. All tools related to some specific tasks are grouped together into *perspectives*.

11.2.2.1.1 Development Configuration Perspective

Development configuration perspective is used as the starting point for working with the JDI as well as projects based on SAP components. For using the central services, it is essential to log on to the JDI from NWDS, which can be enabled by importing a development configuration. This automatically sets up the access paths for the services that are used in the NWDS.

Development Configuration perspective addresses the following tasks:

- Import development configurations.
- Check out entire DC projects and individual project resources.
- Browse contents of components in the central repository and in the local file system.
- Create new DC-based projects for different project types like Web Dynpro and Dictionary.
- Integrate all DTR activities like creating new activities, assigning changes to activities, displaying activities, checking into the repository, or undoing changes.
- Integrate the build and deploy function.
- Activate development components.
- Display properties of objects like development, configuration, software component, DC, development object, and activity.

11.2.2.1.2 Design Time Repository (DTR) Perspective

Development configuration perspective is used for resolving version conflicts and DTR repository administration. The former includes DTR operations like creating new activities, adding changes to activities, viewing changes, and checking into the repository and operations for solving version conflicts, while the later includes activities like managing files within DTR workspaces or configuring the DTR server. Unlike the DC perspective, the DTR Browser offers a pure file and directory-based view of the DTR contents.

DTR perspective groups several views:

- Repository Browser providing a file and directory-based display of DTR contents
- Version Graph displaying the version graphs for the required resources
- Integration Conflicts displaying the version conflicts that have occurred during integration
- Open Activities displaying a list of all activities that are still open
- Closed Activities displaying a list of activities that are already closed
- Command output displaying the Output commands for the operations performed by the users including the failures and error messages, if any

11.2.2.1.3 Dictionary Perspective

Dictionary perspective provides various tools that are required at design time in the Java Dictionary for platform-independent definition of database objects such as tables and indexes and global data types. These are essential for developing portable and high-performance database applications.

Data Type Editor enables the definition of user-defined global data types like *simple* and *structured* data types that contain multiple elements. While defining data types, data characteristics and relevant UI text information can also be recorded along with the data type. The value ranges of the new data types are derived from the predefined native or built-in data types that are in sync with the standard JDBC data types. Each data type can also store texts that can be used as input help, field labels, column headers, or reference information. These texts are used while displaying the corresponding data type in layout of (say) the Web Dynpro applications.

Table Editor enables database-independent definition of tables in terms of the fields (or columns) and key fields. Table indexes can also be defined for specific fields or combination of fields. Similarly, the type of table buffering and the corresponding settings can also be defined. For a specific database environment, the table-related information stored in the Java Dictionary (which is imported into that database environment) is used to create the physical tables in that environment.

Dictionary perspective addresses the following tasks:

- Create Dictionary projects with or without a connection to the SAP component model.
- Create in the Java Dictionary platform-independent database objects like tables and indexes.
- Create in the Java Dictionary user-defined global data types like simple and structured data types.
- Map automatically predefined data types to corresponding JDBC data types.
- Create transportable archives.
- Deploy archives.
- Perform table-related operations like deleting and renaming.

11.2.2.1.4 J2EE Perspective

J2EE perspective provides various tools that are required for uniform access to the development resources within different J2EE project types. J2EE perspective provides views that enable visualization of the J2EE projects in the J2EE Explorer or the J2EE DC Explorer for DC-based projects in the JDI. It provides the logical view of the relevant project structure and is available as the starting point for the main development activities like creating or editing of the corresponding development objects. *EJB Module Project* groups together all of the Enterprise JavaBeans (EJB) resources that are combined into a Java Archive (JAR) file along with the deployment descriptors for the final deployment. *Web Module Project* groups together all of the Web resources that are combined into a Web Archive (WAR) along with the deployment descriptors for the final deployment. Enterprise Application Project groups together all of the J2EE resources in a J2EE application that are combined into an Enterprise Archive (EAR) for the final deployment.

J2EE perspective also provides an alternative diagrammatic view of the declarative steps within a project using graphical editing tools. Diagram views are useful in complex projects to display components and their relationships to each other.

EJB Editor enables easy access to create and edit the individual components of the EJBs (Session Beans, Entity Beans, and Message Driven Beans). Starting from the overview page, it navigates to the bean class and to the corresponding components and the home interfaces of the EJB.

JSP and HTML Editors enable easy access to create and edit Web resources. In addition to the syntax highlighting, code completion, etc., these editors also support preview functionality.

J2EE perspective addresses the following tasks:

- Create J2EE projects with or without a connection to the SAP component model.
- Wizard support for defining and creating EJBs, namely, Session Beans, Entity Beans, and Message Driven Beans.
- Wizard support for defining and creating Web resources like HTML pages, JSPs, Servlets, and listeners.
- Configure the J2EE application using deployment descriptors.
- Create archives (JAR, WAR, and EAR).
- Deploy archives.

11.2.2.1.5 Web Dynpro Perspective

Web Dynpro perspective provides various tools that are required for using the Web Dynpro technology for generating user interfaces of the browser-based applications. It supports developers during the entire development cycle of Web Dynpro applications starting with generating project components, implementing controllers and professional presentation interfaces, and deploying and testing of the finished application. All of the development objects are generated declaratively using wizards or graphical tools that entail minimal manual programming.

Per the MVC design pattern, persistent data are provided in the Web Dynpro by a model layer of the entire application. There are relevant model types for the various back-end scenarios. Web Dynpro provides powerful wizards and generation tools to ensure that the back-end logic is integrated seamlessly.

Web Dynpro perspective addresses the following tasks:

- Create Web Dynpro projects with or without a connection to the SAP component model.
- Design the application using the declarative and graphical facilities of the Data and Application Modelers, for example, displaying relationships between the components of the Web Dynpro project, creating views and view sets, and defining the view sequence using the navigation links.
- Create reusable Web Dynpro application components.
- Design the view layout with the graphical View Designer.
- Define view contexts to store local view controller data and its references (to model data, dictionary types, or to other view contexts).
- Integrate a Java Dictionary to define user-defined global data types like simple and structured data types as well as user-interface-specific texts and messages.
- Import model descriptions to achieve back-end connection.

11.2.2.1.6 Web Service Perspective

Web Service perspective provides various tools that are required for defining Web Service providers or for using Web Service clients. It consists of EJB Explorer, Java Explorer, Client Explorer, Web Service Navigator, and an integrated environment for testing Web Services.

EJB and Java explorers organize all Web Service endpoints and related objects like virtual interfaces, Web Service definitions, and deployment descriptors. Client Explorer generates client proxies corresponding to a Web Service as well as the relevant deployable or stand-alone proxy projects.

Web Service perspective addresses the following tasks:

- Create Web Services as endpoints for Session Beans and Java classes.
- Deploy Web Services on the J2EE Server.
- Integrate UDDI publishing and test environment.
- Integrate UDDI client browser.
- Web Service client proxies.

11.2.2.2 NWDS Development Process

The development environment has been configured first so that it can use the JDI by importing a predefined *development configuration* from the SLD into NWDS. The development configuration enables the local development environment to access the relevant infrastructure services.

An overview of the NWDS development process is described:

1. Developers open the relevant project in the NWDS enabling access to the relevant components and libraries on the local PC.
2. Developers can make the required changes to the project, perform the local build, and test these changes in their local environment. For accessing the relevant test server, only the corresponding details of the J2EE server have to be provided in the NWDS settings.
3. Developers activate their changed objects in NWDS, which entails a successful central build process. NWDS provides developers with error-free components and libraries because only those components get activated that could be built successfully by CBS. In the case of errors during the build process, appropriate messages are displayed for the developers based on which they can again debug, change, and test the component.
4. Once all the tests and subsequent activations are successful, the changes can be released for transport via the NWDS. This enables the CBS to control the transport using the defined transport landscape. CBS processes the release request by incorporating the changes in the assigned consolidation system's import queue. Upon successful completion, CBS marks the corresponding archives as a new version and deployed on a J2EE server and also forwarded to the central consolidation server.
5. Once the test run has been completed successfully, the software application is ready for productive use.

11.2.3 *Java Application Development*

J2EE is the result of Sun's effort to integrate the assortment of Java technologies and API together into cohesive Java development platform for developing complex distributed Java applications. Sun's enhancement of the N-tier development model for Java combined with introduction of specific functionalities to permit easier development of the server-side scalable Web-based enterprise applications has led to a wide adoption of Java for Web-centric applications development.

Enterprise application development entails expertise in host of areas like interprocess communications, memory management, security issues, and database-specific access queries. J2EE provides built-in support for services in all these areas, enabling developers to focus on implementing business logic rather than intricate code that supports basic application support infrastructure.

There are numerous advantages of application development in the J2EE area:

- J2EE offers support for componentization of enterprise applications that enable higher productivity via reusability of components, rapid development of functioning applications via prebuilt functional components, higher-quality test-driven development via pretested components, and easier maintenance via cost-effective upgrades to individual components.
- J2EE offers support for hardware and operating systems (OS) independence by enabling system services to be accessed via Java and J2EE rather than directly via APIs specific to the underlying systems.
- J2EE offers a wide range of APIs to access and integrate with third-party products in a consistent manner including databases, mail systems, and messaging platforms.
- J2EE offers a clear-cut segregation between system development, deployment, and execution, thus enabling independent development, integration, and upgradation of components.
- J2EE offers specialized components that are optimized for specific types of roles in an enterprise application like Entity Beans for handling persistent data and Session Beans for handling processing.

All the aforementioned features make possible rapid development of complex, distributed applications by enabling developers to focus on developing business logic, implementing the system without being impacted by prior knowledge of the target execution environment(s), and on creating systems that can be ported more easily between different hardware platforms and operating systems (OS).

11.2.3.1 Reference Architecture

The objective of the flexibility and reusability can be achieved primarily at two levels: application architecture level and the application component design level. The reference architecture is the vision of the application architecture that integrates the common elements into a component structure modeling the current business and also positioning it to meet the challenges of the future. From a technical point of view, the architecture positions the development organization to automatically meet the benchmark requirements on time-to-market, flexibility, and performance.

A set of key elements drive the definition of the reference architecture that comprises of three layers, namely, business objects, process-oriented or service-based objects, and user interface layer.

The defining elements of enterprise applications are as follows:

■ *Business Entities* are the foci of the enterprise applications. These range from top-level entities such as a customer or a supplier down to bottom-level entities such as purchase orders, sales orders, or even individual level line items of these orders. Entities participate in the business processes, have attributes or properties, have methods for responding to requests for information, and have different sets of enforceable policies or rules applicable to them. The latter include the requirement for persistence of the state of the entities as reflected in the snapshot of all attributes.
■ *Business Processes* carry out the tasks of the enterprise. They have some kind of specified workflow and essentially involve one or more business entities. They must be executed in a secure manner and also be accessible via a host of user interfaces or devices or clients.
■ *User Interactions* carry out the access and display of information related to business entities as an outcome of some business processes for scrutiny by the users of the enterprise application. This essentially involves some kind of screen flow or page navigation, attributes for presentation, user requests, or generated responses, that is, static or dynamic content, form-oriented processing, and error handling. The user interaction could be via a host of user interfaces or devices or clients.

Each of these elements gives rise to the three primary architecture layers of the reference architecture. These layers could reside on the same physical layer or be distributed across a network. Figure 11.2 presents the three architecture layers constituting the reference architecture.

11.2.3.1.1 User Interaction Architecture

User interactions are modeled by user interface components that comprise the User Interaction Architecture. In J2EE platform, this is typically implemented as a combination of servlets and Java Server Pages (JSP). In a Web-based application, this layer would process HTML form submissions, manage state within an application, generate Web-page content, and control navigation between pages. Many of the functions within this layer can be automated through configurable foundation components.

11.2.3.1.2 Service-Based Architecture

Business processes are modeled by service components that comprise the Service-Based Architecture. In J2EE platform, this is typically implemented as a process-oriented object wrapped with a stateless Session Bean. The concept of services allows the front end to be decoupled from the back-end business object components. The service-based layer adds tremendous value in terms of flexibility, reusability, and component design.

11.2.3.1.3 Business Object Architecture

Business entities are modeled by object components that comprise the Business Object Architecture. Each of these components manages the data and business logic associated with a particular entity, including persistence of that data into a relational database. In J2EE platform, this is typically implemented as a combination of regular Java classes and Entity beans in J2EE application. The database access can be implemented by the container in the case of Container-Managed Persistence (CMP) Entity Beans or by the developer in the case of Bean-Managed Persistence (BMP) Entity Beans or regular Java classes. The persistence of each business object is abstracted out to the extent possible so that separate data objects, persistent frameworks, or CMP services can be used to affect the data object persistence in the database.

A major portion of the reference architecture is a generic and configurable implementation of the Model 2 architecture discussed later in the following section.

11.2.3.2 Realization of the Reference Architecture in J2EE

The Java Enterprise Edition (J2EE) platform provides a component-based approach to implement N-tier distributed enterprise applications. Figure 11.2 shows how the J2EE components provide the implementations for the different layers of the reference architecture.

The components that make up the application are executed in runtime environments called containers. Containers are used to provide infrastructure-type services such as life-cycle management, distribution, and security. Containers and components in the J2EE application are broadly divided into three tiers. The client tier is typically a Web browser or alternatively Java application client. The middle tier contains the two primary containers of the J2EE application, namely, Web container and EJB container. The function of the Web container is to process client requests and generate corresponding responses, while the function of the EJB container is to implement the business logic of the application. The Enterprise Information System (EIS) tier primarily consists of data sources and a number of interfaces and APIs to access the resources and other existing or legacy applications.

11.2.3.2.1 JavaServer Pages and Java Servlets as the User Interaction Components

JavaServer Page (JSP) and Java Servlets are meant to process and respond to Web user request. Servlet provides a Java-centric programming approach for implementing Web tier functionality. The Servlet API provides an easy-to-use set of objects that process Hypertext Transfer Protocol

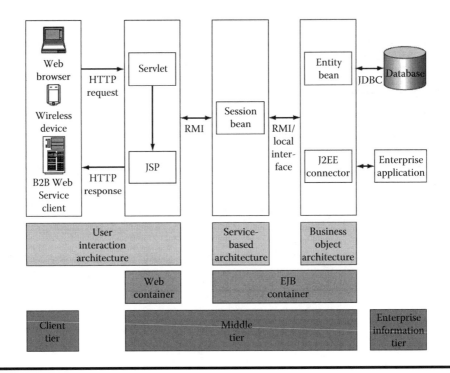

Figure 11.2   Enterprise Application in J2EE.

(HTTP) requests and generate HTML/XML responses. JSPs provide an HTML-centric version of the JavaServlets. JSP components are document based rather than object based and possess built-in access to Servlet API request and response objects as also the user session object. JSPs also provide a powerful custom tag mechanism, enabling the encapsulation of reusable Java presentation code that can be placed directly into the JSP document.

11.2.3.2.2 Session Bean EJBs as Service-Based Components

Session Beans are meant for representing services provided to a client. Unlike Entity Beans, Session Beans do not share data across multiple clients—each user requesting a service or executing a transaction invokes a separate Session Bean to process the request. A stateless Session Bean after processing a request goes on to the next request or next client without maintaining or sharing any data. On the other hand, stateful Session Beans are often constructed for a particular client and maintain a state across method invocations for a single client until the component is removed.

11.2.3.2.3 Entity Bean EJBs as the Business Object Components

Entity Beans are meant for representing persistent data entities within an enterprise application. One of the major component services that are provided to the Entity Beans is that of Container Managed Persistence (CMP). However, in EJB 2.0 specification, CMP persistence is limited to one table only. Any object-relational mapping involving more than a one-to-one table-object mapping is supported only through Bean Managed Persistence (BMP) (see Section 11.2.3.4.1.3 "Entity JavaBeans (EJB)").

11.2.3.2.4 Distributed Java Components

Java Naming and Directory Interface (JNDI) enables naming and distribution of Java components within the reference architecture. JNDI can be used to store and retrieve any Java object. However, JNDI is usually used to look up for component (home or remote) interfaces to enterprise beans. The client uses JNDI to look up the corresponding EJB Home interface, which enables creation, access, or removal of instances of Session and Entity Beans. In case of local Entity Bean, a method invocation is proxied directly to the bean's implementation. While in case of remote Entity Beans, the Home interface is used to obtain access to the remote interface to invoke the exposed methods using Remote Method Invocation (RMI). The remote interface takes the local method call, serializes the objects that will be passed as arguments, and invokes the corresponding remote method on the distributed object. These serialized objects are converted back into normal objects to invoke the method to return the resulting value upon which the process is reversed to revert the value back to the remote interface client.

11.2.3.2.5 J2EE Access to the EIS Tier

J2EE provides a number of interfaces and APIs to access resources in the EIS tier. The use of Java Database Connectivity (JDBC) API is encapsulated primarily in the data access layer or within the CMP classes of the Entity Bean. Data sources that map to a database are defined in JDBC, which can be looked up by a client searching for a resource using the JNDI. This enables the J2EE application server to provide connection pooling to different data resources, which should appropriately be closed as soon as the task is over to prevent bottlenecks.

The various J2EE interfaces and APIs available are as follows:

■ Java Connector Architecture (JCA/JTS) provides a standard way to build adapters to access existing enterprise applications.
■ JavaMail API provides a standard way to access mail server applications.
■ Java Message Service (JMS) provides standard interface to enterprise messaging systems. JMS enables reliable asynchronous communication with other distributed components. JMS is used by Message-Driven Beans (MDB) to perform asynchronous or parallel processing of messages.

11.2.3.3 Model–View–Controller (MVC) Architecture

The Model 2 architecture is based on the model–view–controller (MVC) design pattern. A generic MVC implementation is a vital element of the reference architecture as it provides a flexible and reusable foundation for very rapid web-based application development.

The components of the MVC architecture are as follows:

■ *View* deals with the display on the screens presented to the user.
■ *Controller* deals with the flow and processing of user actions.
■ *Model* deals with the business logic.

MVC architecture modularizes and isolates screen logic, control logic, and business logic in order to achieve greater flexibility and opportunity for reuse. A critical isolation point is between the presentation objects and the application back-end objects that manage the business logic and data. This enables the user interface to affect major changes on the display screens without impacting the business logic and data components.

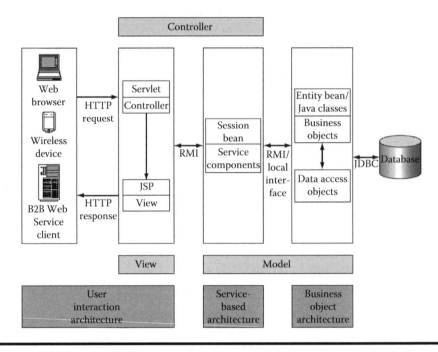

Figure 11.3   MVC and Enterprise Application Architecture.

View does not contain the source of data and relies on the model to furnish the relevant data. When the model updates the data, it notifies as also furnishes the changed data to the view so that it can re-render the display to the user with the up-to-date data and correct data.

The controller channels information from the view on the user actions for processing by the business logic in the model. Controller enables an application design to flexibly handle things such as page navigation and access to the functionality provided by the application model in case of form submissions. Thus, controller provides an isolation point between the model and the view, resulting in a more loosely coupled front end and back end.

Figure 11.3 gives a complete picture of how objects in the MVC architecture are mapped to the reference architecture in J2EE.

11.2.3.4 Overview of J2EE Technologies

These can be subdivided into three main categories, namely, component services, horizontal services, and communication services.

11.2.3.4.1 Component Services

These services assist in expediting and simplifying the development of the enterprise applications. They insulate the resulting applications from the underlying J2EE APIs.

11.2.3.4.1.1 JavaServer Pages (JSP) — As discussed in MVC architecture previously, the objective is to separate the presentation and content from the application logic, with the presentation and content contained in the JSP. JSP is similar to server-side scripting technology, except that

JSP is compiled, whereas scripts are interpreted. JSP utilizes the Java Servlet technology to achieve server-side processing.

A JSP consists of Java code embedded within a structured document such as HTML or XML. The basic idea is to use the markup language for the static portion of the presentation and embed special tags within the page to mark up the dynamic content. The tags are used to process incoming requests from a client and consequently generate a response. As JSP uses additional system resources, wherever the presentation content is static, a plain HTML page should be used. The Use of JSP allows the presentation code to be easily maintained as regular HTML code and shields the Web developer from having to deal with unfamiliar language and tools.

Java Scriptlets can be embedded in a JSP file, though their usage should be kept to the minimum. Sun recommends the use of JSP where there is a significant amount of dynamic content that is envisaged.

11.2.3.4.1.2 Servlets — Servlets are primarily used as a conduit for passing data back and forth between a Web client and an enterprise application running on a server. Servlets are server-side programs that execute in a servlet engine, which often forms a part of the HTTP server, but may also run stand-alone. Servlets run inside the servlet engine or container hosted on a Web server; the servlet container manages the life cycle of a servlet and translates the Web client's requests into object-based requests and, in reverse, the object-based responses back to the Web client via HTTP.

Servlets provide a more effective alternate mechanism to the traditional CGI scripts for interaction between the server-based business logic and the Web-based clients. Servlets are usually employed to handle preliminary tasks like gathering and checking for valid inputs from the entry fields of a Web page. Once the basic checks are completed, the data are then passed on to more suitable component(s) for actual processing.

JSP specification provides the JSP with the same capabilities as the servlet. The basic idea is to leverage JSP for presentation-centric tasks and utilize the servlets for business logic processing-centric tasks. Servlets are preferred for more logical tasks as they are also comparatively easier to debug. Since Java code is embedded within the JSP, it may seem that the separation of presentation from business logic is not realistic. JSP should primarily be focused on presentation, and any Java code embedded within the JSP should primarily be for communication with servlets, other control or data entities, and so on.

JSP development usually adopts the Model 2 architecture based on the Model-View-Controller (MVC) architecture discussed earlier. It uses one or more servlets as controllers; requests received by frontline servlet(s) are redirected to the concerned JSPs. Usually, JavaBeans is used as the model that acts as the conduit to pass information between the controller servlet(s) and the JSPs. The controller fills in the JavaBean based on the request, and the JSP in turn composes the actual page using values from the JavaBean.

11.2.3.4.1.3 Enterprise JavaBeans (EJB) — EJB components encapsulate business logic. EJB defines a comprehensive component model for building scalable, distributed server-based enterprise Java application component.

EJB components have four parts:

1. An implementation class that contains the business logic.
2. Home interfaces that present the EJB methods to the outside world.
3. Remote interfaces that present the EJB methods to the outside world.
4. A deployment descriptor: An XML file that is used to configure the EJB component being deployed in a J2EE server. For example, a deployment descriptor can define the security properties or transaction properties of EJB methods.

EJBs are container-managed components, that is, the container manages their life cycle and, based on the configuration specified in the deployment descriptor, interacts on behalf of the EJBs with various J2EE services.

The success of EJBs is based on a set of key concepts. First, EJBs are deployed within a *container* hosted by an application server, rather than deploying directly onto the application server. A container provides the environment for execution of EJBs, management of their life cycle, and provisioning of additional services. Second, EJBs take an approach based on proxy pattern rather than a monolithic component, which effectively separates out the component into client objects and remote objects. While the EJB user only sees the client object represented by the EJB interfaces, the remote object is free to change in terms of implementation details like location on the network and underlying transport mechanism. Third, EJBs use the concept of deployment descriptors that decouples the development from the deployment aspects.

There are three types of EJBs:

1. *Entity Beans*: Entity beans are EJBs designed specifically to represent data in a persistent store, which is typically a database. They encapsulate persistent data in a data store, which is typically a row or record of data in a database table. Apart from the built-in database access and synchronization capabilities, entity beans automatically provide the ability to share both state and behavior across multiple clients concurrently, disaster recovery facilities, and so on.

   An entity bean consists of a Home interface, a Remote interface, an implementation class, and a primary key class. The Home interface defines create, finder, remove, and home methods. The remote interface defines business methods. It also has a primary key class that contains methods for operating on the primary key for a single or a compounded database table. The implementation class implements all of the life-cycle, finder, select, and business methods. Like all EJBs, entity beans also make use of the deployment descriptor to hold additional information pertaining to the component including transaction settings on business methods, relationships with other entity beans, and persistent filed settings.

2. *Session Beans*: Session beans are the most popular of the EJBs and are used primarily to manage transactions or client sessions. In an enterprise application, they are often used as the main controller connecting servlets or JSPs to entity beans or other components. Apart from the built-in transaction management and state management capabilities, EJB container also provides additional services such as automated resource management, concurrency, and security.

   These are used mainly for transient activities. They are nonpersistent and often encapsulate bulk of the business logic. While *stateful* session beans retain client state between successive interactions with the client, *stateless* session beans do not do so. In the case of a stateless session bean, each successive invocation of the bean is treated as an independent activity.

Entity beans have the option to use two different kinds of persistence mechanisms. First, container-managed persistence (CMP) entails using entity beans, while all database access and synchronization are handled automatically by the EJB container. Second, bean-managed persistence (BMP) entails using entity beans, while all data access and synchronization are handled by hand-crafted custom code.

3. *Message driven Beans (MDBs)*: MDBs are EJBs designed to be asynchronous consumers and processors of JMS messages. These were introduced newly in J2EE 1.3 and are useful for situations where synchronicity is not essential, for example, integrating loosely coupled systems. Session beans employ Remote Procedure Call (RPC)-based communication, which has the disadvantage that the sender must wait for a response before it can undertake the next activity. Message-driven beans are stateless, and unlike session and entity beans, message-driven beans do not have published interfaces.

MDBs are useful for achieving the following:

a. *Efficiency*: Messaging can be used for separating out those elements of the business logic that can be processed independent of the main thread of processing. This enables the main thread to obviate the need to expend resources and time on nonessential operations and move on to the next requests.

b. *Decoupling*: Different subsystems are developed so that they are not tightly integrated with each other.

c. *Flexible integration*: Loosely coupled systems can be composed by using message-driven beans to wrap existing systems.

11.2.3.4.2 Horizontal Services

These are general services that are required across multiple tiers in enterprise application.

11.2.3.4.2.1 JDBC Java Database Connectivity — JDBC enables via database neutral APIs to perform a host of operations like obtaining database connections, executing SQL queries and updates via these connections, and processing the results of such queries. The J2EE extensions also provide support for connections pooling and distributed transactions. The database driver modules in the JDBC are responsible for mapping a database neutral request onto the request expected by a specific RDBMS.

11.2.3.4.2.2 Java Naming and Directory Interface (JNDI) — In J2EE application servers, JNDI provides via neutral APIs a mechanism that is used by the clients, Web components, and EJBs to find J2EE resources using a symbolic naming scheme. Directory and naming services are used to map symbolic names or a set of search attributes onto a resource. For example, the Domain Name System maps symbolic host names onto their Internet addresses. Similarly, a File System maps a symbolic pathname onto a system file identifier like an inode in Unix. Individually, all of these naming and directory services have specific APIs and may be written in a variety of languages.

11.2.3.4.2.3 Java Connector Architecture (JCA/JTS) — JTS is a comprehensive service that supports distributed transactions and consequently two-phase commit protocol. JTA, which is a subset of JTS, is made available as a resource to J2EE application.

11.2.3.4.2.4 XML Processing APIs — XML is a widely accepted way of representing data in a standard format that can be validated against a Document-Type Definition (DTD) or schema.

These data can then be transmitted between various systems that convert the neutral format to system-specific formats, for example, to a relational form. Just as Java provides code portability, XML provides data portability. XML is also used as the configuration language in J2EE.

11.2.3.4.3 Communication Services

11.2.3.4.3.1 HTTP/HTTPS — Hypertext Transfer Protocol (HTTP) is a text-based protocol used for communication across the Internet and supports Web browser interactions with the HTTP servers listening on server machines. The protocol is stateless in that the server does not maintain any client state—every request made by an HTTP client will have to provide all essential information needed to process the request like

- The nature of the client (e.g., kind of browser)
- The kind of request
- The resource target on the server (e.g., a particular HTML page or servlet)
- The data to be sent to the server

Client requests are matched with server responses that provide information about the request like

- The Status of the request
- The MIME type of the response data
- The response data

HTTPS is the secure form of the HTTP in that the HTTP communication is transmitted over the Secure Socket Layer (SSL).

11.2.3.4.3.2 Remote Method Invocation (RMI) — RMI enables communication between distributed objects transparent of their remote locations on the network by communicating with a local proxy or a stub that is generated automatically to communicate with the corresponding remote objects. The code for the proxy is generated automatically and communicates using sockets with the remote object—there is helper code at the remote end that reads from the socket, processes the bytes, and makes the method call on the remote object.

Initially, RMI allowed communication only between java objects. Subsequently, RMI began to support communication with non-Java objects using RMI-IIOP (Internet Inter-ORB Protocol) that is a CORBA transport protocol on top of TCP/IP. RMI enables developers to effectively concentrate on developing the business logic rather than worrying about the details of the distribution.

11.2.3.4.3.3 Java Message Service (JMS) — JMS enables asynchronous communication between producers and consumers in that a producer sends a message to a queue or topic, and, rather than waiting for a response, it moves on to undertake other tasks. As and when they are ready, consumers read messages from queues and topics.

JMS employs two models of communication:

1. *Point to point*: This involves the uses of FIFO queues and supports one-to-one and many-to-one interactions between producers and consumers. Message objects are created by the producers and sent to a named queue. Consumers who wish to read messages from the

head of the queue obtain a reference to the queue head and then listen or wait for messages to be placed on the queue. As and when a message is placed on the queue, it will be read and removed from the queue by the listening consumer.

2. *Publish and subscribe*: This involves the use of topics and supports many-to-many communication between producers and consumers. Topics are analogous to newsgroups and consumers subscribed to one or more topics. As and when producers publish messages to topics, a separate copy of a message is sent to each consumer.

11.2.3.4.3.4 JavaMail — JavaMail enables the sending and receiving of e-mail from within a Java program. It provides APIs that enable creation of MIME message objects that can be sent and received using the underlying mail protocols like SMTP, POP3, and IMAP4. It is a form of an asynchronous mail though slower than JMS and is used mainly for interaction between end users.

11.3 Summary

In this chapter, we discussed tools and techniques for custom development in ABAP and Java. For ABAP custom development, we describe an overview of ABAP, ABAP Objects, Web Applications Builder, and Business Server Pages application development environment. With regard to Java custom development, the chapter gives an overview of SAP Java Development Infrastructure (JDI), NDWS tool and perspectives, and the J2EE platform.

PRE-IMPLEMENTATION STAGE

This part presents the various activities which are prerequisite to starting a SAP CRM project. Chapter 12 discusses various activities and tasks related with the SAP project that needs to be readied for the SAP implementation effort.

Chapter 12

Initiating the SAP Project

This chapter introduces the various issues that are prerequisites for initiating a SAP project. We will discuss the organizational structure recommended for managing a SAP implementation project. This chapter also details the constitution of the various committees and explains the various supporting issues of training and resource management. In the later part of the chapter, it addresses the various kinds of risks that are associated with a SAP project and presents measures recommended by SAP to contain and even minimize their impact. The ground covered here would be covered from the point of view of ASAP methodology in Chapter 13 as well. The objective of dealing the same issues from two different views was to illustrate the importance of adapting a repository-based integrated methodology like AcceleratedSAP.

12.1 SAP Executive Sponsor

The executive sponsor should be the executive with the power to make decisions with respect to processes, finances, and the project timeline. He or she should be a senior member of the organization and represent the business groups of the company. The executive sponsor should also provide resources/infrastructure support and report the project-related issues to the Managing Director (MD) on a regular basis.

12.2 SAP Project Executive Committee

Top management commitment is one of the key factors in a successful implementation of an enterprise resource planning (ERP) system. Hence, it is important that the top management of the company devote adequate time for planning and review of all the activities from the beginning of the project until it is completed. For the success of the project, it is also important that the commitment is visible to all the employees of the company and is exhibited through the direct involvement and actions of the top management.

An executive committee should consist of

- A CMD or CEO (Chief Executive Officer)
- An executive sponsor
- A project general manager
- A COO (Chief Operating Officer) or VP of business operations
- A CIO (Chief Information Officer) or VP of systems
- A Chairman and Managing Director's (CMD's) nominated consultant or any person that CMD may include

Executive committee meetings should be held approximately once every 4 weeks to review the overall progress.

12.3 SAP Project Steering Committee

The steering committee should consist of

- An executive sponsor
- A chief project officer
- A technical team leader
- All key user representatives
- All key consultants
- A technical support project leader
- Senior management representatives
- CMD's nominated consultant

Steering committee meetings should be held every 2 weeks to take stock of the event-based milestones and other project-related issues.

12.4 Roles of the Executive and Steering Committee Members

The roles and responsibilities of the executive and steering committee members should be to

- Provide direction for the entire project
- Approve and control the project scope and implementation strategy
- Approve identified risks and authorize measures to contain them
- Be responsible for milestone deliverables and project delays
- Authorize the staffing plan for the SAP project
- Authorize the training plan and budget for the SAP project
- Help resolve issues, if any, with the implementation partner, coordinate commercial matters, and approve payments on completed milestones
- Authorize and ensure infrastructural support (such as Hardware, Software, network, external software, office space, communication lines, and OSS)
- Resolve the issues raised in business process finalization and standardization
- Resolve administrative issues faced by consultants from time to time

12.5 Mission and Objectives of the SAP Project

The mission of the SAP project should dovetail into the mission and objectives set forth by a company for the following 3–5 years.

12.6 Deciding the Scope of the SAP Project

One of the most important responsibilities to be handled by the executive and steering committees is to decide on the scope of the SAP project. For the Millennium Enterprises under consideration, the approach being recommended here is to adopt the big-bang approach, whereby the company implements most of the standard SAP modules and also any SAP industry-specific solutions if available for its areas of business.

Only in the big-bang approach does the company start utilizing the information captured by the SAP system as a resource like manpower, materials, and money, rather than merely as a recording and reporting system. The traditional systems have been hobbled into playing exactly such a role and have never been able to deliver the productivity gains expected of them.

The company must also decide the phases of implementation following the implementation at the pilot site. The true benefits of an integrated system can be reaped only when all sites and offices of the company are brought on board the SAP platform. Toward this objective, the pilot site team must be staffed by personnel from all future sites of implementations, and the functionality, as implemented at the pilot site, should be as comprehensive as possible, based on the available time frame and business know-how with the members of the team.

12.7 Initiating the SAP Project

Initiating the SAP project primarily involves instituting the project management structure and appointing the chief project officer (CPO). The CPO would have to formulate and initiate the mechanism for the selection or nomination process for the members of the team.

The CPO would also have to formulate and get approval from the project's steering and executive committees on the project policies, the guidelines, the strategies to be adopted for minimizing the identified risks, and the methods for reporting on the project's progress, budget, and resources.

12.8 SAP Project Management Structure

In this section, we look at the organizational structure of a SAP project.

12.8.1 Chief Project Officer (CPO)

The Chief Project Officer (CPO) is also a member of the project's steering committee and has enough responsibility and authority to manage day-to-day operational project-related issues and meet all project-related resource requirements.

The company should appoint a senior manager as the full-time CPO. He or she should be familiar with the business environment and the functional and information technology (IT) to lead a team's key users and technical consultants, who will also participate in the activities of the implementation process and be responsible for the successful implementation of the SAP system.

The CPO performs the following functions:

- Provide supervision of the entire project.
- Be responsible for milestone deliverables and project delays.
- Approve and control the project scope and implementation strategy.
- Prepare and get approval for the staffing plan, including the pilot site and the rollout sites.
- Prepare and get approval for the training plan of the project from the lead super users and end users at various stages of the project.
- Be responsible to get the relevant business users' time and attention at all relevant stages of the project.
- Accept deliverables and give sign-offs.
- Resolve the issues raised in business process finalization and standardization.
- Help resolve issues, if any, with the implementation partner, coordinate on commercial matters, and approve payments on completed milestones.
- Resolve administrative issues faced by consultants from time to time.
- Provide infrastructural support such as Hardware, software, Network, external software, office space, communication lines, and Online Service System (OSS).
- Arrange steering and executive committee meetings and the decisions/clearances required from the committees.
- Provide guidance to SAP and its implementation partner on the company's specific business requirements.
- Provide all data for loading from the relevant business departments.

The CPO also guides the definition and maintenance of the project's Implementation Guide (IMG) for his or her company as a whole.

12.8.2 Site Project Managers

The site project managers (SPMs) are responsible for the SAP implementation at various sites and work under the direct guidance of the CPO. They should be part of the SAP project team for the pilot site from the beginning. This will give them enough exposure and experience on how to handle the implementation at their own respective sites later.

The responsibilities of an SPM include the following:

- Supervise the entire project at their sites.
- Be responsible for milestone deliverables and project delays.
- Assemble the manpower and resources according to the staffing plan for the SAP project.
- Execute the training plan for the site, including training for the Functional and Technical team members, Super Users, and end users at various stages of the project.
- Be responsible to get the relevant site business users' attention at all relevant stages of the project.
- Accept deliverables and give sign-offs.
- Resolve administrative issues faced by consultants from time to time.
- Ensure infrastructural support (such as H/W, S/W, external software, office space, communication lines, and OSS) for the SAP project.
- Provide all data for loading from the relevant business departments.

The SPM is also responsible for maintaining the site project's IMG for their respective sites.

12.8.3 Module Leaders

The project team should include module leaders who are responsible for each of the major SAP modules to be implemented for the company. Module leaders should preferably have requisite prior experience in the concerned functional area and also have undergone adequate functional training in SAP, particularly in his or her module of responsibility.

Module leaders should be identified at the beginning of a project and should be part of the Business Blueprint and Realization phases. They should participate in identifying the processes and documenting them, their gap issues, and their resolutions not only for their modules but for other modules as well. This would enable them to later make a more effective contribution during the module-level and integration-level testing.

12.8.4 Resource Manager

The success of any SAP project is critically dependent on marshalling the right resources at the scheduled time and place. For an IT project with similar scope and investments, SAP projects are usually of a much shorter duration. This requires a person, known as the resource manager, who has previously handled the purchasing and resourcing responsibilities in an IT project. He or she should be conversant with the purchase policies and procedures of the organization, as well as those for reporting on budgets in a SAP project.

In the beginning of the project, and at appropriate stages later, the resource manager could also be a member of the project steering committee. This would enable him or her to escalate issues quickly on resource approval delays, mobilization delays, deliveries, incomplete installations, pending training and support issues, and so on.

12.8.5 Training Manager

Unlike the traditional implementations, SAP implementations involve a much larger number of operational personnel who would be using SAP on a regular basis. The training manager should be able to execute training for the various groups of personnel as per the training plan at appointed sites.

A major responsibility of the training manager is not only to ensure the availability of the instructors but also to release the various personnel from their normal functions at appropriate times so that they can participate in the scheduled training sessions. He or she must also work with the resource manager to complete the installation of the proper software licenses and authorize the training.

In the training of the functional and technical teams, IDES and InfoDB licenses can be obtained and installed with adequate infrastructural support of the PCs, networking, and so on. Similarly, before commencing training for the end users, the latest company-specific user documents for all requisite modules need to be complete and approved specifically for use in the training sessions.

12.9 Project Management Policies and Guidelines

The project management policies and guidelines should be finalized and communicated to all concerned at the earliest time possible.

12.9.1 Project Strategy

As has been mentioned in Chapter 1, Section 1.2.1.4 "Information as the New Resource," implementing SAP will benefit the company only when it starts using the information made available by a productive SAP system as a resource. For this, it is essential that all the base modules are implemented and go into production. Otherwise, the system will function merely as a system for recording and reporting on the past performance.

12.9.2 Project Planning and Monitoring

The issues of reporting the progress of the project can lead to contention among project members. Considering that SAP implementation projects are driven by the business managers, even decisions like whether to employ packaged software for the SAP project can become a major political issue.

12.9.3 Project Resource Requirements

For a successful SAP implementation, especially for the big-bang approach recommended for the millennium enterprise, resources in adequate measures and at the right time are essential. These would be in terms of the following:

- The allocation and disbursement of budget finances at appropriate stages.
- The acquisition and on-schedule installation of the server and PC hardware, the networking and communications hardware, the communications monitoring and network management software, O/S and office automation software at the servers and nodes, and, finally, the SAP software.
- Staffing by recruitment and subcontracting or deputation from the various departments for SAP functional teams, technical teams, resource administration, training and logistics teams, super users, and, lastly, the end users for their orientation training and refresher training just before the go-live phase.
- Data from the legacy system or other systems that are operational within the company or its key business partners. This loading of data could be a one-time exercise before the cutover to the productive SAP system or on a regular basis at predetermined periods during the business cycle every month. The loading process could itself be in the batch mode or be a real-time interface that transfers data and updates between SAP and other systems on an ongoing basis.

12.9.4 Project Training Requirements

SAP implementation projects engender large training requirements. Traditional implementations, however, are closely administered by a centralized computer facility and are confined to smaller numbers of end users. Moreover, these end users are also not actually involved with the operations of the business; on the contrary, often, they are usually personnel only responsible for transcribing transactions and other information into the system.

ERP, in the true sense of the word, brings computerization to the desktops of the operational people. Thus, the training requirements for a SAP project implementation would be huge and may easily involve 10%–20% of the manpower of a company.

A company may have to undertake SAP-related training for three different groups of personnel:

■ The select group of managerial personnel who are key members of their departments and have been nominated as the members of the functional team.
■ The group of key users who form the core of the super users to be entrusted with the task of life-scale testing the system and also training the end users.
■ All other end users who would be using the system as part of their routine operational duties. As an important part of the strategy for post-implementation support, the third group is trained primarily by the members of the second group, the super users.

The managerial personnel group will be trained with an overview of SAP and their module(s) of interest. The key user group will be trained with an overview of their module and all of the critical processes of interest. The end-user group will be trained only in the processes that are routinely used by them on a daily basis.

12.10 Risk Management in a SAP Project

Because the SAP project is an implementation of a standard package, the risks associated with a SAP project are different from those traditionally associated with software implementations. Traditional software projects' major risks are as follows:

■ Lack of resources
■ Lack of appropriate resources
■ Lack of clarity, completeness, and certainty on the scope and functionality
■ Requirements capture and analysis
■ System design that is effective, efficient, and at the same time flexible for changes in the future
■ Development of the system based on this design and testing using this design as a reference
■ Training various groups of users on the new system
■ Interfacing real time with other application systems
■ Loading all relevant and up-to-date data into the new system
■ Parallel runs with the new system
■ Switching to the new system
■ Missing deadlines
■ Disputes regarding roles, responsibilities, and performance criteria
■ User disagreements or nonparticipation
■ Software or infrastructure failures

In addition to these risks, SAP projects have other risks including the following:

■ Requirements capture and analysis
■ Understanding what the SAP system can provide
■ Evaluating and focusing on the gaps in functionality
■ Configuring and customizing the SAP system correctly
■ Integration testing of the SAP system
■ Training all groups of users almost in tandem

■ Loading all relevant and up-to-date data into the new system
■ Switching directly to the new system without the full parallel runs phase

The risks associated with the requirements capture and requirements analysis are no different than those with the traditional projects. Especially for future enterprises of the millennium, it is important to have shorter timelines for the project implementations.

A company implementing SAP can adopt several strategies for minimizing the risks inherent in the project. The most important one is to do away with the requirement analysis phase but at the same time implement functionality that represents the optimal practices for the processes that are critical to business. This is effectively achieved by adopting SAP's recommended best-of-business practices that come bundled along with the system.

12.10.1 Selecting the Most Critical Processes

A company should evaluate and select the processes that are critical to its business and focus on implementing them effectively to add maximum value for optimal effort.

12.10.2 Implementing Best-of-Business Processes

Traditionally, SAP has been known to incorporate a library of 800 of the best-of-business processes derived from companies throughout the world. The success of SAP in providing comprehensive functionality within a shorter time frame compared with traditional implementations is based on the strategy of leveraging the commonality that is found in similar processes prevalent in companies within an industry.

Reusability has been a powerful concept in enhancing productivity and the quality of delivered software in the areas of traditional software development. SAP, in particular, extends this concept of reusability to the design of mission-critical systems. It packages such universal commonalties of functionality for rapid and successful implementations.

Before adding reusability to the library of the best-of-business processes, however, the company should document, rationalize, and standardize the company's select group of processes that are to be implemented using SAP.

12.10.2.1 Documentation of Processes

Documenting the various business processes permits the true comprehension of the characteristic structure and dynamics of the business environment within a company. This involves recording various details on the business processes like name, purpose, responsible function, process description (including inputs and outputs), and subprocesses. This also includes interfaces with other functions and systems, exceptional conditions, areas for improvement, and impact analysis of suggested scenarios.

12.10.2.2 Rationalization of Processes

Many of the systems and procedures adopted by traditional systems were influenced by the architecture of the systems themselves. For instance, these earlier systems were designed to be used by IT-literate personnel managed and supported by a centralized IT function. In contrast, because of the end-user orientation of ERP packages like SAP as well as the online availability of data on all aspects of company operations, SAP permits the rationalizing of many processes. This could be in terms of eliminating sequential wait periods for approvals, acknowledgments prior to further processing, collating status updates from various departments before compiling the latest positions on inventory, and so on.

In enterprise-wide integrated packages like SAP, many of these facilities and features become available automatically as a part of the architecture of the system. Thus, such process steps could be eliminated entirely from the business processes.

12.10.2.3 Standardization of Processes

Every plant or office site of a company develops its own character and culture, which is a result of the company's recommended corporate environment blending with the local situations. Such local practices have strong adherents and generate loyalty and pride. These factors often harm the progress of implementing a fairly uniform system, even if it's a computerized system like SAP, across the organization at all of its sites and offices.

The CPO must take ample measures to ensure the broad acceptance within the organization of standardized implementation. This can be ensured by

- The rapid implementation at the pilot site
- The rapid rollout of SAP at other company sites and offices
- The deputation of key personnel from all sites for the teams at the pilot sites, even at the risk of overstaffing these teams
- The judicious selection and documentation of functionalities for implementation at the pilot sites
- The democratic and transparent process of standardization based on the predefined criteria of value addition in terms of customer friendliness, quality, timeliness, costs, and so on
- Configuring and customizing the maximum possible functionality at the pilot site, keeping in view the businesses and practices prevalent at all other sites and offices

12.10.3 Centralized Base Reference Configuration

A company can experience the real payoff of implementing an ERP like SAP only when it has implemented SAP at all of its plants, facilities, and offices. Traditional computerized systems have a much more difficult time implementing standardized processes across all locations of their organizations. Since a SAP project entails implementing both best-of-business and standardized processes, it leads to fairly standard implementation solutions across all of its sites.

A company should plan to implement a fairly comprehensive functionality at its pilot site. This is termed as the centralized base reference configuration (CBRC). This can simply be transplanted at each of the rollout sites in the subsequent stages of the project. Such an approach engenders faster customization, training, integration testing, and, finally, go-live stages.

12.10.4 AcceleratedSAP (ASAP) Methodology

The AcceleratedSAP (ASAP) implementation methodology is the latest tool introduced by SAP for rapid implementation of the SAP system within an organization. ASAP is a structured implementation approach and can help you achieve a faster implementation with quicker user acceptance, well-defined roadmaps, and efficient documentation at various stages.

The key phases of ASAP methodology are

1. Project preparation
2. Business blueprint
3. Realization
4. Final preparation
5. Go live and support

By promoting the best-of-business practices for implementation, SAP does away with the time-consuming and tedious steps of requirements capture and analysis mentioned previously.

The popularity, effectiveness, and reliability of such an approach were established by the great success achieved by a similar methodology adopted for the traditional software application development in the 1980s. The Structured Systems Analysis and Design (SSAD) methodology introduced by Gane and Sarson essentially skipped the then-popular practice of first analyzing the existing system and went directly to perform the analysis of the proposed system. The design of the proposed system was therefore a radically different interpretation of the future requirements of a company without being encumbered by the constraints, practices, and prejudices of the past systems and procedures prevalent within the organization.

With SAP, as explained, this process is taken a step further by optimizing the traditional design and development stages of the project life cycle by utilizing a library of best-of-business, preimplemented processes for any industry. We will be discussing all these phases of ASAP in detail later in Chapter 13 of this book.

12.11 Change Management in a SAP Project

Initiating change and confronting change are the two most important issues facing companies today. The ability to change business processes contributes directly to your *innovation* bottom line. The traditional concept of change management is understood generally as a one-time event, but if an organization is looking for the ability to not only handle change management, but the management of changes on a continual basis, then SAP is a must. SAP provides a platform for such ongoing changes in the processes that are so critical to the success of a company's business.

As we have stated earlier, business processes that reside or are internalized within the minds of an organizations' employees are difficult to change, simply because we naturally find change difficult. However, processes that reside or are internalized within computerized systems are easy to change. Thus, SAP-supported processes are much more easier to change and execute than the conventional computerized system, because SAP implements a model of the enterprise that is comprehensive and consistent.

Change management is essential and employees are apprehensive because of

- Fear of job reductions
- Fear of losing responsibility and control
- Anxiety arising out of a perceived inadequacy of their background
- Fear of failure
- Loss in the sense of ownership
- Sheer inertia for changing and learning new systems

The issues become further aggravated because of lack of clarity in terms of

- Why changes are needed
- What changes are needed
- Who is accountable for what
- How will the performance and progress be measured

The issues arising because of changes resulting from the implementation of SAP can be resolved by

- Demonstrated support from senior management
- Wide and rapid information dissemination on the SAP project
- Adequate training and refresher programs
- Accelerated progress and effectiveness with the SAP system
- Rotation of job responsibilities or replacement

12.12 Roles of the SAP Project Team Members

In the following sections, we discuss the roles and responsibilities for the members of the SAP team.

12.12.1 SAP Project Team

The SAP project team has the following responsibilities:

- Be responsible for studying and streamlining the business processes.
- Standardize the business processes across all offices.
- Study the system and configure it to suit the business processes with the help of the module consultant.
- Generate necessary documentation.
- Prepare a training manual.
- Identify the roles and responsibilities and required authorizations in the SAP system.
- Set up the authorizations.
- Train users.
- Complete tasks according to the implementation plan.
- Work on data collection and the purification of uploads to the system.
- Support the users after going live.
- Implement at rollout sites.

12.12.2 External Consultants Team

12.12.2.1 Functional Consultants Team

The SAP team of consultants has the following responsibilities:

- Train the SAP team members in respective modules.
- Help the team map processes in the system.

■ Find solutions for the gaps observed after mapping.
■ Guide the team during the integration test.
■ Be responsible for meeting the milestone deadlines of the module.
■ Provide necessary input for programming.
■ Help the team during discussions with users in case of any problems.

12.12.2.2 SAP Technical Team

■ Identifying the list of customizations using user exits, new reports using, and so on
■ Preparing the project SAP programming and documentation standards
■ Writing ABAP programs, user exits, and reports using tools such as Report Painter, Report Writer, ABAP Query, Drilldown Reporting, or ABAP programming
■ Identification of interfaces and data to be uploaded into the SAP system from legacy and non-SAP systems
■ Specification of the interfaces and data uploads
■ Programming the interfaces and data upload programs
■ Unit testing and integration testing

12.12.3 SAP Administration Team

The members of the SAP administration team will have to be skilled in three different areas: basis system administration, database administration, and operating system administration.

The various tasks involved with the SAP Basis area are as follows:

■ Starting and stopping the SAP system
■ Daily administration using Computer Center Management System (CCMS)
■ Performing daily checks
■ Monitoring system logs
■ Monitoring SAP system/database alerts
■ Analyzing Advanced Business Applications Programming (ABAP) dumps and taking corrective actions
■ Process monitoring
■ Update monitoring
■ Batch input monitoring
■ Monitoring lock entries
■ Managing user and system background jobs
■ Print administration
■ Temporary Sequential (TemSe) spool file administration for printing
■ Spool administration and tuning
■ Managing user information, authorization, and profiles
■ Importing transport requests
■ Error analysis and troubleshooting using logs, traces, and program dumps
■ Managing operations and use of the Online Service System (OSS)
■ Planning and managing the disaster recovery site

The database-related tasks are as follows:

- Performing regular SAP database backups as per the backup strategy
- Performing SAP database administration (SAPDBA) activities using utilities like BRBACKUP for backup and BRARCHIVE for archiving logs
- Performing regular archive log backups
- Monitoring and managing table spaces, indices, index extent sizes, and so on

Other operating system- and network-related tasks are as follows:

- Installing upgrades
- Coordinating with the H/W and other vendors for follow-ups on reported problems
- Monitoring network loads and identifying bottlenecks

12.13 Summary

In this chapter, we looked at various aspects preparatory to launching the SAP project. We covered issues dealing with the planning, organization, and managing of SAP projects. We also discussed the various elements of risks that may jeopardize the success of the project as well as measures to mitigate them. In the next chapter, we look into the infrastructure planning and preparation for the SAP implementation project.

IMPLEMENTATION STAGE

This part presents in detail SAP's AcceleratedSAP (ASAP) implementation methodology through all its phases. Chapter 13 introduces the concept and context of ASAP and gives details on the five stages of ASAP, namely, Project Preparation, Business Blueprint, Realization, Final Preparation, and GoLive and Support.

Chapter 13: SAP ASAP Methodology

SAP CRM is very flexible, but in order to configure it correctly, not only is one required to know the business process requirements of the company, but one must also be well acquainted with the SAP functionality even before starting on the configuration. In typical SAP projects, this is right at the initial stages of the project. This is the root cause for the large amount of effort and time required for completing the mapping and configuration of the base SAP system in all SAP projects. Although all the required functionality is already available in SAP all along, it takes some time to discover and use it correctly.

Chapter 13

SAP ASAP Methodology

This chapter introduces the novel implementation methodology devised by SAP to achieve successful implementations in shorter time periods. This is specifically targeted for customers from small and medium enterprises (SMEs).

Notwithstanding the comprehensiveness and flexibility of SAP to address requirements of diverse industries, implementing SAP in a reasonable time frame has become one of the most important issues for companies while evaluating SAP for their organization. Furthermore, as the high end of the market has become saturated, it is evident that SAP's potential for growth in the late 1990s is in the SME market. These are the customers who do not have the resources and time to survive enterprise resource planning (ERP) implementation projects extending for periods ranging from 2 to 3 years.

In 1996, SAP introduced the AcceleratedSAP (ASAP) implementation methodology with the objective of speeding up the SAP implementation projects. ASAP enabled new customers to utilize the experience and expertise gleaned from thousands of implementations worldwide. This chapter introduces the concept and practice of the ASAP methodology for implementation of SAP CRM.

13.1 Introducing the ASAP Methodology

ASAP supports the entire life cycle of the SAP installation; it is not confined to the implementation phase alone. ASAP also provides support for ongoing improvements as well as for efforts during SAP upgrades.

ASAP integrates the following three components that work in tandem to support the rapid and efficient implementation of the system:

1. *ASAP Roadmap*: This is a step-by-step methodology for a successful SAP implementation project.
2. *ASAP tools*: These include project management tools, questionnaires for business process consultants, and numerous guidebooks and checklists.
3. *R/3 services, support, and training*: This includes all consulting, training, and support services such as GoingLive Check and remote upgrades or archives.

ASAP consists of a wealth of checklists, spreadsheets, questionnaires, answers, document templates, and recommendations. It also provides white papers on important issues and includes guidebooks, learning tools, and accelerators on more technical issues related to the SAP infrastructure, installation, and operations. The various reviews and checklists available from ASAP verify not only the implementation project itself but also the stability and integrity of the system along each phase of the project.

The characteristics of the ASAP methodology are as follows:

- It is a proven methodology, having been used successfully in hundreds of projects initially in the United States and subsequently all across the world.
- It is a comprehensive and seamless methodology with integration across the various phases of the project.
- It skips over the as-is problematic phase in the traditional methodologies to directly target the analysis and documentation of the to-be business processes.
- It promotes three distinct roles to guarantee full attention to all aspects of a rapidly moving project: project management, application consulting, and technical implementation.
- The input from the Business Blueprint phase is used as a direct input for configuration in the realization phase.

ASAP methodology consists of five phases:

1. Project Preparation Stage
2. Business Blueprint
3. Realization
4. Final Preparation
5. Go Live and Support

In the following sections, we describe each of these phases in sufficient detail. Figure 13.1 shows SAP's standard schematic on ASAP methodology.

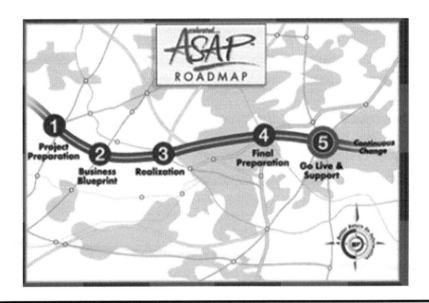

Figure 13.1 SAP ASAP methodology roadmap.

13.1.1 Why Are SAP Implementation Programs So Complex?

The prime reason for the apparently longer duration of SAP implementation projects is due to the peculiar complexity of the product and, hence, its implementation. Let me explain. The contradictory demands of comprehensibility and flexibility are satisfactorily addressable in SAP because of its repository-oriented architecture (in this chapter, we will mainly focus on the functionality aspects of this repository rather than the technical ones, which are also substantial). Fundamentally, this was not much different from the trend of parameterized packages that had been gaining ground among application software packages since the 1980s. The main difference is the extent or degree of parameterization: SAP is parameterized to a much larger extent. It is this property that enables it to be flexible enough to be configurable to the requirements of several industries.

The difficulty in implementing SAP arises from the fact that the success of the implementation project depended on correctly mapping all of the company's customer-facing business process into the SAP system. This entails correct configuration of all the required processes right at the beginning or at the initial stages of the project. As we have seen earlier, SAP addressed the problem of providing usable application software systems by effectively short-circuiting the problematic requirements analysis phase, which is the bane of the traditional software development life cycle (SDLC). Because of the demand for correct configuration right at the beginning, we were back to confronting essentially the same problem.

The majority of the risks for the ultimate success of the project are also dependent on this initial mapping being completed correctly, consistently, and completely. Unlike in the SDLC, where the end users are expected to know only their requirements thoroughly, in the new dispensation, they have the additional burden of having to become quite familiar with the functionality provided by SAP. Thus, SAP is very flexible, but in order to configure it correctly to use its power, not only is one required to know the business process requirements of the company, but one must also be well acquainted with the SAP functionality even before starting on the configuration. In typical SAP projects, this is right at the initial stages of the project. This is the root cause for the large amount of effort and time required for completing the mapping and configuration of the base SAP system in all SAP projects. Although all the required functionality is already available in SAP, it takes some time to discover and use it correctly.

13.1.1.1 Configuration through Implementation Guide (IMG)

Like in SAP's older implementation methodology called Procedure Model, all configuration in SAP is also done through an environment called Implementation Guide (IMG). IMG is not unlike the initialization modules of the traditional computerized systems, except that it is very large by comparison. SAP has more than 8000 configuration tables. All business processes of the company could be mapped onto the SAP system functionality by configuring the parameters in IMG. For implementing any process, one had to identify the parameters that may have to be defined before this process could become operational into the system. For example, for creation of an invoice document, it was important to identify tax parameters and define them first through the IMG. The whole process of specifying the parameters suitable of the specific requirements of a company is also known as customization, which is accomplished using IMG. However, the essential problem was for an integrated system like SAP, there was no systematic way in the earlier methodology to identify all the relevant parameters quickly and completely for implementing these processes.

As noted in the earlier section "Implementation Guide (IMG)," IMG is structured in a manner that does reflect to a certain extent the sequence in which these parameters have to be defined, but for most part, this was not adequate for customizing SAP quickly. For typical SAP implementation teams, locating hundreds of these parameters correctly, completely, in a proper sequence, and also in a timely manner was an intractable problem. Rather than a systematic process, it was more of an experience in discovery, and the number of parameters to be identified and defined was simply overwhelming. To be on the safe side, typical project teams were always on the defensive, invariably confirming and reconfirming every small aspect (although this did not guarantee avoiding missing something) before proceeding further in the effort, and all this simply added to a large time frame for completing the project. And, along the way, the benefit of using the departmental store model of computerization was being lost completely (see Chapter 2, Section 2.1.9 "CRM Represents the New Department Store Model of Implementing Computerized Systems").

The obvious remedy was to address the following two issues for achieving faster SAP implementations:

1. Enable bridging the gap between the know-how of the to-be-mapped company processes and/or requirements, on one hand, and the functionality provided by SAP that was configurable in SAP through IMG, on the other
2. Quick transfer of know-how, expertise, and experience to newer implementation teams on experience gained from numerous earlier implementations

As was seen earlier in this book, repository-oriented systems like SAP is in continuation with the tradition of computer-aided software engineering (CASE) environments. By the same token, the later point truly corresponds to a computer-aided software implementation (CASI) environment, which we consider next.

13.1.1.2 Computer-Aided Software Implementation (CASI)

AcceleratedSAP is a classic illustration of CASI environment that assists in speeding up the implementation effort based on expertise and experience gained from thousands of past SAP implementation projects and will continue the same in the future to improve its performance further. There are two aspects to a CASI: one is CASE and the other is intelligent assistance.

Traditionally, implementing software application systems was constituted of familiar phases like feasibility analysis, requirements analysis, effort estimation, project plan, design, development, testing, integration, documentation, training, data uploads, interfaces, and, finally, cutover to production. Right from the inception of the computerization activity, there have been efforts toward employing computerized systems to aid in this effort at different stages. There has been the usual profusion of software applications addressing the requirements of the various phases of the Software Development Life Cycle (SDLC). Among these program generators, screen painters, report painters, prototyping, and automated/assisted testing tools to assist in the software development have been the most common ones. But there have been solutions for every phase in SDLC. Many of these environments also embodied the corresponding methodologies for speeding up the effort at respective phases of SDLC. Some of these environments or accelerators also became generic that made them adaptable to any methodology deployed for a particular project rather than being confined to specific methodologies including analysis, system design, data modeling, and database design. The history of computerization in the last century has been littered with numerous examples of such environments that, many a time, have followed differing standards and have been incompatible with each other.

13.1.1.3 SAP as Populated CASE Environment

In their most developed form in the later part of the last century, CASE technology was constituted of the following components:

1. Methods
2. Tools Environment

The CASE environment was a set of integrated tools that were designed to work together and to assist or possibly automate all phases of the SDLC.

SAP environments like NetWeaver system, SAP Repository (constituted of advanced tools like the ABAP Dictionary, ABAP Development Workbench, CATT, Workbench Organizer), and Business Engineer (constituted of R/3 Reference Model, Business Navigator, Procedure Model superseded now by ASAP, IMG, International Demo and Education System [IDES], etc.) form a state-of-the-art CASE environment.

However, as noted earlier, SAP is not only one of the best CASE environments, it is also a populated CASE in that its repository is populated with the details of the most comprehensive application system, namely, SAP consisting of Financials, Logistics, and Human Resource systems.

13.1.1.4 SAP Implementations and Expert Systems

Expert systems (ESs) were environments that extended the realm of reusability into the areas of operations and usage of the computerized systems. These knowledge-base-driven systems applied inferences processing to a knowledge base containing data and business or decision rules that matured depending on the veracity of the produced results.

In their most advanced form around the late 1980s, ES technology was constituted of the following components:

1. Knowledge Base
2. Inference Engine that *learned* and fine-tuned its performance based on some predefined criteria with reference to the usefulness of the inferred results (this learning could be in terms of generating new rules or modifying the strengths of the current rules or even updating the knowledge base itself)

AcceleratedSAP is not an expert system in the traditional sense; however, it does have the basic ingredients of a knowledge base and production of inferences or suggested actions. In fact, in certain cases, it affects these actions automatically onto the SAP system. The knowledge base of AcceleratedSAP keeps on getting upgraded based on the latest reported experiences and expertise gleaned from SAP implementations. Presently, this is not an online, dynamic, and automatic update like some of the other services provided by SAP like GoingLive Check or EarlyWatch Alert service; SAP releases periodic upgrade of this knowledge base through CD-ROMs. But it is easy to imagine that AcceleratedSAP may become an online service like GoingLive Check and other services accessible through the Internet in the near future. And it may also become a full-featured expert system with its characteristic features and user interface.

The importance of referring to the original SAP ASAP documentation cannot be overemphasized. What we have presented in this chapter are the essential details of the various stages of the ASAP methodology. However, this chapter is not intended as a replacement for the colossal amount of instructive documentation, guidelines, checklists, templates, samples, questionnaires, and so forth provided and recommended for use by SAP. Those are well-proven instruments, and for an actual project, it is highly recommended that you procure the version of ASAP corresponding to the version of your installation and use it in conjunction with the implementation project.

Some of the material in the following sections may seem repetitive. However, on closer scrutiny, you will note that activities like project management, infrastructure support management, project reviews, etc. are common throughout all the stages of the project, and are referred to appropriately in the beginning and end of each stage. Similarly, since many activities go through the stages of planning and execution, we refer to all such activities through their different stages during the various stages of the project. They are not being repeated, they are only part of the ASAP process checklist recommended by SAP.

13.2 SAP ASAP Methodology

13.2.1 Project Preparation

In this section, we discuss the first phase of the ASAP methodology that covers similar grounds. The objective of dealing the same issues from two different views was to illustrate the importance of adapting a repository-based integrated methodology like AcceleratedSAP. In this chapter, we see SAP's view on preparing for a rapid implementation project that is based on ASAP documentation published by SAP.

In this section, we discuss the setting up of the right context for the SAP project. It addresses the issues of goals, objectives, scope, strategies, and plans for the SAP project. This establishes a framework for all subsequent phases, activities, and tasks performed as a part of the implementation project. This phase deals with instituting the project organization including the teams, roles, and responsibilities. The project infrastructures including hardware and networking issues are determined and finalized. Sizing and benchmarking of the envisaged installation is performed, and the acquisition of the SAP system is initiated. At the end of the preparatory phase, the project starts officially with a kickoff meeting attended by the members of executive and steering committee, project team members, and SAP consultants.

13.2.1.1 Project Planning

This task deals with the preparation and finalization of the project charter, implementation strategy, establishing the project organization, and plans for various activities of the project like the budget, schedule, and resources.

13.2.1.1.1 Prepare Project Charter

This rightly establishes the success-defining criteria for the project. In light of the major investments of time, money, and resources to be expended in the envisaged project, the first step is to seek the business drivers that the SAP implementation aims to assist once it goes in production. These could be knowledgeable responses to customer queries, quick turnaround times, minimization of errors in registering requirements for products and services, making the best pricing available to a valued customer, up-to-the-minute tabs on delivery schedules, error-free dispatches of goods and invoices, proper follow-up on payables, and so forth. Consequently, there is a need to define how the performances will be measured and to define a threshold of performances. It is important to realize that SAP implementation is not an end in itself but toward the achievement of the business objectives of the company, which is not unlike any other similar major effort undertaken within the company:

1. Project Mission
   This helps in orienting company-wide effort toward the success of the implementation as well as ensures focus on the most significant aspects of the project.
2. Project Benchmarks
   This lays down the thresholds of performance that SAP implementation project must deliver in the envisaged time frame. This includes benchmarks for the implementation project itself including milestones for achieving the various phases, but it also includes business benchmarks on the postimplemented business processes in terms of predefined measures in tune with the goals and the objectives of the project.
3. Change Charter
   SAP lays a lot of emphasis on the change-related aspects of SAP and the issues of change management arising out of it. SAP implementation entails many changes in the general operations of the company.

   ASAP does not engender BPR in the conventional sense; the actual business processes do not undergo major changes in design per se. But SAP by its very nature (refer Chapters 1 and 4) triggers major changes in the operational procedures of the company because of
   a. Single-point entry of business transactions
   b. Comprehensive and automatic audit trails
   c. Single Integrated database
   d. Real-time operations
   e. Immediate update and postings of transaction
   f. Immediate access to up-to-the-minute information, queries, reports, etc., to all authorized users

Therefore, ASAP that targets to achieve SAP implementation in extremely reduced time frames has to necessarily address the issue of change management.

13.2.1.1.2 Define Implementation Strategy

This basically addresses the issues of the approach of implementing various functional modules at various sites:

1. Implementation Strategy
   The options are of implementing either as a big bang or in waves. In the former, all relevant modules are implemented at the same time. In this book, we are recommending this approach. The other approach is to implement various modules in succeeding waves of implementations one after the other.

2. Rollout Strategy

This deals with the approach to be adopted for implementation at other than the pilot site chosen for the implementation project. Usually, a base configuration set at the pilot site is rolled out at other places with requisite changes in the master data, additional values in parametric or standard codes data, etc.

3. Implementation of PreConfigured Systems (PCS)

As we have seen in Chapter 12, Section 12.7 "Initiating the SAP Project," these are SAP licenses that come preconfigured for requirements of specific industries including global parameters, process parameters, and reports. This option, if it provides satisfactory functionality that is acceptable to the company, can truly accelerate the implementation to a very large extent.

13.2.1.1.3 Define Project Organization

This task is related with structure and constituents of the project team. It ensures proper allocation, monitoring and managing of resources, resource utilization, and work accomplished by the various subteams:

1. Define Roles.
2. Organize the team.

This task involves identifying, interviewing, and allocating people of these various roles identified. This also includes arranging for the requisite project infrastructure and also administrative support personnel.

13.2.1.1.4 Prepare Project Plan

The aim of this task is to prepare a project plan in light of the goals, objectives, strategies, resources, and budgets allocated for the project. This includes resource utilization plan, budget plan, and a schedule for achieving the project milestones. Evidently, this is not a static plan but a dynamic plan that gets fine-tuned as the project progresses through the various predefined milestones:

1. Project Work Plan
2. Project Budget Plan
3. Project Resource Plan

13.2.1.1.5 Prepare Training Plan

This task is responsible to ensure that all members of the core and the extended team undergo proper training that may have been identified as an essential prerequisite for their roles on the team. It is also essential to ensure that members get trained in their areas of responsibility and in keeping with the role at right junctures; otherwise, too wide a gap between training and the actual delivery of learned skills may deteriorate the performance. In case of the later occurrence, the plan must have provision for refresher courses to ensure meaningful participation of all members in the project effort.

The training programs could be conducted in-house, in SAP training centers, or at the partner's training facilities. The courses may vary depending on the scope and the background of the various members of the team.

13.2.1.2 Project Standards and Procedures

The objective of this task is to lay the ground rules that would be adapted for the project work. A uniform method of working, recording, and reporting permits consistency, avoids redundant effort, and also helps in clear communication.

The SAP project needs to establish two kinds of standards: those applicable directly to the project work and the other dealing with communication with various concerned parties on the status and progress of the project.

13.2.1.2.1 Define Project Management Standards and Procedures

This addresses the task of establishing various standards to be adapted for the SAP project that includes project communications, recording on project activities and milestones, system documentation, application-related quality standards, and issues on change management, team building, etc.:

1. Project Communications
2. Project Planning and Monitoring
3. Project Documentation Standards
4. Scope Management Plan
5. Issues Management Plan
6. Organizational Change Management Plan
7. Team Building Plan
8. Strategy of Using SAP Services
9. Quality Assurance (QA) Plan

13.2.1.2.2 Define Implementation Project Standards and Procedures

The purpose of this task is to establish standards and procedures for both the functional and technical aspects of the SAP project. It relates to the standards applicable in areas of system configuration, testing, authorizations, enhancements, and productive operations:

1. Implementation Project Review Standards
2. System Configuration Standard
3. End-User Documentation Standards
4. Testing Standards
5. Post-Implementation Services and Support Standards
6. System Authorization Standards
7. System Problem Reporting and Error Handling Standards
8. Change Control Management Standards
9. ABAP programming Standards

13.2.1.2.3 Define System Landscape Strategy

The system landscape strategy involves defining the system that will be part of the installation including their purpose and identification. It should deal with the setup and maintenance of the systems and clients both during implementation and post-implementation period. The strategy should also define the release and transport strategy for the distribution of the customizations and development across the landscape to the desired system.

While defining the landscape, the strategy should take into consideration if the customer intends to use Ready-to-Run R/3 system or a Preconfigured System (PCS):

1. Determine and identify Required Systems.
2. Client Deployment Strategy.
3. Release Strategy.
4. Transport System Strategy.

13.2.1.3 Project Kickoff

 In ASAP, this task is the first important milestone of the project.

This task signals the formal initiation of the SAP project. The occasion should be graced by the presence of all the senior management, steering committee members, SAP project managers, SAP team members, SAP consultants, partner representatives, and the change management team and members. This is the platform to elaborate the project charter, the implementation strategy, the project organization, and the overall project plan. It also presents the key roles, requisite skills, time frames, and responsibilities of the various members of the team. The meeting should especially emphasize the change management goals and objectives. In the final analysis, it is basically a forum for get the immediate team motivated and exited about the successful completion of the SAP project in time and on budget.

This meeting also implies the corporate-wide adaptation of the declared goals and objectives, defined strategies and plans, and established standards and procedures by not only the members of the SAP team but also the company as a whole. The kickoff meeting is followed by team standards meeting to adopt all of the relevant standards as well as wide dissemination of the project-related details throughout the organization.

13.2.1.4 Infrastructure Requirements Planning

This task targets gathering of company-specific data to define the requirements of the infrastructure, size and benchmark the hardware and related infrastructure, and procure the hardware keeping in line with the overall time frame of the project:

1. Define Infrastructure Requirements.
2. Benchmark Hardware.
3. Procure Initial Hardware.
4. Order Remote Connection.

It also involves ordering for the remote connection to the nearest SAP servers in that part of the world. This connection acts as the lifeline for specific services provided by SAP at various stages of the project like OSS, GoingLive service, and EarlyWatch service, and this lifeline may become extremely critical at the time of unforeseen problems or emergencies.

13.2.1.5 Quality Check Project Preparation Phase

This is the final verification of the completion of all tasks involved with the project preparation phase.

The SAP-recommended checklist for the Project Preparation Phase is as follows:

1. Review Project Charter and verify completeness.
2. Verify that an implementation strategy has been chosen.
3. Ensure that the project team room has all components.
4. Verify that all needed team roles have been filled.
5. Review the project plan component for completeness.
6. Review the change management plan.
7. Review the project team training plan.
8. Validate that all project management standards and procedures are created.
9. Validate that all implementation standards and procedures are created.
10. Make sure the project kickoff has occurred or is scheduled.
11. Verify that the system landscape strategy is agreed.
12. Validate that the initial system is installed and remote connection is ordered.

13.2.1.6 Sign Off Project Preparation Phase

This task is concerned with obtaining the final sign-off from the project management and approval to proceed to the next phase.

The sign-off on the Project preparation Phase signals the end of the first phase of the ASAP methodology that is also the preparatory phase of the SAP project.

13.2.2 Business Blueprint

The purpose of this phase is to primarily prepare the Business Blueprint phase. The Business Blueprint documents the business process-related requirements of the company. The team members and consultants conduct interviews and workshops in different areas of activity to ascertain the requirements of various business processes. The functionality provided by the R/3 is demonstrated using IDES and supported by questionnaires and process diagrams from R/3 Business Engineer; any gap in addressing functional requirements is identified, and appropriate solutions are explored and devised.

The final outcome of this phase is the Business Blueprint document that details the *TO-BE* processes including written and pictorial representation of the company's structure and business processes. Once this has been approved, the blueprint is taken as the basis for all subsequent phases. This phase also deals with the other central issue addressed by the ASAP methodology for implementing SAP: the change management process. This is related to the organizational and human resource issues that influence the momentum of the R/3 implementation project. The objective of the change management process is to facilitate the timely implementation of SAP within the planned budget and resources.

13.2.2.1 Project Management Business Blueprint Phase

This task deals with the managing and monitoring of the Business Blueprint phase. Using the findings of the study on the requirements of the new organizational structure and the business processes enables identifying where the changes in relationship between the business processes and the organizational structure need to be managed. These act as a major input into refining the implementation plan:

1. Review Project Preparation.
2. Conduct Project Team Status Meetings.
3. Conduct Steering Committee Meetings.
4. Prepare for the Business Blueprint phase.

13.2.2.2 Organizational Change Management

Apart from the tasks related directly with the deliverables of the SAP project, ASAP puts a major focus and attention on the change management issue related to the implementation of SAP. As seen in Section 13.1.1 "Why Are SAP Implementation Programs So Complex?," although not in the conventional sense of a corporate-wide BPR effort, SAP implementation nonetheless has a fundamental and far-reaching effect on the organizational and human resource aspects of the company.

This task deals with a series of change processes that facilitate the change team to diagnose and manage change issues to optimize organizational processes for sustaining the momentum required by the ASAP methodology. To contain the attendant risks, ASAP has devised a full array of processes like impact analysis, assessment of baseline risks, sponsorship strategy, strategy for communications, skills development and knowledge transfer, and the organizational optimization process. We visit each of these aspects of the change management process next.

13.2.2.2.1 Create Business Impact Map

This task is the starting point of the change management process, and its aim is to determine the potential impact of the envisaged SAP implementation. The business impact map helps greatly in assessing the scope, degree, and priority of the anticipated changes.

The business impact map is prepared based on the following inputs:

1. Divisions and units expected to be impacted by the envisaged SAP implementation and, hence, the planned change management process.
2. Perception of the senior personnel in each of these units of the expected changes both within their own and other units.
3. Assess the timing, magnitude, and relative importance of the various changes.

Based on these inputs, the change team compiles a matrix of business units versus degree of anticipated change. An effective and comprehensive change management strategy can be devised based on the critical areas highlighted by the resulting business impact map. This enables the change team to develop the organizational change management plan that is in tune with the overall SAP implementation plan and at the same time is aligned with the perceptions and concerns of the individual departments.

13.2.2.2.2 Complete the Baseline Risk Assessment

This task assesses the degree to which the company operational environment facilitates or inhibits the rapid implementation of SAP. The results of the assessments provide the critical inputs to the change management process.

The risk assessment exercise is performed in three different contexts:

1. Leadership
2. Team
3. Organization

In each of these cases, the change team first devises an appropriate tool, which is administered to a select group of people. The findings are used as an input to generate a risk profile that in turn leads to conducting assessment workshops that basically come up with recommendations that are used to shape the communications and sponsorship programs and other change processes. The Risk Assessment process identifies the key messages that should be disseminated throughout the organization, which are also tailored suitably to the conditions of the individual organizational units:

1. Develop Risk Assessment Tool.
2. Administer the Risk Assessment Tool.
3. Create a Risk Profile.
4. Conduct Risk Workshop.
5. Implement Results of the Risk Workshop.

It must be noted that the Risk Assessment process is not a one-time exercise but an ongoing one. Periodic assessments will need to be performed during the implementation and after the implementation for effective risk mitigation.

13.2.2.2.3 Develop Sponsorship Strategy

The project leadership is the most critical element of a comprehensive change program. There is a need to assess the facilitation or inhibiting factors inherent in the leadership itself that will directly accelerate or undermine the momentum of the implementation project. The baseline leadership risk assessment is the essential input to the sponsorship process. The Sponsor Point is a senior executive champion of change who by his or her actions and communications helps in maintaining project credibility, momentum, and committed support throughout the company.

The leadership risk assessment tool enables the change team to do the following:

■ Get a measure of the risks associated with the envisaged SAP implementation.
■ Uncover the potential implication of these risks on the SAP project.
■ Identify the actions for mitigating these risks to acceptable levels.

The change management team needs to work closely with the Project and Site Sponsors and the Communication Point Person to consistently address the key negatives and reinforce the potential benefits of implementing SAP. Periodic administration of the risk assessment process described earlier helps in ascertaining the effectiveness of the sponsorship process. Any perceived deviation toward increasing risks should be countered immediately by specifically targeted communications and credible actions.

A consistent message, on the organization's demonstrative commitment and focus to see the R/3 implementation through to a successful end, is a powerful enabler for sustaining the right context for achieving the successful completion of the project.

13.2.2.2.4 Establish Communications Framework

This task handles the design of the framework for sharing project-related information and status throughout the organization. While doing so, it incorporates the results of the latest risk assessment processes to address the member's genuine concerns and apprehensions about the SAP implementation and its perceived impact at the organizational level as well as at the individual level. This could be direct communication through formal channels like Project and Site Sponsors or indirectly through the active involvement and participation of a cross section of the members of the company during project-related events, risk assessment processes, focus group sessions, feedback schemes, etc.

This involves identifying the Communication Point person who works closely with the change management team as well as the key Site Sponsors to fine-tune the message and the medium of communication depending on the audience and criticality of the stage and status of the SAP project effort. It is important to ensure that the messages are also customized to the differing ground realities at different sites to discuss how SAP would change jobs, skills, roles, responsibilities, and standards and measurement of performance. Tailoring communications on an organizational unit level also provides the opportunity to enlist the support of the unit-level management or even the line management.

This task also has the responsibility to ascertain the effectiveness of the communications strategy through

1. Informal feedback from focus groups and *influencers* or *opinion leaders* or *thought leaders*
2. Formal feedback through the periodic risk assessment processes wherein specific questions regarding the project communications process can be presented

13.2.2.2.5 Establish the Skills Development Process

This task is related to the formation of the skills development team, identification of the important constituencies of the SAP project effort, compilation of the skills inventory, analysis of the gaps in skills, assessing the training needs, and arranging for the content and logistics of skills development training program. The various constituencies are all members of the SAP core and the extended team, namely, senior executives of the company, project- and site-level sponsors, project team members, SAP consultants, and site-level executives, managers, supervisors, and workers.

The type of training required for the various constituencies are as follows:

1. SAP Implementation Project Impact training
2. Business Process–related training
3. Technical and Functional training on SAP
4. Skills training in use of SAP

The skills development team would decide on the following:

1. Content, for example, prototype, IDES, tutorials, workshops, case study, R/3 testing, or QA client
2. Delivery mechanism for the different kinds of skills training, for example, instructor led or CBTs
3. The delivery vehicle for imparting this training like SAP training partners

It must also set the systems and procedures for assessing the effectiveness of the training for enabling the trained members in performing their identified roles in the SAP project creditably.

13.2.2.2.6 Implement the Know-How Transfer Process

We have spoken about the tacit (or implicit) and explicit knowledge in Chapter 1, Section 1.2.1.4 "Customer Capital: Customer Knowledge as the New Capital" and how SAP act as a medium for converting the tacit knowledge of a company into a valuable resource. Further, in the Note "Information as the New Resource," we have also discussed how information acts as a tangible resource that drives the operational processes faster without expending more conventional resources. ASAP does for the SAP implementation process of the company exactly what productive SAP does for the company as a whole: use all of this relevant information to drive the very process of SAP implementation itself faster!

This task is related to the achievement of the following objectives:

■ Converting and codifying the tacit knowledge scattered across the organization into a coherent and integrated body of knowledge for driving the accelerated implementation of SAP within the organization.
■ Preventing the same history to repeat again in the case of the know-how gained during the SAP implementation itself, that is, codifying and disseminating of knowledge generated during the very implementation of SAP to all the concerned stakeholders as also for use during the next iteration of the SAP implementation. Or it can also be useful for other organizations to leverage on the experience and expertise gained during this implementation.

The valuable experience and insights gained by all members of the SAP team should not lost to other members in the company. All this know-how is an asset, and the organization needs to capitalize on the same. The ASAP Know-how Transfer process taps on the information and experience found both outside and inside the organization. It builds and leverages on the knowledge base that accelerates the SAP implementation by helping the SAP project team and the extended team to take correct decision and also to operationalize these decisions quickly.

ASAP defines the know-how transfer process to be constituted of the following aspects:

1. *Knowledge Drivers*: That relates to the research, collection, authentication, rationalization, standardization, and benchmarking of the information, know-how, and technology
2. *Knowledge Delivery Process*: That relates to the storing, presentation, sharing, and application of the project knowledge

The know-how transfer process is administered and managed by the change team.

13.2.2.3 Project Team Training

The purpose of this task is to plan and conduct training for the SAP team member. This would enable them to map the business process requirements of the company to the functionality provided by R/3 as part of the activities to prepare the Business Blueprint. These are primarily Level 1 and Level 2 courses.

13.2.2.4 Establish Development System Environment

The objective of this task is to install and configure the sandbox client and development system.

13.2.2.4.1 Create Technical Design

SAP recommends the documentation of the technical infrastructure using its template (*IT*) *Infrastructure Document*. This task involves the following:

1. Prepare System Layout and Distribution.
2. Prepare Print Infrastructure.
3. Prepare Network Topology.
4. Prepare Interface Topology.
5. Prepare Change Request Management.
6. Prepare Release Management Strategy.
7. Prepare Desktop Management Strategy.

13.2.2.4.2 Set Up Development Environment

The objective of this task is to use the technical design to set up the development and sandbox client system. This involves the following:

1. Install Initial hardware.
2. Prepare Initial System Landscape.
3. Configure and Test Transport System.
4. Install Desktop Components for Project Members.
5. Prepare User Master Records and Secure the System.
6. Install Initial Printing Services.
7. Set Up Remote Connection to SAP.

13.2.2.4.3 Establish System Administration Functions

This task deals with defining, testing, and establishing the system administration procedures for the development system. It involves the following:

1. Conduct Basis and System Administration Workshop.
2. Define System Administration for Development System.
3. Configure the computer center management system (CCMS) based on the earlier definition.
4. Define Backup Strategy.

13.2.2.4.4 Initialize IMG

The purpose of this task is to create the IMG:

1. Initialize IMG.
2. Create Enterprise IMG.
3. Create Project Header and generate Project IMG.

Please also see Sections 7.3.3.3 through 7.3.3.5.

13.2.2.5 Define Business Organization Structure

This task deals with the concept of the organization structure as defined in SAP using SAP organizational units like the client, company code, controlling area, business area, purchasing organization, and sales organization. This structure defined in SAP structures the processes and processing of the financial and logistics areas of SAP and, consequently, also of the human resource area within SAP.

This task has the deliverable of producing the business organizational structure of the company within SAP based the system organization rules. ASAP provides Structure Modeler documentation and a corresponding Visio template to help a company in completing this task. This task is accomplished by arranging a workshop involving the Project Sponsor, SAP Project Manager, Business Process Team Leader, and key team members. The workshop may have breakaway sessions separately for financial and logistics processes, followed by a session integrating the findings and conclusions of the individual sessions.

ASAP provides organization structure questionnaire that is used as a basic input for the workshop. The questions related to the organizational structure are available in Q&Adb under "Business Overview Questions" and under each process area of the company. Additional related information is available under *Enterprise Modeling-Consultant's Handbook* in Sap Online Documentation CD-ROM.

The workshop achieves the following:

1. Help in identifying the existing business organizational structure including the major business processes and reporting structures by using the Business Impact Map.
2. Understand organization structures in SAP.
3. Map company's organizational structure requirements, including future requirements, in terms of organizational elements provided in SAP.
4. Perform cost–benefit analysis and gap analysis of the newly defined organizational structure in SAP.
5. Iterate and fine-tune the SAP organizational structure.
6. Document the SAP organizational structure.

As a final step, the company approves and accepts the proposed organizational structure across the company.

13.2.2.5.1 Business Process Definition

After defining, the organization structure follows this task for defining the business processes of the company in terms of the business processes supported by SAP. This significant input goes on to the creation of the Business Blueprint document. In the following subsections, we discuss the various subtasks of this important task:

1. Prepare for Business Process Workshops.
2. Conduct General Requirements Workshop.
3. Conduct Business Process Workshops.
   This task is responsible for conducting workshops for gathering business process requirements with all its related requirements as discussed in the following. The information gathered here eventually becomes the Business Blueprint document:
   - Determine Business Process Requirements.
   - Determine Reporting Requirements.
   - Determine Required Interfaces.
   - Determine Conversion Requirements.
   - Determine Enhancement Requirements.

  – Determine Gap Areas.
  – Revise Business Process Descriptions and Models.
4. Conduct Detailed Process Workshops.

These are conducted for the following:

■ Clarify requirements using the Business Process (BP) and Customer Input (CI) information.
■ Clarify and analyze SAP business process implementations, for example, for more efficient or flexible version of the same process.
■ Research deficient areas and gap for possible solutions.
■ Revise business process requirements in terms of processing optimizations, authorization requirements, etc.

13.2.2.5.2 Prepare Business Blueprint

The Business Blueprint document details the business process requirements and serves as the reference document for the subsequent customization and development activities.

As a part of the preparation of the Business Blueprint, the following subtasks are also performed:

1. Perform Organizational Optimization Analysis.
   This subtask performs the fine-tuning of the organizational, reporting relationships, coordinations, etc., resulting from the information gathered in the detailed process workshops. This information is used further to update and prepare the latest
   – Business Impact Maps
   – Process Impact Maps
2. Revise Project Organization and Roles.
   This task deals with refining the project organization roles in light of the information gathered for the Business Blueprint. This information is fed to the change management process. It is also a useful input in the preparation of the
   – Training plan
   – Authorization profiles
3. Compile Business Blueprint.
   This task involves consolidation of all the compiled Q&Adb into a central database and generates the Business Blueprint that is the main deliverable of this phase.
   The generated Business Blueprint consists of the following:
   – Executive Summary
   – Enterprise process area scope document
   – Organization structure
   – Completed Business Process Questionnaires and CI Templates
   – Justifications for enhancements, conversions, and interfaces
   – Completed Technical Questionnaire
   On business processes, the Business Blueprint includes the following details:
   – Requirement Expectations
   – General Expectations
   – Explanation of Functions and Events
   – Special Organizational Considerations
   – Business Model

- Description of Improvements
- Description of Functional Deficits
- Approaches to covering Deficits
- System Configuration Considerations
- File Conversion Considerations
- Reporting Considerations
- Authorization Considerations

4. Business Process Master List (BPML).

The objective of this task is to identify the detailed scope that should be implemented during the Realization phase. The Business Process Master List (BPML) is the R/3 system representation of the total scope of the implementation project. The configuration effort is divided into two parts: Baseline and Final configuration.

ASAP recommends that the Baseline Scope should aim to cover about 80% of the company's requirements. The Baseline scope includes those scenarios, processes, and functions that are priority requirements of the company. All scenarios and business processes that are not included in the Baseline Scope are handled during the Final configuration. To make the final configuration effort easier, ASAP recommends the formation of a series of configuration cycles consisting of a selected set of business processes depending on the degree of their importance.

In Q&Adb, for any business process, on selecting the Business Process Transactions, the associated transactions for this particular business process are displayed. One or more of the eight columns displayed are selected for indicating inclusion in the configuring and integration cycles used during the Realization Phase. The eight column indicators are

SC—In scope
BL—Included in Baseline configuration
C1—Included in Configuration Cycle 1
C2—Included in Configuration Cycle 2
C3—Included in Configuration Cycle 3
C4—Included in Configuration Cycle 4
L1—Included in Integration Cycle 1
L2—Included in Integration Cycle 2

To generate BPML, go to Questions & Answers database (Q&Adb), go to *Report*, and select *BP Master List*, and then choose *Generate*.

In the BPML, *Links* column gives access to the *Customer Input* template for that process as well as to the corresponding Business Process Procedure documents. The BPML also contains the information collected for each of the Business Process Transactions described earlier, or it can be entered in the BPML itself.

13.2.2.5.3 Review and Approve Business Blueprint

 In ASAP, this task is the second important milestone of the project.

This task involves the final review of the Business Blueprint that involves the following:

1. Review of the Enterprise process area scope document
2. Review of the Business Blueprint
3. Review of the Baseline Scope

The Project Manager, Business Process Owners, and the Steering Committee finally approve the Business Blueprint.

13.2.2.6 Prepare End-User Training and Documentation Plan

The objective of this task is to prepare End-User Training and Documentation plan based on the inputs from the Business Blueprint. This also acts as a reference for any future changes in the project decisions on the schedule of the user training and documentation effort.

The plan includes

1. End-User Analysis, that is, number of end users and their job functions
2. Type of End-User Documentation and Training material
3. Preparation of End-User Documentation and Training material
4. Resources required
5. Schedule for conducting the training

13.2.2.7 Quality Check Business Blueprint Phase

This is the final verification of the completion of all tasks involved with the project Business Blueprint Phase.

The SAP-recommended checklist for the Business Blueprint phase is as follows:

1. Validate that the Project Team Status and Steering Committee meeting(s) have occurred.
2. Confirm that successful project team training has been accomplished.
3. Verify that a team building activity has taken place.
4. Ensure user roles and responsibilities are defined.
5. Confirm the development of a technical design.
6. Validate the setup of the development environment and development environment system landscape.
7. Verify the proper systems administration functions have been set up.
8. Validate the IMG initialization.
9. Validate the completion and sign off the Business Blueprint and Baseline Scope.

The Business Blueprint ensures that everybody has an accurate understanding of the final scope regarding organizational structure, business processes, and the technical system environment.

13.2.2.8 Sign-Off Business Blueprint Phase

This task is concerned with obtaining the final sign-off from the project management and approval to proceed to the next phase.

The sign-off on the Business Blueprint Phase signals the end of the second phase of the ASAP methodology that is also the conceptual design phase of the SAP project.

13.2.3 Realization

The goal of this phase is to configure the baseline system using the Business Blueprint. For this, the business processes are divided into cycles of related business processes. The SAP team undergoes Level 3 training. The baseline system prepared here is the basis for the production system. The system is presented to a team of power users who also undergo requisite training in their respective areas of operations; the baseline system is fine-tuned by the validation done by the power users by employing an iterative approach.

In parallel, the technical team sets up the system administration and plans interfaces and data transfer. The interfaces, conversion programs, enhancements, reports, end-user documentation, testing scenarios, and user security profiles are defined and tested. The final integration test is conducted. The final deliverable is a fully configured and tested SAP system that meets the company's requirements.

13.2.3.1 Project Management Realization Phase

The project management task is similar to that for the other phases. This task deals with the managing and monitoring of the Realization phase. Using the findings of the study on the requirements of the new organizational structure and the business processes enables identifying where the changes in relationship between the business processes and the organizational structure need to be managed. This acts as a major input into refining the implementation plan:

1. Review Business Blueprint.
2. Conduct Project Team Status Meetings.
3. Conduct Steering Committee Meetings.
4. Conduct Initial Planning for Production Support and Cutover.
5. Conduct Team Building Activity.
6. Prepare for the Realization phase.

13.2.3.2 Sustaining the Organization Change Management Process

As we have seen in the last chapter, this task deals with a series of change processes that facilitate the change team to diagnose and manage change issues to optimize organizational processes for sustaining the momentum required by the ASAP methodology right through to the end of the project. To contain the attendant risks, ASAP advises continuing with the full array of processes like risk assessment, sponsorship strategy, strategy for communications, skills development, and knowledge transfer as well as the organizational optimization process. Sustaining the organization change management process allows the change team to manage organizational risks, accelerate SAP implementation, and optimize the organizational process:

1. Perform Periodic Risk Assessments and Workshops.
2. Create and Provide Feedback to the Line Managers.
3. Conduct Risk Management Meetings with Key Constituencies.
4. Deliver Key Project Communications.
5. Manage Ongoing Project Sponsorship Process.
6. Manage Ongoing Skills Development Process.
7. Manage Knowledge Transfer Team and Process.
8. Conduct Renewal of the Change Management team.

13.2.3.3 Conduct Project Team Training

The purpose of this task is to plan and conduct training for the SAP team member. This would enable them to configure and test the business process documented in the Business Blueprint. These are primarily Level 3 courses.

13.2.3.4 Systems Management

The purpose of this task is to prepare the system environment for the production. This includes establishing the infrastructure requirements, the performance levels, and the system administration activities and, finally, setting up the production environment:

1. Establish Service-Level Commitments.
2. Develop System Test Plans.
3. Establish System Administration Functions.
4. Set Up Quality Assurance System Environment.
5. Establish Production Systems Management.
6. Set Up Production Environment.

13.2.3.5 Baseline Configuration and Confirmation

The Business Process Master List (BPML) is the SAP system representation of the total scope of the implementation project. The configuration effort is divided into two parts: Baseline and Final configuration.

This task relates to the configuration and confirmation of the settings for the Baseline scope. The Baseline scope includes those scenarios, processes, and functions that are priority requirements of the company. The remaining 20% scenarios and processes are to be considered during the Final Configuration and Confirmation.

ASAP recommends that a company should initially consider processes for the baseline configuration that can be configured without modifying the system.

This involves the following subtasks:

1. Revise the Baseline Scope document prepared during the Business Blueprint phase.
2. Create a baseline configuration plan for the Baseline by doing the following:
   - Choose Business Process Master List (BPML) and select the *Baseline* worksheet.
   - Add global settings in the beginning of the BPML.
   - Add configuration tasks for organizational structure after the global settings.
   - Enter the planned schedule date in the *Plan* subcolumn within *Configuration*.
   - Add sequencing information for dependent processes; this can be done by entering a case number and a sequence number to a group of related processes, in the subcolumns of *Configuration: Case* and *Sequence No.*

   Note: By clicking the *View* cell under the *Configuration* column sorts the processes in the order of case number/sequence no.
   - Save this as the *Baseline Configuration Plan* document MS Excel workbook.
3. Create test cases that are prepared by doing the following:
   - Choose the *Baseline Configuration Plan* document and select the *Baseline* worksheet modified by (2) earlier.
   - This includes the default test cases you can adopt for the project.

- Set the test and sequencing information for dependent processes; this can be done by entering a case number and a sequence number to a group of related processes, in the subcolumns of *Testing: Case* and *Sequence No.*
- Add testing information in the *Baseline Requirements, Notes, and Expectations.*
- For more detailed information on test procedure, select the *Test Procedure* and add details.
- Save.

4. Create test plan for the Baseline configuration by doing the following:
- Choose the *Baseline Configuration Plan* document and select the *Baseline* worksheet modified by (3) earlier.
- Enter the planned schedule date in the *Plan* subcolumn within the *Testing.*
- Save.

5. Allocate resources for the Baseline configuration and testing by doing the following:
- Choose the *Baseline Configuration Plan* document and select the *Baseline* worksheet modified by (4) earlier.
- Determine the skills set needed, confirm availability, and allocate responsibility to process owners, team members, and power users.
- Enter the initials of the team member in the subcolumns of *Responsibilities: Configuration* and *Testing.*
- Save.

6. Approve the *Baseline Configuration Plan* document by the process owners.

7. *Revise Project IMG*: The IMG is modified to record the information about resources and assignments. This can be done either manually in IMG or automatically in case the company is using the ASAP IMG-Link.

13.2.3.5.1 Configure Initial Settings and Organizational Structure

This task refers to the configuration of the global settings and organizational structure that is a prerequisite to the Baseline and Final configuration:

1. Configure Global Settings.
2. Configure Organizational Structure.
3. Configure Predefined Settings.

13.2.3.5.2 Configure and Validate Baseline

This is the heart of the Realization Phase that corresponds to changing the configuration settings for the Baseline scenarios and processes. The completed settings are migrated to the QA environment for testing using the test plans and test cases prepared earlier. The information gathered during this task also helps in revising the Baseline Configuration document as well as the Business Blueprint:

1. Configure Process and Functions.
2. Transport to Quality Assurance System.
3. Test Baseline.
4. Document and Resolve Issues.
5. Revise the Business Blueprint.
6. Verify Completeness of the Baseline Configuration.

13.2.3.5.3 Perform Baseline Confirmation

 In ASAP, this task is the third important milestone of the project.

This task has the responsibility to formulate confirmation scenarios that could be enacted into the system to verify the successful configuration of the system. This involves the following subtasks:

1. Confirmation Scenarios.
   A confirmation scenario (or Process Group) corresponds to a complete business or an end-to-end scenario. It can be subdivided into business cases that make it easier to confirm the complete scenario in incremental steps. A business case includes the critical information flow, associated conditions, and exceptions.
   Compiling a Confirmation Scenario involves the following:
   - Choose the *Baseline Confirmation Plan* document and select the *Baseline* worksheet.
   - Set the confirmation and sequencing information for dependent processes; this can be done by entering a case number and a sequence number to a group of related processes in the subcolumns of *Confirmation: Case* and *Sequence No.*
   - Add information on confirmation procedures by selecting the *Case Procedure* form, and add details.
   - Save.
2. Prepare Confirmation Scenarios agenda by the cross functional process owners, and assign participants.
3. Perform Baseline Confirmation Session.
4. Review and sign off Baseline Confirmation.

13.2.3.6 *Perform Final Configuration and Confirmation*

As referred in the beginning of Section 13.2.3.5 "Baseline Configuration and Confirmation," all scenarios and business processes that are not included in the Baseline Scope are handled during this task. These are the configuration cycles that were mentioned in Section 13.2.2.5.2 "Prepare Business Blueprint."

To make the configuration effort easier, ASAP recommends the formation of a series of configuration cycles consisting of a selected set of business processes depending on the degree of their importance. These are the configuration cycles that were mentioned in Section 13.2.2.5.2 "Prepare Business Blueprint." The cycles are configured sequentially till all issues are resolved and the configured system is ready to be delivered for final integration tests.

A cycle represents an iterative process that systematizes the final configuration effort. The cycles are defined based on the following guidelines:

■ *Cycle 1*: The purpose of this cycle is to tune the configuration of the business processes for the master data and high-priority transactions.
■ *Cycle 2*: The purpose of this cycle is to tune the configuration of the remaining master data and basic transactions.

- *Cycle 3*: The purpose of this cycle is to tune the configuration and master data by running high-priority business processes.
- *Cycle 4*: The purpose of this cycle is to tune the configuration by running the business processes that include exceptions transactions, reports, and user profiles.

The final configuration and confirmation process is similar to that adopted for the Baseline scope except that in the BPML, only those processes are selected that were set to indicate Cycle 1, 2, 3, or 4.

The subtasks involved are listed here:

1. Revise Final Scope.
2. Create Configuration Plan for Final Scope.
3. Prepare Test Cases.
4. Prepare Test Plan for Final Scope.
5. Assign Resources.
6. Approve Plans for Final Scope Configuration.

13.2.3.6.1 Configure and Validate Final Scope (Cycle 1 to *n*)

This involves changing the configuration settings for the Final scenarios and processes. The completed settings are migrated to the QA environment for testing using the test plans and test cases prepared earlier. The information gathered during this task also helps in revising the BPML Configuration document as well as the Business Blueprint.

The task, which is similar to that undertaken for the Baseline scope as explained earlier, consists of the following subtasks:

1. Configure Processes and Functions.
2. Transport Objects to Quality Assurance System.
3. Test Final Configuration.
4. Establish Final Configuration.

13.2.3.6.2 Establish Final Confirmation (Cycle 1 to *n*)

This task has the responsibility to formulate confirmation scenarios that could be enacted into the system to verify the successful configuration of the system. Again, this is similar to approach used for Baseline confirmation except that this is conducted in iterative cycles.

This involves the following subtasks:

1. Prepare Final Confirmation Scenarios.
2. Perform Final Confirmation Scenarios.

13.2.3.7 *Perform ABAP Development*

1. Develop Forms.
2. Develop Reports.
3. Develop Conversion Programs.
4. Develop Application Interface Programs.
5. Develop Enhancements.

13.2.3.8 Establish Authorization Concept

The authorization concepts define the various functions that can be performed by users in different organizational units. The authorization concept maintains a balance between managing access security and assigning privileges to perform jobs on the system as well as the effort expended for administrating this system itself. The aim of this task is to establish an authorization concept or framework that satisfies all these requirements.

In the Business Blueprint, the responsibility of various processes and functions is defined. These responsibility definitions are used for establishing the authorization concept or framework. SAP provides *The System Authorizations Made Easy Guide* as reference for helping with implementing and validating this framework:

1. Compile Authorization Concept-Detailed Design.
2. Management of the Authorization Environment.
3. Validate Authorization Concept.

13.2.3.9 Establish Archiving Management

This task deals with establishing and creating an archival management system. Data that are not needed online in the system should be removed from the system. Large data not only make database administration difficult but also affect performance:

1. Design the Archiving Management system: Archiving system aims at maintaining the balance between an increase in data volume because of the daily transaction and processing, and, a reduction in the data volume because of archiving to ensure optimal performance. The business process owners assist in fine-tuning the archiving cycle for a company.
2. Prepare Archiving Procedures.
3. Implement Archiving Procedures.
4. Validate Archiving Procedures.

13.2.3.10 Conduct Final Integration Test

The purpose of this task is to plan and execute the final integration test. It simulates, in the Quality system, the live operations for functional verification of the productive system:

1. Define Scope of Integration Test.
    The scope of the test is based on the process design for the business areas and the corresponding business areas defined in the Business Blueprint. Like the Final configuration and confirmation tasks, the final integration test is also process oriented. The plan includes the following:
    – Test scope
    – Test scenarios
    – Test processes
    – Resources
    A test scenario (or Process Group) corresponds to a complete business or an end-to-end scenario. It can be subdivided into test processes that make it easier to confirm the complete scenario in incremental steps. A business case includes the critical information flow, associated conditions, and exceptions. This is handled in manner similar to the approach adopted for Final Scope Configuration and Confirmation.

To make the testing effort easier, ASAP recommends the formation of a series of integration-testing cycles consisting of a selected set of business processes depending on the degree of their importance. These are the integration-testing Cycles L1 and L2 that were mentioned in Section 13.2.2.5.2 "Prepare Business Blueprint." The cycles are tested sequentially till all issues are resolved and the tested system is ready to be delivered for final preparation before going into productive phase.

Cycle represents an iterative process that systematizes the final testing effort. The cycles are defined based on the following guidelines:

- *Cycle 1*: The purpose of this cycle is to tune the testing of the business processes for the master data and high-priority transactions, followed by testing the running of high-priority business processes.
- *Cycle 2*: The purpose of this cycle is to tune the testing by running the business processes that include exceptions transactions, reports, and user profiles.

The final integration process is similar to that adopted for the final configuration except that in the BPML, only those processes are selected that were set to indicate integration-testing Cycle 1 or 2.

If one cannot schedule to test everything, the test cases can be prioritized based on

- The frequency of the process
- Failure impact of the process or dependencies of the process
- The probability of occurrence of the test case

ASAP provides a formula to calculate the test priority for test cases; as the test priority increases, the greater is the need to include the test case in the integration testing.

2. Prepare Final Integration Test Plan.

The purpose of this task is to prepare a detailed integration test plan that must include all processes and components like

- Business processes
- Reports
- Interfaces
- Conversions
- Enhancements
- Printer/fax outputs

The scope of the test is based on the process design for the business area and their business processes as defined in the Business Blueprint. The test plan identifies necessary dependencies and ensures that everything in the blueprint is tested.

Again, ASAP provides a list of predefined Test Procedures to help in accelerating this step.

3. Transport All Objects to QA and Freeze System.

The purpose of this task is to freeze the system settings to protect the completed system from changes till the full cycle of integration testing is completed.

This includes

- Configuration Settings
- Client Settings
- Application Data
- Repository Objects

4. Conduct Final Integration Tests.

The purpose of this task is to conduct the final integration test based on the final integration test plan involving usual steps like entering initial setup data, running test cases, recording results, comparing results to expected results, evaluating results and recording issues, resolving issues, and, finally, completing each of the test case one after another.

The team of process owners and power users conducts the final integration test.

 In ASAP, this task is the fourth important milestone of the project.

5. Approve Final Integration Test Results.
6. Finalize System.

The purpose of this task is to resolve all outstanding issues from the final integration testing of the system to ensure that the configured system satisfies all business requirements before going into production.

13.2.3.11 Prepare End-User Documentation and Training Material

The purpose of this task is to define the necessary training to be undertaken by the end users before the Go-Live Phase:

1. Define End-User Documentation Plan.
2. Compile End-User Documentation.
3. Prepare End-User Training Plan.
4. Prepare End-User Training Instructor Material.
5. Prepare End-User Training Material.

13.2.3.12 Quality Check Realization Phase

This is the final verification of the completion of all tasks involved with the project Realization Phase.

The SAP-recommended checklist for the Realization Phase is as follows:

1. Verify the completion of Project Team status and Steering Committee meeting.
2. Validate the completion of the cutover plans.
3. Ensure a team building activity has been undertaken or is scheduled.
4. Validate the completion of the Project Team training.
5. Ensure that System Test Plans are developed and Service-Level commitment defined.
6. Validate the configuration of the Global Settings, Organizational Structure, and the Baseline Scope.
7. Review the Baseline Confirmation approval and sign-off.
8. Confirm setup of the QA system.
9. Confirm the setup of the production system.
10. Validate the configuration of the Final Scope and sign-off of the Final Confirmation.
11. Verify the migration of tested conversions, application interfaces, enhancements, reports, and layout sets.
12. Validate the creation of authorizations, and review the sign-off of the authorization design.

13. Confirm the creation of archiving management.
14. Verify the existence of an integration-tested and finalized system.
15. Ensure the creation of user documentation and training material.
16. Validate the preparation for user training.

This quality check verifies that the final configuration of the R/3 system meets the business requirements specified in the Business Blueprint.

13.2.3.13 Sign-Off Realization Phase

This task is concerned with obtaining the final sign-off from the project management and approval to proceed to the next phase.

The sign-off on the Realization Phase signals the end of the third phase of the ASAP methodology that is also the development and testing phase of the SAP project.

13.2.4 Final Preparation

This phase is aimed at readying the system and the company for the SAP implementation. It consolidates all of the activities of the previous phases to be ready for Go-Live phase including end-user training, system testing, stabilizing systems management, and cutover activities. Any exception and out of turn situations are also addressed and resolved.

The conversion and interface programs are all checked, volume and stress tests are performed, and user acceptance tests are conducted. This is followed with the migration of the data to the new system. The super users under the supervision of the SAP team members conduct end-user training. This phase also strategizes for the next phase including routine periodic uploading of data from non-SAP systems, internal audit procedures, and organization of the help desk support activity.

13.2.4.1 Project Management Final Preparation Phase

The project management task is similar to that for the other phases. The objective is to maintain the momentum as well as focus of the effort throughout the company on completing the remaining phases of the project as per schedule. It also concerns itself with maintaining the motivational level within the organization especially among the end users who are envisaged to play critical role during the cutover phase and, especially, in the post-implementation phase:

1. Review Final Preparation Phase.
2. Conduct Project Team Status Meetings.
3. Conduct Steering Committee Meetings.
4. Continue Team Building Activity.

13.2.4.2 Continuing the Organization Change Management Process

As seen in the earlier phases, this task deals with a series of change processes that facilitate the change team to diagnose and manage change issues to optimize organizational processes for sustaining the momentum required by the ASAP methodology right through to the end of the project.

This task continues with the full array of processes like risk assessment, sponsorship strategy, strategy for communications, skills development, and knowledge transfer as well as the organizational optimization process that were initiated in the Business Blueprint phase. There is an additional importance to these efforts in this phase because this phase initiates the exercise of scaling up the SAP implementation to the enterprise as a whole. This task ensures that especially the skills development, knowledge transfer, and also the communication processes are all geared toward taking on the load of the increased number of participants in the last stages of the project as also in the post-implementation phase.

13.2.4.3 Conduct End-User Training

This task ensures that all end users undergo the requisite SAP training prior to the Go-Live phase. It should be in line with the plan and schedule prepared during the Realization phase.

The basic input for this plan is the Business Process Master List (BPML) compiled during the Business Blueprint Phase and the Job Role matrix prepared during the Realization Phase. Consequently, the training plan ensures adequate coverage of all types of end users but at the same time avoids redundant training. The later is not only a drain of resources but may also lead to losing precious time on a project that may be under tight schedule by this stage of the project.

The end users can be broadly classified into

- Transaction users
- Query and analysis users
- Information users

The various subtasks involved in completing this task are as follows:

1. Prepare for End-User Training
2. Conduct End-User Training
3. Review and Assess Posttraining Skills

13.2.4.4 Systems Management

The objective of this task is to ready the technical infrastructure and establish the system administration for the production system.

13.2.4.4.1 Establish Production System Administration

This subtask aims at establishing the system administration for the production system that entails installation of the CCMS system. The right kind of infrastructure coupled with a matching system administration setup contributes toward high performance of the system and maximization of the availability of the system:

1. Configure CCMS for Production Environment.
2. Configure Production System Printing and Spool Administration.
3. Train System Administration Staff.

13.2.4.4.2 Conduct System Tests

The purpose of this task is to test and validate the configuration of the system infrastructure as well as the system administration procedures devised for managing the system:

1. Conduct System Administration Tests.
2. Conduct Volume Tests.

3. Conduct Stress Tests.
4. Conduct Printing and Fax Tests.
5. Conduct Backup and Restore Procedure Tests.
6. Conduct Disaster Recovery Tests.
7. Conduct GoingLive Check.

13.2.4.5 Refine Cutover and Production Support Plan

The objective of this task is to refine the cutover and support plan devised during the Realization Phase.

 In ASAP, this task is the fifth important milestone of the project.

13.2.4.5.1 Prepare Detailed Cutover Plan

The purpose of this activity is to ascertain the readiness of the system and the company to go into production. As pointed out earlier in this book, SAP implementation does not have any phase analogous to the traditional phase of *parallel runs*. Therefore, it is very important to confirm the readiness of the SAP system to go live not only in terms of the readiness of the SAP system and system administration but also in terms of readiness for timely conversion and uploading of data into the SAP system:

1. Compile Conversion Checklist.
2. Determine Production Readiness.
3. Obtain Approval for Cutover.

13.2.4.5.2 Prepare Production Support Plan

This task targets to refine the production support plan prepared during the Realization Phase in terms of processes and procedures as well as roles and responsibilities of the personnel envisaged to man the help desk:

1. Define Help Desk Procedures.
2. Establish Help Desk Facility.
3. Organize Help Desk Resources and Staff.

13.2.4.5.3 Long-Term Production Support Strategy

This also leads to defining a long-term strategy for supporting the SAP system to address the issues of

■ The post-implementation system changes
■ Subsequent release upgrades
■ Increase of scope resulting from the growth of business of the company
■ Training of new employees resulting from the employee turnover

13.2.4.6 Cutover to Production System

The purpose of this task is to perform the cutover to the production system.

This involves executing the following:

1. Transport to Production Environment of all the customizing settings and the repository objects.
2. Perform Conversions of all master and transaction data.
3. Perform Manual Entries of that category of legacy data that are small in volume or are not easily amenable to data conversion by reason of the complexity of their structure or requires changes in the context of the envisaged SAP system, etc.

13.2.4.6.1 Final Approval for Going Live

The purpose of this task is to make the final decision on the readiness of the system to go live into production.

The decision is based on completion of the following requirements:

1. End-user documentation is complete.
2. End-user training is complete.
3. R/3 System Administration is in place.
4. The technical setup is complete.
5. Conversion of customization settings and master and transaction data is complete.
6. Production Cutover and Support Plan is in place.

The system is cutover into production after

- Obtaining the approval for the Cutover
- Verifying that the users are ready
- The security system is made fully operational

13.2.4.7 Quality Check Final Preparation Phase

This is the final verification of the completion of all tasks involved with the project Final Preparation Phase.

The SAP-recommended checklist for the Final Preparation Phase is as follows:

1. Verify that the project team status and Steering Committee meetings took place.
2. Confirm that a team building activity has occurred or is scheduled.
3. Verify that the user training was completed successfully.
4. Confirm the administration of the productive system.
5. Ensure that the various R/3 system tests yield the required results.
6. Review the production support plan and verify completeness.
7. Verify the cutover was performed successfully.

13.2.4.8 Sign-Off Final Preparation Phase

This task is concerned with obtaining the final sign-off from the project management and approval to proceed to the final phase.

The sign-off on the Final Preparation Phase signals the end of the fourth phase of the ASAP methodology that is also the cutover phase of the SAP project.

13.2.5 Go Live and Support

This phase addresses the issues of the SAP system in production. The GoingLive Check is performed and completed. It involves solving issues of day-to-day operations including problems and security-related issues reported by end users. SAP system and transactions are also monitored for possible optimizations.

The business benefits of the new system are measured to monitor the return on investment for the project. This may be a trigger for further iterations of implementation cycle for improving the business processes. A formal close of the implementation project is also performed.

13.2.5.1 Production Support

The objective of this task is to provide support to SAP system users and maintain optimal system performance. The support issue is very critical especially in the first few weeks of the live operation.

1. Go Live and Support Review.
   This task deals with analysis of the potential risks that are likely to pose problems in achieving the successful completion of the project.
   The review covers issues related to
   – Project Management
   – Technical Project Management
   – IT Infrastructure
   – Change Management Process
   – Member commitment
   It assesses various risks that could affect the successful close of the project.
2. Implement Go live.
   The system goes into production.
3. Provide Production Support.
   The purpose of this activity is to support SAP users. The production support plan devised during the Final Preparation phase is set into operation. The functioning of the help desk itself is monitored and fine-tuned depending on the feedback from the users as well as analysis of the documented problems and their resolutions.
   Power users are also trained in using SAP's Online Service System (OSS).
4. Validate Live Business Process Results.
   The purpose of this task is to confirm that the live SAP system is performing correctly. It confirms the correctness of customizing settings and master data.
   It also monitors the business transactions to ascertain their correctness.
   This task involves the following:
   – Monitor daily transactions.
   – Resolve issues: Ensuring that the issue has been resolved and corrective actions taken and verified.
   The corrective actions could be any of the following:
   – Altering the business process
   – Modifying the ABAP code

    – Modifications of the configurations
    – Refresher training
    – Training on additional modules or functionality

Lastly, the task addresses the obtaining of approval for the production environment. This is the official approval of the live system.

13.2.5.2 Project End

The purpose of this task is to officially close the project. Any open issues that are still pending resolution are reviewed and closed.

13.2.5.2.1 Project Review

This task commences the exercise of measuring the business benefits for the SAP implementation:

1. *Review and close all open issues*: All issues in the issue database are identified, reviewed, resolved, and closed.
2. *Review Business Benefits*: The results of the SAP implementation are compared with the goals and objectives that were set for the implementation project. This also leads to the establishing of an evaluation procedure that can monitor benefits on an ongoing basis.
3. *Evaluate the knowledge transfer process*: The key lessons or conclusions of the project are reviewed and documented. This is done with the help of the information gathered during the course of the project in the Questions & Answers Database (Q&Adb) because that reflects the distillation of the true insight into the functioning of the organization.
4. *Complete Organizational Change Management Process*: The key gains of the organizational change management process are evaluated. Any remaining organizational change management issues are resolved and closed.

13.2.5.3 Project Sign-Off

The purpose of this task is to obtain the formal approval for the close of the project.

When a company adopts ASAP methodology for implementing SAP, their success depends on how quickly the company can implement changes in its business processes that are in line with the best-of-business processes in SAP. While using ASAP, it is advisable that the company should avoid undertaking a Business Process Re-Engineering (BPR) effort in conjunction with the SAP implementation. It is recommended that the company should implement a vanilla SAP functionality initially. Once the implementation stabilizes, then custom functionalities could be introduced later judiciously. The vanilla approach cuts down on maintenance, as well as speeds up the time to production and benefits of the new system.

13.3 SAP ASAP Methodology 7

SAP ASAP Methodology 7 was launched in February 2010. The new methodology brings together the previous ASAP methodology, Business Intelligence Solution Accelerator (BISA) methodology, value delivery principles, business process management methodology, and service-oriented architecture methodology. The ASAP implementation methodology is a phased, deliverable-oriented methodology that streamlines implementation projects, minimizes risks, and reduces the total cost of implementation. ASAP adopts a disciplined approach to project management, organization change management, solution management, business process management, value management, and other aspects related to the implementation of SAP solutions.

There are two highly visible components of the new ASAP Methodology: the ASAP Roadmap 7 core, which covers the entire project lifecycle—from evaluation through delivery to post-project solution management and operations—and, the value, process, and application lifecycle. The new methodology is leaner and more practical, having a clear visibility on the delivered value to ensure efficient guidance for service-oriented architecture (SOA), business process management (BPM), and traditional implementation projects. The second set of visible components of the ASAP methodology is the business add-ons to ASAP that extend the ASAP Roadmap with modular business implementation content. The business add-ons provide proven implementation content for implementation of various industry solutions, solution packages, and other related areas such as agile methodology, BPM, SOA and enterprise architecture (EA) governance, and strategy frameworks.

The various phases of the SAP ASAP methodology 7 are as follows:

1. Project Preparation
2. Blueprint
3. Realization
4. Final Preparation
5. Go Live, Support, and Run SAP

 Since we have already seen an overview of the project management work stream (along with the accompanying deliverables, milestones, key decisions, and so on), we will focus on highlighting how value delivery, business process management, and service-oriented architecture get reflected in the various phases of the ASAP Methodology 7.

13.3.1 Value Delivery Considerations

The objective of *value delivery* is to ensure that the project lives up to the value expectations according to the targets that are stated in the initial business case. This value-based approach serves the following purposes:

■ Execute the project according to the business case or value map targets.
■ Monitor and track the project value delivery based on the initial business case or value map, and, report on the status of value delivery at an early stage of quality gates (Q-Gates).

Value-based solution design plays a critical role in determining value drivers and key process changes for the implementation project. To realize the intended business value for this initiative, it is essential to address key success factors and establish a clear and shared set of expectations for program value creation; achieve a rapid program launch with effective value-based governance; make the business case actionable and measureable by defining design imperatives, key performance indicators (KPIs), and process performance indicators (PPIs); establish ongoing value management discipline to ensure that the Business Blueprint phase and the subsequent implementation reflect design imperatives.

13.3.2 Business Process Management Considerations

The purpose of the business process management work stream is to work with value determination, build a high-level to-be business process map, deliver the business scenario design, and implement.

The work-stream deliverables are enhanced to expand on the business case and ensure that the value drivers are incorporated into the solution design. In addition to identifying the value drivers, key process changes are also identified for input into the solution transformation that is a part of the Business Blueprint BPM work stream. The creation of business process maps helps the project team to verify the agreed-upon scope of the project and provide inputs for the Business Blueprint workshop content. Business process maps provide the framework for business process modeling and, therefore, help to control the scope of the project. Decomposition of the business scenarios during project preparation is the starting point and acts as the foundation for the detailed business process decomposition that takes place during the Business Blueprint stage.

13.3.3 Service-Oriented Architecture (SOA) Considerations

The decision to implement SOA usually represents an important architectural paradigm shift for a company—within both the business and IT organizations. The burden of SOA implementation typically falls most heavily on the organizational side of the business, where new skills and responsibilities have to be introduced along with focused attention to the business requirements including new IT capabilities and to tighter relationship between IT and business.

The enterprise must establish an enterprise service-oriented architecture strategy and governance to ensure the success of your project. Effective enterprise SOA strategy and governance calls for a holistic management approach that integrates and aligns the corporate business strategy, the IT strategy, and the planning and operational activities associated with enterprise SOA solutions—an approach that encompasses people, processes, and technologies. In most companies, IT governance can be used as part of the foundation for enterprise SOA governance. But enterprise SOA governance is much more; it involves organizational structures, skills, and procedures aligned with business needs.

13.4 Success Patterns for SAP Implementation Projects

The concept of patterns was introduced by Christopher Alexander in the late 1970s in the field of architecture. A Pattern describes a commonly occurring solution that generates decidedly successful outcomes.

It is logical at this stage to summarize the lessons learned from past SAP implementation projects in the form of a checklist that can be referred easily. It should be noted that these patterns are applicable for SAP implementations envisaged for the Millennium Enterprises, by which I mean companies that are considered as Small and Medium Enterprises (SMEs) that have annual revenues between $50 million and $1 billion.

In the following is a checklist of Patterns of successful SAP implementation projects:

Success Pattern 1: Direct Involvement of the top management throughout the project

Success Pattern 2: Clear project organization structure and strong project management

Success Pattern 3: Proper visibility and communication throughout the project

Success Pattern 4: A company-wide Change Management plan

Success Pattern 5: Allocation of appropriate budget and resources

Success Pattern 6: Deputation of experienced achievers and key managers on the project and not by people who can be spared from the department

Success Pattern 7: Project driven by the user departments rather than the IT department and implemention of only user-driven functionality

Success Pattern 8: Implementation of the pilot site followed by the rollout sites

Success Pattern 9: Big-Bang implementation of at least the base modules

Success Pattern 10: Clear scope and control on functional creep during the project

Success Pattern 11: Comprehensive Training of SAP team members

Success Pattern 12: Standardizing business processes and preferably implementing SAP standard functionality

13.5 Summary

This chapter introduced the AcceleratedSAP (ASAP) methodology for implementation of SAP CRM. Beginning with understanding why SAP projects tend to be complex, this chapter discussed the background and context of SAP ASAP. We also presented an overview of the various phases of the SAP CRM implementation, namely, project preparation, Business Blueprint, realization, final preparation, and go live and support.

POST-IMPLEMENTATION STAGE

Chapter 14 gives a brief overview of the post-implementation issues associated with the support and enhancement of a SAP CRM system in production.

Chapter 14: Supporting and Enhancing SAP CRM

All front office deployments have performance and scalability requirements that must be met to support efficient business operations and commitments on completing the required workloads on schedule. Good performance is not only important to ensure user satisfaction and the ongoing use of the application but is also critical to the efficiencies and operating costs of the supported business processes. All front office deployments also have application scalability requirements not only in terms of the total number of users, processes, and data volumes that can be supported but also in terms of the deployed network, server, and other resources to control deployment costs.

This chapter also introduces new areas of applications that have significant potential for the future, namely, mobile applications, context-aware applications, big data applications and social networks based applications.

Chapter 14

Supporting and Enhancing SAP CRM

In this chapter, we look at the post-implementation support of SAP within an organization. In traditional application software systems, ongoing maintenance is known to account for more than 50% of the total cost of any system.

SAP simplifies ongoing changes in the delivered functionality of a system because of

- Comprehensive functionality
- Inherent flexibility
- A comprehensive upgrade strategy

In this short chapter, we highlight some of these aspects that are related to supporting and enhancing the performance of the SAP implementation and hence its return on investment (ROI). We end this chapter by looking at the issue of building up consultants and teams for sustaining the momentum and effectiveness of the SAP implementation and then retaining them for maximizing the advantages to the company.

14.1 SAP Deployment

One of the major issues after completing the pilot site implementation of SAP is its implementation at a company's other plant sites and office locations. As touched upon in Chapter 6, "The SAP Implementation Project Cycle," and Chapter 12, "Initiating the SAP Project," SAP deployment at other sites is simplified by adopting the following measures during the pilot site implementation:

- Rationalizing the processes
- Standardizing the processes
- A comprehensive set of processes relevant to all businesses and locations
- The inclusion of members in the implementation from the other sites and offices

The deployment effort involves the following steps:

1. *SAP installation*: This involves the installation of the infrastructure and SAP licenses based on the experience gained from the first-site implementation.
2. *Uploading base configuration*: This involves importing the base configuration prepared, implemented, and stabilized to all other sites.
3. *Uploading data*: This corresponds to the loading of basic data that are common to the operations of the company at all locations. This basic customization data may differ at each site to the extent that the facility addresses different industries, market segments, and so on. This may be reflected in the fact that supplier community may be different at each of these facilities. There may also be differences because of differing rules and regulations at different sites.
4. *Integrated training*: This involves conducting an integrated and tightly scheduled training session conducted for SAP support personnel, power users, and end users at the respective sites. Unlike the case of the pilot site, this training for the rollout sites can be done on the company-specific implementation, an opportunity that is unavailable for the pilot sites.
5. *Integration testing*: This involves conducting integrated and tightly scheduled integration testing using the test scripts that were prepared for the pilot site as the base. This approach makes this exercise highly focused and efficient.

All these apply to cases in which every plant or pilot site has exactly the same configuration.

In reality, this may not be the case. Correspondingly, you may have another step for customizing SAP for the specific requirements of the rollout sites. This customization may involve the configuration of new organization structures such as sales offices or purchasing departments; it may involve configuration of new business processes specific to the new sites; new authorizations may need to be set up to accommodate differing roles or requirements of the rollout sites; and it may involve setting up new reports, new forms, and additional interfaces to the legacy systems of the plant or pilot site. If the pilot site or plant is in a different country (e.g., Canada), there will be significant changes due to different tax regulations, reporting requirements, and other country-specific requirements.

14.2 Continuous Change

This activity deals with ongoing changes that may be adopted in order to enhance the efficiency and effectiveness of the SAP system. This may consist of

◾ Ongoing training
◾ Performance monitoring and fine-tuning
◾ SAP Release upgrade management

This change activity also provides the opportunity to address some of the aspects that were decided to be out of the project's scope for the base implementation. It must be noted that we are not referring to any extensions or enhancements to the functionality provided by SAP per se, but to the functional modules and processes that may not have been implemented during the first wave. Thus, ancillary modules like Plant Management (PM), Quality Management (QM),

Projects System (PS), and even important functionality like HR may get implemented in the second wave of implementation. SAP's Accelerated SAP (ASAP) methodology provides a separate component to address this phase of the life cycle of the SAP implementation.

This activity may also deal with the implementation of functionalities or systems that add value by overlaying on the base modules:

■ SAP Workflow
■ Document management systems
■ SAP Business Information Warehouse
■ Automatic Data Collection (ADC) systems
■ Supply chain Management (SCM) systems
■ Strategic Enterprise Management (SEM) systems

14.3 Customer Center of Expertise (CCOEs) Program

Under this CCOE program, SAP supports setting up the CCOE at valued customer's site. This provides a direct interface between the company and SAP.

The CCOE undertakes the following tasks in the company:

■ Help desk support
■ Training
■ Information services
■ Project implementation and support
■ Coordination of development requests
■ Business support
■ Technical support
■ SAP contract administration
■ Internal marketing for promotion and better acceptance of SAP

14.3.1 Help Desk

The success of a SAP implementation is dependent to a great extent on the deployment of an enterprise-wide and properly resourced help desk. This is especially critical during and immediately after the go-live period, because this is when the system is used by a large number of users for whom the system is new, unfamiliar, and even disorienting. For companies that do not have a history of computerization, this may be a very trying period.

The majority of the problems reported during this period may be due to a lack of knowledge, human errors, system bugs, or technical problems with printers, network connections, and so on.

Some of the issues involved with instituting a help desk include

■ Defining the standards for identifying problems
■ Defining and establishing the method for registering problems
■ Defining the standards and procedures for problem diagnosis and resolutions
■ Defining and establishing the service levels and response times for problem resolution
■ Defining the standards and procedures for communicating the solution

- Defining the standards and procedures for tracking unresolved and pending problems
- Defining the procedure for escalating overdue, unresolved problems
- Establishing help desk logistics
- Implementing a help desk application system
- Defining the help desk team organization and the corresponding requisite skills and resources
- Appointing and training the help desk team

All unresolved problems are finally referred to SAP support services, such as the Online Service System (OSS).

14.4 Upgrading SAP CRM Applications

This deals with the effort that needs to be undertaken to implement the periodic release upgrades provided by SAP. SAP provides upgrades in two categories:

1. *Correction release upgrades*: These are smaller patches released by SAP for rectifying problems that have been reported in the system.
2. *Functional release upgrades*: These primarily extend the functionality of SAP in the concerned areas.

The SAP upgrade effort involves

- Assessing and planning the projected technical downtime
- Upgrading all the systems within the system landscape
- Planning and executing the postupgrade activities
- Skills planning and resourcing for an upgrade

An upgrade is not just a technical procedure. It may involve significant effort and resources of the company. When SAP does an upgrade, it may change the table structures, it may add additional functionality or change the functionality of existing business processes, code may change, and the look of the system may change. When performing an upgrade, additional steps would include

- Integration testing of business processes, reports, interfaces
- Identification and resolution of issues with regard to changes required to reports, interfaces, ABAP programs, authorization, changes, and modifications required as a result of the upgrade
- Configuration and testing of new functionality released in the upgrade
- User documentation and user training as a result of the upgrade (this would be required as a result of a major upgrade where the user's daily tasks would be changed as a result of the upgrade)

The ASAP methodology provides a separate component to address this phase of the SAP implementation life cycle. SAP also provides additional tools like SAP Software Logistics.

14.5 Retaining and Retraining SAP Consultants

Until the recent past, SAP implementations were essentially considered complete after implementing the modules of interest to the organization. However, with the growing importance of virtual corporations or extended enterprises enabled by the Internet, companies are undertaking numerous development efforts. These involve various enhancements and interfacing SAP with supply-chain management systems and customer-facing applications, including sales force automation and call center applications. Thus, retaining the SAP implementation team may be critical for the organization to maintain the momentum of implementing satellite systems that interface with SAP or overlay the operational systems of SAP.

14.5.1 Retention Horizon

If one recalls that companies are advised to nominate their key performers to work as part of the SAP implementation in order to ensure its success, the effect of SAP-trained employees quitting the organization in search of better opportunities is doubly damaging. In such cases, the company not only loses SAP experts who are familiar with the specifics of their implementation, but it may also be deprived of some of its best performers. It is critical for a company to retain its implementation team members at least for twice the period of implementation.

Even if the retention of the core team is achieved at a cost that may double the budgeted figures, it will enable a company to extend its competitiveness further by rapidly implementing additional systems that overlay or interface with SAP. These systems include

- The Web enabling of SAP functionality
- Workflow systems
- SCM systems
- EAI systems
- Performance-enhancement programs like BPR, activity-based management, and Balanced Scorecard

14.5.2 Extending the Boundaries of Expertise

Apart from an increase in remuneration and compensations, training in advanced features and functionalities of SAP and other enterprise applications can be a powerful method of retaining SAP talent within your organization.

An Advanced Business Applications Programming (ABAP) developer's skills could be upgraded by

- Training in Web-based application development projects in HTML, XML, ASP, EJB, Java, JavaScript, VisualBasicScript, and so on
- Training and participation in EAI systems like computerized telephone integration, bar codes, security and access systems, data capture systems, and computer recognition systems
- Training in data warehousing projects using the SAP business information Warehouse solution or even non-SAP solutions that use data from the SAP system
- Training in Workflow for participating in workflow, imaging, and document management projects to be undertaken by the company
- Training in functional modules, depending on background and aptitude

A NetWeaver consultant's skills could be upgraded by

- Training in ABAP development and further opportunities available in that activity
- Training and participation in enterprise infrastructure upgrade projects
- Training and participation in Web infrastructure projects
- Training and participation in enterprise infrastructure management projects including Web-enabled systems management, network management, and performance monitoring systems

A functional consultant's skills could be upgraded by the following:

- Cross-training in different modules. MM and PP consultants could be cross-trained in either module as well as other related modules like QM, PM, PS, and SM. Similarly, FI and CO consultants could be cross-trained in either module as well as other related modules like AM, TR, FM, IM, CCA, PA, and EIS.
- SCM systems.
- Performance-enhancement programs like BPR, activity-based management, and Balanced Scorecard.

14.6 Privacy and Security

The advent of the Internet has transformed the familiar issues of security and privacy beyond recognition. This is primarily because of the following:

- Every computer can be accessed and influenced by any other computer anywhere on the Internet; this effectively eliminates the concept of locality.
- Businesses that are supported on such an extended and open IT substrate are vulnerable to scrutiny and monitoring by interested parties.
- Browsing and visitations of Websites to gather information in turn also expose the visitor's behavior itself to interpretation and analyses.

Consumer privacy issues and concerns have a drastic effect on the enterprise's ability to market to, connect to, and create an ongoing relationship with your customers (see Chapter 1, Section 1.2.6.5 "Permission Marketing" and especially NAOMI KLIEN). Consumers are gravely concerned regarding the abuse of their privacy, but gathering a certain amount of information is necessary for companies to personalize and to serve their customers better. Thus, there is a need for a balance between protecting a consumer's privacy and the need for enterprises to target and personalize their offerings to the customers. In 2000, the US Federal Trade Commission recommended fair information practices of *notice, choice, access,* and, *security.* Enterprises need to adhere to these practices when creating and implementing their privacy policies. Third-party privacy seals are a good way to gain the trust of consumers because these third-party consumer privacy protection organizations certify the enterprise's privacy policy.

There are two types of privacy seal programs. One has strict guidelines that prohibit sites from sharing consumer information they collect with other business partners or from using it for direct marketing programs. Secure Assure, which has 200 member companies, offers an audit program but requires members to adhere to a stringent privacy guideline stating that the e-business will never share a consumer's private information with a third party. Other privacy seal programs award stamps-of-approval to sites that simply stick to whatever privacy policy promises they have made. The oldest and most well-known privacy seal program is Electronic Frontier Foundation's TRUSTe (www.truste.org), which was started in 1997 and has more than 1300 companies as members including AOL and e-Toys.

The threat to information privacy and security can never be eliminated, but controls and technologies can be applied to reduce the risks to acceptable levels. The challenges faced by the various enterprises in this regard are described in the following.

14.6.1 Privacy

There are a number of aspects to privacy:

1. The captured user behavior representing the navigation and interaction of the user with the system(s). To identify a particular user, the Web server writes/updates a small *cookie* file, which is stored on the user system, to record predetermined pieces of information, such as identity of every page visited by the user and every search performed by the user. While this enables enterprises to provide customer-focused services, the compilation of the historic log of searches and Website visits has major implications for privacy-related issues.
2. The transmitted user data as these travel across public networks are vulnerable to being tapped much like telephone calls or being scrutinized at the Web servers much like done for calls passing through telephone exchanges. This is resolved by encrypting that is, employing a special *algorithm* (i.e., a process) for converting a normal *plaintext* message into an apparently unintelligible *ciphertext* message that can be converted back into plaintext by using a deciphering key, which is usually a 40-bit (i.e., a large) number.

   The two basic types of encryption algorithms are the following:

   a. Symmetric key algorithms/schemes rely on a single key to both encrypt and decrypt a message; it is vulnerable to the key being revealed publicly rendering the system unusable or the original message can be tampered with or without being detected playing havoc with the integrity of the system.
   b. Pubic key algorithms/schemes work on the principle that the keys can only work in pairs: one private key (which is maintained private) matches with exactly one public key (which is made public) and that the key used to encrypt a message cannot be used to decrypt it and vice versa. When the user wants to send a message, the message is encrypted with the publicly available public key of the target recipient and, on receipt, only the recipient can decrypt the message using the corresponding private key available solely with the recipient.

 A common compromise solution is to use symmetric keys to encrypt the messages but to use public keys to manage the symmetric keys; consequently, the symmetric key can be used for a set of transactions, also termed as the *session key*.

However, the largest vulnerability is attributable to the use of the public network, which is also the reason for its ubiquity. This is resolved by establishing a *virtual private network* (VPN) between the various nodes of the network. A VPN effectively functions as an extremely secure link via the Internet (termed as a *tunnel*) between these nodes, without the need to lay physical wires between these nodes to create a private network at a great cost. Thus, the VPN between an enterprise and its partners is set up via the Internet with hardware devices at each node on the VPN network; adding another trading partner merely entails adding another security device at their end and configuring the VPN network to include it.

3. The stored user data are discussed in the Section 14.6.3 "Integrity." The protection of access to stored information is dealt in the next subsection.

14.6.2 Intrusion

Intrusion is similar to intruders breaking into a building and likewise is countered by the analog concept of an electronic firewall. The firewall generally sits between the enterprise and the Internet and monitors all traffic coming in (or going out) from your business primarily at two levels, namely,

1. Network level where it does the following:
    a. Restricts access for all, some, or specific users to all, some, or specific applications
    b. Scans e-mails for deleting suspect attachments
    c. Strips ActiveX controls and Java applets from Web pages
    d. Screens access to URLs to prevent nonbusiness and illegal Internet surfing
    e. Scans network activity for irregular activities
2. Application level
    Evidently, a faulty firewall may not only not achieve its objective but is more damaging in that it engenders a false sense of security.

14.6.3 Integrity

This relates to the reliability of the transactions not having been altered without being detected unfailingly.

The common approaches adopted to ensure integrity are as follows:

1. *Secure Socket Layer* (*SSL*) is the most commonly used security schemes on the Internet for the exchange of information between the browser/client and the remote server.
2. VPN is suitable for a community or ecosystem of partners.
3. *Secure Electronic Transactions* (*SET*) is a specialized security protocol for dealing with credit card transactions primarily as a part of the financial transactions.
4. *Electronic signatures* are akin to the total at the end of a column of numbers that is unrelated to the individual numbers but can be used to ascertain the authenticity of the full message. If this number signature is encrypted with a private key, anyone can read the message using the public key for decryption; but if the message has been modified in any way, the signature would no longer match the text. Thus, electronic signatures are direct indicators of the authenticity of the messages.
5. For any encryption, the requisite public key is reliably obtained from a *trusted* third party called the *certification authority* (CA) that provides this information in the form of a *certificate* consisting of
    a. The public key and verification of who the key belongs to
    b. An expiry date indicating period of validity

   c. Level of trust indicating the degree of verification that has been undertaken to ascertain the genuineness of the ownership of the key by a particular individual or party
6. Secure e-mail commonly uses S/MIME (secure multi-purpose Internet mail extensions) that utilizes encryption and certification to provide the needed security to messages.

The totality of infrastructure and system for managing public keys is referred to as a *public key infrastructure* (*PKI*), which includes

   a. A hierarchy of CAs starting with a *root Certification Authority (rootCA)* that focuses only on verifying the veracity of all these layers of CAs
   b. Resolution for a number of issues like Government regulation of CAs, legal admissibility of the Certificates, and liabilities in the case of a failure or fraud

14.6.4 Business Disruption

The common ways in which an electronic attack could disrupt the enterprise's business are as follows:

■ Viruses that are the most common form of attack that can result in incidental damages like wiping of hard disks, overwriting or deletion of files, program crashes, and computers or networks slowing down or even grinding to a halt. Even relatively harmless e-mails/messages in large volumes can also clog the networks and disk spaces to render the system unusable for prolonged periods. E-mail that is the *killer apps* of the Internet is also the most frequent conduit for entry and spreading of viruses within enterprises.
■ Denial of Service (DOS) attacks though not fatal can be equally damaging. This is similar to a telephone exchange or a call center to be swamped by a barrage of spurious calls during a critically timed teleservice event.

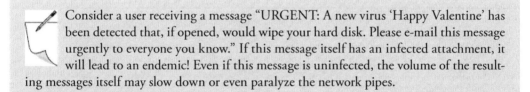

Consider a user receiving a message "URGENT: A new virus 'Happy Valentine' has been detected that, if opened, would wipe your hard disk. Please e-mail this message urgently to everyone you know." If this message itself has an infected attachment, it will lead to an endemic! Even if this message is uninfected, the volume of the resulting messages itself may slow down or even paralyze the network pipes.

14.7 Applications Outsourcing (AO)

Applications are evolving from those that facilitated a single business function (e.g., accounting, payroll) to integrated application environments that facilitate business processes spanning entire enterprises or the extended enterprises. This evolution entails more people, planning, and ongoing management, especially for mission-critical applications that must maintain a high level of availability. With such increasing complexity and the increased amount of time and skill needed to keep up with the rapidly changing technology cycles, organizations are increasingly seeking outside assistance in deploying, managing, and enhancing their applications.

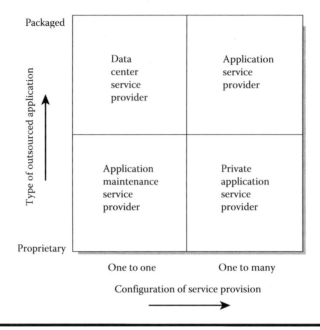

Figure 14.1   Types of application outsourcers.

Application Outsourcing (AO) is a service wherein the responsibility for the deployment, management, and enhancement of a packaged or customized software application is handed off contractually to an external service provider. AO entails specific activities and expertise aimed at managing the software application or set of applications. Contractual service-level agreements (SLAs) are set at the application level and include responsibilities for

- Application availability
- Application performance
- Application enhancement

Figure 14.1 presents the positioning of the various types of application outsourcers based on the type of application being outsourced (proprietary vs. packaged) and the configuration/location of the service provision (one to one or one to many).

The salient characteristics of the various categories are as follows:

1. *Top-left quadrant*: Represents *data center service providers* that provide application hosting services and support to other divisions and are typically managed internally by the enterprises.
2. *Bottom-left quadrant*: Represents the *application maintenance service providers* that provide hosting, maintenance, and support of custom-developed application at the enterprises' site(s).
3. *Top-right quadrant*: Represents the *application service providers* that provide operations and maintenance of both packaged and custom-developed application to disparate enterprises using the same outsourcing infrastructure (hardware, software, networks, operational staff, etc.). We describe this category in Section 14.7.1 "CRM Application Service Providers (ASPs)."

4. *Bottom-right quadrant*: Represents the *private application service providers (ASPs)* that provide operations and maintenance of especially custom applications to an ecosystem of enterprises involved in a particular area of business. We describe this category in Section 14.7.3 "Private ASPs."

Top reasons cited by enterprises for resorting to outsourcing are as follows:

- Free internal resources for more strategic projects
- Offload functions that are difficult to manage
- Receive cash infusion from transfer of assets to outsources
- Replace capital expenditures with pay-as-you-use operational expenses
- Gain access to world-class IT expertise
- Reduce costs for research, development, and successful deployment
- Reduce investment risk in a rapidly changing environment
- Obtain additional manpower on an as- and when-needed basis

In the simplest case, the application is merely hosted for the customer. AO typically does not include responsibility for the underlying business processes or functions; a more comprehensive engagement like Business Processing Outsourcing (BPO) may include operations assessment, process improvement, and change management services. When standard applications are being outsourced, the level of staff and asset transfer to this facility may be minimal, and the application itself may be provided via a license or lease agreement included in the overall service agreement. On the other hand, for more customized applications, the contract may include the transfer of people and assets associated with the outsourced application.

14.7.1 CRM Application Service Providers (ASPs)

The basic idea behind the application service providers (ASPs) computing model is that a provider hosts and manages applications that users can access over networks like the Internet. This is the final step toward software manifesting as a service. The market is evolving toward a state where companies will pay for the software as services on a usage basis, as they do traditionally with utility services like electricity and gas. This market was pioneered in 1998 by start-ups such as Breakaway Solutions, USinternetworking, and Corio. The ASP model typically involves lease-to-own options on software. It entails renting access, at a low rate, to the functionality of ERPs, CRMs, SCMs, etc., over the Internet. In contrasts, traditional outsourcing requires up-front purchase of software licenses and often charges large fees for contracted services. But, recently, many ASPs are also experimenting with other pricing models that involve charges for initial customization, migration, and integration plus a flat monthly fee depending on the use of functionality and services or even a percentage of the customer's revenue. The ASP services could range from infrastructure, colocation, cohosting, dedicated hosting right through, to even hosted businesses such as hosted buying services or even hosted customer relationship management services.

The level of the packaged application could vary from discrete applications (like Web-based transaction application for conducting a commerce-based transaction) to environment applications (like CRM). The level of service provided by an ASP can range from simple hosting of application(s) to also managing the application environment. Hosting is a standardized service that is based on a high-volume and low-cost business model in which applications are hosted at a site and accessed remotely. Managing an application environment goes beyond simple hosting and may include up-front consulting, customization, and extensions of the application and ongoing application technical support.

Factors driving the ASP solutions are as follows:

1. Enabling Technologies:
   a. Pervasiveness of the Internet
   b. Access and declining cost of bandwidth capacity
   c. Shared applications in a client/server environment
   d. Browsers as an accepted GUI application
   e. Potential of e-commerce and e-business solutions
2. Technical Drivers:
   a. Utilization of emerging technologies and *best-of-breed* applications
   b. Accelerated application development
   c. Rapidly changing and increasing complexity of technology
   d. Obtaining business domain, functional and vertical industry expertise
   e. Shortage of skilled IT labor
   f. Transfer of risk regarding application ownership by the super users
3. Business Drivers:
   a. Minimize total cost of ownership (TCO) by at least 30%–50%.
   b. Predictability of cash flows by eliminating the uncertainties of post-implementation software-related expenditures.
   c. Focus on core competencies and strategic objectives.
   d. Improve efficiency of internal IT staff by freeing them to focus on processes and systems to leverage core competencies.
   e. Improve coordination efforts on a global basis.

However, merely hosting and managing an application is not adequate and needs to be augmented for the creation of proprietary and sustainable customer relationships with value-added variations like

■ Domain Expertise Emphasis
■ Vertical Industry Emphasis
■ Vertical Exchange Emphasis
■ Infrastructure Emphasis
■ Security Infrastructure Emphasis
■ Full Service Provider Emphasis
■ Aggregator Emphasis

Some of the challenges faced by the ASP concept are

■ Security of information
■ Scope and flexibility of services
■ Overall quality of service (QoS) and support
■ Adaptability of software

Application Service Providers (ASPs) present a real opportunity to replace the in-house IT department. Smaller companies also need the full functionality of high-end applications such as ERP,

SCM, or CRM that cannot be afforded by them. ASPs meet the needs of MME companies that cannot afford the substantial up-front investments in establishing the infrastructure, knowledgeable and experienced staff, ongoing administration and monitoring services, better backup and recovery methods, and so forth. The top reasons that are cited by companies for renting applications are guaranteed performance levels, high availability, responsive service, and support. The cost of ownership of hosted applications can be 25% cheaper than managing the applications internally. Other criteria for companies to contract ASPs are lower up-front costs, faster implementations, higher redundancy, larger scalability of hardware and bandwidth, automatic upgrades, quicker distribution and deployment, and data storage, backup, and recovery capabilities.

Using application service providers (ASPs) has many advantages, such as

- Enabling a company to concentrate on enhancing the competitiveness of its core functions
- Enabling a company to outsource the enhancing competitiveness of its noncore but still-critical functions like implementing Call Center operations
- Re-engineering critical but noncore functions and processes quickly
- Comprehensive industry-specific and company-specific evaluations
- Rapid prototyping of company-specific implementations
- Lower up-front investments in hardware and software, technical manpower resources, and training
- Reduced risks of initial erroneous decisions in pricing, reliability, scalability, bandwidth, and security
- Flexibility of options like hosting, cohosting, and colocation
- Time to implement at a lower cost
- Time to go live at a lower cost
- Time to benefit at a lower cost
- Time to full ownership at a lower cost
- Time to deploy at other sites at a lower cost
- Higher service-level guarantees
- Better customer service
- Reduced administration, management, maintenance, and support costs

14.7.2 SAP Business ByDesign (BBD)

The newest of SAP's SME offerings, SAP Business ByDesign (BBD), includes preconfigured best practices for managing financials, customer relationships, human resources, projects, procurement, and the supply chain. BBD allows customers to focus on their business, leaving SAP to worry about maintaining hardware and software, running database backups, addressing performance and capacity planning, implementing updates and fixes, and so on. SAP takes care of system installation, maintenance, and upgrades so that you can focus on your business rather than IT. BBD targets to address the market of customers seeking to avoid investing in business software and all the necessary infrastructure and support personnel associated with such an investment.

SAP Business ByDesign solution provides the following advantages:

1. *Hosted solution*: SAP hosts your Business ByDesign system in an enterprise class data center designed to provide high availability and reliability.
2. *Lower efforts and costs*: A company deploying BBD does not necessarily require SAP partners or consultants for implementation.

3. *Increased productivity and ease of maintenance*: A major advantage of BBD is its ease of configuration for changes and maintenance. Nontechnical users can build business processes using visual modeling tools and web services.

14.7.3 Private ASPs

It has been well established that the largest cost component in an application's life cycle is the effort expended on maintenance and upgrades; and this is valid even in the cases of packaged software implementations by reason of the customizations that are indispensable. The key idea underlying the Private ASP is this: *the high cost of maintenance and upgrades (and operations) is spread across the boundary of the enterprise to include the associated ecosystem of at least the exclusive suppliers.* The viability of this business model can be illustrated from the fact that the customization requirements for implementing enterprise systems (ERP, SCM, CRM, etc.) at General Motors's partner/subsidiary Delphi Electronics are going to be similar to or would be heavily influenced by the customization requirements of General Motors itself. From there, it is not very far to see that there will be a major advantage in combining the implementation projects and teams, training programs, testing centers, rollout projects, IT centers, disaster recovery centers, and so on.

We will describe this concept by taking Ford as the hypothetical example. A Private ASP is an extended ASP service, managed and operated by a major player like Ford for itself and its partners—both customers and vendors. All Customization and upgrade issues are dictated mainly by Ford, unlike in the case of a traditional ASP, where they may have to customize for each one of its customers independently—*which basically makes the traditional ASP model unviable*:

> Private ASP = (SCM + CRM like SAP CRMs + Net Markets) on ASP basis for Ford and
> its participating Partners

 None of the partners need to be compelled to join the Private ASP. Ford, however, should mandate that such partners need to integrate and be compatible with its Private ASP at their own cost. Licensing issues are simplified in that all software licenses are owned via the Private ASP instituted jointly by Ford and/or its Partners.

The composite value proposition for Ford and its partners involves the following:

1. Easy to add/integrate new Vendor Partner.
2. Value Proposition of a NetMarket: Ford can service an enlarged base of Vendors for more competitive bidding but within the class of these Preferred Partners/Vendors.
3. Value Proposition of an ASP for reduced application management, operations, and maintenance costs.
4. Value Proposition of implementation, management, and maintenance of a CRM for individual partners who do not have a CRM, which also is the same CRM as used by Ford (at much reduced cost than outside of the Private ASP).
5. Value Proposition of an EAI provider, especially for integrating internal and proprietary applications of Ford and its individual partners (at much reduced cost than outside of the Private ASP).
6. Value Proposition of profitable IT services via the Private ASP for Ford and/or its Partners.

7. Value Proposition of an Outsourcing Service in terms of assets, manpower, support, training, etc.
8. Value proposition of SCM implementation, operations, and management for itself and its Partners—this would be a large benefit in the long term.

14.7.3.1 What Does a Private ASP Offer?

A Private ASP offers the following:

- It Provides Applications Services to a restricted business ecosystem of Ford and its participating partners.
- It provides individual Enterprise-oriented services for Ford and each of the partners through separate instances of each of these applications.
- It also provides individual company-specific services for internal applications like HRMS, CRM, and e-mail to Ford and its partners separately. Thus, if there are 100 partners who have joined Ford's private ASP program, there may be 100 different implementations of HRMS, CRM, etc. (from different vendors), systems for the specific requirements for each of these partners but handled by the same entity—the Private ASP.

Ford can own the Private ASP facility fully and run it as a Profit Center; Ford can charge its Partners on subscription (and/or even transaction basis) along with a possible lump sum enrollment fees. Or Ford can float a separate company along with its participating partners for establishing and run this Private ASP; the Private ASP can then charge via a uniform model for all of its delivered services to all members of the Private ASP.

14.8 Mobilizing the Enterprise and Relationships

Mobilization is fundamentally about extending your enterprise's capacity to do business. The ability to handle and process both personal and public information while mobile is very compelling. Mobilization enables enterprises to extend their networks to mobile enterprises effectively while protecting the investments in legacy systems and current technologies. Mobilizations achieve the following:

- Enable enterprises to distribute enterprise intelligence to wherever, whenever, and whichever device it is needed, enabling accelerated decisions.
- Support the broadest range of enterprise touch points possible. The distinction between PDAs, wireless phones, and handheld PCs (such as Microsoft's Tablet PC) is becoming blurred: PDAs are receiving mobile phone functionality and, in turn, Mobile phones are receiving the functionality of PDAs with calendaring and contact database utilities. And all of them are converging further to access e-mail, Web pages, Internet, and wired and wireless infrastructure from anywhere and anytime.
- Leverage the use of legacy information assets while continuing to maintain their local autonomy, integrity, and relevance.
- Isolate current and future intellectual property and mobile applications from infrastructure and technology innovation and improvements.

Two outstanding benefits of mobilization are increased productivity and real-term gathering and dissemination of information. The mobilized enterprise becomes more productive via the gathering and dissemination of real-term information, enabling the enterprise to respond quickly and appropriately to new problems and opportunities as they arise, for instance, a mobile Sales Force Automation (SFA) application that enables a company to respond to an opportunity quickly. If a salesperson has access to inventory information while he or she is with a customer, the order processing can be handled immediately. Thus, the mobile solutions designed to take into account the needs of the mobile worker enable the enterprise to be more customer focused, more productive, more responsive, more flexible, and more profitable.

The mobile solutions transform the organization from a command-and-control hierarchy into a responsive and adaptive enterprise wherein

- Technology adapts pervasively to the business processes
- Enterprise resources are extended securely to any environment
- Collaboration is supported at all touch points within the workflow
- Distance and time ceases to be impediments to productivity
- Enterprise responds in real term

Mobile technology transforms organizations and has the potential to increase significantly the overall productivity, adaptability, and responsiveness of the enterprise.

14.9 Context-Aware Applications

Most mobile applications are location-aware systems. Specifically, tourist guides are based on users' location in order to supply more information on the city attraction closer to them or the museum exhibit they are seeing. Nevertheless, recent years have seen many mobile applications trying to exploit information that characterizes the current situation of users, places, and objects in order to improve the services provided.

The principle of context-aware applications (CAA) can be explained using the metaphor of the Global Positioning System (GPS). In aircraft navigation, for example, a GPS receiver derives the speed and direction of an aircraft by recording over time the coordinates of longitude, latitude, and altitude. This contextual data is then used to derive the distance to the destination, communicate progress to date, and calculate the optimum flight path.

For a GPS-based application to be used successfully, the following activities are a prerequisite:

a. The region in focus must have been GPS-mapped accurately.
b. The GPS map must be superimposed with the relevant information regarding existing landmarks, points of civic and official significance, and, facilities and service points of interest in the past to the people—this is the context in this metaphor.
c. There must be a system available to ascertain the latest position as per the GPS system.
d. The latest reported position must be mapped and transcribed onto the GPS-based map of the region.
e. This latest position relative to the context (described in b above) is used as the point of reference for future recommendation(s) and action(s).

It should be noted that the initial baseline of the context (described in b above) is compiled and collated separately and then uploaded into the system to be accessible by the CAA.

However, with passage of time, this baseline gets added further with the details of each subsequent transaction.

> We can also imagine an equivalent of the Global Positioning System for calibrating the performance of enterprises. The coordinates of longitude, latitude, and altitude might be replaced by ones of resource used, process performed, and product produced. If we designed a GPS for an enterprise, we could measure its performance (e.g., cost or quality) in the context of the resource used, the process performed, and the product delivered, as compared with its own performance in the past (last month or one year back, etc.) or in particular cases, that of another target organization. Such an approach could help us specify our targets, communicate our performance, and signal our strategy.

Most of the current context-aware systems have been built in an ad-hoc approach, and are deeply influenced by the underlying technology infrastructure utilized to capture the context. To ease the development of context-aware ubicomp (ubiquitous computing) and mobile applications, it is necessary to provide universal models and mechanisms to manage context. Even though significant efforts have been devoted to research methods and models for capturing, representing, interpreting, and exploiting context information, we are still not close to enabling an implicit and intuitive awareness of context, nor efficient adaptation to behavior at the standards of human communication practice.

Context information can be a decisive factor in mobile applications in terms of selecting the appropriate interaction technique. Designing interactions among users and devices, as well as among devices themselves, is critical in mobile applications. Multiplicity of devices and services calls for systems that can provide various interaction techniques and the ability to switch to the most suitable one according to the user's needs and desires. Current mobile systems are not efficiently adaptable to the user's needs. The majority of ubicomp and mobile applications try to incorporate the users' profile and desires into the system's infrastructure either manually or automatically observing their habits and history. According to the perspective being presented here, the key point is to give them the ability to create their own mobile applications instead of just customizing the ones provided.

Thus, mobile applications can be used not only for locating users and providing them with suitable information, but also for

- Providing them with a tool necessary for composing and creating their own mobile applications
- Supporting the system's selection of appropriate interaction techniques
- A selection of recommendation(s) and consequent action(s) conforming with the situational constraints judged via the business logic and other constraints sensed via the context
- Enabling successful closure of the interaction (answer to a query, qualifying an objection, closing an order, etc.)

14.9.1 Decision Patterns as Context

This chapter discusses location-based services applications as a particular example of context-aware applications. But, context-aware applications can significantly enhance the efficiency and effectiveness of even routinely occurring transactions. This is because most end-user application's effectiveness and performance can be enhanced by transforming it from a *bare* transaction to a transaction *clothed* by a surround of a context formed as an aggregate of all relevant decision patterns utilized in the past.

The decision patterns contributing to a transaction's context include the following:

■ Characteristic and sundry details associated with the transaction under consideration
■ Profiles of similar or proximate transactions in the immediately prior week or month or 6-months or last year or last season
■ Profiles of similar or proximate transactions in same or adjacent or other geographical regions
■ Profiles of similar or proximate transactions in same or adjacent or other product groups or customer groups

To generate the context, the relevant decision patterns can either be discerned or discovered by mining the relevant pools or streams of primarily the transaction data. Or they could be augmented or substituted by conjecturing or formulating decision patterns that explain the existence of these characteristic pattern(s) (in the pools or streams of primarily the transaction data). In the next subsection, we look at function-specific decision patterns with a particular focus on financial decision patterns.

 Thus, generation of context itself is critically dependent on employing big data and mobilized applications, which in turn needs cloud computing as a prerequisite.

14.9.1.1 Concept of Patterns

The concept of patterns used in this book originated from the area of real architecture. Alexander gathered architectural knowledge and best practices regarding building structures in a pattern format. This knowledge was obtained from years of practical experience. A pattern according to Alexander is structured text that follows a well-defined format and captures nuggets of advice on how to deal with recurring problems in a specific domain. It advises the architect on how to create building architectures, defines the important design decisions, and covers limitations to consider. Patterns can be very generic documents, but may also include concrete measurements and plans. Their application to a certain problem is, however, always a manual task that is performed by the architect. Therefore, each application of a pattern will result in a differently looking building, but all applications of the pattern will share a common set of desired properties. For instance, there are patterns describing how eating tables should be sized so that people can move around the table freely, get seated comfortably, find enough room for plates and food, while still being able to communicate and talk during meals without feeling too distant from people seated across the table. While the properties of the table are easy to enforce once concrete distances and sizes are specified, they are extremely hard to determine theoretically or by pure computation using a building's blueprint.

In building architecture, pattern-based descriptions of best practices and design decisions proved especially useful, because many desirable properties of houses, public environments, cities, streets, etc. are not formally measurable. They are perceived by humans, and thus, cannot be computed or predicted in a formal way. Therefore, best practices and well-perceived architectural styles capture a lot of implicit knowledge how people using and living in buildings perceive their structure, functionality, and general feel. Especially, the indifferent emotions that buildings trigger, such as awe, comfort, coziness, power, cleanness, etc. are hard to measure or explain and are also referred to *as the quality without a name* or *the inner beauty of a building*. How certain objectives can be realized in architecture is, thus, found only through practical experience, which is then captured by patterns. For example, there are patterns describing how lighting in a room should be realized so that people feel comfortable and positive. Architects capture their knowledge gathered from existing buildings and feedback they received from users in patterns describing well-perceived building design. In this scope, each pattern describes one architectural solution for an architectural problem. It does so in an abstract format that allows the implementation in various ways. Architectural patterns, thus, capture the essential properties required for the successful design of a certain building area or function while leaving large degrees of freedom to architects.

Multiple patterns are connected and interrelated resulting in a *pattern language*. This concept of links between patterns is used to point to related patterns. For example, an architect reviewing patterns describing different roof types can be pointed to patterns describing different solutions for windows in these roofs and may be advised that some window solutions, thus, the patterns describing them, cannot be combined with a certain roof pattern. For example, a *flat rooftop* cannot be combined with windows that have to be mounted vertically. Also, a pattern language uses these links to guide an architect through the design of buildings, streets, cities, etc. by describing the order in which patterns have to be considered. For example, the size of the ground on which a building is created may limit the general architecture patterns that should be selected first. After this, the number of floors can be considered, followed by the above-mentioned roofing style, etc.

14.9.1.1.1 Patterns in Information Technology (IT) Solutions

In a similar way, the pattern-based approach has been used in IT to capture best practices on how applications and systems of applications should be designed. Examples are patterns for fault-tolerant software, general application architectures, object oriented programming, enterprise applications, or for message-based application integration. Again, these patterns are abstract and independent of the programming language or runtime infrastructure used to form *timeless knowledge* that can be applied in various IT environments. In the domain of IT solutions, the desirable properties are portability, manageability, flexibility to make changes, and, so on. The properties of IT solutions become apparent over time while an application is productively used, evolves to meet new requirements, has to cope with failures, or has to be updated to newer versions. During this lifecycle of an application, designers can reflect on the IT solution to determine whether it was well designed to meet such challenges.

14.9.1.1.2 Patterns in CRM

Traditional marketing theory and practice has always assumed that enhancing revenues and maximizing profits can be achieved by expanding the customer base. While this may be a viable strategy, it may not hold true at all times. For instance, in mature industries and mature markets, customer acquisition may not hold the key to better financial performance: higher acquisition rates and retention rates do not necessarily result in higher profitability. While key customer metrics such as acquisition, retention, churn, and win-back are essential for establishing a profitable CRM strategy, merely *maximizing* each of these individual metrics is not necessarily a guarantee for success. Implementing specific and tailored strategies for key customer metrics yields a greater impact on customer decisions and can therefore lead to higher profitability. Prevailing patterns in CRM data can help in developing these specific strategies in each of the four steps of the customer–firm relationship life cycle: acquisition, retention, churn, and win-back.

a. Acquisition: the acquisition strategy involves attaining the highest possible customer acquisition rate by implementing mass-level strategies. Any combination of mass marketing (radio, billboards, etc.) and direct marketing (telemarketing, mail, e-mail, etc.) would be implemented in order to target *eligible* customers rather than *interested* ones. A new approach to CRM pertaining to customer acquisition is gaining ground: there is a conscious move from mass marketing of products to one that is focused on the end consumer. Differentiating and segmenting with regards to demographic, psychographic, or purchasing power-related characteristics became more affordable and possible, and eventually became necessary in order to keep up with competing firms. As firms have become more capable and committed with data analyses, offerings have become more specific, thus increasing the amount of choice for customers. This has in turn spurred customers to expect more choice and customization in their purchases. It is through the continued improvements and innovations in data collection, storage, and analysis that acquisition has moved toward one-to-one acquisition.

b. Retention: since the early 1960s, companies have changed their focus from short-term acquisition and transactions to long-term relationships and CLTV. In fact, retention studies indicate that for every 1% improvement in customer retention rate, a firm's value increases by 5%.

c. Churn or attrition: many firms fail to realize that the majority of customers who are in the churn stage will not complain or voice their concerns. A study on this found that an estimated 4% of customers in the churn stage will actually voice their opinions, with the other 96% lost without voicing their discontent. Further, about 91% of the lost customers will never be won back.

d. Win back: Although reacquiring lost customers may be a hard sell, it has been found that firms still have a 20–40% chance of selling to lost customers versus only 5–20% of selling to new prospects.

14.9.1.2 Domain-Specific Decision Patterns

In the following, we discuss decision patterns for customer relationship management (CRM) which get defined and fine-tuned, across an extended period of operational experience, by the specific requirements of the business, offerings, and geographic region(s) in which the company operates.

14.9.1.2.1 CRM Decision Patterns

This section describes an overview of the statistical models-based decision patterns used in CRM applications as the guiding concept for profitable customer management. The primary objectives of these systems are to acquire profitable customers, retain profitable customers, prevent profitable customers from migrating to competition, and winning back *lost* profitable customers. These four objectives collectively lead to increasing the profitability of an organization.

CRM strategies spanning the full customer lifecycle are constituted of four decision patterns or models:

a. Customer acquisition: This involves decisions on identifying the right customers to acquire, forecasting the number of new customers, the response of promotional campaigns, and so on. The objectives of customer acquisition modeling include identifying the right customers to acquire, predicting whether customers will respond to company promotion campaigns, forecasting the number of new customers, and examining the short- and long-run effects of marketing and other business variables on customer acquisition.

This is a conscious move from mass marketing of products to one that is focused on the end consumer. This is a direct result of increases in data collection and storage capabilities that have uncovered layer upon layer of customer differentiation. Differentiating and segmenting with regards to demographic, psychographic, or purchasing power-related characteristics became more affordable and possible, and eventually became necessary in order to keep up with competing firms. Although segment-level acquisition did not take this theory to the extent that one-to-one customer acquisition has, it reinforced a growing trend of subsets or groups of customers within a larger target market. Being able to collect, store, and analyze customer data in more practical, affordable, and detailed ways has made all of this possible. As firms have become more capable and committed with data analyses, offerings have become more specific, thus increasing the amount of choice for customers. This has in turn spurred customers to expect more choice and customization in their purchases. This continuous firm–customer interaction has consistently shaped segment-level marketing practices in the process to better understand customers.

The decision patterns would incorporate
- Differences between customers acquired through promotions and those acquired through regular means
- Effect of marketing activities and shipping and transportation costs on acquisition
- Impact of the depth of price promotions
- Differences in the impact of marketing-induced and word-of-mouth customer
- Acquisition on customer equity

b. Customer retention: This involves decisions on who will buy, what the customers will buy, when they will buy, and how much they will buy, and so on. During the customer's tenure with the firm, the firm would be interested in retaining this customer for a longer period of time. This calls for investigating the role of trust and commitment with the firm, metrics for customer satisfaction, and the role of loyalty and reward programs, among others. The objective of customer retention modeling includes examining the factors influencing customer retention, predicting customers' propensity to stay with the company or terminate the relationship, and predicting the duration of the customer–company relationship. Customer retention strategies are used in both in contractual (where customers are bound by contracts such as cell (mobile) phone subscription or magazine subscription) and in non-contractual settings (where customers are not bound by contracts such as grocery purchases or apparel purchases).

Who to retain can often be a difficult question to answer. This is because the cost of retaining some customers can exceed their future profitability and thus make them unprofitable customers. When to engage in the process of customer retention is also an important component. As a result, firms must monitor their acquired customers appropriately to ensure that their customer loyalty is sustained for a long period of time. Finally, identifying how much to spend on a customer is arguably the most important piece of the customer retention puzzle. It is very easy for firms to over-communicate with a customer and spend more on his/her retention than the customer will ultimately give back to the firm in value.

The decision patterns would incorporate

- Explaining customer retention or defection
- Predicting the continued use of the service relationship through the customer's expected future use and overall satisfaction with the service
- Renewal of contracts using dynamic modeling
- Modeling the probability of a member lapsing at a specific time using survival analysis
- Use of loyalty and reward programs for retention
- Assessing the impact of a reward program and other elements of the marketing mix

c. Customer attrition or churn: This involves decisions on whether the customer will churn or not, and if so what will be the probability of the customer churning, and when. The objective of customer attrition modeling includes churn with time-varying covariates, mediation effects of customer status and partial defection on customer churn, churn using two cost-sensitive classifiers, dynamic churn using time-varying covariates, factors inducing service switching, antecedents of switching behavior, and impact of price reductions on switching behavior.

Engaging in active monitoring of acquired and retained customers is the most crucial step in being able to determine which customers are likely to churn. Determining who is likely to churn is an essential step. This is possible by monitoring customer purchase behavior, attitudinal response, and other metrics that help identify customers who feel underappreciated or underserved. Customers who are likely to churn do demonstrate *symptoms* of their dissatisfaction, such as fewer purchases, lower response to marketing communications, longer time between purchases, and so on. The collection of customer data is therefore crucial in being able to identify and capture such *symptoms* and that would help in analyzing the retention behavior and the choice of communication medium. Understanding who to save among those customers who are identified as being in the churn phase is again a question of cost versus future profitability.

The decision patterns would incorporate

- When are the customers likely to defect?
- Can we predict the time of churn for each customer?
- When should we intervene and save the customers from churning?
- How much do we spend on churn prevention with respect to a particular customer?

d. Customer win-back: This involves decisions on reacquiring the customer after the customer has terminated the relationship with the firm. The objective of customer win-back modeling includes customer lifetime value, optimal pricing strategies for recapture of lost customers, and the perceived value of a win-back offer.

Identifying the right customers to win back depends on factors such as the interests of the customers to reconsider their choice of quitting, the product categories that would interest the customers, the stage of customer life cycle, and so on. If understanding what to offer customers in winning them back is an important step in the win-back process, measuring the cost of win-back is as important as determining who to win back and what to offer them. The cost of win-back, much like the cost of retention or churn, must be juxtaposed with the customer's future profitability and value to the firm.

14.9.1.2.2 CRM Decision Patterns through Data Mining

CRM systems like SAP CRM are used to track and efficiently organize inbound and outbound interactions with customers, including the management of marketing campaigns and call centers. These systems, referred to as operational CRM systems, typically support front-line processes in sales, marketing, and customer service, automating communications and interactions with the customers. They record contact history and store valuable customer information. They also ensure that a consistent picture of the customer's relationship with the organization is available at all customer *touch* (interaction) points. These systems are just tools that should be used to support the strategy of effectively managing customers.

However, to succeed with CRM, organizations need to gain insight into customers, their needs, and wants through data analysis. This is where analytical CRM comes in. Analytical CRM is about analyzing customer information to better address the CRM objectives and deliver the right message to the right customer. It involves the use of data mining models in order to assess the value of the customers, understand, and predict their behavior. It is about analyzing data patterns to extract knowledge for optimizing the customer relationships. For example,

- Data mining can help in customer retention as it enables the timely identification of valuable customers with increased likelihood to leave, allowing time for targeted retention campaigns.
- Data mining can support customer development by matching products with customers and better targeting of product promotion campaigns.
- Data mining can also help to reveal distinct customer segments, facilitating the development of customized new products and product offerings, which better address the specific preferences and priorities of the customers.

The results of the analytical CRM procedures should be loaded and integrated into the operational CRM front-line systems so that all customer interactions can be more effectively handled on a more informed and *personalized* base.

Marketers strive to get a greater market share and a greater share of their customers, that is, they are responsible for getting, developing, and keeping the customers. Data mining aims to extract knowledge and insight through the analysis of large amounts of data using sophisticated modeling techniques; it converts data into knowledge and actionable information. Data mining models consist of a set of rules, equations, or complex functions that can be used to identify useful data patterns, understand, and predict behaviors.

Data mining models are of two kinds:

1. Predictive or Supervised Models: In these models, there are input fields or attributes and an output or target field. Input fields are also called predictors, because they are used by the model to identify a prediction function for the output or target field. The model generates an *input–output* mapping function, which associates predictors with the output so that, given the values of input fields, it predicts the output values. Predictive models themselves are of two types, namely, classification or propensity models and estimation models. Classification models are predictive models with predefined target field or classes or groups, so that the objective is to predict a specific occurrence or event. The model also assigns a propensity score with each of these events that indicates the likelihood of the occurrence of that event. In contrast, estimation models are used to predict a continuum of target values based on the corresponding input values.

2. Undirected or Unsupervised models: In these models, there are input fields or attributes, but no output or target field. The goal of such models is to uncover data patterns in the set of input fields. Undirected models are also of two types, namely, cluster models, and, association and sequence models. Cluster models do not have predefined target field or classes or groups, but the algorithms analyze the input data patterns and identify the natural groupings of cases. In contrast, association or sequence models do not involve or deal with the prediction of a single field. Association models detect associations between discrete events, products, or attributes; sequence models detect associations over time.

> Segmentation is much more complex than it may seem; simplified segmentation models, when tested in real life, seem to imply that people as customers change behavior radically. If this was really true, there would be no trust, no loyalty, and, consequently, no collaboration. The apparent paradox gets resolved only when it is recognized that while people as customers do not possess multiple personalities, they have differing customs and, hence, play differing roles based on different contexts or scenarios. The problem arises on persisting with the stance of *one-segment-fits-for-all-contexts-for-all-people-on-all-occasions*.

Data mining can provide customer insight, which is vital for establishing an effective CRM strategy. It can lead to personalized interactions with customers and hence increased satisfaction and profitable customer relationships through data analysis. It can support an *individualized* and optimized customer management throughout all the phases of the customer lifecycle, from the acquisition and establishment of a strong relationship to the prevention of attrition and the winning back of lost customers.

a. *Segmentation*: It is the process of dividing the customer base into distinct and internally homogeneous groups in order to develop differentiated marketing strategies according to their characteristics. There are many different segmentation types based on the specific criteria or attributes used for segmentation. In behavioral segmentation, customers are grouped by behavioral and usage characteristics. Data mining can uncover groups with distinct profiles and characteristics and lead to rich segmentation schemes with business meaning and value. Clustering algorithms can analyze behavioral data, identify the natural groupings of customers, and suggest a solution founded on observed data patterns.

Data mining can also be used for the development of segmentation schemes based on the current or expected/estimated value of the customers. These segments are necessary in order to prioritize customer handling and marketing interventions according to the importance of each customer.

b. *Direct Marketing Campaigns*: Marketers use direct marketing campaigns to communicate a message to their customers through mail, the Internet, e-mail, telemarketing (phone), and other direct channels in order to prevent churn (attrition) and to drive customer acquisition and purchase of add-on products. More specifically, acquisition campaigns aim at drawing new and potentially valuable customers away from the competition. Cross-/deep-/up-selling campaigns are implemented to sell additional products, more of the same product, or alternative but more profitable products to existing customers. Finally, retention campaigns aim at preventing valuable customers from terminating their relationship with the organization.

   Although potentially effective, this can also lead to a huge waste of resources and to bombarding and annoying customers with unsolicited communications. Data mining and classification (propensity) models in particular can support the development of targeted marketing campaigns. They analyze customer characteristics and recognize the profiles or extended-profiles of the target customers.
   c. *Market Basket Analysis*: Data mining and association models in particular can be used to identify related products typically purchased together. These models can be used for market basket analysis and for revealing bundles of products or services that can be sold together.

14.10 Big Data Analytics

Along with the data came the problem of how to compute all this volume and variety and how to handle the volume of the data. This is where Google, Facebook, and Yahoo clearly showed the way; the former created a new computing model based on a file system and a programming language called MapReduce that scaled up the search engine and was able to process multiple queries simultaneously. In 2002, architects Doug Cutting and Mike Cafarella were working on an open-source search engine project Nutch, which led to them modeling the underlying architecture based on the Google model. This led to the development of the Nutch project as a top Apache project under open source, which was adopted by Yahoo in 2006 and called Hadoop. Hadoop has in the last few years created a whole slew of companies that are both commercial solutions and commit back features to the base open-source project, a true collaboration-based software and framework development.

   The other technology that has evolved into a powerful platform is the not only SQL (NoSQL) movement. The underpinnings of this platform are based on a theorem proposed by Eric Brewer in 2002 called the CAP theorem. According to the CAP theorem, a database cannot meet all the rules of ACID compliance at any point in time and yet be scalable and flexible. However, in the three basic properties of consistency, availability, and partition tolerance, a database can meet two of the three, thereby creating a scalable and distributed architecture that can evolve into meeting scalability requirements in a horizontal scaling and provide higher throughput, as the compute in this environment is very close to the storage and is a distributed architecture that can allow for multiple consistency levels.

   Facebook was one of the earliest evangelists of the NoSQL architecture, as they needed to solve the scalability and usability demands of a user population that was only third behind China and India in terms of number of people. The popular NoSQL database Cassandra was developed and used at Facebook for a long time (now it has been abandoned by Facebook due to greater scalability needs) and is used across many other companies in conjunction with Hadoop and other traditional RDBMS solutions. It remains a top-level Apache project and is evolving with more features being added.

   The key thing to understand here is the data part of Big Data was always present and used in a manual fashion, with a lot of human processing and analytic refinement, eventually being used in a decision-making process. What has changed and created the buzz with Big Data is the automated data processing capability that is extremely fast and scalable and has flexible processing. If one were to consider all the data, the associated processes, and the metrics used in any decision-making situation within any organization, we realize that we have used information (volumes of data) in a variety of formats and varying degrees of complexity and derived decisions with the data in nontraditional software processes.

We are seeing the evolution of Hadoop, MapReduce, and NoSQL with changes and new features coming out of the woodwork every few months and sometimes weeks. These architectures are being designed and built to handle large and complex data volumes and can process effectively in a batch-oriented environment and have limited real-time or interactive capabilities that are found in the RDBMS.

14.10.1 What Is Big Data?

Big Data can be defined as volumes of data available in varying degrees of complexity, generated at different velocities and varying degrees of ambiguity, which cannot be processed using traditional technologies, processing methods, algorithms, or any commercial off-the-shelf solutions.

Data defined as Big Data include weather, geospatial, and GIS data; consumer-driven data from social media; enterprise-generated data from legal, sales, marketing, procurement, finance, and human resources department; and device-generated data from sensor networks, nuclear plants, x-ray and scanning devices, and airplane engines.

14.10.1.1 Data Volume

The most interesting data for any organization to tap into today are social media data. The amount of data generated by consumers every minute provides extremely important insights into choices, opinions, influences, connections, brand loyalty, brand management, and much more. Social media sites provide not only consumer perspectives but also competitive positioning, trends, and access to communities formed by common interest. Organizations today leverage the social media pages to personalize marketing of products and services to each customer.

Every enterprise has massive amounts of e-mails that are generated by its employees, customers, and executives on a daily basis. These e-mails are all considered an asset of the corporation and need to be managed as such. After Enron and the collapse of many audits in enterprises, the US government mandated that all enterprises should have a clear life-cycle management of e-mails and that e-mails should be available and auditable on a case-by-case basis. There are several examples that come to mind like insider trading, intellectual property, and competitive analysis, to justify governance and management of e-mails.

The list of features for handling data velocity included the following:

- Nontraditional and unorthodox data processing techniques need to be innovated for processing this data type.
- Metadata are essential for processing these data successfully.
- Metrics and KPIs are key to provide visualization.
- Raw data do not need to be stored online for access.
- Processed output needs to be integrated into an enterprise-level analytical ecosystem to provide better insights and visibility into the trends and outcomes of business exercises including CRM, Optimization of Inventory, Clickstream analysis, and more.
- The enterprise data warehouse (EDW) is needed for analytics and reporting.

14.10.1.2 Data Velocity

The business models adopted by Amazon, Facebook, Yahoo, and Google, which became the de facto business models for most web-based companies, operate on the fact that by tracking customer clicks and navigations on the website, you can deliver personalized browsing and shopping experiences. In this process of clickstreams, there are millions of clicks gathered from users at every second, amounting to large volumes of data. These data can be processed, segmented, and modeled to study population behaviors based on time of day, geography, advertisement effectiveness, click behavior, and guided navigation response. The result sets of these models can be stored to create a better experience for the next set of clicks exhibiting similar behaviors. The velocity of data produced by user clicks on any website today is a prime example for Big Data velocity.

The most popular way to share pictures, music, and data today is via mobile devices. The sheer volume of data that is transmitted by mobile networks provides insights to the providers on the performance of their network, amount of data processed at each tower, time of day, associated geographies, user demographics, location, latencies, and much more. The velocity of data movement is unpredictable and sometimes can cause a network to crash. The data movement and its study have enabled mobile service providers to improve the quality of service (Qos), and associating these data with social media inputs has enabled insights into competitive intelligence.

The list of features for handling data velocity included the following:

■ Systems must be elastic for handling data velocity along with volume.
■ Systems must scale up and scale down as needed without increasing costs.
■ Systems must be able to process data across the infrastructure in the least processing time.
■ System throughput should remain stable independent of data velocity.
■ Systems should be able to process data on a distributed platform.

14.10.1.3 Data Variety

Data come in multiple formats as these range from e-mails to tweets to social media and sensor data. There is no control over the input data format or the structure of the data. The processing complexity associated with a variety of formats is the availability of appropriate metadata for identifying what is contained in the actual data. This is critical when we process images, audio, video, and large chunks of text. The absence of metadata or partial metadata means processing delays from the ingestion of data to producing the final metrics and, more importantly, in integrating the results with the data warehouse.

The list of features for handling data velocity included the following:

■ Scalability
■ Distributed processing capabilities
■ Image processing capabilities
■ Graph processing capabilities
■ Video and audio processing capabilities

14.10.2 Big Data Appliances

Big data analytics applications combine the means for developing and implementing algorithms that must access, consume, and manage data. In essence, the framework relies on a technology ecosystem of components that must be combined in a variety of ways to address each application's requirements, which can range from general information technology (IT) performance scalability to detailed performance improvement objectives associated with specific algorithmic demands. For example, some algorithms expect that massive amounts of data are immediately available quickly, necessitating large amounts of core memory. Other applications may need numerous iterative exchanges of data between different computing nodes, which would require high-speed networks.

The big data technology ecosystem stack may include the following:

1. Scalable storage systems that are used for capturing, manipulating, and analyzing massive datasets.
2. A computing platform, sometimes configured specifically for large-scale analytics, often composed of multiple (typically multicore) processing nodes connected via a high-speed network to memory and disk storage subsystems. These are often referred to as appliances.
3. A data management environment, whose configurations may range from a traditional database management system scaled to massive parallelism to databases configured with alternative distributions and layouts to newer graph-based or other NoSQL data management schemes.
4. An application development framework to simplify the process of developing, executing, testing, and debugging new application code. This framework should include programming models, development tools, program execution and scheduling, and system configuration and management capabilities.
5. Methods of scalable analytics (including statistical and data mining models) that can be configured by the analysts and other business consumers to help improve the ability to design and build analytical and predictive models.
6. Management processes and tools that are necessary to ensure alignment with the enterprise analytics infrastructure and collaboration among the developers, analysts, and other business users.

14.10.3 Tools, Techniques, and Technologies of Big Data

14.10.3.1 Big Data Architecture

Analytical environments are deployed in different architectural models. Even on parallel platforms, many databases are built on a shared everything approach in which the persistent storage and memory components are all shared by the different processing units.

A shared-disk approach may have isolated processors, each with its own memory, but the persistent storage on disk is still shared across the system. These types of architectures are layered on top of SMP machines. While there may be applications that are suited to this approach, there are bottlenecks that exist because of the sharing, because all I/O and memory requests are transferred (and satisfied) over the same bus. As more processors are added, the synchronization and communication need to increase exponentially, and therefore the bus is less able to handle the increased need for bandwidth. This means that unless the need for bandwidth is satisfied, there will be limits to the degree of scalability.

In contrast, in a shared-nothing approach, each processor has its own dedicated disk storage. This approach, which maps nicely to an MPP architecture, is not only more suitable to discrete allocation and distribution of the data; it enables more effective parallelization and consequently does not introduce the same kind of bus bottlenecks from which the SMP/shared-memory and shared-disk approaches suffer. Most big data appliances use a collection of computing resources, typically a combination of processing nodes and storage nodes.

14.10.3.2 Row- versus Column-Oriented Data Layouts

Most traditional database systems employ a row-oriented layout, in which all the values associated with a specific row are laid out consecutively in memory. That layout may work well for transaction processing applications that focus on updating specific records associated with a limited number of transactions (or transaction steps) at a time. These are manifested as algorithmic scans that are performed using multiway joins; accessing whole rows at a time when only the values of a smaller set of columns are needed may flood the network with extraneous data that are not immediately needed and ultimately will increase the execution time.

Big data analytics applications scan, aggregate, and summarize over massive datasets. Analytical applications and queries will only need to access the data elements needed to satisfy join conditions. With row-oriented layouts, the entire record must be read in order to access the required attributes, with significantly more data read than is needed to satisfy the request. Also, the row-oriented layout is often misaligned with the characteristics of the different types of memory systems (core, cache, disk, etc.), leading to increased access latencies. Consequently, row-oriented data layouts will not enable the types of joins or aggregations typical of analytic queries to execute with the anticipated level of performance.

Hence, a number of appliances for big data use a database management system that uses an alternate, columnar layout for data that can help to reduce the negative performance impacts of data latency that plague databases with a row-oriented data layout. The values for each column can be stored separately, and because of this, for any query, the system is able to selectively access the specific column values requested to evaluate the join conditions. Instead of requiring separate indexes to tune queries, the data values themselves within each column form the index. This speeds up data access while reducing the overall database footprint while dramatically improving query performance. The simplicity of the columnar approach provides many benefits, especially for those seeking a high-performance environment to meet the growing needs of extremely large analytic datasets.

14.10.3.3 NoSQL Data Management

NoSQL or "Not only SQL," suggests environments that combine traditional SQL (or SQL-like query languages) with alternative means of querying and access. NoSQL data systems hold out the promise of greater flexibility in database management while reducing the dependence on more formal database administration. NoSQL databases have more relaxed modeling constraints, which may benefit both the application developer and the end-user analysts when their interactive analyses are not throttled by the need to cast each query in terms of a relational table-based environment.

Different NoSQL frameworks are optimized for different types of analyses. For example, some are implemented as key/value stores, which nicely align to certain big data programming models, while another emerging model is a graph database, in which a graph abstraction is implemented to embed both semantics and connectivity within its structure. In fact, the general concepts for

NoSQL include schema-less modeling in which the semantics of the data are embedded within a flexible connectivity and storage model; this provides for automatic distribution of data and elasticity with respect to the use of computing, storage, and network bandwidth in ways that don't force specific binding of data to be persistently stored in particular physical locations. NoSQL databases also provide for integrated data caching that helps reduce data access latency and speed performance.

A relatively simple type of NoSQL data store is a key/value store, a schema-less model in which distinct character strings called keys are associated with values (or sets of values, or even more complex entity objects)—not unlike hash table data structure. If you want to associate multiple values with a single key, you need to consider the representations of the objects and how they are associated with the key. For example, you may want to associate a list of attributes with a single key, which may suggest that the value stored with the key is yet another key/value store object itself.

 The key/value store does not impose any constraints about data typing or data structure—the value associated with the key is the value, and it is up to the consuming business applications to assert expectations about the data values and their semantics and interpretation. This demonstrates the schema-less property of the model.

Key/value stores are essentially very long and presumably thin tables (in that there are not many columns associated with each row). The table's rows can be sorted by the key value to simplify finding the key during a query. Alternatively, the keys can be hashed using a hash function that maps the key to a particular location (sometimes called a *bucket*) in the table. The representation can grow indefinitely, which makes it good for storing large amounts of data that can be accessed relatively quickly, as well as allows massive amounts of indexed data values to be appended to the same key/value table, which can then be shared or distributed across the storage nodes. Under the right conditions, the table is distributed in a way that is aligned with the way the keys are organized, so that the hashing function that is used to determine where any specific key exists in the table can also be used to determine which node holds that key's bucket (i.e., the portion of the table holding that key).

NoSQL data management environments are engineered for two key criteria:

1. Fast accessibility, whether that means inserting data into the model or pulling it out via some query or access method
2. Scalability for volume, so as to support the accumulation and management of massive amounts of data

The different approaches are amenable to extensibility, scalability, and distribution, and these characteristics blend nicely with programming models (like MapReduce) with straightforward creation and execution of many parallel processing threads. Distributing a tabular data store or a key/value store allows many queries/accesses to be performed simultaneously, especially when the hashing of the keys maps to different data storage nodes. Employing different data allocation strategies will allow the tables to grow indefinitely without requiring significant rebalancing. In other words, these data organizations are designed for high-performance computing for reporting and analysis.

The model will not inherently provide any kind of traditional database capabilities (such as atomicity of transactions or consistency when multiple transactions are executed simultaneously)—those capabilities must be provided by the application itself.

14.10.3.4 In-Memory Computing

The idea of running databases in memory was used by the business intelligence (BI) product company QlikView. In-memory allows the processing of massive quantities of data in the main memory to provide immediate results from analysis and transaction. The data to be processed are ideally real-time data or as close to real time as is technically possible. Data in the main memory (RAM) can be accessed 100,000 times faster than data on a hard disk; this can dramatically decrease access time to retrieve data and make it available for the purpose of reporting, analytics solutions, or other applications.

The medium used by a database to store data, that is, RAM, is divided into pages. In-memory databases save changed pages in savepoints, which are asynchronously written to persistent storage in regular intervals. Each committed transaction generates a log entry that is written to nonvolatile storage—this log is written synchronously. In other words, a transaction does not return before the corresponding log entry has been written to persistent storage—in order to meet the durability requirement that was described earlier—thus ensuring that in-memory databases meet (and pass) the ACID test. After a power failure, the database pages are restored from the savepoints; the database logs are applied to restore the changes that were not captured in the savepoints. This ensures that the database can be restored in memory to exactly the same state as before the power failure.

14.10.3.5 Developing Big Data Applications

For most big data appliances, the ability to achieve scalability to accommodate growing data volumes is predicated on multiprocessing—distributing the computation across the collection of computing nodes in ways that are aligned with the distribution of data across the storage nodes. One of the key objectives of using a multiprocessing node environment is to speed up application execution by breaking up large *chunks* of work into much smaller ones that can be farmed out to a pool of available processing nodes. In the best of all possible worlds, the datasets to be consumed and analyzed are also distributed across a pool of storage nodes. As long as there are no dependencies forcing any one specific task to wait to begin until another specific one ends, these smaller tasks can be executed at the same time, that is, *task parallelism*. More than just scalability, it is the concept of *automated scalability* that has generated the present surge of interest in big data analytics (with corresponding optimization of costs).

A good development framework will simplify the process of developing, executing, testing, and debugging new application code, and this framework should include

1. A programming model and development tools
2. Facility for program loading, execution, and process and thread scheduling
3. System configuration and management tools

The context for all of these framework components is tightly coupled with the key characteristics of a big data application—algorithms that take advantage of running lots of tasks in parallel on many computing nodes to analyze lots of data distributed among many storage nodes. Typically, a big data platform will consist of a collection (or a *pool*) of processing nodes; the optimal performances can be achieved when all the processing nodes are kept busy, and that means maintaining a healthy allocation of tasks to idle nodes within the pool. Any big application that is to be developed must map to this context, and that is where the programming model comes in. The programming model essentially describes two aspects of application execution within a parallel environment:

1. How an application is coded
2. How that code maps to the parallel environment

MapReduce programming model is a combination of the familiar procedural/imperative approaches used by Java or C++ programmers embedded within what is effectively a functional language programming model such as the one used within languages like Lisp and APL. The similarity is based on MapReduce's dependence on two basic operations that are applied to sets or lists of data value pairs:

1. Map, which describes the computation or analysis applied to a set of input key/value pairs to produce a set of intermediate key/value pairs
2. Reduce, in which the set of values associated with the intermediate key/value pair output by the map operation are combined to provide the results

A MapReduce application is envisioned as a series of basic operations applied in a sequence to small sets of many (millions, billions, or even more) data items. These data items are logically organized in a way that enables the MapReduce execution model to allocate tasks that can be executed in parallel.

 Combining both data and computational independence means that both the data and the computations can be distributed across multiple storage and processing units and automatically parallelized. This parallelizability allows the programmer to exploit scalable massively parallel processing resources for increased processing speed and performance.

14.10.4 SAP HANA

After the requisite background on big data and in-memory computing, we are now ready to get acquainted with SAP HANA.

In 2006, SAP introduced the BW Accelerator (BWA), which was an appliance-based solution specifically targeted to improve the reporting and analytic capabilities for its SAP NetWeaver Business Warehouse (BW). The BWA solution is based on TREX (SAP's Search and Classification Engine) technology to support querying the large amounts of BW data for analytic requirements. BWA as an appliance is a combination of hardware and software that moves identified data onto the BWA, organizes and indexes it differently than done in the core SAP NetWeaver BW database, and then integrates it with the SAP NetWeaver BW reporting tools to read the data via the query engine. BWA is specifically meant for speeding up the responsiveness of queries and reports written against SAP NetWeaver BW. SAP HANA database is an enhancement over BWA.

SAP HANA in-memory database solution is a combination of hardware and software that optimizes row-based, column-based, and object-based database technologies to exploit parallel processing capabilities. SAP HANA is a flexible, data source–independent toolset that enables compressing and handling of large volumes of data in real time, without the need to aggregate or create highly complex physical data models. SAP HANA uses column-based organization for storing and processing data—to update a field in a column-based format, the system has to find the right column and then the right row for the update rendering the process as inefficient. SAP HANA circumvents this problem by inserting a new information instead of updating it. Moreover, using the column structure of data obviates the need to retrieve every possible piece of information in a record for every report requirement, thus making it that much faster and more efficient than traditional row-based access.

SAP HANA has the power to bring together and analyze billions of rows of information in a subsecond. The most common uses for SAP HANA include the following:

- Call detail record analysis
- Point of sale analysis
- Comprehensive understanding of customer's individual needs, habits, and preferences
- Quality and production analysis
- Fraud/risk management and modeling

SAP HANA comes in two versions, namely, stand-alone version and BW version.

14.10.4.1 Stand-alone SAP HANA

This is also known as SAP HANA 1.0 or the enterprise version of SAP HANA. In this version, the organization implements a stand-alone instance of SAP HANA to address a new reporting or analytic need. These stand-alone installations may address a point or single solution and, therefore, could add tremendous value to the organization.

In this case, the organization needs to get the data into SAP HANA via extract, transform, and load (ETL) processes, create the data model, install a BI tool, and create the reports.

14.10.4.2 SAP HANA for BW

This scenario is also known as SAP HANA 2.0 or SAP NetWeaver BW powered by SAP HANA. In this version, the organization is looking to optimize the performance of your existing SAP NetWeaver BW system by replacing their existing database (Oracle, DB2, etc.) with a SAP HANA database.

In this case, the organization is able to leverage all investment of times and efforts expended in implementing the SAP NetWeaver BW system along with the corresponding reports; it has to only replace their existing database with SAP HANA.

This is the long-term direction of SAP: using SAP HANA as the underlying database for existing solutions—removing the existing databases like Oracle and DB2.

14.11 Social CRM via Social Networks

14.11.1 Social Networks

Starting as early as 1995, online social network (OSN) pioneers Classmates.com, SixDegrees.com, and Friendster introduced the notion of profile pages and friend connections. These sites paved the way for today's popular sites, including Facebook, MySpace, LinkedIn, Orkut, Hi5, and CyWorld, each of which boasts tens or hundreds of millions of active members around the world. Facebook, Twitter, MySpace, and an increasing number of other social networks now offer Web services application programming interfaces (APIs), which make it possible for other Web sites and Web applications to tap into profile and social data. These advances are extending the reach and impact of the OSN beyond specific social networking sites to potentially every Web experience.

   a. *Discovery Sites*: The OSN can be manually built up over time by individuals on sites like Facebook or approximated with algorithms. Discovery sites like ZoomInfo, and business/ professional services like LexisNexis, construct a person database by crawling the Web for publicly available information and making associations. They are able to approximate user profiles and social networks without any user participation. Because there is not enough public data available or accessible about people and connections, automated discovery sites are error prone carrying data that is incorrect, incomplete, redundant or out of date.
   b. *Affinity Networks*: Many clubs and organizations, such as university alumni associations, have added online networking capabilities to their Web sites to reach and better engage their membership. Other affinity networks are entirely virtual. For instance, on LinkedIn, the MIT Sloan CIO Network is an exclusive online community of senior IT executives from around the world who are given gated access to one another, in addition to specialized content, discussion boards, and polls. CIOs sign up to network with their peers and access news across the IT community.

14.11.2 Social Network Platforms

Initially, social networking sites were simple communication utilities that let people send messages to one another and share photos and event information. But OSN wanted their members to spend more time on their sites to maximize ad impressions and clicks so that they could make money. For this reason, just about every major social network has unveiled a platform to enable new applications. Social networking platforms expose data, tools, and placement on social networking sites to third-party developers, allowing them to create new functionality that sits on top of the social network. The platform ecosystem is a win-win-win for everyone: Users have access to more functionality, software developers have access to data and users, and the social network becomes more interesting, valuable, sticky, and engaging.

Internet users want applications that are "socially aware" of their identity and relationships; most users do not want to re-enter profile information and re-establish friend connections on every new site they visit. Social networking platforms allow developers and businesses to tap the existing social graph for their applications and Web sites instead of having to reinvent the wheel. Similarly, Social network APIs such as the MySpace API, Facebook Connect, and Google Friend Connect, take the online social network beyond the native social networking sites to external Web sites and applications. Thus, social network is enabling a new Web experience that allows us to bring our online identities and friends with us to whatever site or application we choose to visit on the Internet.

Facebook and LinkedIn established a clear friend request protocol and culture of trust for their networks. Facebook did so through e-mail-based identity confirmation and modeling their online networks off of real offline networks. For example, when you join Facebook, one of the first things you must do is choose one or more networks with which to be associated. Your options include schools, employers, cities, and other real offline networks that have real offline trust. LinkedIn took a different approach to establish protocol. By accepting a LinkedIn connection request, you implicitly agree to share your network and to professionally vouch for this person. Most people aren't willing to vouch for strangers, so they are more careful about accepting LinkedIn connection requests from strangers.

An important precursor to social platforms was the ability to embed YouTube videos on MySpace pages. Prior to MySpace, YouTube struggled to hit a tipping point and really take off. It had a small and scattered community of fans that used its video-sharing service as one-offs. Joining forces with MySpace changed everything overnight–YouTube found itself with a large global audience and infrastructure for word-of-mouth distribution. MySpace saw its pages come to life with rich, multimedia video and its Web traffic shot-up impressively. Naturally, a host of similar successes leads to high degree of heterogeneity in terms of social network platforms. This quickly led to the demand for interfacing standards. In 2007, product managers at Google led an effort, called OpenSocial, to define a set of open source social APIs that could work across any social networking site or other Web site. Having a standard set of APIs would theoretically enable developers to write an application once and have it work on any OpenSocial site. OpenSocial has since spun off from Google as its own independent nonprofit organization and is supported by an industry consortium of social networking sites.

14.11.3 Social CRM

Traditional CRM is effectively a networking tool that lets sales reps view "profiles" of their accounts, capture deal information, track performance, communicate with contacts, and share information internally with sales managers and other members of their account team. However, the social networking sites differ from traditional CRM in one critical dimension—they are conduits for bidirectional visibility and interaction. By making the customer an active participant in CRM, not only will companies benefit from more accurate data and better engagement, but they will also finally achieve a true 360-degree view of their customers across every touch point—whether it is online, on the phone, presales, mid-deal, post-sales, or beyond.

The defining characteristics of social CRM are

- Social experience
- Mobile engagement
- Co-creation
- Gamification

The explosive potential of social CRM in future can only realized on the foundation of relationship-based enterprise. Hence, the rationale for the elaborate relationship-based enterprise architecture and the framework of Management by Collaboration (MBC) established painstakingly in Chapter 1 of this book.

Many of the innovations from social networking are making their way into CRM systems like SAP CRM.

14.12 Summary

In this chapter, we looked at the post-implementation period in the cycle of a SAP implementation. We visited aspects of SAP deployment, configuration changes and enhancements, SAP release upgrades, and Help Desk. Following this, we looked at measures for ensuring the longevity of the SAP team member's association with the company. In the last section, we describe the latest SAP HANA database solution targeted at replacing the existing installed base of Oracle, DB2, and so on.

SAP CRM IMPLEMENTATION AND BEYOND

VI

Chapter 15 presents various aspects related to valuing the ROI of a SAP CRM implementation using the method of Balance Scorecard. In the last chapter of the book, Chapter 16, we visit several aspects of the intelligent customer-centric enterprise and how SAP is gearing up for enabling relationship-based enterprises to address these emerging challenges in the twenty-first century.

An enterprise-wide solution like SAP, which embodies the process-oriented view of the organization, must provide the means for evaluating and maximizing the value delivered by the enterprise to all of its stakeholders. From the perspective of the collaborative enterprise, it is evident that a single stakeholder cannot sustain an appreciable ROI for itself at the cost of the other stakeholders. An ROI for different stakeholders is not in opposition to each other—it is not a "zero-sum game."

Chapter 15

Valuing the Relationship-Based Enterprise

Chapter 1 of this book, "The Relationship-Based Enterprise," dealt at length on the collaborative nature of today's enterprises. In the subsequent chapters, we have seen various aspects of SAP CRM that enable an enterprise to operate as an integrated, enterprise-wide, process-oriented, information-driven, real-time enterprise. We have also seen that as organizational and environmental conditions have become more complex, globalized, and therefore competitive, processes provide a framework for dealing effectively with the issues of performance improvement, capability development, and adaptation to the changing environment.

In turn, continued value addition along every business process has become an essential prerequisite for viability of not only a particular process but also for that of the organization as a whole. Here is the fundamental rationale for measuring and valuing an enterprise in terms of the value determinants that are relevant to all stakeholders of an organization. These include not only the traditionally known stakeholders of a company, like the company's investors and customers, but also the suppliers, managers, and employees of the company as well.

An enterprise-wide solution like SAP CRM, which embodies the process-oriented view of the organization, must provide the means for evaluating and maximizing the value delivered by the enterprise to all of its stakeholders. The first half of this chapter provides a fairly detailed introduction to such a perspective on the value created by an enterprise. It also discusses the now-popular Balanced Scorecard (BSC) approach for valuation of an enterprise or the enterprise of a company. It suggests an interpretation of the scorecard in terms of the value of the five primary stakeholders of an enterprise: customers, vendors, investors, managers, and employees.

15.1 Enterprise Stakeholders

An organization is defined by a constellation of collaborations. All collaborative relationships are truly stakeholder relationships; thus, a company is truly a continuum of collaborative stakeholder relationships. A corporation is embedded in a network of interdependent stakeholder relationships that are defined mutually and dynamically. The competitive response of an organization is the result of all such stakeholder relationships or collaborations. One of the earliest proponents of what is known as the stakeholder theory is R. E. Freeman, who wrote *Strategic Management: A Stakeholder Approach*. The stakeholders are investors, owners, management, political groups, customers, community, employees, trade associations, suppliers, alliance partners, government, competitors, and so forth.

Two kinds of stakeholders exist: primary and secondary. Primary stakeholders are those entities that are affected directly by the success or decline of a company like investors, financial institutions, customers, suppliers/vendors, and employees. Secondary stakeholders like the media, government, and regulatory agencies are affected only indirectly by the varying fortunes of the company, but they definitely exercise influence on the functioning of the company. Sometimes, this influence may not only exceed the influence of the primary stakeholders but may also prove to be decisive for the enterprise.

For the value created by an enterprise, the five stakeholders of primary importance are

1. Customer
2. Investors
3. Vendors
4. Managers
5. Employees

Collaborations are characterized by contracts that can range from explicit to the implicit. These contracts specify or allude to what the company can expect from each stakeholder in achieving its objectives and what each stakeholder can expect in return from the organization. For instance, explicit contracts are contracts whereby a customer pays a predetermined amount of money for availing of the company's products or services. Similarly, implicit contracts are contracts whereby an employee gets a promotion, depending on the performance with reference to the expectations set at the beginning of the concerned period.

It is with reference to these contracts, whether implicit or explicit, that every stakeholder invests capital in the continued and envisaged future success of the company; this capital could be financial, managerial, intellectual, environmental, social, and so forth. The continued involvement, interest, and commitment of the stakeholders are dependent on the stakeholders getting a reasonable *return on investment* (*ROI*). This ROI could be different for different stakeholders. For the customers, it could be in terms of assured competitive products, services, support, and upgrades in the future. For the vendors, it could be in terms of assured supply contracts on favorable terms. For the investors, it could be in terms of an assured dividend in the future. For the managers, it could be in terms of an assured rise up the corporate ladder, and for the employees of the company, it could be in terms of assured security, professional development, and career growth.

15.1.1 From Built-to-Last to Built-to-Perform Organizations

In the early 1980s, Peters and Waterman published a study of 43 major American corporations. The sample included such household names as Disney, Boeing, IBM, Mars, McDonalds, Dupont, Levi-Strauss, Procter & Gamble, 3M, Caterpillar, Hewlett Packard, Kodak, Wang, and Atari. All 43 companies were selected because they had been innovative and adaptable over reasonably long periods, that is, *built to last* organizations. The study reached the conclusion that the cause of the excellence displayed by these companies lay in eight prominent attributes that they shared in common.

The eight attributes were

1. Stick to the knitting
2. Close to the customer
3. Productivity through people
4. Autonomy and entrepreneurship
5. Hands-on and value driven
6. Bias for action
7. Simple form and lean staff
8. Simultaneous loose–tight properties

Each of them had a characteristics pattern of actions, position, posture, and process associated with them. The conclusion drawn was that, if others imitate these eight attributes, they too would become excellent.

The eight-attribute plan proved to be a disappointment because, within 5 years, two-thirds of the companies in the sample had slipped from the pinnacle. A number of other studies followed since then, but none can be judged to have found the best way for all companies to excel in business. For instance, except for General Electric, of the top 12 companies that made up the Dow Jones index in 1900, none survive today. Almost 40% of the names that made up the Fortune 500 10 years ago have disappeared, while of the 1970 list, 60% have been acquired or folded up. Clearly, the best-run and most widely admired companies are unable to sustain their market-beating levels of performance for an extended period of time. The very processes that enable them to survive over the long term thwart them from renewal and reinvention and, finally, fossilize them.

This seems to suggest that one of the fundamental tenets of business that a company should be *built to last* is seriously flawed. Rather than aiming for continuity, enterprises should aim for changes or variations to ensure *built to perform* organizations (see Section 15.6 "Performance Prism"). Analogous to Michael Porter's concept of the value chain that essentially reflects costs at various stages, one can conceive of a casual *performance chain* running from activities to costs to revenues to the valuation of the enterprise in the capital markets. Enterprises should innovate, renew, and reinvent themselves and their businesses to survive in the turbulent market environment.

15.2 Aspects of Enterprise Value

From the perspective of the collaborative enterprise, it is evident that a single stakeholder cannot sustain an appreciable ROI for itself at the cost of the other stakeholders. For instance, shareholder value cannot be maximized indefinitely by reducing product quality or customer service, negotiating arbitrarily lower rates from suppliers/vendors, or cutting down remuneration of the employees. An ROI for different stakeholders is not in opposition to each other; it is not a *zero-sum game*. We have already seen concrete proof of this in the last century when manufacturing quality and cost were mistakenly believed to be in opposition to each other. As it has been shown in the 1990s, an enterprise can achieve excellent quality *at reduced costs*.

Although all companies focus on creating value for all constituencies, these efforts do not or are not able to address all the constituencies simultaneously. An enterprise does not usually have the capabilities to track the information that is essential for maintaining a cross-functional view of the impact of efforts for

- Improving value addition activities at local activity centers
- Minimizing the non-value-addition activities at local activity centers

The apparent improvement in value addition or non-value-addition activities needs to be tracked enterprise-wide across all functions and constituencies. This is because value addition or non–value addition at a local level may not be so for the company as a whole. It has been well accepted by now that output of the organization as a whole cannot be maximized only by maximizing the output of each constituting organizational unit or activity. For overall efficiency and effectiveness, a unit may often have to undertake activities that are essentially non–value added at the operational level of the unit. SAP CRM provides such a system that generates, retains, analyzes, and reports on parameters that can track activity-level measures of performance, revenues, and expenditures. More importantly, SAP CRM highlights cross-functional dependencies of activities across the enterprise.

15.2.1 Value to Customers

Value to customers is one of the most important values that are created by the company. Customers value the product and services not only in terms of its innate use but also in terms of its price relative to the competition. This in turn leads to other satellite criteria that ultimately lead to customers' continued patronage of the company's products. Customers look for

- Responsiveness
- Price
- Quality
- Flexibility
- Utility
- Variability or the range of options
- Reliability
- Standardized interfaces and auxiliary systems
- Durability
- Maintainability
- Upgradability
- Support
- Service
- Innovation

Some of these properties characterizing a product/service may be in opposition to each other; the constellation of values that become applicable may vary from one product to another. Moreover, over the course of time, even the values for one particular product or closely related products may undergo changes. As we have seen in Chapter 7, Section 7.1.1 "Value-Added View of Business Processes," the value shifts may happen because of competitive products, changes in technology, or changes in the regulatory conditions. In fact, in the absence of other causes, value shifts may also occur merely because of the customer's illusive urge for innovation and the need for more than ordinary experiences. Added to this is the complication arising from the fact that the customer base itself is not static and keeps on changing dynamically, depending on the shift in critical value determinants (CVDs).

The customary way to determine the relative importance of value determinants is through customer satisfaction surveys and subsequent customer value analysis to generate normalized customer satisfaction indices. These indices may differ depending on the objectives of the customer value analysis.

15.2.2 *Value to Shareholders*

Shareholders expect a reasonable ROI in the long term. It must be mentioned that whereas none can deny that higher returns are the basic motives for any investment, shareholders also value their contribution in the creation of wealth and job opportunities for their community. They derive immense satisfaction by sharing the created wealth with the community through the employees of the company. If a company demonstrates that it is utilizing its capital competitively and has a viable strategy that will sustain this rate of return or better it in the future, they will continue to maintain their financial interests in the company.

From the traditional earnings point of view, for industrial enterprises geared to mass production strategies, the investors look for Return on Capital Employed (ROCE), Earnings per Share (E/S), Return on Assets (ROA), etc., in terms of integrity and quality of accounting information like

- Relevance
- Reliability
- Neutrality
- Fidelity
- Verifiability
- Comparability
- Consistency

However, the earnings point of view has not proven to be a reliable indicator of the value of a company. It is primarily oriented toward existing and past values and is not geared to address its arc in the future. Earnings are a static concept that uses linear projections based on the figures of the last accounting year. The underlying assumption in the traditional approach is that a company's value can be forecast based on its reported earnings. That this is erroneous has been established beyond doubt by the fact that market values of successful companies have always been greater than twice its book value.

On the other hand, the cash flow perspective sees value as a function of the expected future cash flows, which reflects the company's value in the long term and makes due allowance for the attendant risks. Unlike the accounting approach, in the cash flow approach, a strong correlation has been found to exist between the market price per share and predicted value per share based on cash flow forecasts.

According to the cash flow perspective, the investors look for

- Increased future surplus cash flows
- Assured future cash dividends
- Share price appreciation

For a company with relatively small capital, the earnings and cash flow perspective may not produce appreciably different results, but, even in such cases when we factor in accounts payable and inventories, the two approaches may provide highly divergent views.

15.2.3 Value to Managers

By convention, in the discussions on stakeholders, senior managers are usually grouped with owner/investors, which is incorrect. Managers with their responsibilities for driving the growth and profitability of the company have a different perspective of the values that are important to them vis-à-vis the owner/investors.

Senior managers look for the following:

- The freedom to articulate the vision of the organization and translate the same into objectives for the organization
- The latitude to focus on a select set of strategies and tactics
- The latitude to form the management team that believes in this vision and gels with this approach
- The facility to define the measures of performances for the organization as a whole as well as the individual business and operational managers
- The authority to allocate and deploy systems and resources for executing the plans
- The authority to institute and implement systems for measuring and reporting on the measures of performance for different functions and levels of the organization at predefined time periods or on ad hoc basis
- The latitude to mold the policies and procedures in line with the company's vision
- The latitude to commit research and development (R&D) efforts on technological and managerial issues that they perceive to be of importance for the future
- Remuneration that is commensurate with risks and targeted tasks

With the increase in the pace and pulse of businesses, the leeway available for CEOs and other senior executives has been diminishing continuously. The window of tolerance for failing revenues or periods of executing corrective strategies is progressively becoming smaller. In such circumstances, the hard-driving managers become conscious of the value that is catalyzed by them for the enterprise and the returns that they accrue to themselves. It is a supreme irony of our times that, with their increasing power and prestige, the CEOs and members of a management team are also most vulnerable to being summarily replaced due to perceived nonperformance.

15.2.4 Value to Employees

As described in Chapter 1, Section 1.3 "Management by Collaboration," the dynamic changes in the market and global competition being confronted by companies have resulted in more flexible organizations. These organizations are populated with empowered workers who are multiskilled with enhanced responsibilities. No organization can sustain the generation of value at high levels for extended periods without a corresponding value added to the employees of the company.

Employees value factors like the following:

- Opportunities for participating and contributing significantly to the activities of the enterprise
- Reasonable compensation

- Opportunities to learn, develop skills, and handle challenging roles
- Access to all relevant information and resources for making decisions and discharging their responsibilities creditably
- Opportunities for recognition and rewards
- Opportunities for advancement
- Opportunities for training

The integrated, real-time, and transparent access to relevant data provided by SAP CRM empowers the traditionally deprived members of the organization to make timely decisions and derive the satisfaction of being involved meaningfully in ensuring the well-being of the company.

In many ways, the value for the employees is analogous to the value for the external customers. Like the customers of the company, the effectiveness of employee value is gauged through employee satisfaction surveys that are administered on a periodic basis.

15.2.5 Value to Vendors

In recent times, vendors are getting increased recognition for the value that they add not only to the final output of an enterprise but also to its profitability. Vendors play a major role in enhancing the overall performance of the organization, be it in terms of quality, input costs, overheads, responsiveness to the changes in the market, and so forth. Increasingly, they are perceived more as enterprise partners, rather than as the traditional adversaries to be browbeaten to lower prices.

Vendors in turn look for the following values in the value-creating enterprise of a company:

- Steady order commitments
- Optimal lead times
- Immediate information on deliveries, rejects, returns, and so on in terms of the quantity and control information (such as delivery note numbers and batch numbers)
- Systematic invoice verification
- Prompt payments for verified and accepted invoices
- Interfaces with an enterprise-wide, implemented system like SAP CRM
- Sharing changes in production schedules
- Sharing changes in the positions of inventories vis-à-vis the production orders and so on
- Sharing results and analysis of quality tests on supplied materials
- Participation in plans of new products, models, technologies, and production processes

As mentioned in Chapter 1, Section 1.3.7 "The Virtual Enterprise," only mature Customer Relationship Management (CRM) like SAP CRM can provide the backbone for holding together the virtual value chain across such collaborative relationships with vendors.

15.3 Economic Value Added (EVA)

Economic Value Added (EVA) is a new type of managerial accounting criterion that recognizes that capital, whether equity or borrowed, is simply another resource used in the enterprise.

Traditional accounting methods, which are transaction based, take into account sales (i.e., revenue) and expenses (i.e., purchase and interest payments) for computing profitability that is determined by the measure of the Return on Investment (ROI) defined by

$$Return = (Revenue - Expense)$$

EVA treats both stockholder capital (i.e., equity capital with zero dividends and its average return of about 6% higher than long-term governmental bonds, as its cost) and borrowed capital (with its interest payment as its cost) as expense items. Consequently, if the enterprise uses a combination of the borrowed and shareholder capitals, the cost of capital is a weighted average of the two costs. As EVA is computed as revenue less expenses (including all expenses like purchases, capital, and taxes), the EVA is a genuine measure of the value created from the enterprise operations at various levels.

Once the capital is seen as a resource, the focus shifts from a simplified Return on Investment (ROI) to the Yield on Investment (YOI) that primarily measures revenue generated for the capacity scheduled. The emphasis shifts to minimizing the amount of resources used for generating the revenue, that is, to increase the efficiency with which the stockholder equity is used. Accordingly, the managers are prompted to aim for the following at the operational level:

■ Use less capital.
■ Earn more profit without using more capital.
■ Invest capital in as high-return projects as possible.

Because of the critical role played by employees in the operations of the enterprise, most EVAs incorporate a method for distributing bonuses and dividends to the employees. EVA effectively expands the definition of ownership beyond that of shareholders (who share the risk of the venture) to also include the employees whose participation and commitment also contribute to the success of the enterprise.

15.4 Value-Based Management

For delivering superior stakeholder value, especially shareholder value, a company's management must not only be able to formulate strategies but should also be able to execute them. Value-based management (VBM) ensures the implementation of a corporate strategy by directly linking the strategy, finance, and operations within a company. By linking strategic objectives to resource allocation and performance management, the operational decision making is focused fully on delivering the strategic objectives.

To be effective, VBM entails combining the internal, external, historic, and predicted views with the financial and nonfinancial drivers of the business. Leveraging VBM essentially involves the following four steps:

1. Understanding what factors drive value
2. Finding out where value is created or destroyed
3. Establishing value as the criterion for decision making
4. Embedding value into the corporate culture

The financial-oriented VBMs currently in vogue are primarily aimed at operationalizing the VBM so that individual members of a company can perceive and identify with the shareholder value that is contributed by the various functions and activities within the organization. But, it must be noted that there is already recognition that a financial-oriented view needs to be supplemented also with a value-added view of manufacturing directly. ERP systems basically perpetuate the philosophy of top-down, build-to-stock, and supply-driven mass-producing manufacturing strategy. The value-added view of manufacturing is in line with the increasing emphasis on

- Demand pull reflected in order changes
- Flow manufacturing entailing fast changeovers

Like the Corporate Performance Monitor (CPM) discussed later, it is possible to envisage a Manufacturing Performance Monitor (MPM) that monitors in real-time manufacturing processes in terms of the various technical and economic value drivers.

15.4.1 Time Value of Customers and Shareholder Value

As suggested in Chapter 1, a company's market valuation or shareholder value is the sum total of the envisaged lifetime values (LTVs) of its current and future customers, that is, its customer capital. Customer capital is like a miner's canary—the bird whose death signals dangerous conditions in mines. It is the most accurate (if grisly) leading indicator of the enterprise's competitive advantage as well as that of its partners and competitors.

In this framework, the total value of the company, its market capitalization, is equal to the present value of the total predictable lifetime value (LTV) of its current and future customers, discounted for risk. Figure 15.1 shows the CLTV curve: a graph of Customers-Projected Lifetime Value against Time. The earlier quarters are more accurate as they are based on information on the sales pipelines, work-in-process, and backlog orders that contribute in making these earlier numbers more reliable. But further out on the curve, the envisaged numbers are based more on extrapolations of investments and trends. With the increasing risks associated with the progressive forecasts into the future, the present value placed on them progressively decreases to zero. *The area under the curve represents the customer's market capitalization.* The objective of any management team to increase the shareholder value then translates into increasing the area under this curve.

As evident from looking at the CLTV Curve in Figure 15.2, this is achievable in the following two ways:

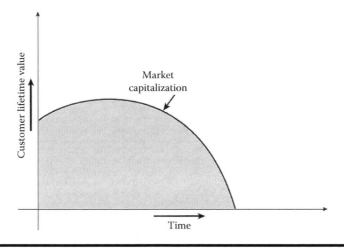

Figure 15.1   Market capitalization in terms of Customer Life Time Value (CLTV).

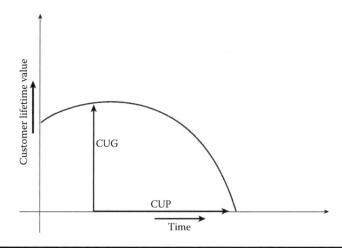

Figure 15.2 Higher market capitalization in terms of higher CUGs and longer CUPs.

1. Increasing the customer-differential gap (CUG) that corresponds to the gap between the enterprise customer's lifetime value (LTV) and those of your closest competitors

    The CUG can be enhanced by
    – Migrating the customers to higher value alternatives of the current offerings
    – Increasing the range/type of offerings
    – Increasing the total quantum of consumption of current offerings
    – Reducing dramatically the cost of serving the existing customers
    – Acquiring new customers!

    The increase in CUG effects the height of the curve because, assuming the cost structure is unaltered, CUG directly impacts both sales and gross margins positively to show up as increased earnings.

2. Increasing the length of the customer-differential period (CUP) for which the enterprise can sustain the CUG once the superior returns generated by the enterprise start attracting additional competition

A long CUP is typically a function of high barriers to entry for competitors' intent on a portion of the same market or high switching costs for customers and partners contemplating defecting to the enterprise's competitors. Long CUPs contribute to higher stock price by increasing the duration of the period of such customer differential. Long CUPs effectively represent a reduction in the long-term risks, resulting in much lower discount rates applied to such risks, which in turn results in extending the curve even further toward the right side.

Thus, the management of shareholder value effectively transforms into sustaining increasingly higher customer lifetime values (LTVs) for longer duration of time, that is, higher CUGs and longer CUPs. Although CUGs and CUPs are interdependent, CUPs primarily represent the sustainability of CUGs, and the enterprise must focus first on CUPs and then on CUGs. This is because while effects on CUGs are short lived and can be corrected easily, the effects on CUPs are more far reaching and have a bigger impact on stock price than CUG. Generally, traditional enterprises with P&L focus already have the tool for managing the CUGs, but they do not have a tool to manage the CUPs.

All line functions need to reevaluate their old metrics to ensure that they are current with the customer-centric and customer-responsive stances of the twenty-first-century enterprises. We discuss these issues next.

15.5 Balance Scorecard (BSC)

The BSC is a VBM system based on four distinct perspectives for evaluating the performance of a company: financial, customer, internal, and learning. The BSC aims to provide a balance between the external and internal measures of performance, between short- and long-term objectives, between financial and nonfinancial measures, and between lagging and leading indicators. It is not limited to being merely a measurement and control system but has actually developed over the course of time into a full-featured management system for the successful implementation of a company's strategy.

As discussed in Chapter 1's "Knowledge as the New Capital," in this postindustrial and postmodern era of information, the focus of capital and investments has changed dramatically. In the industrial era, all measures and managerial assessments were geared toward the efficiency with which financial capital could be allocated for capturing as quickly as possible the economies of scale for maximizing the return on capital employed (ROCE). In this postmodern computerized era, however, a company's competitiveness resides primarily in the collaborative systems, processes, and people that enable it to be flexible and reconfigure rapidly in response to the changes in the marketplace.

It should be noted that a company's emphasis is not on the capability to ingest the latest technology per se, because that would continue to change in future too. The emphasis is related more to the capability to confront any changes in the market with a strategy that will not only make the customers continue to value the company's products and services but also differentiate them effectively from those provided by the competitors. This is the subtle reason why a few years back General Motor's much known foray into highly automated manufacturing facilities to beat the Japanese on productivity and quality was not very successful.

Thus, a company needs a management system to assess and evaluate its strategy in terms of competitiveness and performance in the future. There is also the important need for the company to be able to dynamically monitor the progress and performance of the execution of these strategies, which will then enable the company to administer any corrections or adjustments based on the real-time operational feedback received from such a system. The BSC is precisely such a strategic management system that enables an enterprise to monitor and manage the execution of its value-adding and value-creating strategies effectively. Enterprises also need an information system that would empower them to implement the BSC.

BSC provides companies with a framework for translating the company's vision and strategy into a coherent set of performance measures. BSC derives the objectives and measures of the value determinants or the corresponding performance drivers based on the vision and strategy of the company. As shown in Figure 15.3, the BSC framework is constituted of the following four perspectives:

- Financial
- Customer
- Internal business processes
- Learning and growth

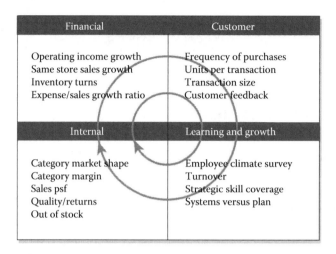

Figure 15.3 The Balance Scorecard (BSC) framework.

BSC retains the financial perspective of the company's performance that is essentially based on past performance and is valid for short-term performance in the immediate future. However, it supplements this traditional perspective with those of the customer and the internal system, process, and people that determine the company's value-generating potential and hence long-term financial performance in the future.

The customer's perspective ensures the continual relevance of the products and services provided by the company. The internal perspective of business processes and the people ensures that the company surpasses the customer's expectations on critical value determinants like quality, timeliness, innovation, and service. It is in this sense that the BSC represents a balance between the external value determinants of the customers and shareholders and the corresponding internal value drivers of the critical systems, business processes, and people.

Two kinds of value drivers exist: outcome and performance. Outcome drivers are lagging indicators like financial measures that are objective, quantifiable, and past facing. On the other hand, performance drivers are leading indicators that link with the company's strategy and provide the rationale for achievements of the outcome drivers. Although performance drivers are future facing, the impact and effectiveness of performance drivers on the outcome drivers are highly subjective. This is compensated by the dynamic nature of the BSC system that treats evaluation and feedback as important elements of the framework. The value drivers are constantly under tests for continued relevance in the market, and any deviations observed in the customer's value determinants are immediately cascaded in terms of the changes in the value drivers' measures or the value drivers themselves. This corresponds to the learning and growth perspective of the BSC framework. It represents the capability of institutional learning, which is the powerful concept of *double-loop* learning that we spoke about in Chapter 1, Section 1.3.6 "Learning Enterprise," which gives tremendous advantages to companies in these times of rapidly changing markets.

In fact, the whole BSC framework is based on a perceived cause-and-effect relationship between the various strategies, organizational elements, and processes of the enterprise. It is in the context of these assumptions that the BSC also incorporates the cause-and-effect relationships in terms of the relationships between the various outcome and performance drivers. For instance, the ROCE driver (in the financial perspective) is dependent on customer loyalty (in the customer's perspective).

Customer loyalty is dependent on the organization's product quality and responsiveness (in the internal business processes perspective), which in turn is dependent on the minimization of product defects, knowledge of the customer's prior transaction history, recorded preferences, and so on (learning and growth perspective). It is due to this that the multiple objectives and measures of BSC do not entail complex trade-offs but can easily be integrated into a consistent framework of 20–25 value drivers that can help navigate the strategy of the company successfully through the turbulent market space.

The strategic management of enterprises using BSC involves the following stages:

■ Mapping the company's strategy into the BSC framework in terms of the strategic objectives and drivers for BSC. This may also involve reconciling or prioritizing among various objectives or defining differing objectives and drivers for different divisions. This stage identifies all processes that are critical to the strategic performance of the enterprise. It must be noted that the BSC is a methodology for implementing a company's strategy and not for formulating one.

■ Communicating the link between the strategic objectives and measures throughout the organization at all levels. This may also involve operationalizing the defined set of measures to the specifics of the local circumstances for the various departmental and functional units of the company. BSCs are usually defined at the level of strategic business units (SBUs), but for a multidivisional company, the defined BSC may incline more toward the financial perspective.

■ Setting targets, devising aligned strategic initiatives, and planning/scheduling initiatives to achieve a breakthrough performance. This may also include financial planning and budgeting as an integrated part of the BSC. From the customer's perspective, this step should include requirements of both existing and potential customers.

■ Enhancing performance through feedback and learning based on operational data and reviews. This may entail reprioritizing or changing the performance thresholds or even the value drivers themselves. The latter may become necessary either because of the changes in the marketplace or because the selected set of value drivers may be ineffectual.

Figure 15.4 shows the BSC approach to create a strategy-focused organization.

In the BSC framework, the financial perspective enables a reality check of the strategic management activity of the enterprise. This is because all strategic initiatives meant for improving the quality, flexibility, and customer satisfaction may not necessarily translate into improved financial results. If the improved operational outcome as seen from the other three perspectives defined by the company does not end in improved financial results, it may be a powerful indicator of the need for reformulation of the strategy itself. All cause-and-effect relationships that knit a BSC program must eventually link to financial objectives. Therefore, the financial perspective is preeminent among all perspectives of the BSC framework.

The standard BSC framework talks of only four perspectives, but, if required, the framework can be supplemented with additional perspectives of stakeholders discussed in the Section 15.1 "Enterprise Stakeholders." In view of the increased importance of supply-chain management (SCM) for the extended collaborative enterprises of today, a prime candidate for addition would be the suppliers/vendors of the company. As we will discuss in the final chapter of this book, the suppliers will play as critical a role in the success of the enterprise as any of its constituent SBUs for the extended collaborative enterprises. In the remaining part of this section, we briefly look at the various perspectives of the standard BSC framework.

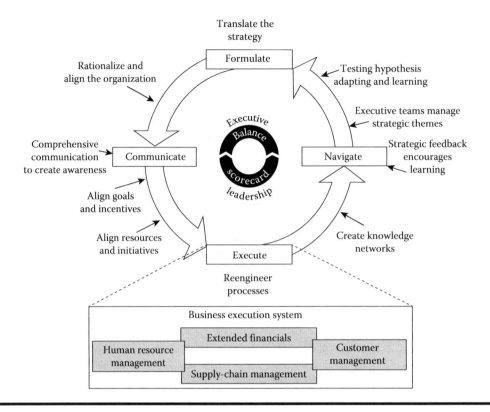

Figure 15.4   BSC Approach to create a Strategy-focused Company.

15.5.1 Financial Perspective

As mentioned earlier, the financial performance measures indicate whether a company's strategy, implementation, and execution are translating into bottom-line financial results. Depending on the business strategy, the financial objectives could be in terms of

- ROCE, economic value add (EVA) or operating income, and maintaining the market share
- Rapid sales growth and increased market share
- Maximize the generation of cash flow

15.5.2 Customer's Perspective

The customer's perspective mainly addresses the customer- and market-oriented strategies that would deliver improved financial results. This involves the identification of the market segments of interest, the value propositions for each of these segments, and the measures that would help in ascertaining the performance of the company in the selected segments.

The basic outcome measures for this perspective could be

- Customer acquisition
- Customer satisfaction
- Customer retention
- Customer profitability

15.5.3 *Internal Business Processes Perspective*

The internal business processes perspective provides focus on the business processes that are critical to the success of the enterprise. These processes selected for improvement could be existing processes (as discussed in Chapter 7, Section 7.2.2 "Selecting Business Processes for BPR"), or they could also be entirely new processes conceived as a consequence of the strategy of the company. For instance, an excellent example of such a process could be a provision for a Web-based procurement of a company's goods and services.

SAP CRM contributes directly to a company's performance in this perspective through its now-familiar library of the best-of-business scenarios and processes as well as its ability to incorporate innovative processes or variations on the existing processes by means of rapid reconfiguration of the IMG.

15.5.4 *Learning and Growth Perspective*

The learning and growth perspective addresses the need to build and maintain an appropriate infrastructure for the long-term growth and success of the company. Contributions from the other perspectives, especially regarding envisaged shifts in customer value, may identify the technologies and products essential to the continued relevance of the company's offerings in the marketplace. These contributions may encompass the following:

1. People's skills
2. Information and support systems
3. Organizational processes and procedures

This perspective comprehensively covers employee-related issues like employee satisfaction, employee training, advancement and promotion policies, employee-friendly policies and procedures, and productivity-multiplying application environments. SAP CRM is an enabling environment for supporting the management of all these perspectives, an aspect that is tackled in the next section.

15.6 Performance Prism

Though the Balance Scorecard takes a far broader view than shareholder value, no mention is made of end users, or employees, or suppliers, or regulators, or local communities. The best way for organizations to survive and prosper in the long term would be to address the wants and needs of all of their stakeholders and deliver value to each of them. Most long-term investors already realize that for companies to be successful over time, they must address multiple constituencies. The only sustainable way of delivering shareholder value in the twenty-first century is to deliver stakeholder value. The Performance Prism provides a framework for ensuring better stakeholder relationships (Neely et al. 2002).

15.6.1 *Performance Prism Framework*

The Performance Prism Framework is based fundamentally on the notion of stakeholder value rather than that of shareholder value. It does not assume that the only stakeholders that matter are the shareholders and customers. It results in the organization being best positioned to deliver the best value to all of its stakeholders by ensuring that the organization's strategies, processes, and capabilities are aligned and integrated with each other.

On the other hand, the Performance Prism also recognizes the fact that organizations are becoming increasingly demanding of their stakeholders too. The following are examples:

- *Investors*: Capital for growth, greater risk-taking, long-term support
- *Customers*: Profitability, retention, loyalty, advocacy, feedback
- *Employees*: Flexibility, multiskilling, cross-training
- *Suppliers*: More outsourcing, fewer vendors, integration
- *Alliance Partners*: Cross-selling, co-development, cost sharing
- *Regulators*: Cross-border consistency, early involvement

The Performance Prism consists of five interrelated perspectives on performance that pose specific vital questions:

- *Stakeholder Satisfaction*: Who are the key stakeholders and what do they want or need?
- *Stakeholder Contribution*: What does the enterprise want and need from the stakeholders on a reciprocal basis?
- *Strategies*: What strategies are needed to satisfy the wants and needs of the stakeholders while satisfying the requirements of the enterprise too?
- *Processes*: What processes need to be in place to enable the enterprise to execute its strategies?
- *Capabilities*: What capabilities need to put in place to allow the enterprise to operate its processes?

15.7 Customer-Centric Activity-Based Revenue Accounting (ABRA)

As indicated in Chapter 7's note "Theory of Constraints (TOC)," a singular drive to minimize costs to the exclusion of all other factors underlies many disastrous managerial decisions. In analogy with ABC, one can conceive of ABRA that involves assigning revenues and costs explicitly to *both* individual customers and processes or activities. Like ABC, ABRA also envisages the enterprise as a collective whole of activities. ABRA would engender the firm to be designed around customer-facing units where activities, costs, and revenues converge on the customer. ABRA would enable the fundamental shift from the enterprise to the customer by shifting the focus from the performance of the *enterprise* as a whole to the *activities* performed by the enterprise (along with their associated costs and revenues).

ABRA is based on the following:

- Activities of the enterprise
- Activity costs
- Revenues resulting from activities
- Measure of performances as the revenues resulting from activities less the cost of performing them

Like ABC, ABRA also identifies activities, activity revenues, revenue drivers, and revenue objects. Because value added for the customer cannot be observed directly, the contribution of activities to customer revenues is estimated by analyzing the relevant data. After assessing the activity costs by using ABC, the profitability of each activity is assessed by comparing activity revenues with activity costs. Ultimately, ABRA separates the offerings contributing to customer profitability from those incurring costs.

ABC is useful wherever the enterprise offerings are clearly separable from the underlying specifications and can also be made to particular specifications known to add value for the customer; the corresponding activities and costs can be identified and optimized (including elimination), and performance can be improved without varying these specifications. In contrast, ABRA may be useful in improving performance in cases like delivery of services (which are innately time dependent and perishable) where the specifications adding value are not fully known and, moreover, are inseparable from the corresponding activity or activities.

1. By allocating costs to customers and revenue to activities and, hence, by enabling comparison of revenues to costs customer by customer and activity by activity, ABRA also provides the rationale for evaluating and compensating individual performance.
2. An ABRA-like approach can also be used for focusing on transactions driving customer loyalty or retention; the costs and revenues will change suitably to aspects that are relevant to the changed context.

15.8 CRM Metrics

Metrics help companies track and assess their performance and, more importantly, evaluate the returns on their CRM initiatives. In the process of implementing CRM, managers have to deal with a huge amount of data with the ultimate goal of evaluating managerial performances based on the value that each individual customer brings to the firm. In order to record and quantify those evaluations, managers need a set of indicators that measure customer values. Metrics perform this role.

The benefits of developing and using metrics are significant to companies. Some of the key benefits that accrue to the firm are

- Tighter control over business processes and CRM activities
- Means to measure changes in revenues, costs, and profits
- Benchmarks and targets to attain certain levels of performance
- Measures on return on investment (ROI)
- Aid in the acquisition and retention, preventing churn, and assisting win-back of profitable customers
- Realigning marketing resources to maximize customer value

There are two broad categories of metrics, brand-level and customer-level. Brand-level metrics are metrics that measure the brand's competitiveness in the market, such as market share, customer equity, sales growth, and so on. Customer-level metrics break down those brand-level metrics to the individual customer, such as acquisition cost per customer, size of wallet, and so on. A combination of brand-level and customer-level metrics gives managers a complete picture of how the firm or the brand fares in the market, as well as how its customer needs differ on an individual level, and how to leverage these differences to enhance the overall competitiveness of the firm. Determining which metric(s) to measure and manage should depend on how each metric relates to the desired short-term or long-term outcome. If the metric(s) chosen cannot be quantifiably related to desired outcome measures such as profitability and shareholder value, the metric(s) generally may not be worth measuring and managing.

Table 15.1 presents some commonly used metrics at both brand-level and customer-level

15.8.1 Enhancement of Measures of Performances by SAP CRM

It is important to define the right measures for assessing a company's performance and its progress toward its declared goals and objectives. SAP CRM assists in monitoring and managing the measures of performances (MOPs) to enhance the company's operational performance. With its integrated and real-time availability of operational data, SAP CRM has the enabling environment to create, monitor, and manage enterprise value. SAP CRM provides the empowered platform for SMEs to address the competitive demands of the rapidly changing marketplace and be successful in terms of

■ Improved customer relations and management
■ Reduced cycle time
■ Improved quality
■ Increased sales volumes
■ Improved margins
■ Reduced product development time
■ Reduced manpower for routine operations
■ Improved market share

The process of monitoring the MOPs can be guided by the value determinants that have been identified for the company. The value determinants can then be prioritized as well as customized suitable for the different activities within the company. Additions and deletions to the selected measures will be likely, depending on the market situations or alterations in the emphasis and focus of the measures already implemented.

The following lists show some of the performance factors that could be considered for measuring the excellence of the processes in SAP CRM.

The sales and distribution performance factors are as follows:

■ The number of new customers
■ The number of one-time customers
■ The number of customers retained
■ The number of repeat orders and type
■ The customer order-to-delivery time
■ The number of nonstandard or customized orders
■ The number of errors per order shipped
■ The percentage of back orders as a percentage of total orders
■ The percentage of on-time first delivery to customers
■ The percentage of on-time complete deliveries to customers

Table 15.1   Brand and Customer Level Metrics

Metric	Definition	Use of Metric
Market share	The percentage of a firm's sales to the sales of all firms in a given market	Brand-level
Sales growth	The increase or decrease in sales volume or sale value in a given period compared to that in the previous period	Brand-level
Acquisition rate	The proportion of prospects converted to customers	Brand-level
Acquisition cost	The acquisition spending of a focal firm per prospect acquired	Brand-level and customer-level
Retention rate	The average likelihood that a customer *makes a repurchase* from the focal firm in period t, given that this customer has purchased in the last period $t - 1$	Brand-level and customer-level
Defection rate	The average likelihood that a customer *defects* from the focal firm in period t, given that this customer has purchased in the last period $t - 1$	Brand-level and customer-level
Survival rate	The ratio of customers who continue to remain as customers (survive) until a period t from the beginning of observing these customers	Brand-level
Average lifetime duration	The average duration customers continue to remain as customers	Brand-level
P-active	The probability of a customer making a repurchase (being active) in a given period	Customer-level
Win-back rate	The ratio of acquisition of customers who had been lost in an earlier period	Brand-level
Share-of-wallet	The ratio of total sales of all customers of the focal firm in a product category to the total spending of those customers in the product category across all different firms	Brand-level and customer-level
Size of wallet	The total spending of a customer on a product category across all different firms	Customer-level
Share of category requirement	The ratio of the sales volumes of a particular product category of the focal firm or brand to the total sales volumes of the product category in the market Also considered the market share of a firm or a brand with respect to a particular product category	Brand-level and customer-level

(*Continued*)

Table 15.1 (*Continued*)   Brand and Customer Level Metrics

Metric	Definition	Use of Metric
Past customer value	The gross contribution of a customer when adjusted for the time value of money	Customer-level
RFM value	RFM stands for Recency, Frequency, and Monetary value: • Recency indicates the most recent purchase date of a customer • Frequency measures how often a customer purchases from the firm • Monetary value measures the average per transaction spending of a customer	Customer-level
Customer lifetime value	The total discounted contribution margins of a customer (excess of recurring revenues over recurring costs to the focal firm) over a specific time period	Customer-level
Customer equity	The total lifetime value of all customers of the focal firm	Brand-level

Table 15.1 lists the various metrics used either at the brand or customer level.

Given the multiplicity of dependencies and influencing factors, the selection of the right measures is a complex task. There is a need for a framework under which multiple measures are integrated and related to each other so that a set of measurements should not be perceived to be in opposition to others. Moreover, there is also a need to have the right balance between the financial and nonfinancial measures, which is the focus of the section on The Performance Prism (see Section 15.6 "Performance Prism").

15.9 Summary

This chapter introduced the perspectives on the value created by an enterprise from the point of view of its five major stakeholders, namely, customers, investors, vendors, managers, and employees. This generated value can be monitored and managed in terms of the measures of performances characterizing the operations of the company. At the end of the chapter, we looked at a sample list of improvements in measures of performances (MOPs) that have been achieved in various companies by the implementation of SAP CRM.

Chapter 16

Beyond the Relationship-Based Enterprise

In this last chapter of the book, we look at the long-term implications and prospects of the *Information Is Relationship* vision. We look at the significance of using customer intelligence to enable highly proactive and customer-responsive *decision on desktops*. Following this, we look at Application Outsourcing and a more refined variation of the Application Service Provider (ASP) model, namely, Private ASP. Web Services are another leading-edge technological solution for creating and delivering cooperative applications over the Internet.

Though gathering a certain amount of information is necessary for companies to personalize and to serve their customers better, consumers are rightly concerned regarding the abuse of their privacy. We discuss various aspects of the customer privacy and security.

In the end, we identify that *Information Is Relationship* leads to the possibility of *Relationships on Demand*, which, in turn, makes possible *Instant Relationships*.

16.1 Intelligent Customer-Centric Enterprise

Business Intelligence (BI) systems must provide business users, trading partners, and corporate clients of an enterprise rapid and easy access to the e-business applications, services, and information that they need in order to compete effectively.

BI systems should provide the following capabilities:

- Channel and cross-channel analysis and campaign applications that measure and analyze the success of the Internet as a sales, marketing, and sales channel
- One-to-one marketing analysis applications that customize and personalize applications, products, services, and information offered to consumers and clients via especially the Internet
- Analysis of content, customer, and merchandise selling applications to track how users navigate the enterprises' websites and use them to buy products

■ Supply-chain analysis applications that enable the enterprise to work with trading partners in optimizing the product supply chain to match the demand for products sold especially through the Internet
■ A singular and integrated Web interface to give internal and external users and applications a secure and managed access to enterprise application, services, and information

16.1.1 How Intelligent Is Your Enterprise?

Each piece of information in the enterprise, including that residing in the company's information systems, has a value. This value is primarily associated with the manner in which this piece of information is utilized by the enterprise for remaining competitive, providing good customer service, and optimizing e-business operations.

In analogy with Metcalfe's Law for networks (see Chapter 1's note "Metcalfe's Law and Network Effects"), the value of customer information can be assessed to be proportional to

$$n^m \times d$$

where
  n is the average number of active users
  m is the average number of employees involved in any business process from different departments
  d is the number of interacting departments involved in the primary business processes of the enterprise

16.1.2 Decisions on Desktops (DoD)

Decisions on Desktops (DoD) is the twenty-first-century analog of Bill Gates' vision of *PCs on every desktop* in the 1980s. The DoD vision in turn is dependent on the attainment of the *Business Intelligence (BI) on Desktops*.

Amid the hypercompetitive environment of the Internet, the systems must enable users to tap the intelligence latent in their data by integrating and analyzing raw data for insights into key business metrics. Desktop-based BI tools should enable real term, interactive access, analysis, and manipulation of mission-critical corporate information to provide user with valuable insight into key indicators to identify business problems and opportunities.

End users from their desktops, especially those involved with customer-facing functions, should be able to probe, slice, skewer, and dice data to assess trends and anomalies in various departments:

■ The finance department needs information on profitability in order to adapt cost structures for maximizing value addition.
■ The product plan department needs information on sales rates in order to optimally plan for production and to negotiate the most advantageous contracts with vendors.
■ The sales department needs information on which products are selling to which demographic population in which market spaces by which channel.
■ The marketing department needs information on who is buying which products in order to create intelligent marketing and advertising programs.

■ The customer relationship department needs information on its customers to retain them, to adapt its customer-facing practices and mechanisms, to drive repeat business, and to win new business.

Enterprise Information Portals (EIPs) like SAP Interactive give users a single Web-based interface to business information and to the applications that generate business information regardless of where they reside. The enterprise can personalize and customize the information and applications accessed through an EIP to match

■ Authorization level of each user
■ Role of the user

EIPs enable complete access to the information flow right from back- to front-office operational applications, to business intelligence and collaborative systems, and back to operational systems as a closed-loop information supply chain.

16.2 Prospects for the Future: Relationships on Demand!

If *Information Is Relationship* is true, then it readily admits of the possibility of *relationships on demand*—with far-reaching implications. Customer and customer interaction–related information available on demand makes it possible for the front-end employees to substitute this information for a possibly intrusive interaction with the customer for ascertaining their routine needs every time.

As we have stated in Chapter 1, companies have a wealth of knowledge in the files and records that customer-facing employees have on customer interactions. The best way to leverage this knowledge would be to free it from the shackles of experience, institutionalize it, and transfer it in real time to all employees, so that they are empowered to leverage or build further on the relationships with particular customers.

But, more significantly, this customer information does not have to be disseminated to everyone on a routine basis but only whenever required. This finally would be the realization of any marketer's dream—*instant relationships*!

16.3 Summary

In this last chapter of the book, we looked at the long-term implications and prospects of the *Information Is Relationship* vision. We also looked at the significance of using customer intelligence to enable highly proactive and customer-responsive *decision on desktops*. In the end, we identified that *Information Is Relationship* leads to the possibility of *Instant Relationships*.

Appendix A: Selecting SAP CRM Implementation Partners

Selecting the right kind of implementation partner is very critical.

For successful implementation of SAP CRM, it is critical for the company to define the objectives and the role of the SAP consulting firm. The prime objectives of the firm should be

- To help and guide the SAP CRM implementation
- To Train the core implementation team of the company
- To educate the members of the implementation team on SAP CRM product and functionality

This will ensure that the company can continue the momentum of the SAP implementation into its subsequent phases even after the exit of the consultants.

SAP CRM implementation partners should be selected on the basis of

a. SAP CRM Implementation Projects Portfolio
b. SAP CRM Consultants and their experience
c. Industry-Specific Expertise
d. Project Consulting Experience
e. Implementation Methodology
f. Location of additional office sites

It should be noted that unlike the case of the earlier projects that were predominantly for Fortune 500 companies, the projects for the Small and Medium Business (SMB) enterprises, with revenues ranging from $25 to $500 million, would require smaller teams with multiskilled consultants. SMB enterprise would not require or be able to afford individual consultant for every functional area.

Appendix B: CRM Industry Analysts

The CRM industry has many consultants and analysts whose sole responsibility is CRM research and reviews. These consultants can provide detailed reviews of any reputable CRM solution on the market. Suggested CRM experts are as follows:

- *ISM-Information Systems Management, Inc.*: It awards the Top 15 CRM Solutions annually. This award is considered the *Oscar Awards* of the CRM industry.
- *Patricia Seybold Group*: The Patricia Seybold Group is customer-centric executives' first choice for strategic insight, technology guidance, and e-business best practices. Founded in 1978 and based in Boston, Massachusetts, the firm offers customized consulting, strategic research, and executive coaching.
- *META Group*: META Group helps companies make technology (IT) decisions by providing research and analyst consultation relevant to their specific business needs. META Group Offers advisory services, consulting/benchmarking, and access to various IT publications. META Group addresses the latest technologies, industry trends, and business challenges
- *OVUM*: Ovum is an independent research and consulting company, offering expert advice on IT, Telecommunications, and E-commerce.
- *Giga Information Group*: Giga Information Group provides research, advice, and coaching on technology for e-business. Giga helps clients make strategic decisions about the technologies, people, and processes needed to excel in the new digital economy.

References

Barabasi A.-L., *Linked: The New Science of Networks* (New York: Perseus, 2002).

Berry M.J.A. and Linoff G.S., *Data Mining Techniques: For Marketing, Sales, and Customer Relationship Management* (Wiley, 2nd edn, 2004).

Blattberg R.C., Getz G., and Thomas J.S., *Customer Equity: Building and Managing Relationships As Valuable Assets* (HBR Press, 2001).

Bligh P. and Turk D., *CRM Unplugged: Realising CRM's Strategic Value* (Wiley, 2004).

Buttle F., *Customer Relationship Management: Concepts and Technologies* (Routledge, 2012).

Cairncross F., *The Death of Distance* (Boston, MA: Harvard Busines School Press, 1997).

Compaine B.M. and Read W.H., *The Information Resources Policy Handbook* (Cambridge, MA: The MIT Press, 1999).

Coveney P. and Highfield R., *Frontiers of Complexity: The Search for Order in a Chaotic World* (New York: Random House, 1995).

Das S., *Computational Business Analytics* (Boca Raton, FL: CRC Press, 2014).

Davis F.W. and Manrodt K.B., *Customer-Responsive Management: The Flexible Advantage* (Cambridge, MA: Blackwell, 1996).

Dawkins R., *The Extended Phenotype: The Long Reach of the Gene* (London, U.K.: Oxford University Press, 2000).

Delmater R. and Hancock M., *Data Mining Explained: A Manager's Guide to Customer-Centric Business Intelligence* (London, U.K.: Butterworth-Heinemann, 2001).

Dove R., *Response Ability: The Language, Structure, and Culture of the Agile Enterprise* (New York: John Wiley, 2001).

Dyche J., *The CRM Handbook* (New York: Addison-Wesley, 2002).

Edvinsson L. and Malone M.S., *Intellectual Capital* (New York: HarperBusiness, 1997).

Goldenberg B.J., *CRM in Real Time: Empowering Customer Relationships* (Information Today, 2008).

Gupta S. and Lehmann D., *Managing Customers as Investments: The Strategic Value of Customers in the Long Run* (FT Press, 2005).

Harper D., *Entrepreneurship and the Market Process* (London, U.K.: Routledge, 1996).

Kadushin C., *Understanding Social Networks: Theories, Concepts and Findings* (New York: Oxford University Press, 2012).

Kalakota R., *E-Business: Roadmap for Success* (Reading, MA: Addison-Wesley, 2000).

Kale V., *Implementing SAP R/3: The Guide for Business and Technology Managers* (Indianapolis, IN: Sams, 2000).

Kale V., *Guide to Cloud Computing for Business and Technology Managers: From Distributed Computing to Cloudware Applications* (Chapman & Hall, 2014).

Kumar V., *Statistical Methods in Customer Relationship Management* (Wiley, 2012).

Kumar V., *Profitable Customer Engagement: Concept, Metrics and Strategies* (Sage Publications, 2013).

Kumar V. and Reinartz W., *Customer Relationship Management: Concept, Strategy, and Tools* (Springer, 2012).

Levinson P., *The Soft Edge* (London, U.K.: Routledge, 1997).

Lowson B. and King R., *Quick Response: Managing the Supply Chain to Meet Customer Demand* (Wiley, 1999).

McGrath M.E., *Product Strategy for High Technology Companies* (New York: McGraw-Hill Trade, 2000).

Naomi K., *No Logo* (New York: Picador, 1999).

Neely A., Adams C., and Kennenerley M., *The Performance Prism: The Scorecard for Measuring and Managing Business Success* (London, U.K.: Prentice Hall, 2002).

Papows J., *Enterprise.com* (London, U.K.: Nicholas Brealey, 1999).

Peppers D. and Martha R., *The One to One Future* (New York: Doubleday, 1997).

Postrel V., *The Future and Its Enemies: The Growing Conflict Over Creativity, Enterprise and Progress* (New York: Free Press, 1998).

Prahalad C.K. and Ramaswamy V., *The Future of Competition: Co-Creating Unique Value With Customers* (HBR Press, 2004).

Reichheld F.F., *The Loyalty Effect* (Boston, MA: Harvard Business School Press, 1996).

Rust R., Zaithaml V., and Lemon K., *Driving Customer Equity: How Customer Lifetime Value is Reshaping Corporate Strategy* (Free Press, 2000).

Sethi V. and King W. (Eds.), *Organizational Transformation through Business Process Reengineering* (Upper Saddle River, NJ: Prentice-Hall, 1998).

Seybold P.B., *Customers.com* (New York: Crown Business, 2001).

Shapiro C. and Varian H.R., *Information Rules* (Boston, MA: Harvard Business School Press, 1999).

Sharp D.E., *Customer Relationship Management Systems Handbook* (Auerbach Publications, 2003).

Shaw C. and Ivens J., *Building Great Customer Experiences* (Palgrave Macmillan, 2005).

Sheth J.N. and Parvatiyar A., *Relationship Marketing* (Thousand Oaks, CA: Sage Publications, 1999).

Siebel T.M., *Taking Care of eBusiness* (New York: Doubleday, 2001).

Slywotzky A.J. and Morrison D.J., *How Digital Is Your Business?* (London, U.K.: Nicholas Brealey, 2000).

Stocker R. and Bossomaier T. (Eds.), *Networks in Society: Links and Language* (Singapore: Pan Stanford Publishing, 2013).

Tapscott D. (Ed.), *Creating Value in the Network Economy* (Boston, MA: Harvard Business School Press, 1999).

Tiwana A., *Knowledge Management Toolkit* (New York: Prentice Hall, 2002).

Trefler A., *Built for Change: Revolutionizing Customer Engagement through Continuous Digital Innovation* (Wiley, 2014).

Vandermerwe S., *Customer Capitalism* (London, U.K.: Nicholas Brealey, 1999).

Index